PARIS & PROVENCE

Directed by
André Gayot

Contributing Editors
Françoise Boisard, Jonell Galloway, Louisa Jones,
Odile Granier, Martine Jacques, Sheila Mooney,
Brigitte du Tanney

Coordination
Sophie Gayot

Publisher
Alain Gayot

Adapted from the
French-Language Guide

published in French by SPES (Paris)

Paris ▪ Los Angeles ▪ New York ▪ San Francisco▪ London ▪ Munich ▪ Turin

GAYOT PUBLICATIONS

Published by GaultMillau, Inc.
5900 Wilshire Blvd.
Los Angeles, CA 90036

Please address all comments regarding
PARIS & PROVENCE to:
GaultMillau, Inc.
P.O. Box 361144
Los Angeles, CA 90036
E-mail: gayots@aol.com

Advertising Sales:
P.M.C.
10 bis rue Jeanne d'Arc
94160 Saint-Mandé, France
Tel (01) 43 28 20 20 Fax: (01) 43 28 27 27

Debbie Eskew
5900 Wilshire Blvd.
Los Angeles, CA 90036
213-965-4841 Fax 213-936-2883

Cover Design & Photos: Alpha Media

ISSN 1099-6265

Printed in the United States of America

CONTENTS

City of Light,
Land of Sunshine

Paris belongs to the world. It's every man's city, rich in history, art, science, architecture, philosophy, and, of course, gastronomy, an essential part of French culture. But *Paris* is also enmeshed in a fabric called *Ile-de-France*, the province which surrounds it. Should you lack the time to journey across France, a trip around Paris and Ile-de-France will provide you with a taste of the diversity that exists throughout the country. Only a few miles outside of Paris, the architecture and the habits begin to vary. The western part of Ile-de-France belongs in spirit to Normandy, the eastern part to Champagne. You will find Brie cheese in the Brie/Champagne area and Camembert near Normandy. The local beverages change as you move around the points of the compass, from the Champagne that makes the east sparkle, to beer in the north and wine in the sunny south.

Provence and *The Riviera* make up a large part of the sunny southeast of France. Once you are south of Lyon, you enter into a profoundly different more exotic France: the universe of La Méditerranée. Forget the Gothic style, the rolling hills, the huge wheatfields, this is the land of Roman churches, olives trees, cypresses and terraces carved on the mountains slopes. The food, the arts, the culture dip their roots down deep into the fabulous soil of the Mediterranean basin, where the very earth and water hold the memory of our Western history and civilization.

We have tailored this book to help you appreciate the differences among these four areas, and to discover some of the many charms of France. Our **Paris, Ile-de-France & Provence and The Riviera** guide, gives you the real lowdown on hundreds of French restaurants and hotels, with inside information that will make you a «traveler in the know», always one step (at least!) ahead of the crowd.

For 33 years, we, at GaultMillau, have scoured the French countryside, visiting urban centers and tiny hamlets, in search of worthwhile places to eat and stay. Contributors from every region of France participate in our national survey of restaurants and hotels. They work to strict standards, ensuring fairness and continuity of the grading system. When, for example, a reviewer spots what appears to be a terrific new place, he or she invariably seeks a second opinion to confirm that the establishment is truly a winner. These thorough, unvarnished appraisals of grand restaurants, bistros, brasseries, auberges and hotels, are presented in a witty, entertaining style that has earned GaultMillau its international reputation. (And thanks to our ever-expanding family of guidebooks, travelers can now rely on Gault-Millau for accurate, up-to-date information on destinations all over the globe. See page 4.)

The purpose of this guidebook is to help you steer a well-informed course through the many restaurants, hotels, gourmet and wine shops, and very «chic» souvenirs in Paris, Ile-de-France & Provence and The Riviera. Naturally, the top establishments tend to be quite expensive, but we also take you into cozy bistros and family-style inns where you can indulge your *gourmandise* without breaking the bank. So whether you are a first-time visitor or a frequent traveler to France, let GaultMillau help you discover the myriad gastronomic pleasures that France has to offer!

André Gayot

A disclaimer

Readers are advised that prices and conditions change over the course of time. The restaurants, hotels, shops, and other establishments reviewed in this book have been reviewed over a period of time, and the reviews reflect the personal experiences and opinions of the reviewers. The reviewers and publishers cannot be held responsible for the experiences of the reader related to establishments reviewed. Readers are invited to write to the publisher with ideas, comments, and suggestions for future editions.

SYMBOL SYSTEMS

RESTAURANTS

We rank restaurants in the same manner that French students are graded: on a scale of zero to twenty, twenty being unattainable perfection. The rankings reflect *only* the quality of the cooking; décor, service, reception, and atmosphere do not influence the rating. They are explicitly commented on within the reviews. Restaurants ranked thirteen and above are distinguished with toques (chef's hats), according to the following table:

Exceptional   4 toques, for 19/20

Excellent   3 toques, for 17/20 and 18/20

Very good   2 toques, for 15/20 and 16/20

Good   1 toque, for 13/20 and 14/20

Keep in mind that these ranks are *relative*. One toque for 13/20 is not a very good ranking for a highly reputed (and very expensive) temple of fine dining, but it is quite complimentary for a small place without much pretension.

• In addition to the standard **carte**, or à la carte menu, you will frequently be offered a choice of all-inclusive fixed-price meals called **menus**, which are generally a very good value. Also common in finer restaurants is the many-course sampling menu, or **menu dégustation**, a good (though not always economical) way to get an overview of a restaurant's specialties. Daily specials, or **plats du jour**, are usually reliable, inexpensive, and prepared with fresh ingredients that the chef found at the market that morning.

• At the end of each restaurant review, prices are given—either *A la carte* (**C**) or *Menu* (**M**) (fixed-price meal) or both. A la carte prices are those of an average meal (a starter, a main course, dessert, and coffee) for one person, including service and a half-bottle of relatively modest wine. Lovers of the great Bordeaux, Burgundies, and Champagnes will, of course, face stiffer tabs. The menu prices quoted are for a complete multicourse meal for one person, including service but excluding wine, unless otherwise noted. These fixed-price menus often give diners on a budget a chance to sample the cuisine of an otherwise expensive restaurant.

• When you go to a top restaurant, let the **headwaiter** suggest some possibilities from the menu (you'll find that many maître d's quite often speak English, though they always appreciate an attempt on the diner's part to speak French). Likewise, the **sommelier's** job is to give diners expert advice on the choice of a suitable wine—regardless of price. Don't be afraid to seek his or her opinion, or to state your budget.

- French law mandates that the **service charge**, 15 percent, always be included in the menu prices. You are not obliged to leave an additional tip, but it is good form to leave a little more if the service was satisfactory.
- The **opening** and **closing times** we've quoted are always subject to change, particularly holiday closings, so be sure to call ahead.
- Many chefs have the bad habit of **changing restaurants frequently**, which means a restaurant can turn mediocre or even bad in just a few days. Chef-owned restaurants tend to be more stable, but even they can decline. A successful owner may be tempted to accept too many diners, which can result in a drop in quality. Should this be your experience, please don't hold us responsible!

HOTELS

Our opinion of the comfort level and appeal of each hotel is expressed in a ranking system, as follows:

 Very luxurious

 Luxurious

 Very comfortable

 Comfortable

🌲🌳 Very quiet

The prices indicated for rooms and half-board range from the cheapest for one person to the most expensive for two.

Sadly, prices continue to creep up, so some places may have become more expensive than our estimates by the time you visit. If you expect to pay a little more—you may end up being pleasantly surprised!

OTHER INFORMATION & ABBREVIATIONS

Rms: Rooms
Seas: Season
Rm ser: Room service
Stes: Suites
Air cond: Air conditioning
Pkg: Parking
Half-board: Rate per person for room, breakfast, and one other meal (lunch or dinner)

How to read the locations:

AIX-EN-PROVENCE	13090
Paris 770 - Avignon 75 - Marseille 31	B./-Rhône

THE CITY	THE POSTAL CODE
Kilometers to Paris and nearby major cities	The regional department

TOQUE TALLY

O-P: Out-of-Paris; **P**: Provence; **R**: The Riviera

Four Toques
19/20

L'Ambroisie, *Paris 4th arr.*
Arpège, *Paris 7th arr.*
Alain Ducasse, *Paris 16th arr.*
Le Louis XV, *Monaco*, (R)

Three Toques
18/20

Apicius, *Paris 17th arr.*
La Bastide Saint-Antoine, *Grasse*, (R)
Les Élysées du Vernet, *Paris 8th arr.*
Pierre Gagnaire, *Paris 8th arr.*
Le Grand Véfour, *Paris 1st arr.*
Ledoyen, *Paris 8th arr.*
Guy Savoy, *Paris 17th arr.*
Taillevent, *Paris 8th arr.*
La Terrasse, *Juan-les-Pins*, (R)

> *The* **ratings** *are based solely on the restaurants' cuisine. We do not take into account the atmosphere, décor, service and so on; these are commented upon within the review.*

Three Toques
17/20

Les Ambassadeurs, *Paris 8th arr.*
Amphyclès, *Paris 17th arr.*
Astor, *Paris 8th arr.*
La Belle Otéro, *Cannes*, (R)
Bistrot des Lices, *Saint-Tropez*, (R)
Le Bourdonnais, *Paris 7th arr.*
Le Bristol, *Paris 8th arr.*
Carré des Feuillants, *Paris 1st arr.*
Chantecler, *Nice*, (R)
Le Clos de la Violette, *Aix-en-Provence*, (P)
Le Duc, *Paris 14th arr.*
Faugeron, *Paris 16th arr.*
La Fenière, *Lourmarin*, (P)
Goumard Prunier, *Paris 1st arr.*
Le Jardin, *Paris 8th arr.*
Laurent, *Paris 8th arr.*
Maximim, *Vence*, (R)
Paul Minchelli, *Paris 7th arr.*
Montparnasse 25, *Paris 14th arr.*
Le Moulin de Mougins, *Mougins*, (R)
L'Oasis, *Mandelieu-La-Napoule*, (R)
La Palme d'Or, *Cannes*, (R)
Passédat, *Marseille*, (P)
Le Pré Catelan, *Paris 16th arr.*
Le Régence, *Paris 8th arr.*
La Table d'Anvers, *Paris 9th arr.*
Les Trois Marches, *Versailles*, (O-P)
La Villa des Lys, *Cannes*, (R)
Vivarois, *Paris 16th arr.*

Two Toques 16/20

Abbaye de Sainte-Croix, *Salon-de-Provence,* (P)

L'Arbousier, *Saint-Raphaël,* (R)

Aubertin, *Villeneuve-lès-Avignon (see Avignon),* (P)

La Bastide de Moustiers, *Moustiers-Sainte-Marie,* (P)

Belles Rives, *Juan-les-Pins,* (R)

Gérard Besson, *Paris 1st arr.*

La Bonne Étape, *Château-Arnoux,* (P)

Jacques Cagna, *Paris 6th arr.*

Le Cagnard, *Cagnes-sur-Mer,* (R)

Le Cap, *Saint-Jean-Cap-Ferrat,* (R)

Le Céladon, *Paris 2nd arr.*

Les Chênes Verts, *Tourtour,* (R)

Chez Bruno, *Lorgues,* (R)

Chiberta, *Paris 8th arr.*

Le Clos des Morillons, *Paris 15th arr.*

Conti, *Paris 16th arr.*

La Côte, *Cannes,* (R)

Le Diamant Rose, *La Colle-sur-Loup (see Saint-Paul-de-Vence),* (R)

La Dinée, *Paris 15th arr.*

Le Dôme, *Paris 14th arr.*

Christian Étienne, *Avignon,* (P)

L'Étoile d'Or, *Paris 17th arr.*

Faucher, *Paris 17th arr.*

La Grande Cascade, *Paris 16th arr.*

Le Grenadin, *Paris 8th arr.*

Les Gorges de Pennafort, *Callas,* (R)

Issautier, *Saint-Martin-du-Var,* (R)

Jamin, *Paris 16th arr.*

Jean-Jacques Jouteux, *Saint-Jean-Cap-Ferrat,* (R)

Le Divellec, *Paris 7th arr.*

Le Lingousto, *Cuers,* (R)

Lucas Carton, *Paris 8th arr.*

La Marée, *Paris 8th arr.*

Le Mas des Herbes Blanches, *Joucas (see Gordes),* (P)

Mas du Langoustier, *Porquerolles (Ile de),* (R)

Bernard Mathys, *Apt,* (P)

Maxim's, *Paris 8th arr.*

Le Meurice, *Paris 1st arr.*

Le Moulin à Huile, *Vaison-la-Romaine,* (P)

L'Olivier, *Saint-Tropez,* (R)

Le Paris, *Paris 6th arr.*

Le Petit Colombier, *Paris 17th arr.*

Paolo Petrini, *Paris 17th arr.*

Le Port Alma, *Paris 16th arr.*

Le Prieuré, *Villeneuve-lès-Avignon (see Avignon),* (P)

Prunier Traktir, *Paris 16th arr.*

Le Relais d'Auteuil, *Paris 16th arr.*

La Réserve de Beaulieu, *Beaulieu-sur-Mer,* (R)

Résidence de la Pinède, *Saint-Tropez,* (R)

Restaurant de Bacon, *Cap d'Antibes,* (R)

Le Restaurant d'Éric Fréchon, *Paris 19th arr.*

Michel Rostang, *Paris 17th arr.*

Les Santons, *Grimaud,* (R)

Le Saule Pleureur, *Monteux (see Carpentras),* (P)

Sormani, *Paris 17th arr.*

Taïra, *Paris 17th arr.*

La Timonerie, *Paris 5th arr.*

La Tour d'Argent, *Paris 5th arr.*

Les Trois Forts, *Marseille,* (P)

La Voile d'Or, *Saint-Jean-Cap-Ferrat,* (R)

PARIS
& ILE-DE-FRANCE

A capital destination

Despite its name, Ile-de-France is not an island. No spot could be less insular than this province at the heart of Europe, since archaic times a strategic crossroads for culture and commerce between Britain and the Mediterranean, Germany and Spain. Home to some twenty percent of France's inhabitants—that comes to about fifteen million souls—Ile-de-France is the nation's richest, most populous and productive region.

What New York, Chicago, Los Angeles, and Washington are to the United States, **Paris** alone is to France. This single city dominates the nation's government and politics, its industry, business, and finance, its media and communications, its artistic and intellectual life. Paris is the biggest consumer market for everything from vacuum cleaners to theater tickets, and the biggest producer of goods. In recent years, the French government has sought to correct the imbalance between the ever-burgeoning capital and the provinces. «Decentralization» is the order of the day: industries and institutions are offered hefty subsidies to set up their headquarters away from the Paris region. Still, the capital remains a dreamed-of destination for many. Nowhere else in France are jobs more plentiful. To this day, ambitious young provincials still «go up» to Paris hoping to make their name and fortune. Foreigners too, especially from France's former colonies in Africa and Asia, pour into Paris dreaming of a better life. They have put their stamp on the capital, establishing ethnic neighborhoods like the North African quarter of the *Goutte d'Or* east of Montmartre, the Southeast Asian «Chinatown» around Place d'Italie, and the Black African enclaves of *Belleville*. Who could recognize the city of the 1950s—the mythical city of *An American in Paris*—in this multicolored metropolis that is hurtling headlong into the twenty-first century?

Some might be tempted to view Paris, with its sumptuous monuments and historic sites, as a shrine to the glories of past kingdoms and empires. But that is not the whole story. Paris is also a high-energy metropolis, a creative world capital. New urban districts have sprung up. La Défense, on the city's western edge, hosts a major modern landmark, the Arche de La Défense. To the east, the Bercy district is home to the pharaonic national library, the recently inaugurated Bibliothèque de France, as well as the mammoth Palais Omnisports. The city's center has been enriched with the Musée d'Orsay and the expanded Grand Louvre, which now houses an ever greater complement of masterpieces.

A new cathedral for a new town

Cars and trucks from all over Europe rumble into the Paris region via a sophisticated network of high-speed autoroutes. The revamped Métro and regional rapid transit system (RER) cross Paris in just minutes and also serve far-flung suburbs. Bullet trains—the TGV—link the capital to the rest of France and Europe. And a third major airport will soon be built to accommodate the millions of air passengers whose numbers are straining the present hubs of Orly and Roissy Charles-de-Gaulle. Central planners have created five *villes nouvelles*, «new towns» complete with schools, parks, and shopping centers, all erected *ex nihilo* in the middle of grain fields. One of them, **Évry**, built on former farmland south of Paris in 1969, even boasts a brand-new (and highly controversial) cathedral designed by Mario Botta.

Since Hugues Capet, count of Paris, was elected King of France in 987 the destiny of Ile-de-France has been shaped by that of the city on the Seine. Royal residences are scattered throughout Ile-de-France, for Hugues Capet and his successors kept their courts on the move: to oversee their lands and subjects; to keep one step ahead of their enemies; and to indulge their passion for the hunt. Even in their present ruined state, the thick-walled fortresses of **Senlis** and **Dourdan**, and the donjon at **Vincennes** (under reconstruction) evoke a feudal age when kings required protection from rivals nearly as powerful as themselves. The Renaissance graces of **Fontainebleau** and **Saint-Germain-en-Laye** mirror a less brutal era, while **Versailles** embodies the brilliance of absolute monarchy at its zenith. With the curious exception of Versailles, most royal châteaux gave onto huge forests teeming with game, where the king could ride to hounds. Even now woodlands covers an astonishing twenty percent of Ile-de-France. The forests of **Fontainebleau** and **Rambouillet**, two of the most splendid in France, count among the region's greatest beauties.

The ire
of the Sun King

Not all of the 3,000 châteaux in Ile-de-France belonged to the Crown. The princely Montmorency and Condé clans, for example, owned vast domains at **Écouen** and **Chantilly**. Their sumptuous dwellings (now home to the Musée de la Renaissance and the splendid Musée Condé, respectively) are set amid gardens and woodlands that impress visitors even today. The seventeenth century was a high-water mark for château construction. The patrician châteaux of **Courances** and **Guermantes** combine brick and stone in a style made popular under Louis XIII; the opulence and classic proportions of **Maisons-Laffitte**, designed by François Mansart in mid-century.

That age dawned in 1661 when Louis XIV attended a *fête* given in his honor by finance minister Nicolas Fouquet, at the latter's new and indescribably luxurious château, **Vaux-le-Vicomte**. Put out by Fouquet's showy splendor (and suspicious of how he had obtained his fortune), Louis had the minister thrown into prison. He then proceeded to hire the same architect, decorator, and garden designer to work on his own royal showplace at **Versailles**. From its completion in 1682 until 1789, Versailles supplanted Paris as the political and artistic capital of the realm. On the eve of the Revolution the château and town counted some 50,000 inhabitants. The Age of Elegance, endures in the eighteenth-century château of **Champs-sur-Marne**, with its Rococo interior (featuring the first dining room ever built for that express purpose) and ravishing *jardin à la française*. The owners of the Renaissance château of **Thoiry** turned the grounds into a wild animal reserve. Visitors drive through the estate (with their windows rolled up...) and watch lions, elephants, monkeys, and rhinos roam free.

The rulers of France, «eldest daughter of the Church», endowed Ile-de-France with a fabulous legacy of religious architecture such as the abbey of **Saint-Denis** where sovereigns are interred, the abbey of **Royaumont**, and the sublime Sainte Chapelle.

Gothic architecture was born in Ile-de-France in the twelfth century. Every nuance of Gothic is represented in the region, from the earliest ogives in the abbey church of **Morienval**, to the vertiginous spires and lacy stonework of the late Flamboyant phase, that grace the church of Saint-Jean Baptiste in **Nemours**. Nowhere else but in Ile-de-France is there such a collection of Gothic cathedrals as those at **Saint-Denis, Paris, Chartres, Pontoise, Senlis, Meaux**...

Just beyond the rose-tinted turrets of Sleeping Beauty's Castle in Disneyland Paris lies the rural **Brie**. A rich agricultural land graced with ancient fortified farms and fine churches, it arcs southward from the town of **Meaux** (famed for Brie cheese and coarsegrain mustard as well as for its splendid architecture) to **Provins**, a well preserved medieval merchant center, once the third largest city in France. And in the wheat-bearing plains of the **Beauce** and of the **Brie** region—still, as always, the breadbasket of France—**Chartres** retains its Gothic serenity despite the throngs of tourists who come to admire the cathedral each year.

While the suburbs of **Asnières** and **Argenteuil**, both close to the capital, are unrecognizable as the arcadian sites painted by Seurat and Monet, **Moret-sur-Loing**, a sleepy town on the edge of the Fontainebleau forest, still bathes in the tender light that Sisley and Renoir captured on canvas. And (in the off-season at least) certain spots of **Auvers-sur-Oise** look much as they did when Cézanne, Pissarro, and Van Gogh planted their easels there.

There are restaurants, *auberges*, and modest eateries aplenty near all the major sites. A few notable exceptions aside (watercress from the Essonne Valley, rabbits and honey from the Gâtinais, cheeses from Meaux, Coulommiers, and Dreux), homegrown foods do not feature prominently in local cuisine. Most ingredients come straight from **Rungis**, the mega-market complex that replaced Paris's Halles in 1969 as the region's supplier of comestibles from France and abroad. There's nothing «provincial» about dishes like the John Dory in curry with melting eggplant cooked to perfection with an oriental twist at Le Régence, or rice pancake with almonds and raw lemon grass juice from Le Clos Morillons. Sophistication and virtuosity are key. Paris, of course, is a magnet for ambitious chefs from all over France. From Normandy's legendary Taillevent, who cooked for King Charles V in the 1300s, to Loire native Pierre Gagnaire contemporary culinary genius, or Landes native Alain Ducasse, Paris is the place where chefs prove their mettle and make their name.

Fine food, ancient monuments, thrilling history: the litany is not exhaustive. Still, it should incite you to venture, as Henry James put it, beyond «the wondrous capital, and the wondrous capital alone» to explore the châteaux and cathedrals, the forests and rivers, the urban and rural treasures of Ile-de-France.

RESTAURANTS

A many-splendored experience

For food-lovers, the lure of Paris's *haute cuisine* is at least as powerful as the temptations of *haute couture* for followers of fashion, or *haute culture* for the high-minded. In fact, we know of one American lady who planned her entire trip abroad around a dinner reservation (made months in advance, of course) *chez* megachef Alain Ducasse, so compelling was her craving for his langoustines aux morilles. Nor is it rare for people who have never even set foot in the French capital to know the names and specialties of all the city's fashionable chefs. Dining out in Paris is a many-splendored experience. Elegance reigns here to a degree not often attained in the restaurants of other cities; Le Grand Véfour, Les Ambassadeurs, and Lucas Carton, for instance, are classified historical landmarks, with interiors of unparalleled beauty. These and the city's other top establishments also offer distinguished service: from the maître d'hôtel and the sommelier to the humblest busboy, the staffs are stylish and professional, a real *corps d'élite*. And the food, on a night when a chef like Michel del Burgo of Le Bristol is particularly inspired, can be memorable, even thrilling, a joy to the eye and a feast for the palate.

If your tastes (or finances!) lead you to prefer less exalted eating houses, we urge you to peruse our reviews for Paris's many marvelous bistros, brasseries, and homestyle restaurants, where prices are—usually—far lower than in *grands restaurants* and where the atmosphere veers more toward relaxed informality. Parisians are fiercely loyal to their neighborhood bistros where they regularly tuck into familiar, traditional dishes with pronounced regional accents (Gascon, Alsatian, Provençal). If you go in for local color, those are the places to try. Brasseries are perfect when you want to eat just a single dish rather than a multicourse meal (but don't try ordering only a salad *chez* Lipp). And they offer sustenance at odd hours—that's important if you're jet-lagged; brasseries also tend to stay open late, and generally do not require reservations.

Restaurant Savvy

- At top Parisian restaurants, you must **reserve a table** far in advance—at least three weeks, sometimes two or three months for such places as L'Ambroisie and Taillevent. Reservation requests from abroad are taken much more seriously if they are accompanied by a deposit of, say, 300 F (about $60). Tables at less celebrated spots can be reserved one or two days ahead, or even on the morning of the day you wish to dine. If you cannot honor your reservation, don't forget to call the restaurant and cancel.
- **Men should wear** a jacket and tie in any Parisian restaurant of some standing. **Women are well advised to dress up**, wearing pantsuits only if they are impeccably tailored. Luxury restaurants do not take the question of dress lightly, so be forewarned. At modest eateries, of course, more casual wear is perfectly acceptable (but jogging suits or running shorts and tank tops are looked at askance).
- **Dinner service** begins around 8pm in most Paris restaurants. People start appearing in the finer restaurants about 9pm. **Luncheon** is served between 12:30pm and 2pm.

1st ARRONDISSEMENT

Zip code	75001

11/20 Joe Allen

30, rue Pierre-Lescot
01 42 36 70 13, fax 01 40 28 06 94
Open daily until 12:30am. Bar: until 2am, Sun 1am. Terrace dining. Air cond.
Relaxed and casual: American, in short. Come to Joe's when you feel the urge to sink a few beers or dig into a chef's salad, chili burger, barbecued spare ribs, or apple pie. C 170-250.

 ## L'Absinthe

24, pl. du Marché St-Honoré - 01 49 26 90 04
Closed Sun. Open until 11:30pm. Terrace dining. Pkg.
What a delight of a location this former bistro with its terrace facing one of Bofill's latest feats of architecture. The à la carte menu is the polished work of the long experience of its new owners, Michel Rostang and Claude Bouillon. What tender morsels: sardine and potato pie, mussel skewers, tomato calamary, or creamy veal, mushroom and onion stew with Basmati rice. The half-bottles of Côtes-du-Luberon and Côtes-de-Ventoux are well worth trying. M 129 (lunch), 148-189.

 ## Armand

6, rue du Beaujolais
01 42 60 05 11, fax 01 42 96 16 24
Closed Sat lunch, Sun, Aug. Open until 11:30pm.
A friendly, intimate restaurant near the Palais Royal gardens, serving traditional fare under an umbrella of stone vaulting. The dishes often make reference to grand names in French history, so it's a delight for history buffs. Delicious crêpe served with warm foie gras, stuffed chicken leg with Diable sauce, or braised salmon dressed up with Italian parsley. The wine menu offers all the grand classics with a smart selection of half-bottles. C 330. M 180 (lunch), 250 (weekday dinner).

 ## Gérard Besson

5, rue du Coq-Héron
01 42 33 14 74, fax 01 42 33 85 71
Closed Sat lunch (dinner Jun 15-Sep 15), Sun. Open until 10:30pm. Air cond. Pkg.
A chic conservatory of cuisine bourgeoise with its sparkling new dining room. Polished classicism, not innovation, is Besson's signature; his only failing is a tendency to overcomplicate (chicken fricassée with sweetbreads and quenelles). Take your choice of oyster flan with escargot fricassée and escargot butter, simply prepared asparagus, an open-face wild game tart, or filet mignon with pineapple chutney and a slice of

roasted mango. Splendid cellar, but too few half-bottles. Delectable desserts. C 450-770. M 200-280 (lunch), 520.

11/20 Café Marly

93, rue de Rivoli
01 49 26 06 60, fax 01 49 26 07 06
Open daily until 1am. Air cond. Terrace dining. Pkg.
Here in the Louvre with a view over I.M. Pei's famous glass pyramind, you may order the most expensive club sandwich in Paris, tuna sashimi, or a well-made *plat du jour*, served in magnificent surroundings. A very dressy crowd of fashion and literary notables has staked out its turf here—you may find yourself sitting next to Karl Lagerfeld! C 200-250.

11/20 Café Véry

Jardin des Tuileries - 01 47 03 94 84
Open daily until 11pm. Air cond. Terrace dining. Pkg.
Good stop on a sunny day in this café tucked away in the Tuileries garden. The bill is sometimes on the hefty side, the fare interesting with the likes of smoked salmon with endives in ginger cream, thin slices of beef marinated in herbs, or lamb and zucchini cake. C 110-150.

 ## Carré des Feuillants

14, rue de Castiglione
01 42 86 82 82, fax 01 42 86 07 71
Closed Sat lunch, Sun, 3 wks in Aug. Open until 10:30pm. Air cond. Pkg.
Authentic ingredients from first-rate producers form the basis of Alain Dutournier's Basco-Béarnaise cuisine. This lover of bull fights (witnessed in the décor) who has defined his own standard of quality in the past recently slipped up on a few occasions, but on our last visit we noted that the reins had been tautened. Pheasant consommé dotted with chestnuts; foie gras spread on warm cornbread; savory Pauillac lamb in a tight, sapid jus; a robust garbure (cabbage soup) with duck confit; slow-simmered veal shank that is lacquered on the outside and meltingly tender within—all these dishes brim over with vigorous, exhilarating flavors. The exciting cellar harbors a mother lode of (mostly affordable) wines accented with all the grand Bordeaux and dotted with some unforgettable Jurançons and Armagnacs. C 600-700. M 285 (weekday lunch), 680.

 ## Les Cartes Postales

7, rue Gomboust - 01 42 61 23 40, fax 01 42 61 02 93
Closed Sat lunch, Sun. Open until 10:30pm. Pkg.
Scores of postcards adorn the beige-and-white walls of this small, pretty, flower-filled restaurant. Yoshimasa Watanabe's dual culinary heritage yields a menu that lists tuna carpaccio or barely cooked brill alongside a sauté of duck and foie gras or a fricassée of langoustines in a

chicken jus. Can be pricey if you don't stick to the 135 F set menu. Nicely balanced cellar. C 300-350. M 135-350.

12/20 Le Caveau du Palais

17, pl. Dauphine - 01 43 26 04 28, fax 01 43 26 81 84
Closed Nov-Apr: Sun, end Dec-beg Jan. Open until 10:30pm. Air cond. Terrace dining.
The atmosphere may be old world in this charming Place Dauphine cellar, but the cooking has taken on a touch of the modern with the arrival of new chef Robert de Lopetegui: St Jean de Luz-style cod, duck breast with thyme flowers or cured Ibaiona ham. Wines by the glass or the pitcher. C 220-260. M 140.

 ## L'Espadon

Hôtel Ritz, 15, pl. Vendôme
01 43 16 30 80, fax 01 43 16 33 75
Open daily until 11pm. Terrace dining. Air cond. Pkg.
A bastion of tradition, cautiously opening itself to the new winds of gastronomy, where you can forget the harsh reality just outside the walls of this prestigious "palace" with its abundant silver, crystal, fresh flowers and trellises—a real enchanted garden in the summer. Better bets are the pan-roasted langoustines or a «mosaic» of sea bass spiced with mustard seeds, or for lunch, lentil cream with ham hock bouillon or red mullet cooked in olive oil and served with a delicious risotto. Sumptuous cellar, and the service is sheer perfection. C 700-900. M 380 (lunch), 600 (dinner).

 ## Fellini

47, rue de l'Arbre-Sec - 01 42 60 90 66
Open daily until midnight. Air cond. Pkg.
Mellow stone walls contribute to Fellini's warmly elegant atmosphere. Appetizing Italian *plats du jour*: fresh pasta with scallops, shrimp and artichoke sauté, calf's liver with a bright lemon sauce. Well selected list of wines from the other side of the Alps (i.e. Italy). C 230-250. M 110 (lunch).

 ## Gaya

17, rue Duphot - 01 42 60 43 03, fax 01 42 60 04 54
Closed Sun. Open until 10:30pm. Air cond. Pkg.
Each day the tide pulls sparkling fresh seafood into this bright and elegant annex of Goumard-Prunier (see below). The catch of the day sometimes features marinated fresh anchovies, pan-roasted red mullet, or tuna with chilis. Be warned, though, that the tab is heftier than you might expect, especially for the wine. C 280-320.

 ## Goumard Prunier

9, rue Duphot
01 42 60 36 07, fax 01 42 60 04 54
Closed Sun, Mon. Open until 10:30pm. Air cond. Pkg.
Jean-Claude Goumard procures the fattest sole and turbot, the sweetest lobsters and prawns, the briniest sea bass and red mullet from his fishermen friends in Brittany and Roussillon. Nothing interferes with the fresh taste of the sea in dishes like scallop carpaccio with oysters, crab with Sherry aspic, or such seasonal delights as sea urchins or baby eels. The cellar spotlights fine white Burgundies. Little remains, alas, of the restaurant's original décor, designed by Majorelle—the only vestiges, it happens, are in the restrooms! C 600-800. M 295 (lunch), 780 (dinner).

11/20 Restaurant Le Grand Louvre

Museum entrance, under the pyramid
01 40 20 53 41, fax 01 42 86 04 63
Closed Tue. Open until 10pm. Air cond.
Something is cooking under I.M. Pei's glass pyramid. The Louvre's restaurant has a chef from the Southwest of France. No wonder his duck foie gras and Pyrenees leg of lamb moistened with Gascon wines light up the pyramid. Non-stop service. C 250-350. M 180.

 ## Le Grand Véfour

17, rue de Beaujolais
01 42 96 56 27, fax 01 42 86 80 71
Closed Sat, Sun, Aug. Open until 10:15pm. Air cond. Pkg.
It's not a wax museum, but you can soak up a bit of French history in this Institution where Bonaparte and Josephine, Victor Hugo, Cocteau and Malraux among a panoply of others have dined, and whose names are to be seen on the engraved copper plates above the terribly appropriate red velvet benches. Guy Martin's menu grows more inventive by the day, with such exceptional creations as almond-milk flan in sorrel bouillon, lightly cooked salmon terrine with eggplant aspic, and basil shortbread topped with candied fennel. The milk-fed calf's sweetbreads studded with truffles and gently cooked with a broad bean jus, though more in keeping with traditional homestyle fare, are a true chef d'œuvre! Hearty Alpine offerings have their place as well (Martin is a native of Savoie): how about a double chop of farm-bred pork swaddled in smoky bacon? As always, the Grand Véfour provides sublime surroundings: carved *boiserie* ceilings, painted allegories under glass, snowy napery, and fragile Directoire chairs. The wine cellar is lavish, and the service is as elegant as the cosmopolitan clientele. C 700-900. M 335 (lunch), 750.

 ## A la Grille Saint-Honoré

15, pl. du Marché-Saint-Honoré
01 42 61 00 93, fax 01 47 03 31 64
Closed Sun, Mon, 3 1st wks of Aug. Open until 10:30pm. Terrace dining. Air cond. Pkg.
The Place du Marché Saint-Honoré, redesigned by Riccardo Bofill, is rather like Place Beaubourg's Pompidou museum. But don't let that discourage you from dropping in at Nicole

and Jean Speyer's Grille for tasty, imaginative «market cuisine»: fragrant crab soup, guinea hen with blackcurrants, smoked haddock with cabbage and chives, etc. Good-priced set meal, especially at lunch. Different wines featured every month. The iron grille, or grating, probably dates from Robespierre's times and is on the list of national monuments. C 300-350. M 180-250.

11/20 Juvenile's

47, rue de Richelieu
01 42 97 46 49, fax 01 47 03 36 93
Closed Sun. Open until 11pm. Pkg.
We've always felt perfectly at ease in Scotsman Tim Johnston's hybrid wine-and-tapas bar, where the Queen's English is spoken, and American understood. The premium Sherries that headline the wine list are ideal companions to the Spanish-style bar snacks (chicken wings, marinated fish, grilled squid, and such) that are the house specialty. His wine list knows no borders—with selections from Spain, Australia, and Mexico among others—and wine by the glass starts as low as 14 F. The menu even sounds a British note with a yummy roast-beef sandwich and nursery desserts. C 150-200. M 98-128.

Kinugawa

9, rue du Mont-Thabor
01 42 60 65 07, fax 01 42 60 45 21
Closed Sun, May 1, Dec 23-Jan 6. Open until 10pm. Air cond.
Perfect sushi, sashimi, and shabu-shabu, charmingly served by an extremely efficient French maître d'hôtel in an intimate setting. Undoubtedly the best Japanese restaurant in Paris, and always glittering with stars. But the prices cut like a samurai's sword. We find their other location on rue Saint-Philippe-du-Roule (see 8th arrondissement) friendlier and more intimate. C 300-500. M 160 (lunch), 245-700.

11/20 Lescure

7, rue de Mondovi - 01 42 60 18 91
Closed Sat dinner, Sun, Aug. Open until 10:15pm. Terrace dining. Air cond.
Tried-and-trusted French fare served in a feverish bistro atmosphere and offering some of the best prices around, with stuffed poule au pot at 42.50 F and a bottle of Cahors at 64 F. Sample the hearty veal sauté or duck confit. Game dishes are highlighted in hunting season. C 150. M 100 (wine incl).

Le Meurice

Hôtel Meurice, 228, rue de Rivoli
01 44 58 10 50, fax 01 44 58 10 15
Open daily until 11pm. Air cond. Pkg.
Rosy nymphs cavort across a ceiling further adorned with gilt and crystal chandeliers, in what is surely one of the city's most sumptuous restaurants. Le Meurice is not all show, however: the food is superb. Marc Marchand eschews pompous cuisine for full-bodied dishes with plenty of rustic flavor: grilled sea bream with fennel chutney, dandelion greens with lamb's brains and a coddled egg, lobster cannelloni in a suave, winy sauce. Faultless service, and a cellar administered by Antoine Zocchetto, an expert sommelier. C 500-600. M 330 (lunch), 430 (dinner, wine incl).

Chez Pauline

5, rue Villedo - 01 42 96 20 70, fax 01 49 27 99 89
Closed Sat (exc dinner May-Sep), Sun. Open until 10:30pm. Air cond. Pkg.
A traditional bistro that perfectly represents a certain ideal of French cuisine. Robust and full of frank flavors, the neo-bourgeois dishes are based on uniformly fine ingredients prepared by a veteran chef. Subtlety is not the strong suit here: braises, sautés, and long-simmered stews are André Genin's stock in trade. The cellar holds memorable (and expensive!) Burgundies. We only wish that the dining room were more comfy, and the staff less chilly. C 300-500. M 220.

12/20 Au Pied de Cochon

6, rue Coquillière
01 40 13 77 00, fax 01 40 13 77 09
Open daily 24 hours. Terrace dining. Air cond.
The atmosphere is effervescent at this Les Halles landmark, renowned for serving thundering herds of pigs' trotters (85,000 annually) and a ton of shellfish every day of the year. Open non-stop. C 200-300. M 123 (wine incl), 178.

Le Poquelin

17, rue Molière - 01 42 96 22 19, fax 01 42 96 05 72
Closed Sat lunch, Sun, Aug 1-20. Open until 10:30pm. Air cond. Pkg.
In the red-and-gold dining room where portraits of Molière look down from the walls, chef Michel Guillaumin wins applause from his regular patrons (many from the Comédie-Française across the street) for his specialities from the Auvergne region: potato pâté, puff pastry stuffed with blue cheese, duck salad and coq au vin, all served with wines from the same region. And this is where what the French call «thin apple tart» was invented back in the days when the restaurant still belonged to Poquelin. A standing ovation for Maggy Guillaumin's cheery welcome. C 280-320. M 189.

12/20 Restaurant Costes

Hôtel Costes, 239, rue Saint-Honoré
01 42 44 50 25, fax 01 42 44 50 01
Open daily until 12:30am. Terrace dining. Air cond.
The only reason to come to this restaurant is the extraordinary setting and décor—certainly not the steep prices or the food. Choose to sit in the little armchairs or on the delightful terrace (in summer) of this Italianate luxury hotel, in a nineteenth-century town house just steps from Place Vendôme. You will dine in trendy dishes surrounded by a trendy clientele, and be served by young waiters who don't really look like waiters. C 350-400.

11/20 Toupary

2, quai du Louvre - 01 40 41 29 29, fax 01 42 33 96 79
Closed Sun. Open until 11:30pm. Terrace dining.
Air cond. Pkg.
Hilton McConnico designed this colorful dining room on the fifth floor of the Samaritaine department store. Along with a splendid view of the Seine, you'll taste essentially classic cooking: cold custard marrow soup with almonds, lamb with pickled lemons, salmon à la niçoise. C 160-260. M 95 & 139 (lunch), 180 (dinner).

The hole in Les Halles

Many Parisians still regret that the city's famous food market, installed here since the twelfth century, was not preserved when the merchants moved out to Rungis in 1969. The **trou** ("hole") **des Halles**, dug after the market was destroyed, became a tourist attraction in its own right during the 1970s, while developers argued with the city over what should be done with it.

One idea was simply to fill it in again; another was to flood it to make a lake linked up to the Seine. A dozen or so architects had their projects rejected before the present Forum des Halles shopping center was approved and built. While indistinguishable from similar emporia worldwide, the Forum at least has the merit of carrying on the centuries-old tradition of trade. Above ground, the site has been attractively landscaped and the surrounding streets are full of echoes of the past for those who care to listen.

11/20 La Tour de Montlhéry

5, rue des Prouvaires - 01 42 36 21 82
Closed Sat, Sun, Jul 14-Aug 15. Open 24 hours.
Here, until the wee hours, you can order up a satisfying plate of stuffed cabbage or warming mutton stew. C 250-280.

Chez Vong

10, rue de la Grande-Truanderie
01 40 26 09 36, fax 01 42 33 38 15
Closed Sun. Open until 12:30am. Terrace dining.
Air cond. Pkg.
Excellent dim-sums, steamed scallops, and shrimp with lotus leaves in this almost mysterious atmosphere with its old stone dining rooms dotted with Buddhas, parasols and bamboo. Although the five-spice duck tongues are quite novel, the gingered lobster lacks spirit, and prices are high. Lovely greeting and the merriest of service. C 250-350. M 150 (weekday lunch).

Willi's Wine Bar

13, rue des Petits-Champs
01 42 61 05 09, fax 01 47 03 36 93
Closed Sun. Open until 11pm. Pkg.
When the English fall for wine, they do it right. Even the best of wine sellers would have trouble living up to the quality (and reasonable prices) of Mark Williamson's wide-ranging wine list (over 200 selections), with its affectionate preference for Côtes-du-Rhônes. Join the customers sitting elbow-to-elbow at the polished white-oak bar, or if you can nab a table in the smallish dining room for a more upscale cuisine, try appetite whetters like pressed duck liver with artichokes, Scottish salmon roasted in salt, or duckling with wine ice cream, followed by unforgettable Stilton blue and their talked-about bitter chocolate terrine. C 200-350. M 145 (lunch), 180 (dinner).

12/20 Yvan sur Seine

26, quai du Louvre - 01 42 36 49 52
Closed lunch Sat & Sun. Open until 4am. Terrace dining. Air cond. Pkg.
Yvan's quayside annex specializes in good seafood, served well into the wee hours. The 148 F prix-fixe meal is just like the one offered at Le Petit Yvan (see *8th arrondissement*). A cheerful mood prevails in the shipshape dining room; indeed, the ambience gets downright gay as the night wears on! Wine available by the glass. C 250-350. M 148 (wine & coffee incl).

2nd ARRONDISSEMENT

Zip code	75002

Café Runtz

16, rue Favart - 01 42 96 69 86
Closed Sat, Sun, 3 wks in Aug, hols. Open until 11:30pm. Air cond. Terrace dining.
An 1880s Alsatian *winstub* serving rich foie gras, excellent choucroute garni, warm potato salad with pork knuckle, and onion tart. Good French Rhine wines and artisanally-brewed beer. Warm atmosphere. Open late, so it makes a perfect stop-off after the theatre or a concert. C 200-240.

12/20 Canard'Avril

5, rue Paul-Lelong - 01 42 36 26 08
Closed Sat, Sun, hols. Open until 10pm.
The menu's just ducky: gizzard salad, confit, and magret de canard feature prominently, alongside a handful of similarly hearty Southwestern dishes. The bargain-priced set meals are sure to quack you up. Moderately priced apéritifs and wines from the Southwest, with a good selection of half-bottles. C 220. M 89-129.

Le Céladon

Hôtel Westminster, 13, rue de la Paix
01 47 03 40 42, fax 01 42 61 33 78
Closed Sat, Sun, Aug, hols. Open until 10:30pm. Air cond. Valet pkg.
Emmanuel Hodencq finally found a jewel box that glitters as much as the bejewelled windows that line the streets of this jewelery district. In the Louis XV décor dotted with Chinese *objets d'art*, and where everything has been shipped up and shaped up, you'll feel as if you're eating in a friend's luxury mansion rather than in a restaurant. The mood is set by the shades of green, which is only appropriate since *céladon* denotes a certain type of green in French. The menu changes with the times, but always remains well balanced and light, with a touch of influence from sunny Provence. Try the savory potato salad with candied tomatoes and truffles, the turbot on a bed of celery root, or the lamb with a candied lemon sauce. Hodencq is also an expert at desserts, so save room for the pistachio shortbread with Amaretto cherry filling. Charm of a wine list presented by the ever-smiling sommelier, Richard Rahard. Is it the new décor which has spruced up the cuisine? In any case, it certainly deserves another point. C 450-500. M 260, 390, 500.

Drouant

18, rue Gaillon
01 42 65 15 16, fax 01 49 24 02 15
Open daily until 10:30pm, midnight at Le Café. Air cond. Pkg.
The cream of the city's biz and show-biz sets meet and greet in the Drouant's grand Art Deco dining room. But the man who we formerly referred to as a «master technician», Louis Grondard, laid out some disappointing surprises this year: overcooked fish lost in a mound of crust and supposedly truffled (we had trouble finding the truffles, and when we did they were tasteless). On another day, the morels did not live up to our expectations. Paradise is not entirely lost however. You'll be pleased with the curried baby lamb compote, accompanied by absolutely marvellous hot potato bread, and the hot chocolate soufflé with saffron sauce. Exceptional wine cellar, young waiters and waitresses always in high spirits. Pricey however, unless you go to the Café Drouant, which draws business lunchers (at noon) and theater-goers (at night) with reasonably priced bourgeois cooking (200 F set menu). C 700-850. M 290 (lunch), 650 (dinner).

12/20 Le Grand Colbert

2, rue Vivienne
01 42 86 87 88, fax 01 42 86 82 65
Closed Aug 10-20. Open until 1am. Air cond.
Classic brasserie cuisine (oysters and shellfish, andouillette ficelle, bœuf gros sel, and poached chicken) served in a sprucely restored historic monument complete with frescoes and ornate plasterwork, brass railings and painted glass panels. Expect a warm welcome and swift, smiling service, but be prepared for the ceiling-height check. C 200-300. M 155.

Au Pays de Cocagne

111, rue Réaumur - 01 40 12 81 81
Closed Sat lunch, Sun, Aug. Open until 10pm. Pkg.
You'll immediately feel at home after the friendly welcome and the just-like-your-mother attentiveness of the service. Can this really be Paris, this must be the country? We are especially fond of the starters—escargots dusted with truffles (a lovely combination) and a green bean salad topped with excellent foie gras. The main dishes won't disappoint you either. Try the flawlessly cooked duck breast with honey vinegar and kasha or the delicately spiced tripe ramekin. We'll let you judge the desserts (don't hesitate!). Cellar entirely made up of Gaillacs at prices easy on your purse strings. M 138-190.

Pile ou Face

52bis, rue Notre-Dame-des-Victoires
01 42 33 64 33, fax 01 42 36 61 09
Closed Dec 23-Jan 1, Aug. Open until 10:30pm. Air cond. Pkg.
Why fiddle with a winning formula? That's the philosophy of the young couple who runs Pile ou Face. The menu continues to showcase fresh produce straight from their own farm in Normandy, and new chef Eric Rogoff successfully draws his inspiration from them. The excellent scrambled eggs with morels have to be tried to be believed. A quiet and unpretentious spot offering a red-and-gold setting with *fin de siècle* touches. Wide-ranging cellar. C 350-450. M 245 (weekday lunch), 280-320 (weekday dinner).

11/20 A Priori Thé

35-37, galerie Vivienne - 01 42 97 48 75
Open until Mon-Fri 6pm, Sat-Sun 6:30pm. Terrace dinning. Pkg.
We'd be hard pressed to come up with a prettier or more charming spot in Paris than the Passage Vivienne. You enter beneath a glass roof supported by bas-relief goddesses and horns of plenty, to reach this honey-colored room (the scrap of a terrace out front is furnished with rattan armchairs). From noon until 3pm fashion mavens, journalists, and intellectuals lunch on cold platters, tempting *plats du jour* (try the Welsh rarebit), and such homey desserts as fruit crumble and pecan pie. Come teatime, you'll find a selection of teas served with scones, muffins, and jam. **Brunch** is served on weekends. C 150. M 135 (lunch Sat), 146 (lunch Sun).

12/20 Rôtisserie Monsigny

1, rue Monsigny
01 42 96 16 61, fax 01 42 97 40 97
Closed Sat lunch, 10 days in Aug. Open until midnight, Sun & Mon 11pm. Air cond. Pkg.
Jacques Cagna is the driving force behind this busy restaurant, where juicy roast lamb and spit-roasted chicken are served forth by an energetic staff under the soft music of a piano. C 220-240. M 100, 160.

12/20 Le Saint-Amour

8, rue de Port-Mahon - 01 47 42 63 82
Closed Sat lunch, Sun. Open until 11pm. Air cond.
Impeccable service and fresh, generous cuisine, heavily inspired by the chef's 10-year stint in Asia. The 150 F set meal and a *carte* delivers (for example) spiced-up versions of French standards: sturgeon in lie-de-vin jelly, parsley-flecked loin of lamb and kidney, and Guanaja chocolate and coriander soufflé. Concise but interesting wine list. C 250-300. M 150.

12/20 Le Vaudeville

29, rue Vivienne - 01 40 20 04 62, fax 01 49 27 08 78
Open daily until 2am. Terrace dining. Air cond. Pkg..
This glittering outpost of the Flo empire is decked out in 1930's-style brass, glass, and wood. Waiters swoop and swirl amid the good-natured clamor (the crowd is often studded with stars, celebrities and stockbrokers from across the street), delivering platters of glossy shellfish, prime meats, the popular house foie gras, and attractively priced little wines. A very Parisian choice for a late bite after the theater. C 200-300. M 123 (lunch, wine incl), 169 (dinner, wine incl).

3rd ARRONDISSEMENT

| Zip code | 75003 |

 ## L'Alisier

26, rue de Montmorency
01 42 72 31 04, fax 01 42 72 74 83
Closed Sat, Sun, Aug, Christmas. Open until 10pm. Air cond. Pkg.
An inviting, old-fashioned bistro (ask for a table upstairs) where you will be greeted with the bubbly hello of the chef's wife. Sit back and enjoy Jean-Luc Dodeman's deft cooking so full of ideas, with a «revolving» fixed-price menu that changes every week, with the likes of cod baked with honey and cumin, warm scallops marinated in not-so-hot Spanish peppers and served with creamed spinach, and millefeuille layered with spiced custard and caramel sauce. And all this for 175 F, including wine and coffee (lunchtime only). Brief but alas wisely selected offering of wines. C 250-350. M 175 (lunch, wine incl).

 ## Ambassade d'Auvergne

22, rue du Grenier-Saint-Lazare
01 42 72 31 22, fax 01 42 78 85 47
Open daily until 10pm. Air cond. Pkg.
Come here for an authentic taste of Auvergne: aged country ham, cabbage and Roquefort soup, and the legendary house aligot (satiny mashed potatoes with cheese). Good desserts—try the mousseline glacée à la verveine du Velay. The cellar holds some little-known Auvergnat wines (Chanturgue, Châteaugay, Estaing) in a wide range of prices. You'll feel you're in Auvergne... C 220-300. M 170.

 ## Au Bascou

38, rue Réaumur - 01 42 72 69 25
Closed Sat lunch, Sun, 3 wks in Aug. Open until 11pm. Terrace dining.
Basque-country native Jean-Guy Loustau (formerly the award-winning sommelier of Le Carré des Feuillants) runs this smart address, all dressed up in the warm colors of the south. The regionally-inspired menu highlights include scallops with fiery Espelette chilis, tiny squid stewed in their ink and presented with a toothsome risotto, and tender tripe en daube with sweet peppers. Top-notch wines, mainly Basque. C 230-250. M 90.

12/20 Le Hangar

12, impasse Berthaud - 01 42 74 55 44
Closed Sun, Mon lunch, Aug 15-beg Sep. Open until midnight. Terrace dining. Air cond. Pkg.
This old shed-cum-restaurant with its over-sized-stone walls offers culture-starved Pompidou-goers something down-to-earth for their stomachs: mushroom and chervil salad, fennel and mozzarella au gratin, asparagus cake with truffle vinaigrette, and little foie gras patties with lentil cream sauce. Good selection of wines, with a different wine by the glass every day. C 180-220.

11/20 L'Imprimerie

101, rue Vieille-du-Temple - 01 42 77 93 80
Open daily until midnight. Terrace dining. Air cond. Pkg.
Picasso museum visitors and artists from the neighborhood galeries drop in here to taste the daily specials. «Bagna-cauda» formula, consisting of salad and carpaccio, for 97 F. C 190-240. M 139.

12/20 Chez Nénesse

17, rue de Saintonge - 01 42 78 46 49
Closed Sat, Sun, hols, 1 wk in winter, Aug. Open until 10pm.
Nénesse puts on the dog for dinner: he covers the Formica tables of his venerable neighborhood bistro with tablecloths and flowers! Fresh, flavorful *plats du jour* based on fine ingredients, carefully prepared. The cellar offers a pleasant selection, but he could go a bit heavier on the

explanations (growers' names and years are often lacking). C 200-250.

 ## Opium Café

5, rue Elzévir - 01 40 29 93 40, fax 01 40 29 93 46
Open daily until midnight. Air cond. Pkg.
Opposite the Musée Cognacq-Jay (home to an exquisite collection of eighteenth-century art and antiques), this spacious, elaborately decorated dining room—lovely armchairs and banquettes, gleaming chandeliers, gilded details everywhere—is a great favorite with the city's gay crowd. Highlights from the clever and appealing menu include fresh vegetables in a blood-orange sabayon and fragrant braised pork with spices. We like the friendly, typically Marais atmosphere, and in the bar, the «party» goes on until two in the morning. Brunch is served on weekends. C 250-300. M 110 (weekday lunch), 100-150 (lunch Sat, Sun).

 ## 404

69, rue Gravilliers - 01 42 74 57 81
Closed 2 wks in Aug. Open until midnight. Air cond. Pkg.
Lively atmosphere with a North African touch. Our meal was a total success—quality ingredients cooked just right: lamb and prune tagine cooked in an earthenware dish, couscous with a chicken shish kebab, and a lovely b'steeya—a pigeon pie with dates, ground almonds, cinnamon and much more. The service is alert but could use some softening around the edges. C 180-250. M 89 (weekday lunch).

4th ARRONDISSEMENT

Zip code	75004

 ## L'Ambroisie

9, pl. des Vosges
01 42 78 51 45
Closed Sun, Mon, Feb school hols, 1st 3 wks of Aug. Open until 10:15pm. Air cond. Pkg.
When Jacques Chirac invited Bill and Hillary Clinton here, he was inviting them to the ultimate in classic French cuisine. With its inlaid stone and parquet floors, book-lined shelves, and sumptuous Aubusson tapestries adorning honey-hued walls, L'Ambroisie has the feel of a beautiful private home, of which Danièle Pacaud is the attentive hostess. Don't expect to see much of Bernard Pacaud, though. He prefers the sizzling sounds of the kitchen to the applause of an appreciative public. His concise *carte* is supplemented by a few *surprises du jour*: marjolaine de foie gras (layered goose liver, truffles, and celery—divine!); flash-cooked sea bass with rosemary-scented artichokes; a majestic poularde en demi-deuil. Some may say he's lack-

ing in inspiration, that he's not overflowing with surprises, but if ever there was a master craftsman in the old-time sense of the word, he is it: tradition at its glorious and soaring heights, tradition which follows the «rules» that gave French cuisine its name. Each dish is flawlessly finished. Faultless cellar, too, run by Pierre Le Moullac, an exemplary maître d'hôtel–sommelier. In keeping with the «deluxe» atmosphere, there is unfortunately no set-price menu. Noblesse oblige! C 1,300.

 ## Baracane

38, rue des Tournelles - 01 42 71 43 33
Closed Sat lunch, Sun. Open until midnight. Pkg.
Tables fill quickly in this tiny Southwestern enclave, because the cooking is full-flavored and generous to boot. Lentil salad with dried goose breast or cassoulet with duck confit precede delectable desserts. Low-priced regional wines wash it all down. Affable service. M 128-215 (wine incl.).

 ## Benoit

20, rue St-Martin - 01 42 72 25 76, fax 01 42 72 45 68
Closed 1 wk in winter, Aug. Open until 10pm.
Benoit is the archetypal Parisian bistro (and surely one of the priciest): velvet banquettes, brass fixtures, lace curtains, and a polished zinc bar compose a seductive décor. Owner Michel Petit (who is anything but!) continues the lusty tradition begun before the Great War by his grandfather: delicious bœuf à la parisienne, good cassoulet, creditable codfish with potatoes and cream. But what's not to be missed is the desserts, every one as good as the other, although we have a slight preference for the divine orange ice cream soufflé. The cellar is stocked with good bottles from Mâcon, Sancerre, Beaujolais, and Saumur. Beware: credit cards are not accepted. C 450-550. M 200 (lunch).

12/20 Bistrot de la Place

2, pl. du Marché Sainte-Catherine
01 42 78 21 32
Open daily until 11pm. Terrace dining. Pkg.
Even though the terrace unquestionably gives onto one of the most charming squares in Paris, in chilly weather, don't hesitate to dine in the Baroque dining room, which is much in keeping with the neighborhood's style. Even though the waiters and waitresses sometimes suffer from a slight superiority complex, and the food, which is mainly Southern and Southwestern in influence, lacks soul for the most part, they still have to turn people away. C 200-250.

 ## Bofinger

3-7, rue de la Bastille
01 42 72 87 82, fax 01 42 72 97 68
Open daily until 1am. Terrace dining. Air cond.
Bofinger's stained-glass ceiling, ceramics, marquetry, mirrors, and tulip-shaped sconces compose a magnificent Belle-Époque décor that has

long been a landmark in the Bastille quarter. Parisians, provincials, tourists, and celebrities throng in for generous assortments of extra-fresh shellfish and hearty choucroute garni. The Flo group, which recently took over this thriving enterprise (the restaurant serves 300,000 meals each year!), is doing a good job of putting the kitchen on a more even keel. The duck foie gras, leg of monkfish with sweet garlic, and lamb tian (Provençal-style au gratin) with summer savory are all thoroughly recommendable. C 200-350. M 169 (wine incl).

Les Fous d'en Face

3, rue du Bourg-Tibourg · 01 48 87 03 75
Open daily until midnight. Terrace dining. Air cond.
Generous, authentic bistro cooking made even more appealing by expertly chosen wines. Enjoy star anise–spiced salmon, scallops en papillote, and pear tart, in a convivial atmosphere. C 190-280. M 88 (weekday lunch), 175(wine incl).

11/20 Jo Goldenberg

7, rue des Rosiers · 01 48 87 20 16
Open daily until 11pm. Terrace dining. Air cond.
The most picturesque of the Goldenberg restaurants in Paris (see *17th arrondissement*). The Central European Yiddish cuisine is served in the heart of the Marais's Jewish district. Prepared foods are sold in the take-out shop. C 150-200.

Le Grizzli

7, rue Saint-Martin · 01 48 87 77 56
Closed Sun. Open until 11pm. Terrace dining. Pkg.
At age 95-plus this Grizzli is still going strong, serving lusty specialties rooted in the Southwest: white-bean salad with duck confit, roast baby lamb, and veal stewed with cèpes, all served in an authentic 1900-style bistro setting. Sprightly service and good quality eating for the money. To drink, try a pitcher of the Côtes-du-Marmandais at the reasonable price of 58 F. C 220-250. M 115 (lunch), 155.

11/20 Mariage Frères

30, rue du Bourg-Tibourg · 01 42 72 28 11
Open daily until 7pm. Terrace dining. Air cond.
At Mariage Frères, tea is to be drunk, or, as you can discover, to liven up what's on your plate: foie gras with Sauternes wine sauce and Oolong orange-flower jelly, chicken breast with Imperial Earl Grey sauce, or sponge cake with green tea sauce. C 150-250. M 125 (weekday lunch), 125 (brunch), 145 (w-e brunch).

Miravile

72, quai de l'Hôtel-de-Ville
01 42 74 72 22, fax 01 42 74 67 55
Closed Sat lunch, Sun, 3 wks in Aug. Open until 10pm. Air cond. Pkg.
Alain Lamaison has slimmed down his tempting single-price menu, and now offers a com-

plete menu—somewhat expensive—at 240 F. As in the past, the chef uses only the best of ingredients to call into action his muses, but, to be quite honest, we found the results just all right, no more. There was one dish that yanked at our heart strings: thin slices of pear and quince with coriander ice cream, simple but truly unforgettable. Each month brings a fresh selection of recommended wines. C 430-520. M 180 (lunch), 240.

Le Monde des Chimères

69, rue Saint-Louis-en-l'Ile
01 43 54 45 27, fax 01 43 29 84 88
Closed Sun, Mon. Open until 10:30pm. Pkg.
A delightful old «island bistro» run by former TV personality Cécile Ibane. The cuisine is reminiscent of Sunday dinner *en famille*—if, that is, your family included a French granny who was also a marvelous cook! Try the crab soup, beef with eggplant and tomatoes, rhubarb pie, or surprising foie gras pan-fried with honey and Sherry and topped with an egg. Yummy homemade desserts. The fixed-price menus are a good buy at lunch, but keep close count if you order à la carte. C 280-340. M 89 (lunch), 160.

L'Ostéria

10, rue de Sévigné · 01 42 71 37 08
Closed Sat, Sun, Aug. Open until 11pm.
Hidden away behind a non-descript façade in the heart of the Marais, this little Italian restaurant plays host to fashion, film, and show-biz luminaries. They delight in the arugula salad showered with Parmesan shavings, spaghetti in a lusty seafood sauce, and potato gnocchi lavished with sage-infused butter, all clemently priced. The cellar is stocked with over 50 great Italian wines, but the prices may leave you dry. C 230-280.

Thanksgiving

20, rue Saint-Paul · 01 42 77 68 28
Closed Sun dinner, Mon. Open until 10:30pm.
American chef Judith Bluysen has recently turned from thoroughly classic American fare to Louisiana Cajun served in a typically Marais-style dining room with its wooden beams and stone walls. Mardi Gras is celebrated New Orleans style with live Cajun music and blues, and the menu offers hard-to-find delicacies such as crawfish boils (in season), chicken filé gumbo, jambalaya, crabcakes and more. Different kind of cheesecake everyday, depending on the chef's inspiration. The weekend brunch is good—try the mouthwatering Eggs Sardou—and you won't go away hungry. Wash it all down with a tasty Frisco beer or a half oak, half grape Cabernet. C 200-240. M 89 (lunch, wine incl), 90 (Sun), 140-160.

Find the address you are looking for, quickly and easily, in the index.

Le Vieux Bistro

14, rue du Cloître-Notre-Dame
01 43 54 18 95, fax 01 44 07 35 63
Open daily until 10:45pm. Terrace dining.
Right next to Notre-Dame, an honest-to-god bistro that the tourist crowds have somehow overlooked. Owner Fernand Fleury cultivates a warm, inviting atmosphere; chef Beaudouin Verlaten's prepares a robust menu of vigorous, homestyle favorites. The cellar is a shade too expensive, but contains all the great classics. C 250-320.

5th ARRONDISSEMENT

Zip code   **75005**

 ## L'Atlas

12, bd St-Germain - 01 44 07 23 66, fax 01 40 46 06 56
Open daily until 11pm. Air cond.
Surprising, slightly cerebral, determinedly modern Moroccan cuisine. The range of options extends beyond couscous and tagines (though a dozen excellent varieties are offered) to such delicacies as peppery mint and bran soup, lamb with mallow, monkfish with thyme flowers, kidneys with sea-urchin butter and an exquisite almond b'steeya. Decorated with mosaics and ornamental plasterwork, the dining room is perfectly lovely; so is the service. C 150-350.

 ## Le Bistrot d'à Côté

16, bd St-Germain - 01 43 54 59 10, fax 01 43 29 02 08
Closed Sat lunch, Sun. Open until 11pm. Terrace dining. Air cond. Pkg.
The new kitchen staff of Michel Rostang's popular bistro annex serves up lively specialties that change with the seasons: mussel shish kebabs with tartar sauce and mushrooms; Dublin bay prawn tempura; fresh goat cheese, melon and aged-ham pancake; spicy honey-coated hog's jowl, and chicken with foie gras macaroni. The wine list offers surprising treasures, or you might want to try the half-bottles of Côtes-du-Ventoux or Côtes-du-Luberon at 59 F. M 129 (lunch), 142, 189.

 ## Les Bouchons de François Clerc

12, rue de l'Hôtel-Colbert
01 43 54 15 34, fax 01 46 34 68 07
Closed Sat lunch, Sun. Open until 11pm. Air cond. Pkg.
Sure, the food is good (snails and gnocchi au pistou, rabbit with foie gras, etc.) but what lures us back again and again is the wine list! Chablis Premier Cru '93 for 72 F, Guigal's Hermitage '92 for 92 F, Boillot's Volnay '88 for 100 F, Grand Puy Lacoste '92 Paulliac for 80 F, Château Giscours Margaux '89 for 192 F, the list goes on: an irresistible deal for wine buffs. M 117 (weekday lunch, wine incl), 219.

La Bûcherie

41, rue de la Bûcherie - 01 43 54 39 24
Open daily until midnight. Terrace dining. Air cond.
After a long absence, Bernard Bosque, built like a Breton buccaneer, and who has been running his Bûcherie for three decades, has finally (and fortunately) returned to tend to his kitchen. Handsome woodwork and modern prints adorn the walls, and there are views of Notre Dame beyond the covered terrace. The cuisine, classic and understated, reflects the seasons. There's game in autumn; baby eels from January to March; asparagus and morels in spring. Service wavers between gracious condescension and outright impropriety. The wine list favors pricey Bordeaux, and there are at least twenty different half-bottles. Fireplace in the winter and pleasant terrace for *les beaux jours*. C 320-500. M 230 (wine incl).

12/20 Campagne et Provence

25, quai de la Tournelle
01 43 54 05 17, fax 01 43 29 74 93
Closed Sat & Mon lunch, Sun. Open until 11pm, Sat & Sun 1am. Air cond. Pkg.
Sunny, unhackneyed Southern cuisine. Sample Patrick Jeffroy's cuisine from his friendly-priced fixed menus: tasty basil ravioli, sea bream with roasted fennel, or salt cod à la niçoise. There's a short but sweet 120 F lunch menu, and an excellent choice of meridional wines, all under 100 F. M 120 (lunch), 180, 215.

11/20 ChantAirelle

17, rue Laplace - 01 46 33 18 59
Closed Sat lunch, Sun. Open until 10:30pm. Terrace dining. Pkg.
Rustic décor and products direct from Auvergne: local salt-cured products, Fourme-d'-Ambert (blue cheese) puff pastry, trout filet with Puy lentils and ox-cheek in sweet garlic. C 160-200. M 75-98 (lunch, wine incl), 140.

 ## Au Coco de Mer

34, bd St-Marcel - 01 47 07 06 64, fax 01 47 07 41 88
Closed Sun, Mon lunch, Aug 10-20. Open until midnight. Pkg.
No, your eyes are not playing tricks: that sandy beach you see is part of the Coco de Mer's exotic décor. The Seychelles Islands inspire the chef's gingery tuna tartare, octopus stewed in coconut milk, grilled pork and duck with tropical fruit. Be daring and try the lime or passion fruit punch. Friendly prices. C 200-250. M 110 (lunch), 135, 170.

Looking for a restaurant? Refer to the **index**.

Les Fontaines

9, rue Soufflot - 01 43 26 42 80
Closed Sun. Open until 11pm. Pkg.
A charmless corner café that draws a smart Rive Gauche crowd with perfectly cooked meat dishes. The butcher-cum-cook of so many years has just hung up his apron, but the new owners are continuing in the same tradition: prime rib, leg of lamb, veal sweetbreads with mushrooms, or Dijon-style kidneys. Excellent wine list; relaxed atmosphere. C 200-260.

12/20 Aux Iles Philippines

9, rue de Pontoise - 01 43 29 39 00, fax 01 44 07 17 44
Closed Sat lunch, Sun. Open until 11:30pm. Terrace dining. Air cond. Pkg.
Nicely crafted Philippine dishes: scrambled eggs with crab on a bed of crispy noodles, glazed pork, and delectable banana cake. Slides down easily with a white Colombelle at 70 F, making for a respectfully priced meal. C 150-250. M 120, 150 (dinner), 250 (dinner, wine incl).

 Inagiku

14, rue de Pontoise
01 43 54 70 07, fax 01 40 51 74 44
Closed Sun, Aug 1-15. Open until 10:45pm. Air cond.
This Japanese restaurant looks like any other one with its geometric black and rosewood décor and its tables with built-in grills, but the food, albeit pricey, proves to be some of the finest Japanese in town. Since we often leave Japanese restaurants as hungry as we came, we ordered a side of sashimi with our Matsu, or «big menu». Well, after putting away the assorted fresh raw fish, sushi with avocado, crisp fried hors d'œuvres, pile of fat shrimp, tender beef fillet, and duo of ginger and chestnut sorbets, we waddled out happy and absolutely stuffed! Excellent vegetables and soya noodles. Wines straight from the growers. C 400. M 88 (lunch), 148-248.

11/20 Le Languedoc

64, bd de Port-Royal - 01 47 07 24 47
Closed Aug, 2 wks at Christmas. Open until 10pm. Air cond.
Chef Pierre Dubois has produced an authentic bistro cuisine for nearly 25 years, and was serving such favorites as marinated herrings and real poached haddock long before they became the rage. C 150-180. M 105 (wine incl).

 Mavrommatis

42, rue Daubenton
01 43 31 17 17, fax 01 43 36 13 08
Closed Mon. Open until 11pm. Terrace dining. Air cond. Pkg.
The Mavrommatis brothers have raised the level of Greek cuisine served in Paris by several notches! There are 30 delicious starters (octopus salad, tuna carpaccio, stuffed eggplant, lamb meatballs, etc.), and worthwhile main dishes, too: red mullet grilled in vine leaves, leg of lamb smothered with herbs, or veal with oaten pasta. Good Greek wines. C 160-240. M 120 (weekday lunch, wine incl), 140.

 Moissonnier

28, rue des Fossés-Saint-Bernard - 01 43 29 87 65
Closed Sun dinner, Mon, 1 wk in Feb, Aug. Open until 10pm. Pkg.
Despite a page of history that turns because of the departure of Louis Moissonnier, nothing has changed, in this landmark Paris bistro. Ex-Troisgros and Senderens chef Philippe Mayet turns out the same robust Lyonnais specialties. Tasty Beaujolais wines are on hand to slake your thirst. C 230-280. M 150 (exc Sun).

12/20 Chez Pento

9, rue Cujas - 01 43 26 81 54
Closed Sat lunch, Sun, Aug 11-24. Open until 11pm. Pkg.
This neighborhood favorite serves generous portions of salt-cured duck with lentils, sausage with butter-braised cabbage, homey chocolate cake and the like, along with astutely chosen wines (some offered by the glass). The waiters are attentive and full of good humor as they caper about in this fifties décor. C 150-220. M 83 (lunch), 104, 140 (dinner).

11/20 Perraudin

157, rue Saint-Jacques - 01 46 33 15 75
Closed Sat & Mon lunch, Sun, last 2 wks of Aug. Open until 10:15pm. Garden dining.
Known to every publisher and professor in the Latin Quarter, this modest eatery provides solid sustenance—roast leg of lamb with scalloped potatoes, bœuf bourguignon, tarte Tatin—in a lively setting. C 130-150. M 63 (lunch).

12/20 Le Petit Navire

14, rue des Fossés-Saint-Bernard - 01 43 54 22 52
Closed Sun, Mon. Open until 10:15pm. Terrace dining.
Anchored not far from the Seine for the past twenty-odd years, Le Petit Navire regales its many regular customers with tapenade, garlicky shellfish soup, grilled sardines, and delightful growers' wines, even though the prices could undergo some revisions. C 250. M 150 (wine incl).

12/20 Rôtisserie du Beaujolais

19, quai de la Tournelle
01 43 54 17 47, fax 01 56 24 43 71
Closed Mon. Open until 11:15pm. Terrace dining. Air cond.
Claude Terrail of La Tour d'Argent (across the road) owns this Lyonnais-style bistro, a nice little place to spend a lively evening with friends over spit-roasted Challans duck, saucisson pistaché, or a salad of boiled beef and lentils. Splendid cheeses and exemplary Beaujolais from Dubœuf. C 230.

La Timonerie

35, quai de la Tournelle - 01 43 25 44 42
Closed Sun, Mon lunch, Aug. Open until 10:30pm. Air cond.
   Philippe de Givenchy continues to surprise us with his streamlined cuisine, based on simple, unpretentious ingredients: mackerel, pollack, inexpensive cuts of meat, offal, and pork. Another chef would make bistro chow out of foods like these, but Givenchy turns them into great modern dishes. What he does with hogs' jowls and a little red wine, or with a mackerel fillet and a handful of herbs, is pure magic. Desserts follow the same vein: a homey repertoire glorified by virtuoso technique. The cellar is not vast, but it is perfectly *à propos*, with a fine range of growers' wines. M 250 (lunch), 350 (dinner).

 La Tour d'Argent

15-17, quai de la Tournelle
01 43 54 23 31, fax 01 44 07 12 04
Closed Mon. Open until 10:30pm. Air cond. Pkg.
   At the ripe age of 78, Claude Terrail is still as savvy as he is charming. He knows that a reputation—no matter how exalted—is not sufficient to survive in the highly competitive world of world-class restaurants. He recently appointed Bernard Guilhaudin to succeed veteran chef Manuel Martinez and infuse some new blood into the Tour d'Argent. The menu is still composed of the legendary specialties of this well-established institution such as canard au sang—over 800,000 have already been served—and the rest, to which Guilhaudin has added some of his own creations, such as gougère with spring vegetables and tomato sabayon, pan-fried red mullet with anchovy butter and parsley purée, and Bresse-chicken tourte with tarragon-speckled pan-fried foie gras. The spark of imagination that made Guilhaudin's cuisine of the past glitter is infusing slowly in the venerable Tour d'Argent. Fabled cellar, with thousands of pricey bottles and a few affordable ones, too. A la carte prices are stuck in the stratosphere, but even this «monument» with all its history has to bow to the times, so the luncheon menu has actually dropped this year, from 395 to 350 F. C 900-1,000. M 350 (lunch).

12/20 Toutoune

5, rue de Pontoise - 01 43 26 56 81
Closed Mon lunch. Open until 10:45pm. Pkg.
   The chefs come and the chefs go, but the regulars know that the welcome warm as the Provençal colors that decorate its walls stays the same. The 168 F single-price menu features fragrant soups, tasty terrines, snails in a garlicky tomato sauce, sea bream with zucchini, and grapefruit gratin with sabayon sauce. Lively atmosphere. M 118 (weekday lunch), 168 (weekdays), 198 (Sun).

Some establishments change their closing times without warning. It is always wise to check in advance.

6th ARRONDISSEMENT

Zip code	75006

12/20 Chez Albert

43, rue Mazarine - 01 46 33 22 57
Closed Sun, Mon lunch, Aug. Open until 11pm. Terrace dining. Pkg.
   Many patrons don't realize that this is a Portuguese restaurant. The menu is mostly French, but the coriander clams, rabbit à la Ranhado, and half-dozen dishes starring salt cod (we like the one with eggs and onions) point clearly to the owner's Lusitanian origins. So does the wine list, with its Douros and Dãos. C 200-250. M 80 (lunch), 135.

 La Bastide Odéon

7, rue Corneille - 01 43 26 03 65, fax 01 44 07 28 93
Closed Sun, Mon, Aug. Open until 11pm. Pkg.
   Gilles Ajuelos impressed us from the start with his sunny Southern cooking. Though we had hesitations about his progress last year, the lacunae are gradually being filled in. We liked his full-flavored red mullet soup and his escargot and white-beet gnocchi so alive with the taste of basil and candied garlic. The walls could use some paint, but the atmosphere is friendly, prices are moderate, and the wine list offers wonderful Provençal wines. C 230. M 139-180.

Le Bistrot d'Alex

2, rue Clément - 01 43 25 77 66
Closed Sat lunch, Sun, Dec 24-Jan 2. Open until 10pm. Air cond.
   Lyon and Provence (with a penchant for the latter) inspire Stéphane Guini's zestful menu. You're sure to like the pistachio-studded saucisson, fragrant daube de bœuf, and tasty orange flan. Delightful welcome by Mamma Guini who looks after her customers with tender loving care in one of the few oases of calm in this sometimes too lively neighborhood. C 220-250. M 140, 170.

 Les Bookinistes

53, quai des Grands-Augustins - 01 43 25 45 94
Closed lunch Sat & Sun. Open daily until midnight. Air cond. Pkg.
   This addition to Guy Savoy's string of bistros sports an avant-garde neo-fifties look that obviously suits the mostly young, mostly Left Bank crowd. Crowded is how you might feel in this elbow-to-elbow eatery, but don't let that diminish your enjoyment of the gnocchi with mussels and spinach, sweetbread fricassée, and gingerbread millefeuille. Snappy service. Scintillating selection of wines, such as Troisgros' Côtes-Roannaises. C 240-260. M 130-160 (weekday lunch), 180 (dinner Sun), 190 (lunch, wine incl).

Bouillon Racine

3, rue Racine - 01 44 32 15 60
Closed Sun. Open until 11:30pm. Pkg.
Olivier Simon, a talented young Belgian chef, presides in the kitchen of this freshly (and beautifully) refurbished Belle Époque jewel. Not only are the surroundings a feast for the eye, the *carte* promises a corresponding treat for the palate: tomatoes stuffed with tiny shrimp, mousse of smoky Ardennes ham with juniper aspic, beef braised in beer à la flamande, pheasant à la brabançonne, and buttery Belgian brioche given the French-toast treatment. Tempting list of Belgian beers, on tap or bottled. **C** 150-200. **M** 88 (lunch, wine incl), 159.

11/20 Brasserie Lutétia

Hôtel Lutétia, 23, rue de Sèvres - 01 49 54 46 76
Open daily until midnight. Air cond. Pkg.
The no-nonsense cooking is prepared with considerable finesse in the same kitchens as Le Paris (see below). The seafood is attractively priced, and the satisfying bourgeois dishes (veal chop with macaroni gratin, poulet au thym) always hit the spot. **Brunch** served on Sundays. **C** 200-250. **M** 135, 295 (wine incl).

 ## La Cafetière

21, rue Mazarine - 01 46 33 76 90, fax 01 43 25 76 90
Closed Sun, 3 wks in Aug, end Dec-beg Jan. Open until 11pm. Air cond. Pkg.
A friendly, open spirit reigns in this French-Italian restaurant blessed with a new kitchen crew trained by none other than Sormani's. Chef Michel Hemmery might be from Picardy, but you'll swear he must have Tuscan or Venetian origins when you savor his bold dishes full of the joy of life: delicious homemade bresaola served with Einkorn and chanterelle mushrooms; scampi and tomatoes on a bed of polenta; crab ravioli, and truly divine taglierini (paper-thin ribbon noodles) in «squid ink». Several choices of fresh fish every day, extra-light tiramisù, and a «developing» cellar of Italian wines. **C** 220-320. **M** 120 (weekday lunch).

 ## Jacques Cagna

14, rue des Grands-Augustins
01 43 26 49 39, fax 01 43 54 54 48
Closed Sat lunch, Sun, 3 wks in Aug, 1 wk at Christmas. Open until 10:30pm. Air cond. Pkg.
Near the Seine, in the refined setting of his wood-paneled sixteenth-century mansion decorated with Flemish paintings, Jacques Cagna keeps turning out the classic dishes that built his success over the years. Sure enough, the products he uses are superb (sea bass from Brittany, fatted chicken from Normandy, lamb from the Pyrenees) but we have known a more audacious Cagna. That's why we give him kudos when he dares adding to his repertoire, dishes like tiny escargots hidden under ground tomatoes in a Charentes potato. The wine cellar is superb and has a fine collection of old Ports. **C** 600-800. **M** 250 (lunch), 470.

 ## Le Caméléon

6, rue de Chevreuse - 01 43 20 63 43
Closed Sat lunch, Sun, 3 wks in Aug. Open until 10:30pm. Pkg.
A pretty and authentic bistro with its fifties-style tile dining room full of regulars. An efficient, charming staff welcomes you as you partake of thinly sliced haddock with fennel, lamb sauté with fresh mint, or pan-fried turbot with eggplant. The 120 F set menu, which includes both wine and coffee, flaunts a hefty mussel flan and a fine chicken curry accompanied by mashed potatoes that could challenge Robuchon's (known as the best). Moderately priced cellar. **C** 120-220. **M** 120 (wine & coffee incl).

12/20 Casa Bini

36, rue Grégoire-de-Tours
01 46 34 05 60, fax 01 46 34 07 32
Closed Sun lunch, Aug 10-20, 1 wk at Christmas. Open until 11pm. Terrace dining. Pkg.
Anna Bini travels all the way to Tuscany to seek out the best ingredients for her little restaurant. The concise menu of carpaccio, crostoni, homemade pasta, and good daily specials suits her trendy Saint-Germain patrons to a T. Reasonably priced Italian wines. **C** 220-250.

12/20 Le Clocher Saint-Germain

22, rue Guillaume Apollinaire
01 42 86 00 88, fax 01 42 60 37 75
Open daily until 11:45pm. Terrace dining. Air cond.
Tourists and locals alike fetch up at this pleasant bistro for such hearty regional classics as warm saucisson lyonnais, salmon with green lentils, and silky blancmange embellished with caramel jam. The frisky wines, offered by the bottle or glass, are ideally suited to the bill of fare. For the neighborhood (just around the corner from the St-Germain-des-Prés church), a pretty darn good deal. **C** 220-345. **M** 148.

12/20 La Closerie des Lilas

171, bd du Montparnasse - 01 40 51 34 50
Open daily until 11:30pm. Terrace dining. Pkg.
The literal translation of the name of this veritable institution is «pleasure garden of lilies», because a Mr. Bullier planted thousands of lilies here in the 19th century. Hangout of the likes of Hemingway and numerous members of the Lost Generation, the charm of its luxuriant bowers does not entirely make up for an over-complicated, out-of-fashion, and high-priced cuisine. You'll get more for your money in the brasserie than in the restaurant: try their famous steak tartare and French fries. Piano music in the evening. **C** 210-250. **M** 220 (lunch, wine incl).

Remember to call ahead to reserve your table, and please, if you cannot honor your reservation, be courteous and let the restaurant know.

Dominique

19, rue Bréa · 01 43 27 08 80, fax 01 43 26 88 35
*Closed Sun, Mon lunch, Jul 20-Aug 20. Open until
11:30pm. Terrace dining. Pkg.*
This famed Montparnasse Russian troika—
take-out shop/bar/restaurant—steadfastly
refuses *perestroika* when it comes to cuisine and
décor. Rostropovitch and Solzhenitsyn have
been spotted here, sampling the delicious
smoked salmon, borscht, and blinis. And there's
vodka, of course, both Russian and Polish, some
60 different ones. C 250-300. M 98 (weekday
lunch, wine incl), 160, 180 (wine incl).

 L'Écaille de PCB

5, rue Mabillon
01 43 26 73 70, fax 01 46 33 07 98
*Closed Sat lunch, Sun, at Christmas. Open until
11pm. Terrace dining. Pkg.*
Marinated sardines with fennel or a salad of
finnan haddie and bacon segue into monkfish
osso buco à l'orientale, John Dory with coarsegrain mustard, or scallops in a creamy garlic
sauce. Our only request would be a tad less
cooking time. The cellar is of only middling interest, save for a fine, bone-dry Jurançon from
Marie de Charles Hours. C 280-350. M 140-210.

 L'Épi Dupin

11, rue Dupin
01 42 22 64 56, fax 01 42 22 30 42
Closed Sat, Sun. Open until 11pm. Terrace dining.
Well-deserved praise has been heaped on
young François Pasteau's cooking. A pupil of
some of the city's finer chefs, he proposes a menu
that includes briefly seared tuna set atop a zesty
onion pizza, scallops paired with celery in a
fragrant Provençal-style broth, breaded calf's
head with saffron potatoes (try it, it's delicious!),
and a bouquet of light, inventive desserts. A
meal here will set you back only 165 F (plus
wine, of course). Remember to book your table
in advance, but don't be in a hurry because the
service is very slow. M 110 (weekday lunch,
wine incl), 165.

Lipp

151, bd Saint-Germain
01 45 48 53 91, fax 01 45 44 33 20
Closed 3 wks in Aug. Open until 1am. Air cond.
Despite often disappointing food (choucroute,
bœuf gros sel) and the cruel whims of fashion,
this glossy brasserie still manages to serve some
400 to 500 customers a day. And one often
catches sight of a powerful politician or a beauty
queen ensconced at a ground-floor table, admiring the gorgeous décor. C 250-300. M 195.

11/20 **La Lozère**

4, rue Hautefeuille · 01 43 54 26 64
*Closed Sun, Mon, Jul 12-Aug 12, 1 wk at Christmas.
Open until 10pm. Air cond. Pkg.*
You can smell the bracing air of the rural
Lozère region in the warming winter soups,

herbed sausages, pâtés, and cheese-laced
mashed potatoes (aligot) served at this crafts
shop-cum-restaurant. C 150-240. M 92 (lunch),
125, 155.

City lights

Admire Paris in all its splendor
during a nighttime visit. Hundreds
of the city's buildings and monuments are cloaked in illuminations
when the sun goes down to show
them at their best. Sparkling fountains, shining façades, glowing
towers—you'll see the city in a
new light.
Monuments: Sun-Fri from dusk to
midnight; Sat & eves of holidays
until 1am.
Fountains: Daytime Apr 1-Dec 31
from 10am to dusk; Nighttime Apr
1-Dec 31 Sun-Fri from dusk to midnight; Sat & eves of holidays until
1am.

12/20 **Marie et Fils**

34, rue Mazarine · 01 43 26 69 49
*Closed Sun, Mon lunch, 2 wks in Aug, 1 wk at
Christmas. Open until 11pm. Terrace dining. Air
cond. Pkg.*
Marie, one of many former wives of the
notorious Eddie Barclay (who long ago beat
Henri VIII's record), and her son have converted
this artist's studio into a pretty, charming restaurant where you can nestle right in with the
regulars. Homestyle dishes such as roast beef
and mashed potatoes, salt cod and potato pie,
farm-raised roast chicken or carmelized suckling
pig. Saturday brunch served. C 250-300. M 78,
120 (wine incl), 110.

 La Méditerranée

Pl. de l'Odéon · 01 43 26 02 30, fax 01 43 26 18 44
*Open daily until 11:15pm. Terrace dining. Air
cond.*
Once a favorite spot of Cocteau and Picasso,
this restaurant known for its seafood had slowly
slipped into a sea of mediocrity in the past few
years. But with new life at the helm—Raphaël de
Montrémy and Geneviève Jabouille—and a
brand new menu custom-created by Japanese
chef Taïra, well known for his sea-inspired creations, the winds are much more favorable. Treat
yourself to pan-fried, herb-flavored cuttle-fish,
to grilled-to-perfection sea bream with fennel, or
to tuna steak au bleu with vegetables and basil.
The desserts and wine list still need some con-
templation, but the prices are now within reach

of normal human beings, and the sail is turned in the right direction. **C** 280-350. **M** 180.

 ## Le Muniche

7, rue St-Benoît - 01 42 61 12 70, fax 01 42 60 37 75
Open daily until 2am. Terrace dining. Air cond.
This sumptuous 1930s-style brasserie, in the past a favorite of numerous writers whose texts adorn the walls and today of the Rue de Seine gallery crowd, offers classic brasserie fare: choucroutes, thick slices of calf's liver à la meunière, and prime rib. **C** 250-300. **M** 99 (lunch), 149.

 ## L'O à la Bouche

157, bd du Montparnasse - 01 43 26 26 53
Closed Sun, Mon, Mar 16-23, 3 wks in Aug. Open until 11pm. Pkg.
This new hot spot sports a creative, thoroughly up-to-date bistro cuisine. Guy Savoy-trained chef Franck Paquier, formerly at La Butte Chaillot, whips up mouthwatering creations like a salad topped with crispy jumbo shrimp cooked in sesame seeds, tuna blackened with mild spices and served with thin rosemary wafers, and pike perch filet with lentils, marrow and red wine. Dishes sure of their intention, precise in their making, with service that matches. Wine by the jug or by the glass. **M** 95-130 (weekday lunch), 140, 180.

 ## Le Paris

Hôtel Lutétia, 45, bd Raspail
01 49 54 46 90, fax 01 49 54 46 00
Closed Sat, Sun, Jul 25-Aug 23. Open until 10pm. Air cond. Valet pkg.
Philippe Renard reigns in the kitchens of Le Paris, one of the best tables on the Left Bank. Rich, well-defined flavors distinguish his terrine of boiled beef and foie gras, turbot cooked in seaweed and sea salt, and rack of pork braised for 36 hours with truffles and leeks. Note the luscious chocolate desserts, and the excellent 260 F prix-fixe lunch. Youthful, prepossessing service which casts aside the often-met «deluxe hotel» attitude. The wine cellar is improving. **C** 400-500. **M** 190-260 (lunch), 360, 565.

12/20 Le Petit Zinc

11, rue St-Benoît - 01 42 61 20 60, fax 01 42 60 37 75
Open daily until 2am. Terrace dining. Air cond.
This picture-perfect little restaurant, with its Arts Déco awning and exquisite faience façade, boasts a good selection of fashionable dishes: young rabbit marbré with foie gras, roast duck with tangerines and pear-gingerbread millefeuille. Don't expect any surprises in the wine list, but the totally drinkable offerings won't empty your pockets. Wide selection of half-bottles. **C** 250-300. **M** 110 (weekday lunch), 168.

12/20 La Petite Cour

8, rue Mabillon - 01 43 26 52 26, fax 01 44 07 11 53

Open daily until 11pm, 11:30pm in summer. Terrace dining. Pkg.
A charming little courtyard—thus the name—brimming with flowers, a carpenter's workshop converted into a Napoleon III style restaurant, and the first-rate, professional welcome by the chef himself add up to a good little address. Chef Patrick Guyader obtains dashing results with an ever-changing menu that mirrors the best products he finds in the market every day: pan-fried cèpes and scrambled eggs with truffles when they are in season, yummy desserts. His Quincy and Reuilly wines are well worth trying. **C** 320-370. **M** 165 (lunch, wine incl), 178 (lunch), 198 (dinner).

11/20 Polidor

41, rue Monsieur-le-Prince - 01 43 26 95 34
Open Mon-Sat until 12:30am, Sun 11pm.
Familiar and soothing blanquettes, bourguignons, and rabbit in mustard sauce are served in a bistro-style dining room that time has barely touched in more than a century. **C** 130-200. **M** 100.

11/20 Le Procope

13, rue de l'Ancienne-Comédie
01 40 46 79 00, fax 01 40 46 79 09
Open daily until 1am. Terrace dining. Air cond.
The capital's oldest café, founded in 1686, restored to its original seventeenth-century splendor, may not be your best bet for a full meal. Tables of tourists feed on unexceptional brasserie fare (shellfish, coq au vin). **C** 250. **M** 109 (lunch), 123 (after 11pm), 178.

 ## Relais Louis XIII

8, rue des Grands-Augustins
01 43 26 75 96, fax 01 44 07 07 80
Closed Sun, Mon lunch, 3 wks in Aug. Open until 10:15pm. Air cond.
Louis XIII was proclaimed King of France in this luxurious tavern with its beams and polished paneling... And today chef Manuel Martinez from La Tour d'Argent is attempting to redefine what was in the past a generally heavy cuisine. We sometimes found he'd gone a little too far in the other direction with, for example, his minuscule portion of the best dish on the menu, the tarte au chocolat. Other dishes won't increase your waistline either: crab salad, faultless young turbot cooked in herbs, John Dory made glorious with splendid Tarbais beans, and carmelized cream with cream cheese and plump slices of mango. The crowd seems more interested in the Louis XIII décor and the urbanity of the reception than the amateurish hit-or-miss service. We can't fault the wine cellar, however, even though a few more half-bottles would balance it out. **C** 300-500.

Le Rond de Serviette ˙

97, rue du Cherche-Midi
01 45 44 01 02, fax 01 42 22 50 10
Closed Sat lunch, Sun, Aug 1-24. Open until 10:45pm. Air cond. Pkg.
The owners cosset their clients in a fresh, pretty setting with lively cuisine full of creativity and savors: marinated scallops on a bed of chopped mangoes and avocado, lobster fricassée with zucchini and basil, knuckle of ham pot-au-feu style with garlic mayonnaise, duckling in sesame seeds, and grapefruit soup with licorice and morello cherry sherbet. You get more than your money's worth with the 168 F fixed-price menu. M 138 (lunch), 168, 270 (wine incl).

 ## La Rôtisserie d'en Face

2, rue Christine - 01 43 26 40 98, fax 01 43 54 54 48
Closed Sat lunch, Sun. Open until 11pm, Sat 11:30pm. Air cond. Pkg.
Jacques Cagna's smart rôtisserie continues to attract Parisians hungry for rousing bistro food at reasonable prices. Sit down to taste duck pâté, Moroccan-style guinea hen with eggplant, and an iced caramel-walnut vacherin. Very nice welcome by Daniel and Olivier. The wine can shoot up the bill, so don't forget to look at the price before you order. M 135-159 (lunch), 210 (dinner).

 ## Yugaraj

14, rue Dauphine
01 43 26 44 91, fax 01 46 33 50 77
Closed Mon lunch. Open until 11pm. Air cond. Pkg.
The best Indian restaurant in the city, hands down. We love the refined surroundings, the smiles of the formally suited waiters, and—especially—the rare delicacies culled from every province of the subcontinent. Savor the cumin-spiced crab balls, tender lamb that is first roasted in a tandoori oven then sautéed with herbs, or cod suavely spiced with turmeric and fenugreek; the subtly harmonized flavors bloom on the palate. In addition, their selection of wines are perfectly suited to food. C 270-300. M 130 (lunch), 170, 220.

7th ARRONDISSEMENT

Zip code	75007

 ## L'Affriolé

17, rue Malar - 01 44 18 31 33
Closed Sat lunch, Sun, 3 wks in Aug. Open until 11pm. Air cond.
They've got it all together: Nicole Atibard's glowing smile when you walk in, the atmosphere, the prices, the market-inspired cooking. Chef Alain Atibard, only 35, has done enough time in the kitchens of the great (Troisgros,

Senderens, Cagna, and Faugeron among others) to understand what makes a restaurant work. His à la carte-style menu, at the reasonable price of 180 F, changes every week and never ceases to coffer up scintillating new dishes. A few examples: sardine tempura with soya béarnaise sauce, lobster chartreuse with grated vegetables and marjoram, guinea fowl and oyster fricassée, flank of beef with white-beets and cèpes, pound cake with candied fennel and chicory blossoms—imagination is not what is lacking. The same magic touch has been applied to the wine list. M 180.

 ## Apollon

24, rue Jean-Nicot - 01 45 55 68 47
Closed Sun (exc Mar-Sep). Open until 11pm. Terrace dining.
First-rate mezes (chopped olives with saffron, meatballs, brochettes) make this one of the city's top Greek eateries. Chummy service. C 200-250. M 79 (lunch, wine incl), 128 (dinner).

 ## Arpège

84, rue de Varenne
01 45 51 47 33, fax 01 44 18 98 39
Closed Sat, Sun lunch. Open until 10:30pm. Air cond.
Although he now sits at the top of the Mount Olympus of gastronomy, Alain Passard has not changed his down-to-earth manner. While some others invest time and money in marble floors and gold faucets, he devotes all his efforts to his twelve tables set in an almost spartan décor of wood and Lalique etched glass, overseen by a portrait of his ancestor. Some call the restaurant cold and stark, but Passard believes in no gimmicks, no tricks, no show off—in the dining room or in his cuisine. Subtle harmonies mark his splendid and delicate compositions, each the result of a reflection on the complementary flavors and textures of the ingredients. If «art cuisine» exists, this is it. Arpège (Arpeggio), a rapid succession of harmonious tones, best describes Passard's virtuosity: fresh spider-crab rémoulade in flat-claw crab-and-sorrel cream; luscious lump of sole stuffed with fresh herbs abed a peppery mussel juice; ultimate-quality lamb T-bone perfumed with tasty tomatoes and eggplant; delicious warm carmelized apricot millefeuille with almond milk sauce. Need we say more? Perhaps one reason Passard's cuisine is so far above the majority of others is because each dish is a reflection of the considerable thought he has put into it, as well as of his utmost respect for the eater. C 700-1,000. M 320 (weekday lunch), 690.

 ## Le Bamboche

15, rue de Babylone
01 45 49 14 40, fax 01 45 49 14 44
Closed Sat, Sun, 2 wks in Aug. Pkg.
David Van Laer seems to be on a roll: two years in business, one toque the first year, two toques

the second. A wee but wildly charming restaurant with Italian décor, tucked away behind the Bon Marché department store. The set-price menu would awaken anyone's curiosity, but the chef puts his real heart and soul into the more upscale à la carte offerings: the ultimate in Dublin bay prawns, served raw in a remoulade sauce and accompanied by a Parmesan pancake; escargot and frog leg fricassée with lentil cream; scallops and foie gras cooked in parchment paper and served with candied turnips, or farm-raised young guinea fowl with pear and fresh truffles (when in season). Named in our list of Grands de Demain 98 (great chefs of the future in 1998). C 350. M 190-320.

11/20 Le Basilic

2, rue Casimir-Périer - 01 44 18 94 64
Open daily until 10:30pm. Terrace dining.
Here's a pretty brasserie across from the stately church of Sainte-Clotilde, where you can count on a warm welcome and a good meal. We can vouch for the saddle of hare en compote, grilled steak with Roquefort, and the fruit gratins offered for dessert. Interesting cellar. C 190-355.

Au Bon Accueil

14, rue de Monttessuy - 01 47 05 46 11
Closed Sat lunch, Sun, Aug. Open until 10:30pm. Terrace dining.
Unbeatable value. Jacques Lacipière's 120 F market-fresh set menu might propose a hearty terrine of calf's foot and kidney, skate with Sherry butter, bœuf bourguignon, or creamy cherry chiboust. A la carte, look for beef fillet à la bordelaise or turbot in an herbal vinaigrette. Just as the sign says, you'll find a friendly welcome. Nice little cellar that we'd like to see expanded. C 250-300. M 120 (lunch), 135 (dinner).

Le Bourdonnais

113, av. de La Bourdonnais
01 47 05 16 54, fax 01 45 51 09 29
Closed Jan 1, May 1, Dec 24-25. Open until 11pm. Air cond. Pkg.
Owner Micheline Coat, a peach of a hostess, greets newcomers as warmly as the politicos and financiers who number among her faithful customers (on the rare occasions when Micheline is absent, however, the ambience is not quite so chic). New chef Jean-François Rouquette, only 31, has readily proven himself (and Micheline's good judgment in choosing her chefs). He demonstrates the mastery of technique he has learned from his mentors at the Crillon and Taillevent, among others, and adds to it his own distinctive touch, resulting in a more than admirable balance between the modern and the classic. Tempt your tastebuds with a delight of a crab in jelly with coral cream, a flawless parsleyed knuckle of veal and foie gras with a green bean salad, or a delectable marjoram-flavored John Dory braised in leeks and potatoes. At lunchtime the 240 F menu (it even includes wine) is a paragon of generosity. The

more expensive set meals also give you quality for your dining dollar, with lobster in brik pastry, spiced langoustines, rosemary-scented Lozère lamb, and a vanilla-berry feuillantine. C 400-500. M 240 (lunch, wine incl), 320, 420.

 ## Écaille et Plume

25, rue Duvivier - 01 45 55 06 72
Closed Sat lunch, Sun, 1 wk in Feb, mid Jul-Aug. Open until 11pm. Air cond.
Seasonal game specialties and seafood are Marie Naël's strong points: try the briny salade océane, shark roasted with lemon grass, hare à la royale or, in its short season, Scottish grouse flambéed with single-malt whisky. Theme menus that change regularly, but which are always an unforgettable celebration of savors and discoveries. The dining room is cozy, the Loire wines well chosen by Philippe Naël. C 260-340. M 180, 195.

11/20 La Fontaine de Mars

129, rue Saint-Dominique - 01 47 05 46 44
Closed Sun. Open until 11pm. Terrace dining. Air cond.
A smiling staff and tasty family-style cooking make this a popular spot. You'll surely relish the warm cèpe pâté, andouillette sausage laced with Chardonnay, or duck breast with cranberries. To drink, look no further than the Brouilly or Mâcon, amiably priced at 50 F a jug. C 180-250.

 ## Gaya Rive Gauche

44, rue du Bac - 01 45 44 73 73, fax 01 42 60 04 54
Closed Sun lunch, Aug. Open until 11pm. Air cond. Pkg.
The smart literary set of the Faubourg Saint-Germain quickly staked out their turf at this annex of the Goumard-Prunier seafood empire. They come here to savor ultrafresh fish in such unfussy preparations as a bracing tartare of tuna and John Dory, tiny deep-fried red mullet, and line-caught sea bass grilled with roasted tomatoes. Pleasant eating at the bar. C 280-320.

 ## Les Glénan

54, rue de Bourgogne - 01 45 51 61 09
Closed Sat, Sun, 1 wk in Feb, Aug. Open until 10pm. Air cond. Pkg.
Christine Guillard manages Les Glénan with energy and charm, while the kitchen is in the capable hands of Thierry Bourbonnais. His sensitive touch brings out all the delicate nuances of seafood and other seasonal ingredients. The 200 F set meal, which includes a half-bottle of Loire Valley wine, features creamy cumin-spiced tomato soup, grilled sea bream with smothered artichokes, and chocolate-swirled pear shortbread, all served in the quiet, intimate décor of a private apartment. C 350-380. M 200 (wine incl).

Looking for a celebrated chef? Refer to the index.

Nouveau Stylo Diabolo de Cartier
Plume or 18 carats* ouvragée à la main.
5 largeurs d'écriture.
Prix indicatif : 1490 F.

CASINO D'ENGHIEN
— PARIS —

"The Number One Table Casino in France"
The only Casino just 20 minutes from Paris
(Take highway A15, 1rst exit to Enghien)

Hôtel du Lac d'Enghien

Grand Hôtel d'Enghien

18 English Roulette, 18 Black-Jack, Chemin de Fer, Banque à Tout-va and Punto Banco

Accomodations on site
Open year round
GRAND HOTEL D'ENGHIEN****** - 47 rms - 670-940 F
Phone : (33) 01 39 34 10 00 - Fax : (33) 01 39 34 10 01
HOTEL DU LAC D'ENGHIEN***** - 109 rms - 550-780 F
Phone : (33) 01 39 34 11 00 - Fax : (33) 01 39 34 11 01
*

Casino opening hours :
Daily from 3 PM to 4 AM (7 days week)
Casino Entrance Fee : 80 - 130 F
ID card or Passport required
3, avenue de Ceinture - 95880 ENGHIEN LES BAINS - FRANCE
Phone (33) 01 39 34 13 00 - Fax : (33) 01 39 34 13 01

LUCIEN BARRIERE
Resorts, Hôtels & Casinos
Enghien

Jules Verne

Tour Eiffel, second floor
01 45 55 61 44, fax 01 47 05 29 41
Open daily until 10:30pm. Air cond. Pkg.
   Dining in this sophisticated room high atop the
Eiffel Tower is a treat in itself. Chef Alain Reix's
menu majors in seafood, but frankly, he has had
more creative periods. The dark disappointment
of the pressed crab and smoked salmon allied
with oysters in jelly was more in keeping with an
upscale deli creation than that of a respected
chef, and we were not convinced by the combination of baby cuttlefish and hot foie gras. The
dainty association of bass and artichokes in
Saint-Emilion sauce somewhat revived our faith
in this craftsman's talent, however. Certain offerings have a pleasing Alsatian accent, and the
desserts are delicious. Perfect service. The wine
cellar is a serious affair. C 650-800. M 290 (weekday lunch), 680 (dinner).

 Le Divellec

107, rue de l'Université
01 45 51 91 96, fax 01 45 51 31 75
*Closed Sun, Mon, Dec 24-Jan 1. Open until 10pm.
Air cond. Pkg.*
   We are still disappointed with Le Divellec,
which was in the past one of the great seafood
restaurants of Paris. The crew will have to steer
a simpler and (if possible) less costly course to
regain its past grandeur. Foie gras, truffles, and
caviar are all noble ingredients, but they are
oftimes capable of standing on their own with no
fuss, no complex combinations, no pretense. But
we have to give Le Divellec credit where it is
deserved: the dishes he managed to keep
simple—the langoustines cooked in white wine
and herbs, the scallops poached to perfection in
seaweed steam, as well as the oysters, sea urchins, clams and shellfish, proved that he still
has more tricks up his sleeve. Classic cellar, and
wine waiter Pierre Laroche will pamper you like
no other; well-bred welcome and service. C 700-
900. M 290-390 (lunch).

 **Maison
de l'Amérique Latine**

217, bd St-Germain
01 45 49 33 23, fax 01 40 49 03 94
*Closed Sat, Sun, hols, Aug 4-25. Open until
10:30pm. Terrace dining. Pkg.*
   Don't come here looking for churrasco or
feijoada—the chef is Japanese and his repertoire
is resolutely French (with a barely discernible
Eastern touch). Among the menu's highlights
are squab ravioli with shiitake aspic, pan-
roasted salmon with sesame seeds and bok choy,
and beef tournedos sparked with preserved
lemon. The garden is a delightful place to dine,
a haven of peace, weather permitting. C 350-370.
M 195-225 (lunch).

11/20 **Le Maupertu**

94, bd de Latour-Maubourg - 01 45 51 37 96

*Closed Sat lunch, Sun, 1 wk in Feb, 2 wks in Aug.
Open until 10pm.*
   Seasonal, market-fresh cooking figures on Le
Maupertu's unbeatable 135 F prix-fixe meal. Try
the lush millefeuille layered with shrimp and
crabmeat, the satisfying daube provençale, and
the bright-flavored orange and almond terrine.
Among the attractive selection of half-bottles in
the cellar, you'll find a tasty '93 Chinon from
Couly-Dutheuil. C 250. M 135.

 Paul Minchelli

54, bd Latour-Maubourg
01 47 05 89 86, fax 01 45 56 03 84
*Closed Sun, Mon, hols, Aug, end Dec-beg Jan. Open
until 10:30pm. Terrace dining. Air cond. Pkg.*
   Remember Paul Minchelli? He's the man who
«reinvented seafood», stripping away meretri-
cious sauces to reveal pure, virginal flavors. He
shipped out of Le Duc, the restaurant he ran with
his late brother, and fetched up here, in Art
Deco–style premises featuring Norwegian birch,
frosted glass, and a huge black bar with a few
stools for casual dining. Minchelli's minimalism
requires fish of optimal quality. He chooses sea
bass that is delectable even in its raw state, just
sliced and drizzled with olive oil, or briefly
steamed to reveal its briny essence. Depending
on what the tide brings in, he might offer lobster
(for example) in several different guises. In one
winning version, the crustacean is flavored with
a touch of honey and chili. Each dish is prepared
to order, so service can be painfully slow. Even
the bread is good! C 450-600.

 L'Œillade

10, rue Saint-Simon - 01 42 22 01 60
*Closed Sat lunch, Sun, last 2 wks of Aug. Open until
11pm. Air cond. Pkg.*
   A rustic atmosphere, but nonetheless air conditioned to keep the politicians and uppercrust
of the neighborhood cool and calm. The single-
price menu is reasonable enough, and the eggplant caviar, duck ballottine, and berry gratin
with Champagne sabayon are good offers for the
price. Coup de Cœur wines around 100 F. C
220-250. M 158.

 Les Olivades

41, av. de Ségur - 01 47 83 70 09
*Closed lunch Sat & Mon, Sun, Aug. Open until
10:30pm. Terrace dining. Air cond.*
   We thought the Paris scene had explored
Provençal cuisine from alpha to omega until
young Flora settled into her little niche behind
Unesco. Her crystal clear, straightforward way
of interpreting the Cuisine of the Sun pulls at
even the most skeptical of heart strings, even in
the fixed-price menu, where she proposes fava
bean soup with aïoli cream, cumin-flavored sardine fritters, sage-flecked lamb rennet, or pieds
et paquets à sa façon. Her boldest statements are
to be found in the à la carte selection: foie gras
and mushroom gnocchi with truffle oil and roast
young pigeon with tapenade and pine nuts. And

despite all this, if you wash it down with a Côtes-de-Provence or a Cairanne, the prices are palatable. **C** 240-300. **M** 125 (weekday lunch), 159, 210.

11/20 Le P'tit Troquet

28, rue de l'Exposition - 01 47 05 49 75
Closed Sun, Mon, 2 wks in Aug, 1 wk at Christmas. Open until 11pm. Pkg.
A real 1920s bistro complete with a collection of period objects. Unpretentious dishes using heartland ingredients such as lamb from Pauillac, woodland duck from the Vendée and scallops from Saint Brieuc. **C** 200-220. **M** 149.

Le Petit Laurent

38, rue de Varenne
01 45 48 79 64, fax 01 42 66 68 59
Closed Sat lunch, Sun, Aug. Open until 10:15pm. Pkg.
Sylvain Pommier turns out an impeccable warm scallop salad enriched with chive butter, terrine of sweetbreads and mushrooms dressed with herbed oil, sea bream roasted with mango and lime, guinea hen intriguingly perfumed with lemon grass, and a luscious apple and chocolate confection laced with Banyuls wine. Diligent service in a comfortable, Louis XVI-style setting. Reasonably priced wine, and the 185 F fixed-price menu is one of the better deals on the Left Bank. **C** 350-450. **M** 185, 250.

Le Récamier

4, rue Récamier - 01 45 48 86 58, fax 01 42 22 84 76
Closed Sun. Open until 10:30pm. Terrace dining. Air cond.
Martin Cantegrit, owner of this elegant establishment, oversees the service of Burgundian classics (jambon persillé, prime rib bourguignon, pike mousse with sauce Nantua) and a few lighter options (John Dory with an herbal emulsion). The clientele—politicians, publishers, media moguls—visibly enjoy tapping the magnificent 100,000-bottle cellar. In summer the comely terrace spills across a pedestrian zone for fume-free outdoor dining. Expect a hefty tab, even though it might not always be matched by quality. **C** 400-500.

12/20 Le 6 Bosquet

6, av Bosquet - 01 45 56 97 26
Closed Sat lunch, Sun, Aug 10-25, Dec 21-Jan 4. Terrace dining. Air cond.
A young couple from Dijon has converted the former (and rather depressing) Duquesnoy into a cheerful bistro serving Burgundy-inspired food. Their set meal formula adds a spark of modernity to the place, but the hefty helping of jambon persillé was not fresh and the coq au vin was served with overcooked pasta. The wines go light on the pocket, with good buys like the Côtes-du-Roussillon at 70 F. **M** 165.

Tan Dinh

60, rue de Verneuil
01 45 44 04 84, fax 01 45 44 36 93
Closed Sun, Aug. Open until 11pm. Pkg.
Tan Dinh's huge wine list has few equals, even among the city's top restaurants—some say it outclasses the food. But the Vifians are justly proud of their innovative Vietnamese menu, which spotlights light, refined dishes like smoked-goose dumplings, lobster toast, chicken with Asian herbs, and veal with betel nuts. If you resist the cellar's pricier temptations, a dinner here amid the stylish Left-Bank crowd needn't lead to financial disaster. **C** 300-400.

11/20 Thoumieux

79, rue St-Dominique - 01 47 05 49 75
Open daily until midnight. Air cond. Pkg.
Regional favorites from the rugged Corrèze region are Thoumieux's stock in trade: chestnut-studded boudin, milk-fed veal, and the rustic fruit flan known as flognarde. Lively atmosphere. **C** 150-250. **M** 170.

Vin sur Vin

20, rue de Monttessuy - 01 47 05 14 20
Closed Sun, lunch Sat & Mon, Aug 1-20, Dec 23-Jan 2. Open until 10pm. Air cond.
Former sommelier Patrice Vidal has assembled a first-rate cellar made up exclusively of growers' wines, from which he selects a few each week to sell by the glass. The quality of the food does not always live up to that of the wine, unfortunately, and prices are high with no prix-fixe relief in sight. It's difficult to find a wine that really suits the stuffed mussels, the foie gras pot-au-feu was pleasant but on the bland side, and we are not out-and-out fans of the farm-raised, honey-coated chine of pork. **C** 320-400.

Le Violon d'Ingres

135, rue St-Dominique - 01 45 55 15 05
Closed Sat, Sun, Aug. Open until 10:30pm. Air cond. Pkg.
Now at the helm of his own ship with no admiral watching over him, Christian Constant, who has left Les Ambassadeurs and set up his own restaurant, is more at ease with his flavorful cuisine, which he constantly refines and simplifies, leaving behind all pomp and circumstance. The ingredients are, as always, superb, and the cooking times are incredibly precise. The result is nearly perfect cuisine that is rustic yet refined. The prices are almost as low as those in an ordinary bistro: mussels and herbs en papillote are priced at only 70 F, and green pollack and chorizo and white-bean purée with aged vinegar at 85 F. His masterpiece, however, is his marvellous dish of pearly scallops roasted in the shell and topped with a pat of parsleyed, salted butter. The limited dessert menu (four simple choices, including rice pudding) deserves to be expanded, as does the wine list. The latter is certainly well chosen, however, and includes a true Bandol (1989, from Château Sainte-

Anne). In the end, quality counts more than quantity. **C** 250-350. **M** 240 (lunch), 290 (dinner).

8th ARRONDISSEMENT

Zip code	**75008**

12/20 Al Ajami

58, rue François-Ier
01 42 25 38 44, fax 01 42 56 60 08
Open daily until midnight. Terrace dining.
Fortunately the menu's perfunctory French offerings are outnumbered by authentic dishes from the Lebanese highlands—assorted mezes, chawarma, keftedes, and sticky pastries. Vegetarians will find a dish specially conceived for them, containing nine different kinds of Lebanese hors d'œuvres. The wines lend a dash of local color to the refined, yellow-and-blue dining room. **C** 220-270. **M** 89 (weekday lunch), 99-140.

Les Ambassadeurs

Hôtel de Crillon, 10, pl. de la Concorde
01 44 71 16 16, fax 01 44 71 15 02
Open daily until 10:30pm. Terrace dining. Air cond. Pkg.
A year and a half after his arrival, Dominique Bouchet—who left La Tour d'Argent in 1988 with an 18/20 rating-—has certainly found his marks at Les Ambassadeurs, one of the most beautiful restaurants in the City of Lights. Laurent Vanhoegaerden, the ultra-efficient restaurant manager, conducts you to one of twenty well-spread tables in this majestic eighteenth-century landmark dining room with its 25-foot ceilings, where you sample a classic, noble cuisine without any frills, a cuisine that proves that marriages between the luxurious and the simple can really work. Green-asparagus Bavarian cream and smoked salmon, suckling pig crisp, pigeon roasted in cabbage leaves, steamed bass: these are just a few choices, where potatoes make happy and morganitic marriages with lobster and caviar. Bouchet is backed up by Christophe Felder, a talented Alsatian pastry chef who is a real expert at preparing light ethereal desserts. The cellar is lined with gold, and the prices are reflective. The service is, of course, perfect. **C** 750. **M** 340 (lunch), 620 (dinner).

11/20 Aux Amis du Beaujolais

28, rue d'Artois - 01 45 63 92 21
Closed Sat dinner, Sun, wk of Aug 15, end Dec-beg Jan. Open until 9pm.
Vigorous French bistro cooking (the menu changes daily) and tasty Beaujolais. Full plates, friendly prices. **C** 150-210.

Androuët

6, rue Arsène-Houssaye - 01 42 89 95 00
Closed Sat lunch, Sun. Open until 11pm. Air cond.
This institution of long repute, known worldwide for its cheese, finally got a face-lift. But though the look has changed in the new lemon-yellow boutique-restaurant with its dignified white tablecloths and pleasing flower arrangements in this more upscale neighborhood near the Champs-Élysées, the theme is the same: cheese, cheese, and just a little more cheese. In all its forms, in all its colors, in all its glory, from the mildest to the sharpest. Some examples: pike perch and sauerkraut with Munster cheese; «epigram» of monkfish with Sainte-Maure cheese; lobster fricassée with Roquefort; lamb noisettes with Saint-Marcellin cheese, or extra-thin pear and Roquefort pie. Good assortment of salads and country breads. **C** 250-350. **M** 175 (lunch), 230-250 (dinner).

12/20 L'Appart'

9, rue du Colisée - 01 53 75 16 34, fax 01 53 76 15 39
Open daily until midnight. Air cond. Pkg.
Decked out to look like a private home—living room, dining room, library—L'Appart' is not just an amusing scene, it's also a pretty good restaurant. You'll enjoy the cheese ravioli, pan-roasted cod with meat juices, and French toast with caramel sauce. **Brunch** is served on Sundays. **C** 180-250. **M** 100 (weekday lunch), 175 (weekday lunch, wine incl), 175 (dinner).

Astor

Astor Westin Demeure Hotel,
11, rue Astorg
01 53 05 05 20, fax 01 53 05 05 30
Closed Sat, Sun. Open until 10pm. Air cond. Pkg.
The restaurant of the Astor Westin Demeure Hotel, with its surprising 1940s décor and Directoire chairs, is under the supervision of none other than Joël Robuchon. He's put one of his star pupils, Éric Lecerf (a two-toque winner in his previous post), in charge of the kitchen, and the disciple is clearly demonstrating that even though he closely follows the master's footsteps, he is now capable of coming into his own. Die-hard Robuchon fans can still partake of the dishes that lent him his renown—cauliflower cream with caviar jelly or spit-roasted Bresse chicken with black truffle macaroni (if you're willing to pay the price of 495 F), but don't hesitate to try the disciple's inventions. You'll find Robuchon-inspired dishes like spider crab in anise jelly with fennel cream and calf's sweetbreads with Parmesan shavings, as well as ideas he's picked up here and there, such as the Pyrenees-inspired sole with baby calamaries and artichokes or the Castillian milk-fed leg of lamb with slowly simmered vegetables. Brilliant wine list with wide choice of half-bottles and regional wines. Service in grand style in a dining room managed by the discerning and gracious Antoine Hernandez, formerly Robuchon's head sommelier. **C** 290-420. **M** 290 (lunch, wine incl).

L'Avenue

41, av. Montaigne - 01 40 70 14 91
Open daily until midnight. Terrace dining. Air cond. Pkg.
If you book a table in the elegant upstairs dining room with its 1950s décor, you can mingle with the chic couture and media crowd that flocks into L'Avenue for such stylish specialties as risotto d'escargots au pistou, spiced scampi fricassée, and lemony veal piccata. Shellfish assortments and a good club sandwich are also on hand, but most noteworthy is the desserts. Wines chosen by the excellent Taillevent winesellers. Considering the classy location in the heart of the Golden Triangle, prices are downright reasonable. C 250-350. M 175 (dinner).

Chic Champs

The cars that long encumbered the **Champs-Élysées** have now been banished to underground lots, and the recaptured space turned into a walkway shaded by hundreds of newly planted plane trees.
Sleek benches and sculptural stoplights designed by Jean-Michel Wilmotte (his credentials include furnishings for the Louvre and the Élysée Palace) also enhance the Champs' refurbished image. And everyone agrees that the new sidewalks, with their subtle tones of gray, are the summum of elegance. There's just one problem: it's nearly impossible to remove chewing gum from the expensive granite paving stones!

11/20 Ma Bourgogne

133, bd Haussmann - 01 45 63 50 61
Closed Sat, Sun, Jul. Open until 10pm. Air cond.
Wine lovers will find a whole gamut of dishes inspired by their favorite crus: the classic œufs en meurette, as well as other more original dishes like monkfish purée in Pouilly wine sauce, coq au Chenas, and Sauternes-based fruit soup. Good selection of Beaujolais and Burgundies that let you stay within your budget. C 260-320. M 165 (lunch), 190 (dinner).

12/20 Le Bistrot de Marius

6, av George-V - 01 40 70 11 76
Open daily until midnight. Terrace dining. Pkg.
If you can't face the prices of the main establishment Marius et Janette, try their bistro right

next door. The chalkboard announces the daily specials, which change with the tides of availability: steamed shrimp, sea bass marinated in olive oil, red mullet a la plancha or sea bream cooked in a thick crust of coarse salt were some of the recent offerings. C 200-250.

Le Bistrot du Sommelier

97, bd Haussmann
01 42 65 24 85, fax 01 53 75 23 23
Closed Sat, Sun, Jul 3-28. Open until 11pm. Air cond. Pkg.
Chef Jean-Michel Descloux invents dishes that keep the wine ever in mind: red mullet marinated in Tandoori spices, young rabbit and Vermouth jelly with fig jam, back of hake with fondue d'épinards, shallot chutney and orange butter, or duck braised in juniper berries and served with wine-flavored pear purée. But it's the cellar that captures the wine buff's interest, with over 900 bottles from all over France—and the world. A special prix-fixe dinner brings six courses paired with compatible wines. C 350-400. M 390 (dinner, wine incl).

Le Bœuf sur le Toit

34, rue du Colisée - 01 43 59 83 80, fax 01 45 63 45 40
Open daily until 2am. Air cond. Pkg.
From a seat on the mezzanine, watch the dazzling swirl of diners and waiters reflected a hundredfold in this mirrored, Art Deco dining room. But don't get so distracted that you can't enjoy classics such as the plentiful shellfish platters, juicy steaks, or choucroutes de poissons, or more surprising fare such as the giant-shrimp ravioli, vegetable anchoïde, or blinis with fennel and berries. The 128 F *Faim de Nuit* menu offers one of the more reasonably priced late-night meals in town. C 200-300. M 123 (weekday lunch), 169 (dinner, wine incl), 128 (dinner, after 10pm, wine incl).

12/20 Boucoléon

10, rue de Constantinople - 01 42 93 73 33
Closed Sat lunch, Sun, 3 wks in Aug, end Dec-beg Jan. Open until 10:30pm. Terrace dining.
An address where value goes hand-in-hand with lively, inventive cooking. Here in a quiet district near Place de l'Europe you'll dine happily on ravigote de joue de bœuf (ox jowls in a tangy sauce), lamb sauté showered with juniper-spiced breadcrumbs, and crème brûlée brightened with mango and passion fruit. Tempting wines featured every month at around 60 F. Smiling reception in what is otherwise a rather stark décor. C 210-250. M 95 (weekdays), 158.

Le Bristol

Hôtel Le Bristol,
112, rue du Fg-Saint-Honoré
01 53 43 43 40, fax 01 53 43 43 01
Open daily until 10:30pm. Terrace dining. Air cond. Pkg.

The Bristol redefined hotel cuisine few years ago, but had recently slipped downhill. With the arrival of culinary troubadour Michel del Burgo, fresh from his three-toque restaurant in Carcassonne, they seem to be racing back uphill. He cooks up a lyrical menu whose inspiration lies where the ultimate quality in products is to be found: duck foie gras from the Landes, langoustines from Loctudy, milk-fed lamb from the Pyrenees. In this high fashion neighborhood, del Burgo skillfully weaves a superbly fine petit point of subtle flavors: «crushed» cauliflower with ewe's cottage cheese and caviar cream for the langoustines, squid ink risotto and pressed-head juice au piquillo for the Breton lobster, stuffed candied tomatoes and braised cèpes in meat juice for the suckling pig stewed with truffled pork rind sausages. The desserts stay in the same realm of wonder—super-thin layers of caramel with coconut whipped cream or poached pineapple with aged-rum syrup and mango nectar—but simplicity might do a power of good. C 600-900. M 360-600.

 ## Café Terminus

Hôtel Concorde Saint-Lazare, 108, rue St-Lazare
01 40 08 44 44
Open daily until 10:30pm. Air cond. Pkg.
A bar/bistro/restaurant in the huge and luxurious Concorde Saint-Lazare hotel where you dine among the velvet and wainscot of Sonia Rykiel's 1900 brasserie-style décor. New chef Guy Pommelet has conjured up a rather unusual «formula» that seems to have taken off. He changes his regional- and foreign-inspired menu once a month, offering delights such as the green-asparagus cake with quail's eggs and parmesan or a juicy tender «Michelangelo» veal chop served with an olive-stuffed tomato. Effective, very attentive service. C 250-400. M 148, 198 (wine incl).

 ## Cap Vernet

82, av. Marceau - 01 47 20 20 40, fax 01 47 20 95 36
Open daily until midnight. Terrace dining. Air cond.
A kitchen crew trained by Guy Savoy runs this show, producing a fresh, flavorful menu that features a zingy dish of sole with lemon and capers and a rack of lamb en petite marmite escorted by Noirmoutier potatoes and tender carrots. Don't overlook the oyster and raw shellfish bar. The wine list is abound with interesting finds and the service surpasses up to par. An address full of life and novel ideas: stop in for the oyster market on Saturdays, or introduce your children to fine French cuisine with the unique tasting menu designed just for children on Sundays. C 240-280. M 200 (lunch, wine incl).

 ## Cercle Ledoyen

Carré des Champs-Élysées
01 53 05 10 02, fax 01 47 42 55 01
Closed Sun. Open until 11:30pm. Air cond. Terrace dining. Pkg.

Jacques Grange is the man behind the elegantly spare interior of this spacious restaurant, a favorite haunt of the city's chic and famous. Jean-Paul Arabian oversees the impeccable service, while Ghislaine Arabian does the same for the menu, which changes practically every day. Zesty starters like a gently poached egg in a sea-urchin shell or finnan-haddie terrine with lentils segue into rabbit en pot-au-feu, sea bass with celery root, or old-fashioned blanquette de veau. Unique pricing system: all hors d'œuvres at 60 F, all main dishes at 110 F, and all desserts at 50 F. Irrigated by modest but tasty little wines, all under 200 F, they add up to perfectly modern meals at a perfectly moderate price. C 280-320.

 ## Chiberta

3, rue Arsène Houssaye
01 45 63 77 90, fax 01 45 62 85 08
Closed Sat, Sun, Aug. Open until 10:30pm. Air cond. Pkg.
Louis-Noël Richard, the soul of this elegant restaurant, passed away. But as he himself would have been the first to say, «The show must go on». The new chef, Éric Croisel, offers a seductive menu waivering between the classic and the height of modernity: exquisite scallops with sea urchins, hot smoked bass lightly cooked with half-cooked, half-raw tomatoes, delight of a Breton lobster cooked in Sauternes, the tenderest of Pyrenees milk-fed lamb with anise-flavored Béarnaise sauce, and chilled grapefruit soup accented with lemon grass. Some rare finds on the more-than-noble wine list. Perfect welcome. C 450-520. M 290.

 ## Le Clovis

Hôtel Sofitel Arc de Triomphe, 4, av. Bertie-Albrecht
01 53 89 50 53, fax 01 53 89 50 51
Closed Sat, Sun, Aug, Dec 23-Jan 2, hols. Open until 10:30pm. Air cond.
The brand new très chic décor in all its abundant luxury is a cut above the cooking this year. Maybe we showed up too early after the post-renovation reopening, because disappointment loomed heavy, first with the over-dominating lemon cream sauce on our faultlessly cooked red porgy filet and then with the tuna tartare, completely overwhelmed by spices. All was not lost, however: the kouing-aman with caramelized apples, rich and buttery, was a pure triumph. Extensive cellar; attentive service. C 400-465. M 195, 235.

 ## Le Copenhague

142, av. des Champs-Élysées
01 44 13 86 26, fax 01 42 25 83 10
Closed Sat lunch, Sun, 1st wk of Jan, Aug, hols. Open until 10:30pm. Terrace dining. Air cond. Pkg.
This Danish enclave is perhaps the last high-class restaurant on the Champs-Élysées, the last to survive the onslaught of hamburger chains, pizzerias, and other fast-food eateries. In the muted atmosphere of the upstairs dining room, salmon is featured in myriad guises, of course,

but there is also smoked eel paired with creamy scrambled eggs, duck à la danoise, and spiced reindeer fillet. And there's plenty of Danish aquavit to wash it all down (but watch the tab!). Elegant but impersonal service. C 400-450. M 250 (wine incl), 280.

La Couronne

Hôtel Warwick, 5, rue de Berri
01 45 63 78 49, fax 01 45 59 00 98
Closed Sat lunch, Sun, Aug, hols. Open until 10:30pm. Air cond. Valet pkg.
La Couronne got new decoration last year. This year, it's the chef who is «renovating» things. He is exploring new territories and working up a new image for his cuisine. This all came too close to press time so we didn't have time to sample them. We will keep you posted! C 350-500. M 260 (wine incl).

11/20 Drugstore des Champs-Élysées

133, av. des Champs-Élysées - 01 44 43 79 00
Open daily until 2am. Terrace dining. Air cond.
Believe it or not, the food at this landmark of 1960s chic is not bad at all. The stayed main-course salads, grills, and crisp pommes frites go very well with the noisy, bustling atmosphere, and there even a few ventures toward finer cooking: cod steak with coriander-perfummed tomato, Limousin leg of lamb and curried pork ribs. Grands crus wines by the glass, ranging from 24 to 36 F. C 160-220.

Chez Edgard

4, rue Marbeuf - 01 47 20 51 15, fax 01 47 23 94 29
Closed Sun. Open until 11:30am. Terrace dining.
Just because the *gratin* of French politics eats here, don't expect to see Jacques Chirac or Alain Juppé seated across from you. «Monsieur Paul» serves up to 500 meals here each day, and in any case the Parisian powers-that-be are always whisked off to the quiet private rooms upstairs. Downstairs, amid the typically Gallic brouhaha, the rest of us can choose from a wide range of good grilled meats and hearty cuisine bourgeoise, prepared with care and skill, even though the prices are on the high side if you steer from the 195 set-price menu, which includes coffee. C 280-420. M 195, 250-355 (wine incl).

Les Élysées du Vernet

Hôtel Vernet, 25, rue Vernet
01 44 31 98 98, fax 01 44 31 85 69
Closed Sat, Sun, Jul 28-Aug 22, Dec 22-26, hols. Open until 10pm. Air cond. Pkg.
Which way to the Riviera, please? We'd suggest this elegant address just off the Champs-Élysées. Although you won't have a view of the Mediterranean, chef Alain Solivérès brings the perfumes and savors of Provence into the Vernet's glass-roofed dining room designed by the great Gustave Eiffel himself. His salt cod with roasted tomatoes, mesclun, and anchoïade

beneath a paper-thin chickpea galette is an eloquent dialogue of Southern flavors. Lately the menu has also made incursions into the Southwest, paying homage to that region's fabulous duck, Chalosse beef, and Pyrenees lamb. Desserts? They're exciting indeed: consider the lemon-bergamot soufflé flanked by quince marmalade, ewe's-milk ice cream, and Szechwan pepper—a clever and delicious conceit. Alain Moser leads the way to impeccable service. The meritorious cellar offers a wealth of wines from Provence, such as the excellent Rondine '92. C 450-650. M 340 (lunch), 390-530 (dinner).

Fakhr el Dine

3, rue Quentin-Bauchart
01 47 23 44 42, fax 01 47 27 11 39
Open daily until 11:30am. Air cond. Pkg.
Delicious Lebanese *mezes* dazzle the eye as they delight the palate: bone-marrow salad, brains in lemon sauce, spinach fritters, fried lamb's sweetbreads, etc. These tidbits are offered in batches of 8, 10, 15, or 20, depending on the size of the company and your appetite. Extra-attentive service (sometimes almost too much) and wonderful welcome; priced accordingly. C 290. M 150-340.

12/20 Finzi

182, bd Haussmann - 01 45 62 88 68
Closed Sun lunch. Open until 11:30pm. Terrace dining. Air cond.
The white-collar crowd that spills out of neighboring offices gladly risks spotting their ties with Finzi's good pasta sauces. Look for lusty Italian hams and salamis, too, and apricot ravioli with custard sauce for dessert. Good wine list. C 220-340.

Flora Danica

142, av. des Champs-Élysées
01 44 13 86 26, fax 01 42 25 83 10
Closed May 1, Dec 24 dinner. Open until 11pm. Terrace dining. Air cond. Pkg.
Salmon—smoked, pickled, marinated, or grilled—and delicious tender herring prepared in every imaginable way are the stars of this once-limited menu which has been lengthened this year with the addition of goodies such as lentil cream with smoked reindeer, cod cooked in spices and celery, and salmon à l'unilatérale, all to be washed down with a Carlsberg or a Cérès on tap. Upstairs at Le Copenhague, more elaborate (and costly) dishes are served (there's an interesting terrine of foie gras and reindeer). If the weather is fine, ask to be seated on the patio behind the Flora Danica. C 300-350. M 170-270.

Fouquet's

99, av. des Champs-Élysées
01 47 23 70 60, fax 01 47 20 08 69
Open daily until 1am. Terrace dining. Pkg.
After a bout of bad publicity, Fouquet's is poised for a fresh departure. This listed

landmark on the Champs-Élysées has acquired the services of Bernard Leprince, formerly at the Ritz and La Tour d'Argent. The fare remains classic brasserie fare, but the quality is moving upwards. We found the green asparagus with its ultra-light mousseline perfection itself; the braised veal sweetbreads and the milk-fed veal chop au jus were equally high on our list. The prices don't match those of the 1899 chauffeurs' eating-house, which has grown up into one of the most deluxe of addresses on the most beautiful avenue in the world. Impeccable service, something that has disappeared on the the Champs. Here's wishing them luck... C 350-450. M 265-450.

 Pierre Gagnaire

Hôtel Balzac, 6, rue Balzac
01 44 35 18 25, fax 01 44 35 18 37
Closed Sat, Sun lunch, 1 wk in Feb, 1 wk in Apr, mid Jul-mid Aug. Open until 11pm. Air cond. Pkg.
The memories of Pierre Gagnaire's harrowing voyage in Saint-Étienne are slowly slipping into oblivion in this chic address off the Champs-Élysées where he chose to resurface two years ago. The former premises of Bice, in the Hôtel Balzac, redone by Michèle Halard in a (to our taste) cold postmodern style with severe blue and gray tones, already has to turn people away. Proof that Gagnaire is a sailor-survivor who knows how to learn from his mistakes and gently float back to the top. The great chef himself admits that the whole experience forced him to work in a more structured manner, but don't worry, the strokes of genius are still there! In fact, it is as if the wisdom of the classic and the wild unexpected pulsations of creative energy for which Gagnaire is so well known have joined hands to form a harmonious balance, giving us two very different perspectives of this most imaginative of imaginative chefs. There are now two distinct parts to his menu: one part offers the fruits of «wisdom», and is classically inspired and theme-oriented, for example, built around eggplant, frog legs, lobster, lamb, squab, duck, etc., the other, the Pierre Gagnaire *menu dégustation* («tasting» menu), gives free rein to his almost limitless imagination. You'll find on it the most unexpected of combinations: tomato «crumpled» with lemon grass served with spider crab cream sauce and fresh almonds; creamed char fish with «heart of beef» cabbage served with a mushroom bouillon flavored with a slighly anise-flavored coffee; poached rock snapper with salted butter with its companion half-cooked rock lobster and red tuna tart flavored with sea fennel; lightly seared pigeon breast with wild rabbit mousse spiced with berberi, a mixture of Eritrea spices. On a more conventional note, you'll find, for example, a chicken-oyster, kidney, cockscomb and lamb sweetbread ragout crowned with grilled foie gras, which will wipe away any doubts one might have had about the gaps in Gagnaire's traditional culinary training. The parade of dishes goes on, and people react to these surprising mélanges one way or another. Do not expect

the desserts to reach new heights—although they wander off the beaten path, they do not match the grandeur of the main dishes. The succinct, well chosen wine list will help you make a quick choice. The refined and unusual experience of dining here is topped off by accommodating, quick and efficient service. For this stellar culinary voyage, be prepared to pay astronomical prices. A lunchtime plat à la carte (230-280 F) at the bar is a more affordable option and does not require a reservation. C 700-1,000. M 480 (lunch), 560 (dinner), 860.

 Le Grenadin

44-46, rue de Naples
01 45 63 28 92, fax 01 45 61 24 76
Closed Sat lunch, Sun, 1 wk in Jul, 1 wk in Aug. Open until 10:30pm. Terrace dining. Air cond. Pkg.
Pungent herbs and bold harmonies are the hallmarks of Patrick Cirotte's repertoire. His affinity for keen, acidulous flavors shows up in the delicious oysters with alfalfa sprouts and lemony cream sauce, and in a pork tenderloin served with quince compote. But he can also strike a suave note, as in the saddle of rabbit cloaked in a mild, creamy garlic sauce. Desserts don't get short shrift either: the ethereal vanilla millefeuille-minute, wine granità, or spiced fruit croûte tempt even flagging appetites. Mireille Cirotte offers reliable advice on wine (note that Sancerres are the pride of her cellar). C 400-450. M 298-330.

 Le Jardin

Hôtel Royal Monceau, 35, av. Hoche
01 42 99 98 70, fax 01 42 99 89 94
Closed Sat, Sun. Open until 10:30pm. Garden dining. Air cond. Pkg.
You step into another world when you enter the candy-pink dining room, its French windows opening onto manicured lawns and flower beds: a garden that seems to have been brought to Paris by the wave of a magic wand. The same spell holds in the kitchen, where Bruno Cirino conjures up a modern, exquisitely delicate menu with a gracious Provençal lilt. Why not order his spider crab in pistou broth—a marvel of subtlety; follow it with sautéed sole escorted by a superb chard gratin, then indulge in the richness of a banana roasted in its skin, laced with amber rum, and flanked by lush Malaga raisin ice cream. Service is impeccable, and a youthful sommelier provides sound advice on a wine list studded with rarities, such as his Côtes-du-Roussillon '91 from Château de Casenove, which could rival a Côte-Rotie. C 500-800. M 290, 350.

Lasserre

17, av. Franklin-D.-Roosevelt
01 43 59 53 43, fax 01 45 63 72 23
Closed Sun, Mon lunch, Aug. Open until 10:30pm. Terrace dining. Air cond. Pkg.
One of the few surviving examples of *le grand restaurant à la française*, Lasserre merits our attention for the ethnological interest it presents.

Nowhere else is the service so minutely choreographed, the atmosphere so well-bred (piano music, soft lights, glowing silver, etc.). But unfortunately the kitchen does not live up to the elegant splendor of these dining rooms once frequented by the likes of Malraux and Dalí and today by the highest of dignitaries, and renders a cuisine that has a few bright moments, but is generally lacking soul. Don't forget to look up as Lasserre's retractable roof brings (weather and visibility permitting) the stars down to you. May the resurrection draw near. C 700-1,000.

Laurent

41, av. Gabriel
01 42 25 00 39, fax 01 45 62 45 21
Closed Sat lunch, Sun, hols. Open until 11pm. Terrace dining. Pkg.
The ever-smiling waiters and the *carte* reflect a sunny trend, with light dishes and sprightly sauces. Philippe Braun executes a menu designed by his mentor, Joël Robuchon, which includes fresh anchovies on a bed of fresh-tasting vegetable brunoise, duck liver set atop black beans fired up with hot chilis, and a superb veal chop set off by tender hearts of lettuce in a savory jus. Now, you may have to sell off a few T-bonds to pay the bill—or else you can do as many of the other high-powered patrons do, and order the excellent prix-fixe menu (available at both lunch and dinner), which in fact includes most of the à la carte selections. Whatever course you choose, sommelier Patrick Lair will advise you on the appropriate wine from his comprehensive wine list. C 800-1,000. M 390.

Ledoyen

Carré des Champs-Élysées
01 53 05 10 01, fax 01 47 42 55 01
Closed Sat, Sun, Aug. Open until 10:30pm. Air cond. Pkg.
Lille's Ghislaine Arabian has made her mark at the luxurious and oh-so-Parisian Ledoyen. After teaching locals to love Flemish flavors—sauces laced with beer and gin, smoked mussels, gingerbread, and pungent Northern cheeses— she is working wonders outside of her regional register. Thus, while signature dishes like Zeeland oysters with smoked ham and buttermilk, smoked sprats on a potato galette, turbot roasted in beer, or potjevleish (a meaty Flemish terrine) with rhubarb chutney hold their own on the menu, she balances them with, for example, lightly salt-cured salmon poached in milk and served with sorrel hollandaise or roasted sweetbreads marinated with smoked garlic and flanked by melting endives. Such marvels have their price, of course, but we say they're worth it! C 600-900. M 290 (lunch), 520, 590.

Lucas Carton

9, pl. de la Madeleine
01 42 65 22 90, fax 01 42 65 06 23
Closed Sat lunch, Sun, 3 wks in Aug. Open until 10:30pm. Air cond. Pkg.

In a magnificent Belle Époque dining room warmed by mellow woodwork, Alain Senderens and his new chef, Frédéric Robert, propose a clever blend of Senderens's most celebrated creations—canard Apicius, foie gras de canard steamed in a cabbage leaf, red-mullet fillets with olives, lemon, and capers—and a (very) few recent inventions. Outstanding among the latter are the pan-roast of frogs' legs and asparagus paired with hot gingered crab and cooling hollandaise sauce; sea bream with thyme-scented potatoes and cuttlefish ravioli; and crisp-crusted veal sweetbreads with crayfish and popcorn. Every recipe is intelligently composed and the execution is invariably faultless. Inspired desserts; legendary cellar with a few nice prices. C 900-1,400. M 395 (weekday lunch).

La Luna

69, rue du Rocher - 01 42 93 77 61, fax 01 40 08 02 44
Closed Sun. Open until 11pm. Air cond.
The tides deposit first-quality fish at La Luna's door, and chef Christian Rocher's modern approach to seafood (brief cooking times, light sauces) enhances its natural flavors. The menu changes from day to day, but you could start out with an ultrafresh carpaccio of sea bream and red mullet, then go on to pan-roasted baby monkfish sparked with lemon, or skate with a lively sauce gribiche. The Zanzibar rum cake is a must for dessert. Summary wine list, though the choices are good. The sparkling Vouvray from Huet for only 94 F washes it all down pleasantly. Charming reception. C 350-400.

12/20 La Maison d'Alsace

39, av. des Champs-Élysées
01 53 93 97 00, fax 01 53 93 97 09
Open daily 24 hours. Terrace dining. Air cond. Pkg.
Since this lively brasserie never closes, any time's a good time for delicious sauerkraut and good Alsatian pork products. Steer away from the not-always-fresh seafood and mediocre Alsatian wines. Expect a hospitable welcome, whatever the hour. C 250-400. M 123 (dinner), 178.

Maison Blanche

15, av. Montaigne
01 47 23 55 99, fax 01 47 20 09 56
Closed Sat lunch, Sun, Aug. Open until 11pm. Terrace dining. Air cond. Pkg.
Here atop the Théâtre des Champs-Élysées, diners look out on the glittering dome of the Invalides, the shimmering Seine, and the handsome buildings that line the quais. In contrast, the dining room sports a spare, vaguely Californian look, one of the most refined in Paris. Bustling service; classic, irreproachable cellar. So far so good, you say, but how about the food? Could we truly expect to be enraptured by chef José Martinez's caramel pork with corn, just one step up from good Tex Mex, especially when you consider the price of 160 F? Even the scallop croque à la ventrèche garnished with candied

quince crisps spiked with sweet potatoes, though of a respectable quality, cannot save his second toque. C 500-650.

 ## Le Marcande

52, rue de Miromesnil
01 42 65 19 14, fax 01 40 76 03 27
Closed Sat, Sun, Aug. Open until 10pm. Pkg.
The well-spaced tables in an elegant setting punctuated by paintings and the good 240 F set menu and revamped *carte* attract discriminating diners. Joël Verron uses top-notch ingredients to turn out tempting treats such as his delectable foie gras and lobster motley, succulent Salers beef filet, and dainty monkfish skewers. Disappointment loomed in other domains, however: the desserts are simply not up to par, and the wine list lacks any note of daring. On nice days, reserve a table near the fountain on the flowery patio and linger long under the arbor. C 350-450. M 240.

 ## La Marée

1, rue Daru - 01 43 80 20 00, fax 01 48 88 04 04
Closed Sat lunch, Sun, Aug. Open until 10:30pm. Air cond. Pkg.
La Marée has finally dropped its old skin: a newly wainscotted dining room decked out with oversize Flemish paintings and a cuisine brimming with new life. Seafood (still) naturally rates top billing at La Marée, a restaurant named for the tide, but the entirely traditional fare of the past has given way to glimpses of modern. Cast your eye down the long menu for classics such as the Belon oysters cooked in Champagne or the rare and divine Colchester flat oysters, or for modern fare such as the bass, John Dory and red mullet tartare, the lemon- and ginger-tinged lobster cassoulet, or the Einkorn with its succulent slice of turbot, simply grilled and served with olive oil. The best of Burgundy and the best of Bordeaux are to be found in the gentleman's club atmosphere with its gentlemanly welcome by Éric Trompier and its old-world, pleasantly abetting service. C 550-600. M 270 (from 6:45pm to 8:15pm).

 ## Marius et Janette

4, av. George-V
01 47 23 41 88, fax 01 47 23 07 19
Open daily until 11:30pm. Terrace dining. Air cond. Pkg.
Not even a fire could destroy the unsinkable Marius et Jeannette, now shipshape again and back afloat with a seaworthy décor of glowing wood and polished brass. A cosmopolitan crowd watches approvingly as waiters flambé fennel-flavored sea bass (270 F per person) and deliver pricey portions of grilled lobster (480 F). Still, ingredients are of pristine quality (note the exquisitely fresh seafood salad), and not every item is stratospherically priced. To drink, try a wine from Bandol or Cassis. *Les beaux jours* on the terrace make you think you're in Monte Carlo. C 450-550. M 300 (wine incl).

 ## Maxim's

3, rue Royale - 01 42 65 27 94, fax 01 40 17 02 91
Closed Sun off-seas, Sun & Mon in Jul-Aug. Open until 10:30pm. Air cond. Pkg.
Pierre Cardin, owner of Maxim's since 1981, decided that he'd served his last plateful of homard à l'américaine and other such culinary chestnuts. He hired Michel Kerever, a respected ex-three-toque Breton chef, to rejuvenate what had become a rather fusty menu. The dining room, thank goodness, is as glorious as ever: Czar Nicholas, the Duke and Duchess of Windsor, Maria Callas and the other legendary denizens of Maxim's in its heyday would surely feel right at home. Kerever's light, exciting menu features rabbit roasted with rosemary and Noirmoutier potatoes, a pan roast of fresh morels and asparagus, and sole on a bed of artichokes, onions, and leeks. Expect to pay a hefty sum, however, to sup in these historic surroundings. Even the cellar's more modest wines are awfully expensive. C 800-1,000.

 ## L'Obélisque

Hôtel de Crillon, 10, pl. de la Concorde
01 44 71 15 15, fax 01 44 71 15 02
Closed Aug, hols. Open until 10:30pm. Air cond. Pkg.
To eat at the Hôtel de Crillon without breaking the bank, try its other, less formal restaurant. You'll still benefit from top-notch service and a menu supervised by Dominique Bouchet, the chef of Les Ambassadeurs (see above). The food is classic bistro fare: traditional joue de bœuf in a wine sauce, sea bream roasted with lemon. Excellent service. Sixteen wines are offered by the glass or half-liter jug. C 300-400. M 270.

 ## Le Patio

Hôtel de Crillon, 10, pl. de la Concorde
01 44 71 15 15, fax 01 44 71 15 02
Open mid May-mid Sep for lunch only until 2:30pm. Pkg.
Another way to enjoy the Crillon's atmosphere is to lunch in the flower-filled inner courtyard, which is open in the summertime and when the weather permits. On offering are such cold dishes as shellfish velouté with asparagus, red mullet atop ratatouille and fruit-of-the-season tart. C 350.

 ## Le Pavillon

Marriott Paris Champs-Élysées - 01 53 93 55 44
Open daily until 10:30pm. Terrace dining. Air cond. Pkg.
This sparkling new deluxe hotel boasts an eighteenth-century décor adorned with lovely stone ballustrades and red-draped bay windows giving onto a gem of a terrace. We noted a few kinks (the asparagus cream was on the salty side, but its accompanying soft-boiled egg was perfectly cooked), but have faith they'll be worked out when the gears are better oiled. Breton Chef Jean-Jacques Macé, given the MOF (best worker

of France) award in 1996, has a soft spot for spices and full flavors: have no hesitation in front of his 9-spice sole or pineapple coated with vanilla butter. C 400-500. M 250 (wine incl).

12/20 Le Petit Yvan

1 bis, rue Jean Mermoz
01 42 89 49 65, fax 01 42 89 30 95
Closed Sat lunch, Sun. Open until midnight. Air cond. Pkg.
Yvan's little annex pulls in a lively, friendly crew with an unbeatable all-in menu that features—for example—scrambled eggs with roasted tomatoes, steak tartare (minced by hand, not by machine) flanked by crispy french fries, and a rum-soaked savarin for dessert. Wine and coffee incur no extra charge. It's all served on bistro tables in a colorful, split-level dining room. M 158 (wine & coffee incl).

Le Régence

Plaza Athénée, 25, av. Montaigne
01 53 67 65 00, fax 01 53 67 66 66
Closed Feb school hols, Jul 21-Aug 10. Open until 10:30pm. Garden dining. Air cond. Pkg.
Changes have not spared the Plaza Athénée among top hotels of Paris. Young chef Éric Briffard, trained by Meneau and Robuchon, blends colors and flavors in perfect harmony, and is thoroughly living up to the expectations we expressed last year. His style of cooking has, in its short stay in this grandest of grand hotels, already proven that it works for the Plaza's clientele; it can already be put in the category of the best Parisian restaurants. And the plates are not always filled with what one might expect in such a luxury establishment. A soft-boiled egg may not get you excited, but when you taste the Greek-style baby vegetables cooked in olive oil and lemon juice and the parsleyed, pan-fried baby squid that go with it, you will change your tune. Same goes for the asparagus cream and coriander-spiced spider crab, the little red mullets in their delicious jelly coated with rosemary cream and partnered with a tapenade «sandwich», the absolutely extraordinary risotto with white-truffle butter, and the exquisite calf's sweetbreads cooked in salted butter and served with candied lemon and parmesan-gratin asparagus. Your spirits will stay high for dessert if you tempt the peach roasted with lavender and almond kernels and escorted by red-currant sherbet. Blown over, none of us questioned whether or not to don him with his third toque—it was a given. We hope he manages to revolutionize his rather old-fashioned, overpriced cellar so that it reaches the level of his cuisine. You can also eat among the chic in the garden in summer. The service has also taken a turn for the better. C 550-750. M 310 (weekday lunch), 585.

Les Saveurs

Sofitel Champs-Élysées,
8, rue Jean-Goujon - 01 40 74 64 64
Closed Sat, Sun, Aug. Open until 10:30pm. Terrace dining. Air cond. Pkg.
If you book a table here, you will able to try Didier Lanfray's fresh style of cooking: vegetable terrine (pressé de légumes) abetted by a truffle infusion, or the bold, full-flavored lotte with green mangos and fresh pasta. Tempting desserts, too, and attentive service. The tables are well-spaced and you can eat in the garden in the summer in this luxurious Empire-style setting once the home of the Princes of Essling. C 300-350. M 165.

12/20 Sébillon Élysées

66, rue Pierre-Charron - 01 43 59 28 15
Open daily until midnight. Air cond.
Excellent but expensive shellfish platters are followed by Sébillon's famous leg of lamb cooked in a salt crust, rosy and tender and carved right before your eyes. Elegant décor, energetic service, all in keeping with grand French tradition. C 220-320. M 180 (wine incl).

Shing Jung

7, rue Clapeyron - 01 45 22 21 06
Closed Sat, Sun lunch, Aug 1-15, Dec 20-Jan 5. Open until 10:30pm.
The owner of this modest establishment will try to convince you that Koreans are more generous than their Japanese neighbors. Indeed, a colossal assortment of raw fish, listed on the menu as «medium», comprised sea bream, salmon, tuna, brill, and mackerel. For the same money most Japanese places would serve about one-quarter the quantity. Also on hand are jellyfish salad, barbecued beef strips, a hotpot of vegetables and beef, and stuffed lentil-flour crêpes. Delicious and incredibly inexpensive. Please note: no credit cards. C 170-295.

Shozan

11, rue de La Trémoille - 01 47 23 37 32
Closed Sat lunch, Sun, Aug. Open until midnight. Pkg.
Show-biz celebrities and fashion honchos have given this new Japanese restaurant their stamp of approval. They settle into the discreetly handsome brown-and-beige dining room to feast on superb sashimi and lightly grilled fish, or the more complex (and most rewarding) ginger-steamed bass with leeks. Meat eaters are not neglected: the beef tenderloin in dashi broth is delectable. Shozan's owners produce saké in Japan, so there is quite a choice on hand for tasting (it's a safer choice than the wine). C 350-420. M 90 (weekday lunch, wine incl), 175-330.

Le Stresa

7, rue Chambiges - 01 47 23 51 62
Closed Sat dinner, Sun, Aug, Dec 20-Jan 3. Open until 10:30pm. Terrace dining. Air cond. Pkg.

Le Stresa's dining room is always full of press, fashion, and movie people (Sharon Stone was spotted here recently) who love the antipasti drizzled with fruity Tuscan olive oil, the spinach ravioli, calf's liver, and smooth tiramisù prepared by Marco Faiola. Claudio and Toni Faiola seat their guests with a sure social sense of who's up, who's in, who's out. Good selection of Alp wines. C 400-450.

 ## Taillevent

15, rue Lamennais
01 44 95 15 01, fax 01 42 25 95 18
Closed Sat, Sun, Aug. Open until 10:30pm. Air cond. Pkg.
Refined yet graceful, elegant but never stiff, the tone at Taillevent is set by Jean-Claude Vrinat, a restaurateur whose sole standard is perfection: each detail of the décor and the menu is calculated to provide utter comfort and well-being. While not boldly creative, the kitchen is far from stodgy. Simpler offerings underscore the pristine quality of the ingredients: seared Breton langoustines, for example, in a lightly creamed broth or sea bass anointed with olive oil and accompanied by slow-roasted vegetables. Still, the classic repertoire provides pleasures of its own: why turn down a chance to savor the rich, resonant flavors of a truffled game pie filled with venison, duck and pheasant? The cheese board is exceptional, and desserts invite you to splurge. Incomparable cellar; silken service. Both the stately dining rooms and the kitchen have just undergone a facelift. C 800-900.

 ## Chez Tante Louise

41, rue Boissy-d'Anglas
01 42 65 06 85, fax 01 45 65 28 19
Closed Sat, Sun, Aug. Open until 10pm. Air cond.
The regulars love being pampered in this snug little spot, where a smiling staff serves Michel Lerouet's lightened versions of traditional and updated French favorites. The single-price menu offers great value, and there is a nicely balanced cellar to boot. C 300-400. M 190.

 ## Tong Yen

1 bis, rue Jean Mermoz
01 42 25 04 23, fax 01 45 63 51 57
Closed Aug 1-25. Open until 12:15am. Terrace dining. Air cond.
The quietly attractive dining room, punctuated with fresh flowers, plays host to personalities from stage and screen, who come to enjoy precisely cooked and seasoned Chinese (and other Oriental) specialties: Peking dumplings, chicken glazed with honey and vinegar, salt-and-pepper shrimp, and the like. Peking duck runs 560 F for 4 people. To drink, order a cool, white Sancerre. Home delivery and carry-out service available. C 250-300.

 ## Le «30»

Fauchon, 30, pl. de la Madeleine
01 47 42 56 58, fax 01 47 42 96 02
Closed Sun. Open until 10:30pm. Air cond.
Whoever dreamed up the name (Le Trente—30—is the building's address) of Fauchon's restaurant won't win any prizes for creativity, but the decorator might, for its «Roman fantasy» interior. Mostly classic, with some bold touches of spice, Bruno Deligne's menu lists very good oysters with celery-root purée (but an otherwise tasty turbot was spoiled by indigestible beans). The stupendous pastries are crafted by Sébastien Gaudard. The luncheon menu seems expensive on first glance, but offers good value for the money. C 300-500. M 259 (lunch, wine incl), 245 (dinner).

 ## Chez Vong

27, rue du Colisée - 01 43 59 77 12
Closed Sun. Open until midnight. Air cond. Pkg.
Here's everyone's dream of a Chinese restaurant: embroidered silk, furniture inlaid with mother-of-pearl, lots of little nooks, an air of mystery, and dishes named «quail in a nest of happiness» or «merry shrimp». The cooking is well crafted. Oddly enough, the cellar is rich in fine (and costly) claret. C 300. M 200 (lunch), 250 (dinner).

 ## Yvan

1 bis, rue Jean-Mermoz
01 43 59 18 40, fax 01 42 89 30 95
Closed Sat lunch, Sun. Open until midnight. Air cond.
Yvan Zaplatilek is café society's darling, but he is also a hard-working chef who gives his customers very good food at moderate prices in a most elegant setting. The menu is primarily French, with an occasional Belgian touch here and there (sole waterzoï, veal kidney braised in dark beer). C 300. M 178 (weekday lunch), 168 & 298 (dinner).

9th ARRONDISSEMENT

Zip code	75009

 ## L'Alsaco

10, rue Condorcet - 01 45 26 44 31
Closed Sat lunch, Sun, Aug. Open until 11pm.
Beyond the unremarkable façade is an authentic Alsatian *winstub*, decked out in traditional painted wood paneling. L'Alsaco serves generous renditions of choucroute garnie, cream and onion tart, and potatoes with melted Munster cheese. To drink, there are Rieslings galore, and a huge cache of clear fruit brandies. C 200. M 79 (lunch), 87 (dinner).

Auberge Landaise

23, rue Clauzel - 01 48 78 74 40
Closed Sun, Aug 10-20. Open until 10:30pm. Air cond. Pkg.
In a rustic setting conducive to a hearty tuck-in, Dominique and Éric Morin treat their customers to cassoulet, foie gras, braised duck with wild mushrooms, and good grills. Full and robust flavors reminiscent of the Southwest of France. High-priced little cellar, but a few affordable wines, such as the Bergerac at 95 F a bottle or the half-bottle of Tursan at 48 F; superb Armagnacs. C 220-300. M 130 (wine incl), 180.

11/20 Le Bistrot des Deux Théâtres

18, rue Blanche - 01 45 26 41 43, fax 01 48 74 08 92
Open daily until 12:30am. Air cond.
A bistro with a British accent, in an improbable neighborhood. The menu is a pretty good deal, what with its duck liver pâté, saffron-spiced scallops, and iced nougatine with raspberry coulis. Perfect stop-off for late-night hunger binges. C 200-300. M 169 (wine incl).

 ## Bistrot Papillon

6, rue Papillon - 01 47 70 90 03, fax 01 48 24 05 59
Closed Sat, Sun, 1 wk at Easter, 3 wks in Aug. Open until 10pm. Air cond.
The cozy ambience fits Jean-Yves Guion's soothing menu, made up of long-standing favorites such as sole filets à l'orange or veal kidneys with morels, and some good market specials—sorrel-scented monkfish shish kebab and rum-flavored pineapple gratin made their appearance on a recent visit. Reliably fine ingredients go into his skillfully crafted preparations. Balanced cellar with good selection of half-bottles. C 240-300. M 140.

 ## La Casa Olympe

48, rue Saint-Georges
01 42 85 26 01, fax 01 45 26 49 33
Closed Sat, Sun, Aug, 1 wk at Christmas. Open until 11pm. Pkg.
Olympe is at home in the former Casa Miguel, long the city's cheapest deal, with a philanthropically priced 5 F set meal. The current menu reflects Olympe at her best. Her fans fall eagerly onto such warming dishes as cumin-spiced calf's foot sausage, pumpkin soup dotted with mussels, and roast shoulder of Sisteron lamb. The premises are small (not to say cramped) though prettily painted in warm tones of yellow and burnt sienna. The wine as well as the mineral water are straight from the «growers». C 250-350.

 ## Charlot

81, bd de Clichy, (pl. de Clichy)
01 53 20 48 00, fax 01 53 20 48 09
Open daily until 1am. Air cond.
A fine view of the Place de Clichy, a warm welcome, and attentive service will take your mind off the overbearing Art Deco interior. Sparkling fresh oysters, plentiful shellfish assortments, bouillabaisse à la marseillaise, and lobsters prepared every possible way are the staples here. It will slide down more easily with Klipfel's Rieseling at 148 F a bottle or Guérard's Tursan at 146 F. C 300-400. M 178.

 ## Chez Catherine

65, rue de Provence - 01 45 26 72 88
Closed Sat, Sun, Mon dinner, Aug, 1 wk beg Jan, Aug. Open until 10pm.
It's no easy feat to find a decent restaurant up here near the major department stores. But we did it! Catherine's sleek bistro provides well-wrought classics based on excellent ingredients: minted lamb terrine, salmon with lentils, spiced sea-bass fillet, and duck confit merit your close attention. Husband Frédéric tends the cellar of astutely selected growers' wines. C 230-300.

12/20 Les Diables au Thym

35, rue Bergère - 01 47 70 77 09
Closed Sat lunch; Apr-Sep: Sun dinner; Aug. Open until 10:30pm. Pkg.
This quiet little straw-yellow dining room is a fortunate find in this neighborhood just off the bustling boulevards. It starts off with a hearty welcome, after which you comfortably settle in for the likes of a potpourri of extra-tender pigeon legs and full-flavored duck breast or a fish pâté with a tangy sauce. The fair-priced cellar offers lots of half-bottles. C 250-280. M 118, 139.

 ## I Golosi

6, rue de la Grange-Batelière - 01 48 24 18 63
Closed Sat dinner, Sun, Aug. Open until midnight. Air cond. Pkg.
Enter this bistro from the picturesque Passage Verdeau to discover two levels decorated in a style we can only call «1950s Italian». From the weekly-changing menu based on ultra-fresh ingredients, you can order imaginative, carefully-prepared dishes such as rabbit with wild thyme, chicken dressed with Balsamic vinegar, and nettle risotto, accompanied by irresistible Italian wines assembled by a passionate œnophile. May well be one of the best Italian restaurants in Paris—no wonder they call it *golosi*, that is to say «gourmets». C 170-200.

12/20 Le Grand Café Capucines

4, bd des Capucines
01 43 12 19 00, fax 01 43 12 19 09
Open daily 24 hours. Terrace dining. Air cond.
The waiter won't pull a face if you order just one course—a shellfish assortment, salmon tartare, or a grilled pig's trotter. The extravagant décor is a replica of a Roaring Twenties *café boulevardier*. C 280. M 123 (dinner, after 11pm, wine incl), 178.

12/20 Menthe et Basilic

6, rue Lamartine - 01 48 78 12 20
Closed Sun, Mon, Aug. Open until 10:30pm. Pkg.
Mint and basil, an appropriate name for a
cuisine emanating sunshine: gently-spiced baby
vegetable tempura, thin veal sweetbread and
mushroom pie, tender little lamb noisettes with
al dente pasta, or flavorful, velvety chocolate
fondant. Service as capable as it is pleasant.
Good apéritifs but the wine list needs some
serious revision to come up to the level of the
food. C 200-250. M 98 (lunch), 148.

 Les Muses

Hôtel Scribe, 1, rue Scribe
01 44 71 24 26, fax 01 44 71 24 64
*Closed Sat, Sun, hols, Aug. Open until 10:30pm. Air
cond. Pkg.*
In the intimate basement setting of the Scribe
Hotel restaurant, young chef Philippe Pleuën
orchestrates a symphony of culinary temptations into a classic but creative repertoire. On his
seasonally changing menu, tempt yourself with
courageous combinations such as cauliflower
cress with roast langoustines, red mullet salmis
(wine-based ragout) with marrow risotto, or
lamp crisp with candied melt-in-your-mouth eggplant. Classic desserts: hazelnut and praline
millefeuille, tangerine ice cream parfait or velvety pear and pistachio macaroon. Eclectic
choice of Bordeaux and Burgundies with a lucky
find from time to time. C 300-400. M 230-290.

 L'Œnothèque

20, rue St-Lazare - 01 48 78 08 76, fax 01 40 16 10 27
*Closed Sat, Sun, hols, 2 wks in Aug. Open until
11pm. Air cond.*
Daniel Hallée was the sommelier at Jamin
before he opened his restaurant-cum-wine shop;
he's just proudly handed over the kitchen to his
son, William. Grand vintages at attractive prices
and interesting lesser-known growths partner
such market-fresh offerings as baby leeks
mimosa, smoked-haddock salad, stewed oxtail
with al dente vegetables, and excellent grilled
fish in this refined little bistro à l'ancienne, an
oasis of peace in this desert of a neighborhood.
Superb collection of Cognacs. C 300-400.

12/20 Au Petit Riche

25, rue Le Peletier
01 47 70 68 68, fax 01 48 24 10 79
*Closed Sun, Jul-Aug: Sat. Open until 12:15am. Air
cond.*
The brass trim, mirrors, and woodwork of this
nostalgic bistro sparkle and gleam. This institution, a hangout for bankers and auctioneers as
well as the after-theater crowd, may be adorned
with a new staff, but the cooking is still of the
honest, satisfying sort: coq au vin de Chinon,
calf's head sauce gribiche, sole meunière. Excellent choice of Loire Valley wines. C 200-300. M
160 (lunch), 135-175 (dinner).

11/20 Pétrelle

34, rue Pétrelle - 01 42 82 11 02
*Closed Sat lunch, Sun, Jul 20-Aug 20. Open until
11pm.*
This charming eatery offers market-fresh
products: chicken-liver confit, juicy lamb, blood
oranges in syrup. The cellar may be small, but
the selection is respectable. C 230-320. M 140.

 Restaurant Opéra

Le Grand Hôtel Inter-Continental, 5, pl. de l'Opéra
01 40 07 30 10, fax 01 40 07 33 86
*Closed Sat, Sun, Aug. Open until 11pm. Air cond.
Pkg.*
Thanks to the efforts of Christian Le Squer, the
cuisine now lives up to the restaurant's opulent
Second Empire setting. Suitably luxurious (and
delicious) are the cream of cèpes with foie gras
and duck cracklings, codfish in a green-olive
cream, roast pigeon, and cinnamon-scented
roasted figs. Rely on the competent sommelier
for help with the wine list, where you might well
fall on some pleasant surprises. C 450-600. M 230
(lunch), 335 (wine incl).

 Sinago

17, rue de Maubeuge - 01 48 78 11 14
Closed Sun, Aug. Open until 10:30pm.
Wonderful Cambodian cooking is served in
this vest-pocket eatery (there's only room for
twenty). Savor the amazing crêpe stuffed with
saffron-stained pork, fish spiced with coriander
and ginger, or broth perfumed with lemon grass
and enriched with plump dumplings. Smashing
buy for such good quality. C 120-200. M 57
(lunch).

 La Table d'Anvers

2, pl. d'Anvers
01 48 78 35 21, fax 01 45 26 66 67
*Closed Sat lunch, Sun. Open until 11:30pm. Air
cond. Pkg.*
While so many chefs fall back on a «safe»,
reassuring repertoire of neo-bourgeois and
bistro dishes to hide their lack of inspiration,
Christian Conticini invents and reinvents flavor
combinations with a wizardry that is nothing
short of staggering. If you're tempted by the
prospect of a real gastronomic adventure, we
suggest you trek up to his Table at the foot of
Montmartre and prepare for a feast! Choose one
of the intriguing «theme» menus (featuring
novel vegetables, rare spices, or «just desserts»...), or explore an exciting *carte* that is keyed
to the seasons. The options are all so enticing that
we usually just close our eyes and pick at ran-
dom! The astonishing desserts are crafted by
Christian's brother, Philippe Conticini, who
managed to lose 120 kg without losing an ounce
of his hearty interest in the sweeter matters of the
palate. A wealth of little-known wines starting
from 100 F. C 500-600. M 180 (lunch), 250 (dinner).

We welcome your questions and comments at our ●-mail address: gayots@aol.com.

Venantius

Hôtel Ambassador, 16, bd Haussmann
01 48 00 06 38, fax 01 42 46 19 84
*Closed Sat, Sun, 1 wk in Feb, Aug. Open until
10:30pm. Air cond. Pkg.*
The composed atmosphere of this dining room
with its marble ionic columns and subtle Directoire style envelops its chiefly banking, insurance and business clientele with
accommodating, irreproachable service at prices
that might make others flinch. We relished the
highly original pig's ear croquettes with Meaux
mustard, a dish which proves that you can make
a noble dish from a not-so-noble ingredient, as
well as the soft-boiled egg with truffle sauce and
the virtuoso Brittany pigeon with country-style
lentils. Both the desserts and the wine list can
hold their own in any competition. C 500-600. M
220 (lunch), 180 (dinner).

 ## Wally le Saharien

36, rue Rodier - 01 42 85 51 90, fax 01 42 86 08 35
*Closed Sun, Mon lunch. Open until 11pm. Air cond.
Pkg.*
Wally has pitched his tent not far from Pigalle,
in a setting accented with carved screens, crim-
son carpets, and Tuareg-style seating. Topping
the list of specialties is his Saharan couscous (no
broth, no vegetables), but you can also sample
mutton with caramelized skin, pigeon pastilla,
and honey cake perfumed with orange-flower
water. Home delivery possible. C 200-300. M
240.

10th ARRONDISSEMENT

Postal code	75010

 ## Brasserie Flo

7, cour des Petites-Écuries
01 42 46 15 59, fax 01 42 47 00 80
Open daily until 1:30am. Air cond. Pkg.
The quintessential Alsatian brasserie, Flo is a
jewel: nowhere else will you find the same vivacious atmosphere, superb décor, lively patrons,
and delicious sauerkraut, best washed down
with carafes of frisky Riesling. C 200-280. M 123
(lunch, wine incl), 128-169 (dinner, wine incl).

 ## Le Canard
Laqué Pékinois

34, bd Bonne-Nouvelle
01 47 70 31 65, fax 01 44 79 00 21
Open daily until midnight. Air cond.
We're usually suspicious of these oversized
Chinese affairs, but Le Canard Laqué is a find.
Good dim-sums, salads, and sautéed shrimp to
start, followed by tasty roasted items and a most
honorable Peking duck. C 130. M 47 (weekday
lunch, wine incl), 58-116 (wine incl).

 ## Le Châteaubriant

23, rue Chabrol - 01 48 24 58 94, fax 01 42 47 09 75
*Closed Sun, Mon, Aug. Open until 10:15pm. Air
cond.*
From the name you'd never guess that this
little dining room tucked away near the Gare de
l'Est is a noted Italian restaurant. Save for the
rotating roster of daily specials, the menu is
immutable. Familiar though they may be, the
sardine lasagne with eggplant and the millefeuille de filet de veau are still perfectly delicious and courteously served. Tempting desserts
such as tiramisù and semifreddo. High prices,
but you might find solace in the new 2-course
lunch «formula» for 118 F. C 250-350. M 159.

12/20 Aux Deux Canards

8, rue du Fbg-Poissonnière
01 47 70 03 23, fax 01 44 83 02 50
*Closed Sat lunch, Sun, Aug. Open until 10:30pm.
Air cond.*
The copper plate out front kindly requests that
you wait for the scholarly looking owner to open
the door for you and escort you to your table; he
will tend to you throughout your meal in this
grand lieu where duck is king: diners can enjoy
the salmon rillettes, magret de canard, canard à
l'orange, and tasty desserts in this naively
charming bistro with great wines to match. C
230-270.

12/20 Julien

16, rue du Faubourg-Saint-Denis
01 47 70 12 06, fax 01 42 47 00 65
Open daily until 1:30am. Air cond. Pkg.
For the pleasure of dining in these exuberant
Art Nouveau surroundings (vintage 1880) with
its exquisite Mucha-style flower girls, we are
willing to put up with mediocre food. But if you
stick to the oysters, the cassoulet, or eggs
poached in red wine, you'll leave with a pleasant
memory. C 200-280. M 123 (lunch, wine incl),
128-183 (dinner, wine incl).

11/20 K.O.H.

67, rue du Fbg St-Martin - 01 42 38 11 23
Open daily until 5am. Pkg.
If you like hot spots where stars trot, this carpet
store-cum-restaurant offers the likes of sole
meunière, tartare, duck confit and upside down
apple tart to ease late-night hunger pangs. C
150-200.

 ## Chez Michel

10, rue Belzunce - 01 44 53 06 20
*Closed Sun, Mon, Aug. Terrace dining. Air cond.
Open until 11:30pm.*
Scion of a family of restaurateurs, Thierry
Breton was just doing what came naturally when
he decided to become a chef. Just as natually, his
preference is for Breton cuisine, the backbone of
his original 160 F single-price menu, which
draws gourmets from all over Paris. It features a
daring andouille terrine with buckwheat crêpes,

kig ha farz (an Armorican boiled dinner of hog jowls and country-cured bacon), and buttery rich kouign-aman cake. He's even unearthed a cheap and cheerful Breton *vin de pays* to wash these good things down with, or try some of the buckwheat or oat beer for a change! M 160.

12/20 Terminus Nord
23, rue de Dunkerque
01 42 85 05 15, fax 01 40 16 13 98
Open daily until 1am. Air cond. Pkg.
Part of the brasserie group of which Flo (see above) is the flagship, the Terminus serves exactly the same food as the rest of the fleet. Enjoy the atmosphere, the gay 1925 décor, and look no farther than the sauerkraut, oysters, and grills for a satisfying meal. Nimble service. Help it all slide down with one of their highly drinkable wines by the pitcher. C 190-280. M 123 (lunch, wine incl), 128 (dinner, after 10pm, wine incl), 189 (dinner, Sun, wine incl).

11th ARRONDISSEMENT

Postal code	75011

12/20 L'Aiguière
37 bis, rue de Montreuil
01 43 72 42 32, fax 01 43 72 96 36
Closed Sat lunch, Sun. Open until 10:30pm. Air cond. Pkg.
Hospitality is the keynote in this flowery, refined décor with its right-at-home atmosphere. The rich cooking, deeply rooted in tradition, sometimes suffers from a little overcooking, but the quality of the ingredients is impeccable. Hungry hunters will do well with the 135 F fixed-price menu with offerings such as scrambled eggs, turkey-wing salad, suckling pig, poached hen stew and varied desserts. Eclectic wine list; elegant setting overseen by owner Patrick Masbatin. C 250-320. M 135-248 (wine incl), 175.

 ## Les Amognes
243, rue du Fg-Saint-Antoine - 01 43 72 73 05
Closed Sun, Mon lunch, 2 wks in Aug. Open until 11pm. Terrace dining.
Thierry Coué has crossed rich and costly ingredients off his shopping list and come up with a single-price menu that offers exceptional quality for the price. The food he serves in his country-style dining room is full of earthy character: warm oysters and leeks ravigote, sweetbreads with cumin-spiced cucumber confit, crêpe stuffed with an eggplant compote redolent of cardamom. The cellar is filled with interesting finds, such as Edmond Vatan's Sancerre or Pierre Overnoy's Arbois-Pupullin. M 190.

 ## Astier
44, rue Jean-Pierre-Timbaud - 01 43 57 16 35
Closed Sat, Sun, 1 wk end Apr, Aug, Dec 23-Jan 2. Open until 11pm. Air cond.
For 135 F (the price hasn't moved an inch in two years!), Jean-Luc Clerc will set you up with a slab of savory chicken-liver terrine, followed by rabbit in mustard sauce or a duo of sea whelks and shrimp, nicely aged cheeses, and rich chocolate mousse for dessert. The bistro atmosphere is good-humored and noisy. Intelligent, wide-ranging cellar worthy of a *grand restaurant* but priced in line with the food. M 135.

11/20 Le Bistrot du Peintre
116, rue Ledru-Rollin - 01 47 00 34 39
Closed Sun dinner, at Christmas. Open until 12:30am. Terrace dining. Pkg.
This authentic 1890s-style bistro, listed on the national historical register, offers unbeatable prices for the likes of egg and puff pastry garnished with piperade, rabbit and asparagus, baby squid ravioli and *coup de cœur* featured wines. C 140-170.

 ## Blue Elephant
43, rue de la Roquette - 01 47 00 42 00
Closed Sat lunch, May 1, 3 days at Christmas. Air cond. Pkg.
Filled with flowers, pagodas, and cheerful waiters, the Thai Éléphant is not your run-of-the-mill Asian eatery. The menu is miles long, and many of the dishes are fiercely fiery (the hottest are marked with three red elephants). The shrimp curry is quite fine, and so are the Fomyang soup and the garlicky pork. For dessert, try the delicious jasmine tart. Director Manuel da Motta Veiga is an avid wine connoisseur and delights in giving wise advice on the matter. First Asian restaurant to receive GaultMillau's famous golden key award. C 250-300. M 150 (weekday lunch), 275, 300.

 ## Khun Akorn
8, av. de Taillebourg
01 43 56 20 03, fax 01 40 09 18 44
Closed Mon. Open until 11pm. Terrace dining. Pkg.
Two brothers, Akorn and Adul, who received the best of English public school educations, suffered immensely from the bad Thai food in England, and considered it their calling to introduce Europeans to authentic, good-quality Thai food. And that's what they've done with rare refinement, served in an evocative, exotic setting. The tong-sai (assorted appetizers) set the mood for what follows. The curries are lighter than their Indian cousins, but Thai chilis make their fiery presence felt elsewhere on the menu. C 200-250. M 129 (lunch), 195-325.

Mansouria

11, rue Faidherbe - 01 43 71 00 16, fax 01 40 24 21 97
Closed Sun, Mon lunch. Open until 11:30pm.
The trendy Bastille crowd comes here for a taste of Morocco: honeyed pumpkin purée, Moroccan crêpes, a light and flavorful couscous, and mellow, long-simmered tagines crafted by Fatema Hal, author of a beautifully illustrated book on Moroccan cooking, who teaches you the subtle differences between the couscouses of various regions. Charming reception and service. Reservations (well in advance) are a must; ask to sit in the Eastern salon at the back of the dining room. C 250-300. M 135 (weekday), 168, 280 (wine incl).

12/20 Jacques Mélac

42, rue Léon-Frot - 01 43 70 59 27
Closed Sat, Sun, Mon dinner, Aug, end Dec-beg Jan. Open until 10:30pm. Terrace dining. Air cond.
One of the city's most popular wine bars. The countrified menu proposes charcuteries from the Aveyron region, good cheeses, and exemplary wines. C 130-160.

12/20 Le Roudoulié

16, rue de la Vacquerie - 01 43 79 27 46
Closed Sat lunch, Sun, Aug 1-15. Open until 10:30pm. Terrace dining. Air cond.
Remember to book in advance (especially for lunch), since Le Roudoulié's charming (but sometimes scatter-brained) service, jolly atmosphere and generous, inexpensive food have plenty of fans. The menu has a rustic Southwestern accent: hot duck pâté studded with cèpes and foie gras, pot-au-feu de canard, and scallops with oyster mushrooms. C 220-280. M 110, 158.

Le Villaret

13, rue Ternaux - 01 43 57 75 56
Closed Sun, 10 days in May, 2 wks at Christmas. Open until 1am. Air cond.
One couldn't say that 26-year-old chef Olivier Gaslain chose the tried-and-true path of traditional cooking. Successful exploration is a more suited term: liver and morels, chops with goat cheese ravioli, skate poached in Epoisses-cheese cream sauce, cod with bacon bits. Original approach to wine as well. The «daily remedies» range from 90 to 260 F, while the «exclusive remedies» go from 300 to 3,500. C 210-240.

12th ARRONDISSEMENT

Postal code	**75012**

11/20 Bistrot du Titi

136, av Daumesnil - 01 43 43 04 22
Closed Sun dinner, Mon, Tue, Aug 15-Sep 7. Open until 10pm. Terrace dining. Air cond. Pkg.
This little bistro is making a big splash with its outstanding luncheon menu. On the 85 F set menu you'll discover quality that is rare at this price: extra-thin carpaccio of scallops on a bed of braised endives, monkfish shish kebab garnished with leeks and mushrooms, and hot apple «lace». C 200-250. M 85 (weekday lunch, wine incl), 130.

La Flambée

4, rue Taine - 01 43 43 21 80
Closed Sun, Aug 3-19. Open until 10:15pm. Terrace dining. Air cond. Pkg.
The dining room shows some signs of wear, but never mind. Michel Roustan warms things up nicely with his traditional Southwestern charcuteries, tasty confit de canard with sautéed potatoes, and excellent warm apple tart. The 199 F set menu affords more imaginative dishes: escargot ravioli with garlic and chervil cream, tarragon sorbet splashed with a swig of Armagnac, bacon-enhanced scallop shish kebab, Pyrenees cheeses and prune sherbet, and includes a half-bottle of Gaillac. The good wines are moderately priced. C 270. M 125, 199 (wine incl).

La Gourmandise

271, av. Daumesnil - 01 43 43 94 41
Closed Sun, Mon dinner, 1 wk in May, Aug 3-25. Open until 10:30pm. Pkg.
Gourmand or gourmet, you'll be tempted to indulge in Alain Denoual's excellent set meals, the less expensive of which delivers fish terrine with shellfish fumet, saddle of rabbit confit with cabbage, and a rich triple-chocolate mousse. A la carte, the langoustines with a red-tea infusion and the zippy mango charlotte are both worthy of note. The fixed-price menus include wine, and the cellar puts forth an admirable selection with Burgundy as star. C 340. M 125 (lunch, wine incl), 165, 199 (wine incl).

12/20 Les Grandes Marches

6, pl. de la Bastille - 01 43 42 90 32, fax 01 43 44 80 02
Closed 3 wks in Aug. Open until 1am. Terrace dining. Air cond.
Restored around the same time as the Opéra Bastille was built, this posh turn-of-the-century brasserie is a fine spot for a post-performance supper. Oysters and other shellfish, steaks, and a splendid sea bream roasted in a salt crust

deserve a round of applause. C 250-300. M 138, 175.

12/20 Le Mange Tout

24, bd de la Bastille - 01 43 43 95 15
Closed Sun, 1 wk in Aug. Open until 11:30pm. Terrace dining.
Uncomplicated cooking, served with a smile and a generous hand. Scrambled eggs with morels, skate with capers, andouillette sausage, and clafoutis are the mainstays of a menu rooted in the provinces of France. Nice assortment of wines which is freshly updated on a continual basis. C 220-260. M 80, 100, 190-195 (wine incl).

 ## L'Oulette

15, pl. Lachambeaudie - 01 40 02 02 12
Closed Sat lunch, Sun. Open until 10:15pm. Terrace dining.
A charmless cohort of office blocks contributes precious little warmth to the surroundings, but happily, Marcel Baudis can be relied upon to kindle a glow with his spirited Southwestern cooking. He ignited our enthusiasm with a spiced duck pâté, tender Pyrenees lamb with country potatoes, and hefty portion of tomme d'Aspe cheese. One of the best cassoulets in town. The cellar is awash in sturdy wines from the Quercy and thereabouts; the service is most attentive. C 300-380. M 160, 240 (wine incl).

 ## La Plantation

5, rue Jules-César - 01 43 07 64 15
Dinner only. Closed Sat lunch, Sun. Open until 12:30am. Terrace dining. Pkg.
Nouvelle cuisine, Creole-style: blaff de bulots (sea whelks marinated in lime juice and chilis), chicken in pan juices deglazed with pineapple vinegar, and fabulous stuffed crab are expertly handled dishes full of vivid tropical flavors. Try the punch. M 148-235.

 ## Au Pressoir

257, av. Daumesnil
01 43 44 38 21, fax 01 43 43 81 77
Closed Sat, Sun, Aug. Open until 10:30pm. Air cond. Pkg.
Forgotten by most Parisians since the Colonial Exposition closed 60 years ago, the Porte Dorée district is home to a covey of fine restaurants. Le Pressoir numbers among them. Chef Henri Séguin cooks with fine ingredients and a generous spirit, shown to advantage in his scallop fricassée with wild mushrooms, codfish brandade with asparagus, or in season a sumptuous hare à la royale. Lavish setting—private air-conditioned dining rooms, cigar cellar, patinated wood paneling, doorman to park your car—all of which you pay for. Expensive cellar. C 500-600. M 400.

*Some establishments change their **closing times** without warning. It is always wise to check in advance.*

 ## Le Quincy

28, av. Ledru-Rollin - 01 46 28 46 76
Closed Sat, Sun, Mon, Aug 15-Sep 15. Open until 10pm. Terrace dining. Air cond. Pkg.
Bobosse, the jovial host, keeps things lively in the dining room, while in the kitchen Jean-Pierre Rouat cooks up zestful bistro dishes rooted in the Berry and Vivarais regions: famously tasty farmhouse terrine, chicken fricassée, boiled crayfish, and the best stuffed cabbage in town. Delicious Rhône and Loire wines topped off with deliciously-aged plum brandy. C 300-400.

12/20 Le Saint-Amarante

4, rue Biscornet - 01 43 43 00 08
Closed Sat, Sun, Mon, Tue dinner. Jul 14-Aug 15. Open until 10:30pm. Terrace dining.
It's too bad about this neighborhood bistro, tucked neatly into a quiet street near the Opéra Bastille. The last time we dropped in we had the disappointment of leathery marinated sardines and undercooked suckling calf (although its potato pancake was excellent). Growers' wines priced under 100 F in a crowded, lively setting. C 200-220.

 ## La Sologne

164, av. Daumesnil
01 43 07 68 97, fax 01 43 44 66 23
Closed Sat lunch, Sun, 2 wks in Aug. Open until 10:30pm. Terrace dining. Air cond. Pkg.
Didier and Virginie Maillet spare no pains to make their patrons feel welcome and well fed in their roomy dining room. The 155 F menu is most attractive (the offerings change often) and the kitchen highlights game in season. Well-rounded wine list; don't hesitate to try the Domaine Gramenon's Viognier. M 155.

11/20 Le Train Bleu

Gare de Lyon, 20, bd Diderot
01 43 43 09 06, fax 01 43 43 97 96
Open daily until 11pm. Pkg.
The feast is for your eyes only: an extravagant, colossal, delirious, dazzling décor. The food? Don't miss your train for it... High prices. C 280-450. M 250 (wine incl).

 ## Au Trou Gascon

40, rue Taine - 01 43 44 34 26, fax 01 43 07 80 55
Closed Sat lunch, Sun, Aug, end Dec-beg Jan. Open until 10pm. Air cond. Pkg.
Time marches on, but here the mellow décor and familiar menu remain unchanged. Year in, year out, you can order well-cured Chalosse ham, a warm pâté de cèpes in a bright-green parsley jus, truffled chop of milk-fed veal with macaroni gratin, or rich duck and pork cassoulet. A few dishes from the Carré des Feuillants can also be spotted on the list (red mullet with potatoes and marrow, chestnut cream soup with bits of pheasant, etc.). To accompany this robust cooking, Nicole Dutournier recommends wonderful wines from Madiran and Jurançon,

and you can cross the finish line in glory with one of her fantastic Armagnacs. C 360-400. M 190 (lunch), 285 (dinner, wine incl).

12/20 Le Viaduc Café

43, av. Daumesnil - 01 44 74 70 70
Open daily until midnight. Terrace dining.
After browsing around the artisans' shops of the Viaduc des Arts, you can enjoy simple French cooking at this arty café. On offer you'll find salmon tartare, grilled duck breast, and vanilla-scented pain perdu (aka French toast). C 160-180.

12/20 Les Zygomates

7, rue de Capri - 01 40 19 93 04
Closed Sat lunch, Sun, Aug, last wk of Dec. Open until 10:30pm.
For starters, there's an earthy salad of pork tongue, followed by grenadier (a firm-fleshed fish) with red-wine butter or pig's tail with morels. The incredible dining room—formerly a pork butcher shop—is full of *fin de siècle* details, but expect to put up with the noise of the tightly compressed crowd. C 210-250. M 75 (lunch), 130.

13th ARRONDISSEMENT

Postal code	75013

 L'Anacréon

53, bd Saint-Marcel - 01 43 31 71 18
Closed Sun, Mon, 1 wk in Feb, Aug. Open until 10:30pm. Air cond.
No-frills surroundings, but the food is full-flavored and unbeatably priced: soy-marinated salmon bundled up in a crêpe purse, veal kidney with mustard sauce and buttery cabbage, light and lively grapefruit gratin. Friendly atmosphere. Well-rounded little cellar with Burgundy by the pitcher, but a bit short on half-bottles. M 120 (lunch), 180.

12/20 Auberge Etchegorry

Hôtel Vert Galant, 41, rue Croulebarbe
01 44 08 83 51, fax 01 44 08 83 69
Closed Sun. Open until 10:30pm. Terrace dining. Air cond.
Come here for hearty Basque food and wines. A cheerful *patron* plates up excellent regional charcuterie, tasty stuffed squid, and generously served quail paupiettes au foie gras. Lots of charm, and a lively atmosphere. Southwest wines, numerous half-bottles. C 280. M 165-320 (wine incl), 175.

12/20 L'Avant-Goût

26, rue Bobillot - 01 53 80 24 00
Closed Sun, Mon, Aug 8-21. Open until 11pm. Terrace dining. Pkg.

When you feel you can eat a wolf, stop by and sample the house specialty, pork pot-au-feu, livened up with a delicate little horseradish sauce, or the chicken and green bean fricassée. Even though the hunger will have been quieted, *gourmandise* may tempt you into ordering the apricot crème brûlée. The space taken up around your beltline on entering will remain about the same on exiting, since the «light» bill leaves your pocket fairly full. The future looks bright for this new addition to our guide. Small cellar of growers' wines. C 150-200.

 La Mer de Chine

159, rue Château-des-Rentiers - 01 45 84 22 49
Closed Tue, end Jul-Aug. Open until 1:30am. Air cond.
The menu features sautéed ducks' tongues, fried soft-shell crabs (imported from Vietnam), oyster fritters, and gingery carp anointed with sesame oil. If chop suey is what you want, look elsewhere! C 180-220. M 78 (weekday lunch), 118.

12/20 Chez Paul

22, rue de la Butte-aux-Cailles
01 45 89 22 11, fax 01 45 80 26 53
Closed Dec 25, Jan 1. Open until midnight. Terrace dining. Pkg.
In the heart of the Butte-aux-Cailles district, a corner of old Paris where tourists never go, Chez Paul serves calf's head gribiche, streaky bacon with lentils, sage-scented suckling pig, and other bistro classics. Do stop to admire the magnificent 1930s bar. Brouilly wine by the pitcher and as much coffee as you can down. C 220-250.

 Le Petit Marguery

9, bd de Port-Royal - 01 43 31 58 59
Closed Sun, Mon, Aug, Dec 24-Jan 3. Open until 10:15pm. Terrace dining. Pkg.
The Cousin brothers aren't sticks-in-the-mud: they're willing to leave the beaten path of bistro fare and offer their patrons crispy ravioli stuffed with langoustines and green apples (delicious!). But they also please their faithful public with down-home favorites delivered by fleet-footed waiters: braised wild mushrooms, black pudding terrine, cod gratin with oysters and asparagus, or compote de coq. The single-price menus help keep costs down, wih a special menu for game lovers. M 165 (lunch), 205, 450.

14th ARRONDISSEMENT

Postal code	**75014**

L'Amuse Bouche

186, rue du Château - 01 43 35 31 61
Closed Sun, 3 wks in Aug. Open until 10:30pm.
A neighborhood crowd comes here for virtuously priced set meals served in a bright, tiny (just 22 seats) dining room. At lunch there's snail fricassée, guinea hen with celery-root purée, and dried fruit-and-nut soup spiced with cinnamon. The cellar is in keeping with the food: unpretentious but sparking the interest. **M** 168.

12/20 L'Angélus

12, rue Joannes (corner of rue Boulitte)
01 45 41 51 65
Closed Sun. Open until 10:30pm.
The two owners used to be magicians, but there's no hocus-pocus going on in the kitchen. The menu is based on prime ingredients handled with a light touch: try the chicken liver terrine, gutsy andouillette sausage with mustard sauce, and frozen honey nougat. Even though the brick-and-stone décor makes for a pleasant atmosphere, the leathery steak and oversweet desserts deprive this restaurant of the toque of the past. Well-annotated wine list dominated by Burgundy and Bordeaux. **M** 132, 163.

L'Assiette

181, rue du Château - 01 43 22 64 86
Closed Mon, Tue, 1 wk in May, Aug. Open until 10:30pm.
If Lulu's success were due merely to the fact that her prices are high, her customers chic, and her dining room determinedly «working class», it would surely have faded long ago. No, the high and the mighty come here year after year because they love the food. So do we: the ingredients are magnificent and the portions huge. When Lulu puts truffles in a dish, you can see, smell, and taste them! Try her justly famous black pudding shepherd's pie, mackerel rillettes, and superb sole meunière (it weighs in at 14 oz). But desserts are not her strong suit, as Lulu owns up herself right on the menu! **C** 250-400. **M** 200 (lunch, wine incl).

11/20 Le Bar à Huîtres

112, bd du Montparnasse - 01 43 20 71 01
Open daily until 1am. Terrace dining. Pkg.
At this popular oyster bar you can, if you wish, order and eat just one oyster—but that would be a shame. Six or a dozen Belons, fines, or spéciales would surely be more satisfying, as are the gargantuan shellfish platters (295 to 600 F). The cooked fish dishes, however, are skippable. **C** 220. **M** 98, 128, 198.

Bistrot du Dôme

1, rue Delambre - 01 43 35 32 00
Open daily until 11pm. Terrace dining. Air cond.
Flipping-fresh seafood is presented with becoming simplicity at this fashionable spot: featured are crispy fried smelts, tuna with sauce vierge, and lotte in a garlicky cream sauce. A price-savvy wine list features all bottles for 99 F, or by the glass at 22 F; merry ambience. **C** 220-260.

12/20 Bistrot Montsouris

27, av. Reille - 01 45 89 17 05
Closed Sun, Mon, wk of Aug 15. Open until 10pm.
Here's a welcoming, unpretentious little seafood spot, situated across from the Parc Montsouris. Jeannine Gaulon greets diners warmly, while in the kitchen her chef cooks up soupe de poissons, langoustine and artichoke salad, fresh tuna en daube (a bit dry on our last visit), and grilled sea bream. A few meat dishes round out the bill of fare. **C** 280-300. **M** 108.

La Cagouille

Opposite 23 rue de l'Ouest,
12, pl. Constantin-Brancusi
01 43 22 09 01, fax 01 45 38 57 29
Open daily until 10:30pm. Terrace dining.
At this *bistro du port*, dishes made from the very freshest fish and shellfish (delivered direct from Atlantic ports) are chalked on a blackboard: depending on the day's catch, they might include tiny squid in a garlicky sauce of their own ink, baked black scallops from Brest, fresh fried anchovies, shad in beurre blanc sauce, herbed brill, mackerel with mustard sauce, or thick, juicy sole. If you are content to drink a modest Aligoté or Quincy, your bill will hover around 300 F. But beware if you succumb to the temptations of the finest Cognac collection in Paris (and maybe the world). **C** 300-350. **M** 250 (wine incl).

Le Caroubier

122, av. du Maine - 01 43 20 41 49
Closed 3 wks in Aug. Open until 10:30pm. Terrace dining. Air cond.
Do you like couscous? Here you'll find the genuine article: homemade, hand-rolled, and fragrant with spices. Also on offer are a lively eggplant salad, savory pastillas, and succulent tagines, simmered in the best Moroccan tradition. Heartwarming welcome. **C** 220-260. **M** 88 (weekday lunch), 140.

La Chaumière des Gourmets

22, pl. Denfert-Rochereau - 01 43 21 22 59
Closed Sat lunch, Sun, 1st 3 wks of Aug. Open until 10:30pm. Terrace dining.
The Chaumière's friendly, provincial dining room still features faded fabric on the walls, the staff carries on with imperturbable diligence, the wine list remains small, and the house repertoire

invariably classic. But in this case, no news really is good news: the flavorful duck terrine, entrecôte bordelaise, and frozen nougat on the 165 F menu attest to Jean-Paul Huc's unfailing consistency and flair. C 325. M 165, 245.

12/20 La Coupole

102, bd du Montparnasse
01 43 20 14 20, fax 01 43 35 46 14
Open daily until 2am. Air cond.
This Montparnasse landmark, respectfully restored and run by the Flo brasserie group, survives with its mystique intact. The menu bears Flo's unmistakable stamp: gigantic shellfish assortments, grilled meats, and carafes of sprightly house Riesling are delivered by friendly waiters perhaps victim of lack of organization in the kitchen—it took us two hours and a half to get through a meal, so don't come here for lunch when you have an important appointment in the afternoon. C 250-350. M 123 (lunch, wine incl), 128 (dinner, wine incl).

 ### Le Dôme

108, bd du Montparnasse
01 43 35 25 81, fax 01 42 79 01 19
Closed Mon. Open until 12:30am. Terrace dining. Air cond. Pkg.
Le Dôme is the capital's top seafood brasserie, with a neo-Art Deco interior, booths that provide cozy comfort and privacy for the high-powered patrons, and an appetizing *carte* prepared by chef Frank Graux. In addition to impeccably fresh oysters and the justly famous lobster salad in a truffled dressing, you can choose bouillon de langoustines aux champignons, turbot hollandaise, sea bass in chive vinaigrette, or bouillabaisse that bears comparison with Marseille's best. Precise, cheerful service, and a cellar filled with bottles that incite you to splurge. C 350-450.

 ### Le Duc

243, bd Raspail
01 43 20 96 30, fax 01 43 20 46 73
Closed Sun, Mon, hols. Open until 10:30pm. Air cond. Pkg.
The respectful, minimalist approach to seafood imposed by Le Duc's founders endures even now that the Minchelli brothers are gone. The kitchen continues to handle only impeccable ingredients, heightening their innate goodness with a little sea salt, a dribble of oil, a brief moment on the fire. A recent dinner brought wild Scottish salmon cured for just a few hours in a bed of salt; perfect raw sardines; expertly grilled sea bream; and red mullet enhanced with fruity olive oil. It deserves another point. C 500-600. M 260 (lunch).

11/20 Giovanna

22, rue Édouard-Jacques - 01 43 22 32 09
Closed Sat lunch, Sun, Aug. Open until 10pm.
You, your companion, and sixteen other diners can tuck into perfectly wrought fresh pasta and

other fine Italian dishes in this minute trattoria, popular with the show-biz crowd. Don't overlook the osso buco. Some Moroccan dishes are also on the marquee. C 160-220.

 ## Lous Landés

157, av. du Maine - 01 45 43 08 04, fax 01 45 45 91 35
Closed Sat lunch, Sun, Aug. Open until 10:30pm. Terrace dining. Air cond.
Hervé Rumen's Southwestern specialties range from the robust to the refined. Taste his truffled foie gras au jus de canard, Landais squab flavored with three kinds of garlic, or his world-class cassoulet. Good news for light eaters: some of the heavier dishes are available in half-portions. Desserts are all you would expect from a former colleague of Christian Constant, and the wine list offers some excellent Cahors, Madirans, and a dry Pacherenc for 130 F. Marie-Thérèse, a charming hostess, welcomes guests into the pretty green dining room. C 300-400. M 195, 320.

 ## Le Moniage Guillaume

88, rue de la Tombe-Issoire
01 43 22 96 15, fax 01 43 27 11 79
Closed Sun. Open until 10:15pm. Terrace dining.
The regulars (and they are legion) just love this long-established seafood spot. Fish and crustaceans are handled with skill—and priced to kill, though the set meals provide some relief. Dessert-wise, the chocolate dumplings with velvety fresh-apricot sauce won't disappoint you. Rich cellar, including a reasonably tariffed Menetou-Salon. C 350-400. M 185, 245.

 ## Montparnasse 25

Hôtel Méridien,
19, rue du Commandant-Mouchotte
01 44 36 44 25, fax 01 44 36 49 03
Closed Sat, Sun, Aug, 1 wk at Christmas. Open until 10:30pm. Air cond. Pkg.
Unlike many hotel restaurants which are little more than a convenience for in-house patrons, the Méridien posts a magnetic menu that draws gourmets from all over Paris. The Art Deco interior opens onto a patio, and the well-spaced tables are just what executives desire for their power lunches. Yet even the most intense negotiations come to a halt when the waiter presents chef Jean-Yves Guého's expressively flavorful dishes. This triple-toque winner cooked for years at the Hong Kong Méridien, and it shows in his spiced sole with fried noodles and baby bean sprouts or stupendous suckling pig served in two courses: the rack and leg rubbed with sesame and satay paste, the shoulder and ribs braised with vegetables. A monumental cheese board presents over 150 choice specimens, and the cellar is awash in remarkable growers' wines. Over 50 fresh-herb teas on hand. C 400-600. M 240 (lunch), 300 (dinner).

Pavillon Montsouris

20, rue Gazan - 01 45 88 38 52, fax 01 45 88 63 40
Open daily until 10pm (11pm in summer). Terrace dining. Pkg.
A walk across the Parc Montsouris at sunset will give you an appetite for a fine feast in this turn-of-the-century greenhouse overlooking the park, once the haunt of the beautiful spy, Mata Hari. Jean-François Sicallac—who just checked out of none other than La Tour d'Argent—puts forth deft cooking that adds still more sunshine to this charming spot: taste the warm Provençal-style shellfish soup, the tangy tongue and calf's head meat roll with ravigote sauce, the well-crafted cod roasted with chitterlings or the potent pot-roasted wild-hare's leg. We find the menu prices portly and the cellar downright expensive. Small tables are balanced by gorgeous desserts and friendly service. C 198-265.

 Les Petites Sorcières

12, rue Liancourt - 01 43 21 95 68, fax 01 42 79 99 03
Closed Sat lunch, Sun. Open until 10:30pm. Terrace dining. Air cond. Pkg.
Christian Teule fills up his pocket-sized restaurant with an appealing lunch menu that offers house-made jambon persillé followed by herb-poached cod, cheese, and bitter-chocolate mousse. A la carte choices are more elaborate but no less savory: yummy chicken terrine, sautéed monkfish with sweet peppers, and spiced pear clafoutis. Good wines are available by the carafe. M 165.

11/20 **Les Phinéas**

99, rue de L'Ouest - 01 45 41 33 50
Closed Sun, Mon. Open until 11:30pm.
You might call this «pie palace». Tarts and pies and quiches galore in a décor totally dedicated to comic strips. A playful atmosphere for dining with friends. C 140.

12/20 **Picrocole**

9, rue Vandamme - 01 43 21 57 58
Closed Sat lunch, Sun, end Jlu-mid Aug. Open until 11:30pm. Pkg.
The relaxed Montparnasse atmosphere of this very Parisian bistro smartened up with a 1930s bar, moleskin booths and an entrancing inner courtyard serves as a merry setting for Jean-Pierre Milan's cooking, which takes on a more serious note: ginger-enhanced blood pudding salad, tartare au couteau (no machine grinding here!), finely textured fennel-flavored cod, and lamb curry with green mangos. The reasonably priced set meals can be accompanied by just as reasonably priced wines, with pitchers running 50 F and all bottles 200. C 200-250. M 90-110 (lunch).

12/20 **Pinocchio**

124, av. du Maine - 01 43 21 26 10, fax 01 43 21 26 37
Closed Sat lunch, Sun. Open until 11pm. Terrace dining.

Step past the wooden statue of Pinocchio on the sidewalk, and settle down for some earthy and satisfying Sicilian fare: spiced octopus, grilled peppers, lamb-stuffed pansotti, and fragrant bollito misto. C 240. M 120.

 La Régalade

49, av. Jean-Moulin - 01 45 45 68 58
Closed Sat lunch, Sun, Mon, mid Jul-mid Aug. Open until midnight. Terrace dining. Air cond. Pkg.
Don't fail to book your table way in advance, for La Régalade fills up fast. Here's why: Yves Camdeborde (ex-Crillon, no less) serves up first-rate cooking at incredible prices. Regionally rooted but modern in outlook, the menu proposes a sapid terrine of oxtail and leek, potato and lobster gratin glazed with Parmesan, succulent wood pigeon barded with bacon, and such delectable desserts as pan-roasted burlat cherries. Appealing Southwestern cellar with prices that match the menu. M 170.

12/20 **La Table et la Forme**

Sofitel Paris Forum Rive Gauche
17, bd Saint-Jacques - 01 45 78 79 60
Closed Sat lunch, Sun, Jul 12-Aug 17. Open until 11pm. Terrace dining. Air cond. Pkg.
That was an idea—gastronomic meals containing less than 1,000 calories, but it's still to be proven. The spanking light wood *boiserie* dining room of the Sofitel hotel hosts dishes such as rabbit in jelly with a low-calorie curd and curry sauce, veal steaks clothed with an insipid (but grease-free) veal stock, and aspartame-sweetened apple charlotte. Not all ideas are good ones... M 195-250.

 Les Vendanges

40, rue Friant - 01 45 39 59 98, fax 01 45 39 74 13
Closed Sat lunch, Sun, Aug. Open until 10:30pm.
Pink napery and antiques lend an old-fashioned charm to this restaurant with its sparkling new façade. Philippe Joubin and Guy Tardif cook up generous classics like pheasant galantine with foie gras, braised beef and vegetables, grilled pike perch with lentils and bacon, and rhubarb-topped shortbread. Tardif, son of a charcutier, also turns out a bang-up andouillette. Interesting cellar, rich in Bordeaux. M 200.

 Au Vin des Rues

21, rue Boulard - 01 43 22 19 78
Closed Sun, Mon, end Feb, Aug. Terrace dining.
Jean Chanrion's robust Lyonnais-style *plats du jour* are served forth in an authentic bistro setting, and are washed down by jugs of wonderful growers' Mâcons and Beaujolais. Don't be in a hurry. C 180-240.

Looking for a celebrated chef? Refer to the **index.**

Vin et Marée

108, av. du Maine - 01 43 20 29 50
Open daily until midnight. Terrace dining. Air cond. Pkg.
Jean-Pierre Durand's first seafood brasserie (on Boulevard Murat in the sixteenth arrondissement) is so successful that he decided to reprise that winning formula here, in premises that formerly housed the Armes de Bretagne restaurant. Durand brings home expertly chosen fish and shellfish from the market at Rungis, so that lucky diners can feast on ultrafresh Breton shrimp, tiny squid sautéed with mild garlic, sole cooked in sweet butter, or grilled turbotin. Briny steamed cockles are offered as an *amuse-bouche*, and for dessert there's a yummy baba au rhum. Well-oiled service. C 200-220.

15th ARRONDISSEMENT

Postal code	75015

 ## L'Agape

281, rue Lecourbe - 01 45 58 19 29
Closed Sat lunch, Sun, Aug. Open until 10:30pm.
Marc Lamic's attractive menu brims with bright ideas and flavors: we gobbled up his delicious confit de canard served beneath a fluffy potato blanket, the tasty turbot roasted with fragrant olive oil, potatoes stuffed with ox tail, and hot pineapple gratin. Down-to-earth prices. C 120.

 ## Bistro 121

121, rue de la Convention
01 45 57 52 90, fax 01 45 57 14 69
Open daily until midnight. Air cond.
Decorated in a now dated «modern» style, but comfortable and bright nonetheless, André Jalbert's bistro is a conservatory of reassuring, traditional French cuisine. You won't leave hungry after feasting on molded anchovies in vinaigrette, veal tenderloin scented with juniper, or the robust game dishes served in season. Attractively priced cellar. C 220-250. M 168, 250 (wine incl).

 ## Le Bistro d'Hubert

41, bd Pasteur - 01 47 34 15 50
Open daily until 11pm. Terrace dining. Air cond. Pkg.
Hubert gets around. It's our good fortune that this cheese specialist turned chef has lighted back on the Paris scene like Roland with a cornucopia of ideas and good things to eat. The delightful dining room is dressed up in a mixture of country inn, bourgeois dining room and old-time general store opening onto the most ultramodern of kitchens, all inspired by Michel Guérard's La Ferme aux Grives. In Paris, it would be hard to match the quality of his set-price menus which allow you to stay the straight path with a thoroughly traditional repertoire or venture into unknown lands with his more inventive offerings such as scallops in oyster emulsion, surprising oxtail nougat adorned with foie gras and curry cream sauce, or Gers chicken fricassée with garlic cloves cooked in their skin. Young bubbly waitresses take jolly care of you in this fun-loving atmosphere. M 100-135 (lunch), 175.

12/20 Casa Alcalde

117, bd de Grenelle - 01 47 83 39 71
Open daily until 10:30pm. Terrace dining. Air cond.
A lively *bodega* offering zesty Basque and Spanish fare. Try the excellent pipérade, marinated anchovies, generously served paella, or codfish à la luzienne. The wine list features fine Rioja and Navarre from beyond the Pyrenees. Reservations strongly recommended. C 200-250. M 150.

 ## Les Célébrités

Hôtel Nikko, 61, quai de Grenelle
01 40 58 21 29, fax 01 40 58 24 44
Closed Aug. Open until 10pm. Air cond. Pkg.
No rough edges mar Jacques Sénéchal's virtuoso handling of flawless seasonal foodstuffs. His 390 F single-price menu presents (for example) clams marinière with garlic and parsley, a lusty boiled-beef salad rémoulade, grilled fish of the day, and pasta fired up with capers, herbs, and chili peppers. Flavors are refined yet definite, cooking times are invariably right. Only the dessert cart needs revising. As for the cellar, it's beyond reproach: astutely assembled, appealing and, all in all, affordably priced. C 400-650. M 290, 390.

 ## Chen

15, rue du Théâtre
01 45 79 34 34, fax 01 45 79 07 53
Closed Sun. Open until 11pm. Air cond.
Inside a shopping mall, aggressively decorated—Chen does not look promising! But the short menu holds lots of wonderful surprises. The fresh, precisely prepared crab velouté with asparagus, dumplings in a fragrant broth, peppery sautéed crab, and exemplary Peking duck may not be cheap, but they're well worth the money. Unquestionably the best lacquered duck in Paris. C 300-500. M 200 (weekdays lunch, wine incl), 280-450.

Le Clos Morillons

50, rue des Morillons
01 48 28 04 37, fax 01 48 28 70 77
Closed Sat lunch, Sun. Open until 10pm.
The French colonial décor of this charming establishment transports you to the tropics. The feeling lingers as you peruse the menu, for 's

repertoire Philippe Delacourcelle is redolent of exotic spices. Among the original, expertly rendered dishes are sole with sweet lime leaves, calf's liver scented with cinnamon, suavely spiced snails, and gingered veal with puréed almonds. The fixed-price menu is truly a find for Paris. Delectable desserts and a fine selection of wines priced under 100 F complete the picture. C 300-350. C 120 (lunch, wine incl), 165, 250.

11/20 Les Coteaux

26, bd Garibaldi - 01 47 34 83 48
Closed Sat, Sun, Mon dinner, Aug. Open until 9:30pm.
The success story started two years ago when Bernard Olry's little restaurant was named GaultMillau's Bistro of the Month and later snapped up the Best Drink award. He continues down the path of success, improving the food as he goes along. This Lyon-style tavern with its oilcloth tablecloths serves up Lyonnais specialities such as silk-weaver's «brains» (herb-flecked curds), grilled pig's ear, sapper's apron (breaded pan-fried tripes), Saint Pourçain andouillette sausage and coq au vin. Imbibe all this with a Beaujolais, Aligoté Burgundy or Ardèche Syrah by the glass, pitcher or bottle—just like in Lyon. M 130.

 ## Philippe Detourbe

8, rue Nicolas Charlet
01 42 19 08 59, fax 01 45 67 09 13
Closed Sat lunch, Sun, Aug. Open until 11pm. Air cond.
Philippe Detourbe's customers never need to wonder about their bill, since the two moderately priced set meals do the figuring for them. Among the adroitly prepared dishes we've noted lately (the menus change every day) are cassolette of snails with bacon and mushrooms, grilled red mullet on a bed of ratatouille, and cod with cabbage and a drizzle of hazelnut oil. Reserve well in advance; Parisians flock into this Orient Express style dining room. Affordable cellar, too. M 180 (lunch), 220 (dinner).

 ## La Dinée

85, rue Leblanc - 01 45 54 20 49, fax 01 40 60 74 88
Closed Sat lunch, Sun. Open until 10:45pm. Air cond. Pkg.
Christophe Chabanel earned his first toque at the tender age of 22. Here in his contemporary yellow-and-blue digs, now hard at work on his third toque in this pluperfect neighborhood restaurant, his finely honed technique and inventive ideas produce a cutting-edge, thoroughly Parisian menu. Among the excellent options on offer are fennel-flavored crab ravioli floating in a licorice-enhanced langoustine consommé, veal sweetbread crisps livened up with candied pepper and horseradish oil, toothsome John Dory fish grilled in buttered paper and highlighted with soya, grapefruit and sage, crusty saddle of lamb flanked with fresh herbs, and chocolate

and banana shortbread companioned with passion fruit. C 350-400. M 220-450 (wine incl), 310.

 ## Fellini

58, rue de la Croix-Nivert - 01 45 77 40 77
Closed Sat lunch, Sun, Aug. Open until 11pm. Pkg.
Giuseppe hails from sunny Napoli, where he learned to cook in a fresh, forthright style. Pull up a seat in his friendly trattoria, and sample a warm salad of baby squid and white beans drizzled with olive oil, or fresh tagliolini with langoustines and tomatoes. His tiramisù is the lightest we've tried. To wash it down, uncork a bottle from the well-stocked well-priced Italian cellar. One of the best Italian restaurants in Paris; be sure and ask about the daily specials. C 250-280.

 ## Le Gastroquet

10, rue Desnouettes - 01 48 28 60 91
Closed Sat, Sun, 2 wks in Aug. Open until 10:30pm.
The *patronne* pampers patrons in the dining room, while her husband, Dany Bulot, cooks up rousing bistro fare in his kitchen. Calf's head, boudin en salade, fresh sausage, and cod marmite are staples on the hearty menu. Moderately priced cellar, with plenty of half-bottles. C 270-330. M 155.

 ## Kim Anh

15, rue de l'Église - 01 45 79 40 96, fax 01 40 59 49 78
Dinner only. Open daily until 11pm. Air cond.
Charming Kim-Anh runs this flower-filled little Vietnamese restaurant while his wife, Caroline, does the cooking in a lilliputian kitchen made for contortionists. Fresh herbs, delectable leaves and shoots, subtle spices enhance her curried shrimp, beef with lemon grass, piquant stuffed crab, and the best egg rolls in town. Steepish prices. C 200. M 150-220 (wine incl).

 ## Restaurant du Marché

59, rue de Dantzig - 01 48 28 31 55
Closed Sat lunch, Sun. Open until 11pm. Terrace dining.
A farmer's cartel sends fresh Southwestern produce straight to Christiane Massia's kitchen door. She transforms this bounty into wonderful cassoulet, beef stewed in Madiran wine, and myriad dishes starring plump Landais ducks. Wash it all down with one of her excellent Bordeaux, and finish off your feast with a tot of fine old Armagnac. C 280-350. M 190.

 ## Morot Gaudry

8, rue de la Cavalerie
01 45 67 06 85, fax 01 45 67 55 72
Closed Sun. Open until 10:30pm. Terrace dining. Air cond.
The thrill is gone. Morot-Gaudry's langoustines with endives, snails with morels and sunchokes, roast lamb with stuffed vegetables, pike perch with tarragon sabayon are all

honorable dishes, but they no longer astonish or surprise. A remarkable chocolate cake en chaud-froid with citrus fruits sounded an optimistic note, however. As always, the cellar holds a trove of moderately priced treasures. From the verdant terrace you can catch a glimpse of the Eiffel Tower. C 370-470. M 230 (lunch, wine incl), 340, 490 (wine incl).

 ## Le Moulin

70, rue de Vouillé - 01 48 28 81 61
Closed Sat lunch, Sun dinner. Open until 10:30pm.
A quiet, unassuming spot where quality ingredients are handled with care. Roger Buhagiar proposes a fine poached foie gras de canard, roast rack of lamb with fresh vegetables, and a rich double-chocolate dessert. Small list of well-chosen wines; cordial welcome. C 250. M 130 (weekday lunch), 150, 175 (dinner).

 ## L'Os à Moelle

3, rue Vasco-de-Gama - 01 45 57 27 27
Closed Sun, Mon, Aug 22. Open until midnight. Terrace dining.
Thierry Faucher gives his customers terrific value for their money, with imaginative menus inspired by whatever looks fresh and fine at the market. The 145 F lunch might bring gingerbread-coated foie gras garnished with spinach and beets, veal kidney with celery root purée and bone marrow, cheese, and a chocolate quenelle with saffron sauce. A *tour de force*, even if portions aren't gigantic. We would hope for a more gracious welcome in the future, however. M 145 (lunch), 190 (dinner).

12/20 L'Ostréade

11, bd de Vaugirard
01 43 21 87 41, fax 01 43 21 55 09
Open daily until 11pm, Sat-Sun 11:30pm. Terrace dining.
While away an hour at this pleasant seafood brasserie before the TGV whisks you out West. Excellent oysters, ultrafresh fish prepared in clever, uncomplicated ways. If you're really in a hurry to catch that train, you can gobble down some of their tasty *tapas*. C 200-250. M 150.

 ## Le Père Claude

51, av. de La Motte-Picquet
01 47 34 03 05, fax 01 40 56 97 84
Open daily until midnight. Terrace dining. Air cond.
Claude Perraudin lives like a monk (albeit of the Rabelaisian type), his existence devoted to feeding his faithful patrons. Seven days a week in his jolly brasserie, Father Claude oversees a gargantuan rotisserie where strings of sausages, plump poultry, beef, and racks of lamb spin slowly on the spit until they're done to a turn. There are oceans of tasty wine to wash it all down. The prices? Blessedly low, of course. C 250-300. M 105-160, 130 (Sat & Sun).

 # Le Petit Plat

49, av. Émile-Zola
01 45 78 24 20, fax 01 45 78 23 13
Closed wk of Aug 15, 1 wk at Christmas. Open until 11pm. Terrace dining. Air cond. Pkg.
A jolly mood pervades this pretty restaurant, owing mostly to the Lampreia brothers' South of France-style cooking: fennel and basil soup, cod with olive oil, tomates provençales, cockles and mussels in a tasty broth, succulent veal breast with slow-roasted vegetables are typical of their light, generous fare. The décor is like the food, simple with no ostentation. The clever wine list was composed by our friend, Henri Gault, and offers a good selection of wines under 100 F. C 180-240. M 135.

 # Le Relais de Sèvres

Sofitel Paris Sèvres, 8-12, rue Louis-Armand
01 40 60 33 66, fax 01 45 57 04 22
Closed Sat, Sun, hols, Aug, Dec 24-Jan 1. Open until 10pm. Air cond. Pkg.
A décor that spells good (but cold) taste in capital letters: blond woodwork; pale-blue fabric on the walls; champagne-colored napery; Louis XVI chairs. Young chef Bruno Turbot is proudly living up to the sterling reputation that Roland Durand left behind. The delicacy of execution is there, but a little less artifice might do his cuisine well. We must give due where its due, however. The langoustine lasagna with ginger butter and melissa, scallops and Belon oysters in sorrel fondue, and roast Bresse chicken with salsify and corn sprouts were worthy dishes. You'll find attention-getting vintages on the carefully selected list of wines, and how original his list of mineral waters from all corners of Europe. C 400-500. M 375 (dinner), 385 (wine incl).

 # Restaurant de La Tour

6, rue Desaix - 01 43 06 04 24
Closed Sat lunch, Sun, Aug. Open until 10:30pm.
Roger Conticini (his sons run the triple-toque Table d'Anvers in the ninth arrondissement) is at the helm of this engaging restaurant. The dishes on his single-price menus change often, but all have an earthy, raffish appeal: hot game pâté, a lusty salad of pig's ear and trotter, tuna braised in red wine with risotto, and ginger-snapped duck breast with honey are typical of the house style. Fine little cellar. Nice going, Roger! C 200-250. M 125 & 138 (weekday lunch), 185.

 # Sawadee

53, av. Émile-Zola
01 45 77 68 90, fax 01 77 57 78
Closed Sun, 10 days in Aug. Open until 10:30pm. Terrace dinning. Air cond.
Sawadee is one of the city's best Thais. Spacious, over-decorated, very lively, it offers an immense list of specialties full of unexpected flavors. The salad of pork rinds and fried rice, skewered shellfish, mussels in a fiery sauce, cod

with seaweed and wild lemon, duck perfumed with Thai basil, and coconut ice cream all come highly recommended. Thai beer is also on hand. C 150-200. M 75 (weekday lunch), 116-175.

12/20 Aux Senteurs de Provence

295, rue Lecourbe
01 45 57 11 98, fax 01 45 58 66 84
Closed Sat lunch, Sun, Aug 4-16. Open until 10pm. Terrace dining.
This temple of bouillabaise also serves up other selections from the delicate, freshly fragrant repertoire of Provençal cuisine. Sun-kissed ingredients lend an authentic savor to the tuna in a tarragon marinade, roast galinette (a Mediterranean fish) à la niçoise, and generous bouillabaisse. The cellar is modest. The salmon-colored crinkled walls, carpet and drapes, all new, make a neat and cheerful setting. C 250-300. M 140.

Pierre Vedel

19, rue Duranton - 01 45 58 43 17, fax 01 45 58 42 65
Closed Sat lunch Oct-Apr, Sun, 1 wk at Christmas. Open until 10:15pm.
Be sure to book your table, because Pierre Vedel's warm Parisian bistro is invariably jam-packed. Little wonder the place is popular, given the delectable house foie gras, authentic bourride de lotte à la sétoise (a garlicky monkfish soup), and lush bitter-chocolate charlotte. If you order one of the more modest growers' wines from the interesting list, the bill won't be too bad. C 300.

16th ARRONDISSEMENT

Postal code	75016

11/20 L'Adresse

4, rue Beethoven - 01 40 50 84 40
Closed Sat lunch, Sun. Open until 11pm. Terrace dining. Air cond.
A bargain-priced menu for 98 F, including wine, offering an array of interesting dishes such as curried mushroom ravioli, navarin d'agneau, and figs served in a peppermint bouillon. C 220-260. M 98 & 158 (wine incl).

12/20 Amazigh

2, rue La Pérouse - 01 47 20 90 38
Open daily until 11pm. Air cond.
A Moroccan restaurant with an enticing bill of fare: savory briouates (deep-fried pastries) filled with shellfish, eggplant salad sparked with coriander (zalouk), lamb tagine with fried eggplant, and sumptuous «grand couscous». Also worthy of interest are the stuffed sardines,

lamb's brains in tomato sauce, and cinnamon-scented oranges. Like the setting, the service is pretty posh. C 250.

11/20 Le Beaujolais d'Auteuil

99, bd de Montmorency - 01 47 43 03 56
Open daily until 11pm. Terrace dining.
Don't let the name mislead you, because you'll find more high-quality reasonably-priced Bordeaux here than you will Beaujolais. These little treasures can be accompanied by friendly-priced classics such as celery root with remoulade sauce, pan-fried onglet steak, kidney fricassée and salmon in all shapes and forms. C 200-250. M 123-143 (wine incl).

Bellini

28, rue Le Sueur - 01 45 00 54 20, fax 01 45 00 11 74
Closed Sat lunch, Sun, 1 wk at Christmas. Open until 10:30pm. Air cond.
Comfy banquettes, mirrors, marble, and chamois-toned walls create a cozy setting for Bellini's somewhat Frenchified Italian fare. Diaphanous slices of prosciutto di Parma lead into such savory dishes as lobster salad with polenta, red mullet with olives, or veal kidney cooked in brawny Barolo wine. The cellar harbors appealing wines from Friulia, Tuscany, and the Veneto. C 250-300. M 180.

Bertie's

Hôtel Baltimore, 1, rue Léo-Delibes
01 44 34 54 34, fax 01 44 34 54 44
Closed 2 wks in Aug. Open until 10:30pm. Air cond. Pkg.
When Bertie's opened, a major London daily ran this tongue-in-cheek headline: «Finally! A good meal in Paris!» The dining room cultivates a clubby British look that Parisians adore. And yes, the menu is English: potted crab, Welsh mussel soup, Scottish lamb with mint sauce, bread-and-butter pudding... The maître d' will astound you with his knowledge of Britain's 400 cheeses; the wine steward will amaze you with his list of prime clarets. And after your meal, you can linger contentedly over a rare whisky or vintage Port. C 280-320. M 160 (lunch), 195.

Bistrot de l'Étoile-Lauriston

19, rue Lauriston - 01 40 67 11 16, fax 01 45 00 99 87
Closed Sat lunch, Sun. Open until midnight. Air cond. Pkg.
This big, bright bistro continues on its successful career. Chef William Ledeuil handles the neo-bourgeois repertoire with admirable ease, offering rabbit persillé or a vibrant vegetable salad showered with Parmesan to start, followed by steak à la bordelaise or stuffed veal shank simmered in a sparky vinegar sauce. For dessert, we warmly recommend the apple-rhubarb crumble. Quench your thirst with a carafe of lusty Chardonnay or Merlot. C 220-250. M 165 (lunch).

La Butte Chaillot

110 bis, av. Kléber
01 47 27 88 88, fax 01 47 04 85 70
Open daily until midnight. Terrace dining. Air cond. Pkg.

Chef and restaurateur Guy Savoy turned an unpromising site (a former bank) into a fashionable restaurant with a star-studded clientele. The keys to his success are a clever contemporary décor, a swift and stylish staff, and—best of all—an ever-changing roster of irresistible dishes: succulent spit-roasted poultry with whipped potatoes, veal breast perfumed with rosemary and olive oil, and lots of luscious desserts. Try Troisgros's highly palatable Côtes-Roannaises or Ostertag's Alsatian Pinot-Noir. C 250-280. M 150-210.

 ## Carré Kléber

Hôtel Paris K Palace,
11 bis, rue de Magdebourg
01 47 55 82 08, fax 01 47 55 80 09
Closed Sat lunch, Sun, 3 wks in Aug, 1 wk at Christmas. Open until 10:30pm. Air cond. Pkg.

Provence, as we know, is furiously à la mode. Christophe Delaunay pays homage to the current fashion with a delicious tart of red mullet and baby mackerel on a bed of tomato fondue and tapenade, and other suitably Southern delights. The very pretty modern dining room opens onto a leafy patio embellished with ornamental ponds and bamboo. Small albeit good collection of wines, but not always served at the right temperature. C 280-320. M 195.

 ## Paul Chène

123, rue Lauriston
01 47 27 63 17, fax 01 47 27 53 18
Closed Sat lunch, Sun, last wk of Dec. Open until 10:30pm. Air cond.

Elbow-room is at a premium in Paul Chène's two faded dining rooms, but the owners are unstinting with their hospitality and the kitchen, too, has a generous spirit. You're sure to relish golden classics such as eggs poached in red wine, quality Parma ham, beef tenderloin béarnaise, and profiteroles napped in chocolate. Both the food and the décor take you back in time to a *Vieille France* which has virtually disappeared. The cellar boasts a varied, judicious selection, yet the house Bordeaux is not to be neglected. C 250-400. M 200, 250.

 ## Conti

72, rue Lauriston
01 47 27 74 67, fax 01 47 27 37 66
Closed Sat, Sun, Aug 4-24, end Dec-beg Jan. Open until 10:30pm. Air cond.

With Sormani's Jean-Pascal Fayet (see seventeenth arrondissement), Michel Ranvier is a leading French exponent of Italian cooking. Perhaps a shade less creative than Fayet, Ranvier still gives his menu a vigorous zest. Examples? Clams and cockles with fennel in a perfumed broth, a perfect risotto with fresh peas and asparagus, and a fabulous bollito misto with pungent mostarda di Cremona. The set-price menu is a gem. The Italian cellar is a wonder to behold, and the staff provides silken service. C 360-460. M 198 (lunch).

 ## Le Cuisinier François

19, rue Le Marois - 01 45 27 83 74, fax 01 45 27 83 74
Closed dinner Sun & Wed, Mon, Aug. Open until 10:15pm. Pkg.

After stints at La Tour d'Argent, Robuchon, and Boyer in Reims, Thierry Conte did not, as one might expect, open a place with his name in large letters over the door. Instead, he settled for an establishment of modest proportions and a menu that is most moderately priced. Sorry to have been so critical the past few years, because this year's visit brings only full and hearty applause. We found him overflowing with imagination. What a novel idea, the red mullet and candied lemon salad with the sweet little sea urchin in its shell resting atop. How terribly original, the scallop fricassée with its gently-dosed ginger butter flanked with old-fashioned vegetables we'd forgotten existed, or the pan-fried cod with garlicky potatoes and a perfectly poignant «wine-inspired» sauce. The upside-down pear and dried fruit pie with licorice ice cream afforded us extreme pleasure. Smiling dynamic reception by Elisabeth Conte. Juguenot's Gouleyant Marsannay '93 is well worth sipping. C 250-350. M 160.

 ## Alain Ducasse

59, av. Raymond-Poincaré
01 47 27 12 27, fax 01 47 27 31 22
Closed Sat, Sun, hols, Jul 4-Aug 4, end Dec-beg Jan. Open until 10:30pm. Air cond. Pkg.

Paris—in geographical as well as in culinary terms—is far from the Mediterranean sea. In the former very chic, a tad solemn, premises of Joël Robuchon in the *beaux quartiers* of Paris, Alain Ducasse felt he had to offer a cuisine somewhat different from the one that made him famous in Monte Carlo (the Louis XV). There is less of the Southern sun in his Parisian dishes, because he is trodding a new (less sunny) territory, which proves the full array of his talent. Here the products of all the French provinces are welcomed, granted, of course, they are the best. In their preparation, Ducasse reveals his parenthood with the great French gastronomic tradition, demonstrating references to Brillat-Savarin and to his owner personal master, Alain Chapel. But he stops just short of total classicism. The menu changes with the seasons. Spring, for instance, is devoted to mushrooms and asparagus. Evidence of the chef's double evolution will be found in his Breton lobster sautéed with morels and asparagus (at Easter time); his half-dried pasta in a rich cream and truffle sauce accompanied by sweetbreads and cockscombs; or his scallops studded with black truffles and fresh Landes foie gras en cocotte. Service is the very model of attentiveness. We were impressed by the monumental cellar and by the equally monumental bill. An elegantly decorated bar on the ground floor is a haven for cigars aficionados and others who appreciate old brandies. C 800-1,200. M 480 (lunch), 780, 890.

Fakhr el Dine

30, rue de Longchamp
01 47 27 90 00, fax 01 47 27 11 39
Open daily until 11:30pm. Air cond. Pkg.
See *8th arrondissement.* C 290. M 150-340.

Faugeron

52, rue de Longchamp
01 47 04 24 53, fax 01 47 55 62 90
Closed Sat lunch off-seas, Sun, Aug, Dec 23-Jan 3. Open until 10pm. Air cond. Pkg.
Henri Faugeron hails from the Corrèze countryside, where a man is judged by his work, not his pretensions. This modest, even self-effacing chef doesn't go in for bold experiments, but he knows how to use an uncommon spice, or mustard, or vinegar to give traditional dishes a pungent, modern zest. Faugeron pays tribute to his rustic roots with seasonal variations on cèpes and truffles, with tender veal shank heightened with a piquant touch of Brive's violet mustard, or a beef daube braised à l'ancienne for a full ten hours and served with truffled pasta. A pastoral apple flognarde is a final flourish to be savored along with the last drops of a great Bordeaux, Burgundy, or more modest Chinon or Sancerre, chosen Jean-Claude Jambon, named World's Best Sommelier in 1986. Madame Faugeron will give you a delicious welcome. C 500-600. M 320 (lunch), 550 (dinner, wine incl)

11/20 Les Filaos

5, rue Guy-de-Maupassant - 01 45 04 94 53
Closed Sun, Aug. Open until 11pm.
Spicy savors from Mauritius: try the palate-tingling stuffed crab seasoned with ginger and coriander, tamarind-flavored codfish beignets, octopus in a saffron marinade, or smoked sausages with a fiery rougail. C 180-210.

Le Flandrin

80, av. Henri-Martin - 01 45 04 35 69
Open daily until 11:30pm. Terrace dining. Pkg.
This chic brasserie now boasts a much-improved *carte*, thanks to the efforts of young Olivier Denis (trained by mega-chef Alain Passard). We like the shrimp beignets, macaroni and ricotta gratin, crab ravioli, langoustines grilled with wild thyme, and the warming lamb curry. Oysters and other fresh shellfish in season; good service. C 230-260.

Le Floridita

19, rue de Presbourg - 01 45 00 84 84
Closed Sat lunch, Sun, 2 wks in Aug. Air cond. Pkg.
Hemingway would have loved this cigar club-bar-restaurant tucked neatly behind the Place de l'Etoile. The leather armchairs and Honduras mahogany woodwork make you think you're in

Cuba. While waiting for your table, light up a *puro* cigar and sip the house cocktail, which is none other than the mighty Mojito, the limy rum-flavored drink invented by Hemingway himself. If you miss those thick New York strips, you'll do well with their juicy melt-in-your-mouth Nebraska beef, the house speciality. C 270-370. M 185 (lunch).

12/20 La Gare

19, chaussée de la Muette - 01 42 15 15 31
Closed Sun. Open until 11:30pm. Terrace dining. Air cond. Pkg.
The quaysides along the former Muette train station now serve as setting for spit-roasted goodies such as poulet-de-Bresse, Limousin lamb and Nebraska beef. A quick stop in a chic neighborhood. C 180-230.

Gastronomie Quach

47, av. Raymond-Poincaré - 01 42 27 98 40
Open daily until 11pm. Air cond.
Aquariums decorate the posh dining room where Monsieur Quach serves Cantonese and Vietnamese dishes that now have more good days than bad: prawns grilled with lemon grass, squid with red peppers, and grilled lamb with five spices are more precisely turned out than in the past. And the fine Peking duck keeps the glossy patrons coming back for more. Good and thoroughly unobstrusive service. C 240-320. M 92 (weekdays lunch), 109.

La Grande Cascade

Bois de Boulogne, near the racetrack
01 45 27 33 51, fax 01 42 88 99 06
Closed end Dec-mid Jan. Open until 10:30pm. Terrace dining. Pkg.
The setting of this former pleasure pavilion is exuberantly Belle Époque, and up until recently, the cuisine was discreetly classic. But super-chef Alain Ducasse has commissioned one of his best lieutenants, Jean-Louis Nomicos, to revamp the menu. As a result, the Cascade now shines with exciting tastes: fine potato ravioli; greens with a Parmesan tuile; sea-bass steak with fennel seeds and black pepper served with ground tomatoes in olive oil; and corn-fed chicken stuffed with fresh herbs sided with succulent mushroom gnocchi. The results are quality, but we are anxious to see more from this young chef once he breaks out of the shell of prestigious influence he was bathed in and starts to trod his own path. Go for the satisfying 295 F menu. C 600-800. M 295.

Lac Hong

67, rue Lauriston - 01 47 55 87 17
Closed Sun, Aug. Open until 10:45pm.
Vietnam's cuisine may be the most delicately flavorful in all of Southeast Asia. To test that proposition, just taste Madame Phan-Tuyêt's preparations full of refinement and magic taste combinations: delectable mussels perfumed

with tamarind and basil; ethereal turbot, gently spiked with ginger and then steamed; regal cockerel, grilled perfecto then removed from the bone and stuffed with seven different spices—worthy of a president's table. Even the Cantonese rice is exquisite: flawlessly cooked and bursting with flavor. C 250-350. M 108 (weekday lunch).

Eau de Wallace

The 50 **Fontaines Wallace** that dot the city are an enduring symbol of Paris. These dark-green iron fountains feature decorative domes upheld by a quartet of female figures, who stand gracefully around an ever-running stream of cool water. Donated to the city in 1873 by the English philanthropist, Sir Richard Wallace, the fountains provided Parisians with pure drinking water, a commodity in dangerously short supply after the devastating Siege of the Commune in 1871.

 ## Jamin

32, rue de Longchamp - 01 45 53 00 07
Closed Sat, Sun, Jul 11-Aug 4. Open until 10:15pm. Air cond. Pkg.
Joël Robuchon's old Jamin is now tended by a former Robuchon pupil, Benoît Guichard. No change in the pink and green candyshop décor, but a definite change in direction. Prices are considerably lower nowadays, with a 375 F set meal served at lunch and dinner, and an à la carte average between 360 and 400 F. The tone of cooking is not that of former days, and Guichard sports a style that resembles good home cooking more than that of the master who worked under this roof in yesteryears. You'll not be disappointed by the ultralight lentil and bacon cream soup or the watercress salad topped with slightly smoked herring. You'll wish there were more of the braised chuckroast with glazy cumin-spiced carrots and the hog jawl and tail ever so gently braised and roasted with marjoram. The pick-of-the-crop wines are sometimes hard on the pocket. C 360-400. M 280 (lunch), 375.

Marius

82, bd Murat - 01 46 51 67 80
Closed Sat lunch, Sun. Open until 10:30pm. Terrace dining.
No frills, no pretense, just good food in record time. This restaurant is almost always packed with regulars, so if you're planning on dropping in after a World Cup game (it's just around the

corner from the Parc des Princes stadium), it may be wise to call ahead. Hearty fare such as herb-flecked grilled sardines, haddock and lentil salad, steamed skate, John Dory and jumbo shrimp with mashed potatoes, and real bouillabaisse. Finish it all off with a super-thin crispy apple pie. Wash it all down with a 1990 Sainte-Roseline Côtes-de-Provence wine. C 250-320.

12/20 Chez Ngo

70, rue de Longchamp - 01 47 04 53 20
Open daily until 11:30pm. Air cond. Pkg.
An elegant Chinese table (pretty décor, lovely dishes) always full to the brim. Only heartbreak this year with the scrappy bits of salt-and-pepper calamari, the sticky steamed dumplings and the eggplant that tasted of soot. In addition, the greeting rather resembles that of a Chinese prison. All that together tips away the toque with no regret on our part. C 200-250.

 ## Oum el Banine

16 bis, rue Dufrenoy - 01 45 04 91 22
Closed Sat & Sun lunch. Open until 10:30pm. Air cond. Pkg.
To enter, knock on the heavy wooden door, just as you would in Morocco. Maria Seguin, who used to teach in Fez, practices authentic Fassi cuisine, whose secrets she gathered from recipes from the last Arab palace cooks. Five types of couscous are on offer, as well as eight tagines (with olives and pickled lemons, peppers and tomato, zucchini and thyme, etc.). More rarely seen, but typically Moroccan, are brains in a piquant tomato sauce, spiced tripe, and calf's foot with chickpeas. For dessert, an almond cream b'steeya. Slosh it all down with a Beni M'tir from the Meknes region. C 250-300.

Le Pergolèse

40, rue Pergolèse - 01 45 00 21 40, fax 01 45 00 81 31
Closed Sat, Sun, Aug. Open until 10:30pm. Air cond.
Local stockbrokers are bullish on Le Pergolèse. They've adopted Albert Corre's plush and intimate (indeed, slightly cramped) dining room as their unofficial headquarters. But it may be that Corre is spending too much time at the tables and not enough at the stove, for the cooking has dipped below its previous high. Perhaps the planned facelift of the dining room will be accompanied by a discerning look at the cooking methods. Our carpaccio of salt-cured lamb lacked character, for instance, and an overcooked sea bass was further marred by a dubious sauce. Happily, an unctuous chocolate dessert saved the toque—but only just! C 400-500. M 230, 380.

 ## Le Port Alma

10, av. de New-York - 01 47 23 75 11
Closed Sun, Aug. Open until 10:30pm. Terrace dining. Air cond. Pkg.
Paul Canal isn't one to blow his own horn, but he has few peers when it comes to cooking fish

and crustaceans. Count on Canal to pick the best of the day's catch, and prepare his prime specimens with a skilled hand and no superfluous sauces to mask their flavors. Bourride and bouillabaisse are featured on Fridays, or upon reservation. Pleasant welcome by the chef's wife, and an atmosphere that lets you forget you're in the busy throng of a large metropolis. Balanced cellar, with plenty of half-bottles. C 350-420. M 200 (lunch).

 ## Le Pré Catelan

Bois de Boulogne, route de Suresnes
01 44 14 41 14, fax 01 45 24 43 25
Closed Sun dinner, Mon, Feb school hols. Open until 10:30pm. Terrace dining. Pkg.
The Pré Catelan comes in two versions: summer, with tables set in a leafy garden amid fluttering parasols; and winter, an elegant dining room warmed by a crackling fire. The versatile talent of chef Frédéric Anton, once right-hand man to the great Robuchon, suits both settings, with dishes that are by turns urbane or rustic. The service may well be the best in Paris, and Jean-Pierre Chauveau is the archetype of what a maître d' should be. In season, you'll discover an extraordinary *menu truffe et cochon*, which demonstrates that with the right perfume—truffles, for example—one can indeed turn a sow's ear into something sublime: in this case a sow's ear crisp with langoustines. Sophisticated spicing marks the black risotto with Thai basil, and lamb's brain salad with its exquisite saffron aspic. This is the testing ground of the ultimate in pastry chefs, Le Nôtre, and divine they are indeed (ah! the hot chocolate-praline pastilla!). The cellar is well served by a first-rate sommelier, and the 550 F set meal will give you a good sampling of the multifarious talents of this chef. C 500-800. M 290 (weekday lunch), 350 (weekday lunch, wine incl), 550, 750.

 ## Prunier Traktir

16, av. Victor-Hugo
01 44 17 35 85, fax 01 44 17 90 10
Closed Sun, Mon lunch, Jul 15-Aug 15. Open until 11pm. Air cond. Pkg.
The rebirth of Prunier Traktir caused great rejoicing among Paris's pearls-and-tweed set, who regarded the demise of this once-brilliant seafood house as a personal loss. The man behind the revival is Jean-Claude Vrinat of Taillevent. From the moment he opened the doors of the gorgeously restored Art Deco interior (the ground floor dining room is on the historical register), Parisians took the dining room by storm. Handsome rooms are fitted up on the second floor as well, and Prunier is regularly packed with the sleek and famous. In the kitchen, Gabriel Biscay balances Prunier classics (lobster bisque, codfish brandade, marmite Dieppoise) with such contemporary items as fish tartare with oysters, red mullet à l'orientale, and langoustines royales au naturel. C 500-700.

Looking for a restaurant? Refer to the **index.**

 # Le Relais d'Auteuil

31, bd Murat - 01 46 51 09 54, fax 01 40 71 05 03
Closed Sat lunch, Sun, 3 wks in Aug. Open until 10:30pm. Terrace dining. Air cond. Pkg.
Patrick Pignol's imaginative, resolutely modern cuisine is a treat to discover. Uncompromising in his choice of ingredients, he follows the seasons to obtain the very freshest, finest produce. In summer, he'll feature zucchini blossoms and other vegetables at the peak of their flavor; in fall, look for sage-scented braised partridge; winter might bring a mammoth sole in a sauce of lightly salted butter and fiery Szechuan pepper. Cozy atmosphere. If only Pignol would keep a tighter rein on his prices...! C 480-550. M 250 (lunch), 420, 530.

 # Le Relais du Parc

Hôtel Le Parc, 55-57, av. Raymond-Poincaré
01 44 05 66 10, fax 01 44 05 66 00
Open daily until 10:30pm. Terrace dining. Air cond. Pkg.
Le Relais du Parc holds a winning hand. Set in the luxurious Le Parc hotel, it sports a British colonial setting and is now under the supervision of Alain Ducasse (who also has taken over Robuchon next door). Ducasse has kept such Robuchon dishes as the aerial creamy soup in a crustacean gelée, but he has also added Southwestern dishes: cod-stuffed bell peppers; tomatoes stuffed with vegetables; John Dory on a bed of fennel; melon soup in Jurançon wine. A vegetable lover's paradise. Reservations are a must. C 320-400.

11/20 Le Scheffer

22, rue Scheffer - 01 47 27 81 11
Closed Sun. Open until 10:30pm.
This retro-style bistro has become a regular stopover for the inhabitants of this ultra-chic neighborhood. Perfect place to sample disappearing home-style classics like leeks with vinaigrette, cod with mashed potatoes or navarin d'agneau. Goes well with a splash of Chinon by the glass. C 180-200.

 # Vivarois

192, av. Victor-Hugo
01 45 04 04 31, fax 01 45 03 09 84
Closed Sat, Sun, Aug. Open until 10pm. Air cond. Pkg.
Claude Peyrot imperturbably polishes a concise, unchanging *carte* which he supplements daily with a half-dozen dishes created on the spur of the moment. In the latter category, we fondly recall a sublime wild-mushroom terrine with foie gras; in the former, we recommend the sweet-pepper bavaroise heightened with an uncommonly fragrant walnut oil. Peyrot's pared-down style leaves little room for error. When a dish is perfectly done, its purity elicits admiration; but the slightest flaw makes simplicity look suspiciously like skimping... Exemplary service in a handsome contemporary dining room. The fine cellar is run by Jean-Claude Vinadier, som-

melier *extraordinaire*. C 600-700. M 355 (weekday).

Woo Jung

8, bd Delessert - 01 45 20 72 82
Closed Sun. Open until 10:30pm. Terrace dining. Air cond.
A Korean restaurant filled with Koreans (a good sign) in the chic Passy district. Adventurous diners can opt for a mustardy jellyfish salad, beef tartare with sesame seeds, or pearly-fresh raw sea bream. Every dish is beautifully served. The green tea or a local beer are complimentary to the food. C 250-270.

12/20 Zébra Square

3, pl. Clément-Ader - 01 44 14 91 91
Open daily until 1am. Terrace dining. Air cond. Pkg.
The reasonably-priced food in this pleasant «American-style» setting is suffering from its own success. Some servings are blatantly skimp—we found all of three olives in our sardines gratinées and hardly more sardines—and the duck breast had that distinctly warmed-over taste. **Brunch** is served on weekends (Sat & Sun noon-4pm). C 220-280.

17th ARRONDISSEMENT

Postal code	75017

Amphyclès

78, av. des Ternes
01 40 68 01 01, fax 01 40 68 91 88
Closed Sat lunch, Sun. Open until 11pm. Air cond. Pkg.
Joël Robuchon imbued his star pupil, Philippe Groult, with a passion for perfection. Superb ingredients, which Groult chooses with discriminating care, are the basis of colorful, flavorful dishes that delight both eye and palate. To wit: a scarlet spider crab stuffed with a blend of its own meat, tourteau crab, and lobster; pearly white John Dory topped with slow-roasted tomatoes and glossy black olives; or golden sweetbreads with dried fruits and nuts and a brilliant green snow-pea fondue. This is cheese-lovers' heaven, with the cheese coming from one of the most noted cheese *affineurs* in France. If you've set your heart on a top-notch meal in Paris, but your pocket is feeling empty, this is the place to set foot. The 260 F set meal is undoubtedly one of the best deals in Paris. The service ventures into chilly waters at times and could use a warm-up. Only the best growers are admitted to the select and expensive wine list, which could however be padded with a few more affordable Rhône Valley, Provence and Loire Valley wines. C 800. M 260 (lunch), 680.

Apicius

122, av. de Villiers
01 43 80 19 66, fax 01 44 40 09 57
Closed Sat, Sun, Aug. Open until 10pm. Air cond. Pkg.
When culinary writer Apicius got into dire debt from his daily gluttony, he chose to poison himself rather than live out the rest of his days eating the food of which ordinary human beings partake. When you want to revel in the gustatory sensuality typical of Apicius's Ancient Rome (excluding the vomitoriums and orgies), just drop in on Jean-Pierre Vigato, the George Bernard Shaw of the kitchen. The party begins from the moment Madeleine Vigato welcomes you into the lavishly flower-decked dining room, and Vigato's Don Juan style, a true *cuisine d'auteur*, contains the sensuality within the bounds of your plate. A high-stepping cuisine with the power to move, continually reviewing and reinterpreting age-old themes: a pepper-coated foie gras, roasted whole, finished off with a paraph of unctuous cocoa sauce; a midriff of turbot, served on the bone like a prime rib, highlighted with an ethereal jus de viande, incensed with a hint of Balsamic vinegar and crowned with a few potatoes à la coppa. The ideas are endless: frothy lemon butters, horseradish confit, visionary desserts—tout-chocolat, blanc-manger with orgeat syrup. His daily inspirations can be sampled through the half-dozen different starters and entrées each day (which Madeleine describes at each table in luscious detail). The eclectic sommelier seduces you with his mixture of great Bordeaux and Burgundies sparked with surprising treasures from lesser known growers. C 750-850. M 520 (weekdays).

Augusta

98, rue de Tocqueville
01 47 63 39 97, fax 01 42 27 21 71
Closed Sun, Aug 4-25. Open until 10pm. Air cond.
Scrupulously seasonal, rigorously precise, based on the freshest seafood: Philippe de Saint-Étienne's cuisine is all this and more. The clear, direct flavors of his sweet-and-sour scampi, rockfish soup, fricassée of sole and artichokes, seared sea bass with sea salt, or roast John Dory with a shellfish jus incite us to unashamed gorging! Remarkable wine list; young, eager staff. But beware: no fixed-price menu. C 400-600.

12/20 Le Ballon des Ternes

103, av. des Ternes - 01 45 74 17 98
Closed Aug 1-21. Open until 12:30am. Terrace dining.
Tuna carpaccio showered with sesame seeds, veal kidney with mustard sauce, and house-made apple tart are served with top-quality wines at this likeable Belle Époque brasserie run by the same family as La Grande Cascade in the Bois de Boulogne. Well-oiled professional service and extensive selection of shellfish from one of the foremost fishmongers in France. C 210-290.

12/20 Baumann Ternes

64, av. des Ternes - 01 45 74 16 66, fax 01 45 72 44 32
Open daily until midnight. Terrace dining. Air cond. Pkg.
A bastion of the Baumann restaurant empire, where you can savor first-class choucroutes and other Alsatian specialties, as well as tasty tartares and grills. Considering that the food is Alsatian, we found the wine list scant on good Alsatian wines. Lively ambience, but service needs to be revised. C 230. M 132, 180 (wine incl).

Billy Gourmand

20, rue de Tocqueville - 01 42 27 03 71
Closed Sat (exc lunch off-seas), Sun, 3 wks in Aug. Open until 10pm. Air cond. Pkg.
Chef Philippe Billy presents his polished, prettily presented cuisine in a spacious dining room decorated with mirrors and plants. On a recent visit we tucked into crab ravioli with mussels and baby broad beans, a tender lamb chop topped with seasoned butter, and a delicate morello cherry cake. The engaging *patronne* oversees a fine cellar of Loire Valley wines. C 250-280. M 165.

Le Bistrot d'à Côté

10, rue Gustave-Flaubert
01 42 67 05 81, fax 01 47 63 82 75
Open daily until 11:30pm. Terrace dining. Air cond. Pkg.
All you want from a bistro: hustle, bustle, and cheeky waiters. This little luxury grocery-cum-bistro, run by Michel Rostang (his main restaurant is right next door, thus the name of the bistro), rather resembles a general store museum full of turn-of-the-century objects. The repertoire is varied—seasonally-inspired dishes, Lyonnais and just plain downhome dishes. A recent visit proffered red-claw crayfish and green bean salad, racy rabbit and pig's foot pâté, macaroni and lobster gratin, oxtail cottage pie with red wine sauce and old-fashioned chocolate pudding. C 250-330.

Le Bistrot de l'Étoile-Niel

75, av. Niel - 01 42 27 88 44, fax 01 42 27 32 12
Closed Sun lunch. Open until midnight. Terrace dining. Air cond. Pkg.
Oyster lovers, here's your heaven: during oyster season, you can choose oysters from an abundance of regions in this typical cheerful neighborhood bistro—except that it's owned and supervised by Guy Savoy. Handily prepared and served with a smile, on hot days, choose the chilled tomato soup with creamy goat's milk cheese or the betterave tartare with marinated cod. When cold days have set in, you might opt for the Aubrac sirloin with gratin dauphinois or with some of the most renowned mashed potatoes in the world, served with jus de veau. The cellar lines its walls with a few bistro-priced grand cru wines. The «flavor discovery»

children's menu at Saturday lunch is a novel way of introducing children to fine eating. There's also a special Sunday night set meal. C 230-250. M 180 (Sun).

Le Bistrot de l'Étoile-Troyon

13, rue Troyon - 01 42 67 25 95, fax 01 46 22 43 09
Closed Sat, Sun lunch. Open until 11:30pm. Terrace dining. Air cond. Pkg.
Guy Savoy can keep a close eye on the firstborn of his bistro annexes, for it stands just across the street from his three-toque restaurant. In the small, convivial dining room, where you'll be coddled by the new manager, Nedra, you can treat yourself to such heartwarming bourgeois classics as leek and chicken-liver terrine, roast veal with onion marmalade, coffee parfait, and lush chocolate quenelles. Good growers' wines; democratic prices. C 200-250. M 160.

Les Bouchons de François Clerc

22, rue de la Terrasse - 01 42 27 31 51
Closed Sat lunch, Sun. Open until 10:30pm. Terrace dining. Air cond.
See *5th arrondissement.* M 117 (weekday lunch, wine incl), 219.

Caves Pétrissans

30 bis, av. Niel - 01 42 27 83 84
Closed Sat, Sun, 3 wks in Aug 4-24. Open until 10:30pm. Terrace dining. Pkg.
Four generations of Pétrissans have overseen this wine shop-cum-restaurant, where patrons linger happily over Denis Bischoff's deft cooking. The quality ingredients are simply prepared and generously served. Try the terrine maison served with onion marmalade, tête de veau sauce ravigote, and flaky fruit tarts. Fabulous wine list, offering weekly and month specials We were particularly fond of Boillot's Meursault and Cuilleron's Côte-Rôtie. C 220-300. M 170.

11/20 Les Cigales

127, rue Cardinet - 01 42 27 83 93
Closed Aug. Open until 10pm.
The décor plays the Provençal card to the hilt (sun-yellow walls, photos of the Riviera...), and so does the bright bill of fare: tomatoes stuffed with creamy goat cheese, grilled sea bream anointed with virgin olive oil, pasta dressed with pistou are all handily turned out. Too bad the cellar is so short on wines from the sunny south. C 190-250. M 90 (lunch, wine incl).

11/20 Le Débarcadère

11, rue du Débarcadère - 01 53 81 95 95
Open daily until 1:15am. Air cond. Pkg.
Housed in the old Sony warehouses, this «unloading dock» as the name denotes, serves as landing for the golden boy crowd. Up-to-date food (lots of olive oil) in a Neo-Baroque décor.

You can sip at the bar while you wait for a table. C 200-250. M 48 (lunch).

Épicure 108

108, rue Cardinet - 01 47 63 50 91
Closed Sat lunch, Sun, Feb school hols, 2 wks in Aug. Open until 10pm.
A quiet restaurant with a pastel interior (in need, we think, of a brush-up) where chef Tetsu Goya presents hearty Alsatian-style dishes. The 175 F menu brings a salad of quail and foie gras, fish simmered with sauerkraut, and chocolate puffs with pear marmalade. Nice little cellar, with some fine Rieslings. M 175, 250.

L'Étoile d'Or

Hôtel Concorde La Fayette, 3, pl. du Général-Kœnig
01 40 68 51 28, fax 01 40 68 50 43
Closed Sat, Sun, Aug. Open until 10:30pm. Air cond. Pkg.
Bold harmonies of flavors, split-second timing, and feather-light sauces are the three solid bases of Jean-Claude Lhonneur's alluring repertoire. We know: it isn't easy to find this handsome, wood-paneled dining room, hidden in the labyrinth of the hotel Concorde La Fayette; paying the bill isn't so simple either. But if you make the effort, your reward will be (for example) meltingly savory duck liver in a Banyuls wine jus, smothered sea bass perfumed with truffled oil, savory stewed ox jowls en ravigote, or a chocolate soufflé that the waiter swears is the best in Paris! Mindful service and exhaustive wine list, with some reasonably priced offerings on hand. C 400-600. M 270.

Faucher

123, av. de Wagram
01 42 27 61 50, fax 01 46 22 25 72
Closed Sat lunch, Sun. Open until 10pm. Terrace dining. Pkg.
Gérard Faucher keeps prices down to keep customers coming. He's crossed a few costly items off his shopping list, but otherwise his menu is as vivid and modern as ever. He's even managed to preserve some signature dishes, like the millefeuille of thinly sliced raw beef and spinach leaves, and the short ribs with a truffled jus. You'll also find a wickedly tasty combination of foie gras, fried egg, and grilled coppa, and a crackling lacquered duck breast. Wines from a revised, less expensive cellar complete the picture. Nicole Faucher greets guests with a smile in the cheerful yellow dining room. Pleasant terrace dining when weather permits. C 320-380. M 390.

11/20 Chez Fred

190bis, bd Pereire - 01 45 74 20 48
Closed Sun. Open until 11pm. Terrace dining.
A good stop-off for home-style classics such as roasted goat cheese, calf's head gribiche, lentil salad, and chestnuts in syrup. Wash it down with some old-fashioned Beaujolais. C 235-300. M 145 (wine incl).

La Gazelle

9, rue Rennequin - 01 42 67 64 18, fax 01 42 67 82 77
Closed Sun. Open until 11pm. Pkg.
The prettiest African restaurant in Paris, La Gazelle boasts a range of intensely tasty dishes prepared by owner-chef Marie Koffi-Nketsin, who comes from Cameroon: try her shrimp fritters, lemon chicken yassa, and marinated kid baked en papillote with African corn. Crocodile also features on the menu—connoisseurs, take note! Heartwarming ambience, and one of the few African restaurants in Paris that offers consistently good quality. C 150-200. M 130, 150.

12/20 Goldenberg

69, av. de Wagram
01 42 27 34 79, fax 01 42 27 98 85
Open daily until 11pm. Terrace dining. Pkg.
Patrick Goldenberg creates a typically Yiddish atmosphere of good humor and nostalgia in which to savor kosher cooking rooted in the traditions of Russia, Hungary, Romania, etc. There's pastrami, corned goose breast, kneidler in chicken broth, veal sausage, and other Central European classics. For dessert, try the poppyseed strudel. Israeli and Hungarian wines on hand to quench your thirst, along with King David kosher champagne for special occasions. C 200-250. M 140 (wine incl).

Graindorge

15, rue de l'Arc-de-Triomphe
01 47 54 00 28, fax 01 44 09 84 51
Closed Sat lunch, Sun. Open until 11pm. Air cond. Pkg.
When Bernard Broux (long-time chef at Le Trou Gascon) opened a place of his own, he forsook the Southwest in favor of the cuisine of his native Flanders. Broux's menu celebrates hearty Northern savors with creamy beer soup, waterzoï of scallops and shellfish in shrimp fumet, carbonnade of ox jowls laced with gin, and strawberries in a sabayon spiked with raspberry-flavored kriek beer. Good wine list, but beer lovers will be knocked out by the selection of rare brews. The 165 F lunch is a bargain. C 250-300. M 135, 165 (weekday lunch), 188, 230.

Guyvonne

14, rue de Thann - 01 42 27 25 43, fax 01 42 27 25 43
Closed Sat, Sun, Aug 3-31, Dec 23-Jan 4. Open until 10pm. Terrace dining.
You'll not find any stereotypical dishes on Guy Cros's menu, because this chef wholeheartedly believes in original, bold combinations. He didn't forget to put the garlic in the escargots, he just thought the asparagus, white nettles and scampi a much more inventive combination. How dare him serve his foie gras fruit-free; you'll change tunes when you taste his thoroughly surprising squash, chervil root and

MUMM
CORDON ROUGE

Since 1827

House founded in 18.

black truffle «sidecar». The cellar proves to be of the same caliber. You can choose a half-bottle of Grippa's 1993 Saint-Joseph at 82 F or Dagueneau's Pouilly-Fumé at 137 F with absolutely no qualms. C 320-450. M 150, 180.

 ## Kifune

44, rue Saint-Ferdinand - 01 45 72 11 19
Closed 2 wks in Aug, Dec-Jan. Open until 10pm. Terrace dining. Pkg.
In the best Japanese tradition, large sums are demanded for tiny portions of food. But at Kifune the quality is irreproachable: sparkling fresh sashimi and sushi, shrimp tempura, whiting in soy sauce, ethereal fried chicken. C 300-400. M 125-135 (weekday lunch, Sat).

 ## Les Marines de Pétrus

27, av. Niel - 01 47 63 04 24, fax 01 44 15 92 20
Closed Aug. Open until 11pm. Terrace dining. Air cond.
The nautical décor charms us less than Souad Barrié, the gracious *patronne,* or the menu of tasty seafood: tartare prepared with a trio of fresh fish, empereur (a mild white fish) au curry, or cod with spicy condiments. Meat-eaters can plump for beef tenderloin béarnaise or pig's trotter en crépinette. A buttery brioche feuilleté served with caramel ice cream rounds things off on a satisfyingly rich note. There are two wine lists: one is modest, the other (which you must ask to see) quite grand. C 240-280.

 ## Le Petit Colombier

42, rue des Acacias
01 43 80 28 54, fax 01 44 40 04 29
Closed Sat, Sun lunch, Aug. Open until 11:30pm. Air cond. Pkg.
With loving devotion, Bernard Fournier watches over his «provincial» inn, a family heirloom which he runs with the energy of three men. The reward for his vigilance is a loyal clientele of contented gourmands who tuck in joyfully to such spirited, full-bodied dishes as hare terrine enriched with foie gras, lobster quenelles, or veal chops tenderly braised en cocotte. Each day also brings a roast—succulent ribs of beef, for example, or poularde truffée aux petits légumes—carved and served at the table. The hunting season brings game. To toast these delights, there is a splendiferous cellar with some 50,000 bottles and some awesome cigars. The set-price luncheon is a feast. C 430-550. M 190 (weekday), 360 (dinner).

 ## Paolo Petrini

6, rue du Débarquadère
01 45 74 25 95, fax 01 45 74 12 95
Closed Aug. Open until 11pm. Pkg.
Paolo Petrini hails from Pisa, he's a genuine Italian chef (Paris has so few)! His cooking is spare and stylized, yet the full spectrum of Italy's seductive savors are present in his warm, basil-scented salad of squid, clams, and cannellini beans, or his delectable risotto ai porcini, grilled beef fillet dressed with Balsamic vinegar, pappardelle napped with a rich, winy hare sauce, or tagliarini swathed in melted Fontina. The new shipshape décor seems to be pushing this self-taught chef to new heights of creativity. Superb Italian cellar to wash down what is probably the best Italian food in town. C 300-350. M 150 (lunch), 190.

 ## Petrus

12, pl. du Maréchal-Juin
01 43 80 15 95, fax 01 43 80 06 96
Open daily until 11pm. Terrace dining. Air cond. Pkg.
Roland Cousin is the skipper aboard the good ship Petrus. He handles seafood with discretion and restraint, serving forth a superb carpaccio of sea bream, bass, and salmon, a golden heap of crisp-fried whitebait, gingered tuna cooked as rare as you like, and a sole of pristine freshness. Summer brings Provence-inspired dishes like curried cod brandade with dried tomatoes, basil-perfumed stuffed Mediterranean squids, or hearty whole bass cooked in a clay pot. Fine selection of white wines: Bonhomme's Macon-Viré Vieilles Vignes or Gripa's Saint-Péray will leave you with precious memories. Service full of attentions and even a doorman to park your car. C 360-460. M 250.

 ## Il Ristorante

22, rue Fourcroy - 01 47 63 34 00
Closed Sat lunch, Sun, 3 wks in Aug. Open until 11pm. Air cond. Pkg.
The Anfuso clan welcomes guests into their Venetian-style dining room to savor Rocco Anfuso's vibrant, high-spirited *cucina,* some of the best in the city. Outstanding features of a recent feast were sea bass ravioli perfumed with basil, beef fillet paired with peppery arugula, and an authentic tiramisù Watch out, though: the fine Italian wines can send your bill soaring! C 260-320. M 165 (lunch).

 ## Michel Rostang

20, rue Rennequin
01 47 63 40 77, fax 01 47 63 82 75
Closed Sat lunch, Sun, Aug 1-18. Open until 10:30 pm. Air cond. Pkg.
Right when we had decided that the answer to Michel Rostang's problem was a simpler approach to cooking, we found ourselves bowled over by a dangerously rich but lusciously delicious crayfish gratin. We stick to our guns, however, because the unpretentious yet beautiful-to-behold bass-and-scallop hash with its savory salt pancakes and the almost austere but succulent roasted milk-fed lamb with ultra-thin tagliatelle livened up with lamb's trotter confirmed our initial impressions: simplicity will be his saving grace. Marie-Claude Rostang remains a gracious hostess in an atmosphere brimming with charm and service that never slips. Alain Ronzatti still presides over a

connoisseur's cellar. C 700-800. M 298 (weekday lunch).

Rôtisserie d'Armaillé

6, rue d'Armaillé - 01 42 27 19 20, fax 01 40 55 00 23
Closed Sat lunch, Sun. Open until 11pm, Fri & Sat 11:30pm. Air cond. Pkg.
Jacques Cagna reprises the bistro formula he successfully inaugurated at La Rôtisserie d'en Face (sixth arrondissement). For 198 F you can choose from a wide array of starters and desserts as well as a main course of spit-roasted poultry or meat. Some recent creations include a fried goose egg napped with oyster sauce, a coriander-spiked rock lobster turnover abed Greek-style veggies, and pork ribs enhanced with chutney and passion fruit. Interesting cellar. M 198.

Guy Savoy

18, rue Troyon
01 43 80 40 61, fax 01 46 22 43 09
Closed Sat lunch, Sun. Open until 10:30pm. Air cond. Pkg.
Guy Savoy is a real cook, a real artisan—a man who likes simple things. The flower arrangements in a bare Japanese style show his taste for simplicity; his cooking follows the same pattern. Savoy has stripped it of unnecessary frills, retaining as much as possible a rustic, yet elegant, style. He likes strong contrasts and does not hesitate, for instance, to serve beets as fingerfood as opposed to cèpe mushrooms. He works magic with what others might consider «less noble» ingredients: calf's trotters, ham hocks, bacon, turnips, beans, all of which render unctuous juices when they are slowly simmered with care. Savoy uses his own products from the *terroir* to create a vivid and robust cooking with a rural accent, which for us is quite a compliment. Just a sample: green garden peas unexpectedly served with exquisite Dublin bay prawns in jelly; artichoke soup topped with truffles and parmesan. Don't let the concise description of the desserts fool you into thinking he's skimping; vanilla-bean millefeuille and warm chocolate tart may sound as simple as peasant food, but are truly regales. Sommelier Eric Mancio passionately champions a fantastic cellar with a large selection of the best. Wines of all regions—with prices in consequence. C 800-900. M 880.

Sormani

4, rue du Général-Lanrezac
01 43 80 13 91, fax 01 40 55 07 37
Closed Sat, Sun, Apr 13-20, Aug 1-24, Dec 23-Jan 5. Open until 10:30pm. Terrace dining. Air cond.
Jean-Pascal Fayet's Italian cuisine is emphatically not the textbook version. His menu fairly crackles with such delectable inventions as diaphanous ravioli stuffed with sea urchins in a creamy ricotta sauce; a «pizza» topped with onion purée, lobster, and arugula; tender tagliatelle enriched with bacon and white beans; a sumptuous white-truffle risotto. True, spooning caviar onto leek ravioli may be a mite decadent, but Fayet's taste is more often faultless and his technique is admirably sure. In the past, he has been known for his over-the-top prices, but he's pared away his overuse of truffles here and truffles there, and come up with an excellent fixed-price meal at 250 F, a true inspiration, with offerings such as his marvellous white-beam soup with cèpe mushrooms, bacon and garlic bread, melt-in-your-mouth risotto dressed up with crunchy asparagus, gnocchi with cod brandade, or ultra-thin veal cutlets surrounded by vegetables from sunnier climates. The cellar boasts fabulous bottles from Piedmont, Sicily, and Tuscany. C 400-600. M 250 (lunch).

La Soupière

154, av. de Wagram - 01 42 27 00 73
Closed Sat lunch, Sun, Aug 11-18. Open until 10:30pm. Terrace dining.
Christian Thuillart pampers his patrons in a pretty *trompe-l'œil* dining room. There's nothing deceptive about Thuillart's classic repertoire, however. A passionate connoisseur of rare and expensive mushrooms, he has built special menus around truffles and morels, served when their season is at its height. His series of menus, some of them based on what's in season, are served at both lunch and dinner, everyday, and offer a solution for every budget. The 168 F set meal recently included lime-marinated cod carpaccio, Guémené andouille sausage with leeks, and poire au vin topped with vanilla ice cream. Nimbly selected wines with a wide choice of half-bottles. C 260-400. M 138, 168 (wine incl), 280.

La Table de Pierre

116, bd Pereire - 01 43 80 88 68, fax 01 47 66 53 02
Closed Sat lunch, Sun. Open until 11pm. Terrace dining.
Pierre Darrieumerlou's table fairly groans beneath the weight of generously served Basco-Béarnais fare. The quality is attested to by the fact that it's a regular rendez-vous for Southwesterners. Bring along a healthy appetite and order the codfish-stuffed peppers, confit de canard aux cèpes, or Pyrenees lamb with beans. Warm welcome; jolly atmosphere. C 280-340. M 210.

Taïra

10, rue des Acacias
01 47 66 74 14, fax 01 47 66 74 14
Closed Sat lunch, Sun, 1 wk in Aug. Open until 10pm. Air cond.
Taïra is not a Japanese restaurant, but its chef is Japanese. What does that mean? Since chef/owner Taïra Kurihara's training is western but his roots are oriental, he has his own unique interpretation of bouillabaisse, and his sardines in oil are a summit. Try the aerial spring rolls stuffed with langoustines, the grilled sea-scallops on a potato purée, the John Dory finished with an unusual prawn sauce, the cuttlefish

scented with basil. One of the the best seafood restaurants of Paris. The cellar offers numerous bottles hand-picked to blend handsomely with seafood: Limoux Chardonnay, Ardèche Viognier, or Provence Blanc de Blancs. And even though he's got two toques, he modestly maintains the 150 and 170 F set-price meals... **C** 300-400. **M** 150, 170, 330 (dinner).

11/20 Timgad

21, rue Brunel - 01 45 74 23 70, fax 01 40 68 76 46
Open daily until 11pm. Air cond. Pkg.
All the fragrant specialties of the Maghreb are on offer in this elegant restaurant, where you can sample hand-rolled couscous, crispy brek turnovers, and a wide range of tagines. **C** 270-350.

 ## La Toque

16, rue de Tocqueville
01 42 27 97 75, fax 01 47 63 97 69
Closed Sat, Sun, Aug 20. Open until 10pm. Air cond. Pkg.
The pretty dining room is tiny and so are the tables at Jacky Joubert's little Toque. Never mind: the good classic cooking is generously apportioned and attractively served, and the fixed-price menus give excellent quality for the money. **C** 250-280. **M** 150, 210.

18th ARRONDISSEMENT

Postal code	75018

 ## A. Beauvilliers

52, rue Lamarck - 01 42 54 54 42, fax 01 42 62 70 30
Closed Sun, Mon lunch. Open until 11pm. Terrace dining. Air cond. Pkg.
If ever a restaurant was designed for celebrations, this is it. Indeed, show-business personalities, celebrities, and politicos regularly scale the Butte Montmartre to toast their triumphs with Beauvilliers's best bubbly. But more care goes into the elegant setting than into the food. Even though we were not moved, we have to admit that you won't be disappointed by the freshness of proven classics like the artichoke bottoms garnished with crab, paupiettes of lamb's brains and œufs à la neige. Adequate desserts; goodish cellar, with a superb selection of Champagnes. **C** 500. **M** 185 (weekday lunch), 285-400 (weekday lunch, wine incl), 300 (Sat lunch, wine incl).

12/20 Le Bouclard

1, rue Cavallotti - 01 45 22 60 01
Closed Sat lunch, Sun. Open until 11pm. Pkg.
The owner's name may be Bonnemort (good dead), but the lively atmosphere here is the creation of someone who relishes life and the good

things it has to offer, especially wine and food. The cooking resembles Southwest farmhouse cooking with hearty offerings such as a hefty crawfish gratin cooked in Mâcon wine, œufs en meurette with an impeccable velvety sauce, genuine Castelnaudary-style cassoulet (some have it that cassoulet was invented there), and as many gratin dauphinois or aligot potatoes as you can eat. Special celebrations when there are soccer games on the tele, when you can count on an endless flow of Burgundy and a goodtime atmosphere that rivals that in the stadium itself. **C** 200-250.

 ## Le Cottage Marcadet

151 bis, rue Marcadet - 01 42 57 71 22
Closed Sun, Apr 13-21, Aug 3-25. Open until 10pm. Air cond.
This little Cottage has nothing in common with the tourist traps farther up the Butte Montmartre. Here, chef Jean-François Canot pleases his patrons with personalized cooking full of bold, frank flavors. We loved the juniper-spiced calf's foot, smoked-fish terrine, grilled sea bream dressed with oyster vinaigrette, and duck confit en chartreuse. The 210 F set meal is practically a gift. Vincent's white Reuilly or Morin's Chinon will undoubtedly please your palate. **C** 300-400. **M** 155 (lunch), 210 (wine incl).

11/20 La Galerie

16, rue Tholozé - 01 42 59 25 76
Closed Sun, hols, 1 wk in Feb, Aug. Open until 10:45pm. Air cond.
This charming street which gently winds up toward the Butte Montmartre plays host to a little fish restaurant offering sweet finds such as shellfish b'steeya, marinated scorpion fish spiked with lemon grass, and pistachio and monkfish curry. **M** 89 (lunch), 139, 179 (dinner).

Langevin

39, rue Lamarck - 01 46 06 86 00
Closed Sun dinner. Open until 10:15pm.
A glassed-in terrace gives patrons a wide-angle view of this picturesque corner of Montmartre. Jean-Paul Langevin serves forth polished country fare such as artichokes stuffed with snails, Barbary duck with baby turnips, and a giant made-to-order raspberry-flavored shortbread cookie. Tempting cellar and fair-priced set meals. **C** 250-300. **M** 115 (lunch), 160.

12/20 Le Perroquet Vert

7, rue Cavallotti - 01 45 22 49 16
Closed 3 wks in Aug. Open until 10:30pm. Terrace dining. Air cond.
On cold wintery evenings, the fireplace chocked right in the middle of the restaurant serves as a warm setting for the 158 F set-price meal offering bay scallops with citrus fruit, milk-fed loin of pork with crystallized endives, and super-thin hot apple pie. **C** 220-230. **M** 98 (weekday lunch), 158.

19th ARRONDISSEMENT

Postal code **75019**

12/20 Dagorno

190, av. Jean-Jaurès - 01 40 40 09 39
Open daily until 11:45am. Air cond. Pkg.
Quite a contrast with the futuristic Cité des Sciences, this opulent brasserie cultivates an old-fashioned image, offering decent, uncomplicated food. You won't be disappointed by the fresh shellfish, calf's head sauce gribiche, or enormous côte de bœuf sauce bordelaise. C 300. M 169 (wine incl).

12/20 La Pièce de Bœuf

7, av. Corentin-Cariou - 01 40 05 95 95
Closed Sat, Sun, Aug. Open until 10:30pm. Terrace dining. Air cond. Pkg.
Well-wrought traditional brasserie fare with a concentration on meat in this former meat district of La Villette. Despite the name, we find that seafood is the menu's strong suit. The wine list favors Bordeaux and Champagnes. Customers who behave well get to visit the kitchen and cellar. C 240-350. M 155.

Le Restaurant d'Éric Fréchon

10, rue du Général-Brunet
01 40 40 03 30, fax 01 40 40 03 30
Closed Sun, Mon, Aug. Open until 11pm. Air cond.
There's nothing mysterious about it: when you serve fine food at reasonable prices, gourmets will beat a path to your door, no matter how remote your restaurant! In his neat and tidy little bistro, Éric Fréchon (a former second-in-command to Christian Constant) proposes a dazzling single-price menu for just 190 F. Market-fresh ingredients, balanced flavors, and cutting-edge technique distinguish Fréchon's cream of white bean soup showered with croûtons and shavings of Spanish ham; his langoustine croquants served with a lovely honey-dressed salad of tender lamb's lettuce; cod stuffed with salt-cod purée and roasted in a spicy herbal crust; or an earthy sausage of pig's trotter enriched with foie gras and presented with whipped potato. For dessert, there's a superb mango feuilleté enhanced by lashings of almond cream. Interesting and selective cellar of growers' wines with prices starting at 80 F; warm welcome from Sylvie Fréchon. In short, this is one of the year's top tables, so we're giving him an extra point. M 190.

12/20 Rendez-Vous des Quais

14, quai de la Seine - 01 40 37 02 81
Open daily until 11pm. Terrace dining.
This is the place to come in the East of Paris. The restaurant area of one of the few remaining buildings from the 1872 Universal Exhibition, used for years as a warehouse, and now converted into a cinema. Clever set menus, such as the 135 F «cinema» menu which comes with two glasses of wine. Good-quality desserts. C 150-180. M 135 (wine incl).

11/20 Au Rendez-Vous de la Marine

14, quai de la Loire - 01 42 49 33 40
Closed Sun, Mon, 1 wk in Aug. Open until 10pm.
Sit down to a hearty omelette aux cèpes, confit de canard, or monkfish fillet at this friendly address by the canal where Marcel Carné's film «Jenny» was made. C 130-140.

Chez Vincent

5, rue du Tunnel - 01 42 02 22 45
Closed Sat lunch, Sun. Open until midnight.
Our friend Henri Gault calls this the «best trattoria in France». Reserve your table well in advance to savor Vincent's beef or salmon carpaccio showered with wonderful vegetables, warm shellfish marinière, deep-fried sardines, squid, and eggplant, or his silky fresh pasta. Animated and picturesque for a goodtime evening with friends. C 180-220. M 130, 180.

20th ARRONDISSEMENT

Postal code **75020**

Les Allobroges

71, rue des Grands-Champs - 01 43 73 40 00
Closed Sun, Mon, Aug. Open until 10pm. Pkg.
It's worth the trip out to the twentieth arrondissement to taste Olivier Pateyron's langoustines with ratatouille, braised lamb with garlic confit, and cherry-pistachio dessert. The little 92 F set meal has its charms, and à la carte prices are clement too, inciting one to splurge on lobster and lotte with tarragon or spiced Barbary duck (order both in advance). Only the wine list needs improvement. C 250-300. M 92, 164.

12/20 Le Baratin

3, rue Jouye-Rouve - 01 43 49 39 70
Closed Sat lunch, Sun, Mon, 1 wk in Jan, 3 wks in Aug. Open until midnight.
This is certainly one of the best wine bars in Paris, so if you're in the mood to see an animated and oft-missed part of the city, Belleville, trot on over and sip some of the treasures of the moment, or ask owner Olivier if you can flip through his wine cellar inventory book—some good (and lengthy) reading and incredibly decent prices. The Argentinian cook offers whatever inspires her on the market every day; try her smashing risotto. C 150-200. M 69 (lunch).

HOTELS

Paris hotel rooms come in every possible style, size, and price range. But whatever the category of the room you seek, remember to book well in advance to get exactly what you want. Our selection ranges from sumptuous suites to far humbler lodgings, but note that certain hoteliers put as high a price on charm or modern facilities as others do on pure luxury, so don't assume that «charming» means «cheap». The prices quoted include taxes and service. Hotels are classified as follows: *Luxury, First Class, Classic, Charming,* and *Practical.*

Reservation service

L'Office du Tourisme de Paris can arrange a same-day reservation at any hotel in Paris or its surroundings. The service costs 20 to 55 F, depending on the hotel. All you need to do is drop in (don't telephone) at one of the locations listed in *Basics* under Tourist Information.

No room at the inn?

If your every attempt to find a hotel room has failed, you needn't panic. Here are two companies that can track down a room for you or even rent you a high-class studio or apartment. The latter come with every guarantee of home comforts, security, and such options as maid, laundry, and repair services. Prices range from 450 to 2,500 F and up, depending on the size and accommodations.
Just contact: *Paris-Séjour-Réservation,* 90, av. des Champs-Élysées, 8th arr., tel. 01 53 89 10 50, fax 01 53 89 10 59, http://www.qconline.com/parispsr, e-mail: parispsr@planete.net; Mon-Fri 9am-7pm, Sat 10am-1pm & 2pm-6pm; or *Parissimo,* 9, av. de La Motte-Picquet, 7th arr., tel. 01 45 51 11 11, fax 01 45 55 55 81, http://www.123france.com; Mon-Fri 9:30am-1pm & 2:30pm-7pm.

Apartment hotels

At the apartment hotels listed below, you'll enjoy the same service you would find in a hotel, for a lower price.
• *Carré d'Or,* 46, av. George-V, 8th arr., 01 40 70 05 05, fax 01 47 23 30 90, http://www.slh.com/carredor/, e-mail: carre-dor@calva.net. 23 stes 2,850-18,950 F. Air cond. Valet parking.
• *Les Citadines-Austerlitz,* 27, rue Esquirol, 13th arr., 01 44 23 51 51, fax 01 45 86 59 76. 2 apts 735-1,180 F. 47 studios 525-925 F. Parking.
• *Les Citadines-Paris-Bastille,* 14-18, rue de Chaligny, 12th arr., 01 40 01 15 15, fax 01 40 01 15 20. 97 apts 450-1,275 F. Parking.
• *Les Citadines-Montparnasse,* 67, av. du Maine, 14th arr., 01 40 47 41 41, fax 01 43 27 29 94. 72 studios 480-1,465 F. Garage parking.
• *Les Citadines-Opéra,* 18, rue Favart, 2nd arr., 01 44 50 23 23, fax 01 44 50 23 50. 76 apts 655-1,525 F. Air cond. Parking. Fitness center.
• *Les Citadines-Trocadéro,* 29 bis, rue Saint-Didier, 16th arr., 01 44 34 73 73, fax 01 47 04 50 07. 97 apts 630-1,685 F. Garage parking.
• *Les Citadines* are also located in the 6th arr., 8th arr., 11th arr., 14th arr., and 18th arr. Central reservation: 01 41 05 79 79, fax 01 47 59 04 70, http://www.citadines.com.
• *Flatotel,* 14, rue du Théâtre, 15th arr., 01 45 75 62 20, fax 01 45 79 73 30. 220 rms & apts 640-2,900 F. Parking.
• *Flatotel Expo,* 52, rue d'Oradour-sur-Glane, 15th arr., 01 45 54 93 45, fax 01 45 54 93 07. 120 rms & apts 680-1,020 F. Parking.
• *Métropole Opéra,* 2, rue de Gramont, 2nd arr., 01 42 96 91 03, fax 01 42 96 22 46. 24 apts 950-1,550 F. 9 studios 650-790 F. Air cond. Conf.
• *Orion Bastille,* 37, bd Richard Lenoir, 11th arr., 01 53 36 22 22, fax 01 53 36 22 00. 30 apts 980 F. 108 studios 650 F. Air cond. Pkg.
• *Orion Italie,* 18, pl. d'Italie, 13th arr., 01 40 78 15 00, fax 01 40 78 16 99. 38 apts 1,010-1,085 F. 129 studios 575-720 F.
• *Orion Louvre,* 8, rue Richelieu, 1st arr., 01 55 35 14 14, fax 01 55 35 14 99. 27 apts 1,220 F. 24 studios 820 F. Air cond.
• *Orion Paris-Les-Halles,* 4, rue des Innocents, 1st arr., 01 40 39 76 00, fax 01 45 08 40 65. 55 apts 1,040 F. 134 studios 730 F. Studios for disabled. Air cond.
• *Résidence du Roy,* 8, rue François-Ier, 8th arr., 01 42 89 59 59, fax 01 40 74 07 92, e-mail: rdr@hroy.com. 28 apts & 7 rms 1,280-2,980 F. Air cond. Valet pkg.

LUXURY

Le Bristol 🌲♟

8th arr. - 112, rue du Faubourg-Saint-Honoré
01 53 43 43 00, fax 01 53 43 43 01
Open year-round. 40 stes 6,500-34,000. 153 rms 2,500-4,600. Restaurant. Rm ser. Air cond. Pool. Valet pkg.
An elegant décor (genuine period furniture, fine pictures), comfortable rooms, lavish suites, and a prestigious clientele make Le Bristol one of the rare authentic luxury hotels in Paris (as well as one of the most expensive). Everything is large in scale and immaculately white. If you feel cramped in big cities, ask for the 1,500 square foot room with its own private gym, and marvel at the enormous Carrara marble bathrooms and the magnificent giant hanging garden terraces. Reception like no other. The swimming pool on the top floor is a work of wonder, and the indoor French-style garden is like an extravagant fantasy world. A very elegant restaurant (Le Bristol) opens in summer onto a formal French garden, see *Restaurants*. The staff is both cordial and impressively trained.

Castille 🌲♟

1st arr. - 37, rue Cambon
01 44 58 44 58, fax 01 44 58 44 00
Open year-round. 21 stes 1,990-3,200. 86 rms 1,690-2,300. Rms for disabled. Restaurant. Rm ser. Air cond. Valet pkg.
Venetian-style elegance, decked out in brocades, damask, and marble, the climax being in the splendid sixth-floor duplex rooms which sport a glimpse of the Vendôme column or the Eiffel Tower. Exquisite *trompe l'œil* wall mural on the Venetian-style terrace. Next door to Chanel, the Castille provides luxurious amenities and impeccably stylish service.

Hôtel de Crillon

8th arr. - 10, pl. de la Concorde
01 44 71 15 00, fax 01 44 71 15 02
Open year-round. 45 stes 4,900-32,500. 118 rms 2,550-4,100. Restaurants. Rm ser. Air cond. Valet pkg.
The Crillon is housed in an honest-to-goodness eighteenth-century palace. Indeed, the accommodations are truly fit for a king, with terraces overlooking the Place de la Concorde, sumptuous public rooms, and an exquisitely trained staff. The guest rooms are beautifully decorated; the suites offer all the splendor one could hope for. Everywhere the eye rests on silk draperies, woodwork ornamented with gold leaf, Aubusson rugs, and polished marble. Restaurants: Les Ambassadeurs, L'Obélisque and Le Patio, see *Restaurants*. Relais et Châteaux.

*For a complete guide to our hotel **ranking system**, see "Symbol Systems", page 8.*

George V

8th arr. - 31, av. George-V - 01 53 53 28 00
The Four Seasons group has just taken over the George V and is investing in a hefty 300 million franc renovation. New additions include a fitness center, spa and pool. Planned reopening spring 1999.

Le Grand Hôtel Inter-Continental

9th arr. - 2, rue Scribe
01 40 07 32 32, fax 01 42 66 12 51
Open year-round. 35 stes 3,500-16,000. 479 rms 1,700-2,800. Rms for disabled. Restaurant. Rm ser. Air cond. Valet pkg.
The monumental Second Empire building has recovered all the splendor it displayed when Empress Eugénie inaugurated it in 1862. The huge central lobby, capped by a glittering glass dome, is a wonder to behold. Guest rooms, unexpectly furnished with quite ordinary oak furniture and antiquated bathrooms, provide everything the international traveler could require in the way of amenities, as well as the most up-to-date business equipment, a health club, and much more. Excellent bar; for the Restaurant Opéra, see *Restaurants*.

Inter-Continental

1st arr. - 3, rue de Castiglione
01 44 77 11 11, fax 01 44 77 14 60
Open year-round. 75 stes 3,000-20,000. 450 rms 2,000-2,700. Restaurants. Rm ser. Air cond. Valet pkg.
The Inter-Continental has just gotten a new look, from top to bottom. It was high time, and the result is amenities abreast of the time, including both a business and fitness center. The gold-leaf ceilings in the sumptuous Imperial hall have survived the renovation, but the 450 some rooms boast a spanking new décor. New bar and new terrace.

Hôtel du Louvre

1st arr. - Pl. André Malraux
01 44 58 38 38, fax 01 44 58 38 01
Open year-round. 32 stes 2,500-4,000. 199 rms 1,350-1,550. Rms for disabled. Restaurant. Rm ser. Air cond. Valet pkg.
The first grand hotel in Paris opened its doors in 1855. Today, it is spruced up in lovely golden yellow fabric, signed by none other than Pierre Frey, and Empire- and Louis XVI-style cherry furniture. The bathrooms could use some revisions however. Unspoilable view of Louvre and Opéra. Warm welcome, from the moment the carman opens the door to the moment you sign in with the charm of a receptionist.

Hôtel Marriott Paris Champs-Élysées

8th. arr. - 70, av. des Champs-Élysées
01 53 93 55 00, fax 01 53 93 55 01

Open year-round. 18 stes 4,000-12,000. 174 rms 1,700-2,800. Restaurant. Air cond. Business center. Fitness center. Sauna. Private pkg.

For its only hotel in France, Marriott has chosen one of the most prestigious addresses in the world. Seventeen of the rooms provide lucky guests with a view of the Champs-Élysées. Rooms are decorated in a traditional style with cherrywood Directoire-style furniture and shot silk fabrics, and all the modern amenities are provided, including two-line telephones and soundproofed windows and floors. The hotel caters to business travelers and provides a modem in every room, as well as a business center, open from 7 a.m. to 10 p.m. Amazing glass atrium that opens onto the sky in better weather. The parking lot is directly beneath the hotel and has direct access to the lobby on the second floor, where there is also a piano bar overlooking the Champs-Élysées. Sauna and gym facilities. Restaurant: Le Pavillon, see *Restaurants*.

 ## Le Meurice

1st arr. - 228, rue de Rivoli
01 44 58 10 10, fax 01 44 58 10 15
Open year-round. 35 stes 6,500-15,000. 142 rms 2,800-4,300. Rms for disabled. Restaurant. Rm ser. Air cond. Valet pkg.

The Meurice has undergone substantial renovation in the past few years to restore its glamour and prestige. The admirable salons on the main floor were refurbished; the guest rooms and suites (which offer a view of the Tuileries) were equipped with air conditioning and tastefully redecorated; and the pink-marble bathrooms are ultramodern. The Meurice ranks as one of the best grand hotels in Paris. The Louis XV- and Empire-style furniture in the rooms may well be the most beautiful of all the Parisian grand hotels, and even though the bathrooms sometimes fall short, the rooms are quiet thanks to the double-glazed windows. An elegant restaurant, Le Meurice, see *Restaurants*, is lodged in the Salon des Tuileries, overlooking the gardens.

 ## Plaza Athénée

8th arr. - 25, av. Montaigne
01 53 67 66 65, fax 01 53 67 66 66
Open year-round. 65 stes 5,300-13,000. 140 rms 2,600-4,000. Restaurant. Rm ser. Air cond. Fitness center. Valet pkg.

Appropriately tucked into the high fashion district and with one of the most prestigious addresses in the world, the Plaza will forever have its diehard fans. This place to see and be seen serves as a luxurious setting for tea in the grandiose Gobelins gallery, for sunny-day lunches on the lavish patio with its «cascades» of ivy, or for a pre-dinner drink in the Scottish bar. The last we heard, the Sultan of Brunei's brother had bought the hotel and planned to completely renovate the upstairs, but the hotel will stay open throughout the work. The welcome is more personal than in some of the other Parisian deluxe hotels. Le Régence restaurant is located across from the patio, where tables are set in the summer among cascades of geraniums and ampelopsis vines, (see *Restaurants*).

 ## Prince de Galles

8th arr. - 33, av. George-V
01 53 23 77 77, fax 01 47 20 61 05
Open year-round. 30 stes 3,650-15,000. 138 rms 1,910-3,485. Restaurant. Rm ser. Air cond. Valet pkg.

Extensive renovations have restored the brilliance of this renowned hotel, built in the Roaring Twenties. Marble expanses stretch as far as the eye can see, walls sport handsome prints, and guest rooms are outfitted with minibars, safes, and a flock of facilities. We only wish that the lovely old mosaics had been preserved. Check out the Chambord suite with its immense bathroom, round bathtub, and gold-leaf tap fittings! As ever, the hotel's open-roofed patio is a delightful place to have lunch on a warm day; the paneled Regency Bar is another pleasant spot, distinguished by excellent service.

 ## Raphaël

16th arr. - 17, av. Kléber
01 44 28 00 28, fax 01 45 01 21 50
Open year-round. 25 stes 3,150-15,000. 75 rms 1,950-2,350. Restaurant. Rm ser. Air cond. Valet pkg.

Built between the wars, the Raphaël has maintained an atmosphere of rare refinement and elegance that you only find in a very few hotels throughout the world. Oriental rugs on the marble floors, fine woodwork, old paintings and period furniture make Le Raphaël a very luxurious place to stay, preferred by a wealthy, well-bred clientele. The spacious rooms are richly furnished in various styles; the wardrobes and bathrooms are immense. A truly extraordinary and splendid new addition is a three-level suite that boasts an eye-popping panoramic view from the terrace (the terrace, by the way, is at the same level as the Arc de Triomphe). Or ask for the duplex suite 515—the bathroom is unbelievable! Top-drawer reception and service, of course. Intimate (and star-studded) English bar, next to the restaurant. Sumptuous conference facilities.

 ## Résidence Maxim's de Paris

8th arr. - 42, av. Gabriel
01 45 61 96 33, fax 01 42 89 06 07
Open year-round. 33 stes 2,750-15,000. 4 rms 2,000-2,250. Restaurant. Rm ser. Air cond. Valet pkg.

Pierre Cardin himself designed the hotel of his dreams, a small but palatial establishment that may well be the world's most luxurious. The landings of each floor are decorated like elegant salons, with beautiful and unusual antique pieces and paintings. Polished stone and sumptuous murals adorn the bathrooms. The suites must be seen to be believed, particularly those on the top floor, which are furnished with pieces designed by Cardin. Obviously, accommodations like these are well beyond the bank balances of most mortals.

 Ritz

1st arr. - 15, pl. Vendôme
01 43 16 30 30, fax 01 43 16 36 68
Open year-round. 45 stes 4,700-49,000. 142 rms 2,800-4,300. Rms for disabled. Restaurant. Rm ser. Heated pool. Valet pkg.
The world's most famous hotel is poised to enter the 21st century with highest-tech facilities, but without having betrayed the character that won the Ritz its reputation. Even if nowadays you can change the video program or make a phone call without leaving your bed or marble bath (Charles Ritz was the first to provide private bathrooms for his clients), nothing has altered the pleasure of stretching out on a wide brass bed surrounded by fine antiques. Add to that an atmosphere of luxury so enveloping that a new word («ritzy») had to be coined for it. Impeccable staff. The health club was modeled on a thermal spa of antiquity, and L'Espadon, (see *Restaurants*), has its own marvelous garden.

 Royal Monceau

8th arr. - 35, av. Hoche
01 42 99 88 00, fax 01 42 99 89 90
Open year-round. 39 stes 3,750-17,000. 180 rms 2,200-3,500. Rms for disabled. Restaurant. Rm ser. Air cond. Heated pool. Valet pkg.
Politicians, foreign business people and entertainers appreciate the Royal Monceau's spacious rooms, magnificent marble bathrooms, and luxurious amenities (excellent room service). Extras include a fashionable piano bar, a prestigious health club, Les Thermes (with sauna, Jacuzzi, swimming pool, and a massage service), ultramodern conference rooms and a well-equipped «business club». The rooms overlooking the charming flowered patio are the most sought-after by the hotel's habitués. Restaurant: Le Jardin, see *Restaurants*.

 Westminster

2nd arr. - 13, rue de la Paix
01 42 61 57 46, fax 01 42 60 30 66
Open year-round. 18 stes 3,600-9,000. 84 rms 1,650-2,600. Restaurant. Rm ser. Air cond. Valet pkg.
To celebrate its 150th birthday, the hotel has completed a total renovation. This charming mid-size luxury hotel is advantageously situated between the Opéra and Place Vendôme. The pink-and-beige marble lobby is splendid and luxurious; the bar, Les Chenets, with piano, is more than comfortable. Conference rooms are superbly equipped. As for the guest rooms, they are handsomely decorated with attractive fabrics, chandeliers, and Louis XV–style furnishings and are fitted with minibars, safes, and satellite TV, with marble bathrooms. Restaurant: Le Céladon, see *Restaurants*. Enquire about the guaranteed dollar rates available throughout the year. Call, within the U.S. only, 1-800-203-3232.

FIRST CLASS

 Ambassador

9th arr. - 16, bd Haussmann
01 44 83 40 40, fax 01 42 46 19 84
Open year-round. 9 stes 2,800-3,800. 279 rms 1,500-2,200. Restaurant. Rm ser. Air cond. Valet pkg.
A fine traditional hotel. The spacious, soundproofed guest rooms have been modernized in excellent taste with sumptuous fabrics, thick carpeting, and the original Art Deco furniture. The lobby and public rooms boast pink-marble columns topped with gilded Corinthian capitals, marble floors, and Aubusson tapestries on the walls. The penthouse suites look out over Sacré-Cœur. Restaurant: Venantius, see *Restaurants*; and a handsome Art Deco bar.

 Astor Westin Demeure Hôtel

8th arr. - 11, rue d'Astorg
01 53 05 05 05, fax 01 53 05 05 30
Open year-round. 5 stes 3,200-10,000. 130 rms 1,790-2,900. Rms for disabled. Restaurant. Rm ser. Air cond. Valet pkg.
After a two-year renovation program directed by architect Frédéric Méchiche, the lobby is resplendent with fine woodwork, and the quiet rooms, arranged around a white courtyard, are decorated in English or Empire style, with striped fabrics in shades of lavender, green, or blue. Though not huge, the guest quarters provide plenty of comfort and luxury. Two mansard duplex suites on the top floor boast a huge terrace with an unforgettable view of Sacré Cœur. Beautiful English-style bar with an atmosphere straight out of a Proust novel. See *Restaurants* for the restaurant Astor.

Baltimore

16th arr. - 88 bis, av. Kléber
01 44 34 54 54, fax 01 44 34 54 44
Open year-round. 6 stes 2,650-3,500. 105 rms 1,790-1,990. Restaurant. Air cond. Pkg.
An English-style hotel near the Trocadéro with a large marble entrance hall decorated with contemporary paintings. The pretty rooms vary in size, and the library is pure elegance. The Viennese pastries are made by Bertie's own pastry chef. Restaurant: Bertie's, see *Restaurants*.

Balzac

8th arr. - 6, rue Balzac
01 44 35 18 00, fax 01 44 35 18 05
Open year-round. 14 stes 3,200-6,000. 56 rms 1,700-2,200. Restaurant. Rm ser. Air cond. Valet pkg.
The arrival of the much-talked-about chef Pierre Gagnaire led to this year's creation of a new bar lined in solid cherrywood, (see *Restaurants*). This quietly luxurious establishment

near the Place de l'Étoile is frequented by celebrities and jet-setters. The huge rooms are completely soundproof and decorated in delicate tones with rather common oak furniture, beautiful chintzes, and thick carpeting. Most have king-size beds, all have superb modern bathrooms. Unobtrusive yet attentive staff.

Château Frontenac

8th arr. - 54, rue Pierre-Charron
01 53 23 13 13, fax 01 53 23 13 01
Open year-round. 4 stes 1,700-1,800. 100 rms 980-1,500. Restaurant. Air cond.
A reasonably priced hotel (given the location), with various sizes of rooms done in vaguely Louis XV style. Superb marble bathrooms. The soundproofing is effective, but the rooms overlooking the Rue Cérisole are still the quietest. Attentive reception staff; excellent service.

Clarion Saint-James et Albany

1st arr. - 202, rue de Rivoli
01 44 58 43 21, fax 01 44 58 43 11
Open year-round. 12 stes 1,800-2,500. 197 rms 980-1,800. Restaurant. Rm ser.
The Clarion Saint-James et Albany enjoys an exceptional location across from the Tuileries, and provides studios, two-room apartments, suites, and bilevel suites. The rooms overlook a courtyard or an inner garden and are perfectly quiet. The seventeenth-century façade is on the historical register, which makes the 1970s-style décor rather out of keeping.

Concorde Saint-Lazare

8th arr. - 108, rue Saint-Lazare
01 40 08 44 44, fax 01 42 93 01 20
Open year-round. 27 stes 2,450-3,500. 273 rms 1,200-1,500. Restaurant. Rm ser. Air cond. Valet pkg.
An enormous hotel, built in 1889 by Gustave Eiffel, with superb rooms and services. The most arresting feature is the lobby, a listed architectural landmark, that soars three storeys up to coffered ceilings aglitter with gilt, marble, and crystal chandeliers. A magnificent billiard room on the main floor is open to the public. Restaurant: Café Terminus, see *Restaurants.*

Édouard VII

2nd arr. - 39, av. de l'Opéra
01 42 61 56 90, fax 01 42 61 47 73
Open year-round. 4 stes 2,150. 65 rms 950-1,500. Restaurant. Rm ser. Air cond.
A luxurious place to stay, with individually styled rooms and beautifully crafted furniture. From the upper storeys there is a wonderful view of the Opéra. Art Deco-style entrance hall, pretty mahogany-paneled bar, and a music-filled atmosphere.

Looking for a hotel? Refer to the **Index.**

Golden Tulip Saint-Honoré

8th arr. - 218, rue du Faubourg-Saint-Honoré
01 49 53 03 03, fax 01 40 75 02 00
Open year-round. 20 stes 2,500-3,900. 52 rms 1,550-1,850. Rms for disabled. Restaurant. Air cond. Pool. Garage pkg.
This comfortable hotel is decorated in modern style using traditional materials (marble, wood, quality fabrics, *trompe-l'œil* paintings). The bright, spacious rooms offer every amenity; all are air conditioned, with splendid marble bathrooms, and some with kitchenettes. Pleasant reception.

Hyatt Regency Paris – Madeleine

8th arr. - 24, bd Malesherbes
01 55 27 12 34, fax 01 55 27 12 10
Open year-round. 5 stes 3,400-12,000. 81 rms 2,400-2,800. Air cond. Restaurants. Rm ser. Fitness center. Pkg.
Ideally located in the «golden triangle», the latest *First Class* hotel to be opened in Paris draws a clientele of informal business men. The lobby's historical glass dome, built in 1901, in the lobby creates the atmosphere right away: noble and sentimental, but with a modern sense of welcome and hospitality. Because you now spend more time working in your room, they are all equipped with a practical desk, two-line telephone, modem, and individal fax. Rooms and bathrooms, all different from each other, are decorated in a sober, modern but with warm tones; some of them offer an exceptional view of Paris rooftops. There is, of course, a business center.

Hilton

15th arr. - 18, av. de Suffren
01 44 38 56 00, fax 01 44 38 56 10
Open year-round. 26 stes 3,300-6,500. 436 rms 1,400-2,200. Rms for disabled. Restaurants. Rm ser. Air cond. Valet pkg.
The city's first postwar luxury hotel is still living up to Hilton's high standards. Rooms are airy and spacious, service is courteous and deft, and children under 16 can share their parents' room at no extra charge. Restaurants, boutiques, and two bars, one with an exceptional panoramic view of the city.

Lancaster

8th arr. - 7, rue de Berri
01 40 76 40 76, fax 01 40 76 40 00
Open year-round. 10 stes 4,050-7,000. 50 rms 1,650-2,650. Restaurant. Rm ser. Valet pkg.
Hints of the Orient intrigue you in this refined hotel riddled with *objets d'art*—Baccarat crystal chandeliers and Boris Pastoukhoff paintings—once a favorite stopoff for Marlene Dietrich. The guest rooms are decorated in silk satin or cotton damask, and the ones on the garden offer the most light.

Littré

6th arr. - 9, rue Littré
01 45 44 38 68, fax 01 45 44 88 13
Open year-round. 4 stes 1,300-1,500. 93 rms 720-1,000. Rm ser. Pkg.
The style and décor of this four-star hotel are stiff and starchy, but the Littré's habitués find the old-fashioned comfort and service entirely satisfactory. In the spacious rooms you'll find high, comfortable beds, ponderous furniture, huge armoires, and big marble bathrooms. English bar.

 Lotti

1st arr. - 7, rue de Castiglione
01 42 60 37 34, fax 01 40 15 93 56
Open year-round. 16 stes 4,900-6,500. 130 rms 1,410-2,620. Restaurant. Valet pkg.
What's known as «the smallest of the Paris grand hotels» is having a hard time keeping up its longstanding reputation. The Louis XVI furniture in the guest rooms is lovely, granted, but the beige fabric with satin stripes is frankly kitsch. No snags in the service and the reception however.

 Hôtel Lutétia

6th arr. - 45, bd Raspail
01 49 54 46 46, fax 01 49 54 46 00
Open year-round. 30 stes 2,200-12,000. 225 rms 990-1,990. Rms for disabled. Restaurants. Air cond. Valet pkg.
A Left Bank landmark, in the Art Deco style. Marble, gilt, and red velvet grace the stately public areas where well-heeled travelers come and go. Leading off the imposing entrance are the lounge, a bar, a brasserie, a restaurant (Brasserie Lutétia and Le Paris, see *Restaurants*), and conference rooms. The large suites are done up in pink, with understated furniture and elegant bathrooms—the overall look is very 1930s.

 Marignan-Élysées

8th arr. - 12, rue Marignan
01 40 76 34 56, fax 01 40 76 34 34
Open year-round. 16 stes 2,800. 57 rms 1,690-1,990. Restaurant. Air cond. Valet pkg.
Strategically situated in the heart of the «Golden Triangle», between the Champs-Élysées and Avenue Montaigne, this charming establishment with its listed Art Deco façade and lobby draws a *haute-couture* crowd. Magnificent rooms done up in marble and expensive fabrics, with every modern comfort; some even boast a little terrace.

 Montalembert

7th arr. - 3, rue de Montalembert
01 45 49 68 68, fax 01 45 49 69 49
Open year-round. 5 stes 2,830-3,700. 51 rms 1,675-2,140. Restaurant. Rm ser. Air cond.
Restored to its former splendor, this 1926 hotel sports luxurious materials (marble, ebony, sycamore, leather), designer fabrics and linens. Guests love the huge towels, cozy dressing gowns, and premium toiletries they find in the spectacular blue-gray bathrooms. The eighth-floor suites afford an enchanting view of the city. The hotel bar is a favorite with writers and publishers.

 Napoléon

8th arr. - 40, av. de Friedland
01 47 66 02 02, fax 01 47 66 82 33
Open year-round. 2 stes 3,500-4,500. 100 rms 1,300-1,500. Restaurant. Rm ser. Air cond. Valet pkg.
The atmosphere is appropriately Directoire, given the name of this deluxe hotel. The beautifully furniture, paintings and sofas dress it up in a slightly stiff Napolean style. Some rooms give onto the Arc de Triomphe. Beautiful, well-equipped terraces.

 Le Parc

16th arr. - 55-57, av. Raymond-Poincaré
01 44 05 66 66, fax 01 44 05 66 00
Open year-round. 18 stes 3,500. 98 rms 2,100-2,750. Rms for disabled. Restaurants. Air cond. Fitness center. Valet pkg.
A magnificent Anglo-Norman style hotel with a glorious indoor garden planted with rare specimens. The ravishing guest rooms are decorated in flowery prints, and don large canopy beds and mahogany bathrooms, all the work of celebrity decorator Nina Campbell. Supreme comfort is on the agenda, as well as every imaginable amenity. The public rooms are accented with beautiful sculpture. Scottish plaids and light woodwork lend a particularly British note to the bar and library. Health center. Restaurant: Le Relais du Parc, see *Restaurants*.

 Pergolèse

16th arr. - 3, rue Pergolèse
01 40 67 96 77, fax 01 45 00 12 11
Open year-round. 40 rms 890-1,620. Air cond.
The Pergolèse provides a top-class address as well as smiling service and first-rate amenities for what are still (relatively) reasonable prices. Elegant furnishings and vivid, modern, décor by Rena Dumas.

 Régina

1st arr. - 2, pl. des Pyramides
01 42 60 31 10, fax 01 40 15 95 16
Open year-round. 28 stes 2,750-4,000. 102 rms 1,650-2,250. Restaurant. Air cond. Valet pkg.
Opposite the Tuileries is one of the city's most venerable luxury hotels, with immense rooms, precious furniture (Louis XVI, Directoire, Empire) and—a practical addition—double-glazed windows. The grandiose lobby is graced with handsome old clocks that give the time of all the major European cities. Pretty indoor garden; English bar.

 Royal Saint-Honoré

1st arr. - 221, rue Saint-Honoré
01 42 60 32 79, fax 01 42 60 47 44

Open year-round. 5 stes 2,350. 67 rms 1,250-1,950. Restaurant. Rm ser.

Soft ochre in the colonnaded entrance hall, warm reds in the cozy new bar. The English-décor guest rooms are small but easy to snuggle in to. Smiling, affable service.

 ## San Régis

8th arr. - 12, rue Jean-Goujon
01 44 95 16 16, fax 01 45 61 05 48
Open year-round. 11 stes 3,200-5,500. 33 rms 1,650-2,850. Restaurant. Rm ser. Air cond. Valet pkg.

This jewel of a hotel, much appreciated by celebrities from the worlds of show business and *haute couture*, provides a successful mix of traditional comfort and the latest technology. Beautiful, newly decorated rooms boast splendid period furniture and paintings, sumptuous bathrooms, and lots of space, light, and character. The staff is irreproachable.

 ## Saint James Paris

16th arr. - 43, av. Bugeaud
01 44 05 81 81, fax 01 44 05 81 82
Open year-round. 27 stes 2,400-3,800. 19 rms 1,650-2,150. Restaurant. Rm ser. Air cond. Valet pkg.

A large staff looks after the 48 rooms and suites—a luxury level of attention with prices fixed accordingly. Some rooms are decorated in a low-key 1930s style with flowers and plants, and feature bathrooms clad in gray mosaic tile; others, which have just been renovated, are decorated in Empire style. Tropical garden under the conservatory-style glass roof and small private terraces. Don't miss the magnificent library (rather like a gentleman's club), which also houses the hotel's piano bar. Very luxurious health club with sauna and a Jacuzzi.

 ## Scribe

9th arr. - 1, rue Scribe
01 44 71 24 24, fax 01 44 71 24 42
Open year-round. 11 stes 1,950-6,400. 206 rms 1,950-2,450. Rms for disabled. Air cond. Valet pkg.

Behind the Scribe's Napoléon III façade stands a prime example of the French hotelier's art. All the rooms, suites, and two-level suites are furnished in classic style, and offer huge bathrooms. A multitude of TV channels is on tap, as well as 24-hour room service. Restaurant: Les Muses, (see *Restaurants*); and a bar.

 ## La Trémoille

8th arr. - 14, rue de La Trémoille
01 47 23 34 20, fax 01 40 70 01 08
Open year-round. 5 stes 5,210-7,410. 106 rms 1,410-2,950. Rms for disabled. Restaurant. Rm ser. Air cond. Valet pkg.

Cozy comfort and balconies with bright flower-filled window-boxes in this private mansion-cum-hotel. The Louis XV drawing room and the eighteenth-century style guest rooms accented with antique furniture are certainly strong points, but frankly, we could do without the spots on the carpet, the depressing (and tacky) neon lights and the grumpy reception—enough to ruin the effect of an otherwise pleasant setting. The delightful dining room/salon is warmed by a crackling fire in winter.

 ## Hôtel Le Vernet

8th arr. - 25, rue Vernet
01 44 31 98 00, fax 01 44 31 85 69
Open year-round. 3 stes 3,900-4,200. 54 rms 1,700-2,550. Restaurant. Rm ser. Air cond. Valet pkg.

An admirable hotel, the Vernet combines the best of modern and traditional comforts. The rooms and suites are handsomely decorated with genuine Louis XVI, Directoire, or Empire furniture, and walls are hung with sumptuous fabrics. Jacuzzi in all the bathrooms. Free access to the beautiful Royal Monceau health club. Restaurant: Les Élysées du Vernet, see *Restaurants*.

 ## Vigny

8th arr. - 9, rue Balzac
01 42 99 80 80, fax 01 42 99 80 40
Open year-round. 12 stes 2,600-5,000. 25 rms 1,900-2,200. Restaurant. Rm ser. Air cond. Pkg.

A romantic hotel, the Vigny offers English mahogany furniture, comfortable beds, and fine marble bathrooms: the virtues of another age simplified and brought up to date. The suites provide all-out luxury. Excellent service. Bar. Relais & Châteaux.

 ## Warwick

8th arr. - 5, rue de Berri
01 45 63 14 11, fax 01 43 59 00 98
Open year-round. 5 stes 4,800-9,600. 142 rms 1,700-3,500. Restaurant. Rm ser. Valet pkg.

Luxurious and modern, just off the Champs-Élysées, this hotel offers bright, spacious, rooms that are being redecorated in classy and sober atmosphere. Efficient soundproofing and air conditioning. Newly refurbished lobby, restaurant, and bar. There is an attractive bar with piano music in the evening, with a jazz band on Thursdays. Restaurant: La Couronne, see *Restaurants*.

 ## CLASSIC

 ## Hôtel de l'Arcade

8th arr. - 9, rue de l'Arcade
01 53 30 60 00, fax 01 40 07 03 07
Open year-round. 4 stes 1,180. 37 rms 790-980. Rms for disabled. Air cond.

Here you'll revel in truly spacious, prettily decorated quarters, conveniently sited in the shoppers' mecca between the Madeleine and the major department stores. The perfectly quiet rooms sport pastel fabrics and cherrywood furniture; bathrooms are clad in white marble.

Commodore

9th arr. - 12, bd Haussmann
01 42 46 72 82, fax 01 47 70 28 81
Open year-round. 11 stes 2,900-3,600. 151 rms 1,600-2,600. Restaurant.
A recently renovated establishment located a few steps away from the Drouot auction house. Good-sized rooms, convenient for business travelers.

 # Concorde La Fayette

17th arr. - 3, pl. du Général-Kœnig
01 40 68 50 68, fax 01 40 68 50 43
Open year-round. 32 stes 3,000-8,000. 938 rms 1,250-1,650. Restaurants. Rm ser. Valet pkg.
The Concorde La Fayette is immense: a huge oval tower that houses the Palais des Congrès, banquet rooms, scores of boutiques, cinemas, and nightclubs. The hotel's rooms meet the chain's usual standards, with all the modern amenities. Panoramic bar, three restaurants, including L'Étoile d'Or, (see *Restaurants*).

 # Frantour-Paris-Suffren

15th arr. - 20, rue Jean-Rey
01 45 78 50 00, fax 01 45 78 91 42
Open year-round. 11 stes 1,990-3,450. 396 rms 890-1,075. Rms for disabled. Restaurant. Air cond. Pkg.
The Frantour-Paris-Suffren is a large, modern hotel located next to the Seine and the Champ-de-Mars. Though somewhat impersonal, the simple rooms are regularly refurbished and offer excellent equipment. Friendly service. Meals are served in the enclosed garden.

 # Grand Hôtel de Champagne

1st arr. - 17, rue Jean-Lantier
01 42 36 60 00, fax 01 45 08 43 33
Open year-round. 3 stes 912-1,242. 42 rms 506-812.
A welcoming hotel, built in 1562, with exposed stone walls and ancient beams for atmosphere. The rooms are individually decorated, sometimes in exuberant fashion; some give onto a pretty terrace.

 # Holiday Inn

19th arr. - 216, av. Jean-Jaurès
01 44 84 18 18, fax 01 44 84 18 20
Open year-round. 8 stes 1,490. 174 rms 890. Rms for disabled. Restaurant. Rm ser. Air cond. Fitness center. Garage pkg.
The contemporary architecture and modern comforts of this Holiday Inn are in keeping with the urban environment of La Villette. Many of the perfectly quiet rooms look out onto the Cité de la Musique, an impressive building by noted architect Christian de Portzamparc.

 # Holiday Inn République

11th arr. - 10, pl. de la République
01 43 55 44 34, fax 01 47 00 32 34
Open year-round. 7 stes 1,950-2,995. 311 rms 1,395-1,625. Rms for disabled. Restaurant. Rm ser. Air cond.
The architect Davioud, who designed the Châtelet, built this former Modern Palace in 1867. Today it belongs to the largest hotel chain in the world, which completely restored and modernized it. The rooms and suites are functional, pleasant, and well soundproofed; the most attractive ones overlook the flower-filled, covered courtyard.

 # Holiday Inn Saint-Germain-des-Prés

6th arr. - 92, rue de Vaugirard
01 42 22 00 56, fax 01 42 22 05 39
Open year-round. 22 stes 1,070-1,230. 112 rms 880-1,050. Rms for disabled. Air cond. Pkg.
This is a quiet, functional establishment. Well-equipped rooms with minibar and satellite TV, some furnished in cruise-liner style. Piano bar filled with plants. American buffet breakfasts, Gregory's Restaurant. Impeccable service.

 # Libertel Terminus Nord

10th arr. - 12, bd de Denain
01 42 80 20 00, fax 01 42 80 63 89
Open year-round. 4 stes 1,500. 239 rms 930-990. Rms for disabled. Restaurant. Air cond.
Conveniently located at the foot of the Gare du Nord, this nineteenth-century hotel is a remnant of the romantic past adorned with Art Nouveau stained glass windows and a glass atrium. The marvels continue after the lounge and into the drawing rooms and cozy English-style bedrooms dressed up in pretty flowered fabrics and mahogany Empire furniture.

 # Méridien Étoile

17th arr. - 81, bd Gouvion-Saint-Cyr
01 40 68 34 34, fax 01 40 68 31 31
Open year-round. 18 stes 3,800-8,000. 1,008 rms 1,350-1,650. Restaurants. Rm ser. Air cond. Valet pkg.
This Méridien is the largest hotel in Western Europe, and one of the busiest in Paris. The rooms are small but prettily furnished. A variety of boutiques, a nightclub, the Hurlingham Polo Bar, and three restaurants liven things up, as does the popular cocktail lounge where top jazz musicians play (Club Lionel Hampton).

 # Méridien Montparnasse

14th arr. - 19, rue du Commandant-Mouchotte
01 44 36 44 36, fax 01 44 36 49 00
Open year-round. 37 stes 3,500-4,000. 916 rms 1,250-1,550. Rms for disabled. Restaurants. Rm ser. Air cond. Valet pkg.
This mastodon of a hotel with its tired rooms, furniture lacking all character, and dreary fabrics, is not what it used to be. The service is,

however, flawless, and the amenities thoroughly up-to-date: voice messaging, multilingual secretaries, faxes and more. Fine dining at the Montparnasse 25, (see *Restaurants*).

Nikko de Paris

15th arr. - 61, quai de Grenelle
01 40 58 20 00, fax 01 40 58 24 25
Open year-round. 12 stes 2,500-8,700. 764 rms 1,480-1,980. Restaurants. Rm ser. Air cond. Heated pool. Valet pkg.
Thirty-one floors piled up to resemble an immense beehive, housing ultrafunctional rooms whose large porthole windows overlook the Seine and the Pont Mirabeau. You'll also find an inviting bar, restaurants (Les Célébrités, see *Restaurants*), and a brasserie within the complex.

Opéra Richepanse

1st arr. - 14, rue de Richepanse
01 42 60 36 00, fax 01 42 60 13 03
Open year-round. 3 stes 1,400-1,950. 35 rms 990-1,400. Rm ser. Air cond.
The cozy, inviting guest rooms are elaborately decorated in shades of blue, with solid-wood furnishings in Art Deco style. Top-floor suites enjoy a wide-angle view of the Madeleine church. On the basement level is a lovely breakfast room, as well as a little sauna.

Paris K Palace

16th arr. - 11 bis, rue de Magdebourg
01 44 05 75 75, fax 01 44 05 74 74
Open year-round. 15 stes 2,610. 68 rms 1,510-2,610. Restaurant. Rm ser. Air cond. Pool. Garage pkg.
Ricardo Bofill designed this sleek, contemporary structure situated between the Trocadéro and Arc de Triomphe. Guests enjoy bright, spacious quarters with sophisticated designer furniture and equipment. There's a fitness center, sauna, and Jacuzzi, too, as well as a covered pool surrounded by a teak deck. For the Carré Kléber, see *Restaurants*.

Rochester Champs-Élysées

8th arr. - 92, rue de la Boétie
01 43 59 96 15, fax 01 42 56 01 38
Open year-round. 10 stes 1,400. 80 rms 900-1,250. Rms for disabled. Air cond.
Renovated from head to toe two years ago, this hotel so near the Champs-Élysées is furnished with period furniture. Some rooms give onto a pleasant courtyard garden.

Sofitel Arc de Triomphe

8th arr. - 14, rue Beaujon or 4, av. Bertie-Albrecht
01 45 63 04 04, fax 01 42 25 36 81
Open year-round. 6 stes 2,450-2,700. 129 rms 1,800-2,300. Restaurant. Rm ser. Air cond. Valet pkg.
This solid, austere building dating from 1925 houses a comfortable hotel that is not long on

charm. But the facilities (ultramodern equipment for the business clientele) are first-rate, and are constantly being updated. The largish, bright rooms are functionally decorated. Restaurant: Le Clovis, see *Restaurants*.

Sofitel Champs-Élysées

8th arr. - 8, rue Jean-Goujon
01 40 74 64 64, fax 01 40 74 64 99
Open year-round. 2 stes 1,800. 38 rms 1,500. Rms for disabled. Restaurant. Rm ser. Air cond. Pkg.
This is the jewel of this large hotel chain; it also has a jewel of a location near the Grand Palais and the «golden triangle». Luxurious decoration, especially in the guest rooms. Good breakfast and pleasant service. Restaurant: Les Saveurs, see *Restaurants*.

Sofitel Forum Rive Gauche

14th arr. - 17, bd Saint-Jacques
01 40 78 79 80, fax 01 45 88 43 93
Open year-round. 14 stes 2,500. 783 rms 1,250-1,500. Rms for disabled. Restaurants. Rm ser. Air cond. Valet pkg.
New name, new look. Cyber-office lounge for those who can't live without the Internet, a new more intimate bar for quiet drinks away from the hustle and bustle, and rooms with a completely new cachet decorated in bright gay designs covered with yellow flowers. La Table et la Forme is probably the only restaurant in Paris serving meals guaranteed to contain only 1,000 calories, including the wine, (see *Restaurants*).

Sofitel Paris Sèvres

15th arr. - 8-12, rue Louis-Armand
01 40 60 30 30, fax 01 45 57 04 22
Open year-round. 14 stes 1,900-2,400. 524 rms 1,550. Restaurants. Air cond. Heated pool. Valet pkg.
The rooms are perfectly functional, very comfortable, with huge bathrooms. A plethora of meeting and conference rooms (with simultaneous translation available in five languages) are connected to a central administration office. Guests enjoy free admittance to the Vitatop gym club on the 23rd floor. Restaurant: Le Relais de Sèvres, see *Restaurants*.

Terrass Hôtel

18th arr. - 12, rue Joseph-de-Maistre
01 46 06 72 85, fax 01 42 52 29 11
Open year-round. 13 stes 1,700. 88 rms 1,260. Restaurant. Rm ser. Air cond. Pkg.
Located at the foot of the Butte Montmartre, this fine hotel offers a majestic view of almost all of Paris. Rooms are comfortable and nicely fitted. Up on the seventh floor, the panoramic terrace doubles as a restaurant in summer.

Prices for rooms and suites *are per room, not per person. Half-board prices, however, are per person.*

Victoria Palace

6th arr. - 6, rue Blaise-Desgoffe
01 45 49 70 00, fax 01 45 49 23 75
*Open year-round. 22 stes 2,000-2,500. 57 rms
1,300-2,000. Air cond. Garage pkg.*
Complete face-lift for this hotel with a new
marble lounge and red damask sitting rooms.
The rooms are bigger, and are furnished in
mahogany Louis XVI and decorated with plaster
columns.

 # La Villa Maillot

16th arr. - 143, av. de Malakoff
01 53 64 52 52, fax 01 45 00 60 61
*Open year-round. 3 stes 2,300-2,600. 39 rms 1,050-
1,800. Rms for disabled. Restaurant. Rm ser. Air
cond. Valet pkg.*
Formerly an embassy, the conversion is
sophisticated and modern: an exemplary establishment. The very comfortable rooms (all with
queen-size beds, some with camouflaged
kitchenettes) have an Art Deco feel. Pink-marble
bathrooms; wonderful breakfasts served in an
indoor garden.

 # Yllen Eiffel

15th arr. - 196, rue de Vaugirard
01 45 67 67 67, fax 01 45 67 74 37
*Open year-round. 1 ste 920-995. 39 rms 500-700.
Rms for disabled.*
Yllen's modern, functional rooms have understated décor and are well soundproofed—but
they are quite small. Corner rooms (those with
numbers ending in 4) on the upper floors are the
best. Energetic management, friendly reception.

 # Waldorf Madeleine

8th arr. - 12, bd Malesherbes
01 42 65 72 06, fax 01 40 07 10 45
Open year-round. 7 stes 1,400. 35 rms 1,100. Air cond.
This handsome freestone building houses an
elegant lobby (notice the exquisite Art Deco
atrium) and rooms of exemplary comfort, with
double glazing and air conditioning. You can
count on a smiling reception.

CHARMING

 # Hôtel de l'Abbaye

6th arr. - 10, rue Cassette
01 45 44 38 11, fax 01 45 48 07 86
*Open year-round. 4 stes 1,900-1,950. 42 rms 900-
1,500. Air cond.*
Set back from the street, this serene eighteenth-
century residence located between a courtyard
and a garden offers well-kept, conventionally
decorated rooms which are not particularly spacious; the most delightful are on the same level
as the garden (number 4 even has a terrace). Very
quiet; lovely public rooms.

 # Alba Opéra

9th arr. - 34 ter, rue La Tour-d'Auvergne
01 48 78 80 22, fax 01 42 85 23 13
Open year-round. 5 stes 900-1,400. 18 rms 450-700.
In the steps of Satchmo, who lived here in 1934.
Kitchen-equipped apartments with flowery
bedrooms or newly added guest rooms for business people.

 # Angleterre

6th arr. - 44, rue Jacob
01 42 60 34 72, fax 01 42 60 16 93
Open year-round. 4 stes 1,400. 23 rms 650-1,100.
Hemingway once lived in this former British
Embassy, built around a flower-filled patio. The
rooms are a speck old-fashioned, but some have
exposed stone walls, canopy beds and Louis XVI
furnishings. Luxurious bathrooms. Charm of a
flower garden. Downstairs, there is a bar.

 # Hôtel d'Aubusson

6th arr. - 33, rue Dauphine
01 43 29 43 43, fax 01 43 29 12 62
Open year round. 49 rms 880-1,900. Air cond. Pkg.
Located in the heart of Saint-Germain on the
Left bank, this intimate new hotel is set in a
handsome seventeenth-century mansion, complete with massive wooden beams, antique furniture and a magnificient Aubusson tapestry.
Romantics will especially appreciate the canopy
beds in the spacious guest rooms.

 # De Banville

17th arr. - 166, bd Berthier
01 42 67 70 16, fax 01 44 40 42 77
*Open year-round. 39 rms 600-860. Restaurant. Rm
ser. Air cond.*
A fine small hotel that dates from the 1930s.
There are flowers at the windows (some of which
open onto panoramic views of Paris) and all
manner of pleasing details in the large, bright
rooms. Marble or tile bathrooms. Excellent
English breakfasts.

 # Beau Manoir

8th arr. - 6, rue de l'Arcade
01 42 66 03 07, fax 01 42 68 03 00
*Open year-round. 3 stes 1,400. 29 rms 995-1,155.
Rms for disabled. Rm ser. Air cond. Pkg.*
A charming hotel near the Madeleine church
with a drawing room doting a magnificent
Gobelins tapestry. The Louis XIII-style
bedrooms are appointed with exquisite turned-
wood, country-style furniture. The fifth-floor
rooms under the mansard roof offer wooden
beams.

Hôtel Bourgogne et Montana

7th arr. - 3, rue de Bourgogne
01 45 51 20 22, fax 01 45 56 11 98
*Open year-round. 6 stes 1,430-1,500. 34 rms 760-
1,500. Air cond.*

Since it is so near the Assemblée Nationale, this hotel has decorated its ravishing rooms with caricatures of turn-of-the-century French parliamentary representatives. English fabrics, Louis XVI furnishings and Italian-tile bathrooms. The same charm does not hold for the standard rooms.

 ## Hôtel de la Bretonnerie

4th arr. - 22, rue Sainte-Croix-de-la-Bretonnerie
01 48 87 77 63, fax 01 42 77 26 78
Closed Aug. 3 stes 950. 27 rms 630-780.
A seventeenth-century town house, charmingly decorated. The rooms are made cozy with exposed wood beams and antique furniture (some canopied beds); the large bathrooms are perfectly modern. Look forward to a friendly reception.

 ## Hôtel de Buci

6th arr. - 22, rue de Buci
01 43 26 89 22, fax 01 46 33 80 31
Open year-round. 24 rms 800-1,200.
Here's a beautiful hotel opposite the Buci street market. The place simply overflows with charm: the cozy rooms are graced with antique furnishings and a wealth of tasteful touches. Excellent breakfasts are served in the hotel's vaulted cellar.

 ## California

8th arr. - 16, rue de Berri
01 43 59 93 00, fax 01 45 61 03 62
Open year-round. 13 stes 4,250-6,250. 160 rms 1,950. Restaurant. Rm ser. Fitness center. Valet pkg.
What sets this hotel apart from other similar establishments near the Champs-Élysées is a collection of some 3,000 artworks. As you might imagine, that's a lot of paintings per square yard (and alas, not all are in the best of taste). But the bright patio, with its tiled fountain, provides a welcome respite.

 ## Caron de Beaumarchais

4th arr. - 12, rue Vieille-du-Temple
01 42 72 34 12, fax 01 42 72 34 63
Open year-round. 19 rms 660-730. Air cond.
Here's a find: a hotel overflowing with charm, set in the heart of the Marais. The lobby's eighteenth-century atmosphere is underscored by a Louis XVI fireplace, beamed ceilings, and handsome antiques. The perfectly comfortable rooms are equipped with air conditioning and double glazing for cool quiet in summer.

 ## Chateaubriand

8th arr. - 6, rue Chateaubriand
01 40 76 00 50, fax 01 40 76 09 22
Open year-round. 28 rms 1,200-1,500. Rms for disabled. Restaurant. Rm ser. Air cond. Garage pkg.
Built in 1991, this luxury hotel tucked away behind the Champs-Élysées boasts a polychrome-marble lobby and a courteous, professional staff. Classically elegant rooms; beautiful bathrooms.

 ## Claridge Bellman

8th arr. - 37, rue François-Ier
01 47 23 54 42, fax 01 47 23 08 84
Open year-round. 40 rms 800-1,350. Restaurant. Rm ser. Air cond.
The controlled luxury of the new bedroom décor is in keeping with the low-key wealth of this neighborhood in the middle of Paris's «golden triangle». Rooms boast modern amenities such as air conditioning, as well as old cherry furniture, ornamental moulding, crystal chandeliers and luxuriously thick carpet.

 ## Comfort Louvre-Montana

1st arr. - 12, rue Saint-Roch
01 42 60 35 10, fax 01 42 61 12 28
Open year-round. 5 stes 1,090. 20 rms 580-1,090.
This very chic little hotel doesn't actually overlook the Tuileries, but they are only a stone's throw away. Rooms are all well equipped. Some rooms have balconies.

 ## Hôtel Costes

1st arr. - 239, rue Saint-Honoré
01 42 44 50 00, fax 01 42 44 50 01
Open year-round. 5 stes 3,250-3,750. 78 rms 1,750-2,750. Rms for disabled. Restaurant. Rm ser. Pool. Fitness center.
An opulent atmosphere prevails at this richly decorated hotel near Place Vendôme, now one of the capital's most sought-after places to stay. Entirely renovated, artistically decorated rooms are both comfortable and blessedly quiet. Duplex suites; gorgeous enclosed courtyard where meals are served in fine weather (see Restaurant Costes in *Restaurants*). There is a beautiful fitness center with a pool on the basement level.

 ## Les Deux Iles

4th arr. - 59, rue Saint-Louis-en-l'Ile
01 43 26 13 35, fax 01 43 29 60 25
Open year-round. 17 rms 720-850. Air cond. Rm ser.
This particularly welcoming hotel, like many buildings on the Ile-Saint-Louis, is a lovely seventeenth-century house. You'll sleep close to the Seine in small, pretty rooms decorated with bright fabrics and painted furniture.

 ## Duc de Saint-Simon ♠♣

7th arr. - 14, rue Saint-Simon
01 44 39 20 20, fax 01 45 48 68 25
Open year-round. 5 stes 1,800-1,850. 29 rms 1,025-1,425. Air cond.
The female presence runs strong in this charm of a hotel run by three perfectly adorable women. Dream rooms with alcove beds and elegant English furnishings. Some have private terraces or give directly onto the bamboo garden.

Warm, quiet atmosphere under the vaulted ceiling of the Napoléon III bar.

Éber Monceau

17th arr. - 18, rue Léon-Jost
01 46 22 60 70, fax 01 47 63 01 01
Open year-round. 3 stes 1,050-1,360. 15 rms 610-660. Rm ser.
A quiet charming hotel, «adopted», so to speak, by people in fashion, photography, and the movies. Rooms are on the small side, and all have cable TV. A large, two-level suite on the top floor has a lovely terrace. The lobby impresses with its Henri II fireplace and Renaissance beams. Breakfast, which can be served in the patio in summer, is wonderful. A bar and a small lounge.

Grand Hôtel Malher

4th arr. - 5, rue Malher
01 42 72 60 92, fax 01 42 72 25 37
Open year-round. 1 ste 880-990. 35 rms 470-720.
This family-owned hotel in the historic Marais sports a welcoming country-style décor. After a good night's sleep in one of the pretty guest rooms, you can go down to hearty breakfast, served with a smile in a vaulted seventeenth-century cellar.

L'Hôtel

6th arr. - 13, rue des Beaux-Arts
01 44 41 99 00, fax 01 43 25 64 81
Open year-round. 2 stes 1,700-3,600. 25 rms 600-2,500. Rm ser. Air cond.
«L'Hôtel» provides top-notch amenities and service, of course, but it's the charm of the place that accounts for its enduring popularity. The décor resembles no other—whether it's number 16, once occupied by Oscar Wilde, the neo-Egyptian Imperial room, the purple-swathed Cardinale room, or number 36, which contains the Art Deco furniture of music-hall star Mistinguett. Bar: Le Bélier.

Hôtel du Jeu de Paume

4th arr. - 54, rue Saint-Louis-en-l'Ile
01 43 26 14 18, fax 01 40 46 02 76
Open year-round. 32 rms 895-1,350. Rms for disabled. Rm ser. Sauna.
This is a seventeenth-century building with a splendid wood-and-stone interior, featuring a glass elevator that ferries guests to bright, quiet rooms with marble baths. There is a pleasant little garden, too, and a music room.

Left Bank Saint-Germain

6th arr. - 9, rue de l'Ancienne Comédie
01 43 54 01 70, fax 01 43 26 17 14
Open year-round. 30 rms 550-990. Rms for disabled. Air cond.
Housed in a seventeenth-century building next to the historic Café Procope, this engaging hotel

offers intimate rooms decorated with Jouy-print fabrics. Some lodgings afford views of Paris rooftops and Notre-Dame; all have nicely equipped little bathrooms.

Lenox

7th arr. - 9, rue de l'Université
01 42 96 10 95, fax 01 42 61 52 83
Open year-round. 2 stes 1,500. 32 rms 650-1,100.
These petite but most attractive rooms are decorated with elegant wallpaper and stylish furniture; numbers 51, 52, and 53 are the most enchanting. On the top floor are two split-level suites with exposed beams and flower-filled balconies. The elegant bar stays open until 2am.

Lenox Montparnasse

14th arr. - 15, rue Delambre
01 43 35 34 50, fax 01 43 20 46 64
Open year-round. 6 stes 980. 46 rms 540-650. Rm ser.
In the heart of Montparnasse, a peaceful hotel with a cozy sort of charm. The penthouse suites are awfully attractive—they even have fireplaces. Rooms vary in size, yet are uniformly comfortable and well maintained. Smiling staff; elegant bar (open until 2am).

Libertel Hôtel d'Argentine

16th arr. - 1-3, rue d'Argentine
01 45 02 76 76, fax 01 45 02 76 00
Open year-round. 40 rms 860-920. Rm ser.
This Napoléon-style hotel near the Arch of Triumph is paradise for Bonaparte admirers. The Neoclassic-style entrance hall recounts the Egyptian expedition, and the smallish bedrooms are decked out in striped fabrics and Empire-style furniture.

Lido

8th arr. - 4, passage de la Madeleine
01 42 66 27 37, fax 01 42 66 61 23
Open year-round. 32 rms 830-980. Air cond.
A laudable establishment, situated between the Madeleine and the Place de la Concorde. The lobby is most elegant, with Oriental rugs on the floor and tapestries on the stone walls. The guest rooms, decorated in pink, blue, or cream, have comfortable beds, modern bathrooms, and double-glazed windows. Thoughtful, courteous staff.

Lutèce

4th arr. - 65, rue Saint-Louis-en-l'Ile
01 43 26 23 52, fax 01 43 29 60 25
Open year-round. 23 rms 850. Air cond.
A tasteful, small hotel for people who love Paris, this handsome old house has some little twenty rooms (there are two charming mansards on the sixth floor), with whitewashed walls and ceiling beams, decorated with bright, cheerful fabrics. The bathrooms are small but modern and impeccably kept. The lobby features lavish

bouquets and a stone fireplace which is often used in winter.

Luxembourg

6th arr. - 4, rue de Vaugirard
01 43 25 35 90, fax 01 43 26 60 84
Open year-round. 33 rms 650-850. Air cond.
Near the Luxembourg Gardens, in the heart of the Latin Quarter. The pleasant rooms have good equipment but small bathrooms.

Madison

6th arr. - 143, bd Saint-Germain
01 40 51 60 00, fax 01 40 51 60 01
Open year-round. 55 rms 700-1,500.
A smart, comfortable hotel in the heart of Saint-Germain. The large lovely guest rooms decked out in cretonne upholstery and curtains are decorated with a sprinkling of antique pieces. Some even have a view of the Saint-Germain-des-Prés church. The bathrooms are done up in pretty Provençal tiles. The Empire-style sitting room is a jewel.

Majestic

16th arr. - 29, rue Dumont-d'Urville
01 45 00 83 70, fax 01 45 00 29 48
Open year-round. 3 stes 1,550-2,000. 27 rms 1,250. Air cond.
The big rooms in this exemplary hotel are redecorated by turns, and all boast comfortable beds, fine furniture, and thick carpeting. On the top floor, a lovely penthouse features a small balcony filled with flowers. Old World atmosphere.

Hôtel Mansart

1st arr. - 5, rue des Capucines
01 42 61 50 28, fax 01 49 27 97 44
Open year-round. 6 stes 1,200-1,500. 51 rms 550-970. Rm ser.
The lobby looks for all the world like an art gallery; the rooms are positively charming, arrayed in elegant furnishings with all the modern comforts and equipment one could wish. If you book well in advance, you can request the «Mansart» room, which overlooks Place Vendôme.

Hôtel de Notre-Dame

5th arr. - 19, rue Maître-Albert
01 43 26 79 00, fax 01 46 33 50 11
Open year-round. 34 rms 690-750.
Some of the beamed rooms are rather small, but all are comfy and prettily fitted out, with impeccable marble bathrooms. Situated on a quiet street near the river, this hotel is managed by a cheerful staff.

Nouvel Hôtel

12th arr. - 24, av. du Bel-Air
01 43 43 01 81, fax 01 43 44 64 13
Open year-round. 28 rms 360-530.
The rooms of the Nouvel Hôtel are peaceful and attractive, and all have been renovated and redecorated (the prettiest is number 9, on the same level as the garden). Good bathrooms; hospitable reception. Old-fashioned hot chocolate is served at breakfast.

Parc Saint-Séverin

5th arr. - 22, rue de la Parcheminerie
01 43 54 32 17, fax 01 43 54 70 71
Open year-round. 1 ste 1,500. 26 rms 510-1,025. Air cond. Rm ser.
The rooms on the sixth and seventh floors of this 1930s-vintage hotel boast balconies with a view over the church and cloister of Saint-Séverin. All the accommodations are bright and spacious, enhanced with antiques and contemporary art objects.

Le Pavillon Bastille

12th arr. - 65, rue de Lyon
01 43 43 65 65, fax 01 43 43 96 52
Open year-round. 1 ste 1,200-1,375. 23 rms 550-955. Rms for disabled. Rm ser. Air cond.
Across from the Bastille opera house, here are all the comforts of a luxury hotel, with the charm of a private town house. The bright rooms and lobby are decorated in a bold, high style; the owner welcomes guests with a glass of white wine. Minibar; sumptuous buffet breakfasts.

Pavillon de la Reine

3rd arr. - 28, pl. des Vosges
01 42 77 96 40, fax 01 42 77 63 06
Open year-round. 22 stes 2,300-3,500. 33 rms 1,500-2,100. Rms for disabled. Rm ser. Air cond.
Part of the hotel dates from the seventeenth century, while the rest is a clever «reconstitution». The rooms and suites, all with marble bathrooms, are tastefully decorated. The furnishings are an artful blend of authentic antiques and lovely reproductions. Accommodations overlook either the back of the Place des Vosges or a quiet inner patio filled with flowers.

Prince de Conti

6th arr. - 8, rue Guénégaud
01 44 07 30 40, fax 01 44 07 36 34
Open year-round. 3 stes 990-1,250. 23 rms 850-990. Rms for disabled. Air cond.
This gem of a hotel, eighteenth century, sports a refined English style in its make-yourself-at-home drawing room as well as in the cozy, flowery guest rooms equipped with satellite television, air conditioning and marble bathrooms. You'll be sure to sleep undisturbed in the rooms giving on to the delightful patio.

Regent's Garden Hotel

17th arr. - 6, rue Pierre-Demours
01 45 74 07 30, fax 01 40 55 01 42
Open year-round. 39 rms 650-940. Garage pkg.
This former gentleman's residence was built by Napoléon III for his private doctor. Set in a

lovely flower garden, the spacious rooms offer peace and quiet and are appointed with ornamental moulding and Louis XV furniture.

 ## Relais Christine

6th arr. - 3, rue Christine
01 40 51 60 80, fax 01 40 51 60 81
Open year-round. 15 stes 2,600-3,200. 36 rms 1,630-1,800. Rm ser. Air cond. Valet pkg.
This Renaissance cloister has retained some of the peace of its earlier vocation, but this luxurious hotel also possesses all the comforts of the present age, from double glazing to perfect service. The rooms are decorated with Provençal prints and pink Portuguese marble baths. The best rooms are the two-level suites and the ground-floor room with private terrace, but all are spacious, quiet, and air conditioned.

 ## Le Relais du Louvre

1st arr. - 19, rue des Prêtres-St-Germain-l'Auxerrois
01 40 41 96 42, fax 01 40 41 96 44
Open year-round. 3 stes 1,000-1,950. 18 rms 480-950. Restaurant. Rm ser.
The original façade of this historic building opposite the Tuileries has been preserved, but the interior is fully modernized. The comfortable rooms, elegantly decorated by Constance de Castelbajac, overflow with charm; they all have marble bathrooms, too. Rooms with numbers ending in 1 are slightly smaller than the rest. Wonderfully hospitable reception.

 ## Le Relais Médicis

6th arr. - 23, rue Racine
01 43 26 00 60, fax 01 40 46 83 39
Open year-round. 16 rms 780-1,495. Air cond.
Bright colors adorn the walls of each room: yellow, blue, red... The effect is cheerful and charming, enhanced by ancient beams, pictures, vintage photos. A quiet patio and fountain are conducive to relaxation. The staff visibly cares about guests' comfort and well-being.

 ## Relais Saint-Germain

6th arr. - 9, carrefour de l'Odéon
01 43 29 12 05, fax 01 46 33 45 30
Open year-round. 1 ste 2,000. 21 rms 1,290-1,800.
All the accommodations are personalized and decorated in luxurious style, with superb furniture, lovely fabrics, exquisite lighting, and beautiful, perfectly equipped marble bathrooms. The tall, double-glazed windows open onto the lively Carrefour de l'Odéon. You are bound to fall in love with Paris staying at this tiny jewel of an establishment. Exemplary service.

 ## Les Rives de Notre-Dame

5th arr. - 15, quai Saint-Michel
01 43 54 81 16, fax 01 43 26 27 09
Open year-round. 1 ste 2,600. 9 rms 1,100-1,650. Rms for disabled. Restaurant. Rm ser. Air cond.

From the roomy, bright accommodations in this seventeenth-century hotel, you'll enjoy a pretty view of the Seine. The rooms all have fresh, personalized décor in Tuscan or Provençal styles.

 ## Rond Point de Longchamp

16th arr. - 86, rue de Longchamp
01 45 05 13 63, fax 01 47 55 12 80
Open year-round. 1 ste 1,500-2,000. 56 rms 600-1,000. Restaurant. Air cond.
Burled-walnut furniture and woodwork fragrant with the smell of wax attract business people who can meet with their customers in the little living rooms/offices adjoining their bedrooms. Splendid scenic view of the Eiffel Tower.

 ## Hôtel Saint-Germain

7th arr. - 88, rue du Bac
01 49 54 70 00, fax 01 45 48 26 89
Open year-round. 29 rms 415-730.
In the best Rive Gauche tradition, this posh yet discreet little hostelry charms guests with beamed and vaulted ceilings, elegant décor, and period furnishings. The atmosphere is somehow provincial (in the best sense of the word); rooms offer space and comfort as well as all modern conveniences. New garden and patio.

 ## Saint-Grégoire

6th arr. - 43, rue de l'Abbé-Grégoire
01 45 48 23 23, fax 01 45 48 33 95
Open year-round. 1 ste 1,390. 19 rms 790-990. Air cond.
The cozy lounge is warmed in winter by a fireplace and there's a small garden for fine days. The rooms are painted in subtle shades of yellow and pink, with matching chintz curtains, white damask bedspreads, and some fine antique furniture. Double glazing and modern bathrooms.

 ## Saint-Louis

4th arr. - 75, rue Saint-Louis-en-l'Ile
01 46 34 04 80, fax 01 46 34 02 13
Open year-round. 21 rms 645-845.
Elegant simplicity characterizes this appealing hotel, where attention to detail is evident in the gorgeous flower arrangements and polished antiques. Small, perfectly soundproofed rooms offer comfortable beds and thick carpeting underfoot. The modern bathrooms are pretty indeed.

 ## Saint-Merry

4th arr. - 78, rue de la Verrerie
01 42 78 14 15, fax 01 40 29 06 82
Open year-round. 1 ste 2,000. 11 rms 400-1,100.
A former presbytery, this seventeenth-century building is home to an original collection of Gothic furniture, which the owner has been

buying at auctions for many years. The telephone booth near the reception desk is a former confessional! Rooms are mostly small, with bathrooms not much bigger than closets, but the charm of the place is such that you have to book well in advance for the summer.

 ## Sainte-Beuve

6th arr. - 9, rue Sainte-Beuve
01 45 48 20 07, fax 01 45 48 67 52
Open year-round. 5 stes 1,550-1,700. 18 rms 700-1,300. Rm ser.
The Sainte-Beuve is a tasteful, harmonious example of the neo-Palladian style of decoration, promoted in particular by David Hicks. In the guest rooms soft colors, chintzes and the odd antique create a soothing atmosphere. Most attractive marble-and-tile bathrooms; elegant lobby with comfortable sofas arranged around the fireplace.

 ## Hôtel des Saints-Pères

6th arr. - 65, rue des Saints-Pères
01 45 44 50 00, fax 01 45 44 90 83
Open year-round. 3 stes 1,650. 36 rms 650-1,250.
Situated in two buildings, with all the quiet, elegantly furnished rooms overlooking a garden. Suite 205 is particularly attractive. Downstairs is a pretty breakfast room, and a bar that opens onto the garden.

 ## Select Hotel

5th arr. - 1, pl. de la Sorbonne
01 46 34 14 80, fax 01 46 34 51 79
Open year-round. 1 ste 890-1,250. 67 rms 530-780.
A glass-roofed atrium with an abundance of plants has been built at the heart of this attractive hotel next door to the Sorbonne. The pleasant, spacious rooms are functionally furnished; some open onto a lively square.

 ## Hôtel Le Tourville

7th arr. - 16, av. de Tourville
01 47 05 62 62, fax 01 47 05 43 90
Open year-round. 2 stes 1,390-1,990. 28 rms 650-1,100. Rm ser. Air cond.
Behind the pretty white façade is a thoroughly modern hotel. The drawing room décor is a balanced play on the right-angle columns, filtered lighting and pure lines of its polished furniture. The guest rooms are decorated in soft, refined colors that take up the tones in the golden yellow, sand and pink upholstery. Some dote Jacuzzis and private terraces.

Vert Galant

13th arr. - 41, rue Croulebarbe
01 44 08 83 50, fax 01 44 08 83 69
Open year-round. 15 rms 400-500. Rms for disabled. Garage pkg.
Now for something completely different: this delightful country *auberge* provides adorable

rooms (with kitchenette) overlooking an indoor garden where grapes and tomatoes grow! Quiet; good value. Restaurant: Auberge Etchegorry, see *Restaurants*.

 ## Vieux Paris

6th arr. - 9, rue Gît-le-Cœur
01 44 32 15 90, fax 01 43 26 00 15
Open year-round. 7 stes 1,650-1,800. 13 rms 1,090-1,470. Garage pkg.
Here's a hotel that wears its name well, for it was built in the fifteenth century. A recent overhaul turned the Vieux Paris into a luxurious stopover, whose comfort and first-rate amenities fully justify the high rates. Rooms are handsomely furnished and perfectly quiet, with Jacuzzis in every bathroom. Warm reception.

 ## La Villa Saint-Germain

6th arr. - 29, rue Jacob
01 43 26 60 00, fax 01 46 34 63 63
Open year-round. 4 stes 1,800-3,000. 28 rms 800-1,800. Rm ser. Air cond.
A laser beam projects room numbers onto the doors; the bathroom sinks are crafted of chrome and sanded glass; orange, violet, green, and red leather furniture stands out vividly against the subdued gray walls: a high-tech environment that attracts a trendy, moneyed clientele. Jazz club on the lower level (La Villa), with name performers.

PRACTICAL

 ## Bastille Speria

4th arr. - 1, rue de la Bastille
01 42 72 04 01, fax 01 42 72 56 38
Open year-round. 42 rms 550-622. Rm ser. Air cond. Pkg.
Modern rooms with mini-bars, trouser presses, safes and satellite television in this prime Marais location between the Bastille and the Place des Vosges.

 ## Bergère Opéra

9th arr. - 34, rue Bergère
01 47 70 34 34, fax 01 47 70 36 36
Open year-round. 134 rms 590-1,090. Rm ser. Air cond.
Just around the corner from the Grands Boulevards, a really pleasant hotel with a flower-filled courtyard and beautiful rooms that are quiet and air-conditioned.

This symbol signifies hotels that offer an exceptional degree of peace and quiet.

Best Western Folkestone Opéra

8th arr. - 9, rue Castellane
01 42 65 73 09, fax 01 42 65 64 09
Open year-round. 50 rms 605-800. Air cond.
The beamed rooms have Art Deco armchairs and comfortable beds. Generous buffet breakfasts; gracious reception.

 ## Hôtel Boileau

16th arr. - 81, rue Boileau
01 42 88 83 74, fax 01 45 27 62 98
Open year-round. 30 rms 370-550.
This establishment is warm and bright, with small, simply furnished rooms. A skylight covers the little garden-courtyard.

 ## Hôtel du Bois

16th arr. - 11, rue du Dôme
01 45 00 31 96, fax 01 45 00 90 05
Open year-round. 41 rms 445-595. Pkg.
Tucked away at the back of a little public square, this quiet little hotel offers smallish rather ordinary rooms.

 ## Hôtel de Châteaudun

9th arr. - 30, rue de Châteaudun
01 49 70 09 99, fax 01 49 70 06 99
Open year-round. 26 rms 620-760. Rm ser. Air cond.
This hotel welcomes a host of regulars who come back for the quiet, air-conditioned rooms and the hospitality of the staff, as well as for its convenient location just a step away from the business district.

 ## Claret

12th arr. - 44, bd de Bercy
01 46 28 41 31, fax 01 49 28 09 29
Open year-round. 52 rms 350-650. Restaurant. Rm ser. Air cond. Pkg.
This old stagecoach inn with its white-beamed ceiling offers some rooms with a view on the terrace-garden.

 ## Hôtel Delambre

14th arr. - 35, rue Delambre
01 43 20 66 31, fax 01 45 38 91 76
Open year-round. 1 ste 650. 29 rms 440-490.
André Breton lived here in 1921, but don't worry, it's been redone since—in fact just last year. Darling rooms with yellow striped upholstery and orangy fabrics.

 ## Ermitage Hôtel

18th arr. - 24, rue Lamarck
01 42 64 79 22, fax 01 42 64 10 33
Open year-round. 12 rms 430. No cards.
This charming hotel occupies a little white building behind the Basilica of Sacré-Cœur. The personalized décor in each room is punctuated by an antique or *bibelot*. Pretty bathrooms; no TV.

There is a garden and a terrace for relaxing, and you can expect a friendly reception.

 ## Étoile Pereire

17th arr. - 146, bd Pereire
01 42 67 60 00, fax 01 42 67 02 90
Open year-round. 5 stes 1,000. 21 rms 560-760. Rms for disabled. Rm ser.
Attention to detail is a priority at this welcoming hotel, owned by a former pianist. Located at the back of a quiet courtyard, the spacious, pastel rooms are most attractive, with garden views. Both the atmosphere and service are charming and cheerful.

 ## Familia Hotel

5th arr. - 11, rue des Écoles
01 43 54 55 27, fax 01 43 29 61 77
Open year-round. 30 rms 370-520.
The management of this modest two-star hotel strives to make guests comfortable. Rooms are small but decently equipped; reasonable rates.

 ## Flaubert

17th arr. - 19, rue Rennequin
01 46 22 44 35, fax 01 43 80 32 34
Open year-round. 37 rms 450-500. Pkg.
Virginia creeper, Aucuba and others types of asparagus hug the exotic-wood galleries that lead you to your room in this hotel near the Parc Monceau. Heartfelt family-style reception.

 ## Forest Hill Paris La Villette

19th arr. - 28 ter, av. Corentin-Cariou
01 44 72 15 30, fax 01 44 72 15 80
Open year-round. 10 stes 1,250. 249 rms 595-940. Rms for disabled. Restaurant. Rm ser. Air cond.
A mammoth concrete structure opposite the Cité des Sciences, the Forest Hill houses functional rooms (with small windows!) that have the virtue of being absolutely quiet.

 ## Hôtel Français

10th arr. - 13, rue du 8-Mai-1945
01 40 35 94 14, fax 01 40 35 55 40
Open year-round. 71 rms 385-470. Garage pkg.
You'll appreciate the good value of this convenient hotel, situated opposite the Gare de l'Est. Old-fashioned charm combines with modern comforts (iron and ironing board, hair dryer, and safe in all the rooms).

 ## Grand Hôtel de Besançon

2nd arr. - 56, rue Montorgueil
01 42 36 41 08, fax 01 45 08 08 79
Open year-round. 10 stes 590-650. 10 rms 560-590.
The Besançon provides soundproofed rooms furnished with Louis-Philippe–style pieces. Convenient to the Louvre and to the Forum des Halles.

Grand Hôtel des Gobelins

13th arr. - 57, bd Saint-Marcel
01 43 31 79 89, fax 01 45 35 43 56 .
Open year-round. 45 rms 390-520.
Situated on the edge of the fifth arrondissement, this hotel offers exceptional value for money. Some of the rooms look out onto the Panthéon. Double-glazed windows; dry cleaning service daily, even on weekends.

 ## Grand Hôtel Jeanne d'Arc

4th arr. - 3, rue de Jarente
01 48 87 62 11, fax 01 48 87 37 31
Open year-round. 36 rms 300-590.
A peaceful seventeenth-century house near the Place des Vosges offering rooms with exposed stone walls where space and rustic-style furniture are slim pickings.

 ## Grands Hommes

5th arr. - 17, pl. du Panthéon
01 46 34 19 60, fax 01 43 26 67 32
Open year-round. 2 stes 860-1,200. 30 rms 635-780.
An eighteenth-century building opposite the Panthéon. The fairly spacious rooms are decorated in ocher and orange tones; room 22 has a canopied brass bed, 60 and 61 boast balconies and pleasant views. The staff is friendly and efficient.

 ## Hameau de Passy

16th arr. - 48, rue de Passy
01 42 88 47 55, fax 01 42 30 83 72
Open year-round. 32 rms 400-600.
Tucked away in a flower-filled cul-de-sac, this hotel is exceptionally quiet. Roughcast walls and stained-wood furniture decorate the comfortable rooms (some connecting) that overlook the garden. Bright, tidy bathrooms; smiling service and reception.

 ## Istria

14th arr. - 29, rue Campagne-Première
01 43 20 91 82, fax 01 43 22 48 4
Open year-round. 26 rms 420-590.
Elm furniture and pastel colors grace the rooms and bathrooms of this well-kept hotel, where Mayakovski, Man Ray, and Marcel Duchamp once slept. The building is fully modernized.

 ## Hôtel Le Loiret

1st arr. - 5, rue des Bons Enfants
01 42 61 47 31, fax 01 42 61 36 85
Open year-round. 31 rms 450-590. Rm ser. Pkg.
Central location just around the corner from the Palais-Royal. Small hotel in a quiet street just off the Faubourg Saint-Honoré. Parisian-size guest rooms, but at a nice price for the neighborhood.

 ## Hôtel du Léman

9th arr. - 20, rue de Trévise
01 42 46 50 66, fax 01 48 24 27 59
Open year-round. 24 rms 390-730.
This charming, out-of-the-ordinary small hotel has been tastefully renovated. Tuscany marble inlays enhance the modern décor in the lobby. The tiny rooms are pleasantly decorated with attractive bedside lamps and original drawings and watercolors. A generous buffet breakfast is served in the vaulted basement. The staff does its utmost to make guests feel at home.

 ## Jardins du Luxembourg

5th arr. - 5, impasse Royer-Collard
01 40 46 08 88, fax 01 40 46 02 28
Open year-round. 25 rms 770-820. Rms for disabled. Air cond.
The ghost of Sigmund Freud, who stayed here often in 1885, will not haunt you in the charming little rooms adorned with wrought-iron beds and smart contemporary Italian furniture.

 ## Hôtel Le Laumière

19th arr. - 4, rue Petit
01 42 06 10 77, fax 01 42 06 72 50
Open year-round. 54 rms 275-380. Pkg.
This meticulously-kept small hotel is located a few steps away from the Buttes-Chaumont park, in a district where modern hotels are not exactly plentiful. Convenient for the La Villette exhibition center. Rooms are small (those on the courtyard are larger), fully renovated, and moderately priced.

 ## Novotel-Bercy

12th arr. - 85, rue de Bercy
01 43 42 30 00, fax 01 43 45 30 60
Open year-round. 1 ste 1,250. 128 rms 690-760. Rms for disabled. Restaurant. Rm ser. Air cond.
This classic chain hotel is located just minutes from the Palais Omnisports and Finance Ministry. Standard rooms and service.

 ## Novotel Les Halles

1st arr. - Pl. Marguerite-de-Navarre
01 42 21 31 31, fax 01 40 26 05 79
Open year-round. 5 stes 1,500. 280 rms 860-1,145. Rms for disabled. Restaurant. Rm ser. Air cond. Pkg.
This ultramodern building constructed of stone, glass, and zinc is located in the heart of the former market district, near the Pompidou Center and the Forum des Halles. The bright, quiet rooms are impeccably equipped. Loads of services on offer; piano bar until midnight.

 ## Novotel Paris Vaugirard

15th arr. - 257-263, rue de Vaugirard
01 40 45 10 00, fax 01 40 45 10 10
Open year-round. 3 stes 1,400. 186 rms 690-835. Air cond. Rm ser. Pkg.

This hotel half-way between the Montparnasse station and the Porte de Versailles convention center offers bright quiet rooms that are in fact much more pleasant than the somewhat careless reception. Sauna and fitness center.

 ## Opéra Cadet

9th arr. - 24, rue Cadet
01 48 24 05 26, fax 01 42 46 68 09
Open year-round. 3 stes 1,500. 82 rms 735-990. Rms for disabled. Air cond. Garage pkg.
A functional, modern hotel in the heart of the city, offering comfortable accommodations. Double-glazed windows; winter garden.

 ## L'Orchidée

14th arr. - 65, rue de l'Ouest
01 43 22 70 50, fax 01 42 79 97 46
Open year-round. 40 rms 456-502. Sauna. Jacuzzi. Garage pkg.
Tucked behind the attractive façade are an inviting lobby furnished with wicker pieces and a small garden-courtyard. Rooms look out over the garden or a square; some have balconies. Impeccable bathrooms.

 ## Orléans Palace Hôtel

14th arr. - 185, bd Brune
01 45 39 68 50, fax 01 45 43 65 64
Open year-round. 92 rms 510-580. Restaurant.
A quiet and comfortable traditional hotel that offers good value. The well-equipped and soundproofed rooms are decorated in contemporary style, and there is a pretty *jardin intérieur.*

 ## Parc Montsouris

14th arr. - 4, rue du Parc-Montsouris
01 45 89 09 72, fax 01 45 80 92 72
Open year-round. 7 stes 490. 35 rms 320-430. Rms for disabled.
This good little hotel features quiet rooms done up in pastel tones and bright, new bathrooms. The lovely Parc Montsouris is just a short walk away.

 ## Paris Lyon Bastille

12th arr. - 3, rue Parrot
01 43 43 41 52, fax 01 43 43 81 16
Open year-round. 1 ste 750-855. 47 rms 495-580.
The location is most convenient (near the Gare de Lyon), and the building is attractive. Comfortable, unpretentious rooms; skimpy breakfasts.

 ## Le Parnasse

14th arr. - 79-81, av. du Maine
01 43 20 13 93, fax 01 43 20 95 60
Open year-round. 79 rms 530-580. Rms for disabled. Air cond.
The Parnasse is lodged in a pretty, white building; it offers large, bright rooms and complete bathrooms. Double glazing ensures peaceful nights. There are views—of the Tour Montparnasse...and the cemetery!

 ## Hôtel de la Place du Louvre

1st arr. - 21, rue des Prêtres-St-Germain-l'Auxerrois
01 42 33 78 68, fax 01 42 33 09 95
Open year-round. 2 stes 812. 18 rms 496-762.
Lodged in a Renaissance building, this hotel is decorated with paintings and sculptures throughout. The fairly large rooms are all comfortably furnished, with good bathrooms, and there are five charming split-level rooms under the eaves. Breakfast is served in a vaulted cellar.

 ## Plaza La Fayette

10th arr. - 175, rue La Fayette
01 44 89 89 10, fax 01 40 36 00 30
Open year-round. 48 rms 595-890. Rms for disabled. Restaurant. Air cond. Pkg.
Conveniently located between with the Gare du Nord and the Gare de l'Est, offering small rooms fitted out for quality comfort, including balneotherapy, fax lines, Numéris modem connection and satellite television.

 ## Hôtel du Pré

9th arr. - 10, rue Pierre-Sémard
01 42 81 37 11, fax 01 40 23 98 28
Open year-round. 41 rms 445-570.
A simple hotel that serves its purpose in this neighborhood bordering the banking district. The rooms are pleasant and well-kept, even though the paint could use refreshing and there is no double glazing.

 ## Queen Mary

8th arr. - 9, rue de Greffulhe
01 42 66 40 50, fax 01 42 66 94 92
Open year-round. 1 ste 1,250. 35 rms 745-915. Rms for disabled. Rm ser. Air cond.
On a quiet street in the Haussmann district, this Queen Mary is an adorable hotel. The cozy little rooms are furnished in the English style, right down to the decanter of Sherry placed on the table.

 ## Regyn's Montmartre

18th arr. - 18, pl. des Abbesses
01 42 54 45 21, fax 01 42 23 76 69
Open year-round. 22 rms 370-445. Pkg.
Best to ask for one of the rooms on the fourth floor, completely redone this year. Swell view of Sacré-Cœur from rooms giving onto rear.

 ## Résidence des Gobelins

13th arr. - 9, rue des Gobelins
01 47 07 26 90, fax 01 43 31 44 05
Open year-round. 32 rms 295-435.
A delightful small hotel in a quiet street not far from the Latin Quarter and Montparnasse with congenial young owners. Rooms are decorated in blue, green, or orange, a different color for each floor. Some give onto a terrace.

Résidence Monceau

8th arr. - 85, rue du Rocher
01 45 22 75 11, fax 01 45 22 30 88
Open year-round. 1 ste 800-880. 50 rms 700. Rms for disabled. Restaurant.
Though it lacks atmosphere, the Résidence Monceau is functional and well kept, and employs a helpful, courteous staff. All the rooms and corridors have just been freshly redecorated.

 ## Résidence Saint-Lambert

15th arr. - 5, rue Eugène-Gibez
01 48 28 63 14, fax 01 45 33 45 50
Open year-round. 48 rms 380-590.
This pleasant, quiet hotel near the exhibition center at Porte de Versailles has tidy, smallish but nicely equipped rooms (double glazing), some overlooking the garden. Laundry and bar on the premises.

 ## Résidence Trousseau

11th arr. - 13, rue Trousseau
01 48 05 55 55, fax 01 48 05 83 97
Open year-round. 2 stes 1,350-1,500. 64 rms 300-550. Pkg.
A modern hotel not far from the Bastille. The suites have been refurbished with kitchenettes, a practical touch. The quiet rooms are set around an enclosed garden.

> Remember to call ahead to **reserve your room**, and please, if you cannot honor your reservation, be courteous and let the hotel know.

Hôtel de Saint-Germain

6th arr. - 50, rue du Four
01 45 48 91 64, fax 01 45 48 46 22
Open year-round. 30 rms 520-695.
This small hotel with its doll-sized rooms and white-wood furniture has finished its renovation. Many services.

 ## Timhôtel Montmartre

18th arr. - 11, rue Ravignan
01 42 55 74 79, fax 01 42 55 71 01
Open year-round. 60 rms 450-550. Rm ser.
Located on a small *place* so typical of Montmartre, where you can practically reach out and touch the five domes of Sacré-Cœur from the small rooms under the mansard roof.

 ## La Tour d'Auvergne

9th arr. - 10, rue de La Tour d'Auvergne
01 48 78 61 60, fax 01 49 95 99 00
Open year-round. 24 rms 500-700. Garage pkg.
Modigliani once lived in this hotel. We wonder how he would feel about its current kitsch décor (don't miss the draped headboards). Nonetheless, a competently run, comfortable establishment.

 ## Le Zéphyr

12th arr. - 31 bis, bd Diderot
01 43 46 12 72, fax 01 43 41 68 01
Open year-round. 89 rms 550-690. Rms for disabled. Restaurant. Air cond. Garage pkg.
Practically next door to the Gare de Lyon, the Zéphyr is a modern hotel with good equipment. Rooms are bright and neat, the welcome is friendly, and service is reliably prompt. Quality breakfasts.

SHOPS

ANTIQUES

Le Louvre des Antiquaires

1st arr. - 2, pl. du Palais-Royal
01 42 97 27 00, fax 01 42 97 00 14
http://www.louvre-antiquaires.com
*Open 11am-7pm. Closed Mon, Jul-Aug: Sun. M°
Palais-Royal.*
 Le Louvre des Antiquaires, a marketplace for
objets d'art, is the greatest success of its kind in
France and probably the world. The former
Magasins du Louvre department store, beautifully remodeled, houses some 250 dealers on
three levels. These merchants are the most select,
professional, and scrupulous in the trade, if not
the most famous. Every piece offered for sale is
absolutely authentic and of irreproachable
quality. Of course, the prices reflect these high
standards.
 Thirty specialties are represented—from archaeological artifacts to eighteenth-century furniture, from nineteenth-century minor masters
to Art Deco ornaments, from antique porcelain
to rare prints, and from animal bronzes to lead
soldiers and ship models, fans, rare books, and
fabulous jewels. In addition, Le Louvre des Antiquaires provides a delivery service, a club, exhibition halls, and bars. Each year two
temporary exhibitions are mounted around
selected themes.

Musée de la Monnaie

The end of the rainbow for numis-
matists: a staggering array of precious coins and medals housed in
the gorgeous Hôtel des Monnaies.
A mere 200 years or so after its
creation (1768 by Louis XV), the
Mint has been reborn as a
museum. On display are coins
from ancient times to the present.
The mansion's court of honor and
the many superb salons are alone
worth the visit.
6th arr. - 11, quai de Conti - 01 40
46 55 33, fax 01 40 46 57 09.
http://www.monnaiedeparis.fr
Open Tue-Fri 11am-5:30pm, Sat-
Sun noon-5:30pm. Closed Mon.
Admission: 20 F, reduced rate:
15 F, Sun: free. M° Pont-Neuf.

Le Marché aux Puces

Marché Biron, 85, rue des Rosiers
01 40 11 59 69, fax 01 40 10 13 08
Marché Serpette, 110, rue des Rosiers
01 40 11 54 14, fax 01 40 12 72 62
Marché Paul-Bert, 104, rue des Rosiers & 18, rue
Paul Bert - same telephone and fax numbers as
Marché Serpette.
Marché Vernaison, 99, rue des Rosiers & 136, rue
Michelet - 01 40 10 27 76
Marché Malassis, 142, rue des Rosiers - 01 49 45 17 38
Marché Dauphine, 138, rue des Rosiers
06 09 48 84 53, fax 01 40 10 07 94
93400 Saint-Ouen
hhttp://www.antiques.tm.fr.
*Open Sat-Mon. Closed Tue-Fri. M° Porte-de-St-
Ouen.*
 Each weekend some 150,000 visitors trek out to
Saint-Ouen, a northern suburb just beyond the
eighteenth arrondissement, to the world's
largest antique market. From dawn on Saturday
through Monday afternoon, dealers sell everything from used kitchen utensils to vintage jeans,
from Art Deco clocks and *bibelots* to signed
eighteenth-century secretaries.
 The **Marché Biron** boasts the classiest merchandise—crystal chandeliers, rare silver, and such;
the **Marché Serpette** draws clients from the
fashion and entertainment fields with trendy
retro and Art Deco pieces; the open-air **Marché
Paul-Bert** is an eclectic treasure trove where
early birds can unearth some terrific finds; the
Marché Vernaison, the heart of the flea market,
numbers 400 stands hawking vintage linens,
crockery, stamps, and miscellaneous collec-
tibles; the tiny, tidy shops of the **Marché Malassis** present cleaned-up, restored merchandise in
a modern, high-tech setting; the **Marché
Dauphine**, offers furniture and objects ranging
from Renaissance to Art Deco, and a unique
concentration of bookstores selling antique
volumes and high-quality papers.

Viaduc des Arts

12th arr. - 9-129, av. Daumesnil - Tél/fax 01 44 75
80 66
http://www.viaduc-des-arts.com
 The viaduct that runs along Avenue Daumesnil from the Bastille to Vincennes no longer sup-
ports a railway line. Instead, it shelters a host of
creative craftspeople and designers—
metalsmiths, jewelers, cabinetmakers, sculptors,
embroiderers, and more—who display and sell
their artistic wares under the viaduct's 60 arches.

Village Saint-Paul

4th arr. - 23-27, rue Saint-Paul
*Open 11am-7pm. Closed Tue-Wed. M° St-Paul Le
Marais.*
 This picturesque congregation of antique
dealers was inaugurated between Rue Saint-
Paul and Rue Charlemagne about fifteen years
ago. Encompassing some 70 stands, the Village
is a good source for jewelry, pictures, glass and
crystal, country furniture, and decorative objects
from the 1900–1930 period.

Village Suisse

15th arr. - 78, av. de Suffren & 54, av. de La Motte-Picquet - 01 43 06 47 87, fax 01 44 49 02 20
http://www.netsud.fr
Open 10:30am-7pm. Closed Tue-Wed, Aug. M° La Motte Picquet-Grenelle.
With 150 dealers offering everything from «junque» to rare and precious pieces, this «Village» is a popular attraction for dedicated antique hounds and Sunday strollers alike. Among the top merchants are Maud and René Garcia, for African art; Michel d'Istria, for sixteenth- and seventeenth-century wooden furniture from France, Spain, Italy, and England; Christian Daniel, for sixteenth- and seventeenth-century French and Italian faïence; and Antonin Rispal, for Art Nouveau glass by Daum, Gallé, Carabin, and Majorelle.

ENGLISH-LANGUAGE BOOKS

The Abbey Bookshop

5th arr. - 29, rue de la Parcheminerie
01 46 33 16 24, fax 01 46 33 03 33
Open 10am-7pm. Closed Sun. M° Cluny-La Sorbonne.
Brian Spence's Abbey Bookshop brings a Canadian point of view to the Paris literary scene. Located in the Latin Quarter opposite the church of Saint-Séverin, the Abbey sells both new and used books: literature, academic works, poetry, philosophy... Half the volumes are devoted to Canadian subjects (travel, art, French-language books from Quebec). Readings and lectures are held regularly. Members of the shop's Club Canadien are entitled to a five percent discount on books and all the coffee or tea they can drink.

Albion

4th arr. - 13, rue Charles-V
01 42 72 50 71, fax 01 42 72 85 27
Open Mon-Fri 9:30am-7pm, Sat 10am-6pm. Closed Sun. M° St-Paul Le Marais.
Let's say you've met a devastatingly handsome Frenchman. He's suave, he's groovy, but he can only *parler français*. Solution: come to Albion for a fast, efficient English-learning method that will have you speaking the same language, pronto! Also on hand: a good selection of English literature and non-fiction.

Brentano's

2nd arr. - 37, av. de l'Opéra
01 42 61 52 50, fax 01 42 61 07 61
Open 10am-7:30pm. Closed Sun. M° Opéra.
Brentano's deservedly remains a favorite among Americans in Paris for its remarkable array of American, English, and French books, periodicals, records, videos, and art books. Bestsellers of the week are always displayed at the entrance. There are also large children's and business sections.

Newsstands

For all you newshounds, kiosks are open 24 hours a day at the following addresses:
8th arr. - 33, av. des Champs-Élysées - tel 01 40 76 03 47. M° Franklin-D.-Roosevelt;
8th arr. - 52, av. des Champs-Élysées - tel 01 42 56 11 16. M° George-V;
8th arr. - 16, bd de la Madeleine - tel 01 42 65 29 19. M° Madeleine;
9th arr. - 2, bd Montmartre - tel 01 45 23 25 34. M° Rue Montmartre;
17th arr. - Place Charles de Gaulle, corner av. de Wagram - tel 01 43 80 10 40. M° Charles de Gaulle-Étoile;
18th arr. - 16, bd de Clichy - tel 01 42 55 97 87. M° Pigalle.

Galignani

1st arr. - 224, rue de Rivoli
01 42 60 76 07, fax 01 42 86 09 31
Open 10am-7pm. Closed Sun. M° Tuileries.
Galignani, purported to be the oldest English bookshop on the continent, was established in 1805 on Rue Vivienne by Giovanni Antonio Galignani, descendant of a famous twelfth-century publisher from Padua, Italy. In the mid-1800s Galignani moved to Rue de Rivoli, near the terminus of the Calais-Paris train, and the shop has passed from father to son and so on down the line. The shop offers a broad selection of English, American, and French hardcovers and paper-backs, lots of children's literature, plus a fabulous international selection of art books.

W.H. Smith

1st arr. - 248, rue de Rivoli - 01 44 77 88 99
Open Mon-Sat 9:30am-7pm, Sun 1pm-7pm. M° Concorde.
This is the closest thing to the perfect self-service bookstore: it is easy to locate almost any item among the over 40,000 English and American titles, from current and classic fiction, biographies, cookbooks, and travel guides to children's books, language methods, history, and English-language videos. The magazine and newspaper section is huge and often very

crowded. As for the staff, it's efficient and friendly...and very British.

Tea and Tattered Pages

6th arr. - 24, rue Mayet
01 40 65 94 35, fax 01 40 56 33 99
Open daily 11am-10pm. M° Duroc.
A charming place to browse through a wide selection of English and American used books, and to enjoy a leisurely cup of tea.

Village Voice

6th arr. - 6, rue Princesse
01 46 33 36 47, fax 01 46 33 27 48
Open Mon 2pm-8pm, Tue-Sat 10am-8pm. Closed Sun. M° Mabillon.
Nowadays the Village Voice controls the turf once so jealously guarded by Sylvia Beach's original Shakespeare and Co.—a mecca for Americans in Paris, especially writers, journalists, and literary types. The Village Voice hosts well-attended poetry readings and book-signing parties, and supplies voracious readers with an intelligently chosen selection of titles. Books special-ordered on request by the knowledgeable staff.

FOOD

Paris is paradise for food lovers, a mecca for gastro-tourists in search of the rarest, the best, the most luxurious *gourmandises*. The capital's pastry shops, chocolate shops, charcuteries, bakeries, and gourmet grocers overflow with temptations to taste on the spot or to pack up and take back home. Specialties and treats from all over France can be tracked down in Paris, where new taste sensations can be discovered around every *coin de rue*.

• *BAKERIES*

Daniel Dupuy

9th arr. - 13, rue Cadet - 01 48 24 54 26
Open 7am-8pm. Closed Tue. M° Cadet.
Daniel's prize-winning pain de campagne, made of natural leavening agents and stoneground flour, lives up to its vaunted reputation. Connoisseurs know that bread with this sort of authentic flavor is indeed worth seeking out. The same can be said of Dupuy's specialty, the Rochetour: he keeps the recipe a closely guarded secret.

Philippe Gosselin

1st arr. - 125, rue Saint-Honoré
01 45 08 03 59, fax 01 45 08 90 10
Open 7am-8pm. Closed Mon. M° Louvre-Rivoli.
In 1996, Gosselin won the competition for the best baguette in Paris. This marvel of freshness is crusty and flavorful. He supplies them to the Élysée Palace, but ordinary customers are still cordially welcomed.

Au Panetier

2nd arr. - 10, pl. des Petits-Pères - 01 42 60 90 23
Open 8am-7:15pm. Closed Sat, Sun. M° Bourse.
Even if you don't want to buy one of the old-fashioned loaves of hazelnut bread, raisin bread, or the house specialty: dense, delicious pain de Saint-Fiacre (all baked in a wood-fired oven), this excellent bakery is worth a visit just for a look at the adorable etched-glass and tile décor.

Au Pétrin d'Antan

18th arr. - 174, rue Ordener - 01 46 27 01 46
Open 7am-1:30pm & 3:30pm-8pm. M° Guy-Môquet.
Philippe Viron, the inventor of the «Rétrodor» baguette, runs this bakery, where you can be sure to find a baguette made according to traditional methods. When you see the Retrodor sign in other bakeries, a good baguette is guaranteed.

Lionel Poilâne

6th arr. - 8, rue du Cherche-Midi - 01 45 48 42 59
Open 7:15am-8:15pm. Closed Sun. M° Sèvres-Babylone.
15th arr. - 49, bd de Grenelle - 01 45 79 11 49
Open 7:15am-8:15pm. Closed Mon. M° Dupleix.
Lionel Poilâne is indubitably the best-known baker on the planet; he can be seen hawking his famous sourdough bread in magazines and on television screens throughout the world. And even though his products are sold all over Paris in charcuteries and cheese shops, goodly numbers of Poilâne fans think nothing of crossing town and standing in line to *personally* buy their favorite bread still warm from his ovens. Poilâne's walnut bread is, in a word, scrumptious, and we are also particularly fond of the shortbread cookies (sablés) and the rustic apple turnover (which makes a delicious and inexpensive dessert, accompanied by a bowl of thick crème fraîche).

Max Poilâne

1st arr. - 42, pl. du Marché St-Honoré
01 42 61 10 53
Open 9am-6:30pm. Closed Sat, Sun. M° Pyramides.
14th arr. - 29, rue de l'Ouest - 01 43 27 24 91
Open 9am-7pm. Closed Sun. M° Gaîté.
15th arr. - 87, rue Brancion
01 48 28 45 90, fax 01 48 28 87 88
Open Mon-Sat 7:15am-8pm, Sun 10am-2pm & 3pm-7pm. M° Porte de Vanves.
Max Poilâne's bread bears a distinct resemblance to that produced by his brother, Lionel (see above). That's natural enough, since their father taught both of them the secrets of the trade. Max bakes big, hearty loaves with a sour-

Seventh heaven for foodies

Ministries, embassies, and well-heeled residents of the posh **seventh arron- dissement** are lucky to live amid some of the best food shops in Paris. Quality is the rule and you can fill your market basket as fast as you empty your pocketbook in Rue du Bac, Rue Saint-Dominique, and Rue Cler. On the way, give your eyes a feast too by peeking into some of the flowered courtyards tucked away behind wrought-iron gates.

Try the **bread** from *Jean-Luc Poujauran* (20, rue Jean-Nicot, see text below), **cheese** from *Marie-Anne Cantin* (12, rue du Champ-de-Mars, see text p. 95), and **chocolates** from *Richart* (258, bd Saint-Germain, see text p. 96).

dough tang, delicious rye bread studded with raisins, and buttery white bread that makes a first-class sandwich. For a teatime treat, try the luscious apple tarts. If you can't wait to try these goodies, just take a seat in the bakery's tea room.

Poujauran

7th arr. - 20, rue Jean-Nicot - 01 47 05 80 88
Open 8am-8:30pm. Closed Sun, Mon. M° Latour- Maubourg.
He's a real darling, that Jean-Luc Poujauran! His bakery may be in a ritzy neighborhood, but he hasn't gone high-hat; food writers regularly wax lyrical over his talent, but his head hasn't swelled an inch. And though he bakes a wonder- ful country loaf with organically grown flour, he's not the type to think he's the greatest thing since sliced bread. Let's just hope he never chan- ges. And let's hope that we will never have to give up his delicious little rolls (or his olive or his poppy seed or his walnut bread), his old- fashioned pound cake (quatre-quarts), his but- tery Basque cakes, or the terrific frangi- pane-stuffed galettes that he bakes for the Epiphany (Three Kings' Day, January 6).

• *CHARCUTERIE & TAKEOUT*

Charcuterie Lyonnaise

9th arr. - 58, rue des Martyrs - 01 48 78 96 45
Open Tue-Sat 8:30am-1:30pm & 4pm-7:30pm, Sun 8:30am-12:30pm. Closed Mon. M° Notre- Dame-de-Lorette.
Lyon's reputed specialties have been holding pride of place here for over 30 years: try the rosette, jésus, or saucisson de Lyon sausages as well as the superb terrines.

Chez Robert

10th arr. - 50, rue du Fg-St-Denis - 01 47 70 06 86
Open Tue & Thu-Sat 7am-1:30pm & 3:45pm- 7:30pm, Wed & Sun 7am-1:30pm. Closed Mon. M° Château-d'Eau.

Just because the price is right does not mean the quality is missing. In fact, the food is so good here that you have to stand in line to get some of it. Everything is housemade, from the sauerkraut, foie gras, onion and parsley sausages and stuffings, to the breaded pigs' trot- ters. If you add the fifteen or so fresh pastas and the ten or so hams, you've got what it takes to back up the good reputation of this artisanal charcuterie.

Coesnon

6th arr. - 30, rue Dauphine
01 43 54 35 80, fax 01 43 26 56 39
Open 8:30am-7:45pm. Closed Sun, Mon. M° Odéon.
Because true practitioners of the charcutier's art are becoming ever harder to find, and be- cause Bernard Marchaudon is one of its most eminent representatives, we recommend that you make a special point of visiting this wonder- ful pork emporium. Marchaudon's boudin blanc and boudin noir are legendary (his chestnut- studded black pudding has won slews of awards); what's more, his salt-and smoke-cured pork specialties are top-notch—especially when accompanied by the crisp yet tender sauerkraut he pickles himself. So step up to counter with confidence, knowing that you will be competent- ly and courteously served.

Flo Prestige

1st arr. - 42, pl. du Marché-Saint-Honoré
01 42 61 45 46
4th arr. - 10, rue Saint-Antoine - 01 53 01 91 91
12th arr. - 22, av. de la Porte de Vincennes
01 43 74 54 32
16th arr. - 61, av. de la Grande-Armée
01 45 00 12 10
& 102, av. du Président-Kennedy - 01 55 74 44 44
Open daily 8am-11pm. M° Pyramides, Bastille, St- Mandé Tourelle, Argentine, Passy.
7th arr. - 36, av. de La Motte-Picquet
01 45 55 71 25
12th arr. - 211, av. Daumesnil - 01 43 44 86 36
14th arr. - 91, av. du Général-Leclerc - 01 53 90 24 50
15th arr. - 352, rue Lecourbe - 01 45 54 76 94

Open daily 8am-9:30pm. M° La Motte Picquet-Grenelle, Daumesnil, Alésia, Sèvres-Lecourbe.
Early or late, every day of the year, you have a sure source of delicious bread, fine wine, yummy desserts—in short, of wonderful meals with Flo Prestige. The selection of foodstuffs is varied and choice, and covers a wide range of prices, from the excellent house sauerkraut to prestigious Petrossian caviar.

Lewkowicz

4th arr. - 12, rue des Rosiers - 01 48 87 63 17
Open Mon 8am-1:30pm & 3:30pm-7:30pm, Tue-Thu 8am-7:30pm, Fri & Sun 8am-1pm. Closed Sat. M° St-Paul Le Marais.
Since 1928 «Lewko» has been serving up authentic Jewish specialties made from old-country recipes. In his expanded and renovated shop, Lewkowicz *Fils* proposes flavorsome corned beef, pastrami, pressed veal, and Krakow sausage, as well as kosher meats and poultry, and a selection of wines, spirits, and canned foods.

Claude Michaux

18th arr. - 125, rue Caulaincourt - 01 42 62 02 33
Open Tue-Sat 8am-8pm, Sun 8am-1pm. Closed Mon. M° Lamarck-Caulaincourt.
A beautiful charcuterie whose shop window leaves your buds tingling. Real variety: over 20 kinds of small sausages, fifteen or so different pâtés, interesting large preserved sausages (pistacho Lyon style, Montbéliards), overflowing bouchées à la reine with an ultra-fine pastry. The crème brulée is a real temptation. Other specialties: quails stuffed with foie gras, galantines, and sole and sea urchin terrine.

Pou

17th arr. - 16, av. des Ternes
01 43 80 19 24, fax 01 46 22 66 97
Open Mon-Fri 9:30am-7:15pm. Closed Sun. M° Ternes.
Pou is divine, an excellent charcuterie whose sober décor and rich displays resemble nothing so much as a palace of earthly delights. A look in the window is an irresistible invitation to buy and taste: black and white boudin sausages, duck pâté en croûte, glittering galantines, cervelas sausage studded with pale-green pistachios, and sumptuous pastries too. Since everything really is as good as it looks, making a choice is quite a task. And given the prices, paying isn't so easy, either.

Vignon

8th arr. - 14, rue Marbeuf - 01 47 20 24 26
Open Mon-Fri 8:30am-8pm, Sat 9am-7:30pm. Closed Sun. M° Franklin-D.-Roosevelt.
Nothing is given away here, but the prices are more justified in the charcuterie section than in the vegetable section. The takeaway dishes are good quality (sautéed veal, potatoes au gratin). Also on hand: Parma hams, pâtés en croute. Ten

or so different kinds of sausage: Lyonnaise, truffled, or with pistachios; quenelles, escargots, bass with fines herbes. Good selection and good quality in a shop that has been here for over twenty years.

• CHEESE

Alléosse

17th arr. - 13, rue Poncelet - 01 46 22 50 45
Open Mon-Sat 9am-1pm & 4pm-7:15pm, Sun 9am-1pm. Closed Mon. M° Ternes.
Father and son Roger and Philippe Alléosse purvey some of the finest cheeses in Paris. With the obsessive zeal of perfectionists, they turn, rinse, brush, and otherwise groom their farmhouse fromages down in the ideally dank depths of their seven maturing cellars. If the shop's astounding stock leaves you at a loss, don't hesitate to seek advice from the staff: they'll introduce you to little-known cheeses from all over France. We understand why so many chefs choose to shop *chez* Alléosse.

Androuët

7th arr. - 83, rue Saint-Dominique - 01 45 50 45 75
Open Mon 4pm-8pm, Tue-Fri 9am-1:30pm & 4pm-8pm, Sat 9am-8pm. Closed Sun. M° Invalides.
8th arr. - 6, rue Arsène-Houssaye
01 42 89 95 00, fax 01 42 89 68 44
Open 9:30am-8pm. Closed Mon, Sun. M° Charles de Gaulle-Étoile.
14th arr. - 19, rue Daguerre - 01 43 21 19 09
Open Tue-Fri 9am-1pm & 3:30pm-8pm, Sat 9pm-8pm, Sun 9pm-1:30pm. Closed Mon. M° Denfert-Rochereau.
This shop, founded in 1909, has three new locations and new owners who carry on the house tradition, offering a wide range of well-chosen, refined cheeses. There is also a restaurant that serves dishes based on the shop's products at rue Arsène-Houssaye, (see *Restaurants*).

Barthélémy

7th arr. - 51, rue de Grenelle
01 45 48 56 75, fax 01 45 49 25 16
Open 7am-1pm & 3pm-7:30pm. Closed Sun, Mon. M° Rue du Bac.
Roland Barthélémy reigns over a treasure trove of cheeses that he selects from farms all over the French countryside, then coddles to perfect ripeness in his cellars. He is also the creator of several marvelous specialties that have the *Who's Who* of French officialdom beating a path to his door (he supplies the Élysée Palace, no less). The Boulamour (fresh cream cheese enriched with crème fraîche, currants, raisins, and Kirsch) was Barthélémy's invention, as was a delicious Camembert laced with Calvados. We also enjoy the amusing Brie Surprise. But not to worry, tradition is never neglected here, witness the rich-tasting Alpine Beaufort, French Vacherin, and other prime mountain cheeses which are a

Barthélémy specialty. The luxuriously creamy Fontainebleau is made fresh on the premises. Take one of the appetizing cheese trays sold here as your contribution to a dinner party: your hostess will love it!

Marie-Anne Cantin

7th arr. - 12, rue du Champ-de-Mars - 01 45 50 43 94
Open Tue-Sat 8:30am-7:30pm, Sun 8:30am-1pm. Closed Mon. M° École Militaire.
The cheeses Marie-Anne Cantin selects and matures herself benefit from unstinting doses of tender loving care. She is an ardent defender of real (read: unpasteurized) cheeses and is one of the few merchants in Paris to sell Saint-Marcellins as they are preferred on their home turf—in their creamy prime, not in their chalky youth. And so it is with the other cheeses she sells, all of which retain the authentic flavors of their rustic origins.

La Ferme Saint-Aubin

4th arr. - 76, rue St-Louis-en-l'Ile - 01 43 54 74 54
Open Tue-Fri & Sun 8am-1pm & 3pm-8pm, Sat 8am-8pm. Closed Mon. M° Pont Marie.
Master cheesemonger Christian Le Lann is a connoisseur in the most lavish of styles. At least 200 cheeses are to be found here, all kept at just the right temperature: Époisses, Langres, Chambertins, Chablis, farmhouse Munsters, Laguioles, Salers, Têtes-de-Moine. Cheeses from other parts of Europe as well: Italy, England, and Switzerland. Vive l'Europe!

La Ferme Saint-Hubert

8th arr. - 21, rue Vignon
01 47 42 79 20, fax 01 47 42 46 97
Open 9am-7:30pm. Closed Sun. M° Madeleine.
16th arr. - Galerie St-Didier, 14, rue des Sablons
01 45 53 15 77
Open Mon-Thu 9am-7:30pm, Fri-Sat 9am-8pm. Closed Sun. M° Trocadéro.
Cheese seller Henry Voy is so passionate about his vocation that he has no time for anything else. Morning and night you can find him tending to his Beauforts (aged for a minimum of two years), his farmhouse chèvres, Corsican sheep cheeses, or his exclusive Délice de Saint-Hubert. He travels all over France, seeking out the most flavorful specimens. For true aficionados, Voy unearths such rarities as unpasteurized butter churned with spring water, and delicate goat's-milk butter. In the adjoining restaurant, at rue Vignon, you can sample cheese-based dishes (open Mon-Sat noon-3:30pm; Mon-Wed 6:45pm-11pm, Thu-Sat 6:45pm-11:30pm).

Fromagerie Boursault

14th arr. - 71, av. du Général-Leclerc
01 43 27 93 30, fax 01 45 38 59 56
Open Tue-Sat 8:30am-12:30pm & 4:15pm-7:15pm, Sun 7:30am-12:30pm. Closed Mon. M° Alésia.

It was here that Pierre Boursault created the triple-creme cheese that bears his name. And it is here, naturally enough, that you will find Boursault at its rich, golden best. Owner Jacques Vernier has made the shop one of the most pleasant in Paris, a showcase for the rare cheeses that he seeks out himself in the French hinterlands. Like incomparable Beauforts aged under his supervision in their native Alpine air; farmhouse goat cheeses (ah, those Picodons!); handcrafted Saint-Nectaire from Auvergne, which has nothing in common with the industrially produced variety; and flawless Camemberts. This is one of the few places on the planet where one can buy Bleu de Termignon, a blue-veined summer cheese from Savoie.

• *CHOCOLATE & CANDY*

Boissier

16th arr. - 184, av. Victor-Hugo - 01 45 04 87 88
Open 9am-7pm. Closed Sun. M° Victor Hugo.
Boissier invented candied chestnuts in 1827, so you can be sure you're getting the real thing here! Also on offer are thirty types of fine chocolates, including the Boissier specialty, a milk chocolate with caramel and nougatine brittle, or try the coffee palace or burned-caramel truffle. Good pastries, too, with two specialties in particular: the Marigny, a macaroon dough filled with bitter-chocolate mousse, and the papillotes (literally, «butterflies»), a praline or chocolate mousse meringue.

Cacao et Chocolat

1st arr. - 13, rue du Marché Saint-Honoré
01 42 61 03 48
Open 10:30am-6:30pm. Closed Sun, Mon. M° Tuileries.
It's not because it's new that it's not good. This place is already a reference in its category thanks to its chocolate *à déguster*, housemade chocolate truffles, «sheet» of cocoa, and almonds coated with Gianduja chocolate and cocoa. Gourmets can sink their teeth into fifty different kinds of chocolate candies, bars and chunks.

Christian Constant

6th arr. - 37, rue d'Assas
01 53 63 15 15, fax 01 53 63 15 16
Open daily 8am-8:30pm. M° St Placide.
Christian Constant, who chooses the best cocoa beans from the West Indies, Tahiti, Ecuador and elsewhere, is a genius with chocolate. His brilliant innovations include a line of flower-scented chocolates (try the ylang-ylang, vetiver, or the jasmine varieties), chocolates filled with delicately spiced creams, others spiked with fruit brandies or cordials, still others incorporating nuts and dried fruit (the Conquistador is loaded with hazelnuts, honey, and cinnamon). Constant recommends that we buy his wares in small

amounts, for optimum freshness and flavor. Well, given the prices (480 F per kilo), for most people quantity purchases are out of the question!

A l'Étoile d'Or

9th arr. - 30, rue Fontaine - 01 48 74 59 55
Open Mon 2pm-8pm, Tue-Sat 10:30am-8pm. Closed Sun. M° Blanche.

Denise Acabo does not make her own chocolate; rather, she is a true connoisseur who selects the very best handcrafted chocolates made in France, and presents them, in a laudable spirit of impartiality, to her delighted customers (while explaining to interested parties the connection between chocolate and eroticism). The famed Bernachon chocolates from Lyon are sold in this beautiful turn-of-the-century shop, as well as Dufoux's incomparable palets (in twelve flavors), and Bonnat's chocolate bars. Don't miss Bochard's mandarin de Grenoble: a glazed tangerine with a chocolate mandarin's hat—it's irresistible!

La Fontaine au Chocolat

1st arr. - 101, rue Saint-Honoré - 01 42 33 09 09
Open 10am-7pm. Closed Sun, Mon. M° Palais-Royal.
1st arr. - 201, rue Saint-Honoré - 01 42 44 11 66
Open 10am-7pm. Closed Sun. M° Pyramides.

Pervading Michel Cluizel's shop is a scent of chocolate so intense that your nose will flash an alert to your sweet tooth, and (we guarantee!) have you salivating within seconds. Whether you try one of the five varieties of palets au chocolat or the croquamandes (caramelized almonds coated with extra-dark chocolate), the mendiants studded with nuts and dried fruit, or the bold Noir Infini (99 percent cocoa, perfumed with vanilla and spices), you're in for an unforgettable treat.

Jadis et Gourmande

4th arr. - 39, rue des Archives - 01 48 04 08 03
Open Mon 1pm-7pm, Tue-Sat 10:30am-7:30pm. Closed Sun. M° Hôtel de Ville.
5th arr. - 88, bd de Port-Royal - 01 43 26 17 75
Open 9:30am-7pm. Closed Sun. M° Port Royal.
8th arr. - 49 bis, av. Franklin-Roosevelt
01 42 25 06 04, fax 01 53 76 00 71
Open Mon 1pm-7pm, Tue 9:30am-7pm, Wed-Fri 9:30am-7:30pm, Sat 10am-7pm. Closed Sun. M° Franklin-D.-Roosevelt.
8th arr. - 27, rue Boissy-d'Anglas - 01 42 65 23 23
Open Mon 1pm-7pm, Tue-Sat 9:30am-7pm. Closed Sun. M° Concorde.

It is delightful indeed to browse around this sugarplum palace, where one is tempted in turn by delicious bonbons, hard candies, caramels, and chocolate in myriad forms (336 F per kilo). The thick slabs of cooking chocolate make one want to rush to the kitchen and whip up a rich devil's food cake! Our favorite confection here is a thick braid of dark chocolate studded with candied orange peel and hazelnuts.

La Maison du Chocolat

6th arr. - 19, rue de Sèvres - 01 45 44 20 40
8th arr. - 52, rue François-Ier
01 47 23 38 25, fax 01 40 70 01 63
& 225, rue du Fg-Saint-Honoré - 01 42 27 39 44
9th arr. - 8, bd de la Madeleine - 01 47 42 86 52
16th arr. - 89, av. Raymond Poincarré
01 40 67 77 83
Open 9:30am-7pm. Closed Sun. M° Rue du Bac, Franklin-D.- Roosevelt, Ternes, Madeleine, Victor Hugo.

There's something of the alchemist about Robert Linxe: never satisfied, he is ever experimenting, innovating, transforming mere cocoa beans into something very precious. His chocolates (490 F per kilo) are among the finest in Paris, maybe even in the world. His renowned buttercream fillings—lemon, caramel, tea, raspberry, and rum—will carry you away to gourmet heaven.

A la Mère de Famille

9th arr. - 35, rue du Fg-Montmartre
01 47 70 83 69
Open 8:30am-1:30pm & 3pm-7pm. Closed Sun, Mon. M° Rue Montmartre.

Perhaps the oldest candy shop in Paris (it dates back to 1761), La Mère de Famille is certainly the handsomest, with a façade and interior from the nineteenth century (note the Second Empire-style cashier's booth). The shop's sweet inventory includes luscious jams, candied fruits, and bonbons from all over France. The chocolates are prepared by the current owner, Serge Neveu, and sell for 380 F per kilo. We love their new creations, the 1761, a pure-Caribbean ganache (a rich blend of chocolate and heavy cream) enhanced with almond mousse, and the orange truffle, which is made fresh every single day.

Richart

7th arr. - 258, bd Saint-Germain
01 45 55 66 00, fax 01 47 53 72 72
Open Tue-Fri 10am-7pm, Mon & Sat 11am-7pm. Closed Sun. M° Solférino.
8th arr. - 36, av. Wagram - 01 45 74 94 00
Open Tue-Fri 10am-7:30pm, Mon & Sat 11am-7:30pm. Closed Sun. M° Ternes.

The Richart brothers may be the most innovative *chocolatiers* around. Not only are their chocolates perfectly scrumptious (filled with single-malt ganache, for example, or wild-raspberry cream, or nutmeg praline, or prune coulis) they are presented in imaginative packages unlike any we've seen. Just look at the Secret Pyramid, a clever box that holds fourteen ultrathin chocolates. Richart's flat Easter eggs are pretty unusual, too! And the Petits Richarts, mini-chocolates that weigh just one-sixth of an ounce, are ideal for nibbling with a clear conscience.

> *Don't plan to do much shopping in **Paris in August**—a great many stores are closed for the entire vacation month.*

EUROPEAN MONUMENTS COIN COLLECTION

A voyage through the 15 countries of the European Union

MONNAIE DE PARIS

http://www.monnaiedeparis.fr

Boutiques : 11, quai de Conti, 75006 Paris - Carrousel du Louvre
Renseignements points de vente France : TEL. 01 40 46 58 96

The Place

2, place du Palais Royal
75001 Paris, open Tuesday to
Sunday from 11a.m. to 7p.m.
Tél : 01 42 97 27 00

The Choice

Jewellery

Objets d'art

Furniture

Paintings

Sculptures

250 antique dealers

LE LOUVRE
des
ANTIQUAIRES
The largest antique centre in the heart of Paris.

Expert consultation

Bureau de change

Bar-restaurant

The Service

Transportation

Car park

• COFFEE & TEA

Betjeman & Barton

8th arr. - 23, bd Malesherbes - 01 42 65 86 17
Open 9:30am-7pm. Closed Sun. M° Madeleine.
11th arr. - 24, bd des Filles-du-Calvaire
01 40 21 35 52
Open 10am-7pm. Closed Sun, Mon. M° Filles du Calvaire.
The name on the sign and the shop's décor are veddy, veddy British, but the firm itself is 100 percent French, directed nowadays by Didier Jumeau-Lafond. An extensive range of premium teas is on offer, comprising over 180 natural and flavored varieties. Indeed, B & B's teas are of such high quality that Harrod's of London (no less) deigns to market them. To help you choose your blend, the staff will offer you a cup of tea—a comforting and highly civilized custom. Excellent jellies and jams and a line of refreshing «fruit waters» intended to be consumed icy-cold in summer, are worth seeking out here. For nibbling with your tea, try the Duchy Originals (sponsored by Prince Charles, don't you know), cookies baked of organic, stone-ground oats and wheat. B & B now produces a line of fine hand-painted china decorated with pretty fruit and flower motifs.

Verlet

1st arr. - 256, rue Saint-Honoré
01 42 60 67 39, fax 01 42 60 05 55
Open 9am-7pm. Closed Oct-Apr: Sun, Mon; May-Sep: Sat, Sun. M° Palais-Royal.
The Verlet family has been roasting and selling coffee beans in their delightful turn-of-the-century shop since 1880. Pierre Verlet imports the finest coffees from Papuasie, Costa Rica, Colombia, Jamaica, Ethiopia, and Brazil, and he also produces several subtle and delicious house blends. He will even create one specially for you, for he is a master at balancing different aromas, different degrees of acidity and bitterness to suit personal taste. If you prefer to sample before you buy, take a seat at one of the little tables and try, perhaps, the Petit Cheval blend, a marvelously balanced and smooth Moka. Verlet also stocks a selection of teas from all over the world and an appetizing array of dried fruits. At lunchtime, crowds pour into the shop for an excellent croque monsieur or a slice of cake and a cup of fragrant coffee.

• ETHNIC FOODS

The General Store

7th arr. - 82, rue de Grenelle - 01 45 48 63 16
16th arr. - 30, rue de Longchamp - 01 47 55 41 14
Open 10:30am-7:30pm. Closed Sun. M° Rue du Bac, Trocadéro.
Tacos, tortillas, and all the other traditional fixings for a Tex-Mex feast may be found in this spic-and-span little shop. But the inventory doesn't stop there: You'll find buttermilk-pancake mix, a selection of California wines (not just Paul Masson), familiar American packaged foods (Karo syrup, cream cheese, canned pumpkin, chocolate chips, Hellmann's mayo), and even fresh cranberries at holiday time. If you crave a sweet snack, look for the delectable pecan squares and cookies whipped up fresh every day. As you would expect, English is spoken, and you can count on a warm welcome.

Goldenberg

17th arr. - 69, av. de Wagram - 01 42 27 34 79
Open daily 10am-11:30pm. M° Ternes.
Familiar deli fare, made measurably more exotic by the fact that it's served within sight of the Arc de Triomphe. There's herring, there's corned beef, there's gefilte fish (stuffed carp), there's pastrami, and that well-known Yiddish dessert, the brownie.

Marks & Spencer

4th arr. - 88, rue de Rivoli - 01 44 61 08 00
Open Mon-Tue 10am-8pm, Wed-Fri 10am-8:30pm, Sat 10am-7:30pm. Closed Sun. M° Châtelet-Les Halles.
9th arr. - 35, bd Haussmann - 01 47 42 42 91

Chinatown, My Chinatown

The developers who built the cluster of Manhattan-inspired skyscrapers around the Avenues d'Ivry and de Choisy (13th arr.) intended them for Parisian buyers; but local investors didn't care for all that concrete. Instead, immigrants from war-torn Southeast Asia who poured into the city in the mid 1970s took over the towers. Today, Chinatown's 40,000 residents have put a vivid Asian stamp on the area's culture, cuisine, and commerce. Sample them all at **Tang Frères**, a multifarious market-cum-restaurant.
Tang Frères, 13th arr. - 44, av. d'Ivry - tel 01 45 70 80 00. Open 9am-7:30pm, closed Mon. M° Porte d'Ivry.

Open Mon & Wed & Fri-Sat 9am-8pm, Tue 9:30am-8pm, Thu 9am-9pm. Closed Sun. M° Chaussée d'Antin.

The food section of this all-British emporium provides ample evidence that English gastronomy is not, as Parisians tend to think, a joking matter. The French are genetically incapable, for example, of producing good bacon. Marks & Spencer's is wonderful: meaty, smoky, with no nasty bits of bone, no inedible rind. The cheese counter carries Stilton, Cheddar, Leicester, and other delicious English dairy products, and the grocery shelves are crowded with all sorts of piquant condiments and chutneys. Teas, biscuits, jams, and marmalades are legion, of course, and special refrigerated cases offer fresh sandwiches for a quick lunch on the run. Prices in the Paris branches are considerably higher than on Marks & Sparks' home turf.

Spécialités Antillaises

20th arr. - 14-16, bd de Belleville - 01 43 58 31 30
Open Tue-Thu 10am-7:15pm, Fri-Sat 9am-7:15pm, Sun 9am-noon. Closed Mon. M° Ménilmontant.

Here's a one-stop shop for Creole fixings and take-out foods. Among the latter, we recommend the scrumptious stuffed crabs, the crispy accras (salt-cod fritters), the Creole sausage, and a spicy avocado dish called *féroce d'avocat*. The grocery section offers tropical fruits flown in fresh from the West Indies, as well as a selection of exotic frozen fish (shark, gilthead, etc.), and an intoxicating array of rums and punches.

• *FRUITS & VEGETABLES*

Le Fruitier d'Auteuil

16th arr. - 5, rue Bastien-Lepage - 01 45 27 51 08
Open 7am-1pm & 3:30pm-7:45pm. Closed Sun. M° Michel-Ange-Auteuil.

Bernard Rapine, president of the Fruit Retailers' Union, has a personal and professional interest in displaying the best produce he can find. He claims—and we have seen it to be true—that any store posting the union label (the word *fruitier* printed over a basket of fruit) is honorbound to provide top-quality merchandise and service. Rapine's vegetables, incidentally, are just as prime. Some are sold peeled and ready to cook. Even less prep is required for the shop's range of take-out dishes that includes delicious soups, eggplant purée, guacamole, fruit salads, and more.

Palais du Fruit

2nd arr. - 62 & 72, rue Montorgueil - 01 42 33 22 15
Open Tue-Sat 8am-7:30pm, Sun & hols 8am-1pm. Closed Mon. M° Sentier.

Superb fruits and vegetables from all over the globe, beautifully presented. Even when skies are gray in France, in Chile or the Antilles gorgeous produce ripens in the sun, then is picked and packed off to this cheerful store. Wide choice, remarkable quality.

• *GOURMET SPECIALTIES*

Faguais

8th arr. - 30, rue de la Trémoille - 01 47 20 80 91
Open 9:15am-7pm. Closed Sun. M° Franklin-D.-Roosevelt.

Yes, Grandmother would feel quite at home in this charming gourmet shop. A dizzying variety of temptations is set out neatly on the shelves. Old-fashioned jams, oils, honeys, cookies, spices, vinegars, and condiments fairly cry out to be bought. As the shop's pervasive fragrance implies, fresh coffee beans are roasted on the premises daily.

Fauchon

8th arr. - 30, pl. de la Madeleine
01 47 42 60 11, fax 01 47 42 83 75
Open 9:40am-7pm. Closed Sun. M° Madeleine.

In 1886, at the age of 30, Auguste Fauchon opened his *épicerie fine* on the Place de la Madeleine, specializing in quality French foodstuffs. The rest is history. After more than a century, Fauchon is the uncontested paragon of what a luxury gourmet emporium should be. The entire staff of 360 employees is committed to the task of tasting, testing, and selling the very finest, the rarest, the most unusual foods in the world. The number of spices alone—110—is enough to make your head spin. And you'll find such delicacies as black-fig or watermelon preserves, lavender or buckwheat honey, Mim tea from India or Kee-yu tea from China, lavish displays of prime vegetables and fruits, and a world-renowned collection of vintage wines and brandies. As for the pastries, well...you try Sébastien Gaudard's creations, which are also featured in Fauchon's on-site restaurants (see Le «30» in *Restaurants*).

La Grande Épicerie de Paris

7th arr. - Le Bon Marché, 38, rue de Sèvres
01 44 39 81 00
Open 8:30am-9:30pm. Closed Sun. M° Sèvres-Babylone.

A deluxe supermarket filled with a huge array of handsomely presented foodstuffs: a lovely place to browse.

Goumanyat et son Royaume

2nd arr. - 7, rue de la Michodière
01 42 68 09 71, fax 01 47 42 27 32
Open 2pm-8pm. Closed Sun. M° Opéra.

Many chefs' culinary secrets start right here. Four hundred products broken down into five «families». The main and oldest one is dedicated solely to saffron, the gold dust of the spice world.

The other «families» include sweets (dried flowers, sugar, jams, vanilla, etc.); over ninety different spices in all shapes and forms; tastes of the earth and regional products (dried mushrooms, truffles, flour, oil, vinegar, etc.); and a new family, products from the sea (seaweed, salt, etc.). The Thiercely family started selecting products back in 1809, so they know their business. You'll be sure to find only the best quality products here, at very attractive prices. Professional knives are also are also on hand.

Hédiard

7th arr. - 126, rue du Bac - 01 45 44 01 98
Open 9:30am-9pm. Closed Sun. M° Sèvres-Babylone.
8th arr. - 21, pl. de la Madeleine
01 43 12 88 88, fax 01 42 66 31 97
Open 8am-9pm (11pm for takeout & confectionery). Closed Sun. M° Madeleine.
16th arr. - 70, av. Paul-Doumer - 01 45 04 51 92
Open 7am-10pm. Closed Sun. M° La Muette.
17th arr. - 106, bd de Courcelles - 01 47 63 32 14
Open 9am-10pm. Closed Sun. M° Courcelles.
Only the most select foodstuffs are deemed worthy of entry into this shrine of epicureanism, founded in 1854. Distinguished smoked salmon from the best «schools», sophisticated sugars and syrups, pedigreed Ports, vintage wines and brandies, and over 4,500 carefully chosen grocery items attract virtually every cultivated palate in town. Even the ordinary is extraordinary here: mustard spiked with Cognac; vinegar flavored with seaweed; opulent fruits and vegetables, always perfect, that hail from the ends of the earth. Many of the items are as costly as they are exotic, but the wines consistently offer excellent value for the money. Hédiard's flagship store on Place de la Madeleine was remodeled and expanded not long ago. It houses a tasting bar in the wine department.

Lafayette Gourmet

9th arr. - 48, bd Haussmann or 97, rue de Provence
01 48 74 46 06
Open Mon-Wed & Fri-Sat 9am-8pm, Thu 9am-9pm. Closed Sun. M° Chaussée d'Antin.
A huge space devoted to the pleasures of gastronomy, with fresh foods, rare condiments, teas, coffees, charcuteries, wines, etc. And there are counters for sampling the wares, so that you can stop for a bite after shopping.

Albert Ménès

8th arr. - 41, bd Malesherbes
01 42 66 95 63
Open Mon 2pm-7pm, Tue-Sat 10am-7pm. Closed Sun. M° St-Augustin.
The Albert Ménès label marks some of the finest handcrafted products of France. The shop offers around 500 regional products, ranging from fine sardines to rare vinegars. There are also cookies, jam, honey and other sweets from each region. The gift presentation is very attractive.

Escargots

L'Escargot de la Butte

18th arr. - 48, rue Joseph-de-Maistre
01 46 27 38 27
Open 9am-7:30pm. Closed Sun, Mon. M° Place Clichy.
«It's really a shame, but there are no more escargots de Bourgogne left in Burgundy», laments Monsieur Marchal. He imports them, therefore, from the Lot and the Ardèche. But his petits-gris come straight from the Provençal countryside, and arrive still frisky at his little shop located at the foot of the Butte Montmartre. He stuffs them with a deliciously fragrant blend of pure butter, garlic, and parsley and they are a remarkable treat!

Foie Gras

Aux Ducs de Gascogne

1st arr. - 4, rue du Marché-St-Honoré
01 42 60 45 31
Open 10am-7pm. Closed Sun. M° Pyramides.
4th arr. - 111, rue St-Antoine - 01 42 71 17 72
Open Mon 3pm-8pm, Tue-Sat 9:30am-2pm & 3pm-8pm. Closed Sun. M° St-Paul Le Marais.
8th arr. - 112, bd Haussmann - 01 45 22 54 04
Open Mon noon-7:15pm, Tue-Sat 10am-7:15pm. Closed Sun. M° St-Augustin.
15th arr. - 221, rue de la Convention - 01 48 28 32 09
Open Tue-Fri 9:30am-1pm & 4pm-8pm, Sat 9:30am-1pm & 2pm-8pm, Sun 9:30am-1pm. Closed Sun. Aug. M° Convention.
16th arr. - 54, av. Victor-Hugo - 01 45 00 34 78
Open Mon-Fri 10am-8pm, Sat 10am-7pm. Closed Sun. M° Victor Hugo.
20th arr. - 41, rue des Gatines - 01 43 66 99 99
Open Mon 3pm-7:45pm, Tue-Sat 9am-12:45pm & 3pm-7:45pm. Closed Sun. M° Gambetta.
This multistore chain specializes in canned and lightly cooked foie gras, as well as other Southwestern favorites (the thick peasant soup—garbure—sold in jars is excellent indeed). Steep prices, but the quality is dependably high.

L'Esprit du Sud Ouest

7th arr. - 108, rue Saint-Dominique
01 45 55 29 06, fax 01 47 53 90 28
Open Tue-Sat 10:30am-1pm & 4:30pm-8pm. Closed Sun, Mon. M° École Militaire.
Here you'll find regional products from the southwest of France made without preservatives. On offer: every type of foie gras (preserved, half-cooked, fresh, etc.), salt-cured products from Lacaune in the Tarn, and a most interesting pure-duck dried sausage. Also try the delicious housemade cassoulet. To help recreate the ambience of this friendly region of France, the shop also sells rugby shirts from the home team.

Foie Gras Luxe

1st arr. - 26, rue Montmartre
01 42 36 14 73, fax 01 40 26 45 50
Open Mon 8am-noon & 2:30pm-4:45pm, Tue-Fri 6am-12:15pm & 2:30pm-4:45pm. Closed Sat (exc Dec: 8am-5pm), Sun. M° Les Halles.
This reliable, long-established shop sells raw foie gras year-round, as well as lightly cooked goose and duck livers. More luxury: Iranian caviar and savory cured hams from Parma, San Daniele, and the Ardennes are also for sale.

Honey & Jams

Le Furet-Tanrade

10th arr. - 63, rue de Chabrol
01 47 70 48 34, fax 01 42 46 34 41
Open 8am-8pm. Closed Sun (exc hols). M° Poissonnière.
Alain Furet is a *chocolatier* first and foremost, but he also makes fabulous jams from recipes developed by Monsieur Tanrade, long the top name in French preserves. Furet took over the Tanrade plant, and now turns out succulent jams (raspberry, strawberry, apricot, blackcurrant, etc.); he also has put the finishing touches on a recipe of his own, for *gelée au chocolat*—a landmark!

La Maison du Miel

9th arr. - 24, rue Vignon - 01 47 42 26 70
Open 9:30am-7pm. Closed Sun. M° Madeleine.
Make a beeline to this «House of Honey» to try over 30 varieties from all over France, and a few imported honeys, too. There's Corsican honey, luscious pine honey from the Vosges mountains (which comes highly recommended for bronchial irritations), Provençal lavender honey, as well as choice varieties from the Alps and Auvergne, all rigorously tested by a busy hive of honey tasters. In addition, you'll find honey «by-

products», such as beeswax, candles, pollen, and royal jelly, as well as a wide range of honey-based cosmetics.

Oils

A l'Olivier

4th arr. - 23, rue de Rivoli - 01 48 04 86 59
Open 9:30am-1pm & 2pm-7pm. Closed Sun, Mon. M° St-Paul Le Marais.
Connoisseurs know that this shop is an excellent source for several fine varieties of olive oil, as well as walnut oil, grilled-almond oil, pumpkin-seed oil, and hazelnut oil. The main attraction, however, is an exclusive, top-secret blend of virgin olive oils. We applaud the store policy of selling exceptionally expensive and perishable oils in quarter-liter bottles. Fine vinegars and mustards are presented too—everything you need to mix up a world-class vinaigrette!

Truffles

Maison de la Truffe

8th arr. - 19, pl. de la Madeleine
01 42 65 53 22, fax 01 49 24 96 59
Open Mon 9am-8pm, Tue-Sat 9am-9pm. Closed Sun. M° Madeleine.
Alongside extraordinary charcuterie, foie gras, smoked salmon, and take-out foods, this luxurious gourmet shop offers truffles (freshly dug or sterilized and bottled) at prices that are emphatically not of the bargain-basement variety. The season for fresh black truffles runs from October to late March; fresh white truffles are imported from Italy from October to December. Owner Guy Monier recently set aside a corner of his shop for tasting: customers may order from a brief menu featuring dishes made

Market culture

A stroll round a Parisian **street market** is one of the best ways to see, smell, and sample French food. Start out early to admire the carefully constructed stacks of fruits and vegetables—and stick around for bargains when stallholders close up shop at about 1pm. The speed with which they dismantle their stalls and pack up their produce is a spectacle in itself. Most markets are held twice a week, some three times a week, and there are 57 sites to choose from. For contrasting views of Parisian shopping and eating habits, visit the resolutely upscale *Point-du-Jour* market in the sixteenth arrondissement (go down the Avenue de Versailles, from rue Le Marois to rue Gudin) held on Tuesday, Thursday, and Sunday, and the funky, multiracial market on the *Place de la Réunion* in the twentieth arrondissement on Thursday or Sunday.
For more information, you can contact **Cellules des Marchés**, tel 01 42 76 34 37.

with the sublime fungus (truffes en salade, truffes en feuilleté, truffles with fresh pasta, in risotto). Look too for the range of oils, vinegars, and mustards all perfumed with—you guessed it!

• ICE CREAM & SORBET

Berthillon

4th arr. - 31, rue St-Louis-en-l'Ile - 01 43 54 31 61
Open 10am-8pm. Closed Mon, Tue. M° Pont Marie.
Berthillon is the most famous name in French ice cream. The firm's many faithful fans think nothing of waiting in line for *hours* just to treat their taste buds to a cone or dish of chocolate-nougat or glazed-chestnut ice cream. Berthillon's sorbets are our particular weakness: pink grapefruit, fig, wild strawberry, etc. The entire repertoire comes to some 100 flavors, including many seasonal offerings.

Glacier Vilfeu

1st arr. - 3, rue de la Cossonnerie - 01 40 26 36 40
Open mid Sep-mid Apr daily noon-7pm; mid Apr-mid Sep: daily noon-1am. M° Les Halles.
Vilfeu's imagination produces some 45 flavors including ice creams flavored with licorice, cinnamon, and ginger, and even an one based on Beaujolais nouveau. We also strongly encourage you to sample the sumptuous frozen desserts, notably the molded cream-cheese sorbet served with a vivid raspberry coulis.

Pascal le Glacier

16th arr. - 17, rue Bois-le-Vent - 01 45 27 61 84
Open 10:30am-7pm. Closed Sun, Mon. M° La Muette.
Michelle and Pascal Combette meticulously select the fruits they use, and they are just as meticulous about the way they greet their customers. It's enough to make a reputation that rivals even Berthillon. No less than 70 flavors are on offer, either inside or on the terrace, and depending on market availability: punch, fig, blood orange, Tahiti vanilla, honey nougat, wild berry, Malibu coco, cranberry, and much more. Excellent quality and quite affordable. Warm atmosphere—you're sure to have a good time.

Raimo

12th arr. - 59-61, bd de Reuilly - 01 43 43 70 17
Open 9am-midnight. Closed Mon. M° Daumesnil.
Sorbets and ice creams produced according to time-honored methods, with strictly fresh ingredients. Raimo's strong suit is concocting seductive flavor combinations; some of the most successful are piña colada, spiced-up three-chocolate, and blueberry and white chocolate.

*Don't plan to shop on **Sundays**—the vast majority of Paris stores are closed.*

• MEAT, GAME & FOWL

Boucheries Nivernaises

8th arr. - 99, rue du Fbg-Saint-Honoré
01 43 59 11 02, fax 01 42 25 92 32
Open Tue-Sat 7:15am-1pm & 3:30pm-7:15pm, Sun 7:15am-12:30pm. Closed Mon. M° St-Philippe-du-Roule.
The Bissonnet family is an institution. It supplies the best restaurants in the neighborhood: beef from Normandy and Simmental, lamb from Pauillac, chickens from Bresse and Landes. Here, quality is what counts, but the prices remain reasonable. Pleasant greeting and good advice from the boss.

Le Coq Saint-Honoré

1st arr. - 3, rue Gomboust
01 42 61 52 04, fax 01 42 61 44 64
Open Mon-Thu 8am-1pm & 4pm-7pm, Fri 3:30pm-7pm, Sat 8am-1pm. Closed Sun. M° Pyramides.
We might as well make it clear right away: For our money, Le Coq Saint-Honoré is one of Paris's top poulterers. It's no coincidence that among its customers are such culinary notables as Bouchet, Savoy, del Burgo, and Dutournier. The refrigerated cases display choice Bresse chickens and guinea hens (fast becoming prohibitively expensive), as well as laudable Loué pullets, Challans ducks, and plump rabbits from the Gâtinais region south of Paris. In season, look for the fine selection of game, including authentic Scottish grouse—a rare and wonderful treat.

• PASTRY

Paul Bugat

4th arr. - 5, bd Beaumarchais
01 48 87 89 88, fax 01 48 87 73 70
Open Tue-Fri 8:30am-7:45pm, Sun 8am-7:30pm. Closed Mon. M° Bastille.
Paul Bugat is a passionate esthete who orchestrates sweet pastry, chocolate, sugar, and cream into exquisite gâteaux. The specialties of the house are delicious, jewel-like petits-fours, along with the Clichy (chocolate buttercream and mocha cream on an almond-sponge base), and the Almaviva (chocolate-mousse cake). Tea room.

Dalloyau

2nd arr. - 25, bd des Capucines - 01 47 03 47 00
Open Mon-Fri 8am-7pm, Sat 9am-7pm. Closed Sun. M° Opéra.
6th arr. - 2, pl. Edmond-Rostand - 01 43 29 31 10
Open daily 8:30am-8:30pm. M° Cluny-La Sorbonne.
7th arr. - 63, rue de Grenelle - 01 45 49 95 30
Open daily 8:30am-8pm. M° Rue du Bac.

8th arr. - 99-101, rue du Fbg-Saint-Honoré
01 42 99 90 00, fax 01 45 63 82 92
Open daily 8:30am-9pm. M° St-Philippe-du-Roule.
9th arr. - Lafayette Gourmand, 48, bd Haussmann
01 53 20 05 99
Open Mon-Wed & Fri-Sat 9am-9pm, Thu 9am-9pm. Closed Sun. M° Auber.
15th arr. - 69, rue de la Convention - 01 45 77 84 27
Open daily 8am-8:30pm. M° Boucicaut.
Deservedly famous, Dalloyau is a temple of *gourmandise* revered by every discerning sweet tooth in town. Among the most renowned specialties are the memorably good macaroons, the chocolate-and-mocha Opéra cake (created in 1955 and still a bestseller), and the Mogador (chocolate sponge cake and mousse napped with raspberry jam, 21 F). Christmas brings succulent candied chestnuts and gluttonously rich Yule logs; Easter calls for chocolate hens and bunnies romping among praline eggs and bells in the adorable window displays.

Duhault

18th arr. - 127, rue Caulaincourt - 01 40 06 13 58
Open daily 8am-8:15pm. M° Lamarck-Caulaincourt.
The velvety black-chocolate cake (Le Moëlleux); the chocolate cookie on chocolate mousse (Le Rêve); the pistachio and chocolate mousse (L'Arlequin); or the passion fruit, mango, and coconut mousse (Le Passoa) are what made the reputation of this pastry shop, where you'll also find twenty different kinds of homemade chocolates and ten delicate but full-flavored ice creams. The vacherin meringue is a must.

Ladurée

8th arr. - 16, rue Royale - 01 42 60 21 79
Open Mon-Sat 8:30am-7pm, Sun 10am-7pm. Closed mid Jul-Aug: Sun. M° Concorde.
8th arr. - 75, av. des Champs-Élysées
01 40 75 08 75
Open daily 8am-1am. M° George-V.
9th arr. - Le Printemps, 64 bd Haussmann
01 42 82 40 10
Open Mon-Wed & Fri-Sat 9:30am-7pm, Thu 9:30pm-9pm. Closed Sun. M° Havre-Caumartin.
16th arr. - at Franck & Fils, 80, rue de Passy
01 44 14 38 80
Open 10am-6:30pm. Closed Sun. M° La Muette.
Among the wonderful pastries sold here, don't miss the sublime macaroons, which are plump and tender on the inside and crispy on the outside. They come in an array of delicate colors and flavors and are now made under the direction of Pierre Hermé, formerly of Fauchon.

Lenôtre

8th arr. - 15, bd de Courcelles - 01 45 63 87 63
15th arr. - 61, rue Lecourbe - 01 42 73 20 97
16th arr. - 44, rue d'Auteuil - 01 45 24 52 52
48, av. Victor-Hugo - 01 45 02 21 21
17th arr. - 121, av. de Wagram - 01 47 63 70 30
Open daily 9am-9pm. M° Villiers, Sèvres-Lecourbe, Michel Ange-Auteuil, Victor Hugo, Wagram.

Normandy native Gaston Lenôtre opened his first shop in Paris in 1957. His pastries and elaborate desserts are now internationally recognized as classics: the Schuss, the Plaisir, the Opéra... His most memorable creation may just be the Passion des Iles—passionfruit mousse on a coconut-meringue base sprinkled with shaved chocolate—a tropical fantasy!

Le Moule à Gâteaux

14th arr. - 17, rue Daguerre - 01 43 22 61 25
Also: 4th arr., 5th arr., 7th arr., 8th arr., 15th arr., 16th arr., 20th arr.
Open daily 8am-8pm. M° Denfert-Rochereau.
This prospering chain specializes in traditional, homestyle cakes fashioned by young pastry cooks who care about their craft. They use time-tested recipes that we wish we still had the leisure (and know-how) to prepare in our own kitchens. We love the apricot feuilleté covered with a golden short crust; the Mamita, a poem in chocolate and crème fraîche; and the flambéed calvados apple tart. Reasonable prices.

Gérard Mulot

6th arr. - 76, rue de Seine - 01 43 26 85 77
Open 6:45am-8pm. Closed Wed. M° Odéon.
Mulot is an endlessly inventive personality, never happier than when he is working out a new idea to complete his line of delectable pastries. Recent creations include the Oasis (almond mousse with an apricot wafer) and the Ardèchois (chestnut custard on a whisky-flavored chocolate cookie filled with candied chestnuts and coated with caramel). In a more down-to-earth vein, Mulot also fashions wonderfully flaky, buttery croissants.

La Pâtisserie Bretonne

16th arr. - 129 bis, rue de la Pompe - 01 47 27 43 55
Open 10am-1:30pm & 3pm-7pm. Closed Sun. M° Rue de la Pompe.
This Breton pastry shop is worth going out of the way for, simply because of the quality of their entirely homemade creations, made with totally natural ingredients: kouing-aman, quatre-quarts, cherry cake, prune pancakes, and excellent cheese shortbread. You always get your money's worth here.

Stohrer

2nd arr. - 51, rue Montorgueil - 01 42 33 38 20
Open daily 7:30am-8:30pm. M° Les Halles.
The rococo shop is decorated with rosy, corpulent allegories of Fame painted by Paul Baudry (he also decorated the Paris Opéra) in 1860. Stohrer was the private pastry chef of Marie Leszczynska, to be Mrs. Louis XV. He set up in Paris in 1730, and was one of the very first pastry chefs/caterers in the city. A long line of artisans have passed through since, including François Duthu, who came on board eleven years ago. He is proud of his turnover made with fresh apples and vanilla cream (so are we), his

wild strawberry puff-pastry tarts, as well as his *puits d'amour*, garnished with vanilla pastry cream caramelized with a red hot iron.

• SEAFOOD

Le Bar à Huîtres

3rd arr. - 33, bd Beaumarchais - 01 48 87 98 92
5th arr. - 82 bis, bd St-Germain - 01 44 07 27 37
14th arr. - 112, bd Montparnasse - 01 43 20 71 01
Open daily noon–1am. M° St Michel, Vavin.
At the outdoor oyster bar, you can purchase dozens of succulent oysters, opened for you free of charge by the nimble-fingered *écaillers* and neatly arranged on disposable trays (no deposit, no return). Just remember to place your order in advance.

Poissonnerie du Dôme

14th arr. - 4, rue Delambre - 01 43 35 23 95
Open Tue & Thu-Sun 8am-1pm & 4pm-7:30pm, Wed 8am-1pm. Closed Mon. M° Vavin.
The lucky residents of Montparnasse can satisfy their urge for seafood at this marvelous fish store, perhaps the best in Paris. Manager Jean-Pierre Lopez admits only «noble» fish (sole, turbot, lotte, sea bass) to his classy emporium. The merchandise, from French (particularly Breton) and foreign waters, is snapped up by such eminent restaurants as L'Ambroisie and Laurent. Need we mention that these delicate denizens of the deep command regally high prices?

• WINE & SPIRITS

Keep in mind that you can purchase a good bottle of wine for your dinner at many of the city's wine bars.

Les Caves Taillevent

8th arr. - 199, rue du Fg-Saint-Honoré
01 45 61 14 09, fax 01 45 61 19 68
Open Mon 2pm-8pm, Tue-Fri 9am-8pm, Sat 9am-7:30pm. Closed Sun. M° Charles de Gaulle-Étoile.
Crack sommeliers—the Vrinat family and their team—select the wines presented by Taillevent. The choice is wide, and the prices are more reasonable than you might expect. They have no qualms about letting their customers taste the lesser known wines of the French soil. They specialize in Burgundy and Languedoc-Roussillon. We eyed (and tasted) the Faugères '94 from Domaine Léon Barral at 39 F a bottle, and the '95 Domaine de la Croix Belle, a «country» wine form the banks of the Thongues, at only 24 F. Their *coups de cœur* are well worth discovering, and can be tasted on Saturdays. New Bordeaux are also available.

Legrand Filles et Fils

2nd arr. - 1, rue de la Banque
01 42 60 07 12, fax 01 42 61 25 51
Open Tue-Fri 8:30am-7:30pm, Sat 8:30am-1pm & 3pm-7pm. Closed Sun, Mon. M° Bourse.
Even if the wines were not half so interesting as they are, Legrand's wine shop would be worth a visit for its old-fashioned charm and warm atmosphere. Francine Legrand offers a fascinating selection of carefully chosen, inexpensive country wines from up-and-coming growers in the South and the Val de Loire, along with a far-ranging inventory of prestigious Alsaces, Burgundies, and Bordeaux (note the many wines from average vintage years, affordably priced). Also, a few uncommon bottlings: luscious Muscat de Beaumes-de-Venise, Vin de Paille du Jura, and some excellent vintage Ports. Legrand's impressive stock of eaux-de-vie is one of the finest in town.

Clos Montmartre

Once upon a time, Montmartre was covered with windmills and vineyards. Today, the sole remaining *vignoble* covers a hillside opposite the celebrated Lapin Agile cabaret, at the corner of Rue Saint-Vincent and Rue des Saules. The wine produced by these Gamay and Pinot Noir grapes is a modest tipple indeed, but the harvest is celebrated with a colorful parade and lots of bacchic bonhomie on the first weekend of October.

Nicolas

8th arr. - 31, pl. de Madeleine
01 42 68 00 16, fax 01 47 42 70 26
http://www.nicolas.tm.fr
Open 9am-8pm. Closed Sun. M° Madeleine.
250 stores in Paris.
Looking better than ever with a spruce gold-and-bordeaux décor, Nicolas's innumerable stores in the Paris area continue to present a wide, diverse, and appealing range of wines for every budget. The chain's monthly promotions are well worth following: featured are (for example) French wines from unfamiliar or under-rated appellations—the Ardèche, Corbières, or Savoie—, imports (Spanish, Italian, and even Lebanese bottlings), and the occasional oenological curiosity, all offered at attractive prices. The multilevel flagship store on Place de la Madeleine has a huge inventory of more than 1,000 different wines, including rare, old Bordeaux. Nicolas is also an excellent source of fine distilled spirits (check out the selection of single-malt whiskies). The Avenue Wagram shop stays open until 10pm (tel 01 42 27 22 07), the An-

cienne-Comédie store until 9pm (tel 01 43 26 61 22). Home delivery service available.

Au Verger de la Madeleine

8th arr. - 4, bd Malesherbes
01 42 65 51 99, fax 01 49 24 05 22
Open Mon 10am-1pm & 3:30pm-8pm, Tue-Sat 10am-8pm. Closed Sun. M° Malesherbes.

Jean-Pierre Legras's staggering collection encompasses such unique and extravagant bottles as an 1811 Cognac Grande Champagne, a Trrantez Madeira from 1789, an 1895 Château Lafite-Rothschild, and the excellent Maastricht white wine. Such treasures are not for everyday drinking, but they make impressive, indeed unforgettable, gifts. Legras also carries various beverage bottles dating from 1900 to the present; they make great birthday presents when you choose one from the year the person was born. All the first growths of Bordeaux (Cheval-Blanc, Pétrus, etc.) are on hand as well, along with superb Burgundies from Montrachet and Meursault, and hard-to-find wines like Château-Grillet and Jasnières. For the faint of wallet, there are inexpensive offerings from the Côtes-d'Au-vergne, Saint-Pourçain, and Saumur.

LUXURY STORES

• HOME

Cutlery

Galerie Laguiole

1st arr. - 1, pl. Sainte-Opportune
01 40 28 09 42, fax 01 40 39 03 89
Open 10:30am-7:30pm. Closed Sun. M° Châtelet-Les Halles.

Philippe Starck designed this contemporary gallery, where the full range of Laguiole knives is on display. Even before they were on the cutting edge of chic, Laguioles were a proud French tradition: crafted with care for a lifetime of use. Once made only of horn, the handles are now available in palmwood, ebony, briar, and other rare woods. The store now carries a new line of copies of Laguiole's traditional knives as well. Don't miss the table knives by Nontron, with their lovely boxwood handles.

Kitchenware

Dehillerin

1st arr. - 18-20, rue Coquillière
01 42 36 53 13, fax 01 42 36 54 80
http://www.edehillerin.fr

Open Sep-Jul: Mon 8am-12:30pm & 2pm-6pm, Tue-Sat 8am-6pm; Aug: Mon-Sat 10am-6pm. Closed Sun. M° Louvre-Rivoli.

Since 1820, the cream of the French food establishment has purchased their *batteries de cuisine* at Dehillerin. More recently, they have been joined by large numbers of American and Japanese culinary enthusiasts. Dehillerin stocks a truly amazing range of cookware, superb knives, copper pots, and every imaginable baking utensil. We suggest you come early in the day to shop here, and above all, don't be in a hurry. Some of the sales clerks speak English and are quite helpful.

Crystal, China & Silver

Atelier Haviland

8th arr. - Village Royal, entrance 25, rue Royale
01 42 66 36 36, fax 01 42 66 45 79
Open 10am-7pm. Closed Sun. M° Madeleine.

Haviland's stunning display windows stop shoppers in their tracks! These imaginative, often fantastical tableaux combine Haviland's newest china patterns (Renaissance, for example, decorated with Italianate motifs, 235 F the dinner plate) with such timeless classics as Louveciennes, Vieux Paris Vert (dinner plate: 375 F), or opulent Impérator Bleu. Speaking of opulence, a new collection features incrustations illuminated with 24-carat gold. And charming gift ideas abound: candy dishes, pillboxes, vases... A line of votives candleholders coordinates with the house's best-known china patterns—they're perfect for creating a romantic table (295 F).

Worth a stroll...

Discount houses stand cheek-by-jowl with the most prestigious names in tableware on the **Rue de Paradis** (10th arr. - M° Château d'Eau). Remember, though, that rooting out a good buy requires considerable time and patience!

Baccarat

8th arr. - 11, pl. de la Madeleine
01 42 65 36 26, fax 01 42 65 06 64
Open 10am-7pm. Closed Sun. M° Madeleine.

Baccarat's flagship store on the Place de la Madeleine boasts a bright, harmonious décor that highlights the extraordinary brilliance of the firm's superbly wrought crystal stemware, decorative accents, and objets d'art. The lastest collections are just introduced: Vega, Lalande, and Lyra include stemware and coordinated candlesticks, vases, and bowls. The Rhine wineglasses in the Vega collection are tinted a stunning sapphire-blue (430 F per stem). The shop's scintillating chandeliers are creation of designers Patrice Butler and Andrée Putman. Another address at: 30 bis rue de Paradis, tenth arrondissement, tel. 01 47 70 64 30.

Bernardaud

8th arr. - 11, rue Royale
01 47 42 82 66, fax 01 49 24 06 35
Open Mon-Fri 9:30am-6:30pm, Sat 10am-7pm. Closed Sun. M° Concorde.
Since 1863, the Limoges-based Bernardaud has been a standard-bearer for French china manufacturers. Following the lead of other prestigious tableware manufacturers, Bernardaud opened a showcase on Rue Royale to display the entire array of its collections. Don't miss the reissue of a service owned by Queen Marie-Antoinette; in a more modern vein, look for Olivier Gagnère's spectacular Ithaque and Lipari cups.

Christofle

2nd arr. - 24, rue de la Paix
01 42 65 62 43, fax 01 47 42 28 51
Open 10am-7pm. Closed Sun. M° Opéra.
Also: 8th arr., 16 th arr.
Christofle was founded in 1830, and began to produce the plated silverware that made the firm's fortune. But silver was just the start: today Christofle designs extend to elegant and functional stainless-steel cutlery, china (the Microgold lines are microwave-resistant), table linens (in gorgeous damask or prints), and decorative gifts. A current bestseller is Christofle's clean-lined Oceano setting, perfect for a contemporary table. Another recent creation, the Talisman line of Chinese-lacquered settings, owes its durable beauty to a jealously guarded secret process. Christofle has also enjoyed notable success with reproductions of its designs from the 1920s (like the coveted tea service in silver plate with briarwood handles).

Cristalleries de Saint-Louis

8th arr. - 13, rue Royale
01 40 17 01 74, fax 01 40 17 03 87
Open 9:30am-6:30pm. Closed Sun. M° Concorde.
This venerable firm (founded in 1586) which long crafted crystal for the kings of France, continues to maintain the highest standards of quality. A visit to Saint-Louis's dazzling showplace on Rue Royale will have you, too, longing to adorn your table with mouth-blown, handcut crystal stemware, decanters encrusted with gold, and filigreed or opaline vases. Don't forget Saint-Louis's creative line of lamps: the Buble model alone is worth a trip to the shop!

Daum

2nd arr. - 4, rue de la Paix
01 42 61 25 25, fax 01 40 20 96 71
Open Mon 11am-7pm, Tue-Sat 10am-7pm. Closed Sun. M° Opéra.

Daum's elegant trilevel showrooms are situated in premises formerly occupied by the great couturier, Worth. Slate-gray walls and green-glazed bronze furniture form an ideal setting for the firm's latest creations. Downstairs you'll find limited-edition (200 or 300 copies) glass pieces, in luminous colors: Claude Lalanne's jewel box, La Diva and carafes with cactus stoppers by Hilton McConnico. The ground floor holds Daum's collections of vases, decorative pieces, and more in crystal and pâte de verre, while the first floor is devoted to Daum's table services.

Gien

8th arr. - 18, rue de l'Arcade
01 42 66 52 32, fax 01 42 65 15 77
Open 10am-7pm. Closed Sun, Mon. M° Madeleine.
The Gien faïence factory, founded in 1821, has been granted a new lease on life. Noted designers have been commissioned to create new patterns that are now on view in Gien's Paris showroom. People who prefer the Gien services that their grandmothers owned will be happy to see that they are still available.

Lalique

1st arr. - Galerie du Carrousel du Louvre
99, rue de Rivoli - 01 42 86 01 51
Open daily 10:30am-7:30pm. M° Palais-Royal.
8th arr. - 11, rue Royale
01 53 05 12 12, fax 01 42 65 59 06
Open 9:30am-6:30pm. Closed Sun. M° Concorde.
Three generations of creative Laliques have earned an international following with their enchanting crystal designs. Marie-Claude Lalique, who succeeded her father, Marc, at the head of the company in 1977, creates marvelous contemporary pieces in the true Lalique spirit—like the Bacchantes vase in transparent satiny crystal. In the courtyard of the Rue Royale shop, Lalique has opened another boutique, devoted to «the art of the table», where you can also find jewelry, perfumes, bags and belts.

Puiforcat

8th arr. - 2, av. Matignon
01 45 63 10 10, fax 01 42 56 27 15
Open Tue-Fri 9:30am-6:30pm, Mon & Sat 9:30am-1pm & 2:15pm-6:30pm. Closed Sun. M° Franklin-D.-Roosevelt.
Victor-Louis Puiforcat founded this prestigious silversmithing firm, and his son, Jean, made its reputation with his distinctive designs in the 1920s and 1930s. (Those pieces and others can be admired in the little museum downstairs from the showroom.) Puiforcat continues to reissue certain vintage designs, but the firm's creativity is alive and well, witness the beautiful Nantes and Don Quichotte settings (the latter combines silver plate and lemonwood). In the gift department, look for the handsome Cyclades boxes (1,412 F) and candy dishes, and the clean-lined Saturne vase (1,342 to 2,428 F).

• *JEWELRY*

Boucheron

1st arr. - 26, pl. Vendôme
01 42 61 58 16, fax 01 40 20 95 39
http://www.boucheron.com
Open Mon-Sat 10am-6:30pm. Closed Sun; Jul-Aug: Sat. M° Opéra.
  Alain Boucheron, the current—dynamic!—bearer of the Boucheron family torch, has led his firm into new areas, including fragrances. But Boucheron's backbone remains prestige jewelry and watches. Beautiful gems are brought forth for inspection on plush trays, in an opulent environment of wood paneling and friezes. The more accessible «Boutique» collections feature (for example) a handsome steel watch with an interchangeable bracelet (9,400 F) and the Parfum ring, in gold and semiprecious stones (from 8,800 F), inspired by the distinctive Boucheron perfume flacon.

Cartier

1st arr. - 7 & 23, pl. Vendôme
01 44 55 32 50/44 55 32 20
2nd arr. - 13, rue de la Paix - 01 42 18 53 70
6th arr. - 41, rue de Rennes - 01 45 49 65 80

La Boutique de la Monnaie

Like the museum (see text, p. 90), La Boutique is a collector's dream. Once or twice a year, a new collection of coins is launched to commemorate a historal, a cultural or sports event. These coins, which bear a face value in French Francs (and sometimes in Euro on one side), can be used, but we don't really recommend it since they are made of silver or gold, and even sometimes in platinum! A fine and large collection of medals are also available, or you can order your own. All the work involved in the production of these pieces is carefully carried out by highly skilled craftspeople. 6th arr. - 11, quai Conti - 01 40 46 58 58, fax 01 40 46 58 00 http://www.monnaiedeparis.fr Open Mon-Fri 9am-5:45pm, Sat 10am-1pm & 2pm-5:30pm. Closed Sun. M° Pont-Neuf.

8th arr. - 23, rue du Fg Saint-Honoré
01 44 94 87 70
8th arr. - 51, rue François-Ier - 01 53 93 95 20
Open Oct-Mar: Tue-Fri 10am-6:30pm, Mon & Sat 10:30am-6:30pm; Apr-Sep: Tue-Fri 10am-7pm, Mon & Sat 10:30am-7pm. Closed Sun. M° Opéra, Concorde, Franklin-D.-Roosevelt.
  «It is better to have authentic junk than fake Cartier», exclaims Alain Dominique Perrin, chief executive of Cartier, the most copied name on earth. Founded in 1847, the firm still produces enviable jeweled ornaments for the big events and for day-to-day life: many are on display, at the Cartier boutique on Rue de la Paix. Not to mention fine timepieces like the celebrated Tank Française, a steel watch (12,900 F for the ladies' version, 15,900 F for the men's) and such nearly affordable trinkets as the famous Trinity ring (3,900 F).

Chanel Joaillerie

1st arr. - 18, pl. Vendôme
01 55 35 50 05, fax 01 55 35 50 08
Open Tue-Fri 10am-1pm & 2pm-6:30pm, Mon & Sat 10:30am-1pm & 2pm-6:30pm. Closed Sun. M° Tuileries.
8th arr. - 40, av. Montaigne - 01 40 70 12 33
Open 10am-1pm & 2pm-6:30pm. Closed Sun. M° Franklin-D.-Roosevelt.
  The décor of Chanel's new boutique on Place Vendôme is reminiscent of Mademoiselle's private apartment. Coromandel screens, luscious suède sofas, and lacquered furniture invite you to admire a dazzling collection of jewels: platinum stars set with diamonds, cascades of pearls, and stunning gold ornaments punctuated with colored gems. Chanel's watches are things of beauty, particularly the square dial on a delicate pearl bracelet and the classic rectangular watch on a leather band (from 8,500 F).

Chaumet

1st arr. - 12, pl. Vendôme
01 44 77 24 00, fax 01 42 60 41 11
Open 10am-6:30pm. Closed Sun. M° Opéra.
  Jeweler in Paris since 1780, Chaumet's creations have beguiled such connoisseurs as Napoléon, Queen Victoria, and countless maharajahs. The firm also produces elegant timepieces, gold jewelry, and writing instruments which are perfectly appropriate for fast-paced modern life. Prices for Chaumet's «Boutique» line start at 4,000 F, and watches at 7,400 F. New this year is a diving watch for both men and women starting at 9,500 F. The Style de Chaumet line of timepieces (models for men and women, from 7,400 F) is stylish. And the Khésis watch for women (from 9,100 F) can be spotted on some of the most fashionable wrists in town.

Mauboussin

1st arr. - 20, pl. Vendôme
01 44 55 10 00, fax 01 44 55 10 09

Open Mon-Fri 10am-6:30pm, Sat 10am-1pm & 2:30pm-6:30pm. Closed Sun; mid Jul-Aug: Sat. M° Opéra.

Founded in 1827, the house of Mauboussin exudes the patrician aura one associates with old-established families, for whom the purchase of fine jewelry is the natural way to celebrate life's big moments. Engagement rings are a Mauboussin specialty: the Nadia ring is a glowing nacre-and-gold band set with a diamond or colored gemstone; the Olympe features a splendid Tahitian pearl surrounded with diamond baguettes mounted on yellow gold.

Mellerio dits Meller

2nd arr. - 9, rue de la Paix
01 42 61 57 53, fax 01 49 27 04 90
Open 10am-1pm & 2pm-6:30pm. Closed Sun; mid Jul-mid Sep: Sat, wk of Aug 15. M° Opéra.

When Queen Marie de Médicis awarded her loyal Lombard chimney sweeps licenses as peddlers, later as street vendors, and finally as jewelers (their reward for having overheard and reported a plot against the Crown), she probably had no idea that she was founding a dynasty. Now, some fourteen generations later, the great house of Mellerio is still not resting on those ancient laurels. The dean of fine jewelers in France, Mellerio combs the worldwide gem markets for outstanding stones that measure up to their noble standards.

Alexandre Reza

1st arr. - 23, pl. Vendôme
01 42 96 64 00, fax 01 42 60 26 90
Open 10am-6:30pm. Closed Sun, Aug. M° Opéra.

The jewels of Alexandre Reza, a major dealer in precious stones, on display in his shop, glow with some of the most beautiful gems around. A master appraiser and collector for over fifty years, Alexandre Reza transformed the boutique's lower level into a gallery that displays opulent and expertly crafted jewelry creations. Admire, for example, the 148.88 carat yellow sapphire pendant framed by pearshaped blue sapphires, cabochon emeralds, round white diamonds and cabochon rubies—based upon an original design by Pouget. Alexandre Reza's workshop on the top floor of his Place Vendôme office turns out settings and designs of a quality and intricacy rarely found in this age.

Van Cleef et Arpels

1st arr. - 22, pl. Vendôme
01 53 45 45 45, fax 01 53 45 45 00
Open Mon-Fri 10am-6:30pm, Sat 10am-1pm & 2pm-6:30pm. Closed Sun; Jul-Aug: Sat. M° Opéra.

The most innovative of Place Vendôme's jewelers, and originator of the gold evening bag set with precious gems, this firm boasts an exclusive mounting technique: the setting fades into the background, thus emphasizing the quality of the stones. Prices reflect this high level of workmanship and creativity, but even rela-

tively modest budgets can find happiness with the Van Cleef «Boutique» line: rings, earrings, and butterfly pendants start at about 4,000 F.

• *LEATHER & LUGGAGE*

Hermès

8th arr. - 24, rue du Fg-Saint-Honoré
01 40 17 47 17, fax 01 40 17 47 18
8th arr. - 42, av. George-V - 01 47 20 48 51
Open Mon 10am-1pm & 2:15pm-6:30pm, Tue-Sat 10am-6:30pm. Closed Sun. M° Concorde, George-V.
15th arr. - Hôtel Hilton, 18, av. de Suffren - 01 45 66 89 29
Open 10:30am-7pm. Closed Sun. M° Bir-Hakeim.

Hermès has purveyed fine leather goods long enough to reign supreme as the undisputed leader of the pack when it comes to saddles, handbags, luggage, and all the accompanying accoutrements of fine living and traveling. But what about the prices? Are they reasonable? Well, take a look at the workmanship. Check the finish on the leather goods: the Kelly (1956) or Constance (1969) or Bugatti bag, all of which come in a dozen different leathers. Think of the meticulous handcrafting that went into the cutting, sewing, and fitting of these bags, or into the voluptuous sets of matched luggage. Now are you ready to whip out your credit card? What's more, if you want something special, such as a leather cover for your bicycle seat or for the cockpit of your private jet, the Hermès custom-craftsmen will gladly oblige.

Didier Ludot

1st arr. - 24, galerie Montpensier - 01 42 96 06 56
Open 10:30am-7pm. Closed Sun. M° Palais-Royal.

Didier Ludot's shop is located under the arcades of the Palais-Royal, which in and of itself is a good reason to come and see how he lovingly reconditions previously owned bags. He also carries some superb 1930s-to-'40s box-calf suitcases lined with suède. Other vintage goodies on sale here are Hermès (Kellys) and Chanel handbags (there are clothes and shoes by those makers, too—all second-hand but in excellent shape). At number 23 next door, you will find vintage couture dating from the 1920s to the 1980s.

Morabito

8th arr. - 55, rue François-Ier
01 53 23 90 40, fax 01 53 23 90 41
Open 10am-7pm. Closed Sun. M° George-V.

Choose between custom-made luggage and handbags in the skin you fancy (crocodile, ostrich, etc.) and the color you prefer, or a sportier line of ready-made bags in textured calf (2,000 to 9,000 F). The made-to-measure bags are generally ready in one week, and prices start at about 8,000 F. Perfect service, of course, from this long-established firm reputed for quality. Custom-made leather-bound desk diaries complete Morabito's elegant inventory.

The *Passages* of Paris

The covered galleries that run like a maze through the heart of Paris are a remote ancestor of today's shopping malls. Popular throughout the first half of the nineteenth century, these arcades afforded protection from the elements as well as from dirt, street noise, and horses run amok.

In these ideal conditions for commerce, shops—and shoppers—poured into the passages, bringing restaurants and theaters in their wake. Suddenly, though, the passages went out of fashion; many were demolished or fell into disrepair and today a total of sixteen remain. In the past decade or so, several have been rescued and refurbished. Weave your way through **Passage Verdeau** (9th arr. - 31 bis, rue du Fbg-Montmartre, M° Richelieu-Drouot), **Passage Jouffroy** (9th arr. - 12, bd Montmartre, M° Richelieu-Drouot), **Galerie Vivienne** (2nd arr. - 4, rue des Petits-Champs, M° Bourse), **Galerie Véro-Dodat** (1st arr. - 19, rue Jean-Jacques Rousseau, M° Louvre-Rivoli), and **Passage des Panoramas** (2nd arr. - 11, bd Montmartre, M° Rue-Montmartre) for a nostalgic taste of "le vieux Paris".

Louis Vuitton

6th arr. - 6, pl. Saint-Germain-des-Prés
01 45 49 62 32
http://www.louisvuitton.com
Open 10am-7pm. Closed Sun. M° St-Germain-des-Prés.
8th arr. - 54, av. Montaigne
01 45 62 47 00, fax 01 45 62 90 43
Open 9:30am-7pm. Closed Sun. M° Franklin-D.-Roosevelt.
8th arr. - 101, av. des Champs-Élysées
01 53 57 24 00
Open 10am-8pm. Closed Sun. M° Franklin-D.-Roosevelt.

Vuitton lovers, here's a test. Put your bag down at the airline counter of an airport. Watch it disappear into a crowd of other Vuittons...now try and identify it! Yet for many, the monogrammed Vuitton bag is a cult object. It consists of printed linen coated with vinyl, reinforced with lozine ribs (which look like leather; Vuitton jealously guards the formula), with untreated leather for handles and straps, copper for rivets and hard corners. Don't like monograms? Then look to Vuitton's Tassili line: the yellow épi leather is winning many fans; or you may be taken with the Alma bag, designed in the '30s for Coco Chanel and recently reissued (2,400 F). And the computer carrying case in green épi leather is the last word in executive chic. All of Vuitton's multifarious collections are now on view in the firm's new Champs-Élysées shop. It is Vuitton's largest European store, and the only one in Paris where you will find Vuitton's ready-to-wear line.

• *TOBACCONISTS*

No Bargains Here

In Paris, you will note, cigars cost an arm and a leg. Why? The state considers them a «drug» and taxes heavily. But take heart: at the shops we have listed in this section you are sure to find a fresh, high-quality cigar and not, as too often happens, a once-choice cheroot that has turned into a roll of stale, bitter-tasting compost.

Dunhill

2nd arr. - 15, rue de la Paix
01 42 61 57 58, fax 01 42 60 63 67
Open Tue-Fri 9:30am-6:30pm, Mon & Sat 10am-6:30pm. Closed Sun. M° Opéra.

The Alfred Dunhill shop remains the domain of men—and women—who have about them the expensive aroma of Havana cigars and fine leather. Foremost among the luxurious items presented in this mahogany-paneled, 1920s-style shop are, of course, the famed Dunhill pipes, among the world's best...and priciest. Collectors will not want to miss the mini-museum of antique Dunhill objects. Dunhill is also a gift shop, with a large selection of costume jewelry, leather goods, and pens. But the lion's share of the shop is given over to smokers' accessories: expensive lighters, cigarette holders, cigar boxes, and humidors in rare woods. In the new ready-to-wear section, men can dress themselves from top to bottom.

A la Civette

1st arr. - 157, rue Saint-Honoré
01 42 96 04 99, fax 01 42 60 44 78

Open 9:30am-7pm. Closed Sun. M° Palais-Royal.
Habitués refer to this venerable establishment as the Civette du Palais-Royal. Founded in 1716, it was the first tobacconist in Paris, for many years *the* place of pilgrimage for cigar and tobacco lovers. Casanova even mentions it in his memoirs. Tobacco goods featured run the gamut from everyday chewing weed to the very best Havanas, including the Hoyo de Monterrey, imported directly from Cuba. La Civette boasts an inventory of 20,000 cigars stored in a climate-controlled vault. Also available is a wide range of accessories: deluxe lighters and pipes (Chacom, Butz-Choquin, Dunhill), humidors in all shapes and sizes, pens, and leather goods.

Lemaire

16th arr. - 59, av. Victor-Hugo
01 45 00 75 63, fax 01 45 01 70 65
Open Mon-Fri 8:30am-7:15pm, Sat 9am-7:15pm. Closed Sun. M° Victor Hugo.
Guy Pihan now presides over one of France's most prestigious tobacconists. Here you will find the cigar of your dreams perfectly preserved and presented with rare flair. Havanas and San Domingos—Zinos, Don Miguels, and Juan Clementes—top the list. Pihan's astonishing vaults accommodate thousands of cases of cigars in ideal conditions. Cigar boxes and humidors sold here are guaranteed for workmanship and reliability (the gamut runs from a solid cedar-wood three-cigar pocket humidor to a vault the size of a writing desk). Pipe smokers will discover the entire range of tobaccos available in France, plus a large selection of pipes (all major brands, with a particularly good collection of meerschaums). Lemaire's vast stock of accessories embraces the finest lighters, cases, and pouches.

OPEN LATE

• BEAUTY & HEALTH

Béati-Corpus

9th arr. - 1, rue Moncey
01 48 74 44 93, fax 01 48 74 10 28
Open daily 24 hours.
Put your feet up at home and have them pampered by professionals. Pedicures and manicures are among the services provided by this very dynamic agency, which also offers massage, body-waxing, make-up, shiatsu, skin-care treatments, and hair-styling, all in the comfort of your own home or hotel, on just a thirty minute's notice.

*Some establishments change their **closing times** without warning. It is always wise to check in advance.*

• DRUGSTORES

Drugstore Champs-Élysées

8th arr. - 133, av. des Champs-Élysées
01 44 43 79 00, fax 01 47 23 00 96
Open daily 9am-2am. M° Charles de Gaulle-Étoile.
Be it premium bubbly or Alka-Seltzer, a little night music or earplugs for a noiseless morning after...the Drugstore Champs-Élysées have got it all. (At 1 av. Matignon, 8th arr., tel. 01 43 59 38 70, you will only find a tobbaco store and a pharmacy.)

• FLOWERS

Élyfleurs

17th arr. - 82, av. de Wagram
01 47 66 87 19, fax 01 42 27 29 13
Open daily 24 hours. M° Wagram.
Open 24 hours, a very convenient place to get a bouquet for that last-minute dinner invitation.

Interflora

0 800 203 204
Open Mon-Sat 8am-8pm.
Minitel: 3615, code Interflora
Open daily 24 hours.
hhttp://www.Interflora.fr
Through its worldwide network, Interflora can send flowers all over the world, including within France of course!

• FOOD & DRINK

A l'An 2000

17th arr. - 82, bd des Batignolles - 01 43 87 24 67
Open Mon-Sat 5pm-midnight, Sun & hols 11am-midnight. M° Rome.
After an evening at the Théâtre des Arts-Hébertot, you can put together a nice post-theater supper with provisions from L'An 2000. All sorts of appetizing dishes are on display at this spacious emporium. From caviar to charcuterie, from bread and fresh-vegetable terrines to wine, cheese, and fresh fruit, you'll find all the makings of a charming midnight feast.

Baskin-Robbins

6th arr. - 1, rue du Four - 01 43 25 10 63
Also: 5th arr., 12th arr., 14th arr.
Open Mon-Sat noon-11pm (8pm off-seas), Sun 2pm-11pm (8pm off-seas). M° Mabillon.
The French tend to find Baskin-Robbins ice creams too sugary-sweet and unnecessarily rich; but they are genuinely intrigued by the flavors: maple-walnut, banana-chocolate swirl, peanut-butter and chocolate. On summer nights, French ice-cream fans come out of the woodwork to join the tourists of every other nationality to sip good ol' American milk-shakes, a Baskin-Robbins specialty.

Le Bar à Huîtres

14th arr. - 112, bd Montparnasse
01 43 20 71 01, fax 01 43 21 35 47
Also: 3rd arr, 5th arr.
Open daily noon-1am. M° Vavin.
See *Food* section, p. 103.

Flo Prestige

See *Food* section for locations, p. 93.
They are perfect places for late-night food
shopping. Temptations include foie gras from
Strasbourg, Norwegian smoked salmon, beautiful cheeses, and irresistible pastries, plus Champagne or a lusty country wine to wash it all
down.

Häagen-Dazs

8th arr. - 49, av. des Champs-Élysées
01 53 77 68 68, fax 01 45 63 10 03
Open Sun-Thu noon-1am, Fri & Sat noon-1:30am.
M° Franklin-D.-Roosevelt.
8th arr. - 144, av. des Champs-Élysées
01 53 75 22 09
Open daily 11am-1am. M° George-V.
Also: 1st arr., 4th arr., 5th arr., 6th arr., 11th arr.,
14th arr., 16th arr., 17th arr.

Goldenberg

17th arr. - 69, av. de Wagram - 01 42 27 34 79
Open daily 10am-11:30pm. M° Ternes.
See *Food* section, p. 97.

La Maison d'Alsace

8th arr. - 39, av. des Champs-Élysées
01 53 93 97 00, fax 01 53 93 97 09
Open daily 24 hours. M° Franklin-D.-Roosevelt.
Beyond the main restaurant, (see *Restaurants*,
p. 40), is a catering service–cum-boutique where
you can purchase essentially Alsatian specialties—sauerkraut, charcuteries, foie gras, etc.
There is a carry-out service should you be
tempted to take home a dish for a midnight
snack.

Raimo

12th arr. - 59-61, bd de Reuilly - 01 43 43 70 17
Open 9am-midnight. Closed Mon, Feb. M° Daumes-
nil.
See *Food* section, p. 101.

• GIFTS

Les Comptoirs de la Tour d'Argent

5th arr. - 2, rue du Cardinal-Lemoine
01 46 33 45 58, fax 01 43 26 39 23
Open Tue-Sat 10am-midnight, Sun noon-mid-
night. Closed Mon. M° Maubert-Mutualité.
Dinner at La Tour d'Argent may be out of
reach, but you can always scrape up a few francs
to purchase a small souvenir bearing the
restaurant's logo! There is a wealth of classic
tableware (crystal, silver, china, embroidered
napery) and lots of determinedly tasteful accessories (how about a Tour d'Argent silk tie?). The
good canned foie gras, duck confit, and the Brut
Champagne also sport the house colors, and like
the rest are high-priced.

• PHARMACIES

Grande Pharmacie Daumesnil

12th arr. - 6, pl. Félix-Eboué - 01 43 43 19 03
Open daily 24 hours. M° Daumesnil.

Pharmacie Internationale

9th arr. - 5, pl. Pigalle
01 48 78 38 12, fax 01 48 78 32 64
Open Mon-Sat 8am-1pm, Sun noon-1am. M°
Pigalle.
See *Basics*, p. 145.

Pharmacie Les Champs

8th arr. - 84, av. des Champs-Élysées
01 45 62 02 41, fax 01 45 63 83 79
Open daily 24 hours. M° George-V.
Note the convenient, *all-day-all-night* hours of
this drugstore.

• RECORD STORES

FNAC Champs-Élysées

8th arr. - 74, av. des Champs-Élysées - 01 53 53 64 64
Open 10am-midnight. Closed Sun. M° George-V.
Music lovers' heaven, it must be, and there's
nearly 30,000 square feet of it! And what a location—on the most beautiful avenue in the world,
under (it's in the basement) one of the most
famous of famous covered walkways, the
Claridge. Other «media» as well: video cassettes
and computer software. You can also purchase
tickets for concerts, the theatre, and other cultural events.

Virgin Mégastore

1st arr. - Galerie du Carrousel du Louvre,
99, rue de Rivoli - 01 49 53 52 90, fax 01 49 53 52 57
Open Sun-Tue 11am-8pm, Wed-Sat 11am-11pm.
M° Palais-Royal.
8th arr. - 52, av. des Champs-Élysées
01 49 53 50 00, fax 01 49 53 50 40
Open Mon-Sat 10am-midnight, Sun & hols noon-
midnight. M° George-V.
Jazz, classical, pop, and rock, on records, CDs,
and cassettes—but that's not all: there are books
(on the lower level) too, video and audio gear,
computer equipment, as well as a ticket agency
for concerts and musical events.

• *24-HOUR POST OFFICE*

Poste du Louvre

1st arr. - 52, rue du Louvre - 01 40 28 20 00
Open daily 24 hours. M° Louvre-Rivoli.
The central post office is open 24 hours a day.
Long-distance telephone calls can be made from
the first floor, ordinary postal transactions on the
ground floor.

PERFUM

L'Artisan Parfumeur

4th arr. - 32, rue du Bourg-Tibourg
01 48 04 55 66
*Open Mon 1:30pm-7:30pm, Tue-Sat 10:30am-
7:30pm. Closed Sun. M° Hôtel de Ville.*
7th arr. - 24, bd Raspail - 01 42 22 23 32
9th arr. - 22, rue Vignon - 01 42 66 32 66
*Open 10:30am-7pm. Closed Sun. M° Sèvres-
Babylone, Madeleine.*
This perfumer's shop looks like a stage set, rich
with gilt and velvet drapery. The fragrances are
equally voluptuous, based on musk, gardenia,
rose, iris...not, we emphasize, the sort of scents
worn by shrinking violets! We like the sensual
Mûre et Musc (385 F). Popular as well are the
aromatic pomanders that diffuse these heady
perfumes, and an exquisite selection of gift
items: jewelry, fans, combs, and other decorative
trifles.

Comptoir Sud-Pacifique

2nd arr. - 17, rue de la Paix - 01 42 61 74 44
Open 9:30am-7:30pm. Closed Sun. M° Opéra.
Josée Fournier has a passion for Polynesia. She
was the first to market monoï oil in Paris some
years ago, and followed up that initial success
with a line of perfumes that recall her beloved
Pacific islands. Their practical packaging (roll-
on perfume, aluminum flasks) make her exotic
scents even more attractive. Fragrances can be
concocted to your specifications for 150 to 950 F,
depending on the ingredients. You'll also want
to try the ginseng shampoo, wild-berry exfoliat-
ing gel, and vanilla body oil. Pretty travel accessories, bath scents, and perfumed candles
complete the Comptoir's range of divinely fragrant merchandise. New store dedicated to men
at 26, pl. Vendôme, first arr., tel. 01 42 61 03 28.

Annick Goutal

1st arr. - 14, rue de Castiglione - 01 42 60 52 82
Also: 6th arr., 7th arr., 17th arr.
Open 10am-7pm. Closed Sun. M° Opéra.
Annick Goutal's unique fragrances are sold in
elegant boutiques decorated in beige and gold
tones. Our favorite scents are the deliciously
citrusy Eau d'Hadrien, romantic Heure Exquise,

and ultrafeminine Rose Absolue. The newest
addition to the range is the intensely fruity Petite
Chérie. Goutal's soaps, bath oils, and scented
pebbles (to scatter in lingerie drawers) make
wonderful gifts.

Guerlain

8th arr. - 88, av. des Champs-Élysées
01 45 62 52 57, fax 01 40 74 09 91
*Open 9:45am-7pm. Closed Sun. M° Franklin-D.-
Roosevelt.*
One of the greatest names in perfume,
Guerlain's reputation is in no way inflated. The
house scents are distinguished, distinctive,
decidedly French. The names alone evoke a
magical, delicately fragranced world: Après
L'Ondée, Samsara, Chamade... For men, Habit
Rouge is a classy, classic scent; lovely too (but far
more expensive) is the sophisticated Mouchoir
de Monsieur. There are seven Guerlain shops in
Paris, but we love to visit the Champs-Élysées
branch, with its sleek Art Deco look. Don't miss
a sophisticated relaxing moment at one of
Guerlain's two beauty salons.

Maître Parfumeur
et Gantier

1st arr. - 5, rue des Capucines
01 42 96 35 13, fax 01 41 19 06 31
7th arr. - 84 bis, rue de Grenelle - 01 45 44 61 57
*Open 10:30am-6:30pm. Closed Sun. M° Opéra, Rue
du Bac.*
Jean-François Laporte's extravagant scents are
for those who like to leave a trail of lingering
fragrance in their wake. Both men and women
can find assertive toilet waters here, with evocative names like Rose Muskissime or Fleurs des
Comores. Laporte's signature scents are also
sold as pot-pourri or room fragrances. Don't
miss his elegant, very dandified perfumed
gloves.

Patricia de Nicolaï

7th arr. - 80, rue de Grenelle - 01 45 44 59 59
*Open 10am-6:30pm. Closed Sun, Mon. M° Rue du
Bac.*
Guerlain's granddaughter, Patricia de Nicolaï,
perpetuates the family tradition of creating
enchanting perfumes. To date, her collection
comprises nine scents for women and four for
men. We especially like Sacre Bleu, Le Temps
d'une Fête, and the new Rose Pivoine, very
flowery of course (347 F for 100 ml). Alongside
perfumed candles, room sprays, and pot-pour-
ris, you'll find delicate carved crystal *flacons*,
which can be engraved with your name.

Jean Patou

8th arr. - 7, rue St-Florentin - 01 44 77 33 00
*Open 10am-1pm & 2pm-7pm. Closed Sat, Sun. M°
Concorde.*
Normandie, L'Heure Attendue, Moment
Suprême, etc. The celebrated creator of Joy per-
fume has reissued a dozen of the house's top

scents, launched between 1925 and 1964 (5,970 F for 30 ml in a Baccarat crystal flacon). They are available once more in this attractive shop, where you can also obtain the famed Huile de Chaldée, an oil that ensures an even, golden tan.

Sephora

16th arr. - 50, rue de Passy - 01 53 92 28 20
Open Mon-Sat 9:30am-7:30pm. Closed Sun. M°
Passy.

Also: 1st arr., 8th arr. (see below), 9th arr., 13th arr., 14th arr.

If you'd rather avoid dealing with salespeople, and prefer to read labels, look at bottles, and decide for yourself what makeup you need, then Sephora, the «beauty supermarket», is for you. Cosmetics and perfumes of every type are on offer: face creams, body-care products, cosmetics, and lots of accessories (hairbrushes, barrettes, mirrors, etc.) from major manufacturers are all neatly displayed.

Beauty on Board

Customers enter via a descending ramp—lined with a «wall of perfume», a veritable museum of beautiful flacons that show off the products to advantage—in a temple dedicated to perfume and cosmetics. Shoppers then arrive in an emporium that exudes luxury and calm, decorated in black and white, like the company's other stores.

The huge shop (1,500 square meters, and 500 meters long!) pays homage to perfume and everything related to it. Browsers can take their time examining the thousand and one new beauty products. In the salesroom, you will find absolutely every brand of perfume available, and almost all brands of cosmetics (altogether, there are more than 13,000 articles) for women, men and children. Adjoining the salesroom are four innovative departments:

- *L'Orge des Parfums*, located at the bottom of the ramp, is a permanent attraction where a specialist is on hand to explain the art of perfume-making, enabling you to deepen your knowledge of perfume instead of just looking at the bottles;
- *Les Sources de Lumière*, where customers can test their makeup in all the different varieties of day and night light;
- *Le Linéaire Culturel*, where you will find everything you ever wanted to know about perfumes and cosmetics through books, magazines, CDs, CD ROMs, videos, etc;
- *Two galleries* with exhibitions that change several times a year.

This is the ultimate in perfume and cosmetics shops, and the prices are actually reasonable. Even if you are not shopping for anything in particular, it is worth a visit just to see the first boutique that unites culture and communications with perfume and cosmetics.

Sephora, 70 av. des Champs-Élysées, 8th arr. - tel 01 53 93 22 50, fax 01 53 93 22 51.

Open Mon-Sat 10am-midnight, Sun & hols noon-midnight. M° Franklin-D.-Roosevelt.

OUT OF PARIS

A ring of forests and meadows

Those lucky Parisians! Not only do they have the rare good fortune to live in a glorious city; that city is ringed with equally glorious woodlands and accessible countryside. Day-trippers from Paris can simply hop on a train and, an hour or so later, alight near one of half a dozen splendid forests complete with magnificent châteaux.

The forests are a legacy of the French monarchy. Avid hunters all, the kings of France naturally took a keen interest in their *chasses royales*, or private hunting grounds close to Paris, the capital of the realm. Thus the woodlands of the Ile-de- France, with their ancient stands of oak, beech, and hornbeam, have been exceptionally well preserved and responsibly managed over the centuries.

Senlis, for example, where Hugues Capet was elected king of France in 987, was a thickly forested royal estate favored for its excellent hunting. It is still hunting country today, as is neighboring **Chantilly**, long celebrated for densely wooded forests, alive with game. Likewise, the châteaux at *Fontainebleau, Rambouillet*, and *Saint-Germain-en-Laye* are still surrounded by vast stretches of woodland, where scions of the royal Valois and Bourbon dynasties once galloped in pursuit of boars and stags. Even **Versailles**, that epitome of regal grandeur, began life as a relatively humble hunting lodge lost amid swamps and trees.

Not everyone, of course, fancies the forest primeval. If more manicured landscapes are your preference, then why not visit the castle gardens at *Écouen* and *Rambouillet*, or Le Nôtre's baroque *jardins à la française* at **Vaux-le-Vicomte, Chantilly, Saint-Germain-en-Laye,** or **Versailles**?

For a rural antidote to urban stress, we recommend that you head for the farmlands of the Beauce region, southwest of Paris. The soothing sameness of these wheat-bearing plains is broken only by grain-gorged silos (this is the bread basket of France) and by the dramatic spires of **Chartres** cathedral. Or you could travel northwest from Paris, along the meanders of the Seine to where the Ile-de-France meets Normandy: here lies the Vexin, a region of farmlands and river valleys brimming with bucolic charm. This is where Claude Monet spent the last years of his life, painting in his garden at *Giverny*.

Plan to travel? Look for GaultMillau/Gayot's other Best of guides to Chicago, Florida, France, Germany, Hawaii, Hong Kong, Italy, London, Los Angeles, New England, New Orleans, New York, Paris, Paris & the Loire Valley, San Francisco, Thailand, Toronto, Washington, D.C., and more to come...

CHANTILLY

About 50 minutes, 50 kilometers north of Paris by the Autoroute du Nord A1, exit No. 7 Survilliers, then D 10, D 16, N 17 to La Chapelle-en-Serval, D 924A to Chantilly.

Thus, by venturing just 20, 30, or 50 miles beyond the Paris city limits and the bleaker *banlieues*, you'll discover serenely beautiful towns and countryside, bathed in the unique light that inspired not only Monet and the Impressionists, but also Corot, the Barbizon painters, Van Gogh, Derain, and the Fauvists. Punctuating these luminous landscapes are fascinating historic monuments and landmarks, as well as masterpieces of religious, civil, and domestic architecture—any of which would make an ideal destination for a fair-weather excursion.

Here, then, are our suggestions for ten easy day trips in the Ile-de-France, all calculated to combine fresh air and greenery with an equally healthy dose of culture. And naturally GaultMillau wouldn't dream of taking you anywhere without first scouting out the best places to dine and spend the night!

Reflected in the shimmering waters of its moat, the château de Chantilly looks like a fairytale castle, almost too perfect to be true. And in a way, it is: the Renaissance-style **Grand Château** isn't much more than 100 years old (although the adjoining **Petit Château** dates from the sixteenth century). The castle that previously stood on this site was razed during the Revolution by angry citizens for whom Chantilly, fief of two ancient warrior families, the Montmorencys and the Condés, symbolized aristocratic privilege and military might.

The Grand Château houses the **Musée Condé**, a jewel of a collection which ranges from the curious—a wax head of King Henri IV, the pink Condé diamond—to the sublime: Piero di Cosimo's *Portrait of Simonetta Vespucci*, Raphael's *Virgin of Loreto*, works by Botticelli, several pictures by Poussin, two masterpieces by Watteau, a splendid series of Renaissance portraits by the Clouet father and son (including the famous *Catherine de Médicis* and *Henri III*), and an admirable collection of illuminated manuscripts. Arranged just as the Duc d'Aumale, the last owner of Chantilly, left it (with orders that it never be changed), the museum has the personal and agreeably eccentric style of a private collection.

Connoisseurs of fine horseflesh know Chantilly as the site of a famous racetrack and Thoroughbred training center. A fascinating «living museum» devoted to horses occupies the colossal eighteenth-century stables. From an architectural viewpoint, these **Grandes Écuries** are more imposing than the château itself. But then that is not so surprising: the Prince of Condé, who built the stables, was convinced that he would be reincarnated as a horse!

The château's majestic **park**, complete with a canal, gardens, and pools planned by seventeenth-century landscape artist André Le Nôtre, is crisscrossed by shady walks and velvety lawns. But the immense (nearly 16,000-acre) Chantilly forest, with its hiking paths and ponds (the Étangs de Commelles), is by far the best choice for a long woodland ramble. Take care, though: between 9am and noon some 3,000 Thoroughbreds thunder into the forest for their morning workout!

The world's biggest hot-air balloon takes 30 visitors at a time up to an altitude of 150 meters for a bird's-eye view of Chantilly.

• *The Château de Chantilly*
is open:
- *Mar-Oct 10am-6pm;*
- *Nov-Feb 10:30am-12:45pm & 2pm-5pm*
- *closed Tue.*
Reservations: 03 44 62 62 62, fax 03 44 62 62 61, Mon-Fri 9am-noon &.2pm-5pm.
Admission: Château and park 39 F, reduced rate: 34 F, under 12: 12 F; park 17 F.
• *The Musée Vivant du Cheval*
is open:
- *Apr & Sep-Oct 10:30am-6:30pm, closed Tue;*
- *May & June daily 10:30am-6:30pm;*
- *Jul-Aug: Mon & Wed- Sun 10:30am-6:30pm, Tue 2pm-6:30pm;*
- *Nov-Mar Mon-Fri 2pm-6pm, Sat-Sun 10:30am-6:30pm.*
Information: 03 44 57 40 40, fax 03 44 57 29 92.
Admission: 50 F, reduced rate: 45 F, under 16: 35 F.
The ticket office closes one hour before the closing times indicated above.

• *RESTAURANTS & HOTELS*

Chantilly

Oise   60500

12/20 **Capitainerie du Château**
Château de Chantilly
03 44 57 15 89, fax 03 44 58 50 11
Lunch only. Open until 2:30pm (3pm Sat & Sun). Closed Tue, Jan-Feb. Pkg.
A convenient spot for lunch after touring the château and Musée Condé. The buffet features

fresh and inviting appetizers and decent desserts, served in two very pretty dining rooms. Friendly staff. C 140-220. M 95, 125 (Sun lunch).

Creil

Oise   *60100*
9 km N by N 16

[13] La Ferme de Vaux

Hameau de Vaux, 11 & 19, route de Vaux
03 44 24 76 76, fax 03 44 26 81 50
Closed Sun dinner. Open until 9:45pm. Terrace dining. Pkg.
　This former farmhouse with its inviting stone-walled dining room plays host to Denis Oudart's finesse-filled cuisine. His salad of pan-roasted red mullets brims with wonderful flavor, his veal kidneys are tender and savory (despite their bland jus), and the fresh fruit gratin served with a delicate Champagne sabayon is a scrumptious way to top off your meal. C 240-400. M 150, 200.

La Ferme de Vaux

(See restaurant above)
Open year-round. 27 rms 295-345. Half-board 450. Rm ser. Pkg.
　Comfortable, well-equipped rooms located in the former farm's outbuildings. Charming welcome.

Gouvieux

Oise   *60270*
3 km W by D 909

Château de la Tour 🌲🍷

Chemin de la Chaussée
03 44 57 07 39, fax 03 44 57 31 97
Open year-round. 41 rms 530-930. Rms for disabled. Restaurant. Half-board 515. Heated pool. Pkg.
　A certain stateliness pervades this turn-of-the-century dwelling; the accommodations and public rooms are hugely comfortable in a way the French describe as «bourgeois». And there are magnificent grounds to stroll in, as well as a delightful heated pool.

Lamorlaye

Oise   *60260*
7 km S by N 16

Hostellerie du Lys 🌲🍷

In Lys-Chantilly, 63, 7e-Avenue
03 44 21 26 19, fax 03 44 21 28 19
Open year-round. 31 rms 300-400. Rms for disabled. Restaurant. Half-board 510. Rm ser. Pkg.

This opulent country inn, situated in large, lush grounds, provides comfortable rooms in a friendly, restful atmosphere. Tennis courts and golf course are within easy reach.

Montgrésin

Oise   *60560*
7 km SE on D 924A

12/20 Relais d'Aumale

37, pl. des Fêtes - 03 44 54 61 31, fax 03 44 54 69 15
Closed Dec 21-28. Open until 10pm. Garden dining. Tennis. Pkg.
　When the weather is fine, you can enjoy the sky and trees as your outdoor dining canopy at this restaurant's forest glade location. Good curried lobster ravioli, beef fillet with a meagerly peppered sauce but an out-of-this-world potato galette, and an impeccable chocolate feuillantine. Let the new sommelier guide you through the extensive offerings in the cellar. C 280-400. M 220-335 (Sun), 210.

Relais d'Aumale

(See restaurant above)
Open year-round. 2 stes 700-900. 22 rms 480-620. Rms for disabled. Half-board 480-740 (oblig in seas). Tennis. Pkg.
　A primeval forest encircles this inviting old hunting lodge boasting sunny, cheerful rooms done up on a modern note. All rooms are exceedingly well-equipped.

Vineuil-Saint-Firmin

Oise   *60500*
1.5 km E by D 924A & D 924

Golf-Hotel Blue Green 🌲🍷

Route d'Apremont, Domaine de Chantilly
03 44 58 47 77, fax 03 44 58 50 11
Open year-round. 2 stes 1,350. 107 rms 590-750. Rms for disabled. Restaurant. Half-board 480. Rm ser. Air cond. Tennis. Golf. Garage pkg.
　Here in the midst of the Chantilly forest is a long, low hotel with a neoclassic colonnade. Rooms are on the small side but are attractively decorated. Most open onto views of the hotel's eighteen-hole golf course.

See also **Senlis** *below.*

CHARTRES

About 1hr10, 90 kilometers southwest of Paris by Autoroute A6 towards Lyon, A10 towards Bordeaux, A11 towards Le Mans, exit No.2 Chartres, then N 10 to Chartres.

Long before Christianity had penetrated the Ile-de-France, before Caesar marched into Gaul—even then, Chartres was a holy place. Legend has it that every year Celtic druids assembled in Chartres to celebrate their mysteries around a sacred wellspring now immured in the cathedral crypt.

What is certain is that from the fourth century on, a sanctuary consecrated to the Virgin Mary brought the faithful to Chartres. When, in 876, Charles the Bald endowed the church with a precious relic (said to be the Virgin's tunic or veil), it gained even greater importance as a shrine, drawing pilgrims from all over Christendom in a steady stream that neither invasions, fires, nor revolutions have stanched. Even today, Catholic students organize a pilgrimage to Chartres each spring in honor of the Virgin.

The ancestor of the current **cathedral**, a Romanesque structure built in the eleventh and twelfth centuries, was ravaged by fire in 1194. The flames spared only the crypt, two towers, and the lower portion of the western façade, with its majestic Portail Royal. But the people of Chartres very quickly set about rebuilding their cathedral, with so mighty a collective will—and generous contributions from rich lords and wealthy townspeople—that it was completed in the impressively short span of just 30 years. It is to the builders' speed that the cathedral owes its exceptional stylistic unity. And it is to their skill in applying new architectural advances—notably the flying buttress—that Chartres owes its soaring height and rare luminosity. Since the buttresses shouldered weight that would otherwise have fallen on the walls, the builders could make the walls higher, with taller windows.

It would be impossible for us to do justice here to the esthetic and spiritual riches of Chartres. A visitor with plenty of time, patience, curiosity, and an observant eye will find innumerable sources of pleasure and interest. Here, however, are a couple of features worth noting, one outside and one inside the cathedral.

The Portail Royal, unscathed by the fire of 1194, is one of the oldest examples of Gothic sculpture in existence. While the emphasis of the ensemble is on the figure of Christ, depicted in infancy and in majesty above each of the three doors, viewers often feel irresistibly drawn to the nineteen elongated figures, a combination of statue and column, that stand aligned on either side of the doors. Interestingly, these Old Testament figures belong to two different eras, the Romanesque and the Gothic; they are the survivors of the old cathedral and, at the same time, heralds of the new sculptural style that first emerged at Chartres. In their extraordinarily sensitive faces, in the contrast between their expressive features and their rigid, stylized bodies, a visitor can trace the mysterious passage from one age—one way of viewing and representing human reality—to another.

Inside the cathedral, among the ravishing, jewel-like shadows and colors of stained glass, there are three windows and a portion of another which, like the Portail Royal, predate the great fire. They are the windows inserted into the western façade, which depict the genealogy, life, and resurrection of Christ, and to the left, the fragment known as Notre Dame de la Belle Verrière (*The Madonna of the Window*), one of Chartres's most venerated images. They merit your special attention because they are the sole remaining examples of the miraculous *bleu de Chartres*, a blue tint rich (as we now know) in cobalt and copper, which for centuries no glassmaker managed to reproduce.

In medieval times, Chartres was a flourishing town, its wealth based on cloth and farming. It was also an intellectual center, with a renowned philosophy school. Investigating the many ancient houses and churches in the **Old Quarter** (the fifteenth-century Maison du Saumon and the Hôtel de la Caige; the medieval church of Saint-Pierre, with its striking stained glass) can be an extremely rewarding way to spend an afternoon.

Agriculture still thrives hereabouts, and the prosperous Beaucerons are fond of the table. Between a tour of the cathedral and a stroll through the town, hungry visitors will find any number of excellent eating places where they may relax and restore themselves.

- *The cathedral*

is open:
- *Mon-Sat 7:30am-7:15pm;*
- *Sun & hols 8:30am-7pm.*
- *Guided tours in English are scheduled regularly.*
- *For additional information,*
  contact the *Office de Tourisme, Pl. de la Cathédrale, tel. 02 37 21 50 00, fax 02 37 21 51 91.*

• RESTAURANTS & HOTELS

Chartres

Eure-et-Loir 28000

 ### Le Buisson Ardent

10, rue au Lait - 02 37 34 04 66, fax 02 37 91 15 82
Closed Sun dinner. Open until 9:30pm. Terrace dining.
To judge by this restaurant's location in the shadow of the cathedral, one is likely to expect yet another tourist eatery with stratospheric prices. Not at all. The menu features nicely crafted dishes made from fresh market produce. Courteous, lively service; worthwhile cellar. C 300. M 128-228.

 ### Le Grand Monarque

22, pl. des Épars - 02 37 21 00 72, fax 02 37 36 34 18
Open daily until 10pm. Terrace dining. Valet pkg.
Is this Chartres or the Loire Valley? You'll wonder as your eyes float down the wine list of over 300 wines where the entire repertoire of Loire Valley wines is represented. The bacchic element is certainly one of the strong points of this veritable institution orchestrated by Georges Jallerat. Generation after generation of bourgeoisie of this region called the Beauce have paraded through these premises. Delight in timeless dishes such as Tours-style egg croustade or pheasant pâté en croûte, or venture to try more timely dishes such as the pike perch roasted in hazelnut oil or the truffled scallops in broth. M 163-294.

 ### Novotel

Av. Marcel-Proust
02 37 88 13 50, fax 02 37 30 29 56
Open year-round. 78 rms 410-485. Rms for disabled. Restaurant. Pool. Pkg.
This modern, functional hotel is located in a leafy setting and provides regularly refurbished rooms. Bar and terrace.

Hôtel de la Poste

3, rue du Général-Kœnig
02 37 21 04 27, fax 02 37 36 42 17
Open year-round. 57 rms 295-330. Restaurant. Half-board 300-330. Garage pkg.
Here's an efficiently modernized hotel close to the cathedral. The soundproofed rooms offer all the comforts one could require, and there is a bar as well as a restaurant on the premises.

 ### La Truie qui File

Pl. de la Poissonnerie
02 37 21 53 90, fax 02 37 36 62 65
Closed Sun dinner, Mon, Aug. Open until 9:30pm. Terrace dining. Air cond.
The fifteenth-century half-timber façade and upper-storey overhang may be some of the oldest in Chartres, but the spacious, comfortable interior is completely contemporary, in keeping with Gilles Choukroun's inspired cuisine. We think that he has a true sense of discovery and refined elegance, both in terms of the combinations of delicate flavors he ventures to put together as well as in the sometimes undreamt-of resources he digs up from this Beauce region. Some of the dishes are musts: the highly original soft-boiled egg with caviar and pig trotter jelly; the vanilla-scented lobster dressed up with artichokes; the succulent tagine-style roast lamb; or the farm-raised guinea fowl and fresh almonds garnished with white-beet leaves. Pilgrims to this mecca of Christians will certainly opt for the reasonably priced 180 F set-price meal in all its perfection. Studied effort towards the wine, cigars, and even the bread, which is a shining example of what bread *should* taste like. C 400-500. M 180-360.

 ### Saint-Hilaire

11, rue du Pont-Saint-Hilaire
02 37 30 97 57, fax 02 37 30 97 57
Closed Sat lunch, Sun, Dec 24-Jan 7, Jul 27-Aug 17. Open until 9:30pm. Terrace dining.
This harmonious cuisine so conscious of the quality of each and every product gets another point this year. On the 145 F menu: scorpion fish in broth livened up with fresh spring herbs, trout stuffed full of vegetables and served with watercress sauce, country-style cheeses, and a Chartres pavé (sliced pain d'épices with cinnamon ice cream) on a bed of seasonal fruits. Solicitous service in a beautifully redone house. The wine waiter is amiable, but the cellar prices less so. M 250. M 198 (lunch, wine incl), 95-245.

 ### La Vieille Maison

5, rue au Lait - 02 37 34 10 67, fax 02 37 91 12 41
Closed Sun dinner, Mon. Open until 9:30pm. Terrace dining.
Chef Bruno Letartre officiates at this fourteenth-century house featuring rustico-bourgeois décor. Food lovers are sure to enjoy his classic cuisine revisited: duck pâté en croûte, tender farm-raised squab with wild mushrooms, delectable pear and chocolate tart. Somewhat costly cellar. C 350-400. M 160-350.

And also...

Our selection of places for inexpensive, quick, or late-night meals.
Café Serpente (02 37 21 68 81 - 2, cloître Notre-Dame. Open daily until 11:45pm, 12:45am in summer.): Located opposite the cathedral, this simpatico bistro draws quite a crowd any time of day or night, eager to tuck into its nicely done (though predictable) brasserie fare. Small, fairly priced cellar. Friendly, quick service—despite the throngs (150).
Les Épars (02 37 21 23 72 - 11, pl. des Épars.

Closed Sun dinner, Mon, Aug 1-10. Open until 10pm.): Just opposite the Grand Monarque. Classic cooking, with simple, sincere set-price menus (80-160).

St-Symphorien-le-Château

Eure-et-Loir   28700
25 km E by N 10 & D 18

 ### Château d'Esclimont

02 37 31 15 15, fax 02 37 31 57 91
Open daily until 9:30pm. Terrace dining. Pool. Tennis. Valet pkg.
   Marie Mon Plaisir 170 (Marie my joy, or shall we say, Marie my beloved mistress) is the motto that the Duc de La Rochefoucauld had engraved above the entrance to this ravishing Renaissance château, a glowing gem tucked into a green, green valley and topped off with fairy-tale towers and moats. And pleasure is what awaits you still, even though our last meal left us a little hungry. It is true that chef Olivier Dupart has a well-honed technique and resourcefully uses deluxe products full of flavors he blends in friendly ways, but even if the oysters chaud-froid with chive cream sauce was finely finished, the pike perch in beer butter sauce was on the simplistic side, and the morello cherry and chocolate fondant was frankly overcooked. The waiters and waitresses carry the platters around on their shoulder just like in a beer hall. The wine cellar is rich, just like the guests. Our faith remains, and so does their mark. C 400-600. M 260 (weekday lunch, wine incl), 320-495.

Château d'Esclimont ♠♥

(See restaurant above)
Open year-round. 5 stes 2,900. 48 rms 650-1,850. Half-board 765-1,415. Rm ser. Pool. Tennis. Valet pkg.
   The 48 rooms and 5 suites of this sixteenth-century château are classic, comfortable, and handsomely situated amid 150 acres of enclosed grounds. The site is at the bottom of a valley traversed by a river, near the road that connects Rambouillet and Chartres. Guests can play tennis, swim in the heated pool, and attend wintertime musical evenings. Perfect for a luxurious, romantic weekend, and only 45 minutes from Paris by car. There's even a helipad. Relais et Châteaux, of course.

ÉCOUEN

About 45 minutes, 19 km north of Paris by Autoroute du Nord A1, exit No.3, then N 1 & N 16.

One needn't travel all the way to the Loire Valley to view a superb French Renaissance château. Just 20 or so kilometers north of Paris, stands Écouen, an admirably preserved castle built between 1538 and 1555 for King François Ier's closest comrade-in-arms, Constable Anne de Montmorency (the same man who commissioned the first château at Chantilly).
   As befitted a great feudal lord and powerful military chief, the constable made Écouen a formidable fortress. Situated on a hill overlooking the broad plain below, surrounded by moats and fortified by steeply sloping walls, Écouen was designed to withstand even artillery fire—a wise precaution on the eve of the Wars of Religion, which ravaged the region in the later sixteenth century.
   Yet the constable and his wife, Madeleine de Savoie, were also humanists and patrons of the arts, who engaged the best architects and sculptors of the day to embellish their home. An equestrian statue of Anne de Montmorency in Roman warrior garb once stood in the portico that leads to the grand courtyard, attesting to the constable's taste for antiquity. That taste is reflected in the château's architecture. Niches in the monumental colonnade of the southern (left) wing once housed Michelangelo's *Slaves* (now in the Louvre), presented to the constable by King Henri II.
   In 1632, the constable's grandson, Henri II de Montmorency, was accused of conspiracy against the Cardinal de Richelieu, and beheaded. Écouen then reverted to the Condé family, but they spent little time there, preferring their estate at Chantilly. During the Revolution, the contents of the castle were confiscated by the state, and eventually dispersed.
   Since 1962, Écouen has housed the **Musée de la Renaissance**, a unique collection of period French, Italian, and Flemish furniture and decorative arts. The most dazzling exhibit is surely the 246-foot-long tapestry displayed in the Galerie de Psyché. Woven in Brussels in the early sixteenth century, this masterpiece of silk, wool, and silver thread relates the story of David and Bathsheba.
   What makes all the objects on view particularly interesting is their setting in the château's authentic, beautifully restored

Renaissance interior. Do take the time to examine and admire the immense fireplaces, decorated with biblical scenes, for which Écouen was famous in its heyday. And nothing gives a better idea of the grandeur of a Renaissance lord's castle than the Grande Salle in the King's apartment. A visitor cannot help but be impressed by the monumental fireplace of stucco and polychrome marble; or with the magnificent gold-and-cerulean tile floor displaying the entwined initials of Anne de Montmorency and Madeleine de Savoie.

We like to wind up a tour of Écouen with a stroll in the garden; the park affords an impressive, sweeping view of the plain below. Hardier souls may prefer to explore the forest that borders the château.

• *The Château d'Écouen*
is open 9:45am-12:30pm & 2pm-5:15pm, closed Tue & some hols.
Information: 01 34 38 38 50, fax 01 34 38 38 78.
Admission: 25 F, reduced rate: 17 F, under 18: free.

ENGHIEN-LES-BAINS

About 35 minutes, 18 km north of Paris by Autoroute A86, then Autoroute A15, exit No.2 Argenteuil/Enghien, N 113.

With its 90-acre lake, its gardens and its flowers Enghien-les-Bains is the oasis of Paris. Only 15 kilometers away from the hustle-bustle of the Place de l'Opéra, its Art Deco architecture and its quiet streets where small châteaux of the past century mingle with contemporary residences attract Parisians in quest of an refreshing break from the Megapole after a 15-minute train ride from the Gare du Nord.

You can go canoeing or sailing on the lake, or rest under the age-old plane trees, shop in the lazy pedestrian lanes. The more active come to watch the famous horse races.

But at 3pm every single day, a very different story commences. At this precise time, the Casino opens its doors until dawn or so. It is the only Casino in the entire Ile-de-France region and gamblers rush in, coming from everywhere to try their luck at roulette, baccarat, or black jack. It's usual to see sheikhs sitting elbow to elbow with luminaries from the international show biz world. Why bother after all going back to Paris in the middle of the night? Top notch hotels stand ready to comfort tired gamblers.

Les Jeux Sont Faits

Feeling lucky? Head for the Casino d'Enghien, a lakeside Art Deco gaming palace just outside of Paris. Ladies, you may don your diamonds (gentlemen, you must wear a tie) to bet on blackjack or baccara: fortunes are won and—mostly—lost as croupiers look on imperturbably.
Casino d'Enghien, 3, av. de Ceinture, 95880 Enghien-les-Bains, tel. 01 39 34 13 00, fax 01 39 34 13 01. Open daily 3pm-4am. Admission: 80 F. Proof of identity required.

Two centuries ago, who could have imagined such sparkling nights in the small hamlet of Enghien? The area was mostly known for its «stinking creek». But it turned out—thanks to the knowledge of a priest—that these malodorous liquids were indeed sulfur waters with strong healing powers. Drinking or spraying the waters was so effective in curing mouth and throat, bronchial and skin disorders, that Louis XVIII, suffering from a leg ulcer, came to Enghien and was almost miraculously cured.

Enghien became Enghien-les-Bains, and thanks to this illustrious patient acquired the status of fashionable resort that it has kept to this very day.

• *RESTAURANTS & HOTELS*

Enghien-les-Bains
Val-d'Oise 95800

12/20 L'Auberge Landaise
32, bd d'Ormesson - 01 34 12 78 36
Closed Sun dinner, Wed, Feb school hols, Aug. Open until 9pm. Terrace dining.
A pleasant little jaunt into the land of the Gascons, where the *patronne* gives quick Parisian-style service in her fun-loving manner. «Today we have pike perch, red mullet and pigeon—poor dumb animals», she said recently. And any restaurant owner who recommends the cheapest wines on the list is to be believed! Healthy servings of dishes such as the little artichoke hearts with Bayonne country ham or the duck breast with green peppercorn sauce, but the crêpes were served in anorexic portions. C 200-250.

Le Grand Hôtel d'Enghien

85, rue du Général-de-Gaulle
01 39 34 10 00, fax 01 39 34 10 01
Open year-round. 3 stes 920. 44 rms 650-720. Restaurant.
This lakeside luxury hotel, right next to the Casino, boasts a handsome wood-paneled lobby and a glass elevator. The superb roomy guest rooms are decorated in Louis XV or Louis XVI style, with room-controlled air conditioning and double glazing. Charming hostesses.

Hôtel du Lac d'Enghien

89, av. du Général-de-Gaulle
01 39 34 11 00, fax 01 39 34 11 01
Open year-round. 7 stes 690-750. 102 rms 530-570. Restaurant. Half-board 715-795. Pkg.
This hotel is the little «brother» of the Grand Hôtel just across the lake. The lovely view enhances the soundproofed rooms with their red and ocher décor.

Montmorency

Val-d'Oise   *95160*
4 km NE by N 311

12/20   Au Cœur de la Forêt

Av. du Repos-de-Diane - 01 39 64 99 19
Closed Mon, dinner Sun & Thu, 10 days in Feb, Aug 16-Sep 7. Open until 9:30pm. Terrace dining. Pkg.
Next time you go walking in the Montmorency forest, ferret around until you find this establishment hidden among the trees. You'll enjoy the family atmosphere and the nicely crafted, seasonal cuisine. Interesting selection of Bordeaux. C 300-380. M 130 (weekdays), 190.

FONTAINEBLEAU

About 1hr, 60 kilometers south of Paris by Autoroute du Sud A6, exit Fontainebleau, then N 37 towards Fontainebleau, N 7 to Fontainebleau.

Just as Versailles was created at the whim of young Louis XIV, Fontainebleau owes its splendor to the sudden caprice of Renaissance monarch François Ier, who in 1528 decided to transform a neglected royal manor near the forest of Bièvre into a personal residence fit for a king. After a humiliating two-year captivity in Madrid, the Roi Chevalier wanted to prove to Emperor Charles V and King Henry VIII of England (who were then erecting spectacular palaces at Grenada and Hampton Court, respectively) that he could equal, indeed surpass, them in magnificence.

Every aspect of the new château in Fontainebleau was calculated to glorify France's first absolute ruler. François Ier was the first French king, for example, to be addressed as «Majesty», a title previously reserved for the emperor. Today, his spirit is still tangibly present at Fontainebleau.

Over the centuries the actual architecture of the palace has undergone considerable alteration. The Galerie François Ier, the most celebrated decorative ensemble of the French Renaissance, was constructed between 1528 and 1530 and embellished with marvelous stuccowork and frescoes by the Florentine artist Il Rosso, a pupil of Michelangelo. Restored not long ago, the frescoes illustrate a complicated and fairly obscure symbolic scheme. One remarkable figure is an elephant emblazoned with fleur-de-lis and sporting a salamander (François Ier's emblem) on its forehead, an allegory of the royal virtue of wisdom. Other scenes commemorate the king's Italian campaigns or his role as a patron of art and literature.

The Salle de Bal (ballroom) is another impressive Renaissance creation. Commissioned by François Ier, it was completed under the supervision of his son, Henri II, by architect Philibert Delorme, who also worked on the Louvre. Here the frescoes—superbly restored—were designed by Il Primatice and executed by Niccolo dell'Abbate, two of the foremost Italian artists of what came to be known as the first Fontainebleau school. The ballroom created such a sensation in its day that painters and engravers came from all over to record its sumptuous decoration. Even now, the room provides a fairly accurate idea of the opulence of the Valois court.

Though Fontainebleau was relatively neglected during the second half of the sixteenth century, it flourished once again under Henri IV. Dating from this era are the Cabinet de Théagène (marvelously preserved, it was the birthplace of Louis XIII) and the Chapelle de la Trinité, decorated with biblical frescoes by Mathieu Fréminet, a French master of the Baroque.

The Bourbons made a habit of spending the autumn at Fontainebleau, and continued to embellish and enlarge the palace even after the court officially took up residence at Versailles. Marie-Antoinette, who loved Fontainebleau, completely redecorated several rooms, including the Salon du Jeu (Gaming Room) and the charming Boudoir de la Reine, which was designed by Mique, her favorite architect.

Napoléon, too, was fond of Fontainebleau, and refurnished the palace entirely. Today it boasts Europe's finest collection of Empire furniture, as well as extensive holdings of Napoleonic relics and memorabilia culled from various national museums. The emperor's private apartments were painstakingly restored: walls hung with silk brocade, precious furniture signed by Jacob Desmalter, and in the bedchamber an extraordinary ceremonial bed dressed in embroidered purple velvet compose a sumptuous ensemble. Among the relics on view is the little table on which Napoléon signed the Act of Abdication in 1814.

The palace is surrounded by what is surely one of the most beautiful forests in France. In autumn and winter, hunters still gallop through the russet groves of oak, riding to hounds just as French kings did centuries before them. Less bloodthirsty nature enthusiasts prefer to explore the innumerable bridle and hiking paths, or scramble around the spectacular rock formations, cliffs, and gorges that make the Forêt de Fontainebleau a challenging and highly popular training ground for aspiring alpinists.

• The *Château de Fontainebleau*
is open:
- Nov-Apr 9:30am-12:30pm & 2pm-5pm;
- May-Jun 9:30am-5pm;
- Jul-Aug 9:30am-6pm;
- Sep-Oct 9:30am-5pm;
- closed Tue, Jan 1, May 1, Dec 25.
The park and gardens are open 9am-5pm/8:30pm depending on the season, and free of charge.
Information: 01 60 71 50 70, fax 01 60 71 50 71.
Admission:
Great Apartments: 35 F, reduced rate: 23 F, under 18: free. The ticket office closes forty-five minutes before the closing times indicated above.
Chinese museum: same ticket. Open occasionally. Call Information the morning of your intended visit
Private Apartments: 16 F, reduced rate: 12 F, under 18: free. Open Mon & hols. On others days, call Information the morning of your intended visit.
• *Musée Napoléon I*
1-hour guided tour, only open upon reservatio. Call Information the morning of your intended visit.
Admission: 16 F, reduced rate: 12 F, under 18: free.
• The *Musée Napoléonien d'Art et d'Histoire Militaire*
88, rue Saint-Honoré, holds collections of uniforms, weapons, and military history.
Open: 2pm-5pm, closed Sun, Mon, & hols.
Information: 01 60 74 64 89.

Admission: 10 F, under 12: free; groups by appointment.

• RESTAURANTS & HOTELS

Fontainebleau

Seine-et-Marne   77300

 ## Le Beauharnais

27, pl. Napoléon-Bonaparte
01 60 74 60 00, fax 01 60 74 60 01
Closed Dec 22-30. Open until 10pm. Garden dining. Air cond. Heated pool. Valet pkg.
Rémy Bidron presents inventive, expertly crafted cuisine in a refined yet relaxed setting. We were mighty impressed by his 180 F set-price meal: spring salad with light flavorful Cabécou goat cheese, excellent scorpion fish steak partnered with light creamy clams, friendly combination of hot genepi soufflé and raspberry sorbet. Even the bread and coffee are first rate. The cellar holds a fine selection, something for every taste and every budget, including some exceptional vintage half-bottles. C 380-420. M 130-150 (weekdays), 180-450.

 ## Hôtel de l'Aigle Noir

(See restaurant above)
Open year-round. 2 stes 1,600-2,000. 55 rms 790-1,050. Rms for disabled. Half-board 685-725. Rm ser. Air cond. Heated pool. Valet pkg.
Opposite the château's gardens stands a peaceful, elegant hostelry, with luxurious rooms decorated in Louis XVI, Empire, or Restoration style. Amenities include satellite TV, books in English, a gym, and a sauna; active types can ride horses or use the indoor driving range. Courteous service.

12/20 Le Caveau des Ducs

24, rue de Ferrare - 01 64 22 05 05
Open daily until 10:30pm. Terrace dining. Air cond.
In a series of superbly vaulted, seventeenth-century cellar dining rooms located in the center of Fontainebleau, the chef serves forth cuisine geared to classic tastes: chausson of Burgundy snails flavored with mild garlic, duck breast cooked in cider vinegar and served with caramelized apples, and a delicate warm apple tart flambéed in Calvados for dessert. C 250-300. M 105 (weekdays), 185 (lunch, wine incl), 175-240.

 ## Grand Hôtel Mercure

41, rue Royale - 01 64 69 34 34, fax 01 64 69 34 39
Open daily until 11pm. Terrace dining. Air cond. Pkg.

Marc Polyte takes his cooking seriously, and the result is well-crafted. That doesn't keep him from offering an array of affordable fixed-price meals, however, such as the 105 F Diana menu. Shoots of young spinach adorn the pan-fried veal sweetbreads, sole filets are napped in a freshwater crayfish sauce, and sage-scented roast lamb médaillons snuggle up alongside a «jealous» potato pancake. Tempt yourself with the Premier Cru Chablis at 123 F. C 170-210. M 105 (weekdays), 150 (Sun lunch, wine incl).

 ### Grand Hôtel Mercure

(See restaurant above)
Open year-round. 6 stes 600-830. 91 rms 510-630. Half-board 350-500. Tennis. Pkg.
Sunny rooms offering tuck-you-in comfort in this hotel with its smiling efficient service. Certain to be a highly pleasing stopoff, viewing the verdancy of the park and its prime location just around the corner from the château. Well-kept place.

 ### Napoléon 🌲🍷

9, rue Grande
01 60 39 50 50, fax 01 64 22 20 87
Closed Dec 21-30. 1 ste 850-1,150. 56 rms 490-800. Restaurant. Half-board 620-910. Rm ser. Garage pkg.
This beautiful hotel in the town center provides good service, excellent bathrooms, and rooms with every comfort. Note that those facing the courtyard are bigger and quieter.

 ### Victoria

112, rue de France
01 60 74 90 00, fax 01 60 74 90 10
Open year-round. 1 ste 670. 19 rms 250-365. Rms for disabled. Restaurant. Half-board 380-510. Rm ser. Garage pkg.
This hotel features quiet rooms on the gardens. Lots of simple, homey atmosphere (this place is a favorite among anglophone guests on extended stays).

Barbizon

Seine-et-Marne 77630
11 km N by N 7 & N 37

12/20 Auberge Les Alouettes

4, rue Antoine Barye
01 60 66 41 98, fax 01 60 66 20 69
Closed Sun dinner. Open until 9:30pm. Terrace dining. Tennis. Pkg.
It's a toss-up as to whether to sit outdoors and enjoy the surrounding flora and fauna, or indoors in the cozy dining room done up with attractive coffered ceilings. But wherever you settle, you're sure to enjoy the resolutely traditional fare on hand here, prepared with panache and served up in generous portions. Smallish, high-priced cellar. C 330-500. M 160, 190.

 ## Auberge Les Alouettes

(See restaurant above)
Open year-round. 22 rms 180-380. Half-board 435-675. Rm ser. Tennis. Pkg.
Lost in the cool calm away from the main thoroughfare, this homey hotel offers hospitable guest rooms. Linger in the lounge chairs in the flowery park, or on colder days, in the little living room, where you can peck out a few notes on the piano.

 ## Le Bas Bréau

22, rue Grande - 01 60 66 40 05, fax 01 60 69 22 89
Open daily until 9:30pm. Garden dining. Heated pool. Tennis. Valet pkg.
This may be a veritable old «institution»; its walls may well speak of the colorful past of the many painters, writers, dignitaries and lovers who have haunted this site, and of the family who has owned it for a century, but that doesn't make its classic cuisine out of date. What in the past had a tendency to be complicated and showy has fine-tuned its act, with a decided return to simpler ways inspired by excellent products. Regal langoustines perfectly roasted in tarragon butter; tender, juicy Corrèze milkfed-veal chop with exquisitely fresh little chanterelles; wildly tasty wild-strawberry shortbread. The cellar is outstanding, the service is of the *grand restaurant* variety, and, you guessed it, it is priced accordingly. The extra point is well deserved. C 500-750. M 350 (weekday lunch, wine incl), 400.

 ## Le Bas Bréau 🌲🍷

(See restaurant above)
Open year-round. 8 stes 1,700-3,000. 12 rms 900-1,500. Rms for disabled. Half-board 1,200. Rm ser. Air cond. Heated pool. Tennis. Valet pkg.
In the past, it was Stevenson and the Fontainbleau School of painters who relished in the luxurious charm of this hunting lodge; today, you can do so, alongside chiefs of state and lovers out for a weekend in the country. The guest rooms are the epitome of good taste. The setting is splendiferous, the service charming, and the breakfasts sublime: wonderful coffee, fresh pastries, and homemade jams. Relais et Châteaux.

 ## Hostellerie Les Pléiades

21, rue Grande - 01 60 66 40 25, fax 01 60 66 41 68
Open daily until 9:30pm. Garden dining. Pkg.
The premises once belonged to the painter Daubigny, and the spacious, nicely decorated dining room, with its cozy hearth and two charming garden extensions, provides a wonderfully relaxing mealtime setting. Owners Yolande and Roger Karampournis' personal touch sets the tone, and chef Paul Gallot's resolutely classical cuisine proves fresh, light, and eminently flavorful. Spot-on cellar. C 300-350. M 185-280.

Hostellerie Les Pléiades

(See restaurant above)
Open year-round. 1 ste 620. 23 rms 270-550. Half-board 390-490. Rm ser. Pkg.
Rooms in the elegant manor house or its extension, La Villa, can be on the smallish side, but all very cozy and prettily decorated and feature nice bathrooms. Charming welcome.

Bourron-Marlotte

Seine-et-Marne   77780
7 km S on N 7

 ### Les Prémices

12 bis, rue B.-de-Montesquiou
01 64 78 33 00, fax 01 64 78 36 00
Closed Sun dinner, Mon. Open until 9:30pm. Terrace dining. Pool. Tennis. Pkg.
Dominique Maës, who had already captivated our attention in Barbizon, has just landed firmly on his feet in the Orangerie of the ravishing Château de Bourron, the former residence of the Montesquiou-Fezensac family. The bright contemporary décor sets the mood for a clear-cut precise style of cooking inspired by the best of products and a slight touch of Provence: pan-fried foie gras with Usson quince brandy sauce; gently-spiced and roasted lobster; galinette (a Mediterranean fish) cooked in a fondue dish with onion greens, sweet peppers and bouillabaisse juice; rack and saddle of milkfed lamb roasted with thyme juice. The cheese comes from the noted Barthélemy's in Fontainebleau. A timid start compared to the daringness he demonstrated in Barbizon. Véronique Maës will welcome you with all her graciousness. C 350-450. M 150-195.

Thomery

Seine-et-Marne   77810
8 km E on N 6 & D 137

 ### Le Vieux Logis

5, rue Sadi-Carnot
01 60 96 44 77, fax 01 60 70 01 42
Open daily until 9:45pm. Garden dining. Heated pool. Tennis. Garage pkg.
The success of Le Vieux Logis stems from a team effort that starts with the way guests are greeted and extends all the way through to the way food is cooked. Madame Plouvier rules the roost here with an iron hand in a velvet glove, and the 145 F price of the short set menu is a real *tour de force*, especially in such a refined setting. Indulge in the wonderful fish and precisely prepared garden vegetables. This is one of those restaurants that's well worth the trip from Moret-sur-Loing or Fontainebleau. The desserts are inventive, and the cellar, presided over by

Monsieur Plouvier, is a reasonably priced work in progress. C 300-350. M 145-240.

 ## Le Vieux Logis

(See restaurant above)
Open year-round. 14 rms 400. Rm ser. Heated pool. Tennis. Garage pkg.
This establishment, located in a peaceful little village renowned for its twelfth-century church, offers sunny rooms, bountiful breakfasts, and great prices. If you're tired (or just in love!), you can dine by candlelight right in your room.

See also **Vaux-le-Vicomte** *below.*

GIVERNY

About 1hr10, 70 km by Autoroute A13, exit No.14 Vernon, then N 15 towards Rouen, D 100, D 201, D 5 to Giverny.

It isn't a palace or royal legend that brings travelers to this tiny village 75 kilometers northwest of Paris, on the border of the Ile-de-France and Normandy regions; what draws crowds to Giverny is the artistic legacy of Claude Monet. From 1883 until his death in 1926, Monet lived and worked in these sublime surroundings, a setting he created largely by and for himself. Giverny provided the light, the landscape, and the meandering Seine that the painter so loved. But Monet himself supplied the grand design, as well as 40 years of unrelenting efforts to make his ravishing garden a reality. It soon became the central motif of his pictures, and in the end, his garden was the only subject that Monet chose to paint.

Shortly before his death, assailed with doubts about the value of his pictures despite public acclaim for them, Monet came to regard the garden at Giverny as his ultimate creation. He employed six full-time gardeners to tend it, day in and day out. Sadly, Monet's beloved garden slowly went to seed after the painter died. Then in 1977 the American Versailles-Giverny Foundation undertook to restore it, along with Monet's house and studio. Well before Europe recognized his genius, America had embraced Monet at his first New York show in 1889. Now, owing in large part to American generosity, Monet's admirers may visit the house where he worked and entertained fellow artist Mary Cassatt, the poet Mallarmé, and many more.

Nothing less resembles a formal French garden than Giverny's glorious, painterly composition of flowers, water, and greenery. Ordinary fruit trees were banished from the orchard where the flower garden now blooms; Monet replaced them with exotic Japanese strains of ornamental cherry and apple. With the arrival of spring, perennial beds lose their disciplined, linear look under an exuberance of bright blossoms. Interestingly, except for the roses and peonies, all the flowers at Giverny are humble varieties: iris, foxglove, poppies, and lupine. Yet they are planted so artfully and their colors, textures, and shapes are arrayed to such advantage that an observer's eye roams over the banks and borders of the garden with as much pleasure as it does over Monet's *Water Lilies*, which hangs in the Orangerie in Paris.

At the far end of the winding central path—take care not to trample the nasturtiums, which grow pretty much wherever they please—is the famous pond that Monet always insisted on showing off to his guests after lunch (he had paid a not-so-small fortune to have it installed). In spring, a curtain of languid wisteria nearly hides the «Japanese bridge», which looks out over a hypnotizing profusion of water lilies. Massed on the surface of the pond, they seem to form a huge artist's palette of delicate tints: white, yellow, pink, blue, and mauve.

The house and studios at Giverny—including one Monet had built specially to paint *Les Nymphéas*—give the haunting impression of being actually inhabited; it's as if the people who lived and worked there have only just stepped out for a moment. Everything is exactly as it was on an ordinary day at the turn of the century, from the pots and pans set out in the kitchen (Monet loved rich, complicated cooking), to the master's fascinating collection of Japanese prints. To borrow a phrase from Marcel Proust, Monet's contemporary and admirer, the evocative atmosphere of Giverny rewards the pilgrims who journey there with a sense of time recaptured.

• *The Musée Claude Monet*
84 rue Claude Monet and the gardens are open Apr-Oct 10am-6pm, closed Mon (exc Easter & Whit-Monday).
Information: 02 32 51 28 21, fax 02 32 51 54 18.
Admission: 35 F for the house and gardens, reduced rate: 25 F, children age 7 to 12: 20 F, under 7: free; 25 F for the gardens.
• *Visit also the Musée d'Art Américain*
99, rue Claude-Monet. Founded in 1992 by American art patrons Daniel and Judith Terra, the museum exhibits the work of American Impressionists who painted in France between 1865 and 1915.
Open Apr-Oct 10am-6pm, closed Mon (exc Easter & Whit-Monday).

Information: 02 32 51 94 65, fax 02 32 51 94 67.
Admission: 35 F, reduced rate 60: 20 F, children age 7 to 12: 15 F, under 7: free; groups by appointment: 20 F.

• RESTAURANTS & HOTELS

Giverny

Eure   27620

12/20 Les Jardins de Giverny

Chemin du Roy - 02 32 21 60 80, fax 02 32 51 93 77
Closed Sun dinner, Mon, Feb. Open until 9pm. Terrace dining. Pkg.
A stone's throw from Claude Monet's house, this fine Norman dwelling sits in a dreamy estate filled with roses and rare species of trees. The elegant white-beamed décor serves as setting for a cuisine inspired by its region, with a special fondness for sauces such as the cider vinegar beurre blanc on the andouille sausage puff pastry, or the cider cream on the braised scallops. C 250. M 130 (weekdays), 170-230.

Les Andelys

Eure   27700
28 km N by N 15, D 316 & D 313

La Chaîne d'Or

27, rue Grande - 02 32 54 00 31, fax 02 32 54 05 68
Closed Sun dinner, Mon, Jan. Open until 9:30pm. Terrace dining. Pkg.
In her superb Norman inn on the banks of the stately Seine, Monique Foucault has put a culinary whiz kid in the kitchen. Francis Chevalliez knows how to bring out the flavors of regional foodstuffs in a modern and exciting way: brill marinated in cinnamon and candied lime, open-air young pigeon infused with soya and served warm as a salad, and royal Dublin bay prawns alongside a potato and Vire andouille sausage crispy. Desserts are original as well: don't miss the warm candied fennel puff pastry served with vanilla ice cream and tomato jam. Flowery little garden-terrace with a view over the river. Warm welcome. C 400-500. M 140-298.

La Chaîne d'Or

(See restaurant above)
Closed Sun pm, Mon, Jan. 2 stes 710-740. 8 rms 400-550. Pkg.
Pleasant, pretty, nicely decorated and irreproachably clean rooms in an eighteenth-century building. All are well equipped, and some have views of the river.

Manoir de Clairval

Le Val-Saint-Martin, 2, rue de Seine
02 32 54 37 17, fax 02 32 54 37 45
Open year-round. 2 stes 590-750. 8 rms 295-400. Restaurant. Half-board 390-480.
A little turn-of-the-century manor house hugging the cliffs overlooking the Seine river. Spacious rooms with a nice view over the restful park. Pleasing reception.

Fourges

Eure 27630
11km E by D 5

12/20 Le Moulin de Fourges

02 32 52 12 12, fax 02 32 52 92 56
Closed Sun dinner & Mon (exc in summer), Jan 2-Feb 12. Open until 10:15pm. Terrace dining.
While the owners pamper customers in the rustic dining rooms of this adorable seventeenth-century mill, the young chef cooks up generous, tasty dishes. Interesting selection of regional wines. C 300-350. M 115 (weekday lunch), 155-295.

Pacy-sur-Eure

Eure 27120
15 km by D 5, D 181 & D 75

12/20 Le Grand Siècle

02 32 52 40 50, fax 02 32 52 69 65
Open daily until 9:30pm. Terrace dining. Heated pool. Tennis. Pkg.
This pure Louis XIII château, complete with 50-acre park and moat, is reminiscent of the Place des Vosges in Paris. You can eat upstairs in front of the gigantic fireplace, under the ancient wooden beams, where you will be served the likes of tough beef carpaccio, overcooked veal médail-lon or delicious Norman tart, all served by a particularly inattentive staff. All this results in the loss the toque. C 350-450. M 140-190 (lunch), 220 (lunch, wine incl), 360 (dinner), 235-350.

Château de Brécourt ♣♨

(See restaurant above)
Open year-round. 5 stes 850-1,680. 25 rms 390-1,040. Half-board 490-1,155. Rm ser. Heated pool. Tennis. Pkg.
A superb seventeenth-century château complete with suits of armor, a multitude of massive fireplaces, moats and a splendid park. The lacklustre, out-of-date rooms do not meet the expectations that the outside might give you, but they are impeccably clean and quiet. Wonderful covered pool with Jacuzzi. Weekend package deals.

*Looking for a restaurant? Refer to the **Index.***

Port-Villez

Yvelines 78270
9 km SE by D 5, D 181 & N 15

La Gueulardière

At Le Village - 01 34 76 22 12
Closed Sun dinner & Mon (exc hols). Open until 9:30pm. Garden dining. Air cond. Pool. Garage pkg.
A pleasant, ivy-covered inn with a warm country décor, a collection of copperware, and bouquets of flowers is just across from Monet's house and gardens at Giverny. There is also a winter garden and sa terrace. Diners can expect to be greeted with a smile before tasting the personalized classic cuisine prepared with a sure hand by Bernard Blondeau. C 320-380. M 150 (weekdays), 240-400.

Vernon

Eure 27200
4 km NW by D 5 & D 181

12/20 Les Fleurs

71, rue Carnot - 02 32 51 16 80, fax 02 32 21 30 51
Closed Sun dinner, Mon, Feb school hols, Aug 1-15. Open until 9:30pm. Terrace dining.
Flowers brighten the walls, the upholstery, and fill vases, too, in the pretty and cheerful dining room. The owner-chef offers an interesting menu of such deftly turned out classics as escargots à la normande, truffled lamb fillet, and parfait au chocolat. C 280-380. M 120-240.

Normandy

1, av. Pierre-Mendès-France
02 32 51 97 97, fax 02 32 21 01 66
Open year-round. 3 stes 550-655. 44 rms 350-390. Rm for disabled. Air cond. Garage pkg.
Located in the town center, this hotel is modern and convenient. The rooms of this hotel at the back are the quietest; all are comfortable, but the '70s-style décor is not to everyone's taste.

12/20 Le Relais Normand

11, pl. d'Evreux - 02 32 21 16 12, fax 02 32 21 32 73
Closed Sun dinner. Open until 9:30pm. Terrace dining.
This pure Normandy-style inn with its country décor and good-natured atmosphere offers cooking that is not always diamond-cut but is precisely cut to the chef's pattern: roasted Normandy oysters, sliced foie gras garnished with apples, or iced apple brandy soufflé. C 270-350. M 120 (weekday lunch), 165-250.

Hôtel d'Evreux

(See restaurant above)
Closed Sun. 15 rms 210-350. Pkg.

This half-timber town house dating from the century of Enlightenment is rather old-fashioned on the inside. The smart rooms are furnished in a myriad of styles scattered among a spruce yellow décor. The reception could certainly be better.

RAMBOUILLET

About 50 minutes, 50 kilometers from Paris by Autoroute A13 & A12, then N 10) the Chartres–Orléans Autoroute A10.

Although it is now the peaceful summer retreat of the president of France, the **château** at Rambouillet has witnessed some of the more dramatic moments in the nation's history. In 1547 François Ier, who enjoyed hunting in the nearby forest, died in a tower of the castle, which then belonged to the captain of his guards. Forty years later, Henri III, driven out of Paris by the League, took refuge at Rambouillet. In 1815, before his departure for exile, Napoléon spent a last night of melancholy reflection at Rambouillet. It was there, too, that Charles X learned of the Revolution of 1830 and announced his abdication. And it was from Rambouillet, in August 1944, that General Charles de Gaulle gave the order for Leclerc's armored division to liberate Paris.

Yet Rambouillet has seen more tranquil times as well. Today, little remains of the sixteenth-century château, save the cool red-and-gray Salle des Marbres (Marble Hall). The eighteenth century and Empire are the periods now best represented at Rambouillet. The Count of Toulouse, a legitimized son of Louis XIV, purchased the château in 1705. He enlarged the existing structures and had the new west wing decorated with enchanting Rococo woodwork. For the garden, he commissioned a system of canals and artificial islands on which magnificent *fêtes* were held throughout the century. The count's son, the Duke of Penthièvre, completed the canals and, in the English garden, had an incredibly kitsch cottage constructed of seashells and slivers of mother-of-pearl; he called it the **Pavillon des Coquillages.**

In 1783, Louis XVI purchased Rambouillet for the exceptional hunting the nearby forest afforded. Marie-Antoinette was less than enthusiastic. She called the place «the toad hole» and longed for her Trianon at Versailles. To appease her, in 1785 Louis had the Neoclassic *Laiterie* constructed, where ladies of the aris-

tocracy came to sip new milk and sample fresh cheese. Today the dairy is no longer in operation, but the *Bergerie*, built the following year, is still home to some 800 sheep, including 120 merinos descended from a flock presented to Louis XVI by the king of Spain (and those *moutons* of course refuse to mix with the other 680 «commoners»).

Rambouillet was virtually abandoned during the Revolution, and its furniture removed and sold, but Napoléon took a fancy to the château and decided to restore it. Visitors may admire the emperor's study, his private apartments ornamented with «Pompeiian» frescoes, and the grand dining room—still used for state dinners—with its enormous, 550-pound bronze chandelier.

The densely treed forest of Rambouillet, a great favorite with hunters, hikers, and mushroom gatherers, covers close to half a million acres, and begins virtually at the door of the château.

• *The Château de Rambouillet*
is open:
- *Apr-Sep 10am-11:30am & 2pm-5:30pm;*
- *Oct-Mar until 4:30pm;*
- *closed Tue & when the president is in residence.*
• *La Laiterie de la Reine Marie-Antoinette*
is open:
- *Apr-Sep 10am-11:30am & 2pm-5:30pm;*
- *Oct-Mar until 3:30pm;*
- *closed Tue.*
Information: 01 34 83 00 25.

• *RESTAURANTS & HOTELS*

Rambouillet
Yvelines   *78120*

12/20 **Le Cheval Rouge**
78, rue du Général-de-Gaulle
01 30 88 80 61, fax 01 34 83 91 60
Closed Sun dinner, Jul 15-Aug 19. Open until 9:30pm. Terrace dining. Air cond.
You won't find a more central location in Rambouillet than this restaurant on the main shopping street, not far from the chbteau. The food is serious and comforting. A 175 F fixed-price menu offers good quality for the price and includes dishes like an excellent home-made foie gras, a good monkfish, pepper steak, and very fine apple tart. C 200-250. M 130, 175.

Cernay-la-Ville

Yvelines   78120
12 km E by D 906 & D 24

12/20   Abbaye des Vaux-de-Cernay

Route d'Auffargis · 01 34 85 23 00, fax 01 34 85 20 95
Open daily until 9:30pm. Terrace dining. Heated pool. Tennis. Pkg.
  This abbey dates back eight centuries, and is set on a vast estate with its own forests. We'd be hard pressed to find a more enchanting site, despite the debatable shade of blue used to paint the doors and window trim! The cuisine is not as delectable as the setting: scrumptious vinaigrette of asparagus with langoustines, foie gras croquette with gingerbread, rhubarb crumble with sweet orange sauce. Celestial cellar. C 350-500. M 160 (weekday lunch), 250-395.

Abbaye des Vaux-de-Cernay 🎋

(See restaurant above)
Open year-round. 3 stes 1,900-3,800. 55 rms 490-1,590. Half-board 650-1,050. Heated pool. Tennis. Pkg.
  This twelfth-century abbey is fairly brimming with mysterious, grandiose atmosphere. The Gothic lounge and music room are true splendors with their vaults and columns. Luxurious, spacious rooms, decorated with genuine period furniture.

Dampierre

Yvelines   78720
16 km E by D 906 & D 91

12/20   Le Belvédère

Château de Dampierre
01 30 52 52 99, fax 01 30 52 59 90
Lunch only, exc Fri & Sat. Closed Tue. Open until 2:30pm & 9pm. Terrace dining. Pkg.
  The name says it all: a panoramic view. A good find perched above the farmlands of the Saône Valley, offering a prudently up-to-date cuisine well worth the price: pike perch braised in red wine or chicken leg with morel cream sauce. C 310-350. M 220-320.

Gazeran

Yvelines   78120
6 km W by D 906 & D 62

12/20   Villa Marinette

20, av. du Général-de-Gaulle
01 34 83 19 01, fax 01 34 83 19 01
Closed Tue, Nov 11-Feb: dinner Sun. Open until 9pm. Terrace dining. Pkg.
  The Villa is a fetching old country house that opens onto a blooming garden. Madame attends to customers, while Monsieur mans the kitchen, producing simple, flavorful dishes based on quality ingredients. M 65 (weekday lunch), 185 (wine incl), 105-145.

See also Saint-Symphorien-le-Château *in* **Chartres** *above.*

ST-GERMAIN-EN-LAYE

About 40 minutes, 20 kilometers west of Paris by the Autoroute de Normandie A13.

In 1862 Emperor Napoléon III, an ardent archaeology buff (his great boast was that he had discovered the site of the Battle of Alésia, where Caesar defeated Vercingetorix, leader of the Gauls, in 52 BC), established the Musée des Antiquités Nationales at Saint-Germain-en-Laye. The oldest artifacts unearthed on French soil are housed in this fascinating museum, which follows the course of French history up to the time of the Merovingians, the first Frankish dynasty. Today, nothing could be simpler than to take this journey back in time, for the RER links Saint-Germain to the center of Paris in a matter of minutes.

On the museum's vast mezzanine, exhibits illustrate the millennia that preceded Rome's occupation of Gaul. It is strangely moving to contemplate these age-old vestiges of human artistry. Most of the pieces are quite small, like the *Dame de Brassempouy*, the oldest known representation of a human face, which is thought to predate Christ's birth by about 20,000 years; or the famous bone carving of a *Bison Licking Its Fur*, from Dordogne (16,000 BC); or the many images that remind us that in France, too, the buffalo roamed and the deer (and antelope) played—at least until the end of the Ice Age.

Even visitors with only a mild interest in archaeology will be riveted by artifacts discovered in the tombs of Celtic princes of the first Iron Age (Hallstatt period), particularly the funeral chariots which indicate that the entombed were of noble rank, the iron swords, carved daggers, and personal ornaments. Other finds verify that Gaulish tribes traded with Greece and Etruria, thus in-

Venez découvrir

Les plus célèbres

Dîner-Spectacles

Du monde !

Discover the world's most famous
dinner & show !

BAL DU
Moulin Rouge
PARIS

Nouveau Chef, nouveaux menus, nouvelles attractions !

Dîner-spectacle à partir de 770F, spectacle à partir de 360F
Montmartre - 82, boulevard de Clichy - 75018 paris

Réservations au 01 53 09 82 82

Brasseries Kronenbourg

- Kronenbourg • 1664 • Kanterbräu •
- Kronenbourg Tradition Anglaise • Kronenbourg
Tradition Allemande • Kronenbourg Légère •
- 1664 Brune • Gold •
- K • Bud • X-Cider •
- Chicada • Kronenbräu •
- Kilkenny • Wilfort •
- Guinness • Carlsberg •
- Tuborg • Grimbergen •
- Kronenbourg Ice • La Réserve de Maître Kanter •
- Obernai • Blanche de Bruges • Mort Subite •
- Kronenpils • Kanterpils • Valstar •
- Tourtel Blonde • Tourtel Ambrée •
- Tourtel Brune • Force 4 • Force 4 Lemon •
- Wel Scotch • Silver • Krony •
- L'abus d'alcool est dangereux pour la santé •
- Consommez avec modération •

BKSA RCS STRASBOURG B 708 502 083

validating the theory that Gaul lived in isolation before the Romans burst onto the scene. The very existence of coins minted by the principal Gallic tribes, of amphoras and other luxury goods, bears witness to the wealth of Gaul's aristocracy, and to their links with the Mediterranean world.

Exhibits on the upper floor document the period of Roman colonization (a model of the Battle of Alisia, which marked the end of Gaul's independence, can be found on the mezzanine). The number of statues representing Gaulish divinities underscores Rome's generally tolerant attitude toward foreign religions, while abundant manufactured goods—ceramics, glass objects—give us a picture of France's earliest industries. The barbarian invasions that followed this period of prosperity are evoked by jewels and impressively worked weapons excavated at Frankish tomb sites.

Though Saint-Germain-en-Laye is now synonymous with prehistory, it holds a significant place in the history of France. A prestigious royal château, it was the birthplace of Kings Henri II, Charles IX, and Louis XIV (who preferred it to all his other palaces until he built Versailles). From the twelfth century through the nineteenth, extensive building and remodeling altered the château's appearance many times over. What the visitor sees today is the Vieux Château, rebuilt under François Ier. This first important example of brick-and-stone architecture in the Ile-de-France was heavily restored in the nineteenth century.

The former splendor of Saint-Germain is perhaps best translated by Le Nôtre's magnificent gardens, and the Grande Terrasse bordered with linden trees. Moreover, with its 8,500 acres of flat, sandy paths, picturesque hunting pavilions, and majestic stands of oak, the forest of Saint-Germain offers ideal hiking terrain within easy reach of Paris.

• The Musée des Antiquités Nationales is open 9am-5:15pm, closed Tue.
Information: 01 39 10 13 00, fax 01 34 51 73 93.
Admission: 25 F, reduced rate: 17 F, under 18: free.

• RESTAURANTS & HOTELS

Saint-Germain-en-Laye
Yvelines   78100

12/20 Brasserie du Théâtre
Pl. du Château - 01 30 61 28 00, fax 01 39 73 98 73
Closed at Christmas. Open until 1am. Terrace dining. Air cond. Garage pkg.

Conveniently sited opposite the château, this 1930s–vintage brasserie provides solid sustenance at nearly any time of the day, just about every day of the year. C 190-360.

 ### Cazaudehore
1, av. du Président-Kennedy - 01 30 61 64 64 (R) 01 30 61 64 64 (H), fax 01 39 73 73 88
Closed Mon (exc hols). Open until 10pm. Garden dining. Pkg.
On the edge of the forest in a setting of lawns and flowers sits this charming establishment decorated with old prints and English chintzes; for summer dining, there's a huge terrace that looks out over the trees. A few Mediterranean touches now grace Philippe Pactol's menu, but for the most part it remains dedicated to pricey French classics and rich Southwestern dishes, all ably handled. Superb cellar, stylish service. C 450-500. M 190 & 290 (weekday lunch, wine incl), 360 (Sat, Sun, wine incl).

 ### La Forestière
(See restaurant above)
Open year-round. 5 stes 1,400. 25 rms 990. Pkg.
Rooms and suites decorated with exquisite refinement, each in an individual style. The forest is close at hand, and is even directly accessible from some of the suites. Guests can count on a warm, attentive welcome. Relais et Châteaux.

12/20 La Feuillantine
10, rue des Louviers - 01 34 51 04 24
Open until 10:30pm. Terrace dining. Air cond.
You'll be charmingly received into this bright, cozy restaurant (it's a popular spot, so remember to book ahead). Save for a flavorless Barbary duck, we have no complaints about the good salmon crêpe, choucroute garnie with seafood, or cold apple dessert laced with Calavados. Extensively annotated wine list. M 75 & 85 (weekday lunch), 130.

 ### Le Pavillon Henri IV
21, rue Thiers - 01 39 10 15 15, fax 01 39 73 93 73
Open year-round. 3 stes 1,350-3,200. 42 rms 400-1,300. Rms for disabled. Rm ser. Pkg.
This is where Louis XIV was born, Alexandre Dumas wrote The Three Musketeers, and Offenbach composed a number of operettas. We don't find the somber blue-gray furnishings very inspiring, but the 45 rooms and suites are huge and airy. The public rooms are magnificent and there's a splendid view over the extensive grounds.

SENLIS

About 50 minutes, 50 kilometers north of Paris by the Autoroute du Nord A1, exit No.8 Senlis, N 324 to Senlis.

When you walk through the narrow medieval streets of Senlis, don't be surprised if you suddenly recognize the set from your favorite French costume drama. This compact, well-preserved town on the border of the Ile-de-France and Picardy offers a fascinating glimpse into the history of pre-Revolutionary France. Understandably, it is a popular location with film-production companies.

North of the town, the **Jardin du Roy** (King's Garden) lies in what was once the moat surrounding a Gallo-Roman defensive wall. The garden affords a marvelous overall view of Senlis, and of one of the best-preserved Roman fortifications in France. About 13 feet thick and 23 feet high, the wall dates back to the barbarian invasions of the third century. It once linked together 28 watch towers, some 16 of which have survived.

The nearby **Château Royal**, despite its grandiose name, is now nothing more than a park scattered with romantic ruins. Built on the site of a first-century Roman fortress, the château was a royal residence from the time of Clovis, in the fifth century, until the reign of Henri IV, early in the seventeenth century. It was there, in 987, that the Capetian line of monarchs took root, with the election of Hugues Capet, duke of the Franks, to the throne of France.

If you cross the pretty square in front of the **cathedral of Notre-Dame**, you can best admire the monumental portal with its celebrated Gothic sculpture. Begun in 1153, ten years before Notre-Dame de Paris, the cathedral at Senlis served as a model for Chartres. Yet by the sixteenth century, recurrent fires had made it necessary to rebuild the northern and southern façades practically from scratch. The work was directed by Pierre Chambiges, who created one of the finest (and last) examples of Flamboyant Gothic architecture. Crowning the northern portal are the initial and emblematic salamander of François Ier.

After visiting the cathedral, we always take the time to wander through the winding, **ancient streets** of Senlis: Rue de la Tonnellerie, Rue du Châtel, Rue de la Treille, and Rue de Beauvais all boast sixteenth-century houses and mansions with splendid carved entrances (many of which are open to visitors in

odd-numbered years, during the month of September for the Rendez-vous de Senlis).

You'll end up at the twelfth-century **church of Saint-Frambourg,** restored through the efforts of pianist and composer George Cziffra, and now used as a concert hall.

If you have time and a car, drive a few kilometers north to the Italianate **château de Raray,** built in the seventeenth century, where Jean Cocteau filmed his magical *Beauty and the Beast.*

Who knows? Perhaps, as you stand admiring the fantastic hunting scenes sculpted on Diana's Gate, your own Beauty—or Prince Charming—will suddenly appear!

- *The Château Royal*
- *Musée de la Vénerie*
- *and the Jardin du Roy*

are open:
- *Feb-Oct 10am-noon & 2pm-6pm;*
- *Nov-Jan until 5pm;*
- *closed Tue & Wed morning.*
- *The cathedral is open daily 7am-7pm.*
- *Information: 03 44 53 00 80, fax 03 44 53 11 99.*

• *RESTAURANTS & HOTELS*

Senlis

Oise   *60300*

12/20 **Chalet de Sylvie**

1, av. Foch - 03 44 53 00 87, fax 03 44 53 80 22
Closed Tue, 3 wks in Jan. Open until 10pm (Fri & Sat 10:30pm). Terrace dining. Air cond.
This bar-restaurant serves up healthy helpings of carefully prepared, prettily presented conventional fare. For 135 F: Beaufort cheese flan wrapped in bacon and tomato-sauced, rack of lamb cooked in coriander, and citrus fruit meringue pastry. If you need peace and quiet, sit on the porch or terrace. C 250-500. M 135 (lunch), 195.

12/20 **Le Scaramouche**

4, pl. Notre-Dame - 03 44 53 16 87
Closed Wed, 1 wk at Feb school hols, 1 wk in Aug. Open until 9:30pm. Terrace dining.
Practically next door to the cathedral, Scaramouche serves honest cooking with its roots in the Picardy *terroir*: goat cheese with Belgian endive, guinea hen à la picarde, fudgy chocolate cake. C 240-280. M 150-280.

The C (A la carte) restaurant prices given are for a complete three-course meal for one, including a half-bottle of modest wine and service. M (Menu) prices are for a complete fixed-price meal for one, excluding wine (unless otherwise noted).

La Chapelle-en-Serval

Oise   *60520*

10 km S by N 17

 Mont Royal 🌲🌸

On D 118, route de Plailly, Le Château
03 44 54 50 50, fax 03 44 54 50 21
Open year-round. 4 stes 1,500-1,800. 96 rms 990-
1,200. Restaurant. Half-board 1,190-1,490. Rm
ser. Air cond. Heated pool. Tennis. Pkg.
  Tucked away in the green Chantilly forest, this
eighteenth-century château is just 15 km from
Roissy airport. You'll live like a lord or lady of
the manor here, amid luxurious amenities (pool,
tennis court, fitness center).

Fleurines

Oise   *60700*

7 km N by N 17

🔲 **Le Vieux Logis**

105, rue de Paris - 03 44 54 10 13, fax 03 44 54 12 47
Closed Sat lunch, Sun dinner, Mon, Feb school hols,
1 wk in beg Nov. Open until 9:30pm. Terrace
dining. Pkg.
  The Vieux Logis's pretty terrace complements
a comfortable dining room brightened up with
bouquets of flowers. A nice relaxing country inn
near Senlis, smack in the park of an old tile
factory near the forest. Yann Nivet proffers an
exacting cuisine, while his wife, Valérie, looks
after the cellar. Roast langoustine and quail filet
salad, monkfish and wild mushroom fricassée,
duck breast with mango. Slip it all down with
Pierre Pouzeau's Chinon at 120 F a bottle. C
250-350. M 140 (weekdays), 180.

Fontaine-Chaalis

Oise   *60300*

9 km SE by D 330 & D 126

12/20   Auberge de Fontaine

22, Grande-Rue
03 44 54 20 22, fax 03 44 60 28 33
Closed Tue off-seas. Open until 9:15pm (10pm in
summer). Garden dining.
  Come here for a pleasant meal in a charming
old village inn. You'll warm up to the homey,
straightforward Provençal cooking, served with
a selection of astutely chosen wines. C 260-340.
M 95 (weekday lunch), 135-240.

 Auberge de Fontaine

(See restaurant above)
Closed Tue off-seas. 1 ste 465-525. 7 rms 245-345.
Half-board 300-350.

A hotel with cozy, well-kept rooms done up in
pretty pastel colors. Big bathrooms.

See also **Chantilly** *above.*

VAUX-LE-VICOMTE

About 1 hr, 60 kilometers southeast of
Paris by the Autoroute du Sud A6, N
104, A5a, A5 exit No.15 Meaux/Vaux-
le-Vicomte, D 126, D 215.

As we stand in the unfinished Grand
Salon of Vaux-le-Vicomte, looking out
over the intricate gardens designed by Le
Nôtre, we can almost picture the scene... The
dog days of August 1661: Nicolas Fouquet,
France's brilliant finance minister, is entertaining his young sovereign, Louis XIV, at an
indescribably lavish reception. A thousand
fountains play in the magnificent *jardins à la
française*, while Molière's troupe performs the
comic ballet *Les Fâcheux*. Courtiers applaud
the water jousts, the concerts, the fireworks...
At dinner—prepared by Vatel, the foremost
chef of his day—the king and his retinue are
served on solid-gold plates. According to
legend, the dinner did not sit well with Louis,
whose suspicions—and envy—were aroused
by such luxury. Historians claim that Colbert,
Fouquet's rival for control of the royal
treasury, had slandered Fouquet, insinuating
that he was raiding the king's coffers. Or it
may have been that the king set Fouquet up
himself: wangling an invitation to Vaux, then
watching the vainglorious minister flaunt his
riches, and thus be hoist by his own petard!
  Whoever laid it, the trap was sprung that
August day at Vaux-le-Vicomte. A few weeks
later, Louis sent d'Artagnan, the captain of his
musketeers, to arrest Fouquet at Nantes. He
then sent workmen to pack up the finest
tapestries, furnishings, and paintings from
Vaux and carry them straight into the royal
collection. Louis summoned Fouquet's architect, Le Vau, his decorator, Le Brun, and
his landscape designer, Le Nôtre, and ordered them all to begin work on the royal
showplace at Versailles.
  After a trial that dragged out over three
years, the courts handed down a sentence of
banishment for Fouquet. Louis, implacable,
overruled them, and condemned his former
minister to life imprisonment. Fouquet was,
in all probability, a rascal. Yet the story of his
fall and miserable end (after nineteen years in

prison) still colors our view of Vaux's splendors with a tinge of melancholy.

It is largely thanks to Alfred Sommier, a sugar-refining magnate who purchased a dilapidated Vaux-le-Vicomte in 1875, that we can now see the château and gardens much as they were on that summer day in 1661. Sommier spent prodigious amounts of money and energy to rebuild sagging roofs and walls, to furnish the nearly empty house with seventeenth-century antiques, and to restore the gardens to their former beauty. That last task alone took a good half-century. Using seventeenth-century engravings, Sommier was able to reconstruct the terraces, pools, and the complex system of pipes that feed the fountains. He planted acres of trees and bushes, and acquired statuary for the garden. Pieces were also commissioned from modern sculptors to replace the statues confiscated by Louis XIV.

In addition to the gardens, three levels of the château are open to the public. On the upper floor are the Fouquets' private living quarters—studies, boudoirs, and bedrooms—handsomely fitted out with period furniture and hung with tapestries and reproductions of paintings from the minister's (confiscated) collection.

For us, the most appealing aspect of the reception rooms downstairs (the Grands Appartements) is Le Brun's decoration. Actually, the term *decoration* is not adequate to describe this virtuoso performance with paint, stucco, carving, and gilt. The scores of rosy nymphs, cherubs, squirrels (Fouquet's emblem), and other allegorical figures that populate the ceilings and woodwork of the Salon des Muses and Cabinet des Jeux (Gaming Room) fill these formal rooms with a rapturous charm. Le Brun's stucco-and-fresco décor in the Chambre du Roi (Royal Chamber) is the model for what later became known throughout Europe as the «French style», which reached its apotheosis at Versailles.

Bereft of its intended decoration, the Grand Salon demonstrates the measure of architect Le Vau's genius; the eye, unsolicited by bright allegories and visions, is naturally drawn outside, to the harmonious perspectives of the gardens, Le Nôtre's masterpiece. In their more modest way, the workrooms and staff quarters on the lower level are also quite interesting. The kitchens (in use until 1956) display a dazzling collection of copper pots and pans scoured to a high polish.

Those in search of rare sensations and exquisite atmospheres will surely want to visit Vaux-le-Vicomte by candlelight on a Saturday evening in summer. The scene is unforgettable— indeed, it is enough to rouse the envy of a king!

• *The Château de Vaux-le-Vicomte*

is open:
- *Mar-Nov 11 daily 10am-6pm;*
- *closed mid Nov-Feb.*
Admission: 30 to 56 F.
• **Candlelight tours**
are held Sat evenings from May to mid Oct (exc Jul 14): 8:30pm-11pm. Admission: 45 to 75 F.
• *Fountain displays*
are scheduled the second and final Sat of each month Apr-Oct: 3pm-6pm.
• *Information: 01 64 14 41 90, fax 01 60 69 90 85. E-mail: chateau@vaux-le-vicomte.com*

• ## *RESTAURANTS & HOTELS*

Les Ecrennes

Seine-et-Marne   77820
16 km E on D 215, D 408 & D 47E

 ### Auberge Briarde

On A 5, exit Châtillon
01 60 69 47 32, fax 01 60 66 60 11
Closed dinner Sun & Wed, Jan 1-15, Aug 1-28. Open until 9:30pm. Terrace dining.
In autumn gourmets come from miles around for Jean Guichard's special game menus, full of rousing, earthy flavors. But at any time of year it's a treat to settle down by the fireplace in this comfortably rustic dining room and savor Guichard's well-wrought classic cuisine. Remarkable desserts; admirable cellar. Monique Guichard greets guests warmly, but the staff is still wet behind the ears! C 250-450. M 135 (weekday lunch), 195-440.

Fontenay-Trésigny

Seine-et-Marne   77610
28 km NE by D 215, D 126, N 36, N 4 & D 402

 ### Le Manoir

Route de Coulommiers
01 64 25 91 17, fax 01 64 25 95 49
Closed Tue (exc hols), Nov 15-Mar 27. Open until 9pm. Garden dining. Pool. Tennis. Pkg.
The warm atmosphere makes guests feel right at home in this Anglo-Norman manor with its pretty veranda overlooking the grounds. And Denis Come's ultraclassic cuisine takes its cue from the finest ingredients worked in an unfailingly precise, refined, and consistent manner. Wonderfully eclectic wine list, and a tempting selection of spirits. Affable welcome. C 300-400. M 180-250 (wine incl), 370.

Looking for a hotel? Refer to the **index.**

Le Manoir

(See restaurant above)
Closed Nov 15-Mar 27. 3 stes from 1,120-1,250. 17 rms 800-880. Rms for disabled. Half-board 825-1,220. Rm ser. Heated pool. Pkg.
This charming manor house set on calm grounds replete with century-old trees offers guests a variety of spacious, inviting rooms decorated in period or contemporary styles. Charming welcome. Relais et Châteaux.

Melun

Seine-et-Marne   77000
6 km W by D 215 & N 36

 La Melunoise

5, rue du Gâtinais
01 64 39 68 27, fax 01 64 39 81 81
Lunch only (exc upon reser for 12). Closed Sat, Sun, Feb school hols, Aug. Open until 2pm. Terrace dining.
Claude and Michel Hinaut's short repertoire has lost its Nordic accent in favor of traditional favorites from the Landes and Provence regions. And we have nary a bone to pick with them on this front, because their hand remains steady, their cooking exact, and their flavors as clean and clear as ever. In addition, a number of their ingredients are homemade. The cellar is well stocked with Bordeaux and the décor is warm in this quaint, flower-bedecked establishment. C 200-260. M 150 & 190 (weekday lunch).

12/20 Le Relais Baltard

8, quai de la Courtille
01 64 39 17 36, fax 01 64 39 85 99
Closed Sun dinner. Open until 11pm. Terrace dining.
This huge corner brasserie right in the middle of town is always overflowing. For 149 F: confit gizzard and liver salad, shark steak on a bed of fennel, or iced nougat with mixed-berry sauce. C 160-250. M 69-149.

Pouilly-le-Fort

Seine-et-Marne   77240
11 km N by D 215, N 36 & N 105

 Le Pouilly

1, rue de la Fontaine
01 64 09 56 64, fax 01 64 09 56 64
Closed Sun dinner, Mon, Aug 10-31, Dec 22-28. Open until 9:45pm. Terrace dining. Pkg.
This beautifully restored farmhouse is replete with sensory delights: a crackling fire in the monumental hearth, prettily laid tables, woody old beams. The food is slipping these days, but we hope it's a passing phase. This year our amuse-bouches were quite ordinary, the mignardises were old, the monkfish undercooked,

and the chicken leg swimming in grease. The reception is highly *courtois* and the service highly professional, but the atmosphere was stiff and the check a harsh surprise. We had gotten accustomed to better. C 400-450. M 165 (weekdays), 220-380.

See also **Fontainebleau** *above.*

About 40 minutes, 25 kilometers west of Paris by the Autoroute de Normandie A13.

Versailles, undoubtedly the world's most famous palace, has been a favorite destination for day-tripping Parisians since 1833, when King Louis-Philippe turned the château, which had been abandoned since the Revolution, into a «museum of the glories of France». Today, Versailles offers pleasures at every season, in every kind of weather. Visitors can amble through parks dotted with romantic statuary, admire a wealth of art, furniture, and architecture—comparing Louis this with Louis that—or simply spread out a blanket and picnic beside the Grand Canal.

It took Louis XIV just 40 years to build the palace and its park around a hunting lodge erected by his father, Louis XIII. And though his successors made many changes, Versailles still bears the unmistakable stamp of the Sun King, who from 1682 on made it the official residence of the court, the sole seat of royal power, and the political capital of France. The court's permanent presence explains the colossal proportions of the palace, which housed the royal family, the princes of the blood, the courtiers, the king's councilors, everyone's servants...it's little wonder, then, that the western façade of the palace stretches out to a width of nearly 2,000 feet.

Lodging his considerable household and entourage was not all that Louis had in mind when he built Versailles. He also saw the palace as a powerful propaganda tool, a monument to the glory of the French monarchy, and a showcase for masterworks by French artists and craftsmen. Versailles was open to all. The humblest subjects of the realm could wander freely through the Grands Appartements to gape at the cream of the royal collections. Classical statues and busts stood in marble-lined halls; paintings from the French and Venetian schools hung on walls covered in velvet, damask, and brocade.

Today's tourists are the descendants of those visitors who, at the end of the seventeenth century, marveled at the dazzling Galerie des Glaces (Gallery of Mirrors) or the Salon d'-Apollon before attending the king's supper or submitting a petition to Louis XIV as he made his way to Mass at the royal chapel.

But we have the advantage over those tourists of long ago, for we can visit parts of Versailles that were then off-limits to the public, even to courtiers. Among the most beautiful of the private quarters is the Petit Appartement, fitted out for Louis XV just above his official suite, a place where he could relax alone—or with friends (like Madame du Barry, who had her own room there).

A similarly intimate mood and scale are evident in the two Trianons, situated about half a mile from the main palace. The Grand Trianon was built in 1687 for Louis XIV, who spent many a quiet summer evening there surrounded by his family. Today it houses heads of state on official visits. The Petit Trianon is an exquisite Neoclassic structure designed by Gabriel in 1764 for Louis XV, who wished to live closer to his beloved botanical garden. It was also the preferred residence of Marie-Antoinette, whose spirit still lingers in the place. There, on October 5, 1789, she learned of the Parisians' march on Versailles.

In fine weather the gardens of Versailles are an irresistible invitation to wander. They cover over 2,000 acres with an enchanting variety of landscapes. The classical French *parterres* (flower beds), with their broad perspectives, pools, and lawns, were designed by Le Nôtre at the height of his powers; his is also the genius behind the marvelous *bosquets* (coppices) that combine thickly massed greenery and spectacular waterworks. Scattered throughout are hundreds of marble and bronze statues, many inspired by the myths of Apollo, with whom the Sun King strongly identified. If you happen to be in Versailles between April and October, make a point of touring the gardens when the Grandes Eaux are scheduled: all over the gardens, in every bed and *bosquet*, the fountains put on a magical display.

And in summer, it is well worth the effort to obtain tickets for a performance at the Opéra Royal, an architectural masterpiece by Gabriel, inaugurated in 1770 for the marriage of the future Louis XVI and the Archduchess Marie-Antoinette. The elegance of its proportions, its superb acoustics, and the splendor of its decoration make it perhaps the most beautiful theater in the world.

• *The Château de Versailles*
is open:
- *May-Sep 9am-6:30pm (last admission 6pm);*
- *Oct-Apr until 5:30pm (last admission 5pm);*
- *closed Mon.*
• *The park and gardens*
are open Oct-Apr daily 8am-dusk; May-Sep daily 7am-dusk.
• *Fountain displays*
are scheduled beg Apr-mid Oct: Sun 3:30pm-5:15pm.
• **Information:** *01 30 84 74 00, fax 01 30 84 76 48.*

• *RESTAURANTS & HOTELS*

Versailles

Yvelines   *78000*

12/20 **Brasserie du Théâtre**
15, rue des Réservoirs
01 39 50 03 21, fax 01 39 50 74 32
Open daily until 1am. Terrace dining.
Classic brasserie food (fresh shellfish, pepper steak, cassoulet), served in a supremely Gallic décor of mirrors, glowing woodwork, and leather banquettes. C 160.

12/20 **Brasserie La Fontaine**
Trianon Palace, 1, bd de la Reine
01 30 84 38 47, fax 01 39 51 57 79
Open daily until 10:30pm. Terrace dining. Air cond. Valet pkg.
This large brasserie with its *belle ambiance* has a gem of a location in the Trianon Palace annexes. But, alas, ambience does not suffice to make a good meal. The lack of consistency in the kitchen as well as up front brought disappointment this year. The sardine millefeuille was superbly savorous and the beurre blanc on the sea perch was favorably flavored. But we didn't like the fact that there was no Grand Marnier in the leathery dessert «packet», when that was what was written on the menu. The superb old-fashioned décor is accented with a series of amusing animal portraits. The servers are nice, but always snowed under. C 200-360. M 120 (weekdays), 165 (Sun).

12/20 **La Flotille**
Parc du Château
01 39 51 41 58, fax 01 39 50 51 87
Open daily for lunch only until 3pm. Terrace dining.
How delightful (and how convenient)! A lovely terraced restaurant planted in the château grounds, just steps away from the boat rental stand. You can't expect lots of fineries on a terrace that serves 500 people, but this restaurant plays its role of nourishing tourists pretty well, merrily serving up haddock lasagne, saddle of lamb, and confit duck leg. Tempt yourself with the white Sancerre at 135 F a bottle. C 180-250. M 132 (lunch).

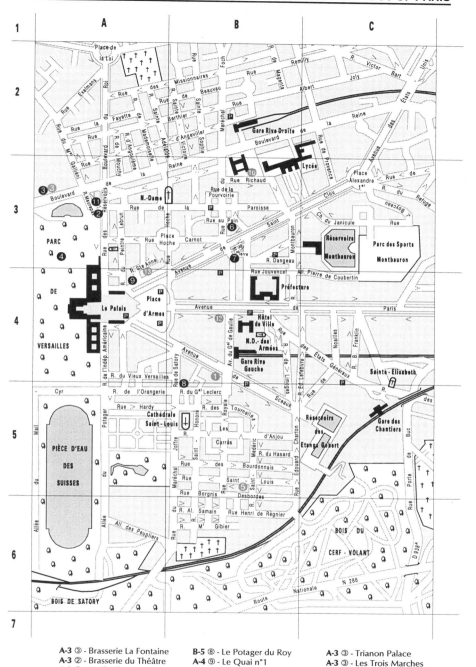

A-3 ③ - Brasserie La Fontaine
A-3 ② - Brasserie du Théâtre
A-3 ④ - La Flotille
B-3 ⑥ - La Marée de Versailles

B-5 ⑧ - Le Potager du Roy
A-4 ⑨ - Le Quai n°1
B-3 ⑩ - Richaud
B-4 12 - Sofitel

A-3 ③ - Trianon Palace
A-3 ③ - Les Trois Marches
A-4 13 - Le Versailles

La Marée de Versailles

22, rue au Pain - 01 30 21 73 73, fax 01 39 50 55 87
Closed Mon dinner, Dec 25-28, Dec 31-Jan 4, Feb school hols, Aug 2-16. Open until 10:30pm. Terrace dining. Air cond.

On the menu tonight: warm Dublin bay prawns served in their shell with acidulated chive cream; thyme-flavored clam fricassée with just a speck of cherry brandy; Breton lobster grilled in coral butter, or iced nougat made with flavorful fir honey. Chef Stéphane Arsicaud was trained by masters like Vigato and Dutournier, and he learned his lessons well, because he turns out flawlessly cooked fish full of flavor. Interesting selection of wines. C 190. M 260.

 ## Le Potager du Roy

1, rue du Mal-Joffre
01 39 50 35 34, fax 01 30 21 69 30
Closed Sun dinner, Mon. Open until 10:30pm. Air cond.

The set meal will pique your appetite, with a soup of mussels and cockles with white beans, a sparky combination of skate and potatoes dressed with capers and lemon, and a smooth guanaja-chocolate dessert (we'd have liked a bit more of that last one). Choosing from the *carte* we encountered bitter oysters and a minuscule portion of scallops, as well as some splendid vegetable dishes. Expensive. The cellar spotlights wines from the Loire. C 300-520. M 120 (weekday lunch), 169.

 ## Le Quai n°1

1, av. de St-Cloud - 01 39 50 42 26, fax 01 39 51 15 45
Closed Sun dinner, Mon. Open until 11pm. Terrace dining. Air cond.

A dependable address for fresh shellfish and decent seafood dishes at reasonable prices. Among the better offerings are a spicy fish soup, a refreshing salad of whelks with mayonnaise, and plaice in a sauce enriched with meat jus. Amusing nautical décor; casual service. C 200-250. M 120, 168.

 ## Richaud

16, rue Richaud - 01 39 50 10 42, fax 01 39 53 43 36
Open year-round. 39 rms 220-360. Garage pkg.

A classic hotel in the center of Versailles, close to the antique dealers. The rooms were all recently modernized and renovated.

 ## Sofitel
Château de Versailles

2 bis, av. Paris - 01 39 07 46 46, fax 01 39 07 46 47
Open year-round. 6 stes 1,850. 146 rms 1,200. Rms for disabled. Restaurant. Rm scr. Air cond. Valet pkg.

This chain hotel is located in immediate proximity to Place d'Armes and the château. Rooms here are spacious and modern, and all of the chain's top-of-the-line services are on offer. Piano bar.

 ## Les Trois Marches

Trianon Palace, 1, bd de la Reine
01 39 50 13 21, fax 01 30 21 01 25
Closed Sun, Mon, Aug. Open until 10pm. Terrace dining. Air cond. Valet pkg.

Gérard Vié is as happy as a king in the splendiferous kitchens of the Trianon Palace, where he and his *brigade* benefit from the state of the art equipment. Vié excels in the «sophisticated country» register that recalls his Languedoc roots: cassoulet with Couïza sausages or hearty Lacaune ham. And his updated French classics are models of the genre: morels braised in cream, asparagus with truffles, turbot with fat Tarbais beans, or a magnificent chop of milk-fed Corrèze veal. The brilliant sommelier can uncork a vintage Pauillac or Margaux to complement Vié's creations, and the maître d'hôtel will ensure that every detail of your meal is memorable. C 480-700. M 270 (weekday lunch), 510, 610.

 ## Trianon Palace

(See restaurant above)
01 30 84 38 00, fax 01 39 49 00 77
Open year-round. 27 stes 2,700-7,500. 67 rms 900-1,800. Rm scr. Air cond. Heated pool. Tennis. P kg.

Spruced up to the tune of $60 million, the Trianon Palace is a stupendously lavish hotel. From video-conference equipment to a medically supervised spa, it is the last word in luxury. Restaurants: Les Trois Marches, Brasserie de la Fontaine, see above.

 ## Le Versailles

7, rue Ste-Anne - 01 39 50 64 65, fax 01 39 02 37 85
Open year-round. 3 stes 520-600. 42 rms 450-550. Rms for disabled. Garage pkg.

Some rooms are located under the rafters, and all are modern, tastefully decorated, and well equipped (satellite TV). This hotel is ideally situated at the entry to the château. Bar, flower-filled terrace where breakfast is served, patio.

• *SIGHTS*

Following is a highly condensed list of Versailles's most noteworthy sights:

The **Château de Versailles** with more than three million visitors per year (from May to September its parks host the Grandes Eaux and the Fêtes de Nuit); the **Trianon Palaces**; the **Salle du Jeu de Paume**; **Notre-Dame** church (designed by Hardouin-Mansart); the **king's vegetable garden** (school of horticulture); the **Carrés Saint-Louis** (modest lodgings dating from the Ancien Régime); the **antique** and **secondhand market** (passage de la Geôle, next to the colorful market at Notre-Dame); the **Hôtel des Ventes** (former home of the Light Cavalry); the delightful **Musée Lambinet** (with beautiful eighteenth-century paintings); the **Couvent des Récollets**.

BASICS

GETTING AROUND

Airport Transportation

Paris is a rationally designed city divided into twenty *arrondissements*, or districts. Essential to getting around Paris is a knowledge of the excellent transportation system and a pocket-size street index called *Paris par Arrondissement*. Available in most bookstores and at major newspaper stands, it includes comprehensive maps of Paris, the subway system (Métro and RER), and bus routes.

• *BUSES*

Riding the bus is a great—and cheap—way to tour the city. The No. 20, 21, 24, 27, 47, 63, 69, 73, 82, and the Balabus buses pass by many historical monuments. Buses take you almost everywhere within the metropolitan area; the one-way fare (no transfers) is one ticket. You can purchase tickets (8 F) on the bus or a block (*carnet*) of ten tickets (48 F—an economical investment) at Métro stations or in *café-tabacs* that display the blue-green Métro ticket sign.

Most bus routes operate from 6:30am to 8:30pm, Monday through Saturday. Others (indicated at bus stops by a colored number inside a white disc) run until 12:30am, and operate every day including Sundays and holidays. *Les Noctambus* is the reliable skeleton service that runs late at night: buses leave Châtelet from special stops marked with the night owl–logo every hour on the half hour from 1:30am to 5:30am.

Every bus stop in Paris posts fares, times, routes, and bus numbers. When you enter the bus, punch your ticket in the machine next to the driver. Do not punch travel passes or Carte Orange coupons: simply hold them up for the driver to see. When you wish to get off, signal the driver by pressing the red button near your seat. Getting around by bus is a good deal easier than it may sound; and listening to an irate Parisian bus driver caught in rush-hour traffic is also an excellent way to learn some interesting French words that you won't find in the dictionary!

Special one- (50 F) two- (80 F) three- (110 F) or five-day (170 F) tourist passes (*Paris Visite*) (half-price under 12), which allow unlimited travel on buses, the Métro, the RER express line, and the SNCF Ile-de-France lines, are sold at major Métro and RER stations. These passes also entitle holders to reduced rates (20 to 35 per cent discount) at certain tourist attractions.

ROISSY CHARLES-DE-GAULLE AIRPORT	
Information	01 48 62 12 12
Luggage claims	
for Air France	01 48 64 92 92
for Paris airport	01 48 62 10 46

ORLY AIRPORT	
Information	01 49 75 15 15
Luggage claims	
for Air France	01 41 75 40 38
for Paris airport	01 49 75 04 55

Roissybus ferries passengers to *Charles-de-Gaulle* airport from Place de l'Opéra (Rue Scribe, in front of the American Express office), with departures every 15 minutes from 5:45am to 8pm, then every 20 minutes until 11pm. The journey to or from the airport takes about 45 minutes if traffic is moving well. The one-way fare is 40 F.

Another convenient way to reach the city's airports is to take the **Air France Bus**. These buses make the same stops on the return journey from the airports. 24-hour information: 01 41 56 89 00 (answering machine in five languages).

From **Paris to Orly** (45 F). It leaves every 12 minutes, starting at 5:50am to 11pm, from: *Aérogare des Invalides*, Esplanade des Invalides, 7th arr.; *Montparnasse*, 1, rue du Commandant-Mouchotte, 14th arr.

From **Paris to Charles-de-Gaulle.**
To **Terminal # 2**: it leaves every 12 minutes, starting at 5:40am to 11pm;
To **Terminal # 1**: it leaves every 20 minutes, starting at 6am to 11pm, from: *Le Palais des Congrès*, bd. Gouvion-St-Cyr, near the Air France agency, (60 F), 16th arr.; *near the Arc de Triomphe* (60 F), in front of 1 av. Carnot, 17th arr.; *Montparnasse*, 1, rue du Commandant-Mouchotte, (70 F), 14th arr., every half hour from 7am to 9:30pm, with a stop at Gare de Lyon, about 10 minutes after the Montparnasse departure, at 2bis boulevard Diderot, 12th arr.

Between **Charles-de-Gaulle and Orly**: from 5:40am to 2pm every 20 minutes; from 2pm to

11pm every 30 minutes (75 F).
Between **Orly** and **Charles-de-Gaulle**: from 6am to 3pm every 20 minutes; from 3pm to 11:30pm every 30 minutes (75 F).

• *LIMOUSINES*

Alliance Autos

94160 Saint-Mandé, 10 bis, rue Jeanne d'Arc
01 43 28 20 20, fax 01 43 28 27 27
E-mail: Allianceau@aol.com
Open daily 24 hours.
The leader in chauffeur-driven limousines, Alliance Autos has conquered a demanding clientele of CEOs, film stars, and media moguls. But you needn't be a celebrity to benefit from Alliance's personalized service. Harried business people and travelers touring the capital are all accorded the «star treatment». Instead of fighting for a taxi, why not arrive in Paris in a chauffeured Mercedes Class S (or a Renault Safrane)? A bilingual driver will be your guide, and facilitate your visit in any way he can. To give you an idea of the prices: transfer from Roissy-Charles de Gaulle to Paris, 700 F (Mercedes), 500 F (Safrane); a half-day (four hours), 1,300 F (Mercedes); a full day (nine hours), 2,800 F (Mercedes). Other types of vehicles (buses, trucks, vans) are also available.

• *MÉTRO*

Getting the knack of the Métro system is a clinch. You'll find a Métro map posted at each station, outside on the street and inside as well. Let's imagine you want to go from the Gare du Nord to Saint-Germain-des-Prés. Locate the two stations on your map and check whether they are on the same line (each line is indicated by a different color). In this case they are, so follow the line from your station of departure to your station of arrival, then note the name of the station at the end of the line (in this instance it's the Porte d'Orléans). That means that Porte d'Orléans is the name of the direction you will be taking. Inside the station, look for signs indicating «direction Porte d'Orléans», and when you reach the platform, check again on the sign located in the middle of the platform. If you must change lines to reach your destination, consult a Métro map to ascertain which stop offers the relevant *corresponda:ce*, or interchange.

> The **R.A.T.P.** runs the Métro, the buses, and the RER. Information line: 08 36 68 77 14 from 6am to 9pm, or 08 36 68 41 14 in English.

Hours: first departure from the terminal: 5:30am; last departure from the terminal: 12:30am.
A single ticket is good for any one-way journey on the Métro system and within zones 1 and 2 of the RER system (see RER, below). Don't forget to keep your ticket until you leave the bus or Métro, for you may be asked to produce it by an R.A.T.P. official. Tourist or not, if you don't have it, you will have to pay an on-the-spot fine if you're caught.

• *RER*

The *Réseau Express Régional* is a network of fast commuter services linking the center of Paris to destinations all over the Greater Paris Region. Quite a number of interesting places to visit are accessible by RER, and you can pick up brochures listing these from any Métro information kiosk.
The flat-rate system on the regular Métro does not apply to the RER unless you are traveling within the city, so you must consult the fee schedules posted on the automatic ticket machines to determine the cost of your journey.

Airport Transportation

> ## Minitel: 3615 HORAV
>
> Departure and arrival times for flights at both Orly and Roissy-Charles-de-Gaulle airports.

The **Orlyval** system is a quick and care-free way to travel to or from Paris-Orly airport. To reach the airport, take the RER B line from, say, Châtelet, then change at Antony for the driverless elevated car that drops passengers off at both Orly terminals. The service operates from 6:30am to 9:15pm Monday through Saturday, 7am to 10:57pm on Sundays. The fare is currently 57 F (28 F for children under 11).

• *TAXIS*

There are some 18,074 taxis available in Paris (until you really need one!). There are three ways of getting yourself a taxi: the first is simply to flag one down (it is available if its roof light is fully illuminated); the second is to go to a taxi stand (*Tête de Station*); the third is to phone a radio taxi that will arrive 5 to 10 minutes later at your address (the meter will already be running, but don't get in if it's more than 35 F). Normally, you pay 13 F to get in the cab and about 3.53 F per kilometer during daytime hours (7am-7pm) and 5.83 F at night (7pm-7am). Rates are higher to the suburbs, on expressways (i.e. to the airports). Supplements are charged if the taxi leaves from a train station (5 F), if a fourth person is aboard (11 F), for each item of luggage (6 F), and for pets (4 F). Though not obligatory, a tip of 10 to 15 percent is customary.

If you wish to report a problem or lodge a complaint, call 01 55 76 20 00, or write to Service des Taxis, 36, rue des Morillons, 75732 Paris cedex 15, indicating the taxi's license number as well as the date and time you were picked up.

Alpha-Taxis

01 45 85 85 85, fax 01 44 24 95 36
Open daily 24 hours.

Artaxi

01 42 03 50 50, fax 01 44 52 23 95
Open daily 24 hours.

G7 Radio

01 47 39 47 39, fax 01 47 37 83 23
Open daily 24 hours.

TOURS

• *BY BUS*

Cityrama

1st arr. - 4, pl. des Pyramides
01 44 55 61 00, fax 01 42 60 33 71
Open daily Apr 1-Oct 31: 6:30am-10pm; Nov 1-Mar 31: Sat-Thu 6:30am-8:30pm, Fri 7:30am-8:30pm. M° Palais-Royal.

Cityrama's double-decker, ultracomfortable tour buses whisk visitors all around Paris morning, noon, and night (for schedules and fares, call or pick up a brochure). A recorded commentary describes monuments, landmarks, and points of interest in the language of your choice Cityrama will also show you around Versailles, Chartres, Disneyland Paris, and many other places of interest.

French Links

20th arr. - BP 41, 29, rue Patrice de la Tour du Pin
Tel/fax 01 44 64 76 26
E-mail: Kaplan@club-internet.fr

Walking tours

Discover the city on foot during a three-hour stroll with a theme. You can choose from luxury fashion, avant-garde fashion, Left Bank fashion, designer fashion, antiques and art galleries, or gift ideas. Cost for a pre-programmed tour (list available at the Office de Tourisme, 127 av. des Champs-Élysées, 8th arr.) is 180 F per person, which includes the services of a bilingual guide and a tea or coffee break.

Full-day tours are also available. You will feel like a real Parisian as you shop in the boutiques and in a food market. As an added bonus, a Cordon Bleu-trained chef will help you cook up the ingredients purchased at the food market (650 F).

Personalized tours may be arranged by request: call **Shopping Plus** at 01 47 53 91 17 for further details, fax 01 44 18 96 68.

Open daily 9am-8pm.

For customized, English-language tours of Paris and its environs—even to the Loire Valley and Giverny—call Rachel Kaplan at French Links. Author of a book on little-known Paris museums, she will guide you to exciting destinations on and off the beaten track. Individuals or groups are chauffered in and around the city in air-conditioned cars, minivans, or small buses. Tell Rachel your interests, and she will compose a personalized tour of cultural sites, the newest restaurants, or the smartest shops.

Paris et son Histoire

9th arr. - 82, rue Taitbout
01 45 26 26 77, fax 01 49 95 94 31
Open 10am-noon & 2pm-6pm. Closed Sat, Sun & hols. Fee: 350 F, 500 F per couple. M° Trinité.

As the name indicates, this association specializes in the history of Paris (and the surrounding Ile-de-France region). Members attend lecture tours throughout the year; and from March to October, bus trips are organized to points of interest in the Paris area. Annual membership fees are 350 F (500 F for couples) and include a monthly bulletin of events. Meeting times and other information are provided by phone, or at tourist offices.

Paris-Vision

1st arr. - 214, rue de Rivoli
01 42 60 30 01, fax 01 42 86 95 36
Open daily Nov 1-Mar 31: Mon 8am-9pm, Tue-Sun 7am-9pm; Apr 1-Oct 31: Mon 8am-10pm, Tue-Sun 7am-10pm. M° Tuileries.
Paris-Vision conducts guided tours of the city in just about any language you can think of. Trips to Versailles, Fontainebleau, Chartres, and more are scheduled as well. For details, consult the firm's brochure, available at the address above or at tourist offices.

R.A.T.P.

8th arr. - Pl. de la Madeleine (beside the flower market) - 01 40 06 71 45
Open Apr 1-Oct 31: Mon-Fri 8:30am-6:45pm, Sat 6:30am-6:45pm; Sun 6:30am-1am; Nov 1-Mar 31: 9am-noon & 1pm-5pm, closed Sat, Sun, hols. M° Madeleine.
Guided bus tours conducted in every imaginable language. Half- and full-day excursions to fascinating sites in the Ile-de-France and even further afield are also offered. For a free brochure listing destinations and prices, drop by the R.A.T.P. tourist office at the Madeleine, or at La Maison de la R.A.T.P. at 191, rue de Bercy in the twelfth arrondissement (tel 01 53 46 43 24, M° Gare-de-Lyon).

• BY BOAT

Step aboard a riverboat for a spectacular view of Paris as you float along the Seine. The city's canals, too, afford a fascinating look at picturesque and *populaire* neighborhoods. The pace is leisurely and there's no hassle with traffic!

Bateaux Parisiens

7th arr. - Port de la Bourdonnais,
Maurice Chevalier landing stage
01 44 11 33 33, fax 01 44 11 33 53
One hour tour. Easter-end Oct: 10am-10:30pm, departures every half-hour; end Oct-Easter: Sun-Fri 10am-9pm, Sat 10am-10pm, departures weekdays every hour, w-e every half-hour. Lunch cruises by reservation only at 12:30pm (2 hours). Dinner cruises at 8pm (2:30 hours). Free pkg. M° Trocadéro.
Don't miss these boats. Bateaux Parisiens' classy all-glass river cruisers offer a memorable guided tour of quayside Paris, wheter you hop on the audio tour, or the commentary one given by a trilingual hostess, both written by a certified professor of history. An illustrated brochure is provided, free of extra charge. Lunch and dinner cruises of reasonable quality are offered, featuring unlimited wine, table service, and even a dance band! Theme cruises can also be arranged; in fact, just tell Bateaux Parisiens what sort of tour you'd like, and they'll custom-design a cruise just for you.

8th
01 42 2
*One hour to
10am-10pm (1
Mar: every hour 11a*
These whales of river
the Seine packed with to
often eliciting a sarcastic smil
But the laugh is on the cynics. Thes
boats provide one of the few ways to
from a new angle. Take an early-morning
dusk cruise, when the light is at its loveliest. O
night cruises, the Bateaux-Mouches' floodlights unveil a phantasmagoric cityscape that fascinates tourists and seen-it-all Parisians alike. Lunch (at 1pm, exc Mon), and formal dinners (daily at 8:30pm) are available on board at reasonable prices, considering the incomparable view that accompanies your meal.

Bat-o-Bus

Discover historical Paris along the Seine on this summer bus trip (no audio commentary). Board at any of these five stops: Tour Eiffel-Trocadéro, Musée d'Orsay, Passerelle des Arts–Musée du Louvre, Notre-Dame, Hôtel de Ville-Centre Georges Pompidou. *From mid Apr to mid Oct, tel 01 44 11 33 44.*

Canauxrama

19th arr. - 13, quai de la Loire
01 42 39 15 00, fax 01 42 39 11 24
1-day cruise Apr-Oct: 8:30am-6pm (exc Wed); 3-hour cruise: daily 9:45am & 2:45pm at La Villette & 2:30pm at Paris-Arsenal. Closed Jan 1, Dec 25. Admission: 75-200 F, reduced rate for children (exc for 1-day cruise). M° Jaurès (La Villette), Bastille (Paris-Arsenal).
Did you know that the Saint-Martin and the Ourcq Canals flow from the Seine in central Paris as far (upstream) as Meaux? Well, now you do. So why go by bus or subway when you can take a boat back from La Villette's Cité des Sciences? Canauxrama's cruises are one of the city's most pleasant, unhurried, uncrowded excursions. The view of Paris and the Ile-de-France from a comfortable canal boat (sunroof, on-board bar, guided tours) has a special charm. Canauxrama offers a day-long trip on the Canal de l'Ourcq through the lovely countryside between Paris and Meaux, with a stopover at Claye-Souilly for a picnic or bistro lunch. Also featured is a tour of the exciting La Villette neighborhood, which includes passage through the deepest lock in the

xurious menu is supervised by
érard Besson. Reservations are in-
! Private parties can also be ar-

AT YOUR SERVICE

• TOURIST INFORMATION

For all the brochures and other «literature» that the sage sightseer might need.

Eiffel Tower Office

7th arr. - 01 45 51 22 15
*Open May 1-Sep 30: 11am-6pm. M° Alma-Mar-
ceau.*

Gare de Lyon Office

12th arr. - 20 bd Diderot - 01 43 43 33 24
*Open 8am-8pm. Closed Sun & hols. M° Gare de
Lyon.*
Located opposite track L/N.

Gare du Nord Office

10th arr. - 18, rue de Dunkerque
01 45 26 94 82
*Open 8am-8pm. Closed Sun & hols. M° Gare du
Nord.*
Located in the suburban (*Banlieue*) lines lobby,
near the entrance to Métro line 5.

Office de Tourisme de Paris

8th arr. - 127, av. des Champs-Élysées
01 49 52 53 54, fax 01 49 52 53 00
*Open 9am-8pm, Sun & Nov-Mar & hols 11am-
6pm. Closed May 1. M° Charles de Gaulle-Étoile.*

24-Hour Information Line

01 49 52 53 56
In English, of course.

• ORIENTATION

Here are a few facts of French life for
foreign visitors.

Remember that in France, the **ground floor**
(*rez-de-chaussée*) is what Americans call the
first floor; the French first floor (*premier étage*)
corresponds to the American second floor,
and so on.

When dining out, the **service charge** (15
percent) is always included in the bill. An

Sein
board th
two comforta
20 and 150 passe
ticularly fine in the
cruises are arranged on re
recommended.

and
.3 on
notier,
etween
is par-
sonalized
servations

Les Vedettes de Paris-Ile-de-France

7th arr. - Port de Suffren
01 47 05 71 29, fax 01 47 05 74 53
http://www.oda.fr/aa/vedettes-paris
*Open daily Apr 1-Sep 30: 10am-11pm; Oct 1-Mar
31: Sun-Fri 10am-6pm, Sat 10am-10pm. M° Bir-
Hakeim.*
A nostalgic dance-hall atmosphere reigns on
these tea-dance cruises with such themes as historic Paris or the Val-de-Marne (1 hour).

Les Vedettes du Pont-Neuf

1st arr. - Square du Vert-Galant, Pont-Neuf landing
stage - 01 46 33 98 38, fax 01 40 26 38 98
*Open daily Apr-Oct: 10am-11pm; Nov-Mar: Mon-
Thu 10:30am-10:30pm, Fri-Sun 10:30am-11pm.
M° Pont-Neuf.*
The Vedettes du Pont-Neuf are medium-size
boats that take passengers on one-hour pleasure
cruises up and down the Seine. Cruises depart
every 30 minutes from 10am to noon and from
1:30pm to 6:30pm in spring and summer, and
every 45 minutes from 10:30am to noon and from
2pm to 6:30pm from late fall through the winter.
Evening cruises along the illuminated banks of
the Seine are conducted from 9pm to 10:30pm
(departures every half hour); off-season at 8pm
and 10pm. Group tours and parties are handled,
too.

Yachts de Paris

15th arr. - Port de Javel-Haut
01 44 37 10 20, fax 01 44 37 10 25
Open daily 9am-11pm. M° Javel.
Dine aboard the elegant *Don Juan,* a 1930s–
vintage motor yacht that cruises nightly along
the Seine. The two-hour cruise includes dinner
with one selection of wine, mineral water and

Les Bateaux-Mouches

TOURS · BASICS

additional tip can be left if you are satisfied with the service. Hairdressers are generally given a 10 to 15 percent tip. Porters, doormen, and room service are tipped a few francs. A hotel concierge makes all sorts of reservations for you (theater, restaurant, plane, train, and so on) and can offer advice about getting around in Paris; don't forget to tip the concierge afterward for his or her considerable services. Ushers at most sporting events, ballets, and concerts expect a tip, and can be vengeful if you fail to shell out a couple of francs.

Note that (most) **telephone numbers** in France have ten digits, beginning with a zero. The initial zero must be omitted if you are calling France from abroad. Within France, dial the entire ten digits.

French and American **voltages** differ, so your electrical appliances (shavers, hairdryers) will require a transformer. You will doubtless also need an adapter for the round prongs of French plugs.
These items can be obtained in many hardware or electrical supply stores, or in the basement of the Samaritaine or BHV department stores.
Hallway lighting systems are often manually operated. Just to one side of the entrance, in a conspicuous place on each landing or near the elevator, you'll find a luminous switch that is automatically timed to give you one to three minutes of light. To enter many buildings, you must press a buzzer or a numerical code usually located at the side of the front door.
The French telecommunications services (FRANCE TELECOM) have created plastic **telephone cards** to be used instead of coins in public phone booths; indeed, a coin-operated phone is something of a rarity nowadays. Phone cards sell for 97,50 F or 40,60 F and may be purchased at the post office, cafés, and some bookstores. Their microchip technology gives you a certain number of units, which are gradually used up as you make your calls. Don't count too heavily on using telephones in cafés and restaurants unless you have a drink or meal there.
Most modern pay phones have instructions in English printed on them. A local call costs 1 F. You can **phone abroad** from most pay phones using either your phone card or (in many booths) a major credit card such as Visa.
Collect calls can be made from pay phones by dialing 0 800 99 00, then the code for the

country you want (Australia, 61; Britain, 44; Canada and the United States, 11).
The Louvre **post office** (52, rue du Louvre, 1st arr., tel 01 40 28 20 00) has a 24-hour international **telephone/telegraph** and fax service which can operates with your credit card.

• *USEFUL ADDRESSES*

Here are some addresses and phone numbers of particular interest to English-speaking travelers:

Churches
American Cathedral in Paris
8th arr. - 23, av. George-V - 01 53 23 84 00
M° Alma-Marceau.

American Church
7th arr. - 65, quai d'Orsay - 01 40 62 05 00
M° Invalides.

Christian Science
14th arr. - 36, bd Saint-Jacques
01 47 07 26 60
M° St-Jacques.

Church of Scotland
8th arr. - 17, rue Bayard - 01 47 20 90 49
M° Franklin-D.-Roosevelt.

Great Synagogue
9th arr. - 44, rue de la Victoire
01 45 26 95 36
M° Le Peletier.

Liberal Synagogue
16th arr. - 24, rue Copernic - 01 47 04 37 27
M° Victor Hugo.

St. George's Anglican Church
16th arr. - 7, rue Auguste-Vacquerie
01 47 20 22 51
M° Kléber.

St. Joseph's Church (Catholic)
8th arr. - 50, av. Hoche - 01 42 27 28 56
M° Courcelles.

St. Michael's English Church
8th arr. - 5, rue d'Aguesseau - 01 47 42 70 88
M° Madeleine.

Remember that if you spend 1,200 F or more in a store, you are entitled to a full **refund of the value-added tax** (VAT). See Basics for details.

Embassies

American Embassy

8th arr. - 2, av. Gabriel
01 43 12 22 22, fax 01 42 66 97 83
M° Concorde.

Australian Embassy

15th arr. - 4, rue Jean-Rey
01 40 59 33 00, fax 01 40 59 33 10
M° Bir-Hakeim.

British Embassy

8th arr. - 35, rue du Fg-St-Honoré
01 44 51 31 00, fax 01 44 51 31 27
M° Concorde.

Canadian Embassy

8th arr. - 35, av. Montaigne
01 44 43 29 00, fax 01 44 43 29 99
M° Franklin-D.-Roosevelt.

New Zealand Embassy

16th arr. - 7 ter, rue Léonard-de-Vinci
01 45 00 24 11, fax 01 45 01 26 39
M° Victor Hugo.

English-Speaking Organizations

American Chamber of Commerce

8th arr. - 21, av. George-V
01 40 73 89 90, fax 01 47 20 18 62
Open 9am-5pm. Closed Sat, Sun. M° Alma-Marceau.

American Express

9th arr. - 11, rue Scribe - 01 47 77 77 50
Open Mon-Fri 9am-6pm, Sat 9am-5:30pm, Sun 10am-5pm.
Here you'll find traveler's cheques and American Express card and travel services. You can also arrange to pick up mail and wire money or have money wired to you. More information can be obtain daily 24 hours at 01 47 77 70 00.

American Library

7th arr. - 10, rue du Général-Camou
01 45 51 46 82
Open 10am-7pm; Aug: Fri noon-6pm, Sat 10am-2pm. Closed Sun, Mon, French hols. M° École Militaire.
This privately run establishment houses the largest English-language library on the continent. There is also a selection of records and cassettes. You must, however, be an official resident of France (with a valid *carte de séjour*) to take books out of the library. An annual membership fee is charged.

Find the address you are looking for, quickly and easily, in the Index.

Postal codes

All Paris postal codes have five digits, beginning with 75 and ending with the number of the arrondissement, with zeros in between. Thus, if a restaurant or shop is in the 8th arrondissement, its postal code is 75008; if it is in the 17th arrondissement, its code is 75017. The zip code is written before "Paris". For example, the address of restaurant in the 8th arrondissement is written out like this: Restaurant name, street name, 75008 Paris, France.

British Council

7th arr. - 9, rue Constantine
01 49 55 73 00, fax 01 49 55 73 15
Open Mon-Tue & Thu-Fri 11am-6pm, Wed 11am-7pm. Closed Sat, Sun. M° Invalides.
The council manages a wide-ranging library of English books and records.

Canadian Cultural Center

7th arr. - 5, rue Constantine
01 44 43 21 00, fax 01 44 43 21 99
Open 10am-6pm. Closed Sat, Sun. M° Invalides.
The Canadian cultural center an art gallery, and offers the services of a library and student-exchange program office.

Hospitals

(English-Speaking)

Hôpital Américain (American Hospital of Paris)

92200 Neuilly-sur-Seine - 63, bd Victor- Hugo
01 46 41 25 25, fax 01 46 24 49 38
M° Pont-de-Neuilly.
More than 40 specialized services are offered. Dental services are also provided, and there is a 24-hour English-speaking emergency service. A consultation here can be paid for in dollars or francs. Many insurance plans honored.

Hôpital Franco-Britannique (British Hospital)

92300 Levallois-Perret - 3, rue Barbès
01 46 39 22 22, fax 01 46 39 22 26
M° Anatole France.
This hospital provides complete medical services.

Pharmacy
Pharmacie Internationale
9th arr. - 5, pl. Pigalle
01 48 78 38 12, fax 01 48 78 32 64
E-mail: Apotec2000@aol.com
*Open Mon-Sat 8am-1am, Sun noon-1am. M°
Pigalle.*
New in Paris: this pharmacy has a unique
database where they can look up the French
equivalents of the medecine you take back home,
no matter where your home! English-speaking
pharmacists, but also German-, Spanish-, Italian-
, Arabic- and even Russian-speaking. One more
plus: you can pay in foreign currency or with
American checks.

• *PHONE DIRECTORY*

EMERGENCY

Fire Department	18
Police Headquarters	17
	or 01 53 71 53 71/73
Lost Credit Cards	
American Express	01 47 77 72 00
Diner's Club	01 47 62 75 75
Eurocard/Mastercard	01 45 67 53 53
Visa	01 08 36 69 08 80

Medical
Assistance Infirmiers Paris
01 47 70 05 05
Open daily 24 hours.
Nurses respond to medical emergencies.

Cardiac Emergency
01 45 27 10 10
Open daily 24 hours.
When heart attack strikes, every second
counts. A call to this number will bring a car-
diologist rushing to the scene.

Centre Anti-Poisons
01 40 05 48 48/48 82/43 31
Open daily 24 hours.
Poison Control Center.

SAMU (Ambulance)
15

Open daily 24 hours.
S.O.S. Crisis Line
01 47 23 80 80
Open daily 3pm-11pm.
In English.

S.O.S. Labo
01 46 08 11 11
Open daily 24 hours.
For emergency blood tests or bacteriological
samples, etc. call this laboratory.

S.O.S. Médecins
01 43 37 77 77 or 01 47 07 77 77
Open daily 24 hours.
These doctors make house calls at any hour of
the day or night, for about 150-350 F.

S.O.S. Psychiatrie
01 47 07 24 24
Open daily 7am-midnight.
Emergency psychiatric care.

Veterinarian
01 42 65 00 91
Open daily 24 hours.
If your pet needs emergency aid, call this number. A vet will be on the scene within 1 hour, for
a charge of about 500 F.

Miscellaneous
Currency
Exchange Office
8th arr. - 140, av. des Champs-Élysées
01 42 89 35 84
Open daily 8am-midnight.
Events
8th arr. - 127, av. des Champs-Élysées
01 49 52 53 53
*Open Apr-Oct: daily 9am-8pm; Nov-Mar: Mon-Sat
9am-8pm, Sun 11am-6pm. M° Charles-de-Gaulle-
Étoile*
Tickets office, and avaibility for plays, concerts, or exhibitions in Paris.

Events
01 49 52 53 56
Open daily 24 hours (answering machine).
Information for plays, concerts, or exhibitions.

Lost & Found
15th arr. - 36, rue des Morillons
01 55 76 20 20, fax 01 55 76 27 11
*Open information by telephone: Mon-Thu 9am-
5pm, Fri 9am-4:30pm; for visits: Mon & Wed
8:30am-5pm, Tue & Thu 8:30am-8pm, Fri*

8:30am-5:30pm. Closed Sat, Sun, hols. M° Convention.
First, say a prayer to Saint Anthony—patron of lost objects—then visit (don't call) this office to see if your plea was answered.

Mayor's Office

1st arr. - 29, rue de Rivoli - 01 42 76 43 43
Open 9am-6pm. Closed Sun & hols. M° Hôtel de Ville.
or 01 42 76 40 40
Open daily 24 hours.
For information on municipal matters in Paris.

Nationwide Traffic

08 36 68 20 00
Open daily 24 hours.
All day, all night, an answering machine will keep you abreast of traffic problems on the highways (and byways) of France.

Paris Traffic

01 42 76 52 52
Open daily 24 hours.
An answering machine reports traffic tie-ups in the capital.

Telegrams

36 55
Open daily 24 hours.
Messages for France are relayed by phone, then the hard copy is sent by mail. The minimum charge is 65 F for 25 words (not including the address) and 12.20 F for each ten-word addition. To send a telegram abroad, call the toll-free number 0 800 33 44 11, (135.24 F for 15 words, including the address, and 27.46 F for each five-word addition).

Time

36 99
Open daily 24 hours.
Feeling disoriented? Call this number to learn the date and time, anytime.

Wake-up Call

55 or 36 88 if 55 doesn't work with the phone you are using.

From any voice-tone phone you can schedule a wake-up call: to be awakened at 7:45am, for example, dial *55*0745#. To cancel, dial #55*0745#. But remember: don't try to schedule a call more than 24 hours ahead! It will cost you 3.71 F.

Weather

08 36 68 00 00
Open daily 24 hours.
No need to stick your head out the window! To find out how the weather is or is likely to be in the Ile-de-France, just pick up your phone.

• *DUTY-FREE SHOPPING*

The bad news is that just about everything in France is subject to **Value Added Tax** (VAT). The charge is 20.6 percent on most items. The good news is that people living outside Europe can get a 100 percent VAT rebate on items they export from France. To qualify for a rebate, you must be at least 15 years of age, and spend more than 1,200 F *in one shop.*

To get reimbursed, have the store fill in the Détaxe Légale form (make sure the shop carries it before you make the purchase). Bring your passport, because you'll be required to show it. Along with the form, the store will supply you with an envelope bearing its address.

When you leave France, show the forms at the Bureau de Détaxe or at Customs and have the Customs officer stamp them. Then seal the forms in the envelope supplied by the shop and mail it back. Keep your receipt. Information can be obtained at *Centre de Renseignements des Douanes*, tel 01 55 04 65 10, fax 01 55 04 65 30.

The rebate can be credited directly to your credit card. Some stores charge a commission for this service, while others (especially the duty-free shops on the Champs-Élysées, Rue de Rivoli, Rue de la Paix, and Avenue de l'Opéra) charge no commission.

French national holidays

They are January 1, May 1, May 8, July 14, and November 11; religious holidays fall on Easter, Easter Monday, Ascension Thursday, Pentecost Sunday and the following Monday, Assumption Day (August 15), All Saint's Day (November 1), and Christmas. A word of warning: banks and some shops will close early the day before a public holiday, and often a three-day weekend will become a four-day weekend when holidays fall on a Tuesday or a Thursday.

PROVENCE
& THE RIVIERA

Welcome to the land of sunshine

Provence! Land of sunshine! Advertisements tout the wines of the Sun, the freeway of the Sun, the fabrics of the Sun... The city of Nice brags of 299 sunny days a year. «Oh, those who don't believe in the sun here are real infidels», wrote Vincent Van Gogh, whose discovery of Provençal light changed his life and the history of painting. The bright, hot Mediterranean summers make aromatic herbs more pungent, give wines a higher degree of alcohol, and draw vacationers from all over the world.

Outsiders have been traveling to Provence since Greek merchants began to set up trading posts around 600 BC, buying metals from tribes settled there in Paleolithic times. Prehistoric sites and caverns remain near **Nice** and **Monaco**, Greek vestiges survive at **Antibes** and in the Hellenes' most powerful center, **Marseille**. A Greek ship lifted from this city's harbor by Jacques Cousteau's team stands proud in the History Museum on Rue Neuve Saint-Martin. The Roman chronicler Tacitus once described Marseille as «a happy mixture of Greek urbanity combined with Gallic temperance». This spirit produced Marseille's most famous culinary specialty, the fish soup sunny with saffron, called *bouillabaisse*.

Next to come were Celtic tribes from the north, fierce headhunters whose capital city stood near **Aix-en-Provence**. They were conquered in the second century BC by the Romans, who left their mark on everything in Provence for centuries after: the language, the legal system, agricultural methods and tools, architecture. **Orange**, **Saint-Rémy-de-Provence**, **Arles**, and **Fréjus** still have impressive and beautifully preserved Roman monuments, and Arles's recent archaeological museum is one of the most fascinating in Europe.

In medieval times, the picturesque perched villages of Provence came into being, houses clustered high up around a church and fortified castle: **Gordes**, **Oppède**, and Peter Mayle's **Lacoste** in the Luberon, **Moustiers-Sainte-Marie** and **Biot** on the Riviera among them. **Les Baux-de-Provence** remains one of the most striking of these vertiginous villages, especially at sunset when one can almost hear the voices of former lords throwing captives off the castle's battlements, or the songs of troubadours courting Alix of the golden hair. In the fourteenth century, **Avignon** became one of Europe's major cities when a series of seven popes chose to live there instead of in Rome, building the majestic Papal Palace where theater festivals are held now every summer. From this time, too, dates the famous Pont d'Avignon, of which only a graceful fragment remains—enough to dance on still, however... Fifteenth-century Provence was dominated by the powerful personality of Good King René; a poet and musician of talent, patron of the arts and an innovative gardener, René lost almost every battle he ever fought. Shortly after his death, Provence became the property of the French Crown.

The seventeenth and eighteenth centuries were prosperous in Provence: the cities filled up with fountains and elegant town houses with wrought-iron balconies. Aix-en-Provence provides one of the most exquisite examples: its summer opera festival is held in the former archbishop's palace. The Riviera mountain town of **Grasse** was also rebuilt in the eighteenth century, though it was already famous for its flowers and perfumes. In that era too, **Tarascon**, Avignon, and Orange began manufacturing Indian-inspired fabrics with great success. The Souleïado company in Tarascon and Les Olivades in nearby **Saint-Étienne-du-Grès** are the two leading examples that remain today.

The birth of the Riviera

Nineteenth-century poets and painters celebrated the romantic charms of the Provençal countryside. In 1834, an English Lord Chancellor set out to take his consumptive daughter to Italy, but was turned back at the border because of a cholera epidemic. He chose to stop in a tiny fishing village called **Cannes**. His friends followed, and thus was founded the French Riviera as it came to be known by cosmopolitans, whose contemporary counterparts still spend part of every year there. **Monaco** made its fortune by opening a casino when the railroad was built in the 1850s. **Nice**, a long-established city, belonged to the house of Savoy until 1860, when a treaty ceded the town to France. Its Italian connections shine through in Niçois cuisine: here pesto is pistou, and is usually stirred into a vegetable soup rather than pasta. In the last hundred years, southern light has drawn wave after wave of painters: Van Gogh, Gauguin, Renoir, later Matisse, Dufy, Picasso, Chagall... Cézanne, of course, was a born Provençal, and devoted his life to celebrating «Nature's infinite diversity» in his native region.

Provence takes its name from the Romans' affectionate nickname for the region, *nostra provincia*, «another Italy», as Pliny called it. In Roman times Provence extended all the way to Spain! The western boundary is for most people marked by the Rhône River—but Arles, on the far side, somehow always finds itself included in Provence. Frédéric Mistral, a nineteenth-century Nobel Prize–winning poet who championed the area's regional culture, established his Provençal museum in Arles. It still has one of the best collections of local antiques, though for antique shopping, the weekend and holiday fairs at Isle-sur-la-Sorgue, east of Avignon, have achieved great renown.

The Camargue, just south of Arles, offers yet another landscape, another world, another cuisine. This is the delta land of the Rhône, a magic blend of fresh and salt water similar to the lower Mississippi. There is nothing else like it anywhere in Europe. Here houses made of mud and straw are surrounded by expansive rice paddies. Here rare birds migrate, shellfish abound, and cowboys called *gardians* herd small, tough bulls around groves of wild tamarisk. These bulls are not killed in the local arenas, where they return to fight many times to the public's enthusiastic applause. But they do sometimes end up as bull stew, with black olives in a heavy, dark sauce.

The northern limit of Provence corresponds roughly to the realm of the olive tree in the west, this symbol of eternity which has nourished the people of Provence since the Greeks showed them how to graft it productively. In the east, however, the Alpes de Haute Provence's high, wild valleys are no longer Mediterranean but mountain country, with good ski resorts. Here, too, nestles the hill town of Moustiers-Sainte-Marie, a producer of colorful faience since the eighteenth century. Nearby, the Verdon River Canyon offers untamed, breathtaking landscapes.

The eastern boundary, the Italian border, was set by the treaty of 1860. Menton, which snuggles up to the frontier, is friendly and picturesque, with an ochre-tinted old town, a lively market, and a lemon festival in February. The sheltered Bay of Garavan at Menton benefits from one of Europe's mildest climates, a boon for the city's famed Belle Époque gardens.

The southern limit of Provence alone poses no problems: it is the great inland sea—*media terra*. Major ports like Marseille and Toulon brim with bustling energy, but there are dozens of smaller fishing villages such as Cassis (famous for its white wine), Le Lavandou, or Saint-Tropez which has lured so many generations of artists and film-makers. Despite problems of overfishing and pollution, the Mediterranean continues to supply an amazing variety of seafood and fish: sea bass (bar or more commonly loup de mer), red mullet (*rouget barbet*), and sculpin (*rascasse*, indispensable in *bouillabaisse*), sea bream (*dorade*), and the «poor man's lobster», the densely fleshed monkfish or anglerfish (*baudroie* or *lotte*).

Enchanted landscapes

Though the coast has much to offer, inland Provence above all has charmed the world with its legendary scenery: «the familiar prospects of vines, olives, cypresses» as British writer Lawrence Durrell puts it, «enchanted landscapes of the European heart».

In the backcountry of course, there is little fresh fish, but dried salt cod has been a staple for centuries, used in dishes like the *grand aïoli* still served in most villages on feast days: platters of poached salt cod surrounded by colorful vegetables with a garlicky mayonnaise. Codfish also appears at Christmas Eve supper...followed by the Thirteen Desserts of Provence, which symbolize Christ and the twelve apostles.

These inland regions where wild limestone ridges contrast with manicured farms and small cities have much diversity: the Var *département* between Nice and Marseille produces charming wines, and is still largely unexplored. On Mont Ventoux, north of Avignon, lavender fields melt into the sky in mid-summer. The lower slopes are decked with vineyards, cherry and apricot orchards, fields of wheat and the winter wheat known as *épeautre*, which local chefs turn into a gourmet treat. The Ventoux is also famous for its truffles, sold at the market town of Carpentras.

Between Saint-Rémy-de-Provence and Arles rise Van Gogh's beloved Alpilles hills. Here a patchwork of irrigation canals and cypress hedging enclose plots of artichokes, oak-leaf and batavia lettuce, early strawberries, zucchini, tomatoes and eggplant, artichokes, melons, asparagus, or pear and apple cordons. On the scrubby hills, redolent of thyme, rosemary, and sage, placid sheep still graze. Today the opulent country life of these vivid valleys proves so attractive to footloose cosmopolitans that Saint-Rémy has recently supplanted the Riviera and the Luberon hills as the most fashionable place to live in southern France.

The keynote of life in Provence today is rustic refinement, a sensual ideal of good yet simple living which has inspired a whole generation of cooks all over France. Chefs from Alsace, Lille, and Brittany are slipping little rougets aux olives in among their local specialties, catering to a clientele more and more insistent on the fresh fish, herbs, and young vegetables which have characterized Provençal cuisine for centuries. Olive oil often replaces butter and cream in Lyon, goose fat in Alsace and the Southwest, as the most elegant—and above all most healthful—enrichment. At a time when many Americans consider French cooking over-elaborate, looking rather to Italy for inspiration, Provence offers the best of both worlds: it combines Mediterranean country roots with French *savoir vivre*.

RESTAURANTS & HOTELS

THE PRESS ACCLAIMS
Gayot Publications

"Their spicy reviews are fun." – **Associated Press**

"For picking restaurants, you can't do better than Gault Millau." – **Travel & Leisure**

"Entertaining... you will enjoy their prose." – **US News & World Report**

"Gault Millau is the toque of the town." – **San Francisco Examiner**

"The best money you'll spend: get a copy of Gault Millau." – **The Star**

"Great fun- An "A" for the authors." – **Daily Herald**

"Gault Millau is the authority on the subject." – **South China Morning Post**

"Witty, breezy, opinionated." – **New York Times**

"Gault Millau is provocative and frank." – **Los Angeles Times**

"Honest and specific. Booksellers are high on Gault Millau." – **The Chicago Tribune**

"They are the top choice." – **Glamour**

PROVENCE

AIX-EN-PROVENCE   13090
Paris 770 - Avignon 75 - Marseille 31   B./Rhône

12/20 L'Aixquis

22, rue Victor-Leydet
04 42 27 76 16, fax 04 42 93 10 61
*Closed Aug 1-20. Open until 10:30pm. Air cond.
Terrace dining.*
New chef Benoît Strohm holds promise of a fine future. He has ideas: salmon and sanguin sausages in a crêpe for a tasty first course, which you could follow with lamb noisettes in a wild-thyme jus. The accoutrements in the dining room are not always on the same note, however. In the two years since Joël Lani ended his «fiefdom», the atmosphere has turned sour; the prissy reception lacks all sense of the eat, drink and be merry attitude of the past, and the food often seems to keep beat with the atmosphere, unfortunately. On a small street away from the Cours Mirabeau. C 420. M 97-138 (lunch), 189-326.

 L'Amphitryon

2-4, rue Paul-Doumer
04 42 26 54 10, fax 04 42 38 36 15
Closed Sun, Mon lunch. Open until 10:30pm. Terrace dining. Air cond.
In an old, charming house right in the heart of a group of streets lined with century-old trees, devil-of-a-cook Bruno Ungaro knows how to whip up conventional fare with a personality all its own. His 145 F «back from the market», Provence-inspired menu is a shining example: half-smoked fresh cod carpaccio scented with rosemary; red mullet pâté en bouillabaisse; Sisteron lamb blanquette livened up with lemon and violet artichokes, and full-flavor chocolate cake. Nice days let you linger under the magnolias on the terrace facing the twelfth-century cloisters. Associate and friend Patrice Lesné has worked up a wine list teeming with growers' wines. Unheard of quality for the money. C 250-300. M 100 (lunch), 145-210.

 Hôtel
des Augustins

3, rue Masse - 04 42 27 28 59, fax 04 42 26 74 87
Open year-round. 29 rms 600-1,200. Air cond.
This beautifully restored twelfth-century convent houses fully renovated rooms with understated furnishings. Magnificent lobby.

12/20 Les Bacchanales

10, rue de la Couronne
04 42 27 21 06, fax 04 42 27 21 06
Open daily until 11pm. Air cond. Terrace dining.
The restaurants on this touristy street are usually more interested in quantity than quality, so this amusing dining room dressed up in Italian clothes is a refreshing find. Henry Flavien offers an impeccable reception and his dining room staff is of an irreproachable quality. Pascal Guillemaud's cooking times are a zig-zag affair, however. On one occasion, our whiting fillet in mullet roe sauce was practically raw, and the next time, the pigeon diodine with baby fava beans was cooked to the hilt. It's a shame, because he starts out with good quality ingredients. M 85 (weekday lunch), 135-285.

12/20 Le Bistro Latin

18, rue de la Couronne
04 42 38 22 88, fax 04 42 38 36 15
Closed Sun, Mon lunch. Open until 10:30pm. Air cond. Terrace dining.
An addition to the Ungaro-Lesné team's list of successes (see L'Amphitryon above). A novel atmosphere with its neo-Greek/Roman decor filled with the scents of Provence. Difficult to find a better menu than their *Menu du Marché*, using the best and most seasonal products found on the market on any particular day and going for less than 100 F. M 75 (weekday lunch), 99, 160.

 Bleu Marine

Route de Galice - 04 42 95 04 41, fax 04 42 59 47 29
Open year-round. 87 rms 420-490. Rms for disabled. Restaurant. Rm ser. Air cond. Pool. Pkg.
A rotunda-shaped building near the center of town, with well-equipped, soundproof rooms, mahogany furniture, and copious breakfasts. Very friendly welcome. Piano bar.

 La Caravelle

29, bd du Roi-René
04 42 21 53 05, fax 04 42 96 55 46
Open year-round. 32 rms 260-420. Air cond. Pkg.
Half of the rooms (the more expensive ones) give onto a lovely succession of indoor gardens. Rooms are renovated regularly.

 Château
de la Pioline

Pôle commercial de la Pioline
04 42 20 07 81, fax 04 42 59 96 12
Closed Sun dinner & Mon off-seas, Feb. Open until 10pm. Garden dining. Air cond. Heated pool. Valet pkg.
When we unearthed this oasis of verdure peacefully tucked away in the middle of a shopping zone, we felt like Robinson Crusoe when he discovered his island. But one most certainly eats

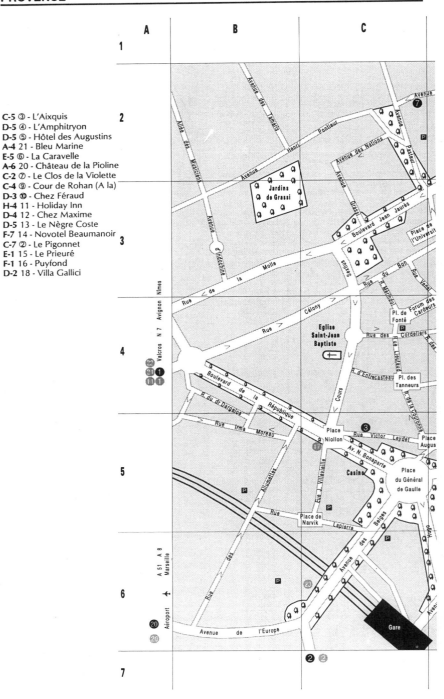

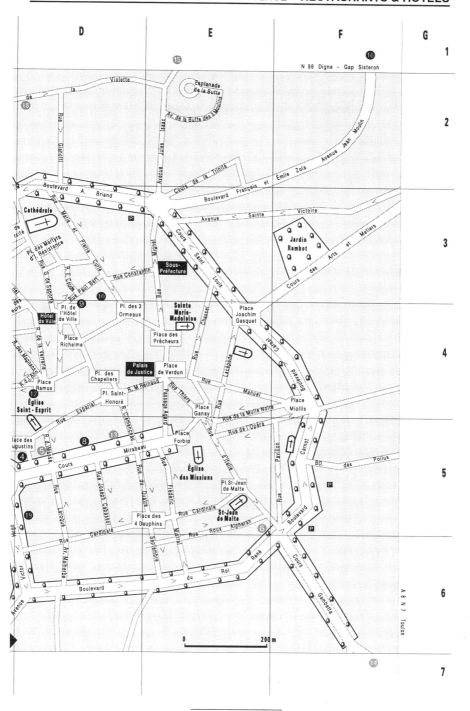

better than Robinson in this superb eighteenth-century castle. A summer lunch on the terrace, under the shade of the age-old lindens, is a source of true contentment. Chef Christophe Gillino did some serious homework at the likes of Senderens and La Tour d'Argent in Paris and the Chèvre d'Or in Eze before stepping off the boat in Aix last March. He quickly found the balance between Provençal *terroir* and his own imagination: ravioli stuffed with baby cuttlefish garnished with a delicate little shellfish cream sauce, glorious pigeon cooked over the coals with alongside a green-lentil risotto bordering on two-toque quality, and an out-of-this-world spicy wine reduction accompanying the blancmange. *La vie du château!* C 430. M 180 (weekday lunch), 230 (weekdays), 250 (Sun), 350 (Sun, wine incl).

 ## Château de la Pioline

(See restaurant above)
Closed Sun dinner & Mon off-seas, Feb. 3 stes 1,300-1,600. 18 rms 800-1,400. Rms for disabled. Half-board 1,120-1,320. Rm ser. Air cond. Heated pool. Valet pkg.

The luxurious guest rooms are faultlessly appointed and decorated with restrained elegance; all have pleasant views, either of the courtyard and fountain or the formal gardens. Exceptional breakfasts.

 ## Le Clos de la Violette

10, av. de la Violette
04 42 23 30 71, fax 04 42 21 93 03
Closed Sun, Mon lunch. Open until 9:30pm. Garden dining. Air cond.

What's going on in this villa with its terrace-garden on the still bonny banks of the Aix? Readers had already forewarned us that trouble was in the air, and our two visits forced us to sound the alarm bell. The consistency of the past seems to be dissolving, both in the dining room and in the kitchen. Surely the charming Madame Banzo has not lost all her capacity to smile, and we find it difficult to believe that Mr. Banzo has entirely lost the tuning fork for the sun-drenched, inventive cooking that, in the past, sung of Provence, but things are certainly off key for the moment. Both our visits started with a cool even haughty welcome. The meal started out on the right note—langoustine shortbread and coral ravioli, an excellent pressed crab served with garbanzo beans—and fell progressively out of tune as the meal progressed. The braised capon speckled with a few slivers of shrivelled up mullet roe and the red mullet fillets full of little bones were the beginning of a steady downhill journey which ended with a rather tasteless mixture of strawberries and raspberries in wine and a pear sweet with sticky caramel. All is not lost, however. The wine list hews to the regional line with a passionate selection of wines, but this is still not enough to keep the

point from dropping while we await a positive response on the part of a normally alert Mr. Banzo. C 500. M 250 (weekday lunch), 400, 500.

12/20 Chez Féraud

8, rue du Puits-Juif - 04 42 63 07 27
Closed Sun, Mon lunch, Aug. Open until 10:30pm. Terrace dining. Air cond.

In a delightful Provençal setting you can lunch or dine on uncomplicated regional fare, washed down by pitchers of tasty house wine. Family-style welcome and fast service. C 220-260. M 100, 135.

Holiday Inn

5-7, route de Galice
04 42 20 22 22, fax 04 42 59 96 61
Open year-round. 4 stes 850-900. 90 rms 470-650. Rms for disabled. Restaurant. Half-board 665-715. Rm ser. Air cond. Pool. Pkg.

A functional member of the famous chain, offering well-equipped, air-conditioned rooms not far from the city center. No-smoking rooms available. Pool with a snack bar. Professional service (including room service).

12/20 Chez Maxime

12, pl. Ramus - 04 42 26 28 51, fax 04 42 26 74 70
Closed Sun, Mon lunch, Jan 15-31. Open until 10:30pm. Terrace dining. Air cond.

Chef Jean-François Cannot just dropped in in fact. Félix Maxime is back in person to watch over his kitchen, his grilled meats and his full-of-fun staff. In the summer, pleasant terrace on the miniature Place Ramus. C 240. M 75-95 (lunch), 125-260.

Le Nègre Coste

33, cours Mirabeau
04 42 27 74 22, fax 04 42 26 80 93
Open year-round. 1 ste 700. 36 rms 350-650. Air cond. Garage pkg.

The oldest (eighteenth century) of Aix's historic hotels right in the center of town still has a real Provence flavor and huge guest rooms. Most of the rooms have been tastefully modernized and soundproofed, but the bathrooms could still use some work. Nicely furnished, with a wonderful old-fashioned elevator and a parking garage service.

Novotel Beaumanoir

Résidence Beaumanoir
04 42 27 47 50, fax 04 42 38 46 41
Open year-round. 102 rms 420-470. Rms for disabled. Air cond. Pool. Pkg.

The hotel, located a couple of miles from the city center, offers all the advantages of the chain: modern, airy, and regularly refurbished rooms.

Le Pigonnet

5, av. du Pigonnet
04 42 59 02 90, fax 04 42 59 47 77

Open year-round. 1 ste 1,650-1,850. 52 rms 600-1,500. Restaurant. Half-board 850-1,100. Rm scr. Air cond. Pool. Garage pkg.

A charm of a hotel lounging in the peace and calm of its two and a half acre park just ten minutes from downtown Aix. Rooms are soundproofed and air conditioned, and the bathrooms are frankly up to par for a king or queen. The prices are rather in the same category.

Le Prieuré

Route des Alpes
04 42 21 05 23, fax 04 42 21 60 56
Open year-round. 23 rms 190-400. Garage pkg.

This exquisitely comfortable, handsomely decorated seventeenth-century hotel was once a priory. Admirably situated opposite Lenfant park, which boasts gardens designed by Le Nôtre. Breakfast is served on the flower-decked terraces.

12/20 Puyfond

7 km N on N 96 & D 13, Rte de Saint-Canadet
04 42 92 13 77
Closed Sun dinner, Mon, Jan 2-10, Feb school hols, 3 wks in Aug. Open until 9:30pm. Garden dining. Pkg.

Anne Carbonel's cooking often resembles a rough draft more than a polished product, even though it is well presented. Well-chosen wines. All served in an ochre-colored dining room decorated with modern furnishings and antique mirrors and paintings, or (weather permitting) on a lovely shaded terrace. Forewarning: the large slightly pretentious house is rather lost (and difficult to find) in its park. C 250. M 130-160.

Villa Gallici

Av. de la Violette
04 42 23 29 23, fax 04 42 96 30 45

Open year-round. 5 stes 2,050-3,000. 14 rms 950-1,950. Rms for disabled. Restaurant. Rm scr. Air cond. Pool. Valet pkg.

Set in a landscaped garden of over two acres dotted with olive trees, oleanders, and cypresses, this exquisite Provençal *bastide* is a highly polished jewel of a hotel. Gilles Dez decorated the interior with verve and style in a manner inspired by the eighteenth century. The rooms are done up with ravishing fabrics and furniture; the bathrooms are dreamy. In fine weather, a lunch buffet is served poolside. Fitness center. Relais et Châteaux.

And also...

Our selection of places for inexpensive, quick, or late-night meals.

À la Cour de Rohan (04 42 96 18 15 - Pl. de l'Hôtel-de-Ville. Open until 10pm, 1:30am in Jul.): With assets like a soothing Provençal décor, a roster of fresh, simple dishes (especially yummy pastries), and a warm ambience, it's no wonder the locals flock here for lunch, tea, and supper. Minuscule cellar of inexpensive wines (200).

Trattoria Chez Antoine (04 42 38 27 10 - 3, rue Georges-Clemenceau. Open until 12:30am. Closed Sun, Jan.): Mediterranean specialties are featured, in a jolly, convivial ambience (190-270).

■ **In Meyreuil 13590**   *5 km SE on D 58h*

 ## Auberge Provençale

On N 7 - 04 42 58 68 54, fax 04 42 58 68 05
Closed Tue dinner, Wed, Feb school hols, 1 wk at Christmas. Open until 9:30pm. Terrace dining. Air cond. Pkg.

Wedged between a busy road and the motorway, this charming inn is warmed by a huge fireplace and a profusion of bouquets. Gabriel Astouric's authentic, robustly flavored Mediterranean menu is based on prime local ingredients,

---

Cruise that barge

Take a leisurely cruise through bucolic Champagne, Alsace/Lorraine, Ile-de-France, Burgundy and the Upper Loire on one of Continental Waterways' luxurious barges. All are handsomely wood-paneled and air-conditioned, and guest cabins boast private showers and bathrooms. By day, use one of the barge's bicycles to explore the countryside, or join a shore excursion to ancient abbeys, châteaux, museums, colorful markets and vineyards. At night, enjoy gourmet dinners, complete with French wines and cheeses. On each seven-day, six-night cruise, all meals, excursions—and wine—are included in the price.
Continental Waterways, 1, promenade du Rhin, 21000 Dijon, 03 80 53 15 45, fax 03 80 41 67 73
In the U.S.A.: 800-332-5332 (West Coast), 800-323-7308 (Rest of U.S.A.).

prepared with an expert touch. And the regional cellar provides perfect foils for the food. Expect a warm welcome from host Jean-Marie Jacquème. C 320. M 100 (weekday lunch), 125-240.

ANGLES (LES) 30   → **Avignon**

APT   84400
Paris 732 - Avignon 52 - Aix-en-P. 55   Vaucluse

Bernard Mathys

Le Chêne, N 100 - 04 90 04 84 64, fax 04 90 74 69 78
Closed Tue, Wed, mid Jan-mid Feb. Open until 9:30pm. Terrace dining.
Bernard Mathys cooks everything to order (so be patient), and the result is neat and clean just like the décor. It's so straight from the oven that he often even brings it to your table himself. He and his brilliant first officer conjure up subtle juxtapositions exhibiting the full range of Provence's rich gallery of flavors: mushroom ravioli, Dublin bay prawn shish kebabs with fresh-oyster sauce or stuffed young rabbit and tiny little Jersey potatoes stewed to perfection. The fixed-priced menu is, as always, an excellent quality for the price at 160 F, but the à la carte prices are another story. The cellar is not enormous, but demonstrates a discerning gustatory selection. C 450-500. M 160-450.

12/20   Café de France

Pl. de la Bouquerie - 04 90 74 22 01
Closed Mar 1-15 & Oct 1-21: Sun, Mon. Open until 9:30pm. Terrace dining.
Locals love this true «market» cuisine, including the smashing scrambled eggs (in season) made with truffles from the region. Try the Richerenches Syrah, which is quite good when it doesn't taste of the cork.

Relais de Roquegure 🌲🍴

Roquefure - 04 90 04 88 88, fax 04 90 74 14 86
Closed Jan 5-Feb 15. 15 rms 210-350. Restaurant. Half-board 250-325. Pool. Garage pkg.
In a ten-acre estate, a country hotel offering a warm welcome. For a holiday far from the madding crowd. Near riding stables.

ARLES   13200
Paris 621 - Marseille 92 - Avignon 40   B./Rhône

12/20   L'Affenage

4, rue Molière - 04 90 96 07 67, fax 04 90 96 56 13
Closed Wed dinner (exc in seas), Sun, 3 wks in Aug. Open until 10pm (10:30pm in summer). Terrace dining.
These old stables converted into a restaurant are the place to be seen for natives of this town. Brimming with life, a simple affordable style of cooking fragrant with the scents of Provence.

The service could add a touch of charm to their sullen repertoire. C 200-250. M 115.

Hôtel d'Arlatan

26, rue du Sauvage
04 90 93 56 66, fax 04 90 49 68 45
Open year-round. 7 stes 950-1,350. 33 rms 465-795. Air cond. Valet pkg.
A nineteenth-century mansion laden with history in a neighborhood saved from urban planning. Archeological treasures are displayed to their full advantage in both the entrance and in the rooms, all of which are air-conditioned and decorated with Frey or Canovas fabrics. Excellent reception.

Brasserie Nord Pinus

Rue du Palais - 04 90 93 02 32, fax 04 90 93 34 00
Closed Wed off-seas, Feb. Open until 10pm (10:30pm in summer). Terrace dining. Pkg.
If there has ever been an homage to bullfighting, this is it. The décor of owner Jean-André Charial's brasserie is a heartfelt dedication to the «art»—it's enough to make you a fan if you're not already. And chef Philippe Lepeltier's cuisine is inspired by his love and respect for something quite different: fresh, high-quality products which he treats with tender loving care, keeping his creative whims well under control. Noteworthy are his pan-fried sea perch, free-range chicken with foie gras and fresh pasta, and tasty raspberry clafoutis. The excellent service and reasonable prices are just one more positive point. C 260. M 120 (lunch, wine incl), 160.

Grand Hôtel Nord Pinus

Pl. du Forum - 04 90 93 44 44, fax 04 90 93 34 00
Closed Feb. 5 stes 1,500. 18 rms 700-900. Restaurant. Half-board 922-1,752. Rm ser. Air cond. Valet pkg.
Wrought-iron details and Venetian candelabra flank handsome Provençal antiques in this gorgeous hotel, part of which is a registered historic landmark. As the many bullfight posters suggest, this is a favorite haunt of local matadors and show-biz celebrities.

Lou Marquès

Bd des Lices - 04 90 93 43 20, fax 04 90 93 33 47
Closed Nov 12-Dec 23. Open until 9:30pm. Terrace dining. Heated pool. Valet pkg.
The cloisters of this seventeenth-century former Carmelite convent now serve as setting to a truly elegant, comfortable, and cheery eating house. Chef Pascal Renaud grows an Epicurean's garden which he nimbly uses to create dishes with a touch of country, such as scallops aside Camargue salt essence, a simple but delicious truffle omelette, John Dory with potatoes and violet artichokes, or wonderful pigeon with candied turnips and bacon partnered with vegetable ravioli, all of which go capitally well with the cellar's regional bottles.

Too bad about the prices. C 350-450. M 150 (lunch), 195-380.

 Hôtel Jules César

(See restaurant above)
Closed Nov 12-Dec 23. 5 sts 1,500-2,250. 50 rms 700-1,250. Rms for disabled. Half-board 875-1,910. Rm scr. Air cond. Heated pool. Valet pkg.
Some fine pieces of Provençal furniture grace the huge, comfortable rooms of this former convent, which sits in a garden on the edge of the old town. Lots of effort to create a quiet atmosphere. Large pool. Charming reception, service, and hospitality are provided in this Relais et Châteaux establishment.

 Mas de la Chapelle

Petite-Route de Tarascon
04 90 93 23 15, fax 04 90 96 53 74
Closed Feb. 1 ste 700. 15 rms 300-400. Rms for disabled. Restaurant. Half-board 400 (oblig in seas). Pool. Tennis. Pkg.
This superbly renovated seventeenth-century *mas* with its refined comfort is located right smack in middle of the marshlands just outside the village of Sambuc. The country-style rooms, beamed and tiled, are decorated in pink ochre and almond green. The cowherd gives «guided tours» of the 1,500-acre estate. The restaurant is housed in a Renaissance chapel.

 Le Mas de Peint

Le Sambuc - 04 90 97 20 62, fax 04 90 97 22 20
Closed Tue (exc Jul-Aug), beg Jan-mid Mar. Open until 9:30pm. Air cond. Terrace dining. Pool. Pkg.
You'll be welcome like long lost relatives in this very pretty kitchen with its old-fashioned caparison of beams, kitchen dressers, coppers and faïences. Everyone sits down together around two farmhouse tables, just like in the old days on the farm, and the feast begins. New chef Danièle Egreteau prepares squids stuffed with ratatouille, sea perch pan-fried with eggplant, leg of lamb and bull's rib teamed with zucchini tian, and a velvety chocolate tart, all using products from this very farm or from the Mediterranean. M 185 (lunch), 230 (dinner).

 Le Mas de Peint

(See restaurant above)
Closed beg Jan-mid Mar. 2 sts 1,750-1,980. 8 rms 1,050-1,500. Half-board 795-1,215. Pool. Pkg.
Lucille and Jacques Bon welcome you to their rustic seventeenth-century farmhouse, just outside the village of Sambuc, as if you were old friends they hadn't seen in years. Stone floors, wooden beams, old furniture and objects from the region, copper beds, white-linen sheets, bathrooms with mezzanines, canopied bathtubs, Canovas and Souleïado drapes: character is not what is lacking. The cowherd organizes walks across the countryside making up this 1,500-acre farm. But watch out for those 300 bulls roaming the same paths as you...

 Mireille

Quartier de Trinquetaille, 2, pl. St-Pierre
04 90 93 70 74, fax 04 90 93 87 28
Closed Nov-mid Mar. 34 rms 320-620. Restaurant. Half-board 379-520 (oblig in seas). Air cond. Pool. Pkg.
Fully remodeled, functional rooms (those in the annex near the swimming pool are less grand), and an outstandingly warm welcome make Mireille a great place to stay. Dining tables are set up on the patio for lunch when the weather is fine. Nearby tennis courts are open to guests, and there's a lovely pool.

12/20 L'Olivier

1 bis, rue Réattu - 04 90 49 64 88
Closed Sun, Mon (exc hols). Open until 9:30pm. Garden dining. Air cond.
In this relaxing environment with plenty of pretty Provençal touches on the lazy banks of the Rhône, the food is slipping in quality. Chef Jean-Louis Vidal disappointed us this year with his over-spiced marinated salmon and tasteless lime-flavored veal kidneys. The welcome is still charming, but the toque is nowhere near. C 350. M 95, 150 (wine incl), 260.

12/20 La Paillote

28, rue du Docteur-Fanton
04 90 96 33 15, fax 04 90 96 56 14
Closed Thu lunch in summer, Sat lunch, end Nov-end Dec. Open until 9:30pm (10pm in summer). Terrace dining.
Jean-Claude Tell offers healthy cooking inspired by the products of the region: aïlo, squid rouille, rack of lamb scented with thyme flowers, and lavender-honey ice cream. Order one of the nice price wines from the good regional selection with the rather short à la carte selections or the attractively priced «chef's mood» fixed-price menu. C 160. M 92.

12/20 Les Saveurs Provençales

62, rue Amedée-Pichot
04 90 96 13 32, fax 04 90 96 54 35
Closed Sun dinner off-seas, Mon. Open until 9:30pm. Terrace dining. Air cond.
This is the Provence you see in pretty picture books in this highly colorful neighborhood near the ampitheatre. First of all, there's the pull-at-your-heartstring accent and sweetness of manner, then there's the fragrances of garlic and basil, then there's that special little touch of Robert Raspail in the gently stewed dishes and salads. You might not be able to figure out just where the flavors come from (apart the olive oil), but you'll like the way this chef so enraptured by good ingredients turns them out in his own unique way. C 270. M 115, 150.

Please excuse us... (and the chefs). Menus are subject to the winds of change, and the dishes we've described may no longer be available when you visit.

Le Vaccarès

Pl. du Forum, entrance rue Favorin
04 90 96 06 17, fax 04 90 96 24 52
Closed Sun dinner & Mon exc in summer, Jan 15-Feb 15. Open until 9:30pm. Air cond. Terrace dining.
This father and son team may not be the Dumas of literary fame, but gee is their cooking poetic. Clever, ably crafted dishes full of sunny regional flavors in this (air conditioned!) dining room overlooking the picturesque Place du Forum. On warm starry nights on the lovely terrace, enjoy dishes such as calamary croquettes à la provençale, sea perch fillet steamed with Maussane olive oil, roast lamb with thyme jus, and the superb always superb pigeon with garlic cloves and foie gras risotto as you mingle with the late-night locals who gather here. Dominique Dumas greets guests with genuine Southern hospitality. Cellar selections have been expanded this year, and the crockery is new. **M** 98 (lunch, exc Sun), 135-280.

And also...

Our selection of places for inexpensive, quick, or late-night meals.
Lou Caleu (04 90 93 44 44 - 27 rue Porte-de-Laure. Open daily until 10pm): It may not be fancy, but it's good home cooking as you dine in this elegant Renaissance manor house overlooking the city. Pleasant staff and reasonably priced (85-220).
Poisson Banane (04 90 96 02 58 - 6, rue du Forum. Open until 12:30am. Closed Sun off-seas.): This terrace restaurant is the place to come on a sunny day. The food is consistently classic with a hint of a Southern accent: sunset shells in cream, scallop salad, and Châteaubriand with morel mushrooms (80-250).

AUBAGNE	13400
Paris 811 - Aix-en-P. 36 - Marseille 17	B./Rhône

12/20 La Ferme

Quartier La Font-de-Mai, chemin Ruissatel
04 42 03 29 67
Closed Mon, dinner Fri & Sat. Open 9:30pm. Terrace dining. Pkg.
This self-taught chef has a special place in his heart for Provençal cuisine. Try his Marseille-style pigs' feet, Provençal-style lamb kidneys, baby squids with fennel, and the fish of the day, always cooked to perfection. **M** 200.

 ## Hostellerie de la Source 🌲🍷

Saint-Pierre-lès-Aubagne
04 42 04 09 19, fax 04 42 04 58 72
Closed Sun, Mon, Feb school hols, Oct. 25 rms 360-1,000. Rms for disabled. Restaurant. Half-board 580-1,120. Rm scr. Heated pool. Tennis. Pkg.
This seventeenth-century manor was restored inside and out a few years back. The discreetly

modern rooms are well equipped. In addition to a bar and salon, the hotel boasts leafy grounds and a shaded terrace.

AVIGNON	84000
Paris 701 - Aix-en-P. 75 - Marseille 100	Vaucluse

 ## Bristol

44, cours Jean-Jaurès
04 90 82 21 21, fax 04 90 86 22 72
Closed Feb 15-Mar 9. 2 stes 800-932. 65 rms 469-786. Rms for disabled. Air cond.
A modern hotel with simple decoration located on a main artery leading to the famous Place de l'Horloge.

 ## Brunel

46, rue de la Balance
04 90 85 24 83, fax 04 90 86 26 67
Closed Sun, Mon, Jul 15-Aug 15. Open until 9:30pm. Air cond. Terrace dining.
Located under the arcades of a street just steps away from the Palais des Papes, Brunel's elegantly simple dining room is a favorite with local gastronomes attracted by the friendly service and fine wines, and, most of all, by the invigorating cuisine proposed by Robert Brunel. For many, self-taught Brunel is the very ebodiment of Avignon tradition. A serious chef who spends his time in the kitchen rather than dancing around the dining room, his devil of a menu at 178 F is a true symphony of market selections: velvety eggplant fondant, sea bream roasted in spices and embellished with lovely Provence-style stuffed artichokes, or golden farm-raised chicken with shallots and candied garlic. The drum roll ends with a plate of assorted pastries. Wash it all down with the amusing local wine from the principality of Orange at 85 F a bottle. **C** 380-430. **M** 120 (lunch, wine incl), 178-300.

 ## Cloître Saint-Louis 🌲🍷

20, rue du Portail-Boquier
04 90 27 55 55, fax 04 90 82 24 01
Open year-round. 3 stes 950-1,090. 77 rms 450-820. Rms for disabled. Restaurant. Half-board 655-1,025. Rm scr. Pool. Garage pkg.
The dignified beauty of this sixteenth-century Jesuit novitiate has been scrupulously respected, in spite of the modern «design» furnishings in the lobby and bar, and the new contemporary wing added by Jean Nouvel, architect of the Arab world institute in Paris, is respectful of this prestigious setting. The rooms are lovely and quiet, with many attractive amenities (cable TV, safes, minibar). A sun lounge has been fitted out on the roof. Delicious breakfasts (and so they should be, at the price).

12/20 Les Domaines

28, pl. de l'Horloge
04 90 82 58 86, fax 04 90 86 26 31
Open daily until 11pm. Terrace dining. Air cond.

MARTELL DEPUIS 1715

L'ABUS D'ALCOOL EST DANGEREUX POUR LA SANTÉ, CONSOMMEZ AVEC MODÉRATION.

Evian.
The natural spring water
on the world's finest tables.

EVIAN, AVAILABLE IN MORE THAN 100 COUNTRIES, ACROSS 5 CONTINENTS.

This anthracite and white dining room in the heart of old Avignon is an intelligent compromise between a wine bar and a family-style restaurant. The menu is simple and generous in portion, with offerings such as pork mignon in garlic cream and sirloin with shallots, which serve as a good pretext for tasting one of the 500 crus from the cellar of this restaurant owned by three brothers wild about wine. C 170-290.

 Christian Étienne

10-12, rue de Mons
04 90 86 16 50, fax 04 90 86 67 09
Closed Sat lunch, Sun. Open until 9:30pm. Terrace dining. Air cond.
Installed in the former residence of the papal chamberlain, Christian Étienne enjoys what may be the best location in Avignon, facing the Palais des Papes, with a panorama of the eponymous *place*. Our hallelujahs of the past were put on standby this year. The staid à la carte menu is frankly not inspirational, and gives you little choice but foie gras or lobster. The best thing is still the slice of monkfish roasted with luscious apples and candied garlic, but it relies too much on the spices to wake up the flavors. The little set menu at 160 F is attractive and offers the famous pieds et paquets, but the tomato-theme menu lacks all luster. A simple tomato salad would have been far better than the bore of a tartare, and the ravioli was served in a thoroughly insipid bouillon. Our hymn books are still open, so we'll see whether songs of praise will be appropriate next year. C 350. M 160-480.

12/20 **La Ferme**

Chemin du Bois (Ile de la Barthelasse)
04 90 82 57 53, fax 04 90 27 15 47
Closed Sat lunch, Nov 4-Mar 4. Open until 9:30pm. Terrace dining. Pool. Pkg.
This old-fashioned Provençal farmhouse with a monumental fireplace and shaded courtyard is an inviting spot for a bountiful but inexpensive lunch. The owner serves forth honest, regional cooking (marinated anchovies, lamb blanquette with cumin, etc.), and there's a small but engaging wine list. Charming welcome. M 110-210.

 La Ferme ⚐♟

(See restaurant above)
Closed Nov 4-Mar 4. 20 rms 330-550. Rms for disabled. Half-board 320-550. Pool. Pkg.
Pleasant hotel on an island in the Rhône River. Cozy, attractive rooms.

 La Fourchette

17, rue Racine - 04 90 85 20 93, fax 04 90 85 57 60
Closed Sat, Sun, Feb 21-Mar 1, Aug 8-30. Open until 9:30pm. Air cond. Terrace dining.
There's feeling put into the cooking here. Try the fresh thyme ravioli with sweet red pepper and capers, or the delicious skate with a slightly acidic ravigote sauce; follow it with the whipped cream-covered rum cake. Walls decorated with—you guessed it!—forks and porcelain crickets. Watch out for the wine list. M 100-115 (lunch), 148.

 Hôtel de Garlande

20, rue Galante - 04 90 85 08 85, fax 04 90 27 16 58
Open year-round. 12 rms 260-440. Rm scr.
The Garlande occupies a well-restored, handsome old house in the center of town. All rooms are redecorated regularly, and have good bathrooms. Convivial atmosphere.

 Le Grangousier

17, rue Galante - 04 90 82 96 60, fax 04 90 85 31 23
Closed Feb school hols, Aug 15-30. Open until 9:30pm. Terrace dining. Air cond.
Chef Philippe Buisson has created a little jewel-box for his seasonal cuisine so full of savors and finesse: an old cobbled courtyard of a medieval town house, now covered by a glass roof, giving it a distinctly modern appearance and located not far from Place de l'Horloge. There is also a distinctly modern side to his cooking: endive and oysters marinated in shallots, green asparagus with black truffle butter, pigeon perfectly roasted in brine with an exquisite au jus, and a very appetizing caramel ice cream with a Madeleine butter cookie livened up with honey and bitter chocolate. The fixed-price menu just under 200 F is a good buy. Excellent choice of Chateauneuf-du-Pape wines. M 140 (weekday lunch), 170 (weekdays lunch, wine incl), 193, 306.

 Hiély-Lucullus

5, rue de la République
04 90 86 17 07, fax 04 90 86 32 38
Closed Mon, Tue lunch (exc Jul-Aug), Jun 23-Jul 2. Open until 9:45pm. Terrace dining. Air cond.
Some think André Chaussy's love of detail and exactitude obsessive, others interpret it as a quest for perfection. No matter what people think, he continues on his merry way lavishing his customers with almost country-style cuisine redolent of herbs from his garden. The 210 F set meal is as young and fresh as ever: clam and scallop marinière, fresh cod roasted with juniper berries, or veal fillet and morels with homemade pasta. Jean-Luc Pamato greets you in a most courteous manner. M 140, 210.

 L'Isle Sonnante

7, rue Racine - 04 90 82 56 01
Closed Sun, Mon, hols, 1 wk in Feb, Aug. Open until 9pm. Terrace dining. Air cond.
If you feel like a tête-à-tête with a friend or a lovesome lunch offering reasonably priced gustatory pleasure, this may well be the place to come. Jérôme Gradassi's spirited cooking turns your tastebuds upside down: pan-fried duck foie gras with Chinese peas, plump green asparagus steam-cooked and lying on a velvety bed of tarragon sabayon, grilled sea bream with candied onion greens in chive butter, rabbit fillet stuffed with Nyons olive purée—a good start,

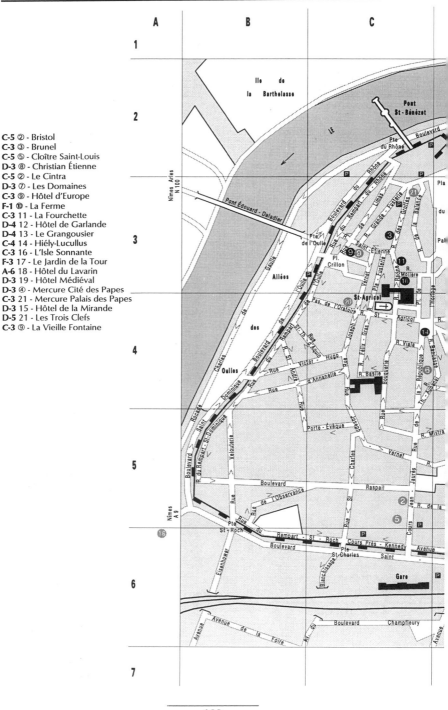

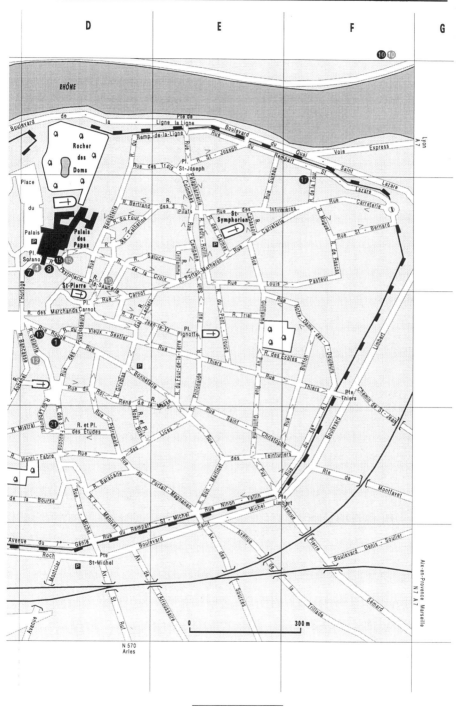

no? All the savors of all the seasons of Provence parade before you plate after plate, just as they are in their full untainted glory. Maria-Cristina Gradassi shows you a cushy time in her motherly way. The cellar is well stocked, and the family's Châteauneuf-du-Pape, the Domaine du Rempart, served in carafes, is certainly not devoid of merit. M 145 (weekday lunch), 220, 310.

12/20 Le Jardin de la Tour

9, rue de la Tour - 04 90 85 66 50, fax 04 90 27 90 72
Closed Sun dinner, Mon, 2 wks in Aug. Open until 10:30pm. Terrace dining.
The postmodern garage-cum-dining room opens onto a courtyard planted with olive trees: it's a setting that captures the spirit of Avignon in the '90s. The chef takes considerable care with his Provençal repertoire: eggplant and tomato in soy sauce and tangerine juice, red mullet matelote stewed in Gigondas wine, or roast duckling with lemon and honey sauce. C 275-365. M 135 (lunch), 165, 265.

 ## Hôtel du Lavarin

1715, chemin du Lavarin
04 90 89 50 60, fax 04 90 89 86 00
Open year-round. 44 rms 290-398. Rms for disabled. Restaurant. Half-board 440. Pool. Garage pkg.
A recently built hotel located outside the city walls, just off the road to Arles, the Lavarin offers quiet, well-equipped though rather aseptic rooms. Pleasant, shaded garden.

 ## Hôtel Médiéval

15, rue de la Petite-Saunerie
04 90 86 11 06, fax 04 90 82 08 64
Open year-round. 35 rms 195-295.
Despite the name, this is actually a seventeenth-century town house near the Palais des Papes, with smartly turned out little salons surrounding a flower-filled patio. Rooms are spacious but not very bright.

 ## Mercure Cité des Papes

1, rue Jean-Vilar - 04 90 86 22 45, fax 04 90 27 39 21
Open year-round. 61 rms 375-575. Rm scr. Air cond. Pkg.
Situated near the Palais des Papes, this hotel boasts large, comfortable, air conditioned rooms in a big, modern building.

 ## Mercure Palais des Papes

Quartier de la Balance, rue Ferruce
04 90 85 91 23, fax 04 90 85 32 40
Open year-round. 87 rms 370-570. Air cond. Pkg.
Situated within the city walls, the rooms of this hotel are comfortable, functional, modern, and well soundproofed, although not long on charm. Breakfast can be taken in the pretty garden.

 # Hôtel de la Mirande

4, pl. de l'Amirande
04 90 85 93 93, fax 04 90 86 26 85
Open daily until 9:45pm. Garden dining. Air cond. Valet pkg.
Set in a superb eighteenth-century town house restored to life with pride and conviction, La Mirande is one of France's most beautiful small hotels, and has a prime location right at the foot of the Palais des Papes. In the dining room (a masterpiece of refined luxury abound with coffered ceilings, tapestries and Old Master paintings), patrons savor Alain Davi's fresh and fragrant cooking. Even if the menu is brief in selections (3 selections per sitting) and the cooking simple and conventional, we made a splendid meal of his gallant goat cheese and basic ravioli, monkfish brazenly accompanied by eggplant caviar, young anise-perfumed sea perch, and young rabbit's leg stuffed with olives. On sunnier days, pleasant dining on the flowery patio or under the glass atrium. Fine selection of Rhône Valley wines. C 315-480. M 135 (weekday lunch, wine incl), 210-380.

 ## Hôtel de la Mirande

(See restaurant above)
Open year-round. 1 ste 3,200. 19 rms 1,700-2,100. Rms for disabled. Rm scr. Air cond. Valet pkg.
Nestled in the heart of Avignon, this stunning little luxury hotel is graced with a delicious secret garden, richly decorated salons, and good-sized rooms whose varied decoration and refined details evoke the luxury and comfort of a bygone era. Views embrace the rooftops of the *vieille ville* and the Palais des Papes. Royal bathrooms.

 ## Les Trois Clefs

26, rue des Trois-Faucons
04 90 86 51 53, fax 04 90 85 17 32
Closed Nov school hols, some wks in winter. Open until 9:30pm (10pm during the Festival). Terrace dining. Air cond.
The three «keys» (as the name denotes) of this restaurant run by Martine and Laurent Mergnac are sincerity, warmth and generosity. Even though monsieur is tiffed with us for dropping a point last year, we still hold that his cooking is an excellent example of exactingness. Bravo for the cherry tomato and pistou puff pastry and the milkfed veal with crushed olives and wine jam on the 120 F set-price menu. Accompany it with a Château Saint-Estève d'Uchaux at only 100 F a bottle. M 120, 145 (weekdays, wine incl), 190.

12/20 Le Vernet

58, rue Joseph-Vernet
04 90 86 64 53, fax 04 90 85 98 14
Closed Sun & Mon off-seas, 2 wks in Feb, 2 wks in Nov. Open until 10pm. Terrace dining.
Near the Vernet museum and one of the most beautiful of the gardens restored in Avignon, the cooking is more ambitious than awash with reflection, with the likes of grilled fish and truffle

omelette. The cellar is tiny but jolly well selected. C 250-350. M 125 (wine incl).

 ## La Vieille Fontaine

12, pl. Crillon - 04 90 14 76 76, fax 04 90 85 43 66
Closed Sun, Mon lunch. Open until 10pm. Terrace dining. Air cond. Valet pkg.
The cool, shaded courtyard, graced by a mossy fountain, is *the* place to dine on a summer's night; the rose and white dining room, stuffed with antiques and landscape paintings, is a bit short on charm for some tastes. Jean-Pierre Robert offers a Provençal cuisine to which he adds his own little spark of originality. Try his fresh minty crab-vegetable tartare with saffron sauce, or his lamb noisettes with sweet peppers and olives, a little tomato stuffed with fresh goat cheese, and garlic purée. Later on, tempt the inventive tomato roasted with lavender honey and dried fruit served with gingerbread toast and creamy lemon-thyme ice cream. Service for a king. Magnificent cellar, but don't bother looking for bargains. C 360-500. M 160 (wine incl), 170 (weekday, wine incl), 210, 350.

 ## Hôtel d'Europe

(See restaurant above)
Open year-round. 3 stes 2,150-2,550. 44 rms 630-1,750. Rm ser. Air cond. Valet pkg.
This luxurious, seductively splendid hotel is replete with Aubusson tapestries, precious *objets*, antique paintings, and artwork. The rooms are grand, with marble bathrooms. Two elegant, spacious rooftop suites have private terraces overlooking the town and the Palais des Papes (which is illuminated by night). Patio-terrace.

And also...

Our selection of places for inexpensive, quick, or late-night meals.
Le Cintra (04 90 82 29 80 - 44, cours Jean-Jaurès. Open daily until 10:30pm, midnight in summer.): Old-fashioned brasserie, with a menu that includes grilled meats, duck breast confit, choucroute (120-200).
Entrée des Artistes (04 90 82 46 90 - 1, pl. des Carmes. Open until 10:30pm. Closed Sat lunch, Sun, Sep 1-15): Chummy, Parisian-bistro atmosphere. Solid sustenance, low prices, and right downtown (120).
Les Félibres (04 90 27 39 05 - 14, rue du Limas. Closed dinner exc Thu, Fri & Jul; Mon; Jul 26-Sep 4.): Bookshop–tea room à la provençale serving honest traditional fare and delicious homemade pastries (120-240).
Simple Simon (04 90 86 62 70 - 26, rue Petite-Fusterie. Open until 7pm, 2am in Jul. Closed Aug.): Thoroughly British restaurant and tea room. Delicious cakes, but also Indian meat loaf, seafood rolls, cottage pies, crumbles and cheesecakes (80-120).

■ **In Les Angles 30133**   *4 km W on N 100*

 ## L'Ermitage Meissonnier

Av. de Verdun (route de Nîmes) - 04 90 25 41 68 (R), 04 90 25 41 02 (H), fax 04 90 25 11 68
Closed Sun dinner, Mon (exc lunch in seas). Open until 9:30pm. Garden dining. Pool. Pkg.
Given a choice, we always prefer a table on the garden-terrace, far more inviting than the rather fusty dining room. But wherever you sit, you're sure to enjoy Michel Meissonnier's fine cooking. This year, we were won over by the classic Avignon bisquebouille, a recipe he inherited from his father, as well as by some of his own creations, such as the lobster and coriander minestrone, the thyme-flavored young rabbit profiteroles and the quail and morel b'steeya. Despite this, we do think the menu could use some new additions. Adjoining the restaurant is a Lyonnais-style bistro where 100 F buys a very attractive meal. C 450-500. M 160-450.

 ## Hostellerie L'Ermitage

(See restaurant above)
Closed Jan-Feb (exc upon reser). 16 rms 230-500. Half-board 350-520. Rm ser. Air cond. Pool. Pkg.
The large trees hide the fact that the paint is peeling off the façade. Rooms are large and traditional for the most part, but some could use a face-lift. Quiet view over the park.

■ **In Montfavet 84140**   *5 km E on D 53*

 ## Le Jardin des Frênes

645, av. des Vertes-Rives
04 90 31 17 93, fax 04 90 23 95 03
Closed Nov-Mar. Open until 9:30pm. Garden dining. Air cond. Pool. Valet pkg.
After a long traipse through a maze of suburbia, you arrive at a stately home enveloped in a verdure of peace and quiet, where you can steep in the endless charm of the terrace under the plane trees and slip slowly into a state of bliss. We have always found the cuisine more staid and stately, like the site, than fresh and full of life; this still holds true. But we have to admit that the cod with mushrooms and truffles turned out to be garnished with summer truffles rather than the black diamond variety from Périgord, and we were not informed of this beforehand. Frankly and to our regret, at these prices, the second toque is not steady on its feet, even though the dessert was a real piece of workmanship. C 400-500. M 195 (weekdays), 295-395.

 ## Les Frênes

(See restaurant above)
Closed Nov-end Mar. 4 stes 1,650-3,000. 16 rms 595-1,590. Half-board 980-1,180. Rm ser. Air cond. Valet pkg.
A gorgeous, supremely comfortable hotel, set in a wooded park with a garden and splashing

fountains. The rooms are spread about in various outbuildings set round a superb swimming pool. The décor ranges from Louis XIII to Empire. Rooms have been redecorated tastefully and equipped with luxurious baths and hydromassage. Capacious parking lot, peerless reception and service. Relais et Châteaux.

■ **In Le Pontet 84130**   *5 km NE on N 7*

Auberge de Cassagne

Avignon North exit on A 6
04 90 31 04 18, fax 04 90 32 25 09
Open daily until 9:30pm. Garden dining. Air cond. Pool. Valet pkg.
   This is bewitching Provence in its full glory, nestled right in the middle of a large garden. A sunny welcome, a decked-out décor, a menu full of great (and voluptuous) expectations: is this paradise? Not quite. It's not for lack of prime ingredients—leek and truffle salad, red mullet pie, lusty lamb—nor for lack of technique. It's just that the dishes are richer than they are poignant, and you're not always sure what effect the chef really meant to make. Some scrutinizing simplification might be what the doctor would order. Grandiose cellar, where every wine lover will find his or her heart's every desire. C 500 and up. M 230-460.

Auberge de Cassagne

(See restaurant above)
Open year-round. 5 stes 1,380-1,880. 25 rms 490-1,240. Rms for disabled. Half-board 670-1,095 (oblig in seas). Rm scr. Air cond. Pool. Tennis. Pkg.
   Peace and quiet are on the menu here. Refined is the word for the Provençal décor of the huge rooms, full of flowers yet toned down in color. Comfort is the word for this newly renovated swimming pool hidden among the verdure, more inviting than ever.

La Table des Agassins

In Le Pigeonnier - 04 90 32 42 91, fax 04 90 32 08 29
Closed Jan. Open until 10pm. Terrace dining. Air cond. Heated pool. Valet pkg.
   A little out-of-the-way haven, just the place to slow down the pace and spend some time lounging by the pool and roaming the park abound with ancient trees. This is the Provence of fairytales, including fountains, plane trees, laurels and palm trees. Provençal cuisine with a modern accent, which has today become almost a given. The difference here is the incredible refinement of flavors, the subtle nuances so expressive that you realize you forgot what things *should* taste like. Just a simple vegetable salad is so redolent of tastes that it approaches operatic drama, the lamb so in harmony with its creamy melt-in-your-mouth fava beans that it resembles a pure elegy. The arrival of Bernard Bordaries in the

kitchen makes La Table des Agassins one of the best restaurants in the region. His wife watches over the discreet service in the dining room. Adequate cellar rich in half-bottles. C 400-460. M 130 (weekday lunch), 230 (wine incl), 280, 340.

 ## Hostellerie des Agassins

(See restaurant above)
Closed Jan. 4 stes 950-1,700. 26 rms 450-850. Rms for disabled. Half-board 660-760. Rm scr. Air cond. Heated pool. Valet pkg.
   A bit of Provence under the pines and the cypresses. Modern Provence-style rooms, all with air conditioning. Tastefully decorated, modern farmhouse that makes you feel right at home.

■ **In Villeneuve-lès-Avignon 30400**   *3 km NW*

 ## Aubertin

1, rue de l'Hôpital
04 90 25 94 84, fax 04 90 26 30 71
Closed Sun dinner & Mon (exc Jul-Aug). Open until 10pm. Terrace dining. Air cond.
   Just 30 guests can gather in this smartly understated dining room to feast on Jean-Pierre Aubertin's simple yet refined cuisine. Split-second timing, well-harmonized flavors, and a passion for Provençal ingredients produce exceptional foie gras, veal sweetbread and langoustine terrine, where every savor is keen and alive. His classic guinea fowl breast is totally metamorphosed by the refinement of the sweet-garlic confit, sided by a spice risotto artfully topped with a few leaves of baby spinach in its jus. Like the food, the regional wines are clemently priced, and Michèle Aubertin offers judicious advice. Attractive set meals. C 350-400. M 100 (weekdays), 160, 240.

 ## Fabrice

3, bd Pasteur - 04 90 25 52 79
Closed Sun dinner, Mon, 1 wk in Feb, 3 wks in Sep. Open until 10pm. Terrace dining.
   Fabrice Guisset likes fish, but he certainly doesn't do injustice to meat with his chicken liver mousse, Charollais beef fillet and mutton stew with potatoes and turnips. And his inventive fish preparations may be enough to tempt even the most die-hard meat-lovers: Italian-style sardines, lightly breaded with herb crumbs and cooked in olive oil; brilliant cod sided with a vegetable tian, and, for dessert, minted fresh-pineapple soup. So simple, but so earnest. Eat in the shade of the garden or in the sunny dining room. C 200. M 90 (weekday lunch), 120 (dinner).

La Magnaneraie

37, rue Camp-de-Bataille
04 90 25 11 11, fax 04 90 25 46 37
Open daily until 9:30pm. Garden dining. Air cond.
Pool. Tennis. Valet pkg.
Charm is not impromptu. In this case it arises out of the deep passion the Prayel family has for entertaining. And wow do they do it well in this lovely residence nested in the middle of a park of rare species of trees. The columns, Louix XV furniture, Tuscan frescoes and rather stately service enhance the setting even further. Unfortunately, Gérard Prayal's cooking has lost a bit of its glitter. The products are still of impeccable quality, but the Dublin bay prawns had lost their crunch, the duo of fish was overcooked, and the fruit gratin was served with a watery sabayon. Sorry, but a toque has to go. C 450. M 170-450.

 La Magnaneraie

(See restaurant above)
Open year-round. 3 stes 1,400-1,800. 25 rms 400-1,200. Half-board 490-930 (oblig in seas). Rms for disabled. Rm ser. Pool. Tennis. Valet pkg.
Luxuriant garden, river of honey, land of plenty: that's the setting. The contemporary drawing rooms are warmly decorated, and some even have character, especially the ones that have managed to keep their nineteenth-century furniture. Sun sports, tennis courts and a splendid pool. Six rooms on the ground floor are handicap-equipped.

 Le Prieuré

7, pl. du Chapitre
04 90 15 90 15, fax 04 90 25 45 39
Closed mid Mar 22-mid Apr: Wed; May 1; Nov 2-mid Mar. Open until 9:15pm. Garden dining. Air cond. Pool. Tennis. Garage pkg.
Thriving under the smiling sun of Provence, in what must be one of the most charming spots on earth, chef Serge Chenet marries Provençal flavors in delicate, beguiling ways. Examples? Try his thoroughly palatable baby-vegetable lasagna with its crispy vegetables cooked in olive oil and tapenade, wonderful veal sweetbreads cooked whole and studded with licorice, or delightful bass roasted in Szechuan pepper. The «natural» caramelized-apple charlotte in mixed-berry sauce was capital. This is good enough to convert even the most dedicated ascetic! Seductive cellar; perfect service. C 480. M 300, 480.

 Le Prieuré

(See restaurant above)
Closed Nov 2-mid Mar. 10 stes 1,450-1,900. 26 rms 570-1,450. Rms for disabled. Half-board 995-2,035. Rm ser. Air cond. Pool. Tennis. Garage pkg.
Whether you book in the old priory, next to the church (smallish rooms), or in the annex by the swimming pool (large rooms with a fine view of the grounds or patios), you'll find the same grand style and luxury, far from prying eyes and the madding crowd. Impeccable reception and service. Relais et Châteaux.

See also: Baux-de-Provence (Les), Noves

BARCELONNETTE	04400
Paris 740 - Nice 209 - Briançon 84	Alpes/H.-P.

 Azteca

3, rue des Trois-Frères-Arnaud
04 92 81 46 36, fax 04 92 81 43 92
Open year-round. 27 rms 330-500. Half-board 255-390. Pkg.
At the junction of two mountain passes, you'll feel yourself in another country, because yes, as the name implies, the guest rooms are decorated in Mexican style. The rooms are well-equipped and you can enjoy the panoramic view from your terrace, or even have your breakfast there in the summer. In off-season, groups and conferences.

 La Mangeoire

Pl. des Quatre-Vents
04 92 81 01 61, fax 04 92 81 01 61
Closed Sun dinner & Mon (exc Jul-Aug, Feb), Apr 20-May 1, Nov 15-Dec 24. Open until 9:30pm. Terrace dining. Pkg.
Built in the seventeenth century, travellers stopped here to pay duties before attacking the mountain pass. You don't have to pay duties today, just the price of an honest meal, and a good one too. The new management has great ambitions, and chef Loïc Balance, formerly at the Pourcel brothers' restaurant in Montpellier, is doing justice. When we were there, he produced a shellfish bouillon with leak ravioli, duck fillet roasted on the bone, and a chocolate soufflé the likes of which we hadn't eaten in years. The future is bright for this country establishment. Cheerful yellow and blue décor, and the dining room opens on to the kitchen so you can watch the chef at work. C 350. M 98 (weekdays), 148, 280.

■ In Pra-
Loup 04400   *8.5 km SW on D 902, D 109*

 Auberge du Clos Sorel

Village de Clos Sorel
04 92 84 10 74, fax 04 92 84 09 14
Closed Apr 11-Jun, Sep-Dec 15. 11 rms 400-800. Restaurant. Half-board 400-600. Heated pool.
This fine old house in a mountain village offers charming, comfortable rooms and an extraordinary view across the valley. Warm welcome.

12/20 La Tisane

04 92 84 10 55, fax 04 92 84 10 55
Closed Apr 15-Jun 27, Sep-Nov (exc Nov school hols & Nov 11). Open until 10pm. Terrace dining.
Tucked into the first floor of a shopping center, you can watch the slopes as you eat in this cozy little dining room. Choose between Roquefort

puff pastry and beef fillet cooked in whiskey, or other more Provence-inspired dishes such as young rabbits with artichokes or pepper-roasted squab. You can count the wines on two hands, but the pleasant service and reception help make up for it. C 220-320. M 85-245.

 In
Sauze 04400   *4 km SE on D 900, D 209*

 Alp' Hôtel   🌲🍴

04 92 81 05 04, fax 04 92 81 45 84
Closed Apr 10-May 25, Oct 10-Dec 20. 5 stes 420-980. 24 rms 320-470. Restaurant. Half-board 290-420 (oblig in seas). Rm ser. Heated pool. Pkg.
This modern complex ideally located near the ski lifts boasts simple, pretty rooms with mountain views, a garden, terrace, and heated pool as well as a bar and a fitness center. Suites have kitchenettes.

BAUX-DE-PROVENCE (LES)   13520
Paris 714 - Avignon 31 - Arles 19   B./Rhône

 La Benvengudo   🌲🍴

On D 78 F - 04 90 54 32 54, fax 04 90 54 42 58
Open year-round. 3 stes 800-930. 17 rms 530-700. Restaurant. Half-board 547-632. Air cond. Pool. Tennis. Garage pkg.
A superb Provençal setting and magnificent antique furnishings make this vine-covered country manor a delightful stop. Rooms are well equipped and offer excellent value for money.

 La Cabro d'Or

Val d'Enfer - 04 90 54 33 21, fax 04 90 54 45 98
Closed Mon & Tue lunch off-seas, Nov 11-Dec 20. Open until 9:30pm. Garden dining. Pool. Pkg.
The little sister of the grand Oustau de Baumanière (see below) is blessed with a colorful garden and a terrace shaded with mulberry trees; the farmhouse also has an absolutely immense fireplace for cool winter evenings. It's a luxurious spot to sample chef Sandro Gamba's cookery which is well crafted and full of ideas, and certainly some of the best of Provençal food to be had: broad bean cream with ewe's milk cottage cheese; extra-thin juicy turnip tart and hot foie gras with a Port reduction; octopus and clam risotto with cuttlefish ink-flavored jus; or frangipane tourte with almond-milk ice cream. Jean-André Charial unearthed this young chef, only 27 years old, at none other than Alain Ducasse's; we must salute his good judgment. Also a new dining room director and sommelier. May the *fête gourmande* begin! C 350-400. M 190 (weekday lunch, wine incl), 270, 395.

 La Cabro d'Or   🌲🍴

(See restaurant above)
Closed Nov 11-Dec 20. 8 stes 1,300-1,700. 23 rms 650-1,100. Rm ser. Air cond. Pool. Tennis. Pkg.

In a dramatic setting of rocks and bright flowers, this hotel offers guests good food, a charming welcome, a rose garden, children's activities, and riding. Tastefully decorated rooms and suites in an understated but luxurious setting. Relais et Châteaux.

 Mas de l'Oulivié   🌲🍴

04 90 54 35 78, fax 04 90 54 44 31
Closed mid Nov-mid Mar. 20 rms 540-1,050. Rms for disabled. Restaurant. Air cond. Pool. Tennis. Garage pkg.
Here is a newly constructed *mas* in the heart of the Vallée des Baux, with bright but smallish rooms, gaily decorated in pure Provençal style. Beautiful landscaped pool grounds, where grilled dishes and salads are served.

 L'Oustau de Baumanière

Val d'Enfer - 04 90 54 33 07, fax 04 90 54 40 46
Closed Wed & Thu lunch off-seas, mid Jan-beg Mar. Open until 9:30pm. Garden dining. Air cond. Pool. Tennis. Valet pkg.
This uniquely charming spot, in what may be the most beautiful village in France, embodies the very essence of Provence. First sight of the amazing Valley of Hell and its chaotic array of boulders over which hangs the village of Baux leaves one utterly spellbound. In the middle of it all is an oasis of peace, verdure and bliss, the enchanting fifteenth-century *mas* with its rosemary-scented terrace girdled with cypresses and Judas trees, with its dream of a pool: the Oustau de Baumanière. Now for gustatory matters. Our marvel is not so all-embracing: «anthology» little red mullets cooked whole with their liver, just like they should be; perfect saddle of lamb accompanied by truly remarkable green beans—a good meal, that time. Another time, a thoroughly unconvincing success for the Dublin bay prawn cappuccino, botched sauce on the brill fillet, and a surprising laxity on the part of staff. Goes to prove that perfection doesn't exist, after all, even when you think you're in paradise. Legendary cellar, where you'll find owner Jean-André Charial's delicious Château Romanin, a wealth of fine Côtes-du-Rhônes, and a cache of vintage Bordeaux collected by Baumanière's founder, Raymond Thuilier. C 450-1,450. M 520 (lunch), 500-780.

 L'Oustau de Baumanière   🌲🍴

(See restaurant above)
Closed Wed off-seas, mid Jan-beg Mar. 8 stes 2,000-2,200. 12 rms 1,300-1,450. Half-board 1,500-1,800. Rm ser. Air cond. Pool. Tennis. Valet pkg.
The captivating beauty of Provence is on full parade here from the swimming pool (which doesn't look like one) surrounded by flowers to the patrician fifteenth-century *mas* itself, with its rooms of varying sizes, some of which are vast suites. For even more peace and quiet, Le Manoir

nearby offers just two suites and two rooms in a lovely garden setting. Nine-hole golf course three kilometers away. Relais et Châteaux.

La Riboto de Taven

Val d'Enfer - 04 90 54 34 23, fax 04 90 54 38 88
Closed Tue dinner & Wed off-seas, Jan 5-Mar 15. Garden dining. Pkg.
The divine setting of this country manor built into the cliffside at the foot of this charming village, the elaborate, refined cooking of Pierre Novi might make you think you're in heaven. Don't worry, this is not heaven, but you're on your way. Take off with the well-prepared, unique slice of foie gras with carrots and shallots cooked in honey, the seafood sausage or the amusing caramelized-fennel tart. The wine goes well with the set menus, the price is right and the service flawless. M 200 (weekday lunch, wine incl), 300-450.

La Riboto de Taven

(See restaurant above)
Closed Tue & Wed off-seas, Jan 5-Mar 15. 3 rms 700-900. Half-board 850. Rm ser. Pkg.
This old manor house rises right out of the cliffs. The troglodytic rooms are huge and breathtaking, and all have everything you could dream of for comfort, including extra-large bathrooms.

BEAUCET (LE) 84 → **Carpentras**

BEAURECUEIL 13100
Paris 783 - Marseille 37 - Aix-en-P. 10 B./Rhône

Relais Sainte-Victoire

04 42 66 94 98, fax 04 42 66 85 96
Closed Sun dinner, Mon, Fri lunch, 1 wk in Jan, Feb school hols, 1 wk in Nov. Open until 9:30pm (10pm in summer). Air cond. Terrace dining. Pkg.
The vigorous, expressive cuisine of René Bergès sums up the gustatory pleasures of Provence, with superb, sun-gorged vegetables and the perfumes of green-gold olive oil and fresh herbs. Notable on the menu are a limpid leek terrine enriched with foie gras, and veal tongue in a concise, aromatic jus. This unique family inn at the heart of Cézanne country is constantly filled with happy customers, who bask in the warm solicitude of Madame Bergès and her staff. C 320-360. M 160, 255 (exc Sun), 450.

Relais Sainte-Victoire

(See restaurant above)
Closed Sun & Mon off-seas, 1 wk in Jan, Feb school hols, 1 wk in Nov. 6 stes 600-800. 4 rms 450-600. Half-board 550-800. Air cond. Pool. Pkg.

At the foot of Mont Sainte-Victoire—so often painted by Cézanne—this hotel provides large, recently renovated and air conditioned rooms with terraces. Some are equipped with Jacuzzis.

BOUC-BEL-AIR 13320
Paris 780 - Marseille 24 - Aix-en-P. 10 B./Rhône

L'Étape des Frères Lani

D 6, exit Gardanne on A 51
04 42 22 61 90, fax 04 42 22 68 67
Closed Sun, Mon, Aug 1-18, Dec 23-31. Open until 9:30pm. Terrace dining. Air cond. Pool. Pkg.
It's easy to zip right by this comfortable inn, but that would be a shame. The entire Lani family lavishes attention on their customers as they enjoy Lucien and Joël Lani's light, delicate dishes prepared with seasonal ingredients. If it's on the menu, do try his farm-raised squab with a tian of winter wheat. Extensive cellar of excellent wines. C 300. M 145 (weekdays), 195, 260.

CARPENTRAS 84200
Paris 683 - Cavaillon 26 - Apt 12 - Avignon 23 Vaucluse

L'Atelier

30, rue des Halles - 04 90 60 20 15, fax 04 90 67 11 56
Closed Sun. Open until 10:30pm. Terrace dining. Air cond.
The owners have changed, but the kitchen of this charming old blue-façade house is still host to Maurice Barnaba's well-mastered but inventive Provence-style cooking. More than ever, we relished in his colossal spicy pan-fried shrimp, his cod fricassée perked up with tomatoes and basil, and his lamb fillet in its sweet-garlic cream. The wine list is limited. C 210-315. M 75 (weekday lunch), 89-240.

Fiacre

153, rue Vigne - 04 90 63 03 15, fax 04 90 60 49 73
Open year-round. 20 rms 190-470. Garage pkg.
Quiet, yet centrally located in an eighteenth-century town house, the Fiacre, with its magnificent wrought-iron staircase, boasts rooms of irregular quality and size, but all are well-kept. Charming atmosphere, beautiful flowery courtyard.

Safari Hôtel

Av. Jean-Henri-Fabre
04 90 63 35 35, fax 04 90 60 49 99
Closed Jan-Feb. 42 rms 250-380. Rms for disabled. Restaurant. Half-board 370-535. Rm ser. Pool. Garage pkg.
Set in pleasant grounds outside of the town's center, this hotel offers perfectly equipped rooms. There are also studios to rent with kitchenettes. «Made in Africa» décor.

 Looking for a hotel? Refer to the **index**.

Le Vert Galant

12, rue de Clapies - 04 90 67 15 50
Closed Sat lunch, Sun, 3 wks in Aug. Open until 9:30pm. Terrace dining. Air cond.

We can't quite figure out what is in the air, but the smell is not so sweet. Jacques Mégean, in whom we banked so much hope a couple years ago, must be tired or preoccupied. We still think him an excellent chef, but the tastelessness of the duckling fillets, Provençal «frivolities», and noisette lamb chops brought only disappointment this year. The price is still right, but we'll stand by for the rest. **M** 138 (weekday lunch), 210, 270.

■ **In Le**
Beaucet 84210 *10 km SE on D 4 and D 39*

Auberge du Beaucet

04 90 66 10 82, fax 04 90 66 00 72
Closed Sun dinner, Mon. Open until 9pm. Terrace dining.

Don't even think about dining (or lunching) here unless you've booked your table in advance. Brigitte Pizzecco can serve only 30 patrons at a time in her exquisite Provençal inn, and her fame is already such that every seat invariably has a taker. Hers is a heartfelt, finely crafted cuisine full of brawny flavors and heady perfumes, set off by house-baked bread and a wonderful regional cellar. Excellent set-price menu with oodles of choices. **M** 165.

■ **In Monteux 84170** *5 km SW on D 942*

Blason de Provence

Route de Carpentras
04 90 66 31 34, fax 04 90 66 83 05
Closed Dec 20-Jan 20. 20 rms 285-410. Restaurant. Half-board 450-525 (oblig in seas). Rm ser. Pool. Tennis. Garage pkg.

A pleasant family-style Provençal establishment set in extensive grounds, featuring comfortable, personalized rooms. Breakfast buffet.

Le Saule Pleureur

Quartier Beauregard, 145, route d'Avignon
04 90 62 01 35, fax 04 90 62 10 90
Closed Sun dinner, Mon, Mar 1-20, Nov 1-15. Open until 9pm. Garden dining. Pkg.

We have observed: the surroundings lack a light note, the garden is still in the embryonic stage, the décor is clean but lacking soul, and the cellar is very selective while at the same time divulging some curious blind spots. So, how do they merit a 16/20 rating? Everything is in the plate and the wonders put upon it. This chef has an incredible talent. He draws his far-reaching inspiration from the scents and savors of the best products of the region (for instance, he has a love affair with truffles) and adds a touch of unselfconscious spontaneity, which can only work when one walks in the halls of the great. Some

examples: foie gras «lost bread» (better known as French toast) and green beans; mussel gratin with a marvellous use of garlic; veal kidneys with panisses, *revues et corrigées*; and still, and we hope forever more, the simple but blissful red mullet pissaladière, his version of a regional tart topped with onions, anchovies, black olives and tomatoes. **C** 300-400. **M** 165-340.

CARRY-LE-ROUET 13620
Paris 768 - Aix-en-P. 40 - Marseille 27 B./Rhône

L'Escale

Promenade du Port
04 42 45 00 47, fax 04 42 44 72 69
Closed Sun dinner, Mon (exc lunch Jul-Aug), Nov-Jan. Open until 9:30pm. Terrace dining. Pkg.

This big white house set on a background of sea blue, girdled with brightly colored flowers and basked in sunlight, resembles a pretty painting of Provence. The hard and fast rule here is the fish, which Gérard Clor buys every morning as he steps down from his terrace, as well as the pleasant reception and the polished ways of the staff. We don't want to call into question the undeniable skill of this chef, but he has been cooking fruit of the sea for so long now that there are fewer and fewer pebbles from elsewhere to cause ripples in his glassy smooth pool of choices. We really doted on the tender, luscious marinated wild salmon (even though we think the caviar adds nothing), but were almost embarrassed about the monkfish pâté garnished with fresh tomatoes because the raw shallots totally overwhelmed the taste of the other ingredients. Other dishes were more successful, such as the Carry red mullets, which went wonderfully with the braised fennel lightly spiked with licorice. Our wish would be for the wine list to be filled in with some more affordable perhaps lesser-known growers' wines, which would keep the bill from drifting too far out to sea. **C** 450. **M** 200 (weekday lunch), 320.

CASSIS 13260
Paris 803 - Toulon 44 - Marseille 23 B./Rhône

12/20 Le Jardin d'Émile

Bestouan beach - 04 42 01 80 55, fax 04 42 01 80 70
Closed Mon off-seas, Jan 4-9, Nov 12-30. Open until 10:30pm. Terrace dining. Pkg.

Romantic terrace giving on to the beach, lovely dining room in yellow and ochre tones, and a winding drive through the corniches to arrive at this lovely red house resting peacefully on the hillside. Olivier Randon puts the «Cuisine of the Sun» before you with his tomato and fresh artichoke heart stew perfumed with fresh herbs, his sapid scallop brochette served on a sprig of rosemary, his delightful stuffed vegetables, and his rich honey-sweetened orange soup. Skip the store-bought chocolate ice cream. **C** 260. **M** 98 (weekday lunch, wine incl), 165 (weekdays), 195, 230 (Sun lunch).

Le Jardin d'Émile

(See restaurant above)
Closed Nov 12-30. 7 stes 300-600. Rm scr. Air cond. Garage pkg.
This old house, beautifully renovated, is perched over a deep creek. The Provençal-style rooms are small but full of charm. Friendly, young staff.

12/20 Nino

1, quai Barthélemy - 04 42 01 74 32, fax 04 42 01 74 32
Closed Sun dinner & Mon off-seas, Dec 15-Feb 1. Open until 11pm. Terrace dining.
Lie back and relax, listen to the waves lapping against the boats in the port, and let yourself partake of a dreamy Provençal-style menu based on top-notch ingredients. Your appetite will be whetted whether you take the grilled bell peppers with anchovy paste dressing the stuffed Mediterranean gurnard, the Provençal fish soup or the fish stew. Local Cassis wines are featured. C 250-300. M 99-140 (weekdays lunch), 180.

 Hôtel de la Plage du Bestouan

Bestouan beach - 04 42 01 05 70, fax 04 42 01 34 82
Closed Nov 12-30. 29 rms 300-650. Pkg.
Well-equipped rooms, eight of which are air conditioned. Excellent reception.

 La Presqu'île

Quartier de Port-Miou
04 42 01 03 77, fax 04 42 01 94 49
Closed Sun dinner off-seas, Mon. Open until 10pm (10:30pm in seas). Terrace dining. Air cond.
Charmingly nestled between Port-Miou, the bay of Cassis, and Cap Canaille, La Presqu'île features elaborate dishes with many a fanciful touch, crafted by Marcel Ricard. His painstaking style calls on an *éventail*, or fan, of fresh, prime-quality products. The red mullet, which had just stepped out of the sea, and was just «sealed» in olive oil, was an unforgettable experience; so was the grouper fillet braised in spices, even though the sauce was on the insipid side and it was garnished with the same vegetable julienne as the previous dish. The raspberry millefeuille was mealy in the mouth. C 450. M 165 (weekdays), 245 (Sun).

 Les Roches Blanches

Route des Calanques
04 42 01 09 30, fax 04 42 01 94 23
Closed Nov 15-Feb 15. 5 stes 1,100-1,200. 20 rms 470-900. Rms for disabled. Restaurant. Half-board 715-1,445. Rm scr. Pool. Valet pkg.
A dreamy, remarkably well-situated establishment on the Cassis headlands with fully renovated rooms and enchanting views. Lovely multi-tiered terraces, sun room and private beach.

*The **prices** in this guide reflect what establishments were charging at press time.*

 Royal Cottage

6, av. du 11-Novembre
04 42 01 33 34, fax 04 42 01 06 90.
Open year-round. 25 rms 500-1,050. Rms for disabled. Rm scr. Air cond. Heated pool. Garage pkg.
A modern building overlooking the town. Pleasant garden with a pool donning a cozy Jacuzzi tucked in the middle. Rooms are capacious and full of light; air conditioned and equipped with everything you need for your comfort and well-being and with private terraces.

CAVAILLON	84300
Paris 704 - Avignon 27 - Aix-en-P. 52	Vaucluse

12/20 La Fin de Siècle

46, pl. du Clos - 04 90 71 12 27
Closed Tue dinner, Wed, Aug 8-Sep 10. Open until 9:30pm. Terrace dining. Air cond. Pkg.
Upstairs in the brasserie, a carefully prepared anxious-to-please cooking offering excellent quality for the money. Not quite as good when the dishes get complicated; better to stick to simple. But real effort is put into this, the price is good, and the décor wants so much to be pretty that it is almost touching. C 300-500. M 89-220.

 Fleur de Thym

91, rue Jean-Jacques Rousseau
04 90 71 14 64, fax 04 90 71 14 64.
Closed Sun, Mon lunch, Jul. Open until 9:30pm (Fri-Sat 10pm). Terrace dining.
Jean-Yves Benoît is from Provence, and everything in his restaurant lets you know it, from the attractive décor to the food replete with sunstruck accents of the region. This pretty 2-storey house with a bright new façade, located on a quiet street right in the middle of town, has two dining rooms: one with an arched ceiling in the basement and another with a large fireplace. The prix-fixe menu offers a good selection of Benoît's light, original cooking, with dishes such as open-faced fresh-scallop ravioli, veal sweetbreads and green asparagus, and Roquefort with pear and walnuts, all for 145 F! The cellar is resolutely regional, offering a good selection of growers' wines. Charming welcome. M 95 (weekday lunch), 145.

 Prévot

353, av. de Verdun
04 90 71 32 43, fax 04 90 71 97 05
Open daily until 9:30pm. Garden dining. Air cond.
Chef Jean-Jacques Prévot's family has a 200-year tradition of feeding people: pastry cooks, makers of sweetmeats, and cooks. Passionately fond of his trade, he is a perfectionist. Every detail of his dainty dining room—the fine china, the Louis XVI décor, the attentive service—reflects the same care that goes into his savory cuisine so rich in the culinary traditions of Provence. That is not to say that he doesn't add his own touch, because creativity is not lacking.

He has a special place in his heart for the famous Cavaillon melons, which he places alongside boar and red mullet, but the bounds of his heart stretch out to all the perfumes of the Mediterranean (beef fillet with stuffed artichokes, roast langoustines with caramelized citrus fruit canapés). Lovely cellar abound with Bordeaux. C 350-400. M 160 (weekday lunch), 215-450.

CHÂTEAU-ARNOUX   04160
Paris 717 - Sisteron 14 - Manosque 38   Alpes/H.-P.

 La Bonne Étape

Chemin du Lac - 04 92 64 00 09, fax 04 92 64 37 36
Closed Mon & Tue lunch off-seas, beg Jan-mid Feb. Open until 9:30pm. Air cond. Heated pool. Valet pkg.
This is the real Provence, not the post card. The dining room décor is in keeping with Pierre and Jany Gleize's cuisine: genuine, staid, lacking affectation. The first time you come, the lamb shoulder roasted on the bone is simply a must: a masterful work of art which brings out the very quintessence of the product, just slightly accentuated with a refined truffle jus. The second or third time, you can try the mallard duck, pigeon or Mediterranean fish. You might start your meal with a subtle-flavored lobster salpicon sided with velvety white-beet ravioli, perfumed with basil and lightly powdered with Parmesan. The cellar lives up to the what's on the plate, and has a respectable number of vintage wines as well as a wide choice of regional wines. Some are even served by the glass. Efficient service. C 380-580. M 225-529, 599 (wine incl).

 La Bonne Étape

(See restaurant above)
Closed Mon eve & Tue off-seas, beg Jan-mid Feb. 8 stes 900-1,500. 10 rms 550-1,100. Air cond. Heated pool. Valet pkg.
Near the olive groves, with whiffs of the nearby lavender, a beautiful interior with a «panoramic» sense of comfort: giant bed, *peignoirs*, etc. Breakfasts are in keeping. And you'll be happy here, because the exquisite *courtoisie* of the Gleize family has (fortunately) worn off on the service staff! Relais et Châteaux.

 Au Goût du Jour

14, av. de Général-de-Gaulle
04 92 64 48 48, fax 04 92 64 37 36
Closed Sun dinner off-seas, Mon, Jan 3-Feb 12. Terrace dining. Air cond.
It's almost catching among great chefs today to open an annex, and the Gleize family has caught the bug. This bistro just opposite the *château* lets you taste a condensed version of the main restaurant at a much-reduced price. With set meals at 85 and 130 F, you can allow yourself to explore dishes such as the smart little fennel, coppa and bacon salad, the «fortifying» veal breast and melon sherbet. Small but spirited selection of wines. The service lacks the luxury of the prim and proper service in the main house, but is efficient. C 210. M 85-130.

 L'Oustaou de la Foun

N 85, Route Napoléon
04 92 62 65 30, fax 04 92 62 65 32
Closed Sun dinner & Mon (exc in seas & hols), Jan 2-12. Open until 9:30pm. Terrace dining. Air cond. Pkg.
The spark is not there yet, but we're confident that the coals are being lit. Gérald Jourdan mixes ingredients from both the land and the sea to give us a perfectly balanced Provençal menu. You may have to wade through the long-winded menu descriptions under the helpful eye of the staff, but the end result is worth it. Among our favorites: delicious sardine fritters and tomato marmelade; laurel-scented potato pancake with bacon bits; roast chicken with candied garlic. Good quality products, correct cooking times, honest, forthright flavors, even though his hand is a little heavy on the herbs at times. We're almost ready to congratulate him, but there's still a little something missing, and that holds us back... C 280. M 110-260.

 Villiard

04 92 64 17 42, fax 04 92 64 23 29
Closed Sat off-seas, Dec 15-Jan 8. 2 stes 365-420. 18 rms 260-360. Pkg.
Cozy, well-kept rooms in the calm of a garden. The rather out-of-date decoration hides the beautiful bathrooms. Family-style reception.

CORNILLON-CONFOUX 13
→ **Salon-de-Provence**

CRILLON-LE-BRAVE   84410
Paris 704 - Carpentras 14 - Avignon 43   Vaucluse

 Hostellerie de Crillon-le-Brave

Pl. de l'Église - 04 90 65 61 61, fax 04 90 65 62 86
Closed weekday lunch, beg Jan-mid Mar. Open until 9:30pm. Garden dining. Pool. Valet pkg.
Philippe Monti gained credentials in such lofty establishments as Pic and Taillevent. His repertoire makes excellent use of local ingredients: chicken livers en brochette, pumpkin soup with parsley, a delicious lamb and eggplant gâteau, and a delectable walnut tart. Courteous welcome and service in a charming restaurant with a pretty terrace that looks out on Mont Ventoux. C 290-380. M 160 (Sun lunch), 340 (dinner), 250, 290.

 Hostellerie de Crillon-le-Brave

(See restaurant above)
Closed beg Jan-mid Mar. 4 stes 1,450-2,400. 19 rms 850-1,650. Rm ser. Pool. Valet pkg.

Overlooking Mont Ventoux and the Comtat vineyards, the rooms are decorated with charming Provençal fabrics and furniture. The Italian-style garden girdled by cypresses and lavender scents speak out for themselves. Luxurious fittings, handsome bathrooms, and expensive but exceptionally delicious breakfasts. Personalized service. Relais et Châteaux.

12/20 Restaurant du Vieux Four

04 90 12 81 39
Closed Mon, Jan-Feb. Open until 9:30pm. Terrace dining.
What a clever idea to turn the village bread oven into a bistro. The *patronne* offers us good home cooking well worth the stop. **M 125.**

DIGNE	04000
Paris 760 - Aix-en-P. 110 - Sisteron 40	Alpes/H.-P.

 ### Le Grand Paris

19, bd Thiers - 04 92 31 11 15, fax 04 92 32 32 82
Closed Sun dinner, Mon, Dec 20-Feb. Open until 9:30pm. Garden dining. Valet pkg.
Jean-Jacques Ricaud set up shop in this twelfth-century convent forty years ago, and though the décor may be a little tired, the chef is still going full force. This is not the place to come for gastronomic adventures, because you are within the walls of a man some call the «pope of regional products», and the very best of homestyle cooking is on the agenda. He knows how to draw the utmost flavor out of every ingredient like no one else can do. His classic pig's snout and foie gras terrine and his «Good Morning, Father» omelette with foie gras and Dublin bay prawns would be nobody's embarrassment. Nor Madame Ricaud's warm welcome and the swarm of waiters and waitresses that hover around. 308 C 400. M 150 (weekday lunch), 195-430.

 ### Le Grand Paris

(See restaurant above)
Closed Dec 21-Mar 1. 4 stes 600-800. 25 rms 380-500. Half-board 440-550. Rm ser. Valet pkg.
The hotel is housed in a seventeenth-century convent, once the home of the Frères de la Trinité. The large rooms are handsomely decorated, and protected from street noise by the terrace's leafy plane trees. Centrally located but quiet.

12/20 Origan

6, rue Pied-de-Ville
04 92 31 62 13, fax 04 92 31 62 13
Closed Sun, Dec 15-28. Open until 9:15pm. Terrace dining.
Heads are nodding, so it's time to sound the wake-up call. Is Philippe Cochet resting on his laurels? This year, his cuisine had lost its lively rapids, even though he had replaced the set

menus with names of other rivers. He still offers real quality at an affordable price, but the cellar is blatantly lacking in half-bottles. C 280. M 98-170.

 ### Tonic Hôtel des Thermes

Av. des Thermes, Vallon des Sources
04 92 31 20 31, fax 04 92 32 44 54
Closed Oct 26-Mar. 58 rms 300-430. Half-board 320-440. Pool.
A cheery, modern building. Colorful, well-equipped rooms, excellent staff. Exercise faciliites and a swimming pool with a pleasant terrace.

See also: **Château-Arnoux**

ENTRECHAUX 84	→ Vaison-la-Romaine

EYGALIÈRES	13810
Paris 715 - Avignon 28 - Cavaillon 13	B./Rhône

 ### La Bastide

Route d'Orgon, chemin de Pestelade
04 90 95 90 06, fax 04 90 95 99 77
Open year-round. 12 rms 390-460. Pool. Pkg.
A modern farmhouse with a breathtaking view of the Alpilles Mountains. Take a leisurely moment by the pool tucked in among the olive trees and rosemary. Comfortable, well-appointed rooms.

 ### Bistrot d'Éygalières

Rue de la République
04 90 90 60 34, fax 04 90 90 60 37
Closed end Feb-beg Mar, end Nov-beg Dec. Open until 10pm (11pm in summer). Terrace dining. Air cond.
There's not much left of the village grocery this once was, only the chalkboard hailing the menu. The bistro has grown up into an elegant restaurant with an entrancing reception and cream-color decoration enhanced by contemporary paintings on the walls. Another ex-employee of Baumanière, chef Wout Bru does scales with regional products, and wanes comfortably between fisherman's pancake, pigeon and candied shallot roll, rack of lamb cooked in sage, and chocolate and wild strawberry millefeuille. The newly donned toque is to be noted. C 300. M 140 (weekday lunch).

 ### Mas de la Brune

04 90 95 90 77, fax 04 90 95 99 21
Closed Dec 15-Jan 15. 1 ste 1,350. 9 rms 750-1,350. Air cond. Pool. Valet pkg.
Behind mullioned windows, the ten rooms of this listed château have real character and are decorated with style. They boast sumptuous bathrooms and perfect appoint-

ments; service is exceptional, too. Outside you'll find a Roman-style pool and a garden fragrant with lavender.

Crin Blanc

3 km E on D 24 - 04 90 95 93 17, fax 04 90 90 60 62
Closed Wed, Nov 15-Mar 15. 10 rms 420. Half-board 395-580 (oblig in seas). Pool. Tennis. Pkg.
Rooms with a view of the Alpilles Mountains giving directly onto a cottage-type garden in this Provençal-style farmhouse sitting tranquilly on the edge of a pine forest.

Mas dou Pastre

Route d'Orgon - 04 90 95 92 61, fax 04 90 90 61 75
Open year-round. 10 rms 320-690. Pool. Pkg.
It is not the Sistine but the Saint-Sixte chapel, and an unusually striking one it is too. This charming little old stone farmhouse is located just across from it, right in the middle of the countryside. Tastefully decorated rooms in Provençal style. Every room is different, but the nicest ones are toward the back giving onto the garden and the pool.

FONTVIEILLE	13990
Paris 745 - Avignon 30 - Arles 10	B./Rhône

Hostellerie Saint-Victor

Chemin des Fourques - 04 90 54 66 00
Open year-round. 1 ste 995-1,295. 11 rms 375-625. Pool. Pkg.
Renovated farmhouse looking down on a village full of charm. The décor is rather hodge-podge, but there are a few nice pieces of furniture. The rooms are commmodious and comfortable. Delicious breakfasts.

La Peiriero

Av. des Baux - 04 90 54 76 10, fax 04 90 54 62 60
Closed Nov-Mar 15. 36 rms 290-560. Restaurant. Half-board 280-415. Rm scr. Air cond. Pool. Pkg.
A traditional Provençal homestead with big rooms that open out onto the surrounding hills.

La Regalido

Rue Frédéric-Mistral
04 90 54 60 22, fax 04 90 54 64 29
Closed Mon (exc dinner Jul-Sep), Jan 2-31. Open until 9:30pm. Garden dining. Air cond. Valet pkg.
Jean-Pierre Michel presents an immutable roster of perennial favorites—innovation is not his style. But his performance never flags. He was ahead of his times when he started his love affair with olive oil, and invented «olive butter», which consists of black locally-grown Fontvieille olives and tapenade, and when it became the pervasive theme of his repertoire: Provence-style omelette with Maussane olive oil; fish fillets «oven-steamed» with vegetables in the local Fontvieille olive oil aside fresh pasta with basil; shepherd's salad (with olive oil, of course); and

even Provençal apple pie with a sugar glaze and, yes, Mouriès olive oil! The food is definitely well oiled, which borders on dull at times, and our dessert was forgotten for just an hour. Of course, this is not the chef's fault, because he spends most of his time in the kitchen. Eat under the vaulted ceiling of the dining room (nice and cool in summer) or when weather permits, in the attractive garden. The checks are well oiled as well. C 390. M 165 (weekday lunch, wine incl), 260-400.

La Regalido

(See restaurant above)
Closed Jan 2-31. 2 stes 1,540-1,570. 13 rms 460-1,190. Rms for disabled. Half-board 860-1,530. Rm scr. Air cond. Valet pkg.
The delightful rooms of this turn-of-the-century hostelry look out over the Alpilles. Breakfast on the charming terraces. An old oil mill, lost among the ivy and the lavender, a pure delight to both eye and nose. Relais et Châteaux.

FORCALQUIER	04300
Paris 790 - Aix-en-P. 66 - Manosque 23	Alpes/H.-P.

Charembeau

Route de Niozelles, 3.5 km on N 100
04 92 70 91 70, fax 04 92 70 91 83
Closed Dec-Jan. 14 rms 290-460. Pool. Tennis. Pkg.
Meadows and hills surround this lovely Provençal dwelling, where intelligently designed rooms look out over the rugged Montagne de Lure. The breakfasts are worth waking up for!

FUSTE (LA) 04	→ Manosque

GIGONDAS	84190
Paris 677 - Avignon 37 - Vaison 15	Vaucluse

Les Florets

Route des Dentelles-de-Montmirail
04 90 65 85 01, fax 04 90 65 83 80
Closed Tue dinner off-seas, Wed, Jan-Feb. Open until 9pm. Garden dining. Pkg.
In the heart of the celebrated Gigondas vineyards, this local institution ages well despite the fact that the old-fashioned country-style dining room is starting to show a few too many wrinkles. On warm days, you'll be better off with a table outside under the linden-treed terrace with its 200 pots of flowers. Jean-Pierre Martin tenders a traditional cuisine that speaks strongly of its Provençal roots: tomate confite with basil, «medley» of monkfish and salmon with sorrel butter, or thinly sliced baron of lamb with eggplant caviar and garlic cream. C 270-330. M 95 (weekday lunch), 120, 220.

Looking for a celebrated chef? Refer to the Index.

GORDES   84220
Paris 734 - Avignon 38 - Cavaillon 17   Vaucluse

La Bastide de Gordes

Le Village - 04 90 72 12 12, fax 04 90 72 05 20
*Closed Nov 15-Mar 15. 1 ste 1,180-1,380. 17 rms
520-1,150. Rms for disabled. Air cond. Pool. Tennis.
Pkg.*
    Nearly a score of spacious and inviting rooms
in a noble Renaissance dwelling, filled with art
works and fine furniture. The lodgings are totally comfortable and unostentatious, done up in
Provençal style. Gym, sauna, and a little swimming pool on the terrace that lets you soak up a
splendid view. Breakfast under twelfth-century
Romanesque-style arches.

Les Bories

2 km NW on D 177, route de l'Abbaye de Sénanque
04 90 72 00 51, fax 04 90 72 01 22
*Closed Mon, Tue lunch, mid Nov-mid Feb. Open
until 9:30pm. Air cond. Heated pool. Tennis. Pkg.*
    New chef Philippe Calandri has just taken over
the reins of this lovely *mas*. Unfortunately, it all
happened so close to press time that we weren't
able to sample the fare. We were however able
to note that the menu reads a good Provençal
rhythm.

Les Bories

(See restaurant above)
*Closed mid Nov-mid Feb. 1 ste 1,580-2,030. 17 rms
830-1,580. Rms for disabled. Half-board 560-1,185
(oblig in seas). Air cond. Heated pool. Tennis. Pkg.*
    A marvelous spot in a magical corner of
Provence. Ten rooms are housed in a little *mas*,
the rest are in authentic dry-stone bungalows
(*bories*). Lavender and cypress trees grow in the
garden, and there are two pretty pools.

Comptoir du Victuailler

Pl. du Château - 04 90 72 01 31, fax 04 90 72 14 28
*Closed Tue dinner, Wed (exc Jul-Aug), Jan 15-
Easter, Nov 15-Dec 20. Dinner upon reservation
only. Terrace dining. Air cond.*
    Easy, convivial dining in the Schmitt family's
bistro set in the heart of the village, opposite the
Renaissance château which houses the Vasarely
Foundation. Joëlle Chaudat serves forth such
graceful, homestyle dishes as herbed rabbit compote, turbot with salicornes (edible seaweed),
and guinea hen with raspberries. Superb wine
list. C 400. M 175 (lunch), 190 (Jul-Sep).

Domaine de l'Enclos

Route de Sénanque
04 90 72 71 00, fax 04 90 72 03 03
*Closed Nov 15-Dec 20. 8 stes 680-1,860. 9 rms
380-980. Rms for disabled. Restaurant. Half-board
390-980. Air cond. Pool. Garage pkg.*
    Just outside of Gordes you'll find this group of
bungalows with airy, comfortable rooms furnished in true Provençal spirit (the bathrooms
are decorated with locally fired tiles). Extras include a fine terrace, a garden, and magnificent
views. Courteous welcome, unobtrusive service.

 12/20   **Ferme de la Huppe**

2 km SE on D 2 and D 156, Les Pourquiers
04 90 72 12 25, fax 04 90 72 01 83
*Closed Thu, Nov-end Mar. Open until 9pm. Terrace
dining. Pool. Pkg.*
    This seventeenth-century farmhouse lost in the
countryside dons a pretty patio dressed up with
wrought iron chairs and perky parasols. The
cooking is pleasing to the tongue, with the likes
of crusty bass fillet, saffron-dusted gingery roast
guinea fowl, and rack of lamb with whole garlic
cloves cooked in their skin. C 210-260. M 150-205.

 Ferme de la Huppe

(See restaurant above)
*Closed Nov-end Mar. 8 rms 400-700. Half-board
370-645. Pool. Pkg.*
    Comfortable well-appointed rooms in rustic
style in the peace and quiet of the Provençal
countryside.

12/20   **La Gacholle**

Route de Murs - 04 90 72 01 36, fax 04 90 72 01 81
*Closed Nov 12-Mar 15. Open until 9:30pm. Terrace
dining. Heated pool. Tennis. Pkg.*
    The spectacle of the Luberon lends consider-
able charm to La Gacholle's dining room and
covered terrace. A pleasant-enough Provençal
repertoire—monkfish osso buco, roast rack of
lamb with thyme vinaigrette, and farm-raised
guinea fowl with garlic cream—but don't go
here if you're famished. C 250-300. M 165-260.

 La Gacholle

(See restaurant above)
*Closed Nov 12-Mar 15. 12 rms 420-650. Half-board
440-590 (oblig in seas). Heated pool. Tennis. Pkg.*
    Set in glorious surroundings, this cozily ap-
pointed *bastide* house proffers well-kept, peaceful rooms furnished with wrought iron furniture
and bright Provençal fabrics, and has just added
balconies lending a glorious view of the
Luberon. A lovely terrace where guests can take
their breakfast on fine summer morns. Facilities
include a very pretty swimming pool and tennis
courts.

Le Gordos

Route de Cavaillon
04 90 72 00 75, fax 04 90 72 07 00
*Closed Nov 15-Mar 15. 19 rms 400-800. Pool. Ten-
nis. Pkg.*
    You only see Provence farmhouses like this in
the movies. Lost in a labyrinth of scents—thyme,
rosemary, lavender, and much more. Well-appointed rooms with private terraces.

*Looking for a winery? Refer to the **index**.*

Le Mas Tourteron

Chemin de Saint-Blaise, Les Imberts
04 90 72 00 16, fax 04 90 72 09 81
Closed Sun dinner, Mon, Nov 15-Mar 1. Open until 9:30pm. Garden dining. Pkg.
Nestled at the foot of Gordes, the Mas is a delightful spot, with its pretty Provençal décor and charming walled garden where you can dine under the trees. Élisabeth Bourgeois handles sun-gorged ingredients with a skilled, inventive touch. Although the confit of lamb is actually just an interesting fancied-up variation on tagine, the vegetable risotto and sea bream with artichokes speak out of freshness and aromas. The tiramisu could use some revision, but the cellar defends its region well. An extra point this year. C 300-400. M 150 (weekday lunch), 200 (weekday dinner), 280 (dinner).

12/20 Le Moulin Blanc

Chemin du Moulin, Beaumettes
04 90 72 34 50, fax 04 90 72 25 41
Open daily until 10pm. Terrace dining. Pool. Tennis. Pkg.
The extremely classic style of cooking goes hand in hand with the traditional-style architecture of this house sitting amidst its own private grounds. Provençal cuisine which would do itself more justice by bringing out the contrasts of the flavors of such dishes as duck breast with peaches and young leg of lamb with garlic. M 160-280.

 ## Le Moulin Blanc

(See restaurant above)
Open year-round. 18 rms 435-975. Half-board 450-690. Rm ser. Pool. Tennis. Pkg.
This house has a history: once a pony-express-type post office, then a flour mill, now a beautiful residence turned hotel. Pretty, well-appointed rooms, some of which give onto the grounds and the stunning pool. Well-furnished sitting room with vaulted ceiling and stone walls.

 ## Les Romarins

Route de l'Abbaye de Sénanque
04 90 72 12 13, fax 04 90 72 13 13
Closed Jan 12-Feb 15. 10 rms 450-750. Rms for disabled. Pool. Pkg.
A fine, traditional *bastide* overlooking the village of Gordes and its château. Fresh, pleasant rooms are furnished with attractive nineteenth-century antiques. Charming reception.

■ **In Joucas 84220** *6 km E on D 2 and D 102*

 ## Le Mas des Herbes Blanches

Route de Murs - 04 90 05 79 79, fax 04 90 05 71 96
Closed Jan 4-Mar 20. Open until 9:30pm. Terrace dining. Pool. Tennis. Pkg.
This bewitching *mas* with its understated luxury affording one of the most beautiful panoramic views of the Luberon has just hit the jackpot with new chef Éric Sapet. Sapet brought along his top-of-the-trade dining room director, so the stars are twinkling in the dining room as well. Some glittering examples: stuffed artichokes on a slightly-licoriced demi-glace; highly original turbot roasted with chicken wings; surprising honey-lacquered suckling pig, and an iced nougat that reinvents nougat. All parading freshness, subtle technical mastery (white-beet tart), and intimate knowledge of his ingredients. Three toques are not far from grasp, and the dire beauty of the view, the frills and the fineries, along with the knowledgeably-selected cellar help move firmly in that direction. A discovery? No, just a scintillating meeting of mind, taste and eye. C 260-400. M 180-300.

 ## Le Mas des Herbes Blanches

(See restaurant above)
Closed Jan 4-Mar 19. 6 stes 1,490-2,150. 13 rms 840-1,530. Half-board 800-1,500. Rm ser. Air cond. Heated pool. Tennis. Garage pkg.
The rooms are air conditioned and offer all modern comforts. Most of the lodgings give onto the Luberon and the hotel's extensive grounds, where *stipas*—the «white grasses» which gave the place its name—grow in profusion. Relais et Châteaux.

Le Phébus

Route de Murs - 04 90 05 78 83, fax 04 90 05 73 61
Closed Oct 15-Easter. Open until 10pm. Terrace dining. Heated pool. Tennis. Valet pkg.
The enticing cooking of Xavier Mathieu, chock-full of ideas, is staged in a country-style dining room replete with Louis XIII chairs, wall tapestries and white upholstery. He pulls delicious surprises out of his bag at every turn, such as his anchovy ice cream with crystallized-vegetable terrine and squash, tomato and fennel sherbet: only the courageous would venture such combinations of taste. Don't worry, there are more conventional selections, such as the pot-roasted pigeon, cooked to perfection, and garnished with diced semolina and soya-tomato jam. C 260-400. M 180-300.

Le Phébus

(See restaurant above)
Closed Oct 15-Mar 15. 5 stes 1,395-1,990. 17 rms 665-1,200. Rms for disabled. Half-board 680-980. Air cond. Heated pool. Tennis. Valet pkg.
Five hugely comfortable suites (two have private pools), lovely rooms, many of which boast stupendous views. The Phébus pampers guests with period furniture, dainty floral arrangements, an alluring terrace, good breakfasts, and efficient service. Extremely quiet.

> *This symbol signifies hotels that offer an exceptional degree of peace and quiet.*

ISLE-SUR-LA-SORGUE (L')   84800
Paris 698 - Avignon 23 - Apt 32 - Carpentras 17   Vaucluse

12/20   Le Carré d'Herbes

13, av. des Quatre-Otages
04 90 38 62 95, fax 04 90 72 09 81
Closed Tue dinner, Wed, Dec 23-Jan 16. Open until 9pm (9:30pm in summer). Terrace dining.
If you eat like a bird, don't drop in at this enormous birdcage amidst its splendid herb garden full of fragrance. Emmanuelle Bourgeois's bistro-style cooking lets you partake of chicken liver shepherd's pie, pig's knuckle and lentils, or roasted thyme chicken. C 150-200. M 120.

12/20   Mas de Cure Bourse

Carrefour de Velorgues
04 90 38 16 58, fax 04 90 38 52 31
Closed Mon, Tue lunch, 2 wks in Jan, 2 wks in Oct. Open until 9:30pm. Garden dining. Pool. Garage pkg.
Real home cooking in a rustic setting or on the shady terrace. We enjoyed the «packet» of crawfish tails with artichokes, the quails stuffed with foie gras, and the pistachio crème brûlée. Well-selected wine list. C 250. M 165-260.

 Mas de Cure Bourse 🍴🌲

(See restaurant above)
Open year-round. 13 rms 290-550. Half-board 365-495. Pool. Garage pkg.
This eighteenth-century postmaster's station is just undergoing renovation...thank goodness! Like that, you can take better advantage of the peaceful charm of the rooms and of the general atmosphere.

 Le Mas des Grès 🍴🌲

Route d'Apt
04 90 20 32 85, fax 04 90 20 21 45
Closed Jan 3-Mar 15. 3 stes 800-1,200. 11 rms 390-600. Rms for disabled. Half-board 395-600. Rm ser. Pool.
There's plenty to charm the eye and soothe the spirit in this fully renovated *mas*, where guests are lodged in large, prettily appointed rooms. The atmosphere exudes simplicity and refinement, and patrons are welcomed as if they were old friends.

 La Prévôté

4, rue Jean-Jacques-Rousseau - 04 90 38 57 29
Closed Sun dinner, Mon (Dec-Jun), Nov. Open until 9:30pm. Terrace dining.
Set in a flower-filled courtyard adjoining the church, this handsome restaurant—the best in town—is built of hewn stone and bare beams warmed by tapestries. Roland Mercier is already a polished pro with more than a little imagination, evident in his deservedly popular 210 F menu. Small but well chosen wine list. C 260. M 125 (weekday lunch), 210-320.

 Le Vivier de la Sorgue

Cours Fernande-Peyre - 04 90 38 52 80
Closed dinner Fri & Sun, Sat lunch, annual closings not availabel. Open until 9:30pm. Terrace dining. Air cond. Pkg.
This peaceful restaurant full of locals is located away from the hustle and bustle of downtown and the multitude of antique shops. The décor is rather oppressive—the colors do nothing to tone down the overly geometrical spaces. The terrace giving onto the water is much more in harmony with new chef's lively but modest Provençal cuisine: anchovy lasagne, flawless thick cod steak, desserts offering unexpected surprises. A worthy new addition; a chef who knows how to add an original flare to a meritorious cuisine without padding the price. M 95 (weekday lunch), 135, 195.

JOUCAS 84   → **Gordes**

LOURMARIN   84160
Paris 754 - Salon 36 - Avignon 56   Vaucluse

 L'Agneau Gourmand

Route de Vaugines
04 90 68 21 04 (R), 04 90 68 30 55 (H), fax 04 90 68 11 97 (R), 04 90 68 37 41 (H)
Closed Wed (lunch in summer), Thu lunch, Nov-end Feb. Open until 9:30pm. Terrace dining. Pool. Tennis. Pkg.
The vaulted dining room of this beautifully restored seventeenth-century *bastide* is the scene of elegant repasts featuring the refined, nicely presented cuisine of Jean-Pierre Vollaire. The sights (the lovely flower garden) and smells (the cooking) of Provence are on hand: scallops and Luberon truffles, Sisteron lamb noisettes with candied garlic cloves, and iced nougat color-specked with crystallized fruit from Apte. There could be more choice however. C 350-480. M 150 (weekday lunch), 185-330.

 Hôtel de Guilles 🍴🌲

(See restaurant above)
Closed Jan 5-Mar 1, Nov-Dec 19. 28 rms 400-620. Rms for disabled. Pool. Tennis. Pkg.
The Provençal-style rooms are quiet and the setting is right for idling around the pool, working out the tension on the tennis courts, or taking a lulling stroll in the wonderfully flowery garden.

 La Fenière

Route du Cadenet, D 942
04 90 68 11 79, fax 04 90 68 18 60
Closed Mon (exc dinner Apr-Sep & hols). Open until 9:30pm. Air cond. Terrace dining. Pool. Garage pkg.
The Sammuts have finally done it. Packed up and moved a mile or so down the road to new quarters. The spanking new vaulted dining room with its warm well harmonized colors and

far-reaching terrace has inspired Reine Sammut to call up the culinary muses with more vim and vigor than ever. What depths does she descend to conjure up such original combinations: grilled red mullet fillets scattered with a mesclun of flowers and tiny crackly violets; carrot and cumin canneloni and marinated sardines with a garlic cake in jelly; risotto primavera (peas and green beans); whole mullet aside candied tomatoes and broiled sweet peppers; roast kid livened up with eggplant caviar and broad beans; lamb's trotter and sweetbread shepherd's pie joined by roast saddle; shoulder slowly cooked in its own fat and classic petits paquets in their jus...the whole gamut of what Provence has to offer, nimbly prepared by a wide-eyed fairy with a thousand and one tricks up her sleeve. The enchantment goes on with the desserts: iced marzipan with apricot and bitter-almond sauce or crusty Brousse goat cheese with zests of candied lemon and honey ice cream. The sun also shines in your glass with a wealth of local wines to choose from. One flaw, however: the lack of half-bottles can run the bill up quickly. And the service is a little slow, but oh so pleasant; after all, we're in the sunny South, so we can take our time! C 460. M 190-490.

 La Fenière

(See restaurant above)
Closed Mon off-seas, Jan 5-Feb 3. 1 ste 900-950. 6 rms 500-750. Pool. Pkg.
Reine and Guy Sammut's new hotel and restaurant blends into the quiet of the Provençal countryside and speaks out for the sweet things that Provence has to offer, and with what taste and refinement! The seven guest rooms are prettily decorated with handmade crafts from the region—baskets, wrought iron, tiles, woven items. The couple also has the good taste to keep the prices moderate. Swimming pool in the park that's being planted.

 Le Moulin de Lourmarin

Rue du Temple - 04 90 68 06 69, fax 04 90 68 31 76
Closed Tue off-seas, Wed lunch, mid Jan-mid Feb. Open until 10pm. Terrace dining. Air cond. Valet pkg.
This superb house with its stones and metal, its tiles and wrought iron, and its refined colorful rooms sings out of Provence in all its elegance. A touch more is added by the fields of lavender and sunflowers a short distance from the house. Swimming pool and shady terrace on the banks of a little brook. C 550-800. M 180 (weekdays), 260-380.

 Le Moulin de Lourmarin

(See restaurant above)
Closed mid Jan-mid Feb. 2 stes 1,600-2,100. 18 rms 500-1,300. Half-board 700-1,000. Rm ser. Air cond. Valet pkg.

A futuristic elevator ferries guests to their luxurious and comfortable lodgings. Magnificent bathrooms; incomparable breakfasts. Note, however, that the pool, sauna, and park are three kilometers away. Good base for jaunts around the Luberon countryside.

MANOSQUE 04100
Paris 767 - Aix-en-P. 53 - Sisteron 52   Alpes/H.-P.

11/20 **Le Gavroche**

21, av. Jean-Giono - 04 92 72 03 36
Closed Sun. Open until 11pm. Terrace dining. Air cond.
A friendly 1930s-style bistro right in the heart of town which is a strong attraction for the lunch crowd. Nice regional fare in a relaxed environment and offering good local wines. The prices have managed to remain modest, and the big parking lot nearby is an added advantage. C 180. M 75, 120.

12/20 **La Rôtisserie**

43, bd des Tilleuls
04 92 72 32 28, fax 04 92 72 92 93
Closed Sun dinner, Mon. Open until 9:30pm. Terrace dining. Air cond. Pkg.
A year ago, Dominique Bucaille came in with a bang to this bastion of broiled meats located along the circle road. But this year, the gears are still not oiled in this modern restaurant, and it's not the daub on the walls, the noisy staff or the overcooked French fries that will help change our opinion. It's time the new master of the house took the horse by the reins... C 300. M 98-174.

 La Source

Route du Dauphin - 04 92 72 12 79
Closed Sat lunch, Mon, Nov. Open until 9pm. Terrace dining. Pool. Pkg.
The modern architecture doesn't really blend in with the surroundings, but the terrace overlooking the firs and the elegant dining room dressed up with painted furniture have a certain charm. Thierry Potignon's cuisine is fragrant with the scents of the Garrigue and the regulars know that you can be sure of the freshness of the products. The fisherman's plate with its lovely beurre blanc is a diamond of a dish. The leg of lamb and pastries are well executed. Fine little-known regional wines and warm welcome.

■ **In La**
Fuste 04210   *6.5 km SE on D 907 and D 4*

 Hostellerie de la Fuste

04 92 72 05 95, fax 04 92 72 92 93
Closed Oct-Apr 15 (exc hols): Sun dinner & Mon. Open until 10:30pm. Garden dining. Heated pool. Pkg.

Set in a luminous Provençal landscape, this *auberge de charme* wears a décor that could be qualified as a mite overloaded. Chef Dominique Bucaille is in love with vegetables, and he handles them with tender and skillful care. He has even conjured up an entire meal based on vegetables. Under the paneled ceiling or on the terrace, under the shade of the age-old chestnuts, revel in the potato and chervil Bavarian cream with its asparagus and tomatoes confites; delight in the hearty flavors of the shoulder of young rabbit stuffed with herbs and variety meat; admire the «variation on an apple» accompanied by its caramel and einkorn cake. Lydia Bucaille is a pleasant hostess, and the sometimes starchy service is professional and courteous. Keep an eye on the price if you order à la carte! C 360-550. M 250-450.

 ## Hostellerie de la Fuste

(See restaurant above)
See restaurant for closings. 2 stes 900-1,400. 12 rms 550-900. Rms for disabled. Half-board 700-900. Air cond. Heated pool. Pkg.
Here's a beatific place to stay, with huge, immaculate rooms and memorably beautiful grounds overflowing with ever-Provençal scents of lavender and rosemary. Warm reception.

MARSEILLE 13000
Paris 771 - Lyon 315 - Nice 188 B./Rhône

 ## René Alloin

8th arr. - 8, pl. de l'Amiral-Muselier
04 91 77 88 25, fax 04 91 77 76 84
Closed Sat lunch, Sun dinner. Open until 10pm. Terrace dining. Air cond.
In his cheerful neo-classic-décor restaurant accented with bright colors, chef René Alloin performs lively interpretations of the Mediterranean repertoire: try the marinated sardines, the extra-large helping of sole with seaweed, the delicious garlic and vinegar chicken fricassée and the homemade Provence-style desserts. Even though the greeting is as cordial as ever, René Alloin has unfortunately lost a bit of the dynamism that made his charm in the past. C 310-400. M 135 (weekday lunch), 195-270.

 ## L'Ambassade des Vignobles

1st arr. - 42, pl. aux Huiles
04 91 33 00 25, fax 04 91 54 25 60
Closed Sat lunch, Sun, Aug. Open until 10:45pm. Terrace dining. Air cond.
This winegrowers' embassy near the city's dockyards presents the rare opportunity to taste perfectly partnered food and wine. The 300 F menu changes every month, to showcase the specialties of a particular region with the wines that match them best—the pairings are most instructive! The cellar is superb, with bottles in every price range. M 150-300 (wine incl).

12/20 Les Arcenaulx

1st arr. - 25, cours d'Estienne-d'Orves
04 91 59 80 30, fax 04 91 54 76 33
Closed Sun, hols. Open until 11:30pm. Terrace dining. Air cond. Pkg.
Pascal Cicchella presides over the kitchens of this famous restaurant-cum-bookshop run by the Laffite sisters. He turns out passable renditions of Mediterranean specialties, like his mouthwatering though heavy winter squash cream soup with anchovy cream, but other dishes, like his baby rabbit tart with its soggy crust and boiled-meat tastes are just down right pretentious. Well-chosen wines. C 260. M 135-280.

 ## L'Assiette Marine

8th arr. - 142, av. Pierre-Mendès-France
04 91 71 04 04
Closed Sun dinner. Open until 10pm. Terrace dining. Garage pkg.
It's hard to find a quiet spot on the terrace of Jean-Luc Sellam's beachfront restaurant, located in a rather brash new shopping district. But the blue and yellow dining room is comfortable, and conducive to enjoying Sellam's light, zesty cuisine. He's a solid technician who knows how to inject a touch of whimsy into the most classic dishes. Seafood is the specialty, but he handles poultry and meat with equal success. C 280. M 140-270.

12/20 Le Carré d'Honoré

1st arr. - 34, pl. aux Huiles
04 91 33 16 80, fax 04 91 33 54 81
Closed Sat lunch, Sun dinner, 2 wks in Aug. Open until 10pm. Terrace dining.
The Italian mosaics and the pretty Provence landscapes on the walls of this pretty restaurant dressed up in yellow and blue resemble a movie set. Unfortunately, the soiled menus, the wine list with more marked out wines than available ones, and the grumpy service put it quickly in the B category. Same goes for the food: the burnt calamaries and the sea bream swimming in a dubious sauce make the B rating firm for this year. C 270. M 95-130.

 ## Concorde Palm Beach

8th arr. - 2, promenade de la Plage
04 91 16 19 00, fax 04 91 16 19 39
Open year-round. 1 ste 1,680. 145 rms 690-870. Restaurant. Pool. Beach. Pkg.
This huge, modern hotel complex offers spacious rooms that all look out to sea. Auditorium for business meetings.

The ratings are based solely on the restaurants' cuisine. We do not take into account the atmosphere, décor, service and so on; these are commented upon within the review.

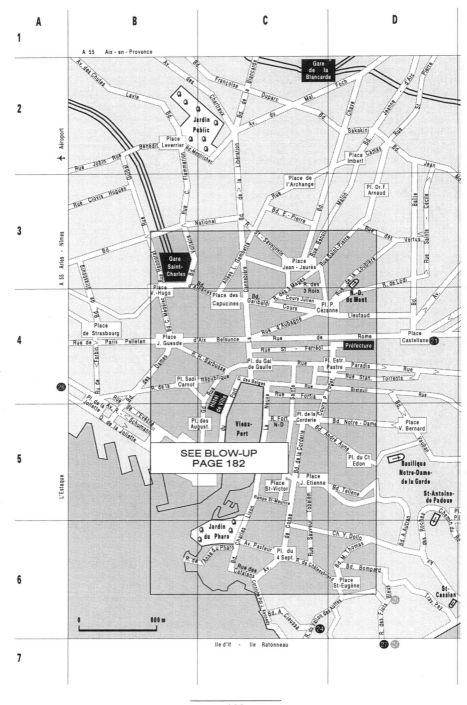

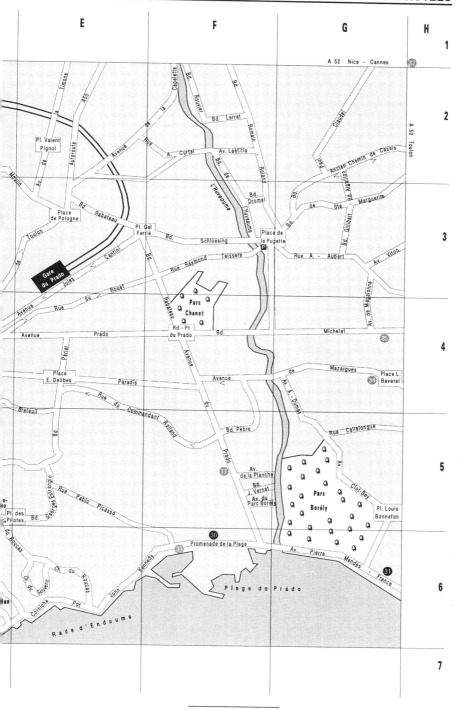

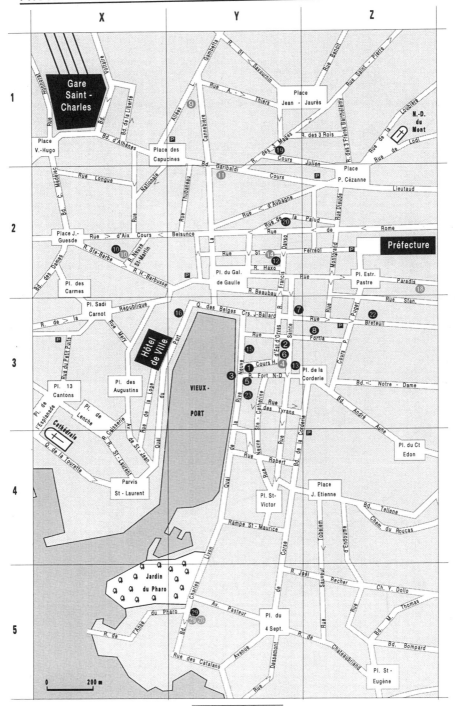

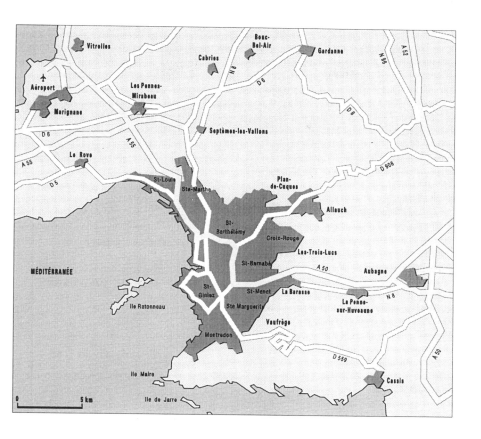

F-6 30 - René Alloin	**Y-3** ⑥ - Les Échevins
Y-3 ① - L'Ambassade	**Y-3** ⑦ - La Ferme
des Vignobles	**C-6** 24 - Chez Fonfon
Y-3 ② - Les Arcenaulx	**F-5** 17 - Holiday Inn
G-6 31 - L'Assiette Marine	**Y-3** 16 - Miramar
Y-3 ⑤ - Le Carré d'Honoré	**X-2** ⑩ - Mercure Euro-Centre
F-6 33 - Concorde Palm Beach	**Y-3** 23 - Les Mets de Provence

D-6 25 - New Hotel Bompard
Y-5 26 - Novotel Vieux-Port
X-2 ⑪ - L'Oursinade
D-7 27 - Passédat
Y-3 13 - Patalain
D-4 21 - Au Pescadou
D-7 27 - Le Petit Nice

Les Échevins

1st arr. - 44, rue Sainte
04 91 33 08 08, fax 04 91 54 08 21
Closed Sat lunch, Sun, Jul 14-Aug 15. Open until 10:30pm. Terrace dining. Air cond.
Take a seat under the 1637 cathedral ceiling of this antique-filled dining room, to savor Jeanne Moreni's polished cooking. She presents a happy blend of her native Southwest and sunny Provence. In particular, don't miss the open-air pigeon, raised the old-fashioned way by Edouard Lamonica, so tender and tasty you want to cry for joy, and one of the most on-the-mark bouillabaisses in all Marseille. Her forté is however the high quality of the ingredients she uses and the «affection» she puts into preparing them. Whisky aficionados, here's one selection that can compete with Harry's Bar! **C** 250-320. **M** 160-300.

 ## La Ferme

1st arr. - 23, rue Sainte
04 91 33 21 12, fax 04 91 33 81 21
Closed Sat lunch, Sun, Aug. Open until 10:15pm. Terrace dining.
Raymond Russo has practically abandoned his kitchen, and much to our dismay, because the customers are swaggering before a cuisine that has its ups and downs. Even though we were served the same heavy sauce with two different dishes, we'll give credit where it's due: the pigeon with foie gras was excellent. We hope this little drop in quality is a passing affair. **C** 300. **M** 250.

12/20 Chez Fonfon

7th arr. - 140, rue du Vallon-des-Auffes
04 91 52 14 38, fax 04 91 59 27 32
Closed Sun dinner, Jan 1-20. Open until 10pm. Terrace dining. Air cond.
Do people come to this homey restaurant tucked away in a rocky inlet for the food, or to pay homage to the patriarch of Marseille's chefs? Both, decidedly. For the bouillabaisse and bour-rides are plentiful and authentic and the fish luminously fresh (monkfish with julienned vegetables, lobster and scallop ravioli). **C** 310-450.

 ## Holiday Inn

8th arr. - Marseille City Center, 103, av. du Prado
04 91 83 10 10, fax 04 91 79 84 12
Open year-round. 4 stes 700-950. 115 rms 510-610. Rms for disabled. Restaurant. Half-board 460-560. Rm ser. Air cond. Fitness. Garage pkg.
Right in the heart of the city, you'll spot the hotel by its smoked-glass façade. Perfectly equipped, air conditioned rooms with neo-Hel-lenic décor.

 ## Maris Caupona

6th arr. - 11, rue Gustave-Ricard - 04 91 33 58 07
Closed Sat, Sun, Aug. Open until 10pm. Air cond. Terrace dining. Air cond.

Pascal Peltier offers surprising combinations using top-quality ingredients and adding his special touch. He's got a bright future. A distinct preference for seafood. We savored the bay scal-lops marinated with five spices, but thought the sardines bleues with olive oil would have been better without the cream cheese mousse. Worthy desserts. Preferable to take a set menu; à la carte prices are over the top. **C** 300-350. **M** 160 (wine incl)

 ## Mercure Beauvau Vieux-Port

1st arr. - 4, rue Beauvau
04 91 54 91 00, fax 04 91 54 15 76
Open year-round. 1 ste 1,500. 71 rms 400-850. Rm ser. Air cond.
This deluxe hotel has welcomed no less than Chopin and George Sand. Exquisite location on the Vieux-Port, this spiffed up luxury hotel from yesteryear now offers modern facilities. Sunny, quiet rooms furnished tastefully with antiques.

Mercure Euro-Centre

See restaurant L'Oursinade

 ## Les Mets de Provence

7th arr. - 18, quai Rive-Neuve
04 91 33 35 38, fax 04 91 33 05 69
Closed Sun, Mon lunch, 2 wks in Aug. Open until 10:30pm. Terrace dining. Air cond.
Raoul Solamito has relaunched one of Marseille's best-known culinary institutions, giving it the most beautiful interior of any res-taurant in town. The director of this orchestra is Rodolphe Badikian, a young chef down from the Maxim's school of music. The mix-and-match table settings are amusing, and the (kitchen) music is confidently crescendoing. **C** 310. **M** 230 (weekday lunch, wine incl), 290 (dinner).

 ## Miramar

2nd arr. - 12, quai du Port
04 91 91 10 40, fax 04 91 56 64 31
Closed Sun, 3 wks in Aug. Open until 10pm. Terrace dining. Air cond.
A strategic address on the Vieux-Port, Miramar is not what it used to be. Only their delicious bouillabaisse, a Marseille classic, keeps it worthwhile. Both the waiters and the décor are tired and need resuscitation. It is only the brave efforts of pastry chef Fabrice Vaquer that save the day (and the toque). **C** 400.

 ## New Hotel Bompard 🌲

7th arr. - 2, rue des Flots-Bleus
04 91 52 10 93, fax 04 91 31 02 14
Open year-round. 46 rms 380-550. Rms for dis-abled. Rm ser. Air cond. Pool. Garage pkg.
Set in quiet grounds just minutes from the old port and the town center, the Bompard houses bright, large rooms that are both functional and comfortable (just avoid those that give onto the

parking lot). The balconies massed with flowers are a nice touch. Studios with kitchenettes available.

Novotel Est La Valentine

11th arr. - Saint-Menet
04 91 43 90 60, fax 04 91 27 06 74
Open year-round. 131 rms 430-480. Rms for disabled. Restaurant. Rm ser. Air cond. Pool. Tennis. Garage pkg.
For the demanding traveller. Huge rooms, extremely well soundproofed. The pleasant 5-acre park offers numerous sports activities. Lively bar.

Novotel Vieux-Port

7th arr. - 36, bd Charles-Livon
04 91 59 22 22, fax 04 91 31 15 48
Open year-round. 90 rms 520-610. Rms for disabled. Restaurant. Rm ser. Air cond. Pool. Garage pkg.
The rooms of this well situated hotel in the Vieux-Port area are comfortable, functional, and airy and sport fine views. Good location for a walking tour of the city.

L'Oursinade

1st arr. - Centre Bourse, 1, rue Neuve-St-Martin
04 91 39 20 00, fax 04 91 56 24 57
Closed Sun lunch, hols, Aug. Open until 10:30pm. Terrace dining. Air cond. Valet pkg.
This hotel dining room may be on the gloomy side, but the food glitters with goodness. Chef Philippe Gaillard knows his business, and his ingredients are of the utmost freshness, which helps make up for the staff that is professional but lacking incentive. Another advantage of this chain: a lot of time and effort has gone into making up this wine list chocked full of nice prices. C 180-260. M 160-245.

Mercure Euro-Centre

(See restaurant above)
Open year-round. 1 ste 1,020. 198 rms 540-650. Rms for disabled. Rm ser. Air cond. Garage pkg.
Ask for an upper-floor room with an enchanting view of the bay. All are comfortable and well appointed. First-class service, gargantuan breakfasts.

Passédat

7th arr. - Corniche Kennedy, Anse de Maldormé
04 91 59 25 92, fax 04 91 59 28 08
Closed Sat lunch & Sun off-seas. Open until 10pm (10:30pm in summer). Garden dining. Air cond. Terrace dining. Pool. Valet pkg.
Nestled in a fold of the corniche with a breathtaking view of the islands across the way (at sunset, it looks like paradise!), this is a most romantic place to dine. The kitchen works exclusively with the freshest ingredients (mainly

seafood), which are used to best advantage in novel, personalized ways: colossal shrimp in carrot and ginger juice or Oriental-style pressed bouillabaisse. Remember to sell a T-bond or two before you reserve your table: the cellar, though stocked well with Burgundies and champagnes, posts dizzying prices, most starters cost over 200, and main courses hover around 300. C 500-800. M 310 (weekday lunch, wine incl), 590-700.

Le Petit Nice

(See restaurant above)
Open year-round. 2 stes 2,900-3,900. 13 rms 1,100-2,100. Half-board 1,210-2,610. Rm ser. Air cond. Pool. Valet pkg.
Set in a stunningly beautiful and peaceful spot overlooking the sea, Le Petit Nice has a handful of lovely, comfortable, and extremely expensive rooms and suites done up in «designer» style (which you'll either love or hate), and superbly equipped bathrooms. Amenities include a saltwater swimming pool, sun room, water skiing, and sea fishing. A nearby villa houses two additional rooms and an opulent suite with a private terrace and sauna. Relais et Châteaux.

Patalain

1st arr. - 49, rue Sainte
04 91 55 02 78, fax 04 91 54 15 29
Closed Sat lunch, Sun, hols, Aug. Open until 11pm. Terrace dining. Air cond.
This favorite of the Marseille bourgeoisie is just a hop away from the port. In this street dedicated to the gustatory senses, Suzanne Quaglia has been cooking up classic Provençal fare for several lustra now, but both the walls of the kitsch thirties-style décor and the cooking have started to show their age. The insipid eggplant terrine resembled a sponge in texture, the sea perch lacked the spices announced on the menu and its side dish of potatoes was practically raw. If you add the fact that the service didn't live up to the grandeur of the check, that the barmaid chain-smoked, and that the *patronne* grumbled and scowled, we have to conclude that old gray mares change too. C 380. M 150 (lunch), 180-370.

Au Pescadou

6th arr. - 19, pl. de Castellane
04 91 78 36 01, fax 04 91 83 02 94
Closed Sun dinner, Jul 21-Aug 31. Open until 10:30pm. Terrace dining.
Here's an elegant bistro where you can down huge platters of fresh shellfish, red mullet en salade, or scallop ravioli anointed with truffle jus, irrigated by a cool white wine from the appealing cellar. We would certainly digest the prices a little better if the staff were more courteous and polished in their ways. C 300. M 158-198.

Le Petit Nice

See restaurant Passédat

Saint-Ferréol's Hotel

1st arr. - 19, rue Pisançon
04 91 33 12 21, fax 04 91 54 29 97
Open year-round. 19 rms 300-500. Air cond.
Here's a hotel with quirky charm in a traffic-free street just 200 yards from the Vieux-Port. The mid-sized rooms sport personalized furnishings; all are efficiently soundproofed. Warm welcome, bar and Jacuzzis.

 ## Les Trois Forts

7th arr. - Vieux-Port, 36, rue Charles-Livon
04 91 15 59 00, fax 04 91 15 59 50
Open daily until 10:15pm. Terrace dining. Air cond. Pool. Valet pkg.
You would come here for the superb view of the old port, even if there were no other attractions. But Dominique Frérard's menu bursts with bold Provençal flavors, enhanced by a capital cellar of regional wines. Sample his pressed lamb tongue, leeks and sweet peppers, served warm and subtly highlighted with a touch of olive oil and tapenade; or the tenderest of pigeon b'steeyas garnished with a ratatouille in a spicy little jus; or the walnut «cracker» with its rattling good aged rum and caramel sauce. Every dish is betwitching without any showing off, offering just that little zest of refinement that transfigures. One of the best buys in town. Another point this year. C 280. M 110-225.

 ## Sofitel Vieux-Port

(See restaurant above)
Open year-round. 3 stes 2,200-3,400. 127 rms 790-1,090. Rms for disabled. Half-board 800-1,000. Rm ser. Air cond. Pool. Garage pkg.
The view of the town across the old port is superb. This renovated hotel offers soundproofed, air-conditioned rooms with functional comfort and modern equipment, but lacking in charm. Excellent breakfast buffet, and a pleasant bar. Good service, too.

And also...

Our selection of places for inexpensive, quick, or late-night meals.
Le Bistrot à Vin (04 91 54 02 20 - 1st arr. - 7, rue Sainte. Open until 11:30pm. Closed Sat lunch, Sun.): This little bistro near the Canebière that attracts *amateurs* with its simple little dishes, pleasant wine by the glass, and pleasant surprises on arrival of the check. (160).
Dock de Suez (04 91 56 07 56 - 2nd arr. - 10, pl. de la Joliette. Open until 10:30pm. Closed Mon dinner, Sat lunch, Sun.): This elegant brasserie, magnificently restored and created just two years ago, is located in the old Joliette docks. Pleasing food and charming reception. (90-250).
New York (04 91 33 60 98 - 1st arr. - 33, quai des Belges. Open daily until 11:30pm.): Red leather décor, located across from the Vieux-Port, and sporting a marvellous view. Show biz stars, politicians and business people rub elbows as they slip down broiled fish and high-quality

tartare. A real plus is Monique Venturini's reception. 467 (160-200).
Toinou (04 91 33 14 94 - 1st arr. - 3, cours St-Louis. Open until midnight. Closed dinner Mon & Tue, Jul-Aug.): In this pleasant atmosphere resembling an auction house, young waiters and waitresses serve the choicest oysters in the region. Good prices on wine (65-240).

MAUSSANE-LES-ALPILLES	13520
Paris 717 - Marseille 85 - Arles 18 - Salon 28	B./Rhône

 ## La Petite France

15, av. de la Vallée-des-Baux
04 90 54 41 91, fax 04 90 54 52 50
Closed Wed, Thu lunch, Jan 3-31, 1 wk in Nov. Open until 9:30pm. Terrace dining. Air cond. Pkg.
This seventeenth-century bread bakery-cum-restaurant breathes *joie de vivre*. The two little vaulted-ceiling dining rooms strewn with beautiful *objets*, the smiling welcome from Isabelle, and the staff that waits on you hand and foot continue in the same strain, as do the talent of Thierry Maffre-Bogé, who just gets better every year. You can still partake of his now classic green-olive and sage ravioli, or you can slip down some of his newer creative renditions of Provence favorites. For example: a splendiforous saddle of young rabbit stuffed with its own liver and fresh herbs, dribbled with a reduction of Baux wines and partnered with broiled artichokes and fennel, or a gossamer-like fig feuillité in a staggeringly good licorice sauce. The wine list might well put you in ecstasy, and the seraphic prices make this one of the best buys in this little area. C 280-350. M 175-350.

 ## Le Pré des Baux

Rue du Vieux-Moulin
04 90 54 40 40, fax 04 90 54 53 07
Closed Oct 15-Mar 15 (exc Christmas-New Year). 10 rms 450-680. Rms for disabled. Pool. Garage pkg.
In a quiet setting, this intimate, modern hotel has sunny, modern rooms with terraces that give onto a swimming pool. Walled garden; attentive service.

 ## Ou Ravi Provençau

34, av. de la Vallée-des-Baux
04 90 54 31 11, fax 04 90 54 41 03
Closed Tue, Nov 20-Dec 20. Open until 9:30pm (10:30pm in summer). Terrace dining.
Jean-François Richard's cheerily decorated Provençal restaurant is warm and welcoming. So is his cuisine, which the locals flock to sample. Try his eggplant papetoun with tomato sauce, escargots à la suçarelle, vegetable and basil crespéu, or old-fashioned beef daube. Nothing goes better with this food than the cellar's excellent, affordable local wines: don't miss the fine Domaine Hauvette. C 300-400. M 190-240.

MEYREUIL 13 → Aix-en-Provence

MONTEUX 84	→ Carpentras

MONTFAVET 84	→ Avignon

MOUSTIERS-SAINTE-MARIE	04360
Paris 875 - Digne 62 - Manosque 48	Alpes/H.-P.

La Bastide de Moustiers

Quartier Saint-Michel
04 92 70 47 47, fax 04 92 70 47 48
Closed mid Nov-mid Mar. Open until 9:45pm. Terrace dining. Air cond. Heated pool. Garage pkg.
If you expect to see the pomp of Monte Carlo or the chic woodwork of Paris, you don't know Alain Ducasse. Here, it is the countryside and the elegant seventeenth-century *bastide* in all its authenticity (although the whole baguette they put on the table is a bit much) that graciously provide the splendor. In this establishment, the dictum is passion for good products, and using them to their utmost potential. Benoît Witz didn't just pop up from nowhere; he was second in line at the Louis-XV, where tongues did speak of his brilliance. The ultra-tender vegetables braised with thin slices of truffles was a brilliant piece of work, as was the spit-roasted herb chicken served with its tender giblets and juice with diced foie gras. It is evident that Ducasse has more than lightly dabbled in the affairs of this kitchen. The rustic bigarreau cherry clafouti is truly sublime, and the vanilla ice cream dumpling and the very warmth of the atmosphere finish off this lovely affair. The 260 F set-price meal is a true godsend. You'll find all the usual vintage *grands crus* wines, as well as a few surprises and discoveries, but half-bottles are not plentiful. The staff is professionally efficient, but a little too boisterous and cheeky. C 350. M 195 (weekdays), 260.

La Bastide de Moustiers 🏰🌳

(See restaurant above)
Closed mid Nov-beg Feb. 7 rms 800-1,300. Rms for disabled. Air cond. Heated pool. Garage pkg.
This is the Provence you dream about: a pretty seventeenth-century ochre-colored house nestled among the olive groves girdled by its little vegetable garden and orchard and doting a pool out back on the terrace. Seven divine rooms decked out in a refined décor which includes old furniture, deep canopy beds, huge spanking white bathrooms, Moustiers faïences, recordings of birds chirping, and much more. Ducasse had a good time doing this, and you might just think you're in Eve's garden. Relais & Châteaux.

La Ferme Rose 🏰🌳

04 92 74 69 47, fax 04 92 74 60 76
Closed Nov 30-Mar 15. 7 rms 390-430. Pkg.

An old farmhouse converted into a hotel, lost in the peace and calm of the Verdon gorge and the Sainte-Croix lake. A lovely collection of post-war objects decorates the rooms, full up with little treasures. Pleasant arbor-covered terrace.

Les Santons

Pl. de l'Église - 04 92 74 66 48, fax 04 92 74 63 67
Closed Mon dinner & Tue (exc in summer), Dec-Jan. Open until 9:30pm. Terrace dining.
Next to the town's Romanesque church you'll find this inviting restaurant with an arbor overlooking the valley and a swift-flowing stream. André Abert, assisted in the kitchen by Christophe Morant, produces regional dishes that are a treat for both the palate and the eye. Appetizing cheese board; alluring Provençal cellar. C 400. M 220-300.

NOVES	13550
Paris 700 - St-Rémy-de-P. 16 - Avignon 14	B./Rhône

Auberge de Noves

2.5 km NW on D 28
04 90 94 19 21, fax 04 90 94 47 76
Open daily until 10:15pm. Garden dining. Air cond. Heated pool. Tennis. Valet pkg.
This *auberge* set high on a hilltop dominates a gorgeous Provençal landscape. On balmy days the garden beckons, while winter feasts take place around the fireplace in a dining room with huge bay windows. Robert Lalleman, son of the chef who put this establishment on the culinary map, interprets a regional cuisine that is more flavorful than refined. His wind is giving out of late, but he's steered his oars toward recovery. The sweet-garlic mousse with petits-gris escargots and pine nuts and the slowly simmered veal kidney are still elegant, well-crafted dishes, even though the kidney was a little dry. This little cocoon of well-being and nostalgia is still a bewitching place that stands up to the test of time. C 490. M 225-525.

Auberge de Noves 🏰🌳

(See restaurant above)
Open year-round. 4 stes 1,700-1,950. 19 rms 950-1,650. Rms for disabled. Rm ser. Air cond. Heated pool. Tennis. Valet pkg.
The best way to take advantage of what this lovely Provence-style house has to offer is to take them up on the off-season «formulas» where everything is included. The recent renovation exposed the handsome timbers and stone façade of this dreamy inn lost among tall pines and cypresses. It is now less austere, and the lovely rooms are more comfortable and spacious than ever. Fabulous breakfasts. Relais et Châteaux.

ORANGE   84100
Paris 678 - Avignon 31 - Carpentras 23   Vaucluse

 Arène

Pl. des Langes - 04 90 11 40 40, fax 04 90 11 40 45
Closed Nov 8-30. 30 rms 340-500. Air cond. Pkg.
Right in the historic city center, on a square
shaded by plane trees. Rooms are well equipped.
There's a nice lounge and terrace, but no
elevator. Impeccable welcome and service.

Le Mas des Aigras

East Russamp, Chemin des Aigras
04 90 34 81 01, fax 04 90 34 05 66
*Open year-round. 11 rms 380-460. Pool. Tennis.
Pkg.*
Let the old stones of this lovely Provence-style
farmhouse lost in the vines and the orchards
seduce you. The comfortable rooms offer you a
peaeful, restful sleep (we hope!).

12/20 Le Parvis

3, cours Pourtoules
04 90 34 82 00, fax 04 90 51 18 10
*Closed Sun dinner & Mon off-seas, Jan 19-27, Nov
11-Dec 3. Open until 9:30pm. Terrace dining. Air
cond.*
Just a step away from the antique theatre, a
sunny cuisine served by an enthusiastic staff in
a cheerful décor. Spring herb cake with broad
beans and snow peas, saffron-scented farm-
raised chicken, suckling pig honey-roasted with
honey from Provence. C 220-320. M 98 (weekdays), 128-225.

PONTET (LE) 84   → Avignon

PRA-LOUP 04   → Barcelonnette

ROCHEGUDE   26790
Paris 663 - Valence 84 - Orange 31   Drome

 **Château
de Rochegude**

04 75 97 21 10, fax 04 75 04 89 87
*Closed Mon & Tue off-seas. 3 stes 1,800-2,500. 26
rms 650-1,700. Restaurant. Air cond. Heated pool.
Tennis. Valet pkg.*
Mont Ventoux and the Montmirail peaks stare
back as you wander in the château's extensive
grounds. This extremely elegant and charming
hotel offers huge rooms furnished with rare antiques. Exemplary staff. Relais et Châteaux.

ROUSSILLON   84220
Paris 742 - Avignon 45 - Bonnieux 12   Vaucluse

 Mas de Garrigon

Route de St-Saturnin-d'Apt, D 2
04 90 05 63 22, fax 04 90 05 70 01
*Closed Mon, Tue lunch, Dec-Jan. Open until
9:15pm. Terrace dining. Pool. Pkg.*
Roussillon's beautiful ochre cliffs stand in full
view of this delightful Provençal *mas* surrounded by pine groves. A simple, straightforward cuisine that does not always have the
character it could (maybe because of the foreign
clientele?). A touch of the fashionable, a healthy
sprinkling of savoir-faire, and a restrained cellar
with a respectable selection of half-bottles. A
good address to give your friends. M 140 (lunch),
185-340.

 Mas de Garrigon

(See restaurant above)
*Open year-round. 1 ste 800-990. 8 rms 590-800.
Rms for disabled. Half-board 595-700 (oblig in
seas). Pool. Pkg.*
This hotel features delightful, Provençal-style
rooms with splendid views of Roussillon and the
Luberon. Pleasant fireside lounge and library;
sheltered swimming pool.

SAINT-RÉMY-DE-PROVENCE   13210
Paris 730 - Marseille 91 - Avignon 21   B./Rhône

 Alain Assaud

Le Marceau, 13, bd Marceau - 04 90 92 37 11
*Closed Wed, Thu lunch, Jan 15-Mar 15. Open until
10pm. Terrace dining. Air cond.*
The long, tall, Provençal dining room is a comfortable place in which to sample Alain Assaud's
sunny, market-fresh cooking. Try the simple but
good fresh-tomato pancake livened up with a
touch of anchovies and slivers of basil, or the
magnificent slice of turbot in a meat jus and
marrow, or the wonderfully authentic soft-
caramel apple gratin. It's simple, but on the
mark. Blatant lack of half-bottles on the wine list.
C 230. M 150-230.

**12/20 Le Bistrot
des Alpilles**

15, bd Mirabeau - 04 90 92 09 17
*Closed Sun, 2 wks in Feb, mid Nov-beg Dec. Open
until 9:45pm (10pm in summer). Terrace dining.
Air cond.*
This «with-it» brasserie lets you taste their
wicked little dishes on the terrace or in the large
dining room dedicated to bullfighting. But the
same old tunes—stuffed artichokes, leg of lamb
and chocolate charlotte (wasn't it without chocolate?)—get old after a while. C 270. M 75 (lunch),
165.

Château de Roussan 🌲🏆

2 km on N 99, route de Tarascon
04 90 92 11 63, fax 04 90 92 50 59
Open year-round. 21 rms 430-750. Restaurant.
Half-board 410-730. Garage pkg.
A delightful eighteenth-century residence surrounded by a huge park dotted with rare trees, flower beds, and ponds. Large, attractively furnished guest rooms; bare-bones bathrooms. Excellent breakfasts. The upkeep could be improved.

 Château des Alpilles 🌲🏆

D 31 - 04 90 92 03 33, fax 04 90 92 45 17
Closed Jan 6-mid Feb, Nov 12-Dec 21. 5 stes 1,320-1,690. 15 rms 900-1,130. Rms for disabled. Restaurant. Half-board 723-847. Rm ser. Air cond. Pool. Tennis.
Serene and lovely, this early nineteenth-century château is surrounded by majestic trees. The rooms are huge and have been redecorated in impeccable taste. One of the most refined hotels in Provence. Sauna. Poolside grill in summer.

12/20 Domaine de Valmouriane

Petite route des Baux
04 90 92 44 62, fax 04 90 92 37 32
Open daily until 10pm. Terrace dining. Heated pool. Tennis. Garage pkg.
The large well-kept park dotes an archery range and a putting green. The pretty house offers scrupulously decorated rooms fitted out with splendid bathrooms and were just redone this year. Some of the rooms even have a terrace and suntrap. Billiards and Turkish bath. C 300-450. M 105 (weekday lunch, wine incl), 200-340.

 Domaine de Valmouriane 🌲🏆

(See restaurant above)
Closed year-round. 2 stes 1,160-1,550. 12 rms 590-1,310. Rms for disabled. Half-board 875-940. Rm ser. Air cond. Heated pool. Tennis. Garage pkg.
This luxurious little hotel has spacious rooms (some with sun rooms and terraces), equipped with all modern amenities and decorated with an attention to detail that is rare. Guests may enjoy billiards, tennis, archery, take a Turkish bath, or practice their putting.

12/20 Le Jardin de Frédéric

8 bis, bd Gambetta - 04 90 92 27 76
Closed Wed, Feb school hols. Open until 9:30pm. Terrace dining. Air cond.
Simone Caloux loves the tastes and smells of Provence and her à la carte set meal, which she calls simply «Provence», speaks out the message loud and clear. She hit a few wrong notes this year with her sauces: flawlessly cooked pan-fried mullet served with practically a ladle of oil, and tarragon rabbit with a watery tarragon infusion. Even if you want to avoid the extra charges for certain dishes, you can still eat a perfectly good meal with the puréed cod soufflé with thin strips of smoked salmon, saffron-flavored Provençal fish soup, saddle-of-rabbit cutlets seasoned with garlic and tarragon, and strawberry soup. All this can be savored on the terrace under the leafy plane trees. C 260. M 135-170.

 La Maison Jaune

15, rue Carnot - 04 90 92 56 14
Closed Sun dinner off-seas, Mon, Tue lunch in seas, Jan 8-Mar 8. Open until 9:30pm (10:30pm). Terrace dining.
Some people get better with age, and François Perraud is proving to be one of them, so the second toque we gave him last year is holding strong. We were particularly impressed with the well-crafted 235 F fixed-price meal. Some of the rattling good items we tasted: crispy Greek-style vegetables with saffron; «brief» marinade of sardines and coriander on a bed of fennel julienne and candied lemons; admirable roast pigeon in Baux wine sauce; and velvety extra-thin walnut pie with tangerine marmelade. The cellar coffers up some real discoveries, but there is an annoying lack of advice on the menu. And the very pleasant welcome can't cover up some of the blunders on the dining room floor. M 120 (weekday lunch, wine incl), 170-275.

 Le Mas des Carassins 🌲🏆

1, chemin Gaulois
04 90 92 15 48, fax 04 90 92 63 47
Closed Nov 5-Mar. 10 rms 400-570. Pkg.
If you savor the idea of sleeping among ancient Roman ruins, this might just be your chance (they're really monuments more than ruins). A nineteenth-century farmhouse slipped quietly in among the olive trees and pepper plants. Attractive rooms.

12/20 Restaurant des Arts

30, bd Victor-Hugo
04 90 92 08 50, fax 04 90 92 55 09
Closed Tue, Feb, Nov-Dec. Open until 9:30pm. Terrace dining. Pkg.
The old village brasserie is now a local institution, where area artists exhibit their work. In summer, Saint-Rémy's entire population seems to throng *en masse* to the terrace to enjoy sautéed cuttlefish à la provençale, bull stewed in wine à la Camarguaise, and tasty house-baked pastries. C 220. M 110 (weekdays), 120, 130 (Sun).

 Vallon de Valrugues

Chemin de Canto Cigalo
04 90 92 04 40, fax 04 90 92 44 01
Open daily until 9:30pm. Terrace dining. Pool. Tennis. Pkg.
This ritzy restaurant offers all the grandeur and trappings that its mainly upper middle class tourist clientele expects: lions rampant on either side of the imposing entranceway, red-coated

carmen, and a plethora of servants to satisfy their every whim. New oarsman Philippe Boucher, at the helm since last year, has brought this place into shipshape order. Not surprising, since he stepped off the ship from the highly reputable Auberge de Cassagne, and his two second-in-commands from Jacques Chibois. The result is a menu that observes the sunny traditions of Provence: Dublin bay prawns in the shell and panisse millfeuille, lamb noisette swaddled in bacon and dressed up with candied tomato petals, or strawberry brioche French toast with mixed-berry sauce. The gears may still need a little running in, but the evident desire to do well still puts this restaurant in the realm of the toques (one toque off the mark). For the moment, the prices make us rather seasick—let's hope that the captain steers them downwards. C 300-400. M 165-195 (weekday lunch), 290-460.

Vallon de Valrugues 🌲🍴

(See restaurant above)
Closed Feb. 18 stes 1,380-4,200. 35 rms 680-1,080. Rms for disabled. Half-board 790-990. Rm ser. Air cond. Heated pool. Tennis. Garage pkg.

Quiet, handsomely appointed, and graced with terraces overlooking olive groves or the Alpilles, the rooms are large and have marble bathrooms. One suite is like a country house, perched on the roof with a spectacular view and complete with a private pool and a kitchen. Leisure facilities include satellite TV, billiards, a sauna, and Jacuzzi. Peerless service.

And also...

Our selection of places for inexpensive, quick, or late-night meals.
Le Café du Lézard (04 90 92 59 66 - 12 bis, bd Gambetta. Open until 10pm. Closed Wed dinner, Thu lunch.): The hot spot in town, this wine bar lets you feast on such goodies as foie gras, the specialty of the day and a superb Saint-Marcellin cheese (180).
Chez Xa (04 90 92 41 23 - 24, bd Mirabeau. Open until 10pm. Closed Wed, Dec-beg Mar.): A simple market-inspired menu with affordable little wines, a pleasant terrace and an informal welcome make up the secret of this little bistro. The flip side of success is that now you need to reserve. (140-230).
Sette e Mezzo (04 90 92 59 27 - 34, bd Mirabeau. Open until 10pm, 11pm in summer. Closed Sun & Mon off-seas, Jan 15-Feb 15.): Best Italian pizza in town. All you can eat of pizza, pasta or meat: you choose which. Another hot spot (75-210).

ST-ROMAIN-EN-VIENNOIS 83
→ Vaison-la-Romaine

12/20 Auberge Cavalière

Route d'Arles - 04 90 97 88 88, fax 04 90 97 84 07
Closed Sun dinner, Mon. Open until 9pm. Terrace dining. Air cond. Pool. Tennis. Pkg.
Regionally-inspired cookery with innovations using prestige ingredients. Eat with the cowboys in this traditional décor equipped for every cowboy's needs. Try the 135 F menu putting before you sunset shellfish in aïoli sauce and bull's meat stew. C 300-400. M 135-320.

Auberge Cavalière 🌲🍴

(See restaurant above)
Open year-round. 42 rms 450-1,000. Half-board 500-750 (oblig in seas). Pool. Tennis. Pkg.
This is the Camargue you see on color postcards, complete with the absolute calm, only broken from time to time by a flock of ducks flying over or some pink flamingos flaunting their beauty. A sprawling farmhouse and charming little bungalows dotted around a pond. Everything is immacuately white, the furniture is rustic, and the bathrooms are fitted out to perfection.

12/20 L'Estelle

4 km on D 38, route du Petit-Rhône
04 90 97 89 01, fax 04 90 97 80 36
Closed Jan-Mar 27, Nov 8-Dec 11. Open until 10pm. Terrace dining. Air cond. Pool. Tennis. Pkg.
Sven Fuhrmann is now beating out the notes in this little restaurant already blessed with a congenial atmosphere. The hardy 135 F set-price meal (moules marinière, bull steak with baked potato and sour cream, and chocolate fondant) gives way to a more elaborate higher echelon: vegetable carpaccio marinated in vinegar, Bouzigues oysters speckled with unrefined sea salt, or sea perch crisp on a bed of spinach napped with a Camargue red-wine sauce. Short but cleverly selected list of wines from the region. C 250-300. M 135 (weekday lunch), 145 (Sun lunch), 190-360 (dinner).

L'Estelle 🌲🍴

(See restaurant above)
Closed Jan-Mar 27. 1 ste 1,190-2,250. 19 rms 640-1,190. Rms for disabled. Half-board 495-675. Rm ser. Pool. Tennis. Garage pkg.
This pretty Camargue-style farmhouse, nestled snuggly in its 5-acre park, offers a pleasant view of the private lake and the Petit-Rhône River. The bright-colored rooms lead onto modern bathrooms and private terraces giving onto the water or the marshes. The numerous plants add to the charm of the garden.

L'Étrier Camarguais

2 km N on N 570, chemin bas des Launes
04 90 97 81 14, fax 04 90 97 88 11
Closed mid Oct-Mar. 27 rms 400-540. Restaurant. Half-board 520-660 (oblig in seas). Pool. Pkg.
A group of small houses in a verdant setting outside Les Saintes-Maries. The nicely furnished rooms are spacious and decorated in bold colors. All have fine terraces opening onto a garden.

 ## L'Impérial

Pl. des Impériaux
04 90 97 81 84, fax 04 90 97 74 25
Closed Tue off-seas, Nov-end Mar. Open until 10pm. Terrace dining.
Unpretentious food prepared just right by Pierre Jay, a former grill room owner. Good quality ingredients are his forté. The menu lists every traditional preparation imaginable for sole, turbot, beef, lamb and much more. A few good Provence-style dishes such as basil-flavored vegetable soup and sunset shells. Fixed-price menus a good buy. Reasonably priced local wines. Lovely terrace under the archway. C 200. M 130-175.

12/20 Le Kahlua

Pl. des Gitans - 04 90 97 98 56, fax 04 90 97 98 56
Closed Tue, mid Jan-mid Feb. Open until 10:30pm. Terrace dining. Pkg.
Interesting mix of traditional and exotic dishes. Located in center of city. We savored the lusty leek terrine embellished with country ham and crushed tomatoes, which actually made us contemplate the addition of a toque. The desserts lack gusto however. C 250. M 85-220.

 ## Lou Mas doù Juge

D 85, route du Bac-du-Sauvage, quartier Pin-Fourcat
04 66 73 51 54, fax 04 66 73 51 42
Open daily until 8:30pm (upon reserv). Terrace dining. Air cond. Pkg.
Renée Granier's set menus attract hearty eaters, with such robust offerings as tourtes filled with meat or cheese, fish grilled over a wood fire, seasonal game, and capon with morels. You'll like the charming welcome, the convivial atmosphere, and picturesque décor of this old Camargue farmhouse. C 500. M 300 (lunch, wine incl), 350 (wine incl), 370 (dinner, Sun, wine incl), 440 (hols, wine incl).

 ## Lou Mas doù Juge

(See restaurant above)
Open year-round. 2 stes 500-800. 5 rms 500. Half-board 1,300 (oblig in seas). Air cond. Pkg.
You can choose between the ferry boat or the bridge to get to this farmhouse. Once there, the horse, donkey and owner lead you up the house. Rather like going to your grandmother's house in the old country. Rooms one hundred percent typical of regional style. Really friendly welcome.

 ## Mas de la Fouque

Route d'Aigues-Mortes, 4 km
04 90 97 81 02, fax 04 90 97 96 84
Closed Tue off-seas, Nov 2-Mar 25. 2 stes 2,300-2,800. 12 rms 1,250-2,120. Rms for disabled. Restaurant. Half-board 1,510-1,850 (oblig in seas). Rm ser. Air cond. Heated pool. Tennis. Garage pkg.
Enjoy your breakfast on the sheltered patio or terrace of your room facing the Étang des Launes. The rooms have an original, elegant décor, dreamy bathrooms.

 ## Mas du Tadorne

3 km N on N 570, Chemin Bas
04 90 97 93 11, fax 04 90 97 71 04
Open year-round. 4 stes 1,100-1,300. 12 rms 650-850. Rms for disabled. Restaurant. Half-board 490-590. Pool. Pkg.
The lodgings are on the small side, but are refined and charming, with balconies overlooking the garden and pool. Contemporary amenities.

 ## Le Pont des Bannes

1.5km N on road to Arles
04 90 97 81 09, fax 04 90 97 89 28
Open year-round. 27 rms 590-860. Restaurant. Half-board 510-1,075. Pool. Pkg.
Simple rooms and cabins surrounded by swamp land, right on the edge of a nature reserve. Good place for those who yearn for a few days of physical activity: horseback riding, hiking, bicycling and boat rentals all available. Pleasing terrace around the pool.

And also...

Our selection of places for inexpensive, quick, or late-night meals.
Les Alizés (04 90 97 71 33 - 36 bis, av. Aubanel. Open until 10:30pm. Closed Dec 5-20.): Shellfish and fish have the seat of honor at this restaurant frequented by tourists and locals alike (65-200).
La Taverne de Marika (04 90 97 80 98 - 9, pl. Mireille. Open until 9:30pm, 11pm in summer. Closed Wed off-seas, mid Jan-mid Feb.): Typical good-quality cooking using olive oil and lemon. Greek specialties in a very pleasant atmosphere (80-180).

 ## Abbaye de Sainte-Croix

3 km NE on D 16, route du Val-de-Cuech
04 90 56 24 55, fax 04 90 56 31 12
Closed Mon lunch (exc hols), beg Nov-mid Mar. Open until 9:30pm. Terrace dining. Pool. Pkg.
An ancient abbey in a spectacular setting, covered with ivy and rambling roses, and doting a lovely terrace shaded by mulberry trees. Pascal Morel, who trained under Roger Vergé and

Georges Blanc, takes a simple yet inventive and delicate approach to his fine ingredients. Curry sole mesclun and leek French toast, red mullet and tapenade sandwiches, eggplant cake in melissa butter: just a few of his creations this year. Splendiforous desserts, a reception and service that serve you hand and foot without getting on your nerves: pure bliss. C 400. M 205 (weekday lunch), 290 (Sun lunch), 390-525.

 ## Abbaye de Sainte-Croix 🏰

(See restaurant above)
Closed beg Nov-mid Mar. 5 stes 1,390-2,310. 19 rms 670-1,330. Half-board 805-1,780 (oblig in seas). Rm ser. Air cond. Pool. Pkg.
The modern additions to this ancient abbey are remarkably faithful to the original. The rooms are furnished with fine antiques, and offer eye-popping views (and all are air conditioned). Leisure pursuits include riding and swimming. Perfect place if you need to get away from absolutely all. Relais et Châteaux.

Le Mas du Soleil

Le Pilon-Blanc, 38, chemin St-Côme
04 90 56 06 53, fax 04 90 56 21 52
Closed Sun dinner, Mon. Open until 9:30pm. Garden dining. Air cond. Pool. Garage pkg.
Despite the name, the sun is not shining so bright on the kitchen of this farmhouse. Apart from the marvellous Banon goat cheese and the cheese platter in general, our last meal was a culinary disaster from start to finish. It started with the waiter masticating away at his gum, and continued with the dried-out rabbit and garlic terrine, the cardboard-textured mushroom and sweetbread fricassée and the dubious medley of fish swimming in an insipid sauce. Shall we continue? The lamb chops were not up to par and the desserts came straight from the fridge. Francis Robin takes your orders with the same pleasant disposition as ever, but half of the menu is the same as it was three years ago. More and more conferences and banquets are held here, so that may explain why the private customer is not the king he once was. C 360-500. M 220 (weekday lunch, wine incl), 170-650.

 ## Le Mas du Soleil 🏰

(See restaurant above)
Open year-round. 1 ste 850-1,000. 9 rms 480-750. Rms for disabled. Half-board 1,350. Rm ser. Air cond. Pool. Garage pkg.
Though not far from the town center, these modern, very comfortable and charming rooms (grouped around the pool or the patio) have a distinctly bucolic feel, owing to the large, shady garden. Guests can expect a kindly welcome.

12/20 La Salle à Manger

6, rue d Maréchal Joffre - 04 90 56 28 01
Closed Sun dinner, Mon, Aug 8-24, Dec 22-Jan 5. Open until 10pm. Terrace dining.

What a dreamy place to dine, this *délicieux* cottage garden behind a lovely nineteenth-century house in romantic «attire». The reception and the service are quite in keeping with the setting, but the unending promises on the menu were not lived up to on the plate, and ended up being more novel than noble. What a pity! C 230. M 89-125.

■ In Cornillon-Confoux 13250   5 km S on D 19

 ## Le Devem de Mirapier 🏰

5 km N on D 19 on D 70
04 90 55 99 22, fax 04 90 55 86 14
Closed Oct-Mar: weekend; Dec 14-Jan 15. 1 ste 720-1,000. 14 rms 380-700. Rms for disabled. Restaurant. Half-board 480-600. Air cond. Pool. Tennis. Pkg.
The surrounding *garrigue* and pine wood make a lovely backdrop for this farmhouse-style hotel. The air conditioned rooms are comfortable and very bright, though a trifle small. Sumptuous suite.

SAUZE 04   → Barcelonnette

SÉGURET 84   → Vaison-la-Romaine

TARASCON   13150
Paris 710 - Arles 18 - Marseille 106   B./Rhône

 ## Les Mazets des Roches 🏰

Route de Fontvieille
04 90 91 34 89, fax 04 90 43 53 29
Closed Nov-Mar. 1 ste 850. 38 rms 300-800. Air cond. Pool. Tennis. Pkg.
Set in a 33-acre park at the foot of Les Alpilles, this agreeable hostelry features comfortable, perfectly equipped, air conditioned rooms with beautiful bathrooms.

VAISON-LA-ROMAINE   84110
Paris 687 - Avignon 46 - Carpentras 28   Vaucluse

12/20 Le Bateleur

1, pl. Théodore-Aubanel - 04 90 36 28 04
Closed Sun dinner, Mon, Nov 15-Dec 15. Open until 9pm (9:30pm in summer). Terrace dining. Air cond.
Pretty bouquets add a colorful touch to this quiet dining room, where you can settle down to a homestyle meal with a fresh, Provençal touch. Short list of wines, mainly from the Côtes-du-Rhône. C 200. M 100 (lunch), 145.

We welcome your questions and comments at our e-mail address: gayots@aol.com.

Richard Hennessy

The

influence

of

eternity.

Hennessy

COGNAC

IN 1765 RICHARD HENNESSY FOUNDED THE COMPANY WHICH BEARS HIS NAME.
EIGHT GENERATIONS OF HIS FAMILY HAVE WORKED TO CREATE A UNIQUE COGNAC FOR YOUR PLEASURE.
"RICHARD HENNESSY", FROM THE WORLD'S LARGEST RESERVES OF AGED COGNACS,
IS THE FINEST TRIBUTE HENNESSY COULD PAY TO ITS FOUNDER.

Hôtel Burrhus

1, pl. Monfort - 04 90 36 00 11, fax 04 90 36 39 05
*Closed Sun (Nov, Jan-Feb), Nov 15-Dec 20. 24 rms
180-320. Pkg.*
This delightful ochre-colored house right in the heart of the village offers quiet, cozy rooms despite the never-ending games of lawn bowls on the square.

 La Fête en Provence

Pl. du Vieux-Marché
04 90 36 36 43, fax 04 90 36 21 49
*Closed Wed off-seas, Nov 15-Feb. Open until 10pm.
Terrace dining.*
A self-taught Scandinavian chef, Niels Christensen, has created a lovely, tranquil restaurant where patrons can savor his unpretentious, regionally rooted cuisine. We tried (and liked) his young rabbit compote spiced with thyme, cod steak with candied zucchini and fresh tomatoes, and lamb and tapenade daube. C 190-250. M 100 (lunch), 150.

 Hostellerie Le Beffroi

Rue de l'Évêché - 04 90 36 04 71, fax 04 90 36 24 78
*Closed Feb 15-Mar 20, Nov 11-Dec 20. 22 rms
330-655. Restaurant. Half-board 405-695. Pool.
Pkg.*
Here's a beautiful Renaissance dwelling, in the heart of old Vaison. Rooms are immense, and furnished with antiques; there are terraced gardens and lovely views. Half the rooms are housed in an equally handsome seventeenth-century annex.

 Hôtel des Lis

20, cours Jean-Henri-Fabre
04 90 36 00 11, fax 04 90 36 39 05
*Closed Sun (Nov, Jan-Feb), Nov 15-Dec 20. 8 rms
250-350. Pkg.*
This centrally-located, 1900-style house with well-decorated, nicely arranged rooms serves as a «gallery» for local painters. Charming reception.

 **Le Logis
du Vieux Château** 🌲🍷

Les Hauts-de-Vaison
04 90 36 09 98, fax 04 90 36 10 95
Closed Nov-beg Apr. 45 rms 235-430. Rms for disabled. Restaurant. Half-board 250-340. Pool. Tennis. Pkg.
A rambling hotel in a verdant setting, with nice big rooms. Some have terraces with views of the town and surrounding vineyards.

 Le Moulin à Huile

Quai du Maréchal-Foch
04 90 36 20 67, fax 04 90 36 20 20
*Closed Sun dinner, Mon, Jan 15-Feb 15. Open until
10pm. Terrace dining. Air cond.*
We tip our hat to Robert Bardotwho has proven himself as adept with the ingredients of

sunny Provence as he was with the products of his native Flanders (formerly at Flambard in Lille, where he had three toques). His *haute cuisine* does justice to this old restored millhouse full of character in the ancient nucleus of Vaison-La-Romaine. We were delighted with the way he poignantly mixed the flavors of dishes like his pigeon risotto with spices from the Isles, sage sea bream, parsleyed ginger John Dory and on-the-spot vanilla cream millefeuille without interfering with the ingredients' natural flavors. Rare to find such quality at this price. C 320-350. M 160 (weekday lunch), 250.

■ **In
Entrechaux 84340** *7 km SE on D 938, D 54*

 La Manescale 🌲🍷

Route de Faucon, D 205
04 90 46 03 80, fax 04 90 46 03 89
*Closed Nov-Easter. 2 stes 550-950. 3 rms 425-620.
Pool. Garage pkg.*
Pretty, cheerful, and well-maintained rooms are provided in this charmingly converted sheepfold. Efficient service in a family atmosphere. Ideal for a restful holiday, but reserve well in advance!

■ **In Saint-Romain-
en-Viennois 84110** *4 km E on D 938 & D 71*

12/20 L'Armourie

Le Village - 04 90 46 43 72
*Closed Tue dinner, Wed (exc Jul-Aug), Dec 15-Jan.
Terrace dining. Pkg.*
This simple village house proffers good food at a remarkable price in this normally pricey region. The duck with ginger and pears was frankly worth two toques; the other dishes merit a point. One thing is for sure: this chef has talent. C 200-250. M 102-235

■ **In Séguret 84110** *10 km SW on D 88*

Domaine de Cabasse

04 90 46 91 12, fax 04 90 46 94 01
*Closed Nov 15-Mar. 12 rms 250-350. Restaurant.
Half-board 365-515. Pool. Garage pkg.*
This establishment is an agreeable stopover in the wine country, at the foot of the Montmirail peaks, with pleasant rooms overlooking a terrace and swimming pool.

12/20 Le Mesclun

Rue des Poternes - 04 90 46 93 43, fax 04 90 46 92 48
*Closed Mon off-seas. Open until 10pm. Terrace
dining.*
Awe-inspiring view of the Rhône Valley and the Ardèche mountains, not so awe-inspiring what you find on your plate. *A la carte* set meal with interesting mixtures from both sea and land: she-crab soup with cream and rabbit *bouillabaisse*. C 160-200. M 90 (weekday lunch).

La Table du Comtat

Le Village - 04 90 46 91 49, fax 04 90 46 94 27
Closed Tue dinner & Wed (exc Jul-Sep 25 & hols), Feb, Nov 27-Dec 11. Open until 9pm. Terrace dining. Air cond. Pool. Pkg.
The sweeping view framed by this fifteenth-century hospice is typically Provençal, and Franck Gomez makes excellent use of the region's bounty in his full-flavored, colorful cooking. If they're on the menu, try the highly harmonious combination of roast lamb with tomatoes and eggplant caviar; the roast turbot with candied lemons and capers; the eggplant charlotte and salt cod brandade, or his simple but «enlightened» version of lime blossom and poached-fruit soup. Interesting selection of Côtes-du-Rhône vintages, with several wines available by the glass. Friendly welcome in a vaguely rustic, slightly overdecorated dining room (but what a view!). Highly professional, smooth service and good wine advice: how could we possibly do otherwise than don him with another toque? C 350-400. M 170 (exc hols), 270-370.

La Table du Comtat ♦♥

(See restaurant above)
Closed Tue & Wed (exc Jul-Sep 25 & hols), Nov 27-Dec 11. 8 rms 460-600. Half-board 620-850. Pool. Pkg.
This stone house, tucked neatly into the hillside and the rocks, overlooks the valley and Rhône wine vineyards. No television in rooms. Carefully prepared breakfast.

Looking for a restaurant? Refer to the index.

VENASQUE   84210
Paris 717 - Avignon 31 - Carpentras 14   Vaucluse

Auberge la Fontaine

Pl. de la Fontaine - 04 90 66 02 96, fax 04 90 66 13 14
Closed Wed, mid Nov-mid Dec. Open until 9pm. Terrace dining. Air cond. Pkg.
Housed in a massive eighteenth-century manor in the heart of an old papal village, this charmingly furnished *auberge* presents a generous single menu full of robust country Provençal flavors, artfully whipped up by chef Christian Sœhlke. A recent visit yielded homemade foie gras, lobster terrine, stuffed roast young goat, and a dish inspired by his Alsatian roots, choucroute with pan-fried foie gras. Game dishes are featured in season. Affable reception and service. Music concerts are held several times a year. M 220.

Auberge la Fontaine ♦♥

(See restaurant above)
Closed mid Nov-mid Dec (exc upon reserv). 5 stes 800. Rm ser. Air cond. Pkg.
Centrally located and pleasantly furnished, with five perfectly equipped, air conditioned suites that include kitchens, dining and living rooms, fireplaces, and terraces. Charming atmosphere. For those who like a décor that is a little different from the run of the mill.

VILLENEUVE-LÈS-AVIGNON 30
→ Avignon

THE RIVIERA

ANTIBES 06600
Paris 913 - Nice 22 - Cannes 11 Alpes-Mar.

 La Bonne Auberge

On N 7, quartier La Brague
04 93 33 36 65, fax 04 93 33 48 52
Closed Sun dinner, Mon, Tue lunch, mid Nov-mid Dec. Open until 10pm (10:30pm in summer). Terrace dining. Air cond. Pkg.
«The times they are a changin'», and Philippe Rostang changes with them; he was one of the first to realize the importance of creating «family-style» prices. This worked wonders, both in terms of attracting business and in terms of gastronomic feats. He has firmly made his mark in this establishment, making it not only chic but sapient, all neatly expressed through his single-price meal offering excellent quality at truly affordable prices: crusty squid tourte, pike dumpling soufflé, or seven-hour lamb. It's not Provençal-style at every turn, yet its inspiration is rooted here. The blue and pink dining room give a contemporary note. The wine list may be short in size but don't think it's lacking in reflection. Delphine Cussac still greets you with her sunny smile. M 200.

12/20 **Chez Olive**

Square Albert-1er - 04 93 34 42 32
Closed Sun dinner, Mon, Dec 17-Jan 4. Open until 10:45pm. Terrace dining. Air cond. Pkg.
With a name like «Olive» you couldn't do any other kind of cooking than the Southern-style cooking she lays before you. Stuffed baby vegetables, sautéed rabbit, daube with cèpes. Nice relaxed atmosphere. M 86 (weekday lunch, wine incl), 126-176.

 La Jarre

14, rue Saint-Esprit - 04 93 34 50 12
Closed lunch, Oct 15-Easter. Open until 10:30pm. Terrace dining.
Charming atmosphere: this is the South of France if there ever was one. Our great regret is the lack of a fixed-price menu, which makes the bill reach heights that are not always kept pace with by the lovingly prepared cooking, sometimes lacking in consistency. Good red mullet tabbouleh, insipid pan-fried scallops with soya, and respectable enough rosemary sea perch steak, and chocolate duo. Pleasant dining under the fig trees in the summer. Good selection of Côtes-de-Provence. C 250-450.

12/20 **Le Marquis**

4, rue de Sade - 04 93 34 23 00
Closed Mon, Tue lunch, Jul. Open until 9:30pm.

A hard core of habitués regularly fills the Marquis's little dining room to see what chef Francis Zany has whipped up that day. Good Provençal homestyle cooking, accompanied by an appetizing choice of local wines. M 90 (weekdays), 130-280.

 Le Relais du Postillon

8, rue Championnet
04 93 34 20 77, fax 04 93 34 61 24
Closed Sun dinner, Nov. Open until 10pm. Terrace dining.
What a «delicious address» (as the French would say). This former coaching inn proves pure Riviera at every turn with a cuisine that is simple but full of savoir-faire and with an amiable hello for its peaceable clientele. Don't hesitate before the pan-fried scallops on a bed of watercress, a mouthwatering sea bream with crushed tomatoes, the charming little goat cheeses, and selection of three-cassonade crème brûlée. The wine is friendly in price, and some are even offered by the glass. Charming service, and excellent quality for the money, even right out from the gate with the 98 F menu. C 300-400. M 98-245.

 Hôtel Royal

Bd du Maréchal-Leclerc
04 93 34 03 09, fax 04 93 34 23 31
Closed Nov 8-Jan. 37 rms 280-640. Restaurant. Half-board 330-440. Pkg.
You can practically dangle your feet in the water in this pleasant hotel offering air-conditioned rooms of passable comfort. The standard is generally high, but light sleepers beware: they lack proper soundproofing. Maybe that's all right, if it's the lapping of the waves you hear. Professional reception and staff.

 Les Vieux Murs

Av. de l'Amiral-de-Grasse
04 93 34 06 73, fax 04 93 34 81 08
Closed Mon off-seas. Open until 10:30pm. Terrace dining. Air cond. Valet pkg.
While other *restaurateurs* fret over half-empty dining rooms, Georges and Suzanne Romano have to turn would-be patrons away. Sure, the lovely covered terrace with its view of the port has something to do with it. The biggest attraction however has long been the excellent 200 F single-price menu. In this vaulted-ceiling dining room just around the corner from the Picasso museum and built into the ramparts signed none other than Vauban, the quality of both the cuisine and the reception have in the past seen low and high tides, but the doctor's medicine seemed to have taken effect on our last visit. The

young, efficient staff was quick-footed, and the full flavors well under the control of the chef's nimble hand (onion and tomato tart topped with thin strips of fresh cod, perfectly-timed cooking of a pan-fried sea bream in Balsamic vinegar sauce, delicious anise pear gratin alongside frangipane). The wine list exhibits a preference for Provençal and Bordeaux wines. C 350-400. M 200.

| ARCS (LES) | 83460 |
| Paris 854 - Draguignan 10 - St-Raphaël 29 | Var |

 Bacchus Gourmand

N 7 - 04 94 47 48 47, fax 04 94 47 55 13
Closed Sun dinner, Mon (exc summer), Dec 22-Jan 13. Open until 10pm. Garden dining. Air cond. Garage pkg.
Philippe Rousselot's delectable cooking (displayed to advantage in the two least expensive set meals) has turned this table into one of the region's most popular restaurants. He may be young, but he has an innate sense of how to subtly and skillfully mix the most unexpected flavor combinations. They'll sometimes surprise you, but never disappoint you, because his skillful hand and high regard for his ingredients make it so. Be tempted by the marvellous Dublin bay prawns in shellfish jelly; the succulent John Dory with savory fennel and white-beet ragoût; a sapid oven-cooked saddle of lamb; or his version of a regional favorite, pieds et paquets, sparked with savory saffron. The dining room is orchestrated by Christian Bœuf, who takes all pains to ensure you absolutely faultless reception and service. Charles Roux is on hand to pass on wise advice *à propos* the lusty list of Provençal wines. Real quality at an affordable price. C 350-500. M 150-265.

12/20 Le Logis du Guetteur

Pl. du Château - 04 94 73 30 82, fax 04 94 73 39 95
Closed Jan 15-Feb. Open until 9:30pm. Garden dining. Pool. Garage pkg.
The good part: This ancient house perches high above a medieval village, affording an impregnable view of the Argens Valley and the Maures massif. In the winter, warm yourself in front of the monumental hearth, in the summer soak up the breathtaking view on the terrace. The other part: ambience is not enough to make a meal good. We started with the sombre reception, and continued with the robot-like service lacking all enthusiasm. The food moves in the same direction with its inconsistent cooking times and its heavy, overwhelming sauces. Prices can soar. The toque has just toppled away. C 260-300. M 135-290.

  Le Logis du Guetteur

(See restaurant above)
Closed Jan 15-Feb. 10 rms 350-520. Half-board 440-520. Pool. Garage pkg.

Ten spacious and pleasant rooms with fabulous views in this eleventh-century fortified castle, perfect for a romantic weekend break. Horseback riding; kayaks for rent nearby.

 Relais des Moines

Route de Sainte-Roseline
04 94 47 40 93, fax 04 94 47 52 51
Closed Sun dinner & Mon (exc Jul-Aug). Open until 9:15pm. Terrace dining. Pool. Pkg.
This is a real haven of peace where the cordial reception and attentive but discreet service tuck you snugly in to a sea of calm. Some lovely specimens such as sea bream in an herb crust, broiled John Dory in a lobster jus, Provence flowers and petits-gris escargot, and duck (yes, duck!) couscous. Tip-top fresh ingredients handled skillfully, although the sauces are vapid at times. Good selection of desserts, for example, the toothesome orange and mint sherbets. Small but good selection of wines, especially local ones. Judicious check. C 300. M 125 (weekday lunch, wine incl), 169 (Sun), 240-300.

| AURIBEAU-SUR-SIAGNE | 06810 |
| Paris 926 - Cannes 16 - Grasse 8 | Alpes-Mar. |

Auberge Nossi-Bé

Pl. du Portail - 04 93 42 20 20, fax 04 93 42 33 08
Closed Mon lunch in summer, Tue dinner off-seas, Wed, Nov. Open until 9:30pm. Terrace dining. Pkg.
Set in the last village near Cannes that hasn't been turned into a craft colony, this welcoming inn serves honest cooking that digs deep into the roots of this region: Provençal rennet in olive oil tomato sauce, good roast cod fillet sided with sautéed potatoes, pork fillet à l'orange garnished with sautéed potatoes, and luscious strawberry crème brûlée. Simple but delightfully tasteful with discerning reception. The set-price meals even include the wine. It's all a joy as you partake of your meal on the terrace overlooking the Siagne flatlands. A real find in this *frou-frou* region! C 250-300. M 145 (weekday lunch, wine incl), 190 (dinner, wine incl).

| BANDOL | 83150 |
| Paris 842 - Marseille 49 - Toulon 17 - Aix-en-P. 74 | Var |

Augerbe du Port

9, allée Jean-Moulin
04 94 29 42 63, fax 04 94 29 44 59
Open daily until 10pm (11pm in summer). Terrace dining. Air cond.
A real taste of the Mediterranean, in every form of the word: seafood, simply broiled, or more dressed-up versions with seafood couscous (semolina topped with a sort of fish stew) and red mullet «cake» with an eggplant tian. Well-respected for classics like bouillabaisse and fish paella. Pleasant terrace but must reserve ahead. Wash it down with one of their fine Bandol wines. C 280-350. M 120-250.

Le Clocher

1, rue de la Paroisse - 04 94 32 47 65
Closed Sun dinner. Open until 9:30pm. Terrace dining.
  Admire the produce of Bandol's open-air market as you head over to the small, sun-drenched dining room of Le Clocher. Alain Gantel's cuisine is uncluttered and precise: he served us thin slices of raw scallops showered with matchsticks of fresh ginger, and monkfish poached in court-bouillon with julienned zucchini, green tomatoes, and tiny pearl onions, lushly accented with garlicky aïoli. Dessert brought a gossamer-light green-apple feuillantine spiced with nutmeg. C 200-380. M 90-190.

 Master Ker Mocotte Hôtel 🌲🍴

103, rue Raimu - 04 94 29 46 53, fax 04 94 32 53 54
Open year-round. 20 rms 290-890. Restaurant. Half-board 300-580. Pool. Pkg.
  A big white house nestled in the pine trees. The famous 1930s actor Raimu had it built in search of some peace and quiet between movies. Lovely rooms looking out over the Renecros Bay.

 Les Oliviers

17, bd Louis-Lumière
04 94 29 33 00, fax 04 94 29 49 49
Open daily until 10pm (10:30pm in summer). Terrace dining. Air cond. Pool. Beach. Tennis. Valet pkg.
  Anchored near the quiet basin, Les Oliviers' big dining room sports a bright, understated Mediterranean décor with a great view of the sea. Chef Laurent Chouviat gives local ingredients an original spin. Try his refreshing pressed eggplant with rock red mullet, or his savory braised John Dory (slightly overcooked). The roasted white asparagus with a poached egg atop is a real temptation. All is not perfection, however, because the jus were often over-salted. The service is prompt and on the mark, but we still find the reception vacuous. Terrific selection of local wines. C 280-450. M 120-245.

 L'Ile Rousse

(See restaurant above)
Open year-round. 2 stes 1,000-1,450. 54 rms 350-1,320. Half-board 425-910. Air cond. Pool. Beach. Tennis. Valet pkg.
  The Provençal-style building designed by Fleury Linossier proffers huge, sunny, well-maintained and modernized rooms, some with views of the sea, but a touch of warmth in the flagging reception would make for a better vacation.

BEAULIEU-SUR-MER　　　　　　06310

Paris 943 - Menton 20 - Nice 10 - Cannes 43　Alpes-Mar.

 Le Métropole

15, bd du Général-Leclerc
04 93 01 00 08, fax 04 93 01 18 51
Closed Oct 20-Dec 20. Open until 10pm. Garden dining. Air cond. Pool. Beach. Valet pkg.
  This Italianate villa is a dreamy spot, one where moneyed patrons find the soul-stirring beauty, distinguished service, and elegant ambience they seek. Last year we worried about the effect of the transition period due to the arrival of new chef Jérôme Coustillas, but his young approach has in fact woken up this old-fashioned institution with its sunny but exacting elegance. Two extra points represent a big jump, but this chef is surely and gradually proving that he is more than comfortable in his starring role, and most of all that he truly masters the culinary art. Merits are in order for the well-judged cooking time of the small calamary and vegetable risotto napped in a green-asparagus emulsion; the admirable effort put into the rock red mullet fillets roasted en barigoule (stuffed); and the savoriness of his herb-flecked lamb with its eggplant and potato cake and aromatic juices à la riquette. An up-to-date Southern cuisine offering pluperfect desserts and a classic cellar, but a staff that needs to be called into action. The wide terrace overlooking Cap Ferrat is delightful. C 600. M 300 (weekday, wine incl), 410, 520.

 Le Métropole 🌲🍴

(See restaurant above)
Closed Oct 20-Dec 20. 3 stes 2,600-5,400. 43 rms 800-2,900. Half-board 900-1,950 (oblig in sea). Air cond. Pool. Beach. Pkg.
  It all starts with the stately appearance of the large white villa itself looking peacefully out to sea and nestled into its two acres of opulent gardens, then proceeds down the path of luxury to the private beach and its floating deck, the seawater swimming pool heated to 84°F all year long, even in winter, and the airy rooms and suites with their ultra-smart décor. Breakfast-lovers' paradise—good quality and hefty quantity. The service is peerless, and no detail is too small for their attention. Off season, the prices are more favorable to social equality. Relais et Châteaux.

 La Réserve de Beaulieu

5, bd du Général-Leclerc
04 93 01 00 01, fax 04 93 01 28 99
Closed Nov-Mar 26. Open until 10:30pm. Terrace dining. Air cond. Heated pool. Valet pkg.
  La Réserve is the sort of place where guests can sip cocktails in a Venetian-style dining room suspended over the sea, and admire a Riviera sunset. The arrival of chef Christophe Cussac in the spring of 1997 rendered a cuisine that took time to get off the ground. By summer, the vague beginnings started to take shape, and his cook-

ing took on sunnier tones, and even a touch of daringness with such dishes as his yellow sweet pepper fondant in pistou sauce dressed up with marinated tuna with red-pepper «crust» and his luscious Dublin bay prawn tian in thyme-flavored crushed tomato and eggplant sauce, although admittedly, the macaroni and fresh-water crayfish turban sided with parmesaned white summer truffles was flavorless. Fine dessert menu: you might try the citrus fruit cookie with zest juice and lime sorbet. We have no doubt about his skill of the trade, we just yearn for more clear-cut flavors and more sharp sensations in his renditions. Jean-Max Haussy's long experience is an invaluable addition to the dining room, the sommelier has pertinent advice with regard to the sumptuous cellar, and the young service puts their best foot forward in this luxurious site so full of history, where even the lowest price set meals are exemplary. C 550-600. M 250 (lunch), 320-490.

La Réserve de Beaulieu

(See restaurant above)
Closed Nov-Mar 26. 10 stes 3,700-5,700. 27 rms 1,800-3,700. Rm ser. Air cond. Heated pool. Pkg.
This mythical luxury hotel looks like a Venetian palace, but was actually built just over a century ago by the owner of the New York Herald Tribune. Guest rooms offer unforgettable refinement and marble bathrooms. Plans are to build a new pool that overflows directly into the sea.

See also: Saint-Jean-Cap-Ferrat

BIOT	06140
Paris 922 - Antibes 8 - Nice 22 - Cagnes 10	Alpes-Mar.

Auberge du Jarrier

30, passage de la Bourgade
04 93 65 11 68, fax 04 93 65 50 03
Closed Mon dinner, Tue (exc dinner in summer), end Jan-beg Feb. Open until 9:30pm (10:30pm in summer). Terrace dining. Air cond.
The Auberge boasts a warm, countrified décor and a devoted following among locals and touring gourmets. Christian Métral's cuisine has lots of character, and even when it gets complicated, the ingredients (all local, all prime) are beautifully balanced. The zucchini flower fritters were excellent. Other dishes breathe of the Southern soil: thyme-flavored roast saddle of lamb, spinach lusciously stuffed with lamb and morels, and pithy pine nut tart with vanilla ice cream. The bread rolls are baked on the premises and the cellar is awash with affordable regional wines. The staff, though prompt, lacks experience, and there is still no wine waiter. The set-price meal at 230 F offers real quality for the money, and will help keep down the sometimes staggering à la carte prices. Flirting seriously with another point. C 450. M 270 (wine incl), 230-300.

Domaine du Jas

625, route de la Mer
04 93 65 50 50, fax 04 93 65 02 01
Closed end Nov-Mar. 2 stes 800-1,200. 15 rms 380-900. Pool. Garage pkg.
Everything you could possibly need for a restful stay by the seaside. Efficient service.

Les Terraillers

11, route du Chemin-Neuf
04 93 65 01 59, fax 04 93 65 13 78
Closed Wed; Jul-Aug: Thu lunch. Open until 10pm. Terrace dining. Pkg.
Planted at the foot of the village since the sixteenth century, this elegantly restored pottery works is now a restaurant, where Claude Jacques presents a rather elaborate cuisine with a Mediterranean accent. Extra-thin vegetable crispy in an herb infusion, local roasted red mullet and a little canapé with zucchini «spaghetti», out-of-this-world John Dory roasted and stuffed with Provence-style vegetables and saffron-flavored panisse. On a sweeter note, a lemon gratin partnered with mixed berries and napped in an apricot sauce. Lots of discoveries to be made in the adventurous cellar, and excellent gourmet coffees, a rarity in the Riviera. Our most recent meal was a savory success from start to finish, but the rising prices are on the verge of stifling our enjoyment. Wise ones will stick to the friendly-priced, good-quality set meal at 250 F. Delightful welcome and service, and summer eating under the arbors is a purely Mediterranean delight. C 380-500. M 220 (weekday lunch, wine incl), 180 (weekday lunch), 250-360.

12/20 Galerie des Arcades

16, pl. des Arcades - 04 93 65 01 04
Closed Sun dinner off-seas, Mon, Nov 15-Dec 15. Open until 9:30pm. Terrace dining.
This fifteenth-century setting offers you generous helpings of Provençal cuisine served in a jovial yet well-polished atmosphere. C 200-220. M 160 (lunch), 180 (dinner).

BORMES-LES-MIMOSAS	83230
Paris 890 - Toulon 40 - St-Tropez 35 - Le Lavandou 5	Var

La Cassole

Ruelle Moulin - 04 94 71 14 86
Closed Oct-Nov 15 & Feb-Easter: Sun dinner; Easter-Jun & Sep: Mon & Tue lunch; summer exc Sun & hols: lunch; Nov 15-Jan 24. Open until 9pm (10pm in summer). Terrace dining. Air cond.
A warm, intimate little restaurant tucked into a tiny street right in the heart of the old town and run by two women. New chef Daniel do Vale whips up a bountiful cuisine with a Mediterranean note: juicy good pan-fried scallops, a happy marriage between sea and land with the sea perch and sweetbreads, and a super crackling sea bream. Local wines of good quality. Enthusiastic reception and service. C 250-300. M 150-250.

12/20 L'Escoundudo

2, ruelle du Moulin - 04 94 71 15 53
Closed Mon off-seas, Tue, Wed. Open until 11pm. Terrace dining.
Take time out on this flower-filled terrace right in the heart of this medieval village. The Dandines' open-arm reception and the simple but good cooking using products from the region are just one more reason to stop here. We were partial to the bell pepper salad and tomatoes with little slices of bread spread with anchoïade (anchovy paste). C 230-260. M 100 (lunch), 160.

 ## Le Mirage

38, rue Vue-des-Iles
04 94 05 32 60, fax 04 94 64 93 03
Closed Nov 1-Mar 26. 1 ste 970-1,150. 35 rms 430-860. Rms for disabled. Restaurant. Half-board 430-645. Rm ser. Air cond. Pool. Tennis. Pkg.
The well-equipped rooms have mezzanines and superb views of the bay. Great breakfasts. Children will love the game room and garden; business types will be happy to find complete conference facilities.

 ## Les Palmiers

6 km S on D 559, in Cabasson, 240, chemin du Petit-Fort - 04 94 64 81 94, fax 04 94 64 93 61
Closed Nov 15-Dec 20. 2 stes 1,000-1,280. 18 rms 380-600. Rms for disabled. Restaurant. Half-board 450-520 (oblig in seas). Rm ser. Tennis. Pkg.
Surrounded by greenery and just a five-minute walk from the sea, this holiday hotel proposes quiet, attractive rooms.

 ## La Reine Jeanne

N 98, Forêt Domaniale
04 94 15 00 83, fax 04 94 64 77 89
Closed Sun dinner & Mon off-seas, Jan 5-Feb 5. Open until 9pm (10pm in summer). Terrace dining. Pkg.
A brand new team has brought this hundred-year-old restaurant back to life. The chef is tired of gastronomy for the sake of gastronomy, and prefers to offer a cuisine that is heftily invigorating yet refined. Splendid spit-roasted suckling pig and milkfed lamb, fit-for-a-king pot-au-feu (doesn't resemble the usual peasant fare!), stewed young rabbit, or crusty quick-cooked pigeon. Fish on hand for those who prefer the fruits of the sea. The cellar is tiny, but good local wines are on offer at reasonable prices. Warm welcome and a staff that looks after you well. M 150-280.

12/20 Chez Sylvia

872, av. Lou Mistraou - 04 94 71 14 10
Closed Wed (exc school hols), Dec-Jan. Open until 10:30pm. Garden dining. Pkg.
Sylvia serves Sicilian pizzas, savory brochettes, and sweet cannoli on her shady terrace. C 180-260. M 135.

12/20 La Tonnelle des Délices

Pl. Gambetta - 04 94 71 34 84
Closed Wed, Oct 15-Dec 15. Open until 10pm. Terrace dining.
Take a seat on the hanging garden-terrace or in the dining room filled with pretty bric-à-brac to sample Alain Pasetto's fresh Provençal cooking: mussels with garlic and parsley, fish soup, anchoïade, rabbit in pistou sauce, daube à l'ancienne. The execution is better than in the past, putting forth good seafood soups and stews and vegetables oozing with flavor. The very feminine reception and service is pleasant indeed. Fixed-price menus of quality, wine priced to drink. C 200-250. M 75-160.

CADIÈRE D'AZUR (LA)   83740
Paris 821 - Marseille 46 - Toulon 22 - Aix-en-P. 63   Var

 ## René Bérard

Rue Gabriel-Péri - 04 94 90 11 43, fax 04 94 90 01 94
Closed Sun dinner, Mon, Jan 10-Feb 20. Open until 9:30pm. Air cond. Pool. Garage pkg.
René Bérard is holding hands with the muses, inspired by the ingredients around him to create classics in the manner of the masters as well as truly original works of art, such as his divine nougat de bœuf, perfectly-prepared foie gras with roasted figs, and tiny red mullets in pistou sauce. Delicious vegetables. Some disillusionment with the overcooked veal chop, but made up for with the mixed-berry fritters. The à la carte prices are often high and heavy, but the set-price meals are in a more down-to-earth realm. Evidence corroborates the second toque awarded last year, even though there were a few slip-ups in cooking times. Good selection of local Bandol wines at nice enough prices. Splendid welcome. C 300-450. M 160-450.

  ## Hostellerie Bérard

(See restaurant above)
Closed Sun, Mon, Jan 10-Feb 20. 4 stes 890-1,200. 36 rms 415-810. Half-board 500-700. Air cond. Heated pool. Garage pkg.
This Renaissance-era hostelry provides rooms decorated thoughtfully in neo-Provençal style. An annex overlooks the garden and swimming pool. Flanked by vineyards and olive trees.

CAGNES-SUR-MER   06800
Paris 920 - Cannes 22 - Nice 13 - Antibes 11   Alpes-Mar.

 ## Le Cagnard

Haut-de-Cagnes, rue du Pontis-Long
04 93 20 73 21, fax 04 93 22 06 39
Closed Thu lunch, Nov-mid Dec. Open until 10:30pm (11pm in summer). Terrace dining. Air cond. Valet pkg.
This ravishing medieval dwelling affords a stupendous view of the coastline all the way to Antibes. You can enjoy that sweeping panorama

from a terrace equipped with a sliding paneled ceiling, which protects you from bad weather or opens to let you admire the stars. Supplied with superb raw materials and uncommon skill, Jean-Yves Johany can turn a simple poulet grand'mère, stuffed vegetables à la niçoise, or soupe au pistou into a feast of rare refinement. The *carte* is devilishly expensive, but at lunchtime, the 275 F set meal includes a kir, wine and coffee. Divine desserts. The wines will add further freight to an already hefty bill, even though they express little curiosity in terms of local fare. C 450-600. M 275 (lunch, wine incl), 300 (dinner), 380-500.

 ## Le Cagnard

(See restaurant above)
Open year-round. 4 stes 1,300-1,500. 23 rms 750-1,100. Half-board 760-1,100. Valet pkg.
Some of the rooms and suites are situated in beautifully renovated village houses. The balconies and private terraces look out to sea. Inside, you'll find flawless appointments and gorgeous marble bathrooms. Delightful staff. Relais et Châteaux.

 ## Entre Cour et Jardin

Haut-de-Cagnes, 102 montée de la Bourgade
04 93 20 72 27, fax 04 93 20 24 60
Closed Tue, Jan 5-31. Open until 11pm. Terrace dining.
Jacques Madina and Patrice Reignault are holding their own in this hillside street where even good restaurants can tumble down. Don't look for wild extravagances here, because all you will find is good quality, ultra-fresh ingredients and sure-fired execution: polenta, parmesan, mesclun greens and crushed tomatoes perfumed with basil; gingery pan-fried scallops on a bed of zucchini «spaghetti» poached in cream; original desserts that work (roasted apple in gingerbread butter served with honey ice cream). Too bad about the uninspired cellar. Spanking reception and service in the light-colored dining room; really pleasant in summer. C 250. M 140-200.

 ## Josy-Jo

Haut-de-Cagnes, 8, pl. du Planastel
04 93 20 68 76
Closed Sat lunch, Sun, Jan 15-30, Aug 1-15. Open until 10pm. Terrace dining. Air cond.
For 30 years Jo and Josy Bandecchi have been serving seasonal Provençal fare to appreciative customers. There are artichokes à la barigoule, stuffed zucchini blossoms, charcoal-grilled meats and fish, and delectable fresh-fruit tarts. Not to mention friendly service and an adorable terrace massed with flowers. C 300-350.

 ## Restaurant des Peintres

Haut-de-Cagnes, 71, montée de la Bourgade
04 93 20 83 08, fax 04 93 20 61 01

Closed Mon lunch & Wed (exc Jul-Aug). Open until 10pm (10:30pm in summer). Terrace dining. Air cond.
Former chef Alain Llorca took the train to the Negresco in Nice, which could have tolled the knell for this restaurant which had quickly made itself a name with its fine lively Italian-Provençal cuisine. But Jacques Madina and Patrice Reignault, already well-established just up the street, deftly stepped in, and made a whoppingly smooth transition. The cheeriness of this dining room seems to have had its effect on Reignault's craftsmanship; he has found a better ground onto which he can stamp out his well-turned cuisine. Exquisite indeed were his cèpe and tiny Jersey potato upsidedown tart in a rosemary-flavored meat jus, and his royal sea bream cooked to utter perfection, partnered with a onion-green butter and sautéed artichokes. The cheese board proved to have been hand-selected, and the fig shortbread was interestingly embellished with a savory Port reduction, which turned out to be a little too dry. The top-notch ingredients are handled with amazing dexterity, and the resulting dishes bear witness to this chef's sense of discernment when it comes to matters of the palate. The reception is extremely *courtois*, but the cellar blatantly lacks Provence wines, so it does not live up to the quality of the rest. C 450-480. M 135 (weekday lunch), 200-240.

■ **In Cros-de-Cagnes 06800**   2 km SE

 ## La Bourride

Port de Cros-de-Cagnes
04 93 31 07 75, fax 04 93 31 07 75
Closed Wed, Feb school hols. Open until 10pm. Garden dining. Air cond.
A dreamy summer restaurant with a pine-shaded patio opposite the port is a perfect setting for a leisurely lunch or dinner. Hervé Kobzi's bracing seafood repertoire is absolutely in tune with the scenery: tender sautéed squid à la provençale, excellent lobster in warm vinaigrette, and lusty versions of the region's traditional seafood soups, bourride and bouillabaisse. Friendly welcome and efficient service. C 300-350. M 170-320.

CALLAS   83830
Paris 870 - Draguignan 15 - Castellane 61   Var

 ## Les Gorges de Pennafort

In Perroport, route du Muy
04 94 76 66 51, fax 04 94 76 67 23
Closed Sun dinner & Mon lunch off-seas, Jan 15-Mar 15. Open until 10pm. Terrace dining. Air cond. Pool. Tennis. Pkg.
The site is sensational (magnificent gorges just opposite), the restaurant is comfortable, and Philippe da Silva's cooking is polished to a high sheen. He and his other half returned this smart *bastide* in its *délicieux* park from the dead. Locals

and foreigners alike flock to partake of this cuisine so highly perfumed yet based in the classics; they like it for its extreme munificence, of course, but above all for its incredible consistency of quality. Langoustine ravioli, roast lobster with simmered vegetables and pistou, pluperfect roast lamb fillet and eggplant, and simply amazing desserts (tangerine rum cake and sorbets). The cellar boasts more regional fare than ever, the service is full of attention, and Mrs. da Silva's welcome is engaging and accompanies you right through the meal, making you feel the full gracious effect of this big bourgeois house in the middle of the country. Eat on the lime-tree terrace in summery weather. C 350-400. M 160 (weekday lunch), 205-275.

 ### Les Gorges de Pennafort

(See restaurant above)
See restaurant for closings. 4 stes 800-950. 12 rms 500-650. Rms for disabled. Half-board 560-720. Rm ser. Air cond. Pool. Tennis. Pkg.
   Welcoming, air-conditioned rooms and small, well-appointed marble bathrooms. An annex offers four very attractive larger rooms. Charming welcome; excellent service.

CANNES	06400
Paris 910 - Marseille 165 - Nice 33	Alpes-Mar.

 ### Amarante

78, bd Carnot - 04 93 39 22 23, fax 04 93 39 40 22
Open year-round. 1 ste 650-1,900. 70 rms 380-790. Rms for disabled. Restaurant. Half-board 300-400. Rm ser. Air cond. Pool. Beach. Garage pkg.
   A modern hotel decorated in Provençal style, with smallish but very well equipped and soundproofed rooms. Sun room and outdoor pool. Restaurant serves regional specialities.

11/20 Athènes

18, rue des Frères-Pradignac - 04 93 38 96 11
Closed Sun lunch & Wed (exc hols & Aug-Sep), 2 wks in Jun, Dec 15-25. Open until 10:30pm. Air cond.
   The chef once lived in Istanbul and knows how to mix both Turkish and Greek cuisine. Delicious skewered meats, authentic moussaka and stuffed vegetables. Friendly service. Expensive. C 200-300. M 150, 190.

The Beaches

Lunch only.
Long Beach (04 93 38 17 47 - 8, bd de la Croisette. Closed dinner.): Family and friends gather for fish soup, salmon with basil, and mussel casserole at this popular beachside restaurant opposite the Noga Hilton. C 180-240. M 110.
Martinez (04 92 98 74 22 - 73, bd de la Croisette. Open until 4pm. Closed end Sep-Easter.): Not only does the Martinez occupy the largest strip of beach in Cannes, it lays on a lavish Provençal-

style buffet in a setting dotted with parasols and a plethora of plants. C250-350. M 195.
Miramar Beach (04 93 94 24 74 - 67, bd de la Croisette. Open until 4:40pm. Closed Oct 15-Apr 15): A shady terrace where you can dip your feet in the water as you gobble up the fresh sea-inspired food: Nice-style sea perch fillet, red mullets with tartar sauce, pan-fried langoustines, etc. C 200-300. M 115.
Ondine (04 93 94 23 15 - 15, bd de la Croisette. Open until 9:30pm. Closed Nov 15-Dec 15.): Facing the sea, near the Carlton, a perfect spot for a ridiculously expensive lunch with friends. Get them to treat... C 350-500.
Plage des Dunes (04 93 94 14 99 - 15, bd de la Croisette. Closed dinner, Dec.): A convivial spot with a pretty terrace, where you can feast on typical Mediterranean specialties. C 220-300.

 ### Beau Séjour

5, rue des Fauvettes
04 93 39 63 00, fax 04 92 98 64 66
Open year-round. 45 rms 330-750. Restaurant. Half-board 490-715. Rm ser. Air cond. Pool. Pkg.
   A modern, perfectly equipped residence 300 yards from the beach. All rooms have terraces leading into the garden and swimming pool. Efficient service. Good value, for Cannes.

 ### La Belle Otéro

Carlton Inter Continental,
58, bd de la Croisette
04 93 68 00 33, fax 04 93 39 09 06
Closed Sun & Mon (exc Jul-Aug), Jun 8-Jul 7, Nov 16-Dec 1. Open until 10:30pm (midnight in summer). Terrace dining. Air cond. Valet Pkg.
   Beneath the low wood-paneled ceiling of a Louis XV dining room that could hardly be less Mediterranean, Francis Chauveau imparts his professional touch to dishes that make the most of premium Provençal produce. Some dishes push too far into the realm of invention, however, and lose track of their essential aim. Such was the case with the royal langoustine mesclun hugged tightly by its eggplant «melt» garnished with panisses and marinated in tapenade marinade; the excellent petits farcis and scampi, each of which would have been even better on its own; the flawlessly cooked baked bass with its carousel of tomatoes, lemon and mushrooms, partnered with a quite ordinary tomato and zucchini au gratin and an utterly unbecoming risotto. The desserts are of fine quality, and the cellar is slight but offers a balanced selection. High-class service, of course. C 650-750. M 290 (lunch, wine incl), 390 (dinner), 620.

12/20 Le Bouchon d'Objectif

10, rue de Constantine - 04 93 99 21 76
Closed Mon, Nov 15-Dec 15. Open until 10:30pm.
   This restaurant-cum-photo gallery serves unpretentious, low-priced dishes like crab and marinated salmon tartare with blinis, aïoli, fish soup, monkfish bourride, and tiramisù. C 195-300. M 88, 135.

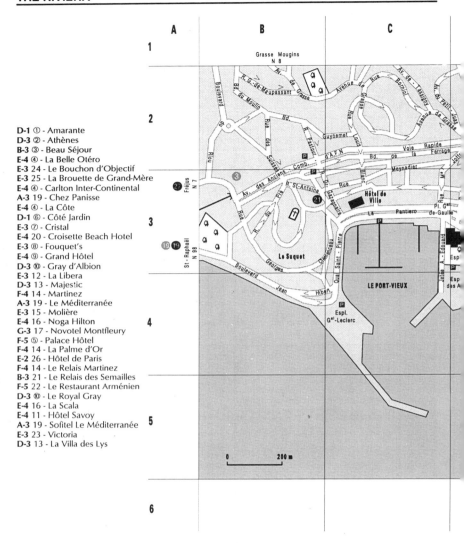

12/20 **La Brouette de Grand-Mère**

Rue d'Oran - 04 93 39 12 10
Dinner only. Closed Sun, Jul 1-12, Nov 1-Dec 15. Open until 11:30pm. Terrace dining. Air cond. Pkg.
This legendary bistro continues to draw enthusiastic crowds with its single menu: an apéritif with a few pre-dinner tidbits, followed by a good hearty pot-au-feu, andouille sausage in Muscadet wine sauce, tarragon chicken, and Crottin-de-Chavignol goat cheese. You can drink as much house wine as you like, but it won't be from Provence. C 200. M 195 (wine incl).

 La Côte

Carlton Inter Continental, 58, La Croisette
04 93 06 40 06, fax 04 93 06 40 25
Closed Oct-May. Open until 11pm. Terrace dining. Air cond. Pool. Beach. Valet pkg.
This hotel restaurant follows the colors of the seasons with its continually renewed menus, al-

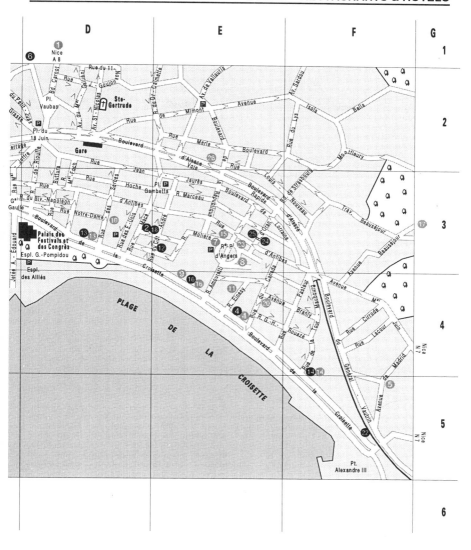

ways resolutely Provençal in tone. Slip into bliss with the Canne-style seafood stew enhanced with saffron pistils; the capon bourride with its hearty potatoes and squid; the red mullet brandade dressed up with tapenade and zucchini; the rack of lamb in garlicky brown sugar. Clever too how they serve the bouillabaisse bouillon and fish in several different courses. Cheese from the celebrated Ceneri's, and all the best of Provence crus are on hand. Young prepossessing service. C 480. M 260 (lunch).

 Carlton Inter-Continental

(See restaurant above)
Open year-round. 30 stes 2,900-40,000. 308 rms 1,020-3,800. Rms for disabled. Rm ser. Air cond. Pool. Beach. Valet pkg.
The constantly renovated, luxurious rooms are extremely comfortable, and the hotel's thirteen-room penthouse is unquestionably the most «Imperial Suite» on the Riviera. Superb service; perfectly equipped fitness center.

Côté Jardin

12, av. St-Louis - 04 93 38 60 28, fax 04 93 38 60 28
*Closed Sun off-seas, Mon lunch in summer, Feb.
Open until 10pm. Garden dining. Air cond.*
In this little out-of-the-way restaurant near the Palais de Justice, chef Alexandre Walger concocts a cuisine full of stimulating ideas which sometimes miss their mark. Exquisite squash and morel cake, good pike perch fillet with melt-in-your-mouth leeks and pan-fried squids, or original oxtail wrapped in cabbage leaves and braised with carrots. The crème brûlée deserves an honorable mention. A restaurant full of vitality and joy, and decked out with an arbor in the little garden. Comely service and wise-priced wines. C 240-350. M 105 (lunch, wine incl), 185.

 ## Cristal

13, rond-point Duboys-d'Angers
04 93 39 45 45, fax 04 93 38 64 66
Open year-round. 7 stes 950-1,950. 44 rms 550-1,350. Rms for disabled. Restaurant. Half-board 445-755. Rm scr. Air cond. Valet pkg.
This candy-colored luxury hotel, with its elegantly decorated interiors, provides rather small, but well-designed rooms with comfortable, modern furniture. The sixth floor boasts a panoramic restaurant and bar, as well as a swimming pool, Jacuzzi, and veranda. Centrally located near the Croisette.

 ## Croisette Beach Hotel

13, rue du Canada
04 93 94 50 50, fax 04 93 68 35 38
Closed mid Nov-mid Dec. 7 stes 1,200-1,900. 93 rms 560-1,750. Rms for disabled. Rm scr. Air cond. Pool. Pkg.
Located near the prestigious Rue d'Antibes, this hotel offers all the services one would expect from this level of quality. The walls in the guest rooms are covered with fabric and offer quite adequate comfort.

 ## Fouquet's

2, rond-point Duboys-d'Angers
04 93 38 75 81, fax 04 92 98 03 39
Closed Nov-Mar 15. 10 rms 440-1,400. Rm scr. Air cond. Garage pkg.
Strategically situated about 100 yards off the Croisette, this uncommonly comfortable hotel offers irresistible rooms with boudoirs and little balconies.

 ## Grand Hôtel

45, bd de la Croisette
04 93 38 15 45, fax 04 93 68 97 45
Closed Nov 1-Dec 10. 78 rms 550-1,600. Restaurant. Half-board 720-1,470. Rm scr. Air cond. Beach. Valet pkg.
A remarkable modern little luxury hotel set amid verdant gardens. Among the assets are large, perfectly comfy rooms with terraces, high-quality reception and service, and a private beach. Panoramic restaurant.

Gray d'Albion

See restaurant Le Royal Gray

 ## Hôtel Savoy

5, rue Fr.-Einesy - 04 92 99 72 00, fax 04 93 68 25 59
Open year-round. 5 stes 2,200-5,600. 101 rms 600-1,500. Rms for disabled. Restaurant. Half-board 550-950. Air cond. Pool. Valet pkg.
The lobby displays a disconcerting mix of styles, with its colorful antique columns and deep, 1930s–style armchairs. As for the rooms, they are smaller than one would expect, but thoroughly soundproofed, with marble baths, sea views, Art Deco décor and irreproachable service.

12/20 La Libera

17, rue du Commandant-André - 04 92 99 00 19
Open daily until midnight. Terrace dining. Air cond.
Come here for a relaxed meal of Italian food in a convivial atmosphere: fresh scampi salad with balsamic vinegar, carpaccio, fritto misto, gnocchi, delicious cod à la vicentina. Nice selection of Piedmontese wines. C 350.

Majestic

See restaurant La Villa des Lys

Martinez

See restaurant La Palme d'Or

 ## Le Méditerranée

Plage du Midi, 2 bd Jean-Hibert
04 92 99 73 10, fax 04 2 99 73 29
Closed Nov 25-Dec 15. Open until 10:30pm. Terrace dining. Air cond. Heated pool. Valet pkg.
Come here for the best view in town! A sort of seventh heaven with its panoramic view, a sure inspiration to chef Guy Santoro, who wholeheartedly gets another point this year. It's the kind of Provençal food we like: flawless cooking times, simple but polished preparations. Check out the original candied sweet peppers in pistou sauce with thin slices of roast cod, the excellent rack of lamb with crispy baby green vegetables and onion jam, or the top-notch crème brûlée. Smiling service, and a classic cellar with some highly affordable Provence wines. C 300. M 180 (weekday lunch), 230 (weekday dinner & Sun).

 ## Sofitel Le Méditerranée

(See restaurant above)
Closed Nov 25-Dec 15. 6 stes 1,710-2,500. 143 rms 730-1,780. Half-board 955-2,230. Rm scr. Air cond. Heated pool. Valet pkg.
Provence has gained a little ground in this chain hotel: half of the guest rooms are done up in the sunny colors of the South—ochre, lavender blue and olive green. Bright, and comfy too. A specimen of good taste and character, from the entrance hall all the way up the seventh

floor. Solarium and terrace looking out on the port.

Molière

5, rue Molière - 04 93 38 16 16, fax 04 93 68 29 57
Closed Nov 15-Dec 20. 42 rms 400-620. Rms for disabled. Air cond.
A conveniently located hotel, not too far from the center of town, offering bright rooms with balconies. Pleasant garden.

Noga Hilton

See restaurant La Scala

Novotel Montfleury

25, av. Beauséjour
04 93 68 91 50, fax 04 93 38 37 08
Open year-round. 1 ste 1,500-4,500. 180 rms 450-1,250. Restaurant. Half-board 340-540. Rm ser. Air cond. Heated pool. Tennis.
Set in the heart of the ten-acre François-André Park, with a view of the bay, this contemporary luxury hotel has unusually spacious rooms, with terraces from the fourth storey up. Fitness center on the premises.

Palace Hôtel

14, av. de Madrid - 04 93 43 44 45, fax 04 93 43 41 30
Closed Nov 20-Dec 20. 3 stes 1,200-1,795. 98 rms 530-1,595. Restaurant. Half-board 720. Rm ser. Air cond. Pool. Pkg.
This modern hotel stands in a quiet residential district 200 yards from the beach. The spacious rooms are perfectly equipped and air conditioned. Coolish service. Numerous facilities; garden.

La Palme d'Or

73, bd de la Croisette
04 92 98 74 14 (R), 04 92 98 73 00 (H),
fax 04 93 39 67 82
Closed Mon, Tue (exc dinner mid Jun-mid Sep), mid Nov-mid Dec. Open until 10:30pm. Terrace dining. Air cond. Pool. Valet pkg.
We never tire of Christian Willer's cuisine, which has, for twelve years now, been breathing of life and the lust for living, which remains light of touch and taste with wonderful wisps of elegance, so terribly appropriate for the climate and mood of the Croisette. The scents and smells of gardens and orchards mix with the sea breeze to create a «symphony» of Provence vegetables in pistou sauce, garnished with shellfish, and gently braised rock octopus and squids, or a «scenario» of lobster and foie gras aside a zucchini rémoulade embellished with lemon and orange zests, or rock red mullet fillets (we do prefer them whole, however) with potato and zucchini fritters in olive cream. Despite the portraits of Marilyn and Marlene, the glamour of the cinema world has not had much effect on this cuisine, which never overdoes it. Same goes for the service, which is highly attentive without ever getting in the way. The stars of the cellar are

the grand names of Provence. C 600-800. M 295 (weekday lunch, wine incl), 350, 580.

Martinez

(See restaurant above)
Open year-round. 12 stes 5,760-14,900. 418 rms 800-4,120. Rm ser. Air cond. Pool. Beach. Tennis. Valet pkg.
After a period of decline, the world-famous Martinez, which in the 1930s was a world-renowned hotel with a glittering guest list, has undergone a total renovation. Now the equal of the Carlton and Majestic hotels, it boasts refined and luxuriously comfortable rooms decorated in «Roaring Twenties» style. In the garden is a sumptuous swimming pool, while on the other side of the Croisette an elegant private beach is reserved for hotel guests. General manager Patrick Sicard has infused the hotel with a dynamic new attitude (now if he could just improve the breakfasts, all would be perfect).

Hôtel de Paris

34, bd d'Alsace - 04 93 38 30 89, fax 04 93 39 04 61
Closed Nov 21-Dec 29. 5 stes 1,000-1,400. 45 rms 350-720. Air cond. Pool. Garage pkg.
This dwelling has the charm of a manor house, and its old-fashioned rooms prove to be functional even though they are rather small. A green, green lawn. The lovely reception gives you the impression you've just arrived at a long lost friend's instead of a hotel. Pleasant terrace.

Le Relais Martinez

Hôtel Martinez, 73, bd de la Croisette
04 92 98 74 12, fax 04 93 39 67 82
Open daily until 10:30pm (midnight in summer). Terrace dining. Air cond.
A market-inspired cuisine à la Méditerranéenne: simple but brimming with flavor. We liked the chilled vegetable gazpacho enhanced with broiled shrimp, the broiled sea perch with vegetable risotto, the fromage blanc dressed up with onion greens and fines herbes, and the Tropez-style pie. The food is well-crafted, and the prices more accessible than in the past, but we didn't appreciate the slow service and the lack of conviction on the part of the staff. And we especially disliked the overpriced wine list, short on local wines. Just a half-bottle of Côtes-de-Provence knocks you back 110 F. If you want to eat nearer the sea, try La Ginguette on the hotel's beach, which specializes in seafood and broiled fish. C 250. M 130-165.

Le Relais des Semailles

9, rue Saint-Antoine
04 93 39 22 32, fax 04 93 39 84 73
Closed Sun off-seas, Wed (Jul-Aug). Annual closings not available. Open until 11pm. Terrace dining. Air cond.
The décor is delightful, almost too much so, but it's a good place for intimate little dinners in this mostly tourist neighborhood. The evening meals

have gone back to being consistent, and it merits more points. Shrimp salad in shellfish cream sauce topped with candied tomatoes, sea bream cooked in full-flavored oil and served up with panisses, and fruit mousse were some of our more successful choices. Beware of à la carte prices; it is wiser to choose the *Gourmand* menu. Cellar offering sober-minded selections, but harboring some novelties and regional selections as well. C 300-400. M 155-180.

 ## Le Restaurant Arménien

82, bd de la Croisette
04 93 94 00 58, fax 04 93 94 56 12
Closed Wed off-seas. Open until 10pm. Terrace dining. Air cond.
Armenian food in a brasserie décor, why not? Lucie and Christian Panossian bring you all the essentials: taste, consistency and a horn of plenty. Along with all the time you need for explanations about the ins and outs of their delicious steamed cuisine. Regulars line up for the tarama, meat tourte, mint ravioli and cinnamon and walnut puff pastry. Good selection of wines, adorable reception. Another point is well merited. M 250.

 ## Le Royal Gray

38, rue des Serbes - 04 92 99 79 79, fax 04 93 99 26 10
Open daily until 10:30pm. Terrace dining. Air cond. Beach. Valet pkg.
It wouldn't be just to forget the Royal Gray. After all, Jacques Chibois left behind some good memories as well as his second-in-command, Michel Bigot, who offers a serious-minded sunny cuisine in a chic brasserie décor with no special charm. It's a bit set off from the Croisette, but we liked the prepossessing reception and the undeniable quality for the money of the à la carte set meal, which offers, for example, lobster, mussel and squid soup with wild mushrooms, broiled sea perch with baby legumes and anise butter, and a warm pear tart. So what if there's no sea view. C 390-520. M 190-290.

 ## Gray d'Albion

(See restaurant above)
Open year-round. 14 stes 2,600-6,350. 172 rms 600-1,700. Rms for disabled. Rm ser. Air cond. Beach. Tennis. Valet pkg.
Although it isn't on the Croisette, the Gray d'Albion affords pleasant views of the hills (from the upper floors) or of the sea from the ninth floor where there is a suite with a huge balcony. The rooms are spacious and well equipped, with modern furnishings. Direct access to a shopping mall; very chic discothèque (Jane's) on the premises, piano bar, underground parking. Lovely private beach with a restaurant.

*Some establishments change their **closing times** without warning. It is always wise to check in advance.*

 ## La Scala

50, bd de la Croisette
04 92 99 70 00, fax 04 92 99 70 11
Closed Sun dinner & Mon (exc Jlu-Aug). Open until 10:30pm (11pm in summer). Garden dining. Air cond. Pool. Beach. Pkg.
One of the nicest terraces in town awaits you here, as well as a classically done up dining room. Slide down some respectable pan-fried red mullet fillets, tasty sage veal scallop, sautéed cèpes and ricotta pancake, or a savory dome of nougatine abricots and blackcurrant purée. Southern-inspired wine list with some Italian and Provençal wines. Good-natured service, and the luncheon menu offers a good buy. C 350-500. M 210 (lunch), 295 (dinner).

 ## Noga Hilton

(See restaurant above)
Open year-round. 47 stes 1,950-25,500. 182 rms 790-3,390. Rms for disabled. Rm ser. Air cond. Beach. Pkg.
This Hilton offers absolutely comfortable accommodations in a building that sports a splendid modernist façade. Every conceivable amenity has been provided, including wonderful marble bathrooms. Also on the premises are restaurants, a piano bar, a shopping arcade, and a rooftop swimming pool with a panoramic view. Private beach.

Sofitel Le Méditerranée

See restaurant Le Méditerranée

 ## Victoria

Rond-point Duboys-d'Angers
04 93 99 36 36, fax 04 93 38 03 91
Closed Nov 20-Dec 27. 25 rms 350-1,250. Rm ser. Air cond. Pool. Valet pkg.
A modern hotel with quiet, comfortable, tastefully decorated rooms, located next to the former Palais des Festivals. Pleasant English bar and tea room; stylish service. Lovely terrace.

 ## La Villa des Lys

14, bd de la Croisette
04 92 98 77 00, fax 04 93 38 97 90
Closed mid Nov-Dec. Open until 10:30pm. Terrace dining. Heated pool. Beach. Tennis. Valet Pkg.
The boardwalk is no longer the maker of great chefs as it was a few seasons ago. Many are gone now, but there are still the trio leaders of the large luxury hotels, the Carlton, Majestic and Martinez, which make up the essential base of Cannes cuisine. In just two seasons, Bruno Oger has confidently leapt right up to the front of the class, and that's why we're donning him with another point this year. In the chic décor of the Majestic, extended by the long terrace well protected from the rumors that raid the Croisette, his cuisine has come into its own, and is, more than ever, his own personal version of Mediterranean cuisine. Delicious monkfish fondant with eggplant, shellfish ragoût and ravioli, perfect roast lamb

with braised vegetables in jus, savory expertly-prepared sea perch and black-olive oil risotto. Delicate desserts with a statement, like the caramelized orange gratin with a reduced citrus fruit juice and lemon sherbet. The service is more attentive, but there are still gaps to be filled in, and the cellar does not come up to par with that required by a deluxe hotel such as this. One of the young Riviera chefs with the most promising futures, named one of Tomorrow's Greats in 1998. C 480-700. M 240-540.

 Majestic

(See restaurant above)
Closed mid Nov-Dec. 23 stes 3,150-13,700. 264 rms 1,050-4,100. Half-board 1,570-2,480. Rm ser. Air cond. Heated pool. Beach. Tennis. Valet pkg.
The Majestic has long been a symbol of luxury and refinement in Cannes. Movie stars love to stay here during the film festival, and soak up the sumptuous atmosphere. Gorgeous rooms look out on the garden and pool or on the Croisette and the hotel's private beach. Roaring Twenties-style décor. Five tennis courts.

And also...

Our selection of places for inexpensive, quick, or late-night meals.
La Mère Besson (04 93 39 59 24 - 13, rue des Frères-Pradignac. Open until 10:30pm. Closed Sun, lunch Mon & Sat.): The scent of garlic emanates perpetually from the kitchen of this well-known restaurant. Unvarying *plats du jour* include frogs' legs à la provençale, fish soup, Niçois monkfish, veal kidney in aigrelette sauce. Good choice of Provençal wines. Expensive (95-300).
Chez Panisse (04 92 99 73 10 - Plage du Midi, 2 bd Jean-Hibert. Open until 10:30pm. Closed Nov 25-Dec 15): The Sofitel brasserie is playing Pagnol with its olive tree, crickets and apéritifs d'époque. It may be colorful, but it's not always tasteful. The rosemary young rabbit marble and the tuna noisette with savory spices proved to be quite mediocre. The accent is there, but the flavor is missing (150-320).
La Papille (04 93 39 27 28 - 38, rue Georges-Clemenceau. Open until 10pm. Closed Sun dinner, Mon.): The *patronne* may defend her food, and yes it's inexpensive, but oh it's inconsistent, too. Yes to the melt-in-your-mouth fennel with walnuts, ricotta ravioli and olive daube. No to the just so-so petits farcis. Amusing selection of wines, much more than the dining room (98-270).
La Poêle d'Or (04 93 39 77 65 - 23, rue des États-Unis. Open until 10pm. Closed Sun dinner in winter, Mon, Tue lunch in summer, Feb school hols, 1 wk in Jul, last wk of Nov.): It's too bad that you never know what kind of meal you're going to get here. The roast John Dory, zucchini and ratatouille met the mark with flying colors; so did the pigeon and fava bean «sandwich». The cooking times are left to the wind, don't even think of ordering the tiramisù, and the service is

a catastrophe. Cellar lacking representation of its region (150-500).

■ **In Le Cannet 06110**   *3 km N*

12/20 **La Magnanerie**
6, rue des Muriers - 04 93 46 44 22
Closed Sun dinner & Mon off-seas. Annual closings not available. Open until 10pm (10:30pm in summer). Terrace dining. Air cond.
The rustic walls of this eighteenth-century house have a few stories to tell. The owner hands out a fine hello, but the cook could use a refresher course in the classics. There's quality to be had for the money, however, especially in the first fixed-price menu: baby Romans ravioli in mushroom sauce, osso buco garnished with pasta in basil sauce, and a fine rendition of his coconut and caramelized-peach Bavarian cream give this restaurant a foothold in this neighborhood far from the Croisette. Respectable quality Côtes-de-Provence starting at 70 F. Flowery terrace, but parking is difficult. C 160-220. M 100-145.

CAP D'AIL	06320
Paris 967 - Nice 18 - Monaco 1	Alpes-Mar.

 Ramada Hotel
In the harbour - 04 92 10 67 67, fax 04 92 10 67 00
Open year-round. 12 stes 1,200-1,600. 174 rms 695-990. Air cond. Rm ser. Pool. Pkg.
The nearby helicopter pad makes this a handy stopover for business people. The rooms are well appointed and boast capacious bathrooms. Some give onto the marina. The small pool sports a terrace bar offering a wide range of refreshments.

CAP D'ANTIBES	06600
Paris 905 - Nice 22 - Antibes 2	Alpes-Mar.

 Beau Site
141, bd Kennedy
04 93 61 53 43, fax 04 93 67 78 16
Closed Nov-Feb. 30 rms 290-659. Air cond. Pool. Pkg.
This holiday home between Antibes and Eden Roc is right on the road, but is well protected by the tree-filled garden surrounding it. Rooms freshened up in Provençal style. Small *déjeuner sur l'herbe...*

 Hôtel Castel Garoupe Axa
959, bd de la Garoupe
04 93 61 36 51, fax 04 93 67 74 88
Closed Nov 10-Mar 15. 2 stest 950-1,350. 27 rms 510-810. Pool. Tennis. Pkg.
This Provençal house is chocked full of country-style furnishings and dotes a handsome garden. Lovely rooms with private terrace.

Restaurant de Bacon

Bd de Bacon - 04 93 61 50 02, fax 04 93 61 65 19
Closed Mon (exc Jul-Aug), Nov-Jan. Open until 10pm (10:30pm in summer). Terrace dining. Air cond. Valet pkg.

Since the Sordello brothers shell out top dollar (or franc...whatever) for their locally caught seafood, patrons, too, pay a pretty penny (centime?) for the ultrafresh sea bass, sea bream, and other Mediterranean fish offered here. These prize specimens will be brought to your table for inspection, then prepared as you wish: grilled, steamed, baked in parchment paper, etc. We're fond of the tiny red mullet cooked whole and ungutted, and of the justly celebrated bouillabaisse. To drink, why not uncork a cool bottle of white Cassis or Bandol wine? **C** 500-700. **M** 250-400 (exc dinner Jul-Aug).

COLLE-SUR-LOUP (LA) 06

→ St-Paul-de-Vence

CROIX-VALMER (LA) 83420

Paris 879 - Toulon 62 - St-Tropez 12 - Grimaud 12 Var

La Brigantine

Plage de Gigaro - 04 94 79 67 16 (R)
04 94 79 60 35 (H), fax 04 94 54 37 05
Dinner only. Closed beg Oct-beg May. Open until 10pm (10:30pm in summer). Garden dining. Pkg.

Enjoy a lazy, holiday atmosphere on this shady seaside patio, with its restful view of beach umbrellas and Cavalaire Bay. The single set menu (you can even pass up certain courses and reduce the price) offers vivacious dishes made from ultrafresh ingredients. **C** 250. **M** 260.

Hôtel de Gigaro

(See restaurant above)
Closed end Sep-mid Apr. 38 rms 570-1,110. Half-board 580-870. Pool. Tennis. Pkg.

Airy, comfortable rooms (some can accommodate two parents and two children) in a pleasant hotel that sits in verdant grounds. The leisure center includes both a bar and a reading room. Just 150 yards away there is a private beach.

Château de Valmer

Route de Gigaro - 04 94 79 60 10, fax 04 94 54 22 68
Closed Nov-Mar. 1 ste 1,670-1,785. 41 rms 770-1,400. Rms for disabled. Restaurant. Half-board 700-1,015 (oblig in seas). Air cond. Pool. Beach. Tennis. Garage pkg.

For a quiet stay even at the height of the season, choose this old Provençal farmhouse situated at the far end of a splendid palm grove, on a working wine-growing concern. Direct access to the beach.

Les Moulins de Paillas

Plage du Gigaro - 04 94 79 71 11, fax 04 94 54 37 05
Closed end Sep-mid Apr. 30 rms 590-1,110. Half-board 600-890. Pool. Tennis. Pkg.

Highly attractive, renovated rooms in this long, Provence-style building lying atop a private beach. Well-appointed.

La Pinède

Plage du Gigaro - 04 94 54 31 23, fax 04 94 79 71 46
Closed Oct-Apr. 40 rms 525-1,470. Half-board 715-1,050 (oblig in seas). Pool. Tennis. Pkg.

The main attraction of this hotel is its exquisite location right on a private beach, almost hidden among the pines. Modern rooms full of sunlight, often with a pleasant terrace. Smiling service.

Souleias

Plage de Gigaro - 04 94 79 61 91, fax 04 94 54 36 23
Closed Oct-beg Apr. Open until 10pm. Garden dining. Heated pool. Tennis. Garage pkg.

What a gorgeous place this is: a splendid *mas* clinging to a remote hillside, set amid flowers and olive trees. Though the site, setting and view are as magnificent as ever, the alarm bells have gone off recently. It starts with the reception, which has turned cold and half-hearted. In the opposite direction, the decidedly young dining room staff is so enthusiastic that it wears you out dealing with them. Our fish panaché was made with fresh ingredients, but prepared all-thumbs (botched cooking time) and was swimming in its excess of oversalted bouillabaisse jus. The roast tuna served as *amuse-bouche* and the codfish aïoli suffered the same haphazard preparation (the insipid fish was swimming in an equally insipid broth lopped in the middle of overcooked vegetables). The discomfort is added to further by the long waiting time. We had grown accustomed to better. **C** 300-400 **M** 245, 360.

Souleias

(See restaurant above)
Closed mid Oct-beg Apr. 7 stes 1,370-2,300. 39 rms 400-1,470. Half-board 635-1,095. Air cond. Heated pool. Tennis. Garage pkg.

Large, sunny, amazingly comfortable rooms are housed in little cottages nestled in foliage and flowers, with heavenly views of the sea and coastline. The hotel's catamaran takes guests to the Iles d'Or for outings and picnics.

CROS-DE-CAGNES 06 → Cagnes-sur-Mer

CUERS 83390

Paris 856 - Toulon 22 - Hyères 25 Var

Le Lingousto

Route de Pierrefeu
04 94 28 69 10, fax 04 94 48 63 79
Closed Sun dinner (exc Jul-Aug), Mon (exc dinner Jul-Aug), Jan-Feb. Open until 9:30pm. Terrace dining. Garage pkg.

Alain Ryon's light, expertly wrought cooking is worth a trip into the hill country behind Toulon, to this imposing *bastide* surrounded by vineyards. Ryon wins full marks for his braised monkfish médaillons, pig's trotter and eggplant crépinette sausage, and lamb tournedos served with an artichoke tagine. As is the ritual here, the dessert assortment features no fewer than five scrumptious sweets. Intelligently composed cellar with some affordable selections. Really nice Mentor fixed-price meal which includes five different wines. Impeccable service and warm-hearted reception, making this all and all a magic stopoff. C 320. M 290 (wine incl), 198-380.

EZE	06360
Paris 959 - Nice 11 - Menton 18 - Monaco 7	Alpes-Mar.

 ### Richard Borfiga
Pl. du Général-de-Gaulle
04 93 41 05 23, fax 04 93 41 26 79
Closed Mon, Jan. Open until 10pm. Terrace dining. Air cond.
Discredit has fallen on this once-lovely restaurant on the edge of the old town, but it is still a sure choice. Richard Borfiga has spread himself a little too thin with the addition of the catering operations, and unfortunately his restaurant has suffered the consequences. Classic flavors and correct cooking times. Friendly reception in this dining room towering over the shady Eze parking lot. Cellar rich in regional crus. M 180-300.

Château de la Chèvre d'Or
Moyenne-Corniche, rue du Barri
04 92 10 66 66, fax 04 93 41 06 72
Closed Wed off-seas, Dec-Feb. Open until 10:30pm. Terrace dining. Air cond. Pool. Valet pkg.
Nature has provided a breathtaking panorama for this aerie perched more than 1,300 feet above the sea. To our dismay, the air in this ethereal dwelling with its pluperfect Mediterranean décor has grown stale. Perhaps Elie Mazot is thinking of retiring early after more than twenty years of loyal and exacting service to his kitchen? In any case, on our last visit, everything went haywire. The oxtail and caviar consommée was bland, the decent langoustines accompanied by a chanterelle mushroom fricassée were decent and no more, the herb velouté and celery root mousseline garnished a dried-out turbot, and the lamb noisettes were embarrassingly overcooked (we asked for them medium rare). The meal was only saved by the gingery chocolate with mint sherbet. We'll put it all down to an absence (physically or metaphorically?). To top it all off, the service was cavalier and forgot how to play their role (the wine waiter never did show up—too bad, he had ample material to comment upon on the superb wine list). All this is problematic for a restaurant of this caliber. C 500-600. M 250 (weekday lunch), 360 (lunch), 590.

 ## Château de la Chèvre d'Or
(See restaurant above)
Closed Dec-Feb. 8 stes 2,600-4,000. 21 rms 1,400-2,750. Rm ser. Air cond. Pool. Valet pkg.
The jet set makes up the clientele of this neo-Gothic refuge (which might be more aptly named the «golden calf»), built in the 1920s. The hotel is made up of several delightful houses that cling to the cliff; inside are personalized rooms and luxurious fittings. Superb swimming pools. Private parking lot. Relais et Châteaux.

 ### Château Eza
04 93 41 12 24, fax 04 93 41 16 64
Closed Dec 25-Apr 9: Tue & Wed, Nov 1-Dec 25. Open until 10pm. Terrace dining. Air cond. Valet pkg.
The site is as spectacular as ever, the building (where William of Sweden once dwelled) has lost none of its seductive charm. The view over the Mediterranean makes one giddy—you might feel like flying right out over the sea, but please don't. It would be a shame to miss such gastronomic pleasures as are on offer in this lap of luxury where you dine among the beautiful people in an oasis of calm. Thierry Bagnis and his young team help you nestle right in to this aerie where you can delve in to giant shrimp salad topped with candied fennel and sweet peppers, irreproachable crusty roast John Dory alongside a potato pancake dashed with tomatoes and topped with a creamy pistou jus, and rhubarb pyramid and raspberries in an unfortunately overly sugary orange sauce. No critique of the flawless welcome, a cellar brimming with feisty finds from the region, and the fixed-price meals (especially lunch) are truly discerning affairs, all in a setting that makes you feel you really have wings. C 550. M 250 (lunch, wine incl), 350 & 490 (dinner).

 ### Château Eza
(See restaurant above)
Closed Nov 2-Apr 9. 5 stes 3,200-3,500. 5 rms 1,600-3,200. Air cond. Valet pkg.
This cluster of medieval dwellings was made into a château by Prince William of Sweden. Each of the luxurious rooms is decorated and furnished differently (and sometimes a bit over the top). They afford mind-boggling views of the sea. Panoramic view of the village as well, enthusiastic welcome, and *grande maison* service. Footpath entrance. Prices are as lofty as the site.

 ### Le Grill du Château
Moyenne-Corniche, rue du Barri
04 92 41 00 17, fax 04 93 41 06 72
Closed Thu, Sun dinner. Open until 10:30pm. Terrace dining.
Robert Guilloux, formerly at the Épicuriens in Nice, has added some pizzazz to the second restaurant of La Chèvre d'Or, as well as a return to the roots of this region so rich in flavors. The

tables near the bay windows provide panoramic views. Savory zucchini and pine nut salad, flawlessly cooked cod napped with spiced-up tomato sauce (generally too salty however), or fettucini and fresh scampi (too much oil). Tasty, full of ideas, a small regional cellar, and pleasant service, but conspicuously lacking professionalism. C 200-340.

Restaurant le Troubadour

Rue du Brec - 04 93 41 19 03
Closed Sun, Mon lunch, Feb school hols, 1 wk beg Jul, Nov 25-Dec 15. Open until 9:30pm. Terrace dining.
So winsome an inn is naturally clogged with tourists in the high season, but the crush has no adverse effects on the kitchen. Gérard Vuille is an accomplished *saucier* who enhances his classic cooking with wonderfully well wrought jus, essences, and emulsions. Costly cellar, with a few affordable wines from the region. C 300-450. M 118 (weekday lunch), 165, 245.

Les Terrasses d'Eze

Route de La Turbie
04 93 41 24 64, fax 04 93 41 13 25
Open year-round. 6 stes 1,050-2,850. 75 rms 600-1,000. Rms for disabled. Restaurant. Half-board 850-1,150. Rm ser. Air cond. Pool. Tennis. Valet pkg.
A pretty, contemporary residence built in to the mountainside and facing out to sea. Large, sunny rooms with pretty decoration. Newly done, luxurious bathrooms. Extremely attentive staff.

FRÉJUS   83600
Paris 890 - Cannes 40 - Ste-Maxime 21 - Hyères 76   Var

Port Royal

In Port-Fréjus - 04 94 53 09 11, fax 04 94 53 75 24
Closed Wed, mid Jan-mid Feb. Open until 9:30pm (10:30pm in summer). Terrace dining.
Fréjus's yacht port seems to want to remain a secret; there are no signs directing you there! But if you manage to find it, your reward is this friendly restaurant offering the flavorful, generous cooking of Marcel Chavanon. His repertoire is traditional and prepared with whole-hearted effort: try the John Dory with eggplant caviar or sweetbreads paired with oyster mushrooms in a luscious sauce. Good cellar, but expensive local wines. Courteous welcome. C 300-350. M 195.

12/20 Les Potiers

135, rue des Potiers - 04 94 51 33 74
Closed Tue. Open until 10pm. Terrace dining. Air cond.
It's worth the trek through the charmless old town to fetch up in this pretty dining room. Owner Hubert Guillard has moved in the right direction: original, unpretentious cooking using

market-fresh products from Provence. We liked the pumpkin soup with mussels and the monkfish with bell pepper sauce. Make sure to reserve before going. C 220-290. M 95-105 (weekday lunch), 120-165.

GASSIN   83580
Paris 877 - Le Lavandou 33 - St-Tropez 8   Var

Le Micocoulier

Pl. des Barrys - 04 94 56 14 01, fax 04 94 56 44 85
Closed Mon. Open until 11:30pm. Terrace dining.
The church square is perched and Provençal, just to our taste. The restaurants line up to take advantage of the lovely backdrop, but this one, despite the fact that it keeps changing chefs, manages to offer a regional selection. Rennet with citrus fruit vinaigrette, ravioli à la daube, red mullet fillets with artichokes and onion greens, a few Gulf wines. Polished service, but the à la carte prices will wake you up if you're snoozing. C 300-450. M 110 (weekday lunch), 160-260.

12/20 La Verdoyante

866, VC de Coste-Brigade
04 94 56 16 23, fax 04 94 56 43 10
Closed Wed off-seas, Oct-Mar. Open until 9:30pm (10pm in summer). Garden dining. Pkg.
Soft vineyard breezes and the gentle pace of another era stir this exquisite terrace where yesterday, today, and—we are certain—tomorrow patrons feed on an unvarying menu of mussels and spinach au gratin, Provençal beef stew, garlicky sautéed rabbit, iced nougat, and other perennial favorites. Wash them down with a Château de Minuty, made right nearby. C 250-350. M 140, 185.

 ## Hôtel Villa Belrose

Lotissement Grande Bastide
04 94 55 97 97, fax 04 94 55 97 98
Closed Oct 15-Apr. 2 stes 5,500-11,500. 38 rms 1,200-3,600. Restaurant. Half-board 1,650-4,050. Air cond. Rm ser. Pool. Pkg.
In the hills of Gassin, a brand new location right in the heart of a magnificent private estate. Rooms and suites are luminous, airy and very well fitted out. Italian restaurant, large pool, pool house. Perfect reception and service. Excellent continental and American breakfasts.

GIENS   83400
Paris 875 - Toulon 27 - Hyères 12 - Carqueiranne 13   Var

12/20 L'Eau Salée

Port Niel - 04 94 58 92 33, fax 04 94 58 92 33
Closed Sun dinner & Mon off-seas, 3 wks in Apr. Open until 10pm. Terrace dining.
The site makes you dream: the most wonderful terrace imaginable, overlooking the beach and the port of Niel. The food less so, even if an ex-Verger chef sparks a little hope. But alas! the

cooking times for the fish were fine (good spree scallop, pan-fried and served alongside candied shallots), approximative flavor for the white fish chartreuse in coral cream sauce, and desserts far too pretentious for a place that calls itself «salty water». We like the wise-priced regional wines, the second prix-fixe menu, and the shade the terrace afforded. We liked less the service, which is «just so», but lacks soul. C 250-350. M 130, 185.

 Le Provençal

Pl. St-Pierre - 04 94 58 20 09, fax 04 94 58 95 44
Closed Oct 25-Apr 3. 45 rms 275-665. Restaurant.
Half-board 400-610. Pool. Tennis. Pkg.
At the tip of the peninsula you'll find this hotel with simple rooms and sumptuous sea views (that same sea water, by the way, feeds the swimming pool).

GOLFE-JUAN   06350
Paris 929 - Nice 27 - Cannes 6 - Antibes 5   Alpes-Mar.

 Le Bistrot du Port

53, bd des Frères-Roustan - 04 93 63 70 64
Closed Sun dinner, Mon. Open until 9:30pm. Terrace dining. Pkg.
The attractions here are a series of small glassed-in rooms overlooking the port, an enjoyable summer terrace, and simple cuisine based on fresh seafood and fine meats. Decent cellar. M 80 & 100 (lunch), 125-200.

GRASSE   06130
Paris 938 - Nice 39 - Draguignan 56   Alpes-Mar.

12/20 Pierre Baltus

15, rue de la Fontette - 04 93 36 32 90
Closed Wed dinner, Sat lunch. Open until 10pm. Terrace dining.
The cozy dining room can hold only fourteen guests—the rest of the space is given over to a large bar and an upright piano. Traditional but passé cuisine full of heavy sauces, but good-priced set meals. C 220-350. M 95-170.

 La Bastide
Saint-Antoine

48, av. Henri-Dunant
04 93 09 16 48, fax 04 93 42 03 42
Open daily until 10pm. Terrace dining. Air cond. Pool. Valet pkg.
Jacques Chibois, awarded cook of the year in 1987, is a quiet, cool-minded man, but don't think he's lacking in spirit. He's simply not the kind to rush into hazardous improvisations. Chibois is a virtuoso who orchestrates the region's vivacious tastes and aromas to create endlessly fascinating flavor harmonies. He knows how to exalt the true savors of the sea, land and forest through a democratic union of produce, spices and herbs, rather than drowning them in problematic alliance. Consider these compositions: chanterelle and trumpet squash, fresh-water crayfish salad in a tomato crust; honest-to-goodness ravioli à la Nissarte in a baby fava bean broth; fat Fario trout sprinkled with fresh herbs and served on a bed of mashed potatoes and peas. The show goes on: pistachio macaroon filled with wild strawberries and napped with licorice sauce, a «testimonial» of the same finesse of execution and of taste. The cellar bravely speaks out (and well) of all the regions of France, starting, of course, with Provence. The 210 F set luncheon menu is practically a philanthropic effort in this magnificent *bastide* girdled by olive trees. C 400-600. M 210 (weekday lunch), 380, 550.

La Bastide Saint-Antoine

(See restaurant above)
Open year-round. 3 stes & 8 rms 700-1,600. Air cond. Rm serv. Pool. Pkg.
So that your pleasure can be total, so that you can continue your pleasure to infinity (or until tomorrow at least), eleven rooms are being added to this eighteenth-century *bastide*. No need to say that they are all the model of luxury, including the bathrooms, which have two sinks, and sometimes even a vintage bathtub. We can't wait to see them finished so we can rate them (certainly to be classified in the *Luxurious* category).

 Charme Hôtel du Patti

Pl. du Patti - 04 93 36 01 00, fax 04 93 36 36 40
Open year-round. 50 rms 330-420. Rms for disabled. Restaurant. Half-board 310-420. Rm ser. Air cond. Garage pkg.
Marvelously situated in the heart of the old town, this charmless modern hotel houses small, quiet rooms with individual heating and good bathrooms. There's an adorable terrace on the little square out front.

■ **In Opio 06650**   *8 km SE on D 2085 & D 3*

12/20 Mas des Géraniums

7, rte de Nice, quartier San-Peyre
04 93 77 23 23, fax 04 93 77 76 05
Closed Tue dinner, Wed, Oct 24-Nov 24, Dec-Jan 5. Open until 9:30pm. Terrace dining. Pkg.
A charm of a Provençal *bastide* swathed in green and quiet and boasting an arbor, a view over the golf course, and an immense parking lot. Creamed scorpion fish garnished with chilled ratatouille, good shoulder of lamb stuffed with herbs, or chicken breast stuffed with morel mushrooms. A cuisine that is more classic than sunny. The cellar is not for mean ones, as the Scots might say. The service is delightful. C 250-300. M 145-185.

See also: **Mougins**

For a complete guide to our restaurant **ranking system**, *see* "Symbol Systems" *page 7.*

GRIMAUD 83310
Paris 857 - Hyères 45 - Saint-Tropez 10 Var

 Athénopolis

Quartier Mouretti - 04 94 43 24 24, fax 04 94 43 37 05
Closed Nov-Easter. 11 rms 490-660. Rms for disabled. Half-board 413-498. Rm ser. Pool. Tennis. Pkg.
On the outskirts of town but well worth the detour. Fine, large rooms, well-equipped and modern. Charming, heartfelt welcome. The sea is five minutes away by car.

 La Boulangerie

Route de Collobrières
04 94 43 23 16, fax 04 94 43 38 27
Closed Oct 10-Mar. 1 ste 960-1,420. 10 rms 500-820. Rms for disabled. Half-board 560-820. Rm ser. Air cond. Pool. Tennis. Pkg.
An attractive and cozy hotel with a capital view of the Massif des Maures. Video library. In fine weather, lunch is served to guests (many are return visitors) around the superb swimming pool.

 La Bretonnière

Pl. des Pénitents - 04 94 43 25 26
Closed Sun dinner & Mon off-seas. Open until 10:30pm (midnight in summer). Terrace dining. Air cond.
Overflowing with old Provence-style furniture and paintings and offering a magnificent view of the Grimaud vineyards. The highly refined service and one of the nicest and most polished receptions you'll find, added to the *douceur* of the setting make up the magic charm of this place. The ingredients are always of the utmost freshness, especially the fish and the vegetables, the cooking times are absolutely fault-free (for the grouper as well as the other fish we sampled), and Marcel Mannoy reachs heights of perfection with his jus. The desserts are also worth making a detour, in particular the incredibly refreshing mixed-berry soup. The little house-made cakes served with the various gourmet coffees also receive very honorable mention. C 250-300. M 155 (exc Sun) 190-225.

Le Coteau Fleuri

Pl. des Pénitents - 04 94 43 20 17, fax 04 94 43 33 42
Closed Tue (exc Jul-Aug), Jan 6-31, Dec 1-18. Open until 9:30pm (10:30pm in summer). Terrace dining. Pkg.
Flowers, flowers everywhere engulf this wonderful villa next to the Penitents' Chapel. From the terrace you'll discover a mind-blowing view of the Massif des Maures and the Provençal hill country. Chef Jean-Claude Paillard favors local ingredients for his always flavorful cooking, which he's finally learned to simplify to take better advantage of the natural flavors. C 300-350. M 150 (lunch), 190.

 Le Coteau Fleuri

(See restaurant above)
Closed Jan 6-31, Dec 1-18. 14 rms 275-550. Half-board 370-445. Pkg.
Picturesque setting in the heart of the old town. Breathtaking view of the Massif des Maures. Rooms are not all the same size but are comfortable enough.

 Les Santons

Route Nationale - 04 94 43 21 02, fax 04 94 43 24 92
Closed Wed (exc dinner Jul-Aug), Jan 2-Mar 15, Nov 2-Dec 23. Open until 10:30pm. Terrace dining. Air cond. Pkg.
Santons—those terracotta figurines which adorn the Christmas crèche—fill this Provençal dining room, the fief of gentle giant Claude Girard. Here's a chef who goes in for classic cuisine with lots of Mediterranean flavor, characterized by prime ingredients, rigorous technique, and delicate sauces. You'll love his succulent lobster risotto, but we must admit that the sauce was a little too creamy, and some of the other jus were of the same approximative nature. Good gently-simmered farm-raised chicken and sumptuous desserts to finish off the affair. Some à la carte prices shoot straight through the roof, such as the truffle omelette at 260 F. Perfecto reception and service. Girard is a winemaker himself, so trust his choices when it comes to picking a winning bottle. C 400-500. M 215 (lunch, wine incl), 260, 420.

HYÈRES 83400
Paris 866 - Fréjus 76 - Toulon 18 Var

 La Colombe

La Bayorre - 04 94 65 02 15, fax 04 94 35 36 68
Closed Sun dinner, Mon in seas, Sat lunch off-seas. Open until 9:45pm. Terrace dining. Air cond.
Even though located away from town, over the years, this little inn managed to make a name for itself as being the best restaurant in the «city of palm trees». Unfortunately, this year, we noted some downright careless ways. The ingredients have dropped in quality and the cooking lacks the mastered craftsmanship of the past: both the scallop tartelette and the pan-fried sea perch with savory were not as good as in former days. The *patronne* dispenses a cold reception and the service is devoid of all passion. The second toque topples away into the wild blue yonder. C 250-300. M 135.

 Les Jardins de Bacchus

32, av. Gambetta
04 94 65 77 63, fax 04 94 65 71 19
Closed Sun dinner off-seas, Sat lun & Mon in seas. Open until 10pm (10:30pm in summer). Terrace dining. Air cond.
Bacchus beams benevolently down from the huge mural that adorns the dining room, and he inspires the wine list (rich in local treasures) that

Claire Santioni has put together. Jean-Claude Santioni's bracing menu takes its cue from the culinary traditions of the Rhône and the Mediterranean. His sometimes over-complicated ways of the past have been honed down for the better. Some regal dishes this year: lobster ravioli with zests of candied orange, pan-fried capon fillets, and sesame lamb hand in hand with its toothsome eggplant cake. Flawless cooking times, beautifully made-up plates, and absolutely first-rate ingredients. The perfection continues to the very end with successes such as the praline chocolate crispy. Irreproachable service. A second toque well-deserved. C 250-300. M 200 (weekday lunch, wine incl), 145-300 (weekdays).

 Mercure

19, av. Ambroise-Thomas
04 94 65 03 04, fax 04 94 35 58 20
Open year-round. 84 rms 445-595. Restaurant. Half-board 485-650. Air cond. Pool. Pkg.
A convenient hotel, located on the bypass road, that is up to par with the chain's standards. Rooms are well-kept and well fitted out. Pleasant atmosphere in bar and restaurant.

ISSAMBRES (LES)   83380
Paris 884 - Toulon 32 - Hyères 15   Var

 Chante-Mer

Village provençal - 04 94 96 93 23
Closed Sun dinner & Mon (exc in summer). Open until 9pm. Terrace dining. Air cond.
The name tells all. Mario Battaglia has a love affair with the sea and your tastebuds will prove it to you. His sea perch, sea bream and bass with fennel are faultless. His steamed salmon simply makes you want to stay and savor more. Enjoyable lemon-tree terrace. Not a large selection of wines, but all the sought-after «gems» of Provence are available. C 250-350. M 120, 205.

 Villa Saint-Elme

N 98, at L'Arpillon
04 94 49 52 52, fax 04 94 49 63 18
Closed Wed mid Oct-mid Mar, Jan 6-25, Nov 16-Dec 14. Open until 10pm. Terrace dining. Air cond. HOTEL: 3 stes 2,000-4,600. 13 rms 750-2,900. Pool. Beach. Sauna. Garage pkg.
This white Italian-style villa from the 1930s, standing between the superhighway and the sea, offers a splendid view of the Golfe de Saint-Tropez through large bay windows overlooking the terrace. Locals flock here (especially in the evening) to indulge in appetizing pistou fava bean soup and rock red mullet or the even better sea bream with clam ravioli en barigoule. Desserts are classic but delicious; the rhubarb and rosemary puff pastry tart was a pure delight. Chef Laurent Picharles, who came down from Normandy, is quickly learning his way around the repertoire of Southern cuisine; he is taking the curves well, and started racing full speed ahead at the beginning of last summer. His

precision and skill of the trade led us to name him one of the great chefs of the future last year. After imbibing a bottle of the many Bordeaux or Burgundies on hand, you might want to book one of the three lovely air conditioned suites (the rooms in the more modest annex are a bit noisy), or one of the new rooms with a Jacuzzi. C 350. M 230, 350.

JUAN-LES-PINS   06160
Paris 920 - Nice 22 - Cannes 9   Alpes-Mar.

 Ambassadeur

50-52, chemin des Sables
04 92 93 74 10, fax 04 93 67 79 85
Open year-round. 6 stes 1,900-2,200. 235 rms 750-1,200. Rms for disabled. Restaurant. Half-board 545-715. Air cond. Pool. Beach. Valet pkg.
Not far from the pine grove you'll find this luxurious modern hotel, where cozily decorated rooms boast balconies and the very best bathrooms. All the usual amenities are on hand, as well as some delightful extras. Zealous, professional service.

 Belles Rives

Bd du Littoral - 04 93 61 02 79, fax 04 93 67 43 51
Closed Oct 15-Apr 1. Open until 10:30pm. Garden dining. Air cond. Beach. Valet pkg.
Formerly a holiday villa occupied by the likes of Scott and Zelda Fitzgerald, for the last 60 years Belles Rives has been a family-run luxury hotel,

The toque, circa 1700

Have you ever wondered about the origin of that towering, billowy (and slightly ridiculous) white hat worn by chefs all over the world? Chefs have played an important role in society since the fifth century B.C., but the hats didn't begin to appear in kitchens until around the eighteenth century A.D. The **toque** is said to be of Greek origin: many famous Greek cooks, to escape persecution, sought refuge in monasteries and continued to practice their art. The chefs donned the tall hats traditionally worn by Orthodox priests, but to distinguish themselves from their fellows, they wore white hats instead of black. The custom eventually was adopted by chefs from Paris to Peking.

with a guest register signed by the Windsors, Édith Piaf, Josephine Baker, Miles Davis, and loads of other celebrities. A breath of new life with Thierry Grattarola, who recently arrived in the kitchen. A rather contemporary cuisine (compared to the setting, at least) offering goodies such as lobster chaud-froid with zucchini blossoms in shellfish butter, broiled scallops in spicy sauce (which hides the taste of the scallops), delicious orange supreme roasted in honey and green anise, and old rum and vanilla cream sabayon. The cellar does not offer the grandeur of the rest of this paradise, and is especially lacking in Bordeaux. The service is uneven—sometimes of Pink Panther speed, other times turtle-like. Exquisite Art Deco dining room with views of the sea. C 520. M 180-350.

 ## Belles Rives

(See restaurant above)
Closed Oct 15-Apr 1. 4 stes 1,690-4,450. 41 rms 700-2,550. Half-board 390 (oblig in seas). Air cond. Beach. Valet pkg.
With superb views over the bay, these 1930s–style rooms are all different and extra comfortable (not to mention expensive), with lovely marble bathrooms. Some rooms have views of the sea. Business services available, as well as a private beach and landing dock.

 ## Beauséjour

Av. Saramartel - 04 93 61 07 82, fax 04 93 61 86 78
Closed Oct-Apr 15. 30 rms 500-1,000. Pool. Pkg.
This pretty contemporary villa enveloped in its very Provençal grove of olive trees, cedars and laurels and chock-full of flowers, is located in a quiet neighborhood. The vast rooms offer a terrace and unostentatious, relaxing appointments, all adding up to a stay full of repose.

 ## Bijou Plage

Bd Charles-Guillaumont
04 93 61 39 07, fax 04 93 67 81 78
Open daily until 9:30pm (midnight in summer). Terrace dining. Air cond. Beach. Valet pkg.
Here's a rarity: a real «bijou» of a Riviera beach restaurant, open year round to boot. The Japanese chef deftly selects and prepares utterly fresh fish for a gilt-edged clientele: salmon and asparagus terrine, grouper au pistou, and tarragon-scented fricassée of monkfish and scampi with smoky bacon are excellent choices. Appealing Provençal cellar. C 350. M 100 (weekday lunch), 165-280.

 ## Garden Beach Hotel

La Pinède, 15-17, bd Baudoin
04 92 93 57 57, fax 04 92 93 57 56
Open year-round. 16 stes 1,000-3,300. 156 rms 650-1,800. Rms for disabled. Restaurant. Half-board 490-1,530. Rm ser. Air cond. Beach. Valet pkg.
Housed in a modernist cube constructed on the site of the former casino, this luxurious hotel offers every comfort and service. The rather chil-

ly interior of red and black marble and granite is warmed by photos of jazz greats who have graced the local festival, and by the great sea views from the rooms. Impeccable service. Lunch buffet and dinner grill service in summer on the lovely private beach.

 ## Hélios

3, av. du Docteur-Dautheville
04 93 61 55 25, fax 04 93 61 58 78
Closed Nov-Mar. 5 stes 1,500-2,500. 60 rms 600-1,500. Rms for disabled. Restaurant. Half-board 550-900. Rm ser. Air cond. Beach. Valet pkg.
Another luxurious hotel, this one with its own private beach (breakfasts are served by the water). Some of the lovely, large, modern rooms have splendid balconies, while others are smaller with plain-vanilla furniture and only the merest sliver of a sea view. Piano bar.

 ## Les Mimosas

Rue Pauline - 04 93 61 04 16, fax 04 92 93 06 46
Closed Oct-mid Apr. 34 rms 470-650. Pool. Pkg.
An agreeable white house with a garden in a residential area 500 yards from the sea. The bright rooms all have balconies and have been refurbished. Huge swimming pool.

 ## Pré Catelan

22, av. des Lauriers (corner av. des Palmiers)
04 93 61 05 11, fax 04 93 67 83 11
Open year-round. 18 rms 250-550. Air cond. Pkg.
A little house in a quiet, palm-shaded garden 200 yards from the sea. Good, traditional rooms.

 ## La Terrasse

La Pinède, av. Georges-Gallice
04 93 61 20 37 (R), 04 93 61 08 70 (H), fax 04 93 61 76 60
Closed Wed (exc in summer), Nov-Easter. Open until 10pm (10:30pm in summer). Garden dining. Heated pool. Beach. Valet pkg.
Light beige and rich green marble floors, straw yellow wainscoting on the walls, alternating smoked and transparent beveled glass: a spanking new *luxe de luxe* décor, no doubt to reward the chef for the spectacular reputation he has made for this place. Chef Christian Morisset shuns the limelight: he prefers to stick close to his stoves, working away on a dazzling *carte*. Glistening Mediterranean fish, perfumed Provençal vegetables and herbs, and prime foodstuffs from all over the map are transformed into triple-toque dishes that shun the over-complicated and relish clear-cut flavors, like the local John Dory simply pan-fried with eggplant and fresh tomatoes and livened up with oregano. It's difficult to find any fault; it's slam-bang from start to the finish: remarkable *amuse-bouche*, young rabbit terrine in coriander vegetable jelly, crayfish à la Bordelaise, or rare and delicious meagre fish accompanied by a sumptuous risotto. Desserts carry on with the theme of exquisiteness. Tempt yourself with the roast apricot and wild strawberries, vanilla, almond and pistachio

ice cream. This is the work of a perfectionist: disciplined, precise cooking that defines and enhances each nuance of flavor. Cooking of this caliber doesn't come cheap, of course, but there's always the 270 F lunch, which is as carefully crafted as the rest. Lovely cellar with the *grands crus* from here and elsewhere. C 600-800. M 270 (lunch), 410-630.

Juana

(See restaurant above)
Closed Nov-Easter. 5 stes 1,600-3,500. 45 rms 650-2,050. Rms for disabled. Half-board 580-660. Rm scr. Air cond. Heated pool. Beach. Valet pkg.
Small but luxurious, run by the same family since the 1930s, the tradition of elegance is expressed through its stylish façade and wrought-iron elevator shaft. Ultra comfortable rooms, tastefully modernized using lofty materials such as mahogany. Some have a terrace looking over the marble pool and the pine forest, where there is a jazz festival in August. Pleasant American-style bar, beach and private floating deck just 500 feet away.

LAVANDOU (LE)	83980
Paris 887 - Toulon 41 - St-Tropez 38 - Cannes 104	Var

L'Algue Bleue

62, av. du Général-de-Gaulle
04 94 71 05 96, fax 04 94 71 20 12
Closed Wed exc off-scas or upon reserv. Open until 10pm. Air cond. Garden dining. Pool.
The view is positively appetizing: the dining room's arched windows frame a dreamy perspective of the port and the Hyères Islands beyond. The plate-side view is just as good: prime-quality ingredients, faultless cooking times, all dressed up in a picture perfect presentation. Luscious langoustine salad—the prawns literally melt in your mouth—and excellent sea perch supreme sautéed in truffle oil (despite the weakly vegetable garnish). Well-wrought desserts and well-informed selection of wines. Refined reception and service. The bill is not too salty, despite the name «blue alga». C 280-380. M 200-320.

Auberge de la Calanque

(See restaurant above)
Closed Nov, Jan. 2 stes 950-1,200. 35 rms 400-750. Half-board 430-785. Rm scr. Air cond. Pool.
Overhanging the new port, pleasant rooms, some with their own little gardens. Inviting pool, which makes you forget going to the beach. Good breakfasts.

Belle Vue

In Saint-Clair, bd du Four-des-Maures
04 94 71 01 06, fax 04 94 71 64 72
Closed Nov-Feb. 19 rms 300-600. Restaurant. Half-board 350-600 (oblig in scas). Pkg.

Overlooking the sea and coast, this quiet, charming hotel offers rustic but comfortable rooms. You'll love the beautiful flower garden and the genial reception.

Le Club de Cavalière

Plage de Cavalière - 04 94 05 80 14, fax 04 94 05 73 16
Closed Oct-May 10. Open until 10pm. Terrace dining. Air cond. Heated pool. Beach. Tennis. Valet pkg.
First, there's the private beach, beautifully tended to and free of charge for those staying in the hotel (which is not always the case in the Riviera!). Then there's the enormous rooms, beautifully kept up and furnished in a smashing Provençal style that really works. Then the breakfast, which gives preference to regional specialities. C 350-400. M 300.

Le Club de Cavalière ♨♥

(See restaurant above)
Closed Oct-May 10. 3 stes 1,275-1,725. 39 rms 950-2,900. Rms for disabled. Half-board 700-2,700 (oblig in scas). Air cond. Heated pool. Beach. Tennis. Valet pkg.
One of the rare luxury hotels on the coast with a private sandy beach. All of the rooms are freshly renovated in beautiful Provence style, and boast terraces where breakfast is served. Wonderful location, between Cap Bénat and the rocky spur of Cap Nègre.

Le Sud

In Aiguebelle, av. des Trois-Dauphins - 04 94 05 76 98
Open daily until 9:30pm (11pm in summer). Terrace dining. Air cond. Pkg.
Cristophe Pétra has set up shop just a few lengths away from his old address. The ship has shifted course, dropping the pure gastronomic tendency and opting for a more rustic yet still refined cuisine. Superb sea perch roasted in fig leaves; stuffed capon à la Provençal; broiled lobster or colossal shrimp; or succulent spit-roasted pigeon. The cellar offers a few thoroughly palatable local *cuvées* at friendly prices. Incredibly enthusiastic reception and attentive service. C 250-320. M 190-220.

Les Roches

In Aiguebelle, 1, av. des Trois-Dauphins
04 94 71 05 07, fax 04 94 71 08 40
Closed Oct-Easter. Open until 10:30pm. Terrace dining. Air cond. Pool. Pkg.
There are things that never change in this paradisiacal site: its majesty and sublimeness, the magic setting and exceptionlly fine view, the irreproachable welcome and service. There are other things that do change, unfortunately, namely, what's on your plate. Gone are the glorious days of the Tarridec period. A certain slackness is evident from the outset: products are sometimes fresh, but then sometimes they're not; cooking times are sometimes right, and sometimes totally botched; sauces do not always meet

the good intentions of the chef. Our last meal saw a sea bream alongside duck foie gras, both over-cooked and oversalted. No set meal in sight, and a rather brief à la carte menu announcing over-the-top prices—fish soup at 165 F! All is not lost in paradise, however, because the cellar is well-lined and varied. C 350-500.

Les Roches

(See restaurant above)
Closed Oct-Easter. 5 stes 2,700-3,500. 40 rms 1,300-2,500. Half-board 1,845-2,845. Air cond. Pool. Valet pkg.
Les Roches is unquestionably one of the most refined recent constructions on this stretch of coast. The sunny, antique-filled rooms, with ter-races overlooking the sea, are furnished with taste, the bathrooms are clad with marble and Salerno tiles. Shady footpaths wind through a garden planted with cactus and rare trees, lead-ing to the private beach and freshwater swim-ming pool. Tennis and boating facilities are close at hand, and there's a golf course nearby. Relais et Châteaux.

Les Tamaris

Plage de Saint-Clair
04 94 71 07 22, fax 04 94 71 88 64
Closed mid Jan-mid Feb. Open until 10:30pm. Ter-race dining. Air cond. Pkg.
Lounge a while under the rose laurels on the terrace just off the beach, fall into one of those comfortable armchairs. The locals call it «Raymond's place», how suitable. Raymond Viale still looks after his seaside restaurant, even if he's not in the kitchen anymore. This is certain-ly one of the best fish restaurants in the Var region, even if the summer onslaught plays havoc with the cooking times. During off-season, you can order ahead such taste-tinglers as shellfish au gratin or the ultimate in fish and bouillabaisse cooked over a wood fire. The cellar is blatantly lacking in regional bottles, but the white wine from Domaine de Saint-Baillon (Côtes-de-Provence) is excellent. Pleasant, laid-back reception. C 250-400.

See also: Bormes-les-Mimosas, Por-querolles (Ile de), Port-Cros (Ile de)

LEVANT (ILE DU)	83400
Boarding at Cavalaire, Lavandou or Hyères	Var

La Brise Marine

Pl. du Village - 04 94 05 91 15, fax 04 94 05 93 21
Closed Nov 2-Apr 15. 20 rms 240-320. Restaurant. Half-board 395-475. Pool.
Situated at the high point of the island, over-looking the sea, the Brise boasts handsome, com-fortable, well-equipped rooms set round a delightful, flower-filled patio. Superb swim-ming pool and sun terrace.

Hôtel Gaétan

04 94 05 91 78, fax 04 94 36 77 17
Closed Sep 20-Apr 15. 14 rms 220-300. Restaurant. Half-board 300-330 (oblig in seas).
Set in a pleasant garden, the Gaétan's rooms are very simple (all have showers, not all have toilets) and are quite well kept. Solarium, bar.

LORGUES	83510
Paris 850 - Draguignan 13 - St-Raphaël 43	Var

Chez Bruno

Route de Vidauban
04 94 73 92 19, fax 04 94 73 78 11
Closed Sun dinner & Mon. Open until 10pm. Gar-den dining. Pkg.
The phrase *bon vivant* seems to have been coined just for Bruno Clément, a generous, sen-sual chef with a passion for truffles. Now mind you, these are not the Périgord variety, but the summer truffles found in the earth of the Haut-Var region. Bruno's single menu, priced at 280 F, is constantly revamped, but allows you to ex-plore the world of truffles—enveloped in puff pastry or raw and dipped in salt with a touch of olive oil. The fête can continue with perfect shoulder of milkfed lamb baked gently in its own fat and a double dessert with strawberry pie and strawberry sherbet. There's still no wine list—just a selection of wines grown by Bruno's winegrowing friends. Lively service in the spirit of the master. Gourmet boutique (truffles and wine), library, *boiseries*, fountains. Live the good life with all they might, everything you need is here—a marvellous backdrop and a myriad of tastes and good taste. M 280.

MANDELIEU-LA NAPOULE	06210
Paris 850 - Cannes 8 - La Napoule 2	Alpes-Mar.

Acadia

681, av. de la Mer - 04 93 49 28 23, fax 04 92 97 55 54
Closed Nov 19-Dec 25. 6 stes 450-840. 29 rms 250-440. Rms for disabled. Heated pool. Tennis.
This pleasant villa, recently built on the banks of the Siagne, was built with your vacation in mind. Sunny, comfortable rooms, a quiet gar-den, and good sports facilities. Package deals include hotel and green fees on the numerous golf courses in the area.

L'Armorial

Bd Henry-Clews - 04 93 49 91 80, fax 04 93 93 28 50
Closed Wed off-seas, Nov 15-Dec 20. Open until 10pm. Terrace dining. Air cond.
On the waterfront, this restaurant is genuine and gracious and offers good middle-class com-fort and traditional food. Quality seafood, fish broiled or cooked in a salt crust, and a few saucier dishes. Creamed scorpion fish, tooth-some crab-stuffed capon, pan-fried scallops, and saddle of sea perch à l'unilatérale. The desserts are less scintillating. The service is not very

fashionable and you wait a long time between courses, but they look after you well. The owner tries to meet your every need. The regionally-focused wine list is interesting and offers a number of half-bottles. C 200-300. M 140-185.

 ## Domaine d'Olival

778, av. de la Mer - 04 93 49 31 00, fax 04 92 97 69 28
Closed Nov-mid Jan. 11 stes 680-1,780. 7 rms 435-925. Air cond. Pool. Tennis. Pkg.
Superb 20,000 square foot plus garden. The rooms are quite in keeping: polished décor, private kitchen, appointments, and much more. On the banks of the Siagne river, a floating dock awaits you for a little boating party.

 ## L'Ermitage de Riou

Bd Henry-Clews - 04 93 49 95 56, fax 04 92 97 69 05
Open daily until 10pm (10:30pm in summer). Terrace dining. Air cond. Pool. Pkg.
The dining room of this lovely Provençal hotel near the convention center belongs to a Var wine grower, Elie Sumeire. The recent face-lift gave birth to a beautiful covered terrace extension. The chef whips up dashing ideas inspired by his deep South(west) roots (superb foie gras) and Mediterranean variations (rabbit terrine speckled with little olives, sea bream and eggplant, and fish cooked in a salt crust). Charming and highly professional reception. The wine list is a quick read, offering Côtes-de-Provence howbeit. C 300-450. M 230 (wine incl), 450.

 ## Hostellerie du Golf

780, bd de la Mer - 04 93 49 11 66, fax 04 92 97 04 01
Open year-round. 16 stes 600-860. 39 rms 330-640. Restaurant. Half-board 370-480. Pool. Tennis.
A gay Provençal-type hotel on the banks of a river and snuggled in to a beautiful park. Enormous, particularly pleasant rooms with a pretty little terrace. The decoration is unostentatious and well turned out in pretty pastels.

 ## L'Oasis

La Napoule - Rue Jean-Honoré-Carle
04 93 49 95 52, fax 04 93 49 64 13
Closed Sun dinner & Mon (exc Apr-Oct). Open until 10pm. Garden dining. Air cond. Valet pkg.
Stéphane Raimbault took time to give his own twist to Outhier's signature mix of Mediterranean and Asian flavors—hot, herbal, highly perfumed dishes that require every element to be in perfect balance—but now he's found the right note. His main trump card is the way he mixes exquisitely fresh fish with the very best of the Provençal repertory of vegetables. His stint in Japan left him with a fondness for spices. Purists who prefer their fish simply broiled or pan-fried to perfection may find the spices overwhelming, but that is a matter of personal taste. The dessert cart is terribly conventional; there are more exciting alternatives in today's world. C 550-650. M 275 (weekday lunch, wine incl), 210 (lunch), 290-550.

 # Royal Hôtel Casino

605, av. du Général-de-Gaulle
04 92 97 70 00, fax 04 93 49 51 50
Open year-round. 30 stes 2,500-6,000. 180 rms 690-1,800. Restaurant. Half-board 560-810. Rm ser. Air cond. Heated pool. Tennis. Valet pkg.
The contemporary rooms with sea views sport a fresh, attractive look. The hotel provides an hourly shuttle service to Cannes and excellent facilities for business meetings, but the soundproofing is not up to par on the street side. Piano bar and many deluxe services.

See also: Cannes

MENTON	06500
Paris 961 - Nice 31 - Cannes 63	Alpes-Mar.

 ## L'Aiglon

7, av. de la Madone
04 93 57 55 55, fax 04 93 35 92 39
Closed beg Nov-mid Dec. 3 stes 780-1,050. 28 rms 350-770. Restaurant. Half-board 395-565. Air cond. Heated pool. Pkg.
A beautiful nineteenth-century mansion situated not far from the center of Menton, and just 50 yards from the sea, presents big, well-outfitted rooms and delightful gardens. The furniture, though, is oddly mismatched.

 ## Ambassadeurs

2, rue du Louvre
04 93 28 75 75, fax 04 93 35 62 32
Closed Jan 5-Feb 13. 9 stes 1,200-1,500. 40 rms 525-950. Rms for disabled. Restaurant. Half-board 260-275. Rm ser. Air cond. Valet pkg.
Modern comforts in a romantic, nineteenth-century hotel (note the beautiful wrought-iron staircase). The rooms are large and tastefully decorated, with all the amenities one might require. Piano bar; excellent welcome and service.

Chambord

6, av. Boyer - 04 93 35 94 19, fax 04 93 41 30 55
Open year-round. 40 rms 400-580. Air cond. Tennis. Pkg.
Close to the sea, this hotel features fairly spacious, sunny rooms next to the municipal gardens and casino.

12/20 Darkoum

23, rue Saint-Michel - 04 93 35 44 88
Closed Mon, Tue lunch, 1st 2 wks of Jun. Open until 10pm (11pm in summer & weekend). Terrace dining. Air cond.
In these parts, you expect to eat Italo-French, so this amiable cooking brimful of perky Moroccan flavors is a pleasant surprise. Phyllo savory pies, delightful tagines (Tangier-style fish) and sweet pastries. All-smiles welcome. C 160-180. M 98-138.

Napoléon

29, porte de France
04 93 35 89 50, fax 04 93 35 49 22
Closed Nov-Dec 8. 40 rms 350-600. Restaurant.
Half-board 335-460. Pool.
You will enjoy a view either of the mountains or the sea, depending on which of these well-outfitted rooms you occupy. Panoramic restaurant.

 ## Hôtel Riva

600, promenade du Soleil
04 92 10 92 10, fax 04 93 28 87 87
Open year-round. 2 stes 1,000-1,220. 40 rms 440-620. Pkg.
Modern appointments for this classy hotel giving onto the sea. Old-fashioned charm in a lemon-tree estate pleasantly mixed with well-designed comfort in guest rooms full of light, where nothing has been looked over in terms of fitting out. Agreeable rooftop pool and sun solarium.

 ## Le Royal Westminster

1510, promenade du Soleil
04 93 28 69 69, fax 04 92 10 12 30
Closed Nov. 92 rms 310-720. Rms for disabled. Restaurant. Half-board 340-610. Rm ser. Air cond. Pkg.
A turn-of-the-century luxury hotel with pleasant, bright rooms and Pompeian bathrooms! The blooming garden looks out to sea. Peace and quiet assured.

MONACO (PRINCIPALITY OF) **98000**
Paris 955 - Nice 18 - Menton 9 - San-Remo 44   Monaco

 ## Abela Hôtel Monaco

Quartier Fontvieille, 23, av. des Papalins
(377) 92 05 90 00, fax (377) 92 05 91 67
Open year-round. 18 stes 1,080-1,320. 174 rms 640-1,110. Rms for disabled. Restaurant. Half-board 610-785. Rm ser. Air cond. Pool. Garage pkg.
The very attractive and comfortable rooms overlook the Princess Grace rose garden and the harbor. Excellent service and equipment; delicious breakfasts.

Balmoral

12, av. Costa
(377) 93 50 62 37, fax (377) 93 15 08 69
Open year-round. 7 stes 1,200-1,500. 68 rms 450-900. Rm ser. Air cond. Garage pkg.
This hotel, facing the marina, just turned one hundred, and unfortunately you can tell. Even though the sitting room is old-fashioned, you'll admire the tasteful period antiques.

12/20 Café de Paris

Pl. du Casino
(377) 92 16 20 20, fax (377) 92 16 38 58
Open daily until 2am. Garden dining. Air cond. Garage pkg.

A wide, sun-washed terrace opens in front of this enormous brasserie decorated in Belle Époque style. Despite the crowds, the service is smiling and the cooking fresh and good. Some decent Provençal wines are also on hand. C 285-495.

 ## Côté Jardin

Hôtel de Paris, pl. du Casino
(377) 92 16 68 44, fax (377) 92 16 38 40
Closed Jul 4-Aug. Open lunch only until 3pm. Terrace dining. Air cond. Valet pkg.
If you'd like to soak up a magnificent view of the port and the Rocher but you just want simple Riviera favorites cooked in a crafted manner, drop in on chef Mario Muratore. Artichoke risotto, broiled fish and vegetables, spit-roasted leg of milkfed lamb, jolly good salad bar and dessert cart (the tiramisù is delectable). The dispassionate welcome gives way to prompt and careful service. The cellar walls are well lined in *à propos* local offerings, such as the Château Rasque. Cheerful atmosphere at poolside luncheons. The reasonable prices are not at all in keeping with the Monaco tradition. C 370.

 ## La Coupole

1, av. Princesse-Grace
(377) 92 16 65 65, fax (377) 93 50 84 85
Closed lunch, Jul-Aug. Open until 10pm. Terrace dining. Air cond. Heated pool. Valet pkg.
Joël Garault had difficulty finding the right balance for his wide-eyed, perfectionist style of cuisine in the not-so-cheerful atmosphere of this well-kept and polished grand hotel, but he manages to maintain his high standards. Thoroughly toothsome vegetable preparations, and the dishes with sauces are first rate. Delectable squid risotto donned with shreds of oxtail and slivers of Parmesan, aiguillettes of lamb and baby vegetables. Purely choice desserts prepared by Benoît Perruchon-Monge, Garault's indispensable right-hand man in the domain of studied elegance (caramel Chiboust cream au gratin with chocolate sauce), and one of the top pastry chefs in the Riviera. Quality cellar offering some surprisingly reasonable prices for Côtes-de-Provence. Service full of attention. C 550-700. M 260 (weekday lunch), 300, 450.

Mirabeau

(See restaurant above)
Open year-round. 10 stes 2,100-6,800. 83 rms 1,100-2,400. Half-board 1,040-2,390. Air cond. Heated pool. Beach. Tennis. Golf. Valet pkg.
The well-equipped rooms have individual air conditioning and terraces overlooking the sea. Heated swimming pool. Free access to activities sponsored by the *Société des Bains de Mer*, reduced prices on tennis and golf fees. Note that the Coupole restaurant closes in July and August, but the Café Mirabeau is open for lunch.

Looking for a chic souvenir? Refer to the index.

Hermitage

Thermes Marins, square Beaumarchais
(377) 92 16 40 00, fax (377) 92 16 38 52
Open year-round. 34 stes 6,000-10,000. 197 rms 1,300-3,300. Restaurant. Air cond. Heated pool. Valet pkg.
A stunning Belle Époque hotel perched on a cliff and doting a dome built by none other than Eiffel of Eiffel Tower fame: stay here and you'll be just a few yards from the beach and a minute from the casino. Splendid swimming pool; seawater spa.

 L'Hirondelle

Thermes Marins, 2, av. de Monte-Carlo
(377) 92 16 49 47, fax (377) 92 16 49 49
Closed Sun dinner. Open until 9:30pm. Terrace dining. Air cond. Pool. Valet pkg.
It's not because it's diet food that it lacks taste, and here's the place to prove it. In a thermal bath setting with a terrace doting an impregnable view of the port, both dieters and gourmets will dance with light delight. Philippe Girard offers an exacting cuisine brimming with life: squid salad, sapid spicy red mullet gazpacho, crusty saddle of turbot, and mango ravioli with almonds. Dieters can choose from the list of mineral waters, while the less calorie-conscious can imbibe one of the select Southern wines. Smiling service that looks after your every need. C 350-480. M 285.

 Hôtel Loews Monte-Carlo

Av. de Spélugues
(377) 93 50 65 00, fax (377) 93 30 01 57
Open year-round. 40 stes 2,600-5,400. 579 rms 1,250-2,000. Rms for disabled. Restaurants. Rm ser. Air cond. Pool. Valet pkg.
As well as its luxurious suites and bright, welcoming rooms and broad terraces, this prestigious hotel offers a host of facilities: five restaurants, bars, cabaret, casino, boutiques, swimming pool, and a fitness club with unparalleled equipment.

 Le Jardin

4, av. de la Madone
(377) 93 15 15 15, fax (377) 93 25 24 44
Open daily until 10:30pm. Terrace dining. Air cond. Pkg.
This is neither luxury hotel food nor gastronomic delight. In fact, they can't decide whether they want to run with the hare or hunt with the hounds: salmon millefeuille with spice and chervil butter, scorpion fish fillet in a tomato emulsion, and a surprise plate for dessert (we had little fritters stuffed with chocolate and apples). Attentive service and reasonable prices. In the summer, lunch is buffet only. C 250-350. M 350 (dinner in summer).

 Le Louis XV

Hôtel de Paris, pl. du Casino
(377) 92 16 30 01 (R),
(377) 92 16 30 00 (H)
fax (377) 92 16 69 21 (R), (377) 92 16 38 50 (H)
Closed Tue & Wed (exc dinner Jun 17-Aug 26), Feb 17-Mar 4, Dec 1-27. Open until 10pm. Terrace dining. Air cond. Valet pkg.
Can the famous Alain Ducasse really be in two places at the same time (Monaco and Paris) and remain at the top? A *tour de force* such as that would need a maestro conductor, true, but also musicians who can play their scores backward and forward without keeping their eyes riveted on the conductor's baton. This certainly seems to be the case, because we have dropped in on several occasions—sometimes when he was there, sometimes when he was away—and frankly, we can't see the difference. The symphonic crescendos we noted this year included an appetizing chilled lobster bouillon dressed up with caviar, an exceptional-tasting quick-cooked miniature Mediterranean lobster sided by Val Noria fava beans, and a sumptuous John Dory fish served alongside zucchini crushed with olive oil, mesclun salad and a crostini. Before the final act of the show, the table dressing plays Cinderella and turns to white, blue and gold to announce the coming arrival of stars like the delightful chocolate cake garnished with a praline crispy or a rum baba cake just like grandma's. Ducasse summed it all up himself: «The chef's role is to turn something already handsome into something really good.» The sommelier's role is not bad either, with a cellar boasting 250,000 bacchanalian gems to work with. C 800-1,400. M 480 (lunch, wine incl), 810, 920.

 Hôtel de Paris

(See restaurant above)
Open year-round. 59 stes 3,000-10,600. 141 rms 1,900-3,200. Air cond. Heated pool. Beach. Tennis. Valet pkg.
The last of Europe's really grand hotels has been welcoming the rich and famous since it opened in 1865. Completely modernized, it has divinely comfortable rooms, a chic bar, and a lovely indoor pool. But don't expect a warm reception unless you roll up in a...Rolls. The hotel shops are less classy than they seem to think, and the breakfasts are quite ordinary.

 La Pergola

22, av. Princesse-Grace
(377) 93 30 98 80, fax (377) 93 50 23 14
Closed Sun, Mon, Dec. Open until 11pm. Terrace dining. Air cond. Pool. Beach. Valet pkg.
The full flavors of the South of France enlightened by the touch of Raffaele Lauriola: mouthwatering risotto wrapped in country ham and first-rate osso-buco cooked in Dolcetto red wine. Meanwhile in the dining room, the pleasant Italian staff has a good eye for who's who. C 350. M 250 (weekday dinner).

*The **prices** in this guide reflect what establishments were charging at press time.*

Méridien Beach Plaza

(See restaurant above)
*Open year-round. 9 stes 1,600-5,500. 304 rms 800-
2,500. Rms for disabled. Restaurant. Half-board
750-1,600. Rm ser. Air cond. Heated pool. Beach.
Valet pkg.*
This elegant hotel has a private beach, three
swimming pools, and a «sea club» offering a
range of sporting activities. The rooms are spacious and prettily decorated. Private beach. Just
undergone complete renovation, including
swimming pools.

 Le Saint-Benoît

10ter, av. de la Costa
(377) 93 25 02 34, fax (377) 93 30 52 64
*Closed Mon lunch, Dec 22-Jan 5. Terrace dining.
Air cond.*
Marcel Athimon has the distinct advantage of
offering one of the most breathtaking views of
the port and the palatial house, especially for
summer dining on the terrace. Classic cooking
redolent of the sea, but not always on the mark.
Broiled scampi, roast capon with baby
vegetables, seafood fettuccine, dessert cart and
affordable cellar. Prepossessing reception, but
the service has a tendency to drag its feet. M 200
(lunch, wine incl), 165-230

 Sans Soucis

42, bd d'Italie - (377) 93 50 14 24
*Closed Sun off-seas. Open until 11pm. Terrace
dining. Air cond.*
Join the many Italians who flock to this convivial bistrot for uncontrived dishes made with
luminously fresh ingredients. Frisky Italian
wines accompany assorted frittatas, risotto with
cèpes, pasta with dried mullet roe and *tutti quan-
ti.* Good selection of Italian wines. Jolly, swift
service. C 250-400.

And also...

*Our selection of places for inexpensive,
quick, or late-night meals.*
Le Pinocchio ((377) 93 30 96 20 - 30, rue Comte-
Félix-Gastaldi. Open until 11pm, midnight in
summer. Closed Wed off-seas, Dec 10-Jan 20.):
The tiny terrace, near a small square, provides an
attractive setting for supping on freshly-made
ravioli with sage or carpaccio with Parmesan
(100-250).
Polpetta ((377) 93 50 67 84 - 2, rue du Paradis.
Open until 11pm. Closed Tue, Sat lunch, 3 wks
in Feb, 2 wks in Oct.): Everybody who's anybody
shows up here to taste this simple but carefully
prepared, Italian-inspired cooking. You can eat
on the terrace or in the rather small vaulted-ceiling dining room (150-250).
La Piazza ((377) 93 50 47 00 - Rue du Portier.
Open until 11pm. Closed Mon.): A new Italian
restaurant offering pasta with pistou sauce, octopus and bean salad, good basil and tomato
gnocchi, veal scallop, scampi with salt essence,

and a so-so tiramisù. Amiable service and some
nice-price wines, but the décor is lack-lustre.
Pleasant lunching on terrace. (250-320).
Pulcinella ((377) 93 30 71 61 - 17, rue du Portier.
Open daily until 11pm.): An appetizing menu
and fair prices make this one of Monaco's most
popular trattorias (150-220).
Sass Café ((377) 93 25 52 00. 11, av. Princesse-
Grace. Open until 11:30pm. Closed 2 wks in
Nov.): (350).
Il Triangolo ((377) 93 30 67 30 - 1, av. de la
Madonne. Open until 11pm. Closed Sat lunch,
Sun.): The only real trattoria up on The Rock,
offering such fare as basil spaghetti, fettucine
with cèpe mushrooms, and gorgonzola gnocchi.
Smiling staff and a lively time to be had by all
(100-200).

**See also: Cap d'Ail, Roquebrune-Cap-Mar-
tin**

MOUANS-SARTOUX	06370
Paris 910 - Nice 35 - Cannes 13 - Grasse 7	Alpes-Mar.

12/20 **Le Palais des Coqs**

By CD 409, 107, chemin Plan-Sarrain
04 93 75 61 57, fax 04 92 92 91 71
*Closings not available. Open until 9:30pm
(10:30pm in seas). Terrace dining. Pkg.*
The subdued countryside and the peace and
quiet of the flowery park around this house serve
as setting for Honoré Boulicaut's classic cuisine
rather short on imagination. Pâté en croûte,
chicken liver terrine, petits farcis, roast rack of
lamb and classic crêpes Suzette. The wine list
offers little selection of local bottles. M 98 (weekday lunch, wine incl), 135-255.

12/20 **Le Relais de la Pinède**

Route de la Roquette - 04 93 75 28 29
*Closed Wed, Feb. Open until 9:30pm. Terrace
dining. Pkg.*
A modest log cabin in a pine grove, with a
simple, savory menu of inexpensive dishes: try
the veal sweetbreads in mushroom cream sauce,
beef fillet with cèpes, and nougat glacé with
peach coulis. Tiny wine list. M 99 (weekdays),
149-170.

 Le Relais de Sartoux

400, route de Valbonne
04 93 60 10 57, fax 04 93 60 17 36
*Closed Wed off-seas, Nov. 12 rms 295-440. Res-
taurant. Half-board 310 (oblig in seas). Pool. Pkg.*
This *mas* offers a resolutely Provençal atmosphere. The rooms give on to a flower garden and
the decoration pays tribute to the bright colors of
the South.

MOUGINS   06250
Paris 902 - Nice - Cannes 8 - Grasse 11   Alpes-Mar.

12/20   Le Bistrot de Mougins

Pl. du Village - 04 93 75 78 34, fax 04 93 75 25 52
*Closed Wed lunch, mid Nov-mid Dec. Open until
10pm. Terrace dining.*
    A dinner under the vaulted ceiling of one of the
two flowery dining rooms is perfect for a romantic escape. The tune is Provençal, and even
though you get good enough quality for the
money, there are false notes from time to time.
White-beet tourte, pistou soup, saddle of lamb
fondant and old-fashioned apple pie. The second
fixed-price meal offers a wide selection and the
wine list offers well-studied choices. M 125
(lunch), 175.

Clos Saint-Basile

351, av. St-Basile - 04 92 92 93 03, fax 04 92 92 19 34
*Closed Wed, Mar. Open until 10pm. Terrace
dining. Pkg.*
    Charming restaurant-art gallery combined
where Claude Muscatelli expresses his origins
with tasty dishes like fresh cod with tomate confite and saddle of rabbit with goat cheese and
thyme—enough to tingle the tastebuds of even
the tiredest of tourists. Flower-embellished terrace, real Provence-style décor. Refreshing
choice of wines. C 200. M 120 (weekday lunch),
140 (weekday), 185.

La Ferme de Mougins

10, av. St-Basile - 04 93 90 03 74, fax 04 92 92 21 48
*Closed lunch; Mon (exc lunch in summer); winter:
Sun dinner; mid Jun-mid Sep: Wed, Sat. Open until
10pm. Terrace dining. Pkg.*
    The new young chef still needs a little time to
find his bearings after the departure of Thierry
Tiercelin, but he is diligently working in the right
direction. The pan-fried Dublin bay prawns,
herb salad and tomato pistou jus demonstrated
a distinct lack of resolute character, but the turbot in minestrone and cooking jus enhanced
with olive oil were flawlessly cooked. Desserts
were less interesting. We'll refrain from making
harsh judgements awaiting a fresh start, which
has already taken off from the gate with the
surefire ways of the service. Highly attractive
luncheon menu and well-composed wine list. C
400-600. M 165 (lunch), 250-360.

Le Manoir de l'Étang

66, allée du Manoir, route d'Antibes
04 93 90 01 07, fax 04 92 92 20 70
*Closed Mon off-seas, Nov-end Dec, beg Jan-beg Mar.
Open until 9:30pm. Garden dining. Pool. Pkg.*
    Picture a luxurious poolside terrace next to a
splendid manor house. Makes you want to take
a vacation? This is the place for it. There are ups
and downs in the food, however. Last year, we
had to search hard for the merits; they seemed to
have gotten their feet back on the track. Charming welcome, service full of attention, and

cuisine that has come back to life: good lobster
ravioli, excellent lamb and eggplant aumônière,
and iced honey nougat. Wisely well-constructed
wine list, market-inspired set meals (150 F including a half-bottle of Côtes-de-Provence), and
good quality for the price. C 200. M 150 (weekday lunch, wine incl), 190.

Le Manoir de l'Étang

(See restaurant above)
*Closed Nov-end Dec, beg Jan-beg Mar. 2 stes 1,350-
1,600. 15 rms 800-1,000. Pool. Pkg.*
    This sumptuous Provençal dwelling dates
from the nineteenth century; it is set in handsomely groomed grounds and offers airy rooms
(some are huge) with personalized décor and
antique furniture. Five golf courses nearby.

12/20   Le Mas Candille

Bd Rebuffel - 04 93 90 00 85, fax 04 92 92 85 56
*Closed Tue & Wed lunch (exc Jul-Aug), Nov-Mar.
Open until 10pm. Terrace dining. Air cond. Heated
pool. Tennis. Garage pkg.*
    Although this eighteenth-century farmhouse
offers an irresistible charm, the cooking didn't
quite live up to our expectations. The dishes are
well-crafted but uninspired. Quality cellar and
cordial reception. Charming place, especially for
terrace dining on summer evenings. C 350-450.
M 165 (weekday lunch), 195-270.

Le Mas Candille

(See restaurant above)
*Closed Nov-Mar. 2 stes 1,800-2,300. 21 rms 680-
1,180. Restaurant. Half-board 620-795. Rm ser.
Air cond. Heated pool. Tennis. Garage pkg.*
    Bright, comfortable rooms with excellent
facilities look out onto a delightful green
landscape dotted with cypresses, olive trees, and
umbrella pines. Absolute, blessed quiet. Heated
pool; tennis courts. Rather stiff welcome.

Hôtel de Mougins

205, av. du Golf - 04 92 92 17 07, fax 04 92 92 17 08
*Open year-round. 1 ste 1,650. 50 rms 800-1,020. Res-
taurant. Half-board 620-680. Pool. Tennis. Pkg.*
    Scents of lavender and rosemary permeate
these four Provençal *mas* done up like new.
Flower terraces and sunny balconies facing the
pool. Bright attractive rooms.

Le Moulin de Mougins

Quartier Notre-Dame-de-Vie
424, chemin du Moulin
04 93 75 78 24, fax 04 93 90 18 55
*Closed Mon (exc dinner Jul 20-Aug 31), Jan 25-
Mar 9. Open until 8:45pm. Terrace dining. Air
cond. Valet pkg.*
    It would be too easy and in the swim to forget
about Roger Vergé, stellar figure he is on the
other side of the Atlantic, right when he has
decided to revamp his act. He chaperones chef
Serge Chollet who has stamped out a solid path

that brings back celebrities from across the globe again and again, like prodigal sons returning home to wide-open arms. Ultra-fresh artichokes, toothsome sea perch on a bed of honey carrot caramel and earthy wild thyme cream and sweet-garlic croquettes, but we had a special fondness for the farm-raised duckling roasted with baby turnips and served in its jus. Desserts prove more conventional, such as the lemon soufflé with mango sauce. Impeccable, well-oiled service. Bills tend to dig deep into the pocket, but this is still one of the better restaurants in the Riviera. C 1,000. M 520-740.

 Le Moulin de Mougins

(See restaurant above)
Closed Jan 25-Mar 9. 4 stes 1,300-1,500. 3 rms 800-900. Air cond. Valet pkg.
The three rooms and two small suites are delightful and much cheaper than a grand hotel, but harder to book than a place in paradise. Relais et Châteaux.

 Les Muscadins

18, bd Courteline - 04 92 28 28 28, fax 04 92 92 88 23
Closed Tue off-seas, mid Feb-mid Mar, 1 wk in Dec. Open until 10pm. Terrace dining. Pkg.
The bay of Cannes serves as backdrop on the flower-massed terrace of Les Muscadins. Chef Noël Mantel is the «little prince» of Mougins. Picasso used to paint the walls of this modest little hotel on the edge of town, which has now grown up into a quality restaurant offering food rich in its South of France roots. Delicious creamy risotto with baby vegetables, cappuccino-style lentil cream soup with braised-oxtail croutons, stuffed young rabbit, polenta in olive jus, and exquisite langoustines with crispy parsleyed vegetable and a fava-flavored bouillon. Delicate desserts, such as bitter chocolate fondant and almond-milk ice cream. A rare find in the Riviera where the love of the «table» and charming décor are often short-listed. The staff seems to sense your every desire and they try to fulfill it. The cellar rolls in great Bordeaux and they've managed to ferret out some Provence treasures as well. The starting-price set menu makes this one of the best buys in the region. The dining rooms are to be redone this year. C 350. M 175, 240 (in summer), 290.

 Les Muscadins

(See restaurant above)
Closed mid Feb-mid Mar, 1 wk in Dec. 1 ste 1,200. 7 rms 750-950. Half-board 575-800. Rm ser. Air cond. Pkg.
Eight delightful rooms, each one individually decorated and attractively furnished. Sensational marble bathrooms. Charming, intimate bar and lounge.

NANS-LES-PINS
83860
Paris 811 - Toulon 61 - Aix-en-P. 43 - Marseille 41 — Var

 # Domaine de Châteauneuf

N 560, Logis de Nans
04 94 78 90 06, fax 04 94 78 63 30
Closed beg Dec-beg Mar. Open until 10pm. Garden dining. Heated pool. Tennis. Valet pkg.
Beware of the charm: once you arrive, the attraction may be so strong that you might have trouble leaving this eighteenth-century *bastide*, hidden away in its mass of luxuriant peace and quiet. The spell doesn't seem to have any effect on the chefs however, who seem to follow one after the other. Bruno Gazagnaire has been here for a year now, but he hasn't quite managed to eclipse the sometimes inaccurate cooking times, even though he has good quality products to work with, and is backed up by impeccable reception and service and a divine setting. The check for à la carte venturers is a heavy affair. Splendid cellar. It's a shame about the restaurant, because the site, an ocean of green, is truly exceptional, and offers an 18-hole golf course, a huge pool and tennis courts in a sumptuous setting. C 280-350. M 170 (weekday lunch), 230-380.

 # Domaine de Châteauneuf

(See restaurant above)
Closed beg Dec-beg Mar. 5 stes 1,270-2,300. 25 rms 580-1,210. Half-board 570-1,430. Rm ser. Heated pool. Tennis. Valet pkg.
Surrounded by wooded grounds and a superb eighteen-hole golf course, this eighteenth-century residence is decorated in infinite taste with clear, bright colors and fine antiques. Excellent breakfasts and perfect reception. Relais et Châteaux.

NICE
06000
Paris 943 - Lyon 475 - Marseille 188 — Alpes-Mar.

12/20 Actair

Nice Airport, Terminal 1, 2nd floor
04 93 21 36 36, fax 04 93 21 35 31
Lunch only. Open until 3pm. Terrace dining. Air cond. Pkg.
The departure of chef Francis Delucq did not help matters in this restaurant which had never really gotten off the ground. Rich brasserie décor and attentive service. Salmon marinated in dill, zucchini blossoms, fish panaché, apple pie and a few regional wines. M 170-300.

 # L'Allégro

4, pl. Guynemer - 04 93 56 62 06, fax 04 93 56 38 28
Closed Sat, Sun. Open until 10:30pm. Terrace dining. Air cond.

Frescoes depicting the Commedia dell'Arte grace this eating house near the port. No pizzas here: L'Allegro specializes in «real» Italian food. Good, but not to die for, and the prices have leapt up the ladder, so use a calculator when you order if you want to avoid (unpleasant) surprises. C 250. M 120-200 (wine incl), 350 (dinner).

 ## L'Ane Rouge

7 quai des Deux-Emmanuel
01 93 89 49 63, fax 04 93 89 49 63
Closed Wed, Jan 8-15. Open until 10:30pm. Terrace dining. Air cond.
Everything's spiffier here these days. The bright new décor seems to have lit a spark in the kitchen as well, rendering a cuisine that is more exacting than in the past. It was time. Nice-inspired, using products from the sea: roast sardines in racy orange butter sided by semolina cake, palatable sea bream braised with crushed olives and homemade pasta, gently simmered young rabbit and baby vegetables, and refreshing iced marzipan in apricot sauce. The first fixed-price menu offers excellent quality at a very reasonable price. Lunching on the terrace facing the Lympia port. Too bad about the lackadaisical service and brevity of the wine list. C 300. M 148-248.

 ## L'Auberge des Arts

9, rue Pairolière - 04 93 85 63 53, fax 04 93 80 10 41
Closed Sun & Mon lunch (exc hols). Open until 11pm. Terrace dining. Air cond. Garage pkg.
This is one of the best «tables» in Nice. Recent arrival David Faure renders his own well-revised version of the Niçois repertoire, adding two points right out the gate. The renowned bagna cauda is thoroughly à la Faure: crispy celery with lobster, and he has added a plethora of new dishes: marinated sardines and sweet peppers, delectable half-salted cod alongside white-beets in bouillabaise jus, and a lively array of desserts with poignant flavors, such as the hazelnut and rosemary crispy. The *patron* is always around (almost too much). Interesting wine list. C 250-300. M 130 (weekday lunch).

 ## Beau Rivage

24, rue Saint-François-de-Paule
04 93 80 80 70, fax 04 93 80 55 77
Open year-round. 10 stes 1,300-1,800. 108 rms 650-1,000. Rms for disabled. Restaurant. Half-board 880-1,230. Rm ser. Air cond. Beach.
Near the opera and favored by prima donnas. The rooms are charming, air conditioned, and soundproof, and have lovely marble bathrooms. Very warm welcome.

 ## Café de l'Horloge

12, av. Félix-Faure - 04 92 17 53 00 (R)
04 93 80 62 52 (H), fax 04 93 80 40 02
Open daily until 11:30pm. Terrace dining. Air cond. Pkg.

Good brasserie fare with a personal touch from time to time, located in the Aston hotel. Luxury furnishings and decorated in rich, warm colors. Well-wrought «return-from-the-market» dishes: asparagus puff pastry and calamaries, luscious roast John Dory fillet, perky pan-fried artichokes sided with sage Bavarian cream, and delicate desserts such as the warm little hazelnut-praline crêpe. The set meal at 170 F is respectably priced. C 220-260. M 120, 170.

 ## Grand Hôtel Aston

(See restaurant above)
Open year-round. 155 rms 450-1,300. Half-board 575-1,425. Air cond.
Some of the rooms of this plush, modern hotel overlook a square with floodlit fountains. Among the Aston's assets are a beautiful lobby, richly decorated public rooms, and well-equipped (though slightly noisy) accommodations, as well as a rooftop terrace that affords a view of the Mediterranean.

Chantecler

37, promenade des Anglais
04 93 16 64 00, fax 04 93 88 35 68
Closed mid Nov-mid Dec. Open until 10:30pm. Terrace dining. Air cond. Valet pkg.
You may feel you're taking part in *la vie du château*, but you don't have to pay the price, because the 255 F set meal (including wine) is one of the godsends of this pricey city. When chef Alain Llorca moved from his village vantage point to this seaside *palace*, he changed not only his life, but also his cuisine. Though his Italo-Provençal cuisine doesn't always try to take front stage, it rings true in our ear, proffering lilts like the polenta and salt cod velouté topped with pan-fried Perrugini sausage, a really fine Italian-style risotto, grated black truffles, and roasting jus. Also on hand, cooked-to-perfection turbot, fava bean purée, asparagus tip and onion green ragoût, or tender baked lamb with ricotta and sweet marjoram ravioli, artichokes dressed up with fava beans, and tomato en persillade. The show goes on with the dessert—we savored a delectable mango and pineapple au gratin with mango sherbet—and the service is always graciously restrained yet thoroughly attentive. C 500-700. M 205-250 (lunch), 395-560.

Negresco

(See restaurant above)
Open year-round. 21 stes 3,250-7,800. 122 rms 1,300-2,350. Rms for disabled. Half-board 925-1,450. Rm ser. Air cond. Beach. Valet pkg.
Witness to turn-of-the-century wealth and extravagance, the Negresco still oozes luxury and style. The fine old paintings and period furniture would fill an auction room several times over, and there's even a huge chandelier that is listed as a historic monument (its twin hangs in the Kremlin). The 6,000 square meters of rooms and suites require constant maintenance, and the owners spare no efforts to keep them freshly

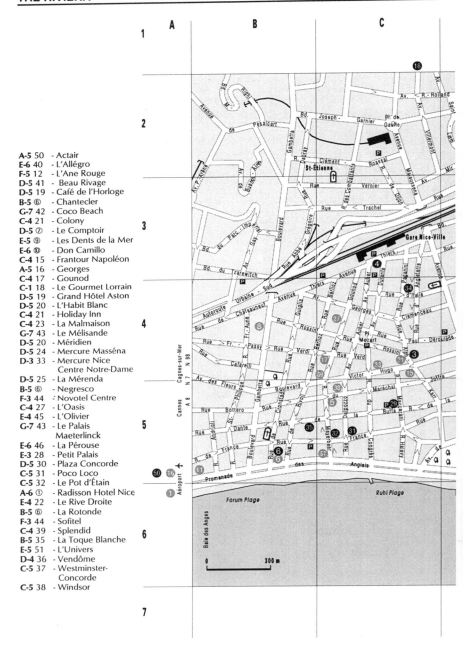

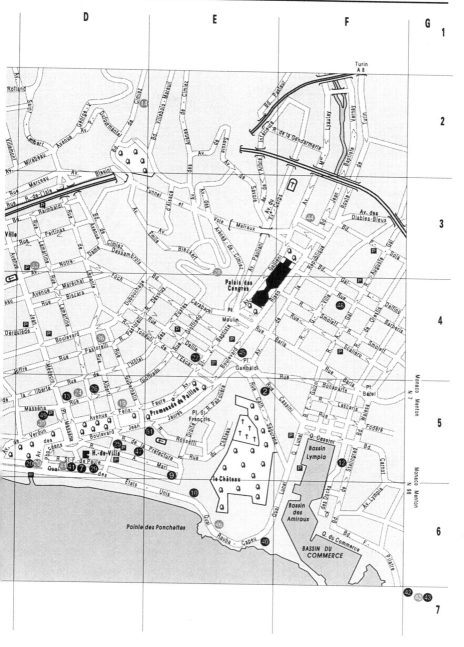

decorated. The riot of color in the guest rooms may not be to everyone's taste but these opulent lodgings provide a glimpse of a more leisured era (as does the much-photographed car attendant in his jaunty plumed hat).

 ## Château des Ollières

39, av. des Baumettes
04 92 15 77 99, fax 04 92 15 77 98
Open year-round. 4 stes 1,350. 4 rms 950-2,800. Rm ser. Air cond. Garage pkg.
If you want to go back in time, say to the Belle Époque, stay at this château, nestled snuggly into its two and one half-acre park, among its multitudinous rare species of trees. It was bought by Prince Lobanov-Rostowsky in 1885 and converted to a hotel in 1990 by current owner Robert Fontana. Overflowing with exquisite wainscoting, silk, ceilings decorated with Pompeii-style frescoes, and objets d'art, the only word to describe this setting is grandiose. Each of the eight rooms are unique and some of the bathrooms resemble theatre decor more than bathrooms. Unfortunately, some of the secret enchantment of the park is ruined by the noise from the expressway. Centrally located around the corner from the Chéret museum.

12/20 Coco Beach

2, av. Jean-Lorrain
04 93 89 39 26, fax 04 92 04 02 39
Closed Sun dinner, Mon, Dec. Open until 10pm. Terrace dining.
The Cauvain family keeps their weather eye open on this promontory towering above the port of Nice and titivates the marine paneling in their restaurant. This fashionable dive serves up baskets of salads, zucchini fritters, broiled fish, and bouillabaisse on special order. The fixed-price menu allows you to stay safely berthed. C 265. M 220 (lunch).

12/20 Colony

20, bd Victor-Hugo
04 93 16 55 00, fax 04 93 16 55 55
Open daily until 10pm. Terrace dining. Air cond. Pkg.
The Holiday Inn restaurant, right smack in the middle of town, doesn't do too badly. Sunny dining room on the ground floor, and a mixture of both classic and Provençal food. You might try the sardine fillet fritters garnished with marinated raw tomatoes or the pan-fried saddle of sea perch and homemade pasta. C 280. M 125-155 (lunch), 178 (dinner).

 ## Holiday Inn

(See restaurant above)
Open year-round. 2 stes 1,600-2,200. 129 rms 550-1,050. Rms for disabled. Rm ser. Air cond. Pkg.
This hotel of recent vintage stands on a broad boulevard in the heart of Nice. It offers fine, thoughtfully equipped rooms (satellite television, minibar, air conditioning) furnished with wicker pieces. Steam bath and sauna.

12/20 Le Comptoir

20, rue St-François-de-Paule - 04 93 92 08 80
Closed Sun dinner. Open until 11:30pm. Terrace dining. Air cond.
A shady terrace just a few steps away from the Cours Sleya, the sea and the Opéra, but you can soak up the beauty of the Arts Déco style dining room on cooler days. Foie gras au torchon, pan-fried colossal shrimp and duck breast.

 ## Les Dents de la Mer

2, rue Saint-François-de-Paule
04 93 80 99 16, fax 04 93 85 05 78
Open daily until 11pm. Terrace dining. Air cond.
A cool terrace shaded by an awning, an upturned boat, and tanks full of fish compose the décor of this chic, popular restaurant strategically located to serve up fish practically straight from the sea: small calamary salad, John Dory fillet, roast sea bream cake and eggplant, and Grand Marnier soufflé. Cellar with strong regional accent, starting from 100 to 120 F. Professional reception. The 148 F set meal helps you save for your retirement. C 300-350. M 148, 199.

 ## Don Camillo

5, rue des Ponchettes
04 93 85 67 95, fax 04 93 13 97 43
Closed Sun, Mon lunch. Annual closings not available. Open until 9:30pm. Terrace dining.
Here in the chic Ponchettes district near Nice's flower market, you'll discover a bright, unassuming restaurant. The Italo-French cuisine lets you sample delectable little ravioli à la daube and white-beets, saddle of lamb speckled with slivers of Parmesan served aside sautéed potatoes, exquisite Tende ewe with fava beans, and citrus fruit chaud-froid. It's not always thoroughly rooted in the region, but always in the spirit of the Niçois countryside and invariably made with superb ingredients. Wide selection of Italian (Piedmont) and Provence wines. The atmosphere is as ever, not very gay... C 300-500. M 200, 320.

 ## Fleur de Sel

18, bd Dubouchage - 04 93 13 45 45
Closed Sun dinner, Mon, Dec 20-Jan 20. Open until 10:15pm. Terrace dining. Air cond.
We almost skipped the 600-calorie meal, but we would have been wrong to do so. The elegant simplicity and culinary astuteness, the considered prices, the highly professional welcome and the short little wine list all give rise to curiosity. Patrice Couderc's cooking is exacting, yet knows how to continually recharge its battery: smoked salmon and chanterelle ravioli, sea bream crépinette sausage with candied garlic and lemon cream, thyme-flavored angler and velvety sweet pepper lasagne, and iced tiramisù with honey caramel. The sunny terrace is a rare find in this downtown area, but the dining room lacks that little cheerful note. This quality at this price livens up the neighborhood, and rightly so. C 200. M 79 (weekdays), 140.

Frantour Napoléon

6, rue Grimaldi - 04 93 87 70 07, fax 04 93 16 17 80
Open year-round. 2 stes 790-1,120. 81 rms 515-1,020. Rms for disabled. Half-board 465-630. Air cond.
This imposing 1930s hotel a stone's throw from the Promenade des Anglais offers good-sized, fairly quiet renovated rooms and a wide array of services.

 Georges

3, rue Henri-Cordier
04 93 86 23 41, fax 04 93 44 02 30
Open year-round. 18 rms 300-450. Rms for disabled. Air cond. Garage pkg.
A little white villa crouched in between the modern buildings near the Promenade des Anglais. Good quality at a reasonable price. Hearty welcome. Hotel customers can take advantage of the Florida beach.

 Gounod

3, rue Gounod - 04 93 88 26 20, fax 04 93 88 23 84
Closed mid Nov-mid Dec. 6 stes 500-790. 42 rms 370-600. Air cond. Pool. Garage pkg.
This pink Belle Époque hotel provides huge, nicely equipped rooms. Friendly reception; a certain old-fashioned charm lingers still.

12/20 Le Gourmet Lorrain

7, av. Santa-Fior - 04 93 84 90 78, fax 04 92 09 11 25
Closed Sun dinner, Mon, Jan 5-12, mid Jul-mid Aug. Open until 9:30pm. Terrace dining. Air cond.
Come into the spacious, tidy dining room of this old-fashioned villa for traditional country cooking based on first-rate ingredients. The cheese board and wine list are sensational, and the welcome is friendly. C 160-250. M 95 (weekday lunch), 150 (Sun).

Grand Hôtel Aston

See restaurant Café de l'Horloge

12/20 L'Habit Blanc

1, promenade des Anglais - 04 93 82 69 16 (R), 04 93 82 25 25 (H), fax 04 93 88 91 29
Open daily until 10:30pm. Terrace dining. Air cond. Pool. Valet pkg.
Even if you normally flee hotel restaurants, give this one a chance. The light and airy dining room looks out to sea, the staff coddles guests with unobtrusive attentions, and the chef makes inventive use of superbly fresh market ingredients. Taste his langoustine salad flavored with vanilla seeds and his zucchini blossoms stuffed with salmon and strewn with baby fava beans, then finish it all off with a strawberry crispy with poignant tastes of lemon and thyme. Cellar rich in costly Southwest wines. Considerable selection of gourmet coffees, teas and herbal infusions. C 300-350. M 240, 280.

 Méridien

(See restaurant above)
Open year-round. 30 stes 2,500-3,000. 290 rms 950-1,450. Rm ser. Air cond. Pool. Valet pkg.
The very modern, well-furnished rooms all boast sea views. There's a piano bar, tea room, admirably appointed fitness center—and the service is perfect.

Holiday Inn

See restaurant Colony

 La Malmaison

48, bd Victor-Hugo
04 93 87 62 56, fax 04 93 16 17 99
Closed Jan 5-Feb 5. 2 stes 550-800. 50 rms 350-650. Restaurant. Half-board 238-334. Air cond. Garage pkg.
A late-nineteenth-century bourgeois house offering velvety-lush drawing rooms, an at-home atmosphere, and a good location near the Promenade des Anglais. The soundproofing needs to be improved, however, as well as the upkeep of the rooms, which are otherwise rather pretty.

 Le Mélisande

Basse corniche, 30, bd Maeterlinck
04 92 00 72 00, fax 04 92 04 18 10
Open daily until 10pm. Terrace dining. Air cond. Pool. Valet pkg.
The splendiferous isolation of this site suited Maurice Maeterlinck to a tee, and he certainly left his mark. The hotel, which sits like a ship anchored between Nice and Villefranche-sur-Mer, captivates a beautiful people audience. So does the food. Laurent Broussier, a former Maximin brigadier, has woken up the hot Southern blood of this restaurant, which has once again turned into an animated spot. Rabbit in jelly and olive salad, tomatoes stuffed with a «mini» ratatouille and goat cheese, red mullets with granulated apples, and macaroni with fresh Parmesan and artichoke shavings. On-the-mark ideas, vivacity and bills that continue to move in the downward direction. This luxury liner hotel is more and more within reach of mere mortals, and even though the service has fallen into decline, we are giving back the point they lost last year. The terrace-patio facing the sea is a pure delight. C 470-600. M 200 (weekday lunch, wine incl), 200 (Sun lunch), 240-700.

 Le Palais Maeterlinck

(See restaurant above)
Closed Jan-mid Mar. 22 stes 2,700-10,000. 14 rms 1,450-2,500. Rm for disabled. Rm ser. Air cond. Pool. Beach. Valet pkg.
Designed by a Swiss financier for his friends and the occasional wealthy traveler bored by the average luxury hotel. Here you can admire a profusion of murals and *trompe-l'œil* paintings

by Serge Megter. Huge terraces, and a private beach, landing stage, and helipad. The superb swimming pool is surrounded by Ionic columns; the amenities include private safes, minibars, VCRs, and satellite TV. Pricey.

Mercure Nice Centre Notre-Dame

28, av. Notre-Dame
04 93 13 36 36, fax 04 93 62 61 69
Open year-round. 1 ste 1,500. 200 rms 525-695. Rm ser. Air cond. Pool. Valet pkg.
A remarkably soundproofed modern hotel in the center of town. The comfortable, redecorated rooms have various amenities that can be conveniently operated by remote control from the bed. The rooftop terrace hosts a bar, swimming pool, and sauna, with a poolside grill from May to October.

Mercure Masséna

58, rue Gioffredo - 04 93 85 49 25, fax 04 93 62 43 27
Open year-round. 116 rms 440-795. Rms for disabled. Pkg.
This fine traditional hotel 500 yards from the sea boasts renovated bathrooms. Modern facilities, plenty of amenities, and meals served in the rooms at all hours. Many deluxe services.

La Mérenda

4, rue de la Terrasse - No phone
Annual closings not available. Open until 9:30pm. Terrace dining. No cards.
You can't book a table here because there's no telephone, the bar-stool seating is uncomfortable, and they don't take credit cards. Nonetheless, Dominique Le Stanc's small restaurant is packed all year with customers eager to taste his racy return-to-roots cooking. Really delicate pizzas, eggplant fritters, tripes à la niçoise, pasta with pistou sauce, and trulle (Niçoise-style black pudding); there's also mesclun salad and daube, of course. A few new dishes, and even a few more wines (before there was only red, white or blush). New ideas include raw fava beans, pancetta and poached egg, and lemon pie. It all sings of olive oil, baby vegetables and simple ideas. Full of flavors and shining with emotion. Authentic cooking at bargain prices. C 180-230.

Méridien

See restaurant L'Habit Blanc

Negresco

See restaurant Chantecler

Novotel Centre

8-10, esplanade du Parvis-de-l'Europe
04 93 13 30 93, fax 04 93 13 09 04
Open year-round. 2 stes 800-850. 171 rms 480-550. Restaurant. Half-board 500-790. Rm ser. Air cond. Pool. Garage pkg.

Situated in the city's new shopping and cultural center. The rooms have been redone, along with the bar and terrace. Pleasant reception, eager service, and a free shuttle service to the airport.

L'Oasis

23, rue Gounod - 04 93 88 12 29, fax 04 93 16 14 40
Open year-round. 38 rms 300-430. Garage pkg.
An oasis of greenery in the center of Nice. The little rooms are clean, quiet and comfortable. Very pretty terrace for relaxing after a long day.

12/20 L'Olivier

2, pl. Garibaldi - 04 93 26 89 09
Closed Wed dinner, Sun, Aug, 1 wk at Christmas. Open until 9:30pm. Terrace dining. Air cond.
This tiny bistro under the most beautiful arcades in Nice serves up hefty portions of Niçois and heartier cuisine. The daily offerings are listed on the blackboard, and include vegetable fritters, tripes, pieds et paquets, green cabbage and Toulouse sausage, daube ravioli and delectable desserts. Short wine list. Eager reception and service looked after by Christian Musso. You can lunch under the arches in the summertime. C 150-200.

Le Palais Maeterlinck

See restaurant Le Mélisande

La Pérouse

11, quai Rauba-Capeu
04 93 62 34 63, fax 04 93 62 59 41
Open year-round. 3 stes 1,690-2,260. 61 rms 415-1,370. Air cond. Pool. Valet pkg.
Set back from the corniche, and just a few steps away from old Nice, yet quiet. The rooms have been redone in cheerful Provençal style and some have a sumptuous view.

Petit Palais

10, av. Emile-Bieckert
04 93 62 19 11, fax 04 93 62 53 60
Open year-round. 1 ste 890-1,290. 25 rms 390-780. Rm ser. Garage pkg.
This Petit Palais sits majestically on a hilltop overlooking Nice. The interior décor follows the lead of the building's handsome Belle Époque architecture: the attractive, well-equipped rooms—with terrace or private garden—boast fine paintings, comfortable armchairs, and superb bathrooms. Very attentive service. Near museums.

Plaza Concorde

12, av. de Verdun - 04 93 16 75 75, fax 04 93 82 50 70
Open year-round. 10 stes 1,300-2,500. 176 rms 600-1,300. Restaurant. Half-board 530-880. Rm ser. Air cond. Beach.
Wonderful rooftop terrace and well-equipped, air conditioned conference rooms. Rooms just redecorated in contemporary style. Bar, grill,

and various shops and services are on the premises.

12/20 Poco Loco

2, rue Dalpozze - 04 93 88 85 83, fax 04 93 88 35 51
Closed Sat & Sun lunch, May 1. Open until 11:30pm (midnight in summer). Terrace dining.
Sip expertly mixed tequila cocktails in a convivial atmosphere, then order from the Mexican menu: enchiladas, nachos, and fajitas are all tasty and inexpensive. C 150. M 50-75 (lunch).

12/20 Le Pot d'Étain

12, rue Meyerbeer
04 93 88 25 95, fax 04 93 87 75 04
Open daily until 11pm. Terrace dining. Air cond.
The price is not the problem, nor the cozy dining room. The problem is the thoroughly bad duck-breast salad and the truly disappointing melon roll stuffed with spinach and smoked salmon. The desserts are worthy and the cellar offers an interesting selection of Provences. C 270-320. M 95.

Radisson Hotel Nice

223, promenade des Anglais
04 93 37 17 17, fax 04 93 71 21 71
Open year-round. 12 stes 1,800-3,500. 321 rms 640-1,290. Air cond. Pool. Valet pkg.
The huge, extremely comfortable rooms of this seafront palace on the Baie des Anges boast loggias with superb views.

12/20 Le Rive Droite

29, rue Saint-Jean-Baptiste - 04 93 62 16 72
Open daily until 11pm. Terrace dining. Air cond.
Authentic Niçois dishes—socca, air-dried beef, onion pizza, great gnocchi, daube and polenta—are featured on a copious 190 F set meal. C 160-250. M 190.

12/20 La Rotonde

Hôtel Negresco, 37, promenade des Anglais
04 93 16 64 00, fax 04 93 88 35 68
Open daily until 11:30pm. Terrace dining. Air cond. Beach. Valet pkg.
This is *the* place to go in the Riviera and what a place with its merry-go-round décor where wooden horses circle round you as you dine. The little 135 and 155 F single-price meals valiantly struggle against the competition next door (Chantecler). Loyal regulars wouldn't change their habits for the world: petits farcis, parsleyed rack of lamb, and sole meunière, nor the bubbly welcome of Jean-Pierre. C 200-250. M 115-155 (weekdays).

Sofitel

2-4, parvis de l'Europe
04 92 00 80 00, fax 04 93 26 27 00
Open year-round. 15 stes 1,100-2,500. 137 rms 860-1,600. Rms for disabled. Restaurant. Rm ser. Air cond. Pool. Garage pkg.

This six-story building just opposite the exhibition center dons a swimming pool and rooftop bar overlooking Nice. High-grade service and comfort, offering in addition a workout room and sauna.

Splendid

50, bd Victor-Hugo
04 93 16 41 00, fax 04 93 87 02 46
Open year-round. 12 stes 1,300-1,750. 115 rms 695-1,190. Restaurant. Half-board 570-820. Air cond. Pool. Garage pkg.
This lovely marble and smoked-glass building on a tree-lined main artery offers rooms with perfect appointments. From the swimming pool to the Jacuzzi on the terrace, you'll discover the rooftops of Nice, and, like a poster, a palm tree with a Mediterranean background.

12/20 La Toque Blanche

40, rue de la Buffa
04 93 88 38 18, fax 04 93 88 38 18
Closed Sun, Mon, Jul-Aug. Open until 9:30pm. Terrace dining. Air cond.
Too bad, because the food is good, but the expensive à la carte menu, the lack of choice on the fixed-price menus, and a stymied atmosphere don't help. Lobster salad, fish panaché with bouillabaisse jus and veal chop with morels. Tasty desserts, such as the two-chocolate cake. Feeble wine list. Amiable reception. C 330-400. M 145-290.

L'Univers

54, bd Jean-Jaurès - 04 93 62 32 22
Closed Sat lunch, Sun. Open until 11:30pm. Terrace dining. Air cond.
Christian Plumail fights like a devil in this Niçois party site in all its splendor of the past, where he tried to make gastronomy and brasserie food live happily side by side. It's difficult to play two tunes at once, and he's tired indeed. But that doesn't mean he's lost his lust for cooking, because his is one of the most straightforwrd and Provençal of any cuisine you'll find. His sardine and zucchini blossom fritters, spiced-up sabayon sea bream with gingery baby broccoli, and stuffed squid à la niçoise sided with baked sweet peppers are devilishly good. The service sometimes drags its feet in this décor that definitely needs resuscitating. Cellar disappointingly devoid of Provence wines. He may fight like a devil to make it good, but his set meal prices are angelic. C 270-320. M 160 (weekday lunch, wine incl), 170.

Vendôme

26, rue Pastorelli - 04 93 62 00 77, fax 04 93 13 40 78
Open year-round. 5 stes 600-900. 51 rms 350-590. Rm ser. Air cond. Garage pkg.
This former town house with its superb staircase, built in the nineteenth century, has been restored in the best of taste. The pleasant rooms are decorated in attractive colors and have hand-

somely designed furniture. Room service (including meal trays); garden.

 ## Westminster-Concorde

27, promenade des Anglais
04 93 88 29 44, fax 04 93 82 45 35
Open year-round. 5 stes 1,000-1,200. 100 rms 500-1,000. Restaurant. Half-board 750-950. Rm ser. Air cond.
Ideally located on the Promenade des Anglais, the majestic Westminster has plenty of character and charm, as well as all the modern conveniences. The service has remained soothingly old-fashioned. Bar.

 ## Windsor

11, rue Dalpozzo - 04 93 88 59 35, fax 04 93 88 94 57
Open year-round. 60 rms 400-670. Restaurant. Half-board 390-640. Air cond. Pool.
A lovely tropical garden and moderate prices make the Windsor a standout. This elegant hotel with superb frescoes in some rooms also boasts modern facilities such as offices for business meetings and a fitness club. Very pleasant bar.

And also...

Our selection of places for inexpensive, quick, or late-night meals.
L'Auberge de Théo (04 93 81 26 19 - 52, av. Cap-de-Croix. Open until 11pm. Closed Mon, Aug 20-Sep 10.): Close to the Matisse and Chagall museums, a charming restaurant that served robustly flavorful Italian food (150-200).
La Cervoiserie (04 93 88 07 71 6 50, rue Trachel. Open until 10:30pm. Closed Sun, Jun, hols.): A real brasserie offering over 150 different kinds of beer. Happy reception and hearty fare: andouillette sausage, carbonade stew, and other beer-based dishes. (92-200)
Chez Pipo (04 93 55 88 82 - 13, rue Bavastro. Dinner only. Open until 10pm. Closed Mon off-seas, Jan 1-15.): A 70-year-old institution serving socca (chickpea pizza), baked in a wood-fired oven and washed down with a glass of red. Picturesque (160).
Choupette (04 93 80 28 69 - 20, rue Barillerie. Open until 10pm. Closed Sun, Jul.): Rustic charm with Southwest (good duck breast) and Southeast (zucchini fritters) inspirations. Interesting cellar and charming reception. (120-220).
Fjord (04 93 26 20 20 - 21, rue François-Guisol. Open until 5pm. Closed Mon.): Refreshing spot, adorable welcome, Scandinavian dishes, carryout available. (90-110).
Le Vendôme (04 93 16 18 28 - 1, pl. Grimaldi. Open daily until 11:30pm.): An authentic bistro serving tasty homestyle cooking (120-150).

OPIO 06 → **Grasse**

*Looking for a restaurant? Refer to the **Index**.*

PEILLON 06440
Paris 953 - Nice 18 - Contes 13 Alpes-Mar.

 ## L'Authentique

04 93 79 91 17, fax 04 93 79 99 36
Closed Wed, Jan 7-24, Oct 20-Dec 20. Open until 9pm (or upon reserv). Terrace dining. Pkg.
After an appetite-rousing trek among the villages perchés of the Niçois hill country, here is a delightful place to regather your strength. At their adorable *auberge* set in a blooming garden, the Millo family welcome walkers with open arms. Sample the chicken liver terrine with onion confit, red mullet fillet with new potatoes, sea bass with wild fennel and a vegetable fondue, and thyme-scented roast lamb. Good cellar, too. C 280-300. M 140 (weekday lunch, wine incl), 200 (weekdays), 240, 280-350 (hols).

 ## Auberge de la Madone

(See restaurant above)
See restaurant for closings. 3 stes 800-1,200. 17 rms 440-800. Half-board 460-700. Rm ser. Tennis. Pkg.
Discover superb scenery at this comfortable country inn, where rooms are attractively decorated with Provençal fabrics. Perfect peace and quiet are assured.

PORQUEROLLES (ILE DE) 83400
Boarding at Cavalaire, Hyères or Toulon Var

 ## Auberge des Glycines

Pl. des Armes - 04 94 58 30 36, fax 04 94 58 35 22
Closed Jan-mid Feb. 12 rms 450-650. Restaurant. Half-board 450-850 (oblig in seas). Garage pkg.
Sprightly, refined country décor, in the true style of Provence, set off with dainty fabrics and light-colored woodwork. All rooms give onto a delight of a patio, shaded by a single fig tree; as you enjoy the comfort of your room, you'll appreciate that someone has thought of not only your every desire, but your every need.

 ## Mas du Langoustier

04 94 58 30 09, fax 04 94 58 36 02
Closed mid Oct-end Apr. Open until 9pm. Garden dining. Tennis. Garage pkg.
Day trippers seldom venture here, for the Mas du Langoustier shelters behind a screen of umbrella pines and eucalyptus trees. This magical site is the preserve of the hotel's residents and moneyed mariners from Le Lavandou or Saint-Tropez, whose yachts weigh anchor in the turquoise-tinted creek below. But you can join them, if you book ahead, on the Mas's lovely terrace or in the big, bright dining room, to savor Joël Guillet's sun-struck cuisine. The menu is a rhapsody of barely tamed Mediterranean flavors: olive oil lemon and violet snail tartare, pan-fried red mullet fillets, sublime almond purée, candied tomato and sea purslane salad,

tuna steak, zucchini gnocchi, candied sweet peppers with baby shrimp, piquant Espelette-pepper onion jus, surpising delicate desserts. We like the beautifully orchestrated dining room management, the incredibly attentive waitresses, and the prudent prices of the wine. Land here in off-season and lose yourself in the peace and quiet among the creeks and the garrigue. C 400.

 ## Mas du Langoustier 🌲♥

(See restaurant above)
Closed mid Oct-end Apr. 3 stes 1,464-1,552 half-board incl. 47 rms 963-1,289 half-board incl. Full-board 158. Tennis. Garage pkg.
An island of Edenic tranquility, pierced only by the murmur of the wind in the pines or the cicadas' creaking song. The 50-odd rooms and suites have been further refurbished; those on the ground floor have private terraces overlooking the water. Air conditioning is provided by the sea breezes, and there's a sandy beach instead of a pool. Two tennis courts; and a heliport, of course.

PORT-CROS (ILE DE) 83145
Var

12/20 Le Manoir

04 94 05 90 52, fax 04 94 05 90 89
Closed Oct-Apr. Open until 9pm. Terrace dining. Pool.
The garden facing the bay is a lovely sight, with its huge white parasols, eucalyptus trees, and dancing butterflies. The immaculate big nineteenth-century *bastide* bordered by a lusciously fragrant garden serves as sapid setting for Sylvain Chaduteau's carefree cuisine rooted in its Mediterranean soil, but which doesn't hesitate to pay friendly visits to other regions from time to time. M 300. M 250 (dinner).

 ## Le Manoir 🌲♥

(See restaurant above)
Closed Oct-Apr. 4 stes & 18 rms 750-1,100, half-board incl.
A charming white colonial-style hotel with large, quiet rooms (cars are banned on the island). Some rooms have private terraces.

PORT-GRIMAUD 83310
Paris 884 - Toulon 32 - Le Lavandou 13 Var

 ## L'Amphitrite

Grand-Rue - 04 94 56 31 33, fax 04 94 56 33 77
Closed Oct 31-Easter. Open until 10:30pm. Terrace dining. Air cond. Heated pool. Beach. Valet pkg.
Chefs come and chefs go (Laurent Carlier only stayed one season). Is it the Gulf or the mistral that blows them hither and there? In any case, it makes it difficult to make a lasting judgment. The predominantly sea-inspired cuisine somehow manages to remain up-to-date and of good

quality, and the beachside site is quiet and highly pleasing, especially if you sit poolside on the terrace on starry evenings. C 250-390. M 135 (lunch), 180-250 (dinner).

 ## Giraglia

(See restaurant above)
Closed Oct 31-Easter. 7 stes 1,600-2,100. 42 rms 650-1,600. Rm ser. Air cond. Pool. Beach. Valet pkg.
A very attractive set of Provençal-style buildings which blend in well with the village. Rooms are spacious, comfortable, and remarkably well appointed. A fine sandy beach, water sports, and excursions into the hills are additional attractions. Magnificent swimming pool and terrace.

RAMATUELLE 83350
Paris 892 - Hyères 54 - St-Tropez 10 Var

12/20 Auberge de l'Oumède

Chemin de l'Oumède, route des Plages
04 94 79 81 24, fax 04 94 79 81 24
Dinner only. Closed end Oct-end Mar. Open until 10:30pm (11:30pm in summer). Terrace dining. Pkg
Lose yourself in the carressing quiet of the vineyard in a flowery Provence *mas* decked out with rush-bottomed chairs and a blue and white décor. The cooking portrays the same country image, but has a few growing pains. On occasion, there's so much time between the dishes that it ruins the whole meal. On offer are sardine and fresh tomato tart, good beef fillet dressed up with candied shallots, and roast sea bream garnished with tapenade and mild peppers. The terrace is very pleasant, but the whole thing is pricey for a place that makes itself out to be a country inn. M 200.

 ## Les Bergerettes 🌲♥

Route des Plages, quartier des Marres
04 94 97 40 22, fax 04 94 97 37 55
Closed Oct-Easter. 29 rms 510-980. Air cond. Pool. Pkg.
This charming hotel, which looks rather like a Provençal *bastide*, is set in a pine wood, facing the beach. The rooms are very appealing, and some have terraces.

Les Bouis 🌲♥

Route de la Plage de Pampelonne
04 94 79 87 61, fax 04 94 79 85 20
Closed Nov-Mar 20. 4 stes 800-1,300. 13 rms 600-1,180. Rms for disabled. Air cond. Pool. Garage pkg.
A group of luxurious buildings in a pine grove dotted around the swimming pool. The attractive rooms have rattan furniture, tiled floors, and private terraces with a sea view. All are air conditioned and have satellite TV.

*For a complete guide to our restaurant **ranking system**, see "Symbol Systems" page 7.*

12/20 Chez Camille

Quartier de Bonne-Terrasse - 04 94 79 80 38
*Closed Tue (exc dinner Jul-Aug), Oct 10-Apr 1.
Open until 9:30pm. Terrace dining. Pkg.*
An excellent bouillabaisse (order it in advance) and perfectly good grilled fish are sufficient reason to stop for a meal and a view of the Bonne-Terrasse Bay. It's not great gastronomy, but the vacation crowd eats it right up. **M** 185-420.

12/20 Chez Madeleine

Route de Tahiti - 04 94 97 15 74
Closed Oct 15-Easter. Open until 10:30pm. Garden dining. Pkg.
Madeleine Serra's children somehow manage to grab the best of the catch from their fishermen friends, even at the height of summer. Wonderful bouillabaisse (order in advance) and bourride, and the fresh fish. Saint-Tropez prices, but an institution worth visiting. **C** 300. **M** 160-230.

Dei Marres

Route des Plages - 04 94 97 26 68, fax 04 94 97 62 76
Closed Nov-mid Mar. 2 stes 550-1,400. 22 rms 300-1,100. Pool. Garage pkg.
Comely modern structure with sunny, well-appointed rooms. Pleasant setting among the cypresses and the olive trees, and just 500 yards from the Lices beach. Some rooms have terraces. Reasonably priced.

La Ferme d'Hermès

Route de l'Escalet - 04 94 79 27 80, fax 04 94 79 26 86
Closed Jan 10-Mar, Nov 3-Dec 27. 8 rms 600-890. Pool. Pkg.
A charming little *mas* in wine country, offering rooms with kitchenettes and a swimming pool set amid the vineyards.

12/20 Ferme Ladouceur

Quartier La Roullière
04 94 79 24 95, fax 04 94 79 12 14
Dinner only. Closed Tue (exc in summer), Oct 20-beg Apr. Open until 10:30pm. Terrace dining.
The food here is concocted by an ex-Moulin de Mougins cook. A charming house girdled by vineyards and a pretty garden serves as backdrop for a cuisine that merits respect. All the more in that the à la carte-style fixed-price meal (sole option) is a very reasonable affair. **M** 165 (wine incl).

La Figuière

Le Pinet, route de Tahiti
04 94 97 18 21, fax 04 94 97 68 48
Closed Oct 6-Apr 3. 3 stes 1,400-1,500. 39 rms 420-950. Rms for disabled. Air cond. Pool. Tennis. Garage pkg.
An old farmhouse set among vineyards, just 300 yards from the sea. Peace, comfort, and an elegant clientele of regulars.

12/20 La Forge

Rue Victor-Léon - 04 94 79 25 56
Closed Tue, Nov 15-Feb 15. Terrace dining.
In a wood and white-wall décor, Pierre Fazio serves up a cuisine full of vigor where fish (broiled or spit-roasted) and shellfish make up the lion's share: langoustine-tail salad in truffle vinaigrette, flavored-up «leaves» of fresh cod, or steamed sea bream fillet. Good selection of Côtes-de-Provence wines. **C** 240-360. **M** 165.

La Garbine

Route de Tahiti - 04 94 97 11 84, fax 04 94 97 34 18
Closed Jan 3-Mar, mid Oct-Dec 25. 20 rms 450-950. Rms for disabled. Air cond. Pool. Tennis. Pkg.
Nice setting: 500 yards from the beach with a little stream running alongside it. With the tile roof and the olive grove, you really get the feeling you're in Provence, even though all the rooms are air conditioned and have a private terrace giving onto the pool.

⌂ L'Hacienda

Quartier des Marres
04 94 56 61 20, fax 04 94 97 05 24
Open year-round. 8 rms 600-1,200. Restaurant. Rm ser. Pool. Pkg.
An attractive Provençal house and veritable oasis of luxury and calm, right near Saint-Tropez and the beaches. The rooms are very comfortable and tastefully furnished. Meals are served only upon request (they're good) in the lovely poolside garden. Very warm welcome and service.

12/20 Moorea

Route de Tahiti - 04 94 97 18 17, fax 04 94 97 24 72
Lunch only. Closed mid Nov-Mar. Open until 4pm. Terrace dining. Garage pkg.
So you want to eat a real meal on the beach? Here's the place to come for tomatoes and mozzarella, Niçoise salad, broiled sea bream, sea perch or lamb chops, on the most sought-after beach in Europe. You even get to sit under a red umbrella... Not a lot of thought put into the wine list, but the local wines are good enough. **C** 250-350.

Tahiti

Le Pinet - 04 94 97 18 02, fax 04 94 54 86 66
Closed mid Oct-Easter. 8 stes 1,180-1,320. 14 rms 660-1,210. Restaurant. Air cond. Pool. Beach. Tennis. Garage pkg.
Leftover hippies will relish this darling little hotel. The owner Félix will greet you in his most graphic manner. Muscle building, boutiques, you name it: everything you need to take you back a few decades.

⌂ La Terrasse

Av. Gustave-Étienne
04 94 79 20 48, fax 04 94 79 28 36
Closed Oct 15-Mar 30. Open until 9:30pm. Terrace dining. Heated pool. Pkg.

The pleasant terrace looks out over the hilltops, vineyards and sea and makes an ideal stop for a dinner in the cool of the evening far from the maddening crowd. The restaurant is recovering its renown of the past with the arrival of Sylvain Humbert. His cooking gets better with age, but remains resolutely Provençal and free of excess—how fitting for this house hanging tightly to its hillside. Both the food and dining room exude radiance: sardine and ratatouille petits farcis in phyllo pastry, squid with tomatoes and polenta, and cumin-spiced pieds et paquets. The wine list may be short, but it is brimming with good taste, especially for the local Provence wines. C 240-350. M 180-270.

Hostellerie Le Baou 🌲♣

(See restaurant above)
Closed Oct 15-Mar 30. 2 stes 1,350-1,600. 39 rms 500-1,250. Half-board 491-1,041. Heated pool. Pkg.
On summer nights, you can eat grilled foods around the beautiful swimming pool. This modern hotel—sitting smack on the edge of a hillside covered in olive trees, cypresses and aromatic herbs, located at the foot of the old village of Ramatuelle—proposes comfortable, sunny, spick-and-span rooms, all with a terrace.

La Vigne de Ramatuelle

Quartier Audrac, route des Plages
04 94 79 12 50, fax 04 94 79 13 20
Closed Nov-Mar. 14 rms 450-1,350. Air cond. Pool. Garage pkg.
The sweet smells of the pine forest envelop you from your private terrace, and all you see round you are vineyards and lawn. This hilltop hotel, a mile and a half from the beach, proposes small but luxurious rooms with relaxing décor. Efficient, charming reception.

ROQUEBRUNE-CAP-MARTIN   06190
Paris 953 - Nice 26 - Menton 5   Alpes-Mar.

12/20 La Dame Jeanne

1, chemin Sainte-Lucie - 04 93 35 10 20
Open daily until 10:30pm. Terrace dining.
Century-old arches put you in the mood for Claude Nobbio's good downhome, Provence-style eating in this house full of old-world character and charm. Try the cèpe risotto, the beef fillet with garlic cream sauce, or the rabbit with rosemary essence on a starry night on the terrace and wash it down with one of the many wines from his well-rounded cellar. C 250-300.

12/20 Au Grand Inquisiteur

18, rue du Château - 04 93 35 05 37
Closed Mon, Tue lunch, Nov 11-Dec 26. Open until 10pm. Terrace dining. Air cond.
The name promises torture, but the only torture you'll find here is having to choose from among Max Valente's tempting dishes, such as squash and mussel casserole, knuckle of ham

with mushroom cream sauce, or red mullet with liver and anchovies. Respectable enough wine cellar. Village sheep-fold converted into restaurant, charming is the only word for the décor. C 200. M 145-215.

Monte-Carlo Beach Hotel 🌲♣

Av. Princesse-Grace
04 93 28 66 66, fax 04 93 78 14 18
Closed Nov 30-Apr 3. 4 stes 2,700-5,500. 41 rms 1,650-2,550. Rms for disabled. Restaurant. Rm ser. Air cond. Heated pool. Beach. Tennis. Valet pkg.
Billionaires lurk behind the splendid curved façade of this luxury hotel with its Olympic-sized swimming pool and service reminiscent of a more leisurely age. The magnificently restored rooms all have loggias overlooking the sea. The luncheon buffet is served on the «La Vigie» covered terrace which affords glorious sweeping views of the Riviera.

Le Roquebrune

100, Corniche-Inférieure
04 93 35 00 16, fax 04 93 28 98 36
Closed Jun-Aug: lunch Mon-Thu; Sep-May: Tue & Wed lunch; Nov 17-Dec 12. Open until 10:15pm. Terrace dining. Valet pkg.
From the terrace or the spacious dining room, well-heeled patrons ooh and aah over the view of Roquebrune Bay. Daniel Tessier handles his magnificent seafood and produce with respect, creating dishes with intense, well-balanced flavors. Warm welcome and excellent service. The cellar is distinguished, but the à la carte prices are crippling. C 500-650. M 170 (lunch), 360.

Le Vistaero

Grande-Corniche - 04 92 10 40 20 (R)
04 92 10 40 00 (H), fax 04 93 35 18 94
Closed Nov 15-Dec 22, Jan 20-Mar 15 (exc groups). Open until 10:15pm. Terrace dining. Air cond. Heated pool. Valet pkg.
This hilltop hotel with its wide-screen view of Monte Carlo and the Italian Riviera is the perfect backdrop for a romantic evening. Jean-Pierre Pestre crafts a lively cuisine served in a newly spiffed up dining room. The broiled John Dory fillet with its macerated fresh herbs, tomatoes, olives and fava beans was exquisite and of the utmost freshness. The beef fillet with morels and truffles was a thoroughly worthy effort, and the chocolate and Cointreau mousse was a delight. The three set-price meals offer discerning choices and are intelligently devised, even though the 350 F menu doesn't even offer cheese. If you venture away from the set path of the fixed-price menus, take an oxygen mask (slip it on before you look at the bill). The cellar is an overwhelming affair that we found difficult to maneuver, since the sommelier didn't show up at our table at order-taking time. Really good service and a Southern cuisine full of intelligence. C 500-800. M 250, 350, 560.

Vista Palace ⚓🍴

(See restaurant above)
See restaurant for closings. 26 stes 1,750-6,000. 42 rms 1,050-1,850. Rms for disabled. Half-board 370. Rm ser. Air cond. Heated pool. Valet pkg.
This exquisitely luxurious hotel pampers guests with large, bright rooms and suites and with what just might be the best view in the Riviera; some have private swimming pools and Jacuzzis. Divine nine-acre garden «suspended» over the sea. Charming, experienced staff; fitness center.

SAINT-JEAN-CAP-FERRAT	06230
Paris 945 - Nice 14 - Monaco 11	Alpes-Mar.

 ## Brise Marine ⚓🍴

58, av. Jean-Mermoz
04 93 76 04 36, fax 04 93 76 11 49
Closed Nov-beg Feb. 16 rms 670-730. Air cond.
This hotel, 100 yards from the beach, has large, rather antiquated rooms, a garden, and terraces for summer breakfasts. Some rooms look out to sea. Pricey.

 ## Le Cap

Bd du Général-de-Gaulle
04 93 76 50 50, fax 04 93 76 04 52
Closed Jan-Feb. Open until 9:45pm (10:15pm in summer). Terrace dining. Air cond. Pool. Beach. Tennis. Valet pkg.
This beautiful establishment, with its glorious veranda and terrace and fifteen acres of peace, happiness and sensual delight, is one of the last remaining grand hotels dating from the Riviera's heyday. Chef Jean-Claude Guillon pampers guests with fresh, light dishes that are luxurious but still identifiably Southern. The cooking times are faultless for dishes such as the pan-fried John Dory fillets sided with sautéed chanterelles and artichoke ragoût and the lovely roast chicken full of the aroma of tarragon. Other dishes are more in tone with the voluptuous setting, yet intelligently up-to-date: broiled red mullets with zucchini blossoms in ratatouille and green gnocchi. Magnificent desserts, and a capital cellar. The reception and service are less attentive and professional than in the past. The check reflects the setting. C 450-580. M 420, 490.

 ## Grand Hôtel du Cap-Ferrat ⚓🍴

(See restaurant above)
Closed Jan-Feb. 11 stes 2,950-10,000. 48 rms 950-3,900. Rms for disabled. Half-board 1,300-3,900. Rm ser. Air cond. Pool. Beach. Tennis. Valet pkg.
This majestic hotel from the Belle Epoque is hidden away in fifteen acres of lawns, copses, and flower beds, but overlooks the sea. A plethora of money has turned this hotel into one of the Riviera's top luxury hotels, complete with an Olympic-size swimming pool. The British decorators who embellished the lounges and rooms have done a bang-up job, creating an atmosphere that is elegant yet relaxed. Rooms offer heavenly comfort with a dream of a balcony. The clientele is younger and less flashy than one might expect. The Le Dauphin restaurant offers poolside dining. Piano bar.

 ## Jean-Jacques Jouteux

2, av. Daniel-Semeria
04 93 76 03 97, fax 04 93 76 05 39
Closed lunch Mon-Wed. Open until 11pm. Terrace dining. Air cond.
There are those times in life when you are moved by what you see before you because never in your wildest dreams did you think such things could become reality. It takes a visionary, a magician, an artist not bound by the limits of convention to create the food you'll relish here: that is our label for Jean-Jacques Jouteux. Need more adjectives? Overcome with emotion at the wild but successful juxtaposition of ingredients we partook in this lovely dining room adorned with walls painted in classic Italian style. God touched his hand when he cooked the foie gras and iced rabbit with figs and Balsamic vinaigrette. He was still present when he prepared the monkfish and eggplant, Provençal au gratin and basil-scented veal jus and the saddle of lamb in a crust of spices garnished with on-the-spot potatoes au gratin, and was still certainly hovering over him when he deftly crafted the full-flavored acidulous mixed-berry au gratin in orange and Grand Marnier butter. Turning dreams into reality never comes cheap though...unless you try the admirable 190 F set meal, which gives a glimpse of this chef's brilliance. The (costly) cellar you dream of owning, but you'll have to search hard for Provence wines. Efficient attentive service. C 450-600. M 190-350.

 ## Panorama

3, av. Jean-Monnet
04 93 76 31 00, fax 04 93 01 23 07
Closed Dec-Feb. Open until 10:30pm. Garden dining. Air cond. Pool. Beach. Tennis. Valet pkg.
The views of the bay and the Villa Kerylos are so spectacular, especially at night, that it is easy to be distracted from your food. Which would be a pity, because Yves Merville's cooking is a marvel of harmony and balance. A recent feast here brought country-style with the peasant-style vegetable soup with lard and pistou and the Riola farm-raised chicken roasted with aromatics and accompanied by white-beets in jus, and sea-inspired with the delicious small strips of roast John Dory, clam broth and basil gnocchi. Desserts by Christian Faure, one of the best pastry chefs in the Riviera: divine citrus fruit tart with semi-candied orange supreme and tangerine sherbet. The cellar holds a trove of fine regional wines. Service is full of attention but sometimes shy. Discover the 230 F return-from-the-market menu for *la vie du château* at a working man's price. C 400-600. M 230 (wine incl), 290 (Jul-Aug), 390.

Royal Riviera

(See restaurant above)
Closed Jan-Feb. 5 stes 3,100-5,000. 72 rms 790-2,990. Rms for disabled. Rm ser. Air cond. Pool. Beach. Tennis. Valet pkg.
This superb Belle Époque hotel has been impeccably renovated and is one of the choicest on the coast. The best of these luxuriously appointed rooms overlook the garden and the magnificent pool. Private beach.

 Le Sloop

At the marina - 04 93 01 48 63
Closed Wed off-seas, Nov 15-Dec 15. Open until 9:30pm (10:30pm in summer). Terrace dining. Pkg.
A nice surprise to find this right on the seaside. Extremely charming welcome, well-kept dining room, and excellent quality for the money for the set-price meals. Chef Alain Therlicocq steers a straight course in this fashionable but dreary port. Delicious langoustine sauté dressed up with asparagus salad in Balsamic vinaigrette, flawlessly cooked sea perch, chilled lobster risotto and fried Italian parsley, a more conventional tulip pastry filled with vanilla ice cream and local strawberries, and a cellar offering good regional samples starting from 145 F. All well turned-out, inexpensive, beautifully presented and served with care. C 270-400. M 155.

 La Voile d'Or

At the marina
04 93 01 13 13, fax 04 93 76 11 17
Closed Nov-Mar. Open until 10:30pm. Garden dining. Air cond. Pool. Beach. Valet pkg.
With Denis Labonnein the kitchen, this traditional establishment can keep its letters patent of nobility and hold on to its image of family luxury hotel, lending it a noble clientele made up of captains of industry, rich families and crowned sovereigns. Labonne is in step with the rhythm of this Florentine universe with its superb terrace jutting dramatically out over the sea, especially his seasonally-inspired set-price meal at 340 F. Delicious foie gras with acidulous sauce (although the scampi right in the middle was not a welcome addition) and roast asparagus barded in lard; cooked-to-perfection breast of roast pigeon with garden delights—string beans, bacon bits and pearl onions; and chocolate and orange marmalade with Grand Marnier sauce. Your money is wisely spent, despite the fact that the heights of these cliffside cellar prices might give you vertigo, but the sommelier proffers wise advice. We had an exceptional Château Lagrande 1989. Discreet service that takes extra-good care of you. C 400-800. M 250 (lunch), 290-340.

 La Voile d'Or

(See restaurant above)
Closed Nov-Mar. 4 rms 4,260. 41 rms 580-2,660. Half-board 360. Air cond. Pool. Beach. Valet pkg.

An Italian villa and its luxuriant gardens overlooking the harbor. The interior is highly decorative, with *trompe-l'œil* paintings, fine fabrics, and marble everywhere you look. Countless services and amenities.

***See also:* Beaulieu**

ST-MARTIN-DU-VAR   06670
Paris 970 - Nice 27 - Antibes 34   Alpes-Mar.

 Issautier

3 km S on N 202 - 04 93 08 10 65, fax 04 93 29 19 73
Closed Sun lunch Jun 28-Sep 13, Mon, Jan 5-Feb 3, Oct 12-20. Open until 9:30pm. Terrace dining. Air cond. Pkg.
Sun-gorged seasonal produce from the hilly Niçois hinterland is the keynote of Jean-François Issautier's full-bodied cooking. His 260 F prix-fixe menu is unbeatable. The peasant's bliss, for example, consists of exquisite fava beans served as a warm salad, sautéed calamaries, and country-style salt pork, or creamy Parmesan polenta, fish of the day and chicken jus with cèpes, or a flawlessly cooked roast John Dory with tomato jus, olive oil mashed potatoes, and pistou sauce. Desserts remain country with a fruit chaud-froid au gratin topped with lemon sorbet. The accessibly priced cellar holds a wonderful cache of Provençal wines (the Clos Saint-Joseph is a sure bet). Excellent coffee. Madame Issautier greets you with a smile, and the service is reliable and low-key. C 435-585. M 250 (lunch, wine incl, exc Sun & hols), 320, 515.

SAINT-PAUL-DE-VENCE   06570
Paris 925 - Cannes 27 - Nice 20 - Antibes 16   Alpes-Mar.

 La Brouette

830, route de Cagnes - 04 93 58 67 16
Closed Sun dinner, Mon, 2 wks in Feb, 2 wks in Oct. Open until 11pm. Garden dining. Air cond. Garage pkg.
Brigitte, Ole Bornemann, and their son Michel, serve authentic Danish specialties in a lively, pleasant atmosphere. Opt for a seat near the fireplace in winter, or in the garden when the weather warms up, for its great view of the village and a barbecue where fish are smoked. Sample the tasty liver terrine with cucumber confit, trout smoked with dill, and leg of Greenland reindeer. Expansive welcome. C 170. M 95 (weekday lunch), 148.

12/20 La Colombe d'Or

Pl. du Général-de-Gaulle
04 93 32 80 02, fax 04 93 32 77 78
Closed beg Nov-Dec 20. Open until 10pm. Terrace dining. Heated pool. Valet pkg.
Picture a paradise for art lovers, with works by Picasso, Rouault, Léger, Miró and others adorning the walls. Come here to enjoy the leafy terrace and garden, and some very simple but

pricey Provençal food (rack of lamb, chicken fricassée with morels, almond tart spiked with sweet Beaumes-de-Venise wine). C 350-450.

La Colombe d'Or

(See restaurant above)
Closed beg Nov-Dec 20. 10 stes 1,550. 16 rms 1,350. Rms for disabled. Half-board 1,750-1,950. Air cond. Heated pool. Sauna. Valet pkg.
This warmly welcoming Provençal hotel is very tastefully decorated. The rooms are delightful. Superb swimming pool.

La Grande Bastide

1350, route de la Colle
04 93 32 50 30, fax 04 93 32 50 59
Closed Jan 8-Mar 15, Nov 15-Jan 8. 4 stes 750-950. 6 rms 550-750. Air cond. Heated pool. Pkg.
This bastide sits happily on the hilltop on the road leading into the village. Beautifully renovated, it offers rooms of varying sizes, all decorated with bright Provence-style fabrics. Some have mezzanines. Friendly welcome. Too bad the pool and garden are so small.

Le Hameau

528, route de La Colle-sur-Loup
04 93 32 80 24, fax 04 93 32 55 75
Closed Jan 8-Feb 15, Nov 16-Dec 22. 3 stes 730-800. 14 rms 410-640. Pool. Pkg.
The old village towers over this absolutely charming Provence-style farmhouse offering prettily-decorated rooms and small independent apartments. Surrounded by a plum orchard.

Hostellerie des Messugues

Domaine des Gardettes, impasse des Messugues
04 93 32 80 12, fax 04 93 32 94 15
Closed Oct-Mar. 15 rms 450-650. Rms for disabled. Pool. Pkg.
Just outside the village, deep in a pine grove, stands this comfortable, attractively decorated hotel. Good rooms, pretty baths.

Mas d'Artigny

Route de La Colle
04 93 32 84 54, fax 04 93 32 95 36
Open daily until 10pm. Garden dining. Heated pool. Tennis. Valet pkg.
The largest dining room in this huge, rambling building sports a warm and colorful Provençal décor. All the better to put diners in the mood for Francis Scordel's subtle, sunny cooking with a personality all its own. Delectable marinated mussels, tomato sauce bound with cream, olive oil and basil; toothsome panaché of five fish; young rabbit round and semolina gnocchi; wonder of a cheese platter; and cherry clafouti. The cellar is amply lined and the service impeccable. All this together adds two points well deserved. C 450-600. M 290, 395.

Mas d'Artigny

(See restaurant above)
Open year-round. 29 stes 1,760-2,700. 55 rms 525-1,850. Half-board 730-1,335. Rm ser. Air cond. Heated pool. Tennis. Valet pkg.
The rooms and poolside suites have all it takes to make you feel like a millionaire. There are several marvelous multi-room villas scattered among the twenty acres of pines.

Le Saint-Paul

86, rue Grande - 04 93 32 65 25, fax 04 93 32 52 94
Closed Nov-Easter: Wed & Thu lunch. Open until 10pm. Terrace dining. Air cond.
Olivier Borloo made the right choice when he set up shop in this sixteenth-century house in the heart of town—his exquisite renovations and the flowery terrace on the edge of the ramparts make this a madly charming place to slide down a midsummer night's meal. Frédéric Buzet holds strong with the excellent price-quality ratio of his first set meal, even if the Provençal simplicity sometimes slips away. Insipid salt cod brandade and broiled apples, duck breast in gibier sauce, rosemary crème brûlée, fresh cheese and mixed berries and a gigantic almond tuile wafer cookie. Handsome selection of cheeses, ready and willing service (but sometimes overworked), and harshly priced wine. The house is lovely—fireplace in the drawing room, collection of ceramic barbotines—and the good efforts should continue, because they've already added a point this year. C 300-500. M 185 (weekday lunch), 290-420.

Le Saint-Paul

(See restaurant above)
Open year-round. 3 stes 1,300-2,500. 15 rms 750-1,500. Rms for disabled. Half-board 1,245-1,890. Rm ser. Air cond.
This delightful hotel dates from the Renaissance. Its freshly refurbished rooms are most attractive and comfortable (those with a view of the countryside are the best), and the service is very good indeed. There's also a library, and a bar. It's not easy to get to, but the receptionist will know how to make it all work out fine, even the parking. Relais et Châteaux.

■ **In La Colle-sur-Loup 06480**   *3 km SW on D 7*

Le Diamant Rose

Route de St-Paul - 04 93 32 82 20, fax 04 93 32 69 98
Closed Nov 15-Dec 20. Open until 10pm (11pm in summer). Terrace dining. Air cond. Pool. Valet pkg.
Antoine Versini transformed a sumptuous villa at the foot of Saint-Paul-de-Vence into a restaurant with a princely dining room and a luxurious panoramic terrace. Chef Daniel Ettlinger takes immense pains with his classic cuisine—check out his eggplant and season's vegetable gazpacho; his faultlessly cooked broiled sea perch with spinach, candied onions

and asparagus; the roast porgy (on the dry side); and the delectable chocolate fondant, nougatine and crème caramel. Beautiful dining on the terrace on starry summer nights. All the best Provençal wines are represented in the costly cellar, but there is no sommelier to give you advice. The prices remain viable if you stick with the country-style dishes. C 300-600. M 240 (wine incl).

 ## Domaine du Diamant Rose ★♣

(See restaurant above)
Open year-round. 15 stes 960-2,500. Rm for disabled. Half-board 950-1,750. Rm ser. Air cond. Pool. Valet pkg.
The accommodations are housed in a cluster of independent Provençal-style villas, all impeccably equipped and luxuriously decorated in the best of taste. The peace and quiet of a golden pond. Gorgeous swimming pool.

SAINT-RAPHAËL	83700
Paris 892 - Cannes 44 - Toulon 96	Var

 ## L'Arbousier

6, av. de Valescure
04 94 95 25 00, fax 04 94 83 81 04
Closed Tue, Wed (exc dinner in summer), Dec 17-Jan 3. Open until 10pm. Terrace dining. Air cond.
Happily ensconced in a pretty town house with a garden and terrace. Madame greets you with a bubbly welcome and the service is deft and on the ball, but too bad about the sad sick green backdrop of the dining room. Chef Philippe Troncycombines keen flavors with inventive flair: his is a resolutely modern version of Provençal cuisine. The 140 F fixed-price menu is unsurpassable, offering ewe's milk Brousse cheese and country ham ravioli in pistou sauce, or gently roasted leg of young rabbit. Not only wise prices, but exactingess of technique: remarkable potato pancake and Upper Var truffles with broiled scallops, racy pan-fried red mullet canneloni with squid ink and chanterelles, and flawlessly cooked rack of lamb roasted with browned garlic and potatoes livened up with salt essence. Desserts of a delicate nature, like the black sesame crisp or strawberry and lime millefeuille, and handsome selection of cheese. Summer dining is delightful on the garden terrace. Capital cellar, fairly priced, with many half-bottles. C 340-390. M 140 (weekday lunch), 180-310.

 ## Golf-Hôtel de Valescure ★♣

Valescure Golf course, av. Paul-Lhermite
04 94 52 85 00, fax 04 94 82 41 88
Closed Jan 7-31, Nov 15-Dec 22. 40 rms 470-970. Rms for disabled. Restaurant. Half-board 545-840. Air cond. Pool. Tennis. Pkg.

Snuggled into the peace and quiet of a lovely forest of umbrella pines and facing the greens, you'll curl up comfortably in these enormous rooms full of light and offering all the appointments necessary. Archery courses and practice in the park.

 ## Le Jardin de Sébastien

595, av. des Golfs - 04 94 44 66 56, fax 04 94 82 40 55
Closed Sun dinner & Mon off-seas, 2 wks in Jan, 2 wks in Nov. Open until 10:30pm. Terrace dining. Garage pkg.
On a starry summer's night, reserve a table on the terrace by the fountain and dine to the soothing sound of the water. Chef Sébastien Arfeuillère has grounded himself here after a long stay in one of the finer kitchens of France. He is following in his master's footsteps by offering market-fresh ingredients crafted with the tenderest of loving care and a skilled and nimble hand: toothsome clam and red mullet risottos, delectable pan-fried saddle of cod, saddle of young rabbit, or lobster lasagne. The wine list evokes mainly local bacchanal delights; we liked the Domaine des Planes and the Châteaux Sainte-Roseline. The set-price meals are extremely meritorious. C 250-300. M 150 (weekday lunch, wine incl), 190-295.

 ## Pastorel

54, rue de la Liberté
04 94 95 02 36, fax 04 94 95 64 07
Closed Sun dinner, Mon lunch in Aug. Open until 10pm. Terrace dining.
Take a terrace table if you can. There you'll enjoy even more Charles Floccia's updated traditional dishes from the Provençal repertoire, available on a variety of well-designed, fairly priced set meals. Lots of customers in season, but the welcome is always cordial. Good selection of local wines. M 100 (weekday lunch, wine incl), 160, 195.

 ## La Potinière ★♣

5 km E on N 98, Boulouris
04 94 19 81 71, fax 04 94 19 81 72
Open year-round. 4 stes 560-1,350. 24 rms 290-790. Restaurant. Half-board 430-535 (oblig in seas). Heated pool. Garage pkg.
A large villa lazing in the middle of eucalyptus and umbrella pines. Peace and quiet are on the agenda in this little corner a little away from the seaside. The major renovation has made this into a pleasant place.

Les Arcades

Hôtel Byblos, av. Paul-Signac
04 94 56 68 00, fax 04 94 56 68 01
*Closed mid Oct-mid Mar. Open until 10:30pm
(11:30pm in summer). Terrace dining. Air cond.
Heated pool. Valet pkg.*
　The Byblos has finally had a face-lift (it was
time!). No revolution in the kitchen, however.
One can still depend on chef Philippe Audibert,
because he's steadfastly no-frill and serious
about what he does. This is the way it should be,
even if we did find his cooking a little less incisive than in the past. The tastes are marked by
steady continuity from the roasted verbena John
Dory, citrus fruit jus and spinach buds, to the
more successful capon fricassée with chanterelles, white-beets and fennel, and still with the
fresh figs with almonds napped with wine and
red currant sauce (lacking all contrast). One
point less for the animation and simplicity that
has gently slipped under the rug, but perhaps
not forever lost. Well-selected regional wines,
but few in number. C 450-550. M 190 (lunch),
240-410.

 Byblos

(See restaurant above)
*Closed mid Oct-mid Mar. 55 stes 2,700-6,500. 47
rms 900-2,950. Half-board 415. Rm ser. Air cond.
Heated pool. Valet pkg.*
　A mythical venue, where everyone who's
anyone in Saint-Trop' eventually shows up,
either at the magnificent pool or the trendy disco.
The hotel's layout is so skillful that customers are
not bothered by the bustling attendance of Saint-
Tropez's gilded set. Extremely luxurious appointments.

 Auberge des Maures

4, rue du Docteur Boutin
04 94 97 01 50, fax 04 94 97 18 35
Closed Jan-Feb. Open until 11pm. Terrace dining.
　Modern, light cooking in this lovely little inn
with simple but well-prepared, regionally-inspired dishes such as steamed monkfish with a
really fine-tuned aïoli sauce, first-rate broiled sea
bass and velvety frozen nougat. The reception is
only skin deep, but the service proves to be
relaxed yet efficient. Friendly prices for Saint-
Tropez. C 250-300. M 220 (wine incl), 300.

Bastide de Saint-Tropez

See restaurant L'Olivier

 La Bastide des Salins ⚏♨

Route des Salins - 04 94 97 24 57, fax 04 94 54 89 03
*Open year-round. 1 ste 1,200-2,200. 14 rms 750-
1,400. Air cond. Rm ser. Pool. Garage pkg.*
　A nineteenth-century *bastide* just spiffed up
this year and located in an enormous park just
300 yards from the beach. Spacious well-appointed rooms.

The Beaches

***Generally open from Easter to October,
for lunch only.***
Bora-Bora (04 94 97 19 75 - Plage de Pampelonne.
Lunch only. Closed mid Oct-beg May.): A
relaxed atmosphere where you can eat a hearty
lunch on La Mandarine's private beach as you
twitter your toes in the water...(160-180).
Club 55 (04 94 79 80 14 - Plage de Pampelonne.
Lunch only. Closed Nov 11-Mar, exc Christmas
& Feb school hols.): Fried fish combo plates and
broiled fish. Local wines. Lost in the pine trees
behind the bamboo arbor (250-350).
Tropicana (04 94 79 83 96 - Chemin de Bonne
Terrasse. Lunch only. Closed Oct 10-Mar 21.):
Wide selection of regional specialities at reasonable prices (considering where you are!) in this
simple little restaurant full of good cheer (250).
La Voile Rouge (04 94 79 84 34 - Plage de
Ramatuelle.): This restaurant serves well-
prepared food made from market-fresh ingredients and served by a youthful (and
beautiful) staff. Salads, artichokes with parsley
sauce, etc. (300).

 Bistrot des Lices

3, pl. des Lices
04 94 97 29 00, fax 04 94 97 76 39
*Closed Sun dinner, Wed off-seas, Jan 15-Mar 15,
Nov 15-Dec 15. Open until 10:30pm. Garden
dining.*
　From the terrace, diners can admire the skill of
local *boules* players; inside, there's an intimate
dining room that leads out to a walled garden
and tables shaded by parasols. Breton native
Laurent Tarridec presides over this smart, *très
tropézien* scene. One of our taste testers had an
unexplicably botched meal, and others noted
inconsistencies—thus the drop of a point. That
doesn't mean we've changed our mind about the
capabilities of this great chef whose cuisine is full
of wholehearted devotion and personality.
While so many menus in the Riviera are redun-
dant copies of a fashionable but commonplace
Provençal cuisine, Tarridec brings forth genuine,
intense flavors, brought to life again and again
in new and different ways, ever digging into his
bottomless well of creativity. On our last
anonymous stop, he more than made up for the
inexplicable lapses and proved with vim and
vigor that his talent is still intact, whether it be
foamy buckwheat soup with shellfish; sautéed
vermicelli and freshwater crayfish; porgy steak
with olives, lemon, candied tomatoes, garlic,
potatoes and artichokes; or rabbit compote—
dishes that are brimming with inventiveness yet
full of motherly savors—he is the king of slowly
simmered vegetables. A model cellar flowing in
regional crus, a thoroughly Saint-Tropez atmosphere, but not too pretentious...there's not really
any reason to worry. C 600. M 195 (lunch), 150
(wine incl), 325.

Le Byblos
See restaurant Les Arcades

 Les Capucines

Domaine du Treizain
04 94 97 70 05, fax 04 94 97 55 85
Closed Nov-Mar. 24 rms 400-1,100. Pool. Pkg.
A complex of little Provence-style houses perched on a pine-covered hilltop and overhanging the sea. Each house is modern and set apart from the others. Quiet.

12/20 Le Carpaccio

N 98, chemin de Gassine
04 94 97 48 98, fax 04 94 97 16 01
Closed mid Oct-beg May. Open until 10:30pm. Terrace dining. Air cond. Pool. Tennis. Pkg.
We prefer the carpaccio version by the pool, under the shade of the palm trees—an oasis offering exotic charm in absolute peace and quiet—to the fancy *boiseries* of the hotel dining room. The cooking is summery and light, Italo-Provençal style with no affectation. Basil beef carpaccio, broiled scampi, broiled sea perch and artichokes, and perfecto anise ice. For those moments when you need to get away from the folies of Saint-Tropez. C 250-350. M 190 (dinner, wine incl), 290.

 Domaine de l'Astragale

(See restaurant above)
Closed mid Oct-beg May. 34 rms 1,150-2,250. Rms for disabled. Rm ser. Air cond. Pool. Beach. Tennis. Pkg.
Luxurious accommodations set in beautiful grounds around the pool; rooms on the upper floor have balconies, while those below give directly onto the garden. Access to the private Bouillabaisse beach and restaurant.

 Château de la Messardière

Route de Tahiti - 04 94 56 76 00, fax 04 94 56 76 01
Closed beg Nov-end Mar. Open until 10:30pm. Terrace dining. Air cond. Heated pool. Valet pkg.
Once shipwrecked on the shoals of ambition, this curious, enormous turn-of-the-century villa is now seaworthy again. The cuisine served in the chintz-decked dining room (and on the terrace with a splendid view of the Bay of Pampelonne) is the work of Franck Broc, who is starting to stand firm on his feet. We're sorry about the crispy chicken: the sage and savory can't hide the flawed cooking time. All is not lost, however, because the desserts are delightfully scrumptious. The reception is still a pure delight, but it gives way to a cold, mechanical team of robot-like waiters and waitresses. Even if we live in a world chock-full of robots, this is over the edge. Some quick emergency repair is definitely in order. C 500-600. M 240-420 (dinner), 280.

 Château de la Messardière

(See restaurant above)
Closed Nov-end Mar. 20 stes 2,600-12,000. 70 rms 800-3,100. Rms for disabled. Half-board 380. Rm ser. Air cond. Heated pool. Valet pkg.
A pastiche of different styles—Disney-style belfries, Moorish arcades, and Florentine columns—set in a 20-acre park towering proudly over the Gulf of Saint-Tropez, the Ramatuelle vineyards and the Pampelonne beaches. All decorated in interesting ochre, yellow and pink cameo style. Magnificent pool.

Domaine de l'Astragale
See restaurant Le Carpaccio

12/20 L'Échalote

35, rue du Général-Allard
04 94 54 83 26, fax 04 94 97 18 71
Closed Thu lunch off-seas, Nov 15-Dec 15. Open until 11:30pm. Terrace dining. Air cond.
A certain laxity has set in in the classic cooking of François Calderon; he watches less closely over his cooking times. Still on offer are foie gras au torchon, house-made black pudding, beef steak with shallot sauce, fresh cream cheese and blue cheese straight from the churn. The food from «foreign» regions proves heavy at times. Amiable welcome and splendiferous little inner courtyard where you can eat in the summer. C 210-350. M 98-150.

 Ermitage

Av. Paul-Signac - 04 94 97 52 33, fax 04 94 97 10 43
Open year-round. 1 ste 590-990. 25 rms 290-890. Valet pkg.
From the garden of this white 1930s villa on Place de Lices at the foot of the citadel, guests enjoy a sweeping view of old Saint-Tropez. The smallish rooms are decorated in a plush, comfortable style.

12/20 Le Girelier

Quai Jean-Jaurès - 04 94 97 03 87, fax 04 94 97 43 86
Closed Oct 10-Mar. Open until 10:30pm. Terrace dining. Air cond.
With its lovely navy-blue terrace giving on to the port, you can slip down sinfully fresh grilled fish and other sagely classic Provençal fare. The cellar rings of Provence, and is fairly well in tune, in a rather tourist-free environment. C 250-450. M 180.

Les Lauriers

Rue du Temple
04 94 97 04 88, fax 04 94 97 21 87
Closed mid Jan-mid Feb. 18 rms 275-575.
Here's a quiet little establishment near Place des Lices, with a garden and freshly redecorated rooms.

 ## Le Levant

Route de Salins
04 94 97 33 33, fax 04 94 97 76 13
Closed Oct 11-Mar 22. 28 rms 395-875. Pool. Garage pkg.
Sweet little bungalows offering charming, tastefully renovated rooms and located on a country road. Direct access to the sea.

 ## Hôtel des Lices

Av. Augustin-Grangeon
04 94 97 28 28, fax 04 94 97 59 52
Closed Jan 5-Feb school hols, Nov 12-Dec 26. 41 rms 300-1,600. Restaurant. Half-board 530-1,070. Air cond. Pool. Valet pkg.
All-new bathrooms, a freshly renovated terrace, a brand-new Jacuzzi, solarium, and outdoor bar, and renovated rooms add to the attractions of this impeccably kept hotel just steps away from Place des Lices.

 ## Lou Troupelen

Chemin des Vendanges
04 94 97 44 88, fax 04 94 97 41 76
Closed end Oct-Easter. 45 rms 330-499. Pkg.
These two roomy neo-Provençal buildings are located between the shore and the town center. Lodgings are comfortable and pleasantly decorated, with attractive views. Breakfast is served in the quiet, shady garden.

 ## La Maison Blanche

Pl. des Lices - 04 94 97 52 66, fax 04 94 97 89 23
Open year-round. 1 ste 1,200-1,800. 7 rms 550-1,800. Rm ser. Air cond. Valet pkg.
This turn-of-the-century residence in the center of town is flanked by a tiny garden, where a bar is set up in summer. Pleasant, tasteful décor and atmosphere, antique furniture. Very attentive service.

12/20 La Maison de Marie

26, rue des Charrons - 04 94 97 09 99
Closed Mon off-seas, Jan. Open until 10pm. Terrace dining.
A typically Saint-Tropez style house with its two magnolias in the yard, although the prices are not all so typical as that. A must. Savor this totally Mediterranean cooking made from only the highest quality ingredients: soupe au pistou, stuffed squids, lasagne, garlic chicken, honey and almond cake. And it's so inviting, you might forget whether you're in a restaurant or at home in your own kitchen. C 230-270. M 89 (lunch, wine incl), 150.

 ## La Mandarine

Route de Tahiti - 04 94 76 06 66, fax 04 94 97 33 67
Closed mid Oct-beg May. 4 stes 2,180-3,050. 39 rms 960-1,960. Restaurant. Half-board 820-1,865. Rm ser. Air cond. Pool. Beach. Pkg.
Accommodations consist of several pink neo-Provençal bungalows scattered around five acres of idyllic grounds. Luxurious rooms, impeccably tended, with views of vineyards and mountains. Pool on the premises; the hotel's private beach is Bora-Bora (see *The Beaches*), at nearby Pampelonne.

12/20 Nioulargo et Kailargo

Bd Patch - 04 94 79 82 14, fax 04 94 79 90 42
Closed Oct 9-Easter. Open until 10:30pm. Terrace dining. Air cond. Pkg.
Exotically-inspired cooking in a restaurant you can drive right up to in your boat. Sample the shrimp and green mango salad, the shrimp and squids sautéed in hot-pepper basil, or the ginger-spiced fish broiled in a banana leaf. Located on the Pampelonne beach, with a floating deck serving as entrance bridge. C 280-350.

 ## L'Olivier

Route des Carles, 1 km
04 94 97 58 16, fax 04 94 97 21 71
Closed Mon & Tue lunch off-seas (exc Easter weekend), Jan 5-Feb 13. Open until 11pm. Garden dining. Heated pool. Valet pkg.
Just minutes away from Place des Lices you find yourself among verdant fields and vineyards, in a lush garden planted with palm, olive, and fig trees. This is the realm of new young chef, Franck Putelat, who worked one year at Taillevent and four years at Blanc. It's never easy to get started in this little «planet» all on its own, but this boy seems to have landed with his feet fairly firmly on the ground. He quickly understood that Provençal and sunny ingredients are the rhyme and reason here. A sunny start: the little tomato, lobster, calamary and mussel soup redolent of the sunny flavors of the South and marked by flawless craftsmanship; the tangy twice-cooked red mullets in warm Roma tomato vinaigrette; the perfecto cooking time for the sea bream on a bed of zucchini, jus and lard crisp. A less sunny interlude: the chicken rounds with crackling rice and baby vegetables in a foie gras jus. Putelat mixes sea and countryside in an exacting clear-cut manner which only shows signs of getting better. His pastry chef also came along from Vonnas, and kneads up delights such as velvety bitter-chocolate cake with lavender-honey ice cream, a delicious lime-theme creation, and cardamom-scented jelly. The sommelier whispers sweet nothings about the wines of his Provence, and he has good literature to work with. The waiters and waitresses are young but very well behaved. Heaven on earth on summer evenings tucked in between the fashionable conservatory and the flower-decked terrace. The excellent 260 F set-price meal is really not to be missed. A place to

discover, far from the madding crowd. C 600. M 220 (lunch), 290 (dinner).

Bastide de Saint-Tropez

(See restaurant above)
Closed Jan 5-Feb 13. 8 stes 1,800-3,500. 18 rms 980-2,350. Rms for disabled. Rm ser. Air cond. Heated pool. Valet pkg.
Well away from the buzzing crowds of Saint-Tropez, in an enchanting garden, you can stay in delightful rooms and suites, all of which have either a terrace or a private garden where you can invite your friends in to lunch or dine just as if you were at L'Olivier. Gorgeous pool; really perfect service.

Les Palmiers

Pl. des Lices, 26, bd Vasselot
04 94 97 01 61, fax 04 94 97 10 02
Open year-round. 23 rms 390-600. Rms for disabled.
The rooms are unexceptional, but pretty inexpensive by local standards. What's more, the garden is a delight. You can take your breakfast there, amid orange trees and jasmine.

Le Petit Charron

6, rue des Charrons - 04 94 97 73 78
Closed Wed & Sun dinner off-seas, Nov-Feb. Open until 10pm. Terrace dining. Air cond.
A pearl of a place in Saint-Tropez. Anne-Violaine and Christian Benoît welcome guests into their tiny dining room and serve them simple, eminently satisfying food: a crisp-crusted tomato and sweet-pepper tart, tiny red mullets given a quick turn on the grill and served with their briny juices intact, and a rich crème brûlée perfumed with lavender. The cellar's prices are as friendly as the service. One of the best buys to be had on this most fashionable of fashionable peninsulas. C 210-270. M 150-180.

12/20 La Ponche

Port des Pêcheurs, 3, rue des Remparts
04 94 97 02 53, fax 04 94 97 78 61
Closed Nov-Mar. Open until midnight. Terrace dining. Air cond. Valet pkg.
A cosmopolitan crowd haunts La Ponche's terrace overlooking the old fishing port, to sample seafood salads, turbot with tomato-butter sauce, and simple Provençal dishes prepared with obvious care. Regional cellar; attentive staff. C 240-350. M 130 (lunch), 180-240.

La Ponche

(See restaurant above)
Closed Nov-Mar. 5 stes 750-2,300. 13 rms 750-1,680. Half-board 950-1,940. Rm ser. Air cond. Valet pkg.
Charming, remodeled, well-equipped rooms with sea views. You'll find elegant décor and

excellent comfort. Breakfast is served on the terrace that overlooks the port.

12/20 Le Relais des Caves du Roy

Hôtel Le Byblos, av. Paul-Signac
04 94 56 68 20, fax 04 94 56 68 01
Closed mid Oct-mid Mar. Open until 1:20am. Terrace dining. Air cond. Valet pkg.
If you're itching to see and be seen, here's the place to go. For night owls only. A charming bistro where you can dine with as well as under the stars if you choose the terrace. Standards such as tomato and mozzarella, risotto, and even pizza, but all done with care and precision. C 200.

Résidence de la Pinède

Plage de la Bouillabaisse
04 94 55 91 00, fax 04 94 97 73 64
Closed mid Oct-beg Apr. Open until 10:30pm. Terrace dining. Air cond. Pool. Beach. Valet pkg.
Hervé Quesnel is versatile. He can come up with a deluxe poolside snack for a billionaire guest who's feeling peckish, or for more stately occasions, lusty summer-truffle ravioli in a cèpe emulsion, pan-fried langoustine cracknel on a bed of eggs (not like any you've eaten!) scrambled with candied tomatoes and basil, or Bresse-chicken breast roasted with sage. The fiesta continues with a crispy super-thin fig tart. This is serious-minded work that undergoes constant evolutionary change. Outright innovation isn't his strong suit, but he knows how to get a bead on culinary trends (like the current fashion for Mediterranean flavors) and use them to enliven his repertoire. The young wine waiter hands out deft advice about the enticing cellar, rich in regional wines and fine Bordeaux. The service is fault-free. How much? You'll feel so good you won't think about it, but if you do, try the excellent «glance at Provence» set-price meal. C 500-700. M 250 (lunch), 380, 450.

Résidence de la Pinède

(See restaurant above)
Closed mid Oct-beg Apr. 7 stes 2,200-7,480. 39 rms 1,300-3,300. Rms for disabled. Half-board 900-2,050. Rm ser. Air cond. Heated pool. Beach. Tennis. Valet pkg.
A screen of greenery keeps road noise out, and the Bay of Saint-Tropez spreads seductively below—direct access to the private beach. Umbrella pines shade the huge, extremely comfortable rooms. Kidney-shaped swimming pool, and spectacular views from the balconies of each room and suite overlooking the sea. Exemplary service. Relais et Châteaux.

We welcome your questions and comments at our e-mail address: gayots@aol.com.

Hôtel Sube

On the harbor - 04 94 97 30 04, fax 04 94 54 89 08
Open year-round. 30 rms 390-1,500. Air cond. Pkg.
Behind the renovated façade are some expensive, though pleasant little rooms with views of Saint-Tropez's quays, yachts, and crowds.

 ## La Tartane

Route de la plage des Salins
04 94 97 21 23, fax 04 94 97 09 16
Closed Oct 15-Mar 15. 12 rms 450-900. Rm ser. Air cond. Heated pool. Tennis. Garage pkg.
La Tartane's thirteen handsome bungalows, nestled in a verdant setting, form a sort of hamlet, with superb, well-equipped rooms and comfortable terraces. The beach is 800 yards away.

 ## Le Yaca

1, bd d'Aumale - 04 94 97 11 79, fax 04 94 97 58 50
Closed Oct 15-Mar 27. 2 stes 2,900-3,200. 24 rms 900-2,300. Rm ser. Air cond. Heated pool. Pkg.
In the heart of Saint-Tropez, Le Yaca is an elegant, expensive hotel with a score or so of rooms (the nicest are on the upper floors). There's also a lovely enclosed garden.

See also: Gassin, Grimaud, Port-Grimaud, Ramatuelle

SAINTE-MAXIME 83120
Paris 880 - St-Raphaël 23 - Cannes 61 Var

 ## Calidianus

Bd des Hortensias
04 94 96 23 21, fax 04 94 49 12 10
Closed Jan 4-Feb 6. 33 rms 490-930. Restaurant. Half-board 1,000-1,140. Pool. Tennis. Pkg.
Nestled in leafy grounds near the sea, the Calidianus comprises a group of small buildings in the local style. The rooms are spacious and well furnished; most have balconies or terraces giving onto the swimming pool.

 ## Golf Plaza

Golf de Sainte-Maxime
04 94 56 66 66, fax 04 94 56 66 00
Closed Feb-Mar 1. 13 stes 1,500-2,500. 93 rms 690-1,350. Rms for disabled. Rm ser. Air cond. Pool. Tennis. Golf. Pkg.
This hotel with its garish façade, a developer's dream, dominates the Sainte-Maxime golf course. The attractive, super-comfortable rooms are nicely equipped, with south-facing terraces that look out onto the Bay of Saint-Tropez. Lots of sporting facilities: eight tennis courts, fitness club, private beach.

Hostellerie de la Belle Aurore

4, bd Jean-Moulin
04 94 96 02 45, fax 04 94 96 63 87

Closed Wed lunch off-seas, end Sep-Mar. Open until 10pm. Terrace dining. Air cond. Pool. Beach. Tennis. Garage pkg.
Get away from it all in this rotunda-shaped dining room with large bay windows giving onto the bay, with Saint-Tropez as backdrop. Charm is not lacking, and the food is not bad either. Good-quality local ingredients are carefully crafted into tasty showpieces: delectable roast langoustines aside artichoke and green-asparagus Bavarian cream and taste-tingling duck breast in honey juice. The excellent desserts, wide in variety, also deserve special mention. You may want to steer clear of some of the pricey options on the à la carte menu. Perfecto service—low-key yet efficient. Discerning wine list, but short on half-bottles. C 400. M 160 (weekday lunch), 240-450.

 ## Hostellerie de la Belle Aurore

(See restaurant above)
Closed Jan 5-Feb, Oct 10-25, Nov 15-Dec 26. 1 ste 1,300-2,500. 16 rms 600-1,900. Rms for disabled. Half-board 600-1,300. Rm ser. Air cond. Pool. Beach. Tennis. Pkg.
An azure blue location with Sol looking straight down on it and facing the mighty Gulf as it hangs above the rocks. Pleasant rooms spiffed up to Provence taste, with rattan furniture and pale-colored fabrics on the walls. The windows open out onto the ridges and the swells. The cloud-free welcome makes this address even sunnier.

 ## Hostellerie La Croisette

2, bd des Romarins - 04 94 96 17 75, fax 04 94 96 52 40
Closed Nov-Mar 1. 17 rms 390-890. Rms for disabled. Air cond. Garage pkg.
The Provençal-style rooms are attractively decorated and well equipped, with views either of the sea or the charming garden out back. Cheerful reception.

12/20 La Maison Bleue

24 bis, rue Paul-Bert
04 94 96 51 92, fax 04 94 96 71 69
Closed Tue off-seas, Jan 10-Feb school hols, Oct 20-Dec 26. Open until 10pm (10:30pm in summer). Terrace dining. Air cond.
This little restaurant is almost lost among the many bars and coffee houses of this pedestrian street, but has kept its head up over the years thanks to good-quality downhome cooking using fresh ingredients. Warm reception. C 240. M 90, 135.

Parc-Hôtel du Jas Neuf

71, route du Débarquement
04 94 96 51 88, fax 04 94 49 09 71
Open year-round. 1 ste 600-940. 26 rms 300-400. Restaurant. Half-board 365-535. Air cond. Pool. Pkg.

Several modern, Provence-style buildings arranged in stairsteps around the fresh-water swimming pool. Pleasant rooms with Provence-style décor, most of which give onto the pool and garden. Located on the Nartelle beach.

Hôtel de la Poste

7, bd Frédéric-Mistral
04 94 96 18 33, fax 04 94 96 41 68
Closed Oct 15-May 15. 24 rms 300-620. Pool. Pkg.
Just 100 yards from the harbor, in the center of town, this outstanding modern hotel is elegant and bright, with handsome rooms (some connecting, for families). Breakfast is served on the poolside terrace.

SOPHIA-ANTIPOLIS 06 → Valbonne

TOULON	83000
Paris 833 - Nice 152 - Aix-en-P. 81 - Marseille 66	Var

 La Chamade

25, rue Denfert-Rochereau - 04 94 92 28 58
Closed Sat lunch, Sun. Annual closings not available. Open until 9:30pm. Terrace dining. Air cond.
Véronique Bonneau's warm welcome adds to the charm of La Chamade's new décor. Her husband Francis, an alumnus of Taillevent, has composed a very up-to-date menu based on top-quality ingredients: taste his lusty brochette of snails and lamb's tongue à la provençale, grouper roasted with rashers of smoky bacon and a touch of rosemary, and delectable date craquelin spiked with gentian liqueur. Charming service. C 320-420. M 185 (weekdays).

 La Corniche

17, littoral Frédéric-Mistral
04 94 41 35 12, fax 04 94 41 24 58
Open year-round. 4 stes 400-650. 19 rms 350-450. Rms for disabled. Restaurant. Air cond.
This hotel provides well-equipped, distinctive, comfortable rooms, half of which have balconies or terraces overlooking the sea. All are air conditioned and offer cable TV.

12/20 Le Gros Ventre

Corniche du Mourillon, opposite Fort St-Louis
04 94 42 15 42, fax 04 94 31 40 32
Closed Wed (exc Jul-Aug), Thu lunch. Open until 11pm. Terrace dining. Pkg.
Maybe Alain Audibert should take a bit of time off from the kitchen and see what's going on in the dining room. The welcome is far from cordial and the waiters and waitresses are noisy and disorganized. The cooking is not without reproach, either. The defunct 194 F menu only offered two first courses—meat (rack of lamb) and fish (salmon fillet)—and both were disconcertingly commonplace. The salmon was overcooked and the truffle sauce was unrefined and

dripping of grease. C 250-300. M 95 (weekday lunch), 120-224.

Holiday Inn Garden Court

1, av. Rageot-de-la-Touche
04 94 92 00 21, fax 04 94 92 08 15
Open year-round. 7 stes 600-750. 74 rms 380. Rm for disabled. Restaurant. Half-board 420-430. Air cond. Pool. Garage pkg.
Central location just around the corner from the train station. Good quality hotel with prettily decorated, big rooms. Efficient reception and service. The rooms cost the same for up to four people.

 Le Jardin du Sommelier

20, allée Courbet - 04 94 62 03 27, fax 04 94 09 01 49
Closed Sat lunch, Sun. Open until 11pm. Terrace dining. Air cond. Pkg.
This little dining room is elegance itself with its exquisite floral compositions. In this prime location right next to the Place d'Armes, Gilles Oliviero tempts you with his skillfully executed cooking full of inventiveness and ingenuity. Let yourself be seduced by the first-rate, cooked-to-perfection lobster pistou served with a delectable stuffed-squid salad. Surprise yourself with the duck tournedos and chanterelle mushrooms served with potatoes in oil. The owner used to be a sommelier, thus the name, and thus the cleverly selected wines of his ever-evolving wine list. Professional, attentive service. We told you last year that you should keep your eye on this restaurant, that its future looked bright. It seems that we were right since we are giving it an extra point this year. C 250-300. M 220.

 Au Sourd

10, rue Molière - 04 94 92 28 52, fax 04 94 91 59 92
Closed Sun, Mon lunch. Open until 10:30pm. Terrace dining.
This is the oldest restaurant in town—it dates from 1862—and probably one of the best places to slip down fish. Jean-Pierre Martellotto practically dips his hand in the nets of the last Bandolais fishermen. Pageot sea bream, porgy, sole, Daurade sea bream, mullet, calamaries and squill of a freshness rarely encountered. We would like the cooking times to be more perfectly calculated however. Cordial reception and enthusiastic service. When you count the pennies, you come out all right if you stray away from some of the slightly overpriced wines. C 280-350. M 140.

And also...

Our selection of places for inexpensive, quick, or late-night meals.
Le Bistrot (04 94 41 35 12 - Hôtel La Corniche, 17, littoral Frédéric-Mistral. Open until 10pm.

Closed Sun dinner, Mon.): Go here for the superb view over the Porquerolles and the freshness of the seafood, because the overpriced checks are certainly no attraction. (120-300).

Chez Mimi (04 94 92 79 60 - 83, av. de la République. Open until 11pm.): If you've always been curious about spices, here's the place to come to enhance your knowledge. Traditional dishes such as deep-fried egg turnovers (*brik à l'œuf*), couscous and tagines (Moroccan meat and chicken stews) served with a smile (160).

TOURTOUR	83690
Paris 860 - Draguignan 20 - Aups 10 - Salernes 11	Var

 ## Bastide de Tourtour 🏰♟

04 94 70 57 30, fax 04 94 70 54 90
Closed Nov-Mar 1. 25 rms 320-1,200. Rms for disabled. Restaurant. Half-board 550-1,000 (oblig in seas). Rm ser. Pool. Tennis. Garage pkg.
You can take in a hundred kilometers of magnificent Var scenery from this luxurious mountain fastness among the pines. Jacuzzi, exercise room.

 ## Les Chênes Verts

2 km on route de Villecroze
04 94 70 55 06, fax 04 94 70 59 35
Closed Tue dinner, Wed, Jan 1-15, Jun 15-30. Open until 9:15pm. Terrace dining. Garage pkg.
Can a chef follow the same path for twenty years, yet continue to improve? Paul Bajade shows that it is indeed possible: he refines his beautifully designed set menus year by year, adding ever more full-flavored regional dishes. On a recent visit, the 250 F market menu brought little escargot spring «crust», brimming with flavor; green asparagus with morel and olive oil cream (the olive oil came from the Tourtour oil mill), and perfect duck liver flavored up with juniper berries. Follow on with melt-in-your-mouth baked Sisteron lamb chops, sage Einkorn risotto, then fresh goat cheese simply dipped in salt. Truffles are right at home here (of course). Good selection of regional crus and service of the utmost discretion. The dining rooms (no air conditioning) are decorated in a minimalist fashion, and include some Bernard Buffet paintings. Three comfortable enough rooms if you need to rest after the meal. C 450. M 1 (weekdays), 250-600.

TRIGANCE	83840
Paris 818 - Draguignan 44 - Grasse 72 - Castellane 20	Var

12/20 Château de Trigance

04 94 76 91 18, fax 04 94 85 68 99
Closed Wed lunch off-seas, Nov 2-Mar 21. Open until 9:30pm. Terrace dining. Garage pkg.
At the doors of the city of Verdon, a tenth-century fortress sitting atop a rocky crag and converted into a stunning restaurant and hotel. The vaulted ceiling and stone walls of the dining

room serve as sword and buckler setting, where you'll partake of char-fish roll with onion greens, duck leg with foie gras, and mullet stuffed with tapenade. The superb terrace on top of the keep offers a smashing panoramic view. C 300-370. M 150 (lunch), 210, 270.

 ## Château de Trigance 🏰♟

(See restaurant above)
Closed Nov 2-Mar 21. 2 stes 900. 8 rms 600-900. Half-board 550-730 (oblig in seas). Garage pkg.
These beautiful rooms are handsomely furnished (canopied beds), and equipped with excellent bathrooms. Relais et Châteaux.

VALBONNE	06560
Paris 913 - Cannes 13 - Grasse 9 - Nice 30	Alpes-Mar.

 ## Les Armoiries

Pl. des Arcades - 04 93 12 90 90, fax 04 93 12 90 91
Open year-round. 16 rms 450-850. Air cond.
This hotel, on the national register of historical monuments, goes back a long way—to the seventeenth century, to be exact. Located on a most bewitching square and offering simple but well-appointed rooms.

L'Auberge Fleurie

1016, route de Cannes
04 93 12 02 80, fax 04 93 12 22 27
Closed Sun dinner, Mon, Dec 15-Jan 30. Open until 10pm. Terrace dining. Pkg.
Jean-Pierre Bataglia's traditional cuisine is polished and precise. Sample his à la carte specialties, or choose a set menu, accompanied by one of the well-chosen wines from the regional cellar. Guests are welcomed with a smile into the comfortable, modern dining room (in fine weather, ask for a terrace table). C 250-330. M 115-185.

12/20 Bleu Lavande

28, chemin de Pinchinade - 04 93 12 28 01
Closed Tue dinner. Open until 10pm. Terrace dining. Garage pkg.
Classic Provençal fare in a classic Provençal décor (almost too much). Ratatouille and tapenade flan, tournedo with morels, lavender crème brûlée. Not enough color and flavors to really feel you're down home. C 220. M 135-180.

 ## Novotel

Rue Dostoïevski - 04 93 65 40 00, fax 04 93 95 80 12
Open year-round. 97 rms 450-480. Rms for disabled. Restaurant. Rm ser. Air cond. Pool. Tennis. Pkg.
In front of the big Sophia-Antipolis industrial park, this is an excellent hotel for conferences.

12/20 Relais de la Vignette

Route de Cannes - 04 93 12 05 82
Open daily until 10:30pm. Terrace dining. Garage pkg.

The stained glass and armour serve as medieval setting just down the street from the high-tech paradise of Sophia-Antipolis. The cooking is rather old-fashioned as well: lacklustre guinea fowl and veal sweetbread terrine, black fettucine, good young rabbit in puff pastry, and pear Bavarian cream. It's a little too old-fashioned (for our taste) to drink your wine out of tin cups, though! C 250-300. M 99 (weekday lunch, wine incl), 125-175.

 In Sophia-Antipolis 06560 _7 km SE on D 3, D 103_

12/20 L'Arlequin

3550, route des Dolines
04 92 96 68 78, fax 04 92 96 68 96
Closed Sat lunch & Sun in winter, Dec 23-Jan 6. Open until 10:15pm. Terrace dining. Air cond. Pool. Pkg.

The toque has just toppled off this year for the lack of flavor and the over-minimalist reception and service. Lamb daube in fresh-herb jelly, dried-out honey and lemon guinea fowl fricassée, rubbery ravioli, chocolate truffle, almond-milk ice cream and no cheese on the 185 F fixed-priced meal. It's a shame, because the atmosphere is extremely pleasant and there are numerous godsends on the wine menu— Gruaud Larose's Saint-Julien '91 or Carbonnieux's Pessac-Léognan '93 under 200 F. C 200-250. M 185.

 Grand Hôtel Mercure ♨♥

(See restaurant above)
Open year-round. 2 stes 800-1,600. 105 rms 600-780. Rms for disabled. Rm ser. Air cond. Pool. Pkg.

An immense leisure complex set in extensive grounds just a few minutes from the sea (free shuttle bus to the beach). Guest rooms are well appointed, soundproofed, and have private balconies. Among the many services on tap are a masseur, exercise classes, a beauty salon, gift shop, and car-rental agency. Piano bar.

VALLAURIS 06220
Paris 929 - Nice 25 - Cannes 6 Alpes-Mar.

12/20 Le Manuscrit

224, chemin Lintier - 04 93 64 56 56
Closed Mon, Tue off-seas, mid Jan-beg Feb, mid Nov-beg Dec. Open until 9:45pm. Garden dining. Garage pkg.

Once a perfume distillery, Le Manuscrit offers simple, bountiful meals at prices unheard-of for Cannes and its environs. Just 95 F buys pistachioed rabbit terrine, veal kidney and sweetbreads en cassolette, and a refreshing fruit gratin. Moderately tariffed cellar; smiling staff—

what more could you ask? M 95 (lunch), 120 (dinner), 175.

VENCE 06140
Paris 925 - Nice 22 - Antibes 19 - Grasse 27 Alpes-Mar.

 ## Château Saint-Martin

Av. des Templiers - 04 93 58 02 02, fax 04 93 24 08 91
Closed end Oct-Apr. Open until 9:30pm. Garden dining. Air cond. Heated pool. Tennis. Valet pkg.

The Knights Templar, who founded this castle, rode two to a horse as a sign of poverty. Saint Martin is said to have cut his mantle in two to share with a beggar here. The patrons of Château Saint-Martin have plenty of horsepower under the hoods of their fancy cars, and they are also willing to sacrifice half the price of a mink coat to spend a weekend admiring the Château's stupendous views while gorging on Dominique Ferrière's impeccable, classic cuisine. Starchy service; excellent cellar, supervised by René Leroux. C 450-650. M 300 (weekday lunch), 375 (dinner), 430, 490.

 ## Château Saint-Martin

(See restaurant above)
Closed end Oct-beg Apr. 10 stes 3,000-4,000. 25 rms 2,800-4,000. Half-board 500. Air cond. Heated pool. Tennis. Valet pkg.

Sumptuous view of the sea or the back-country hills. Sumptuous like the rooms in this _bastide_, with their period furniture, fully-equipped and refined bathrooms, and _grand luxe_ breakfasts. The thirty-five acres of parkland around the château ensure you a quiet sleep. Highly professional reception. You have to pay for all this, of course. Relais et Châteaux.

12/20 La Farigoule

15, rue Henri-Isnard - 04 93 58 01 27
Closed Fri (exc lunch in seas), Sat lunch, Nov 10-Dec 15. Open until 9:15pm (10pm in summer). Terrace dining.

Georgette Gastaud entices you with large helpings of downhome Provençal cooking. From her farigoule rabbit (farigoule is the word in these parts for «thyme»), her Niçois veal sauté, to her roasted herb-coated duckling, you will taste all the sunny flavors of the South. We really like the prices. M 120, 145.

 ## Hôtel Floréal

440, av. Rhin-et-Danube
04 93 58 64 40, fax 04 93 58 79 69
Closed Nov-Mar 15. 43 rms 350. Half-board 490-590. Pool. Garage pkg.

A modern building set in pretty grounds. The rooms are bright and cozy, with tasteful decoration and a view over the countryside. Snacks are served round the swimming pool. Garden with exotic plants.

Maximin

689, chemin de la Gaude
04 93 58 90 75, fax 04 93 58 22 86
Closed Sun dinner, Mon, Jan 12-Feb 12. Open until 10:30pm. Terrace dining. Air cond. Valet pkg.

Right when you think there's nothing more that can be said about Maximin—about his strokes of genius, his moodiness and his *enfant terrible* pranks—he puts us off track with his devish art of counter-attack and panache. No wonder they call him the Bonaparte of the kitchen. He was said to be less inventive, more settled down, but the amazing hot squash flower tea, the incredible association of truffles, tripes and squill-fish with poached egg, the astonishing young-rabbit aspic with ravigote oyster sauce, and the sea perch with cuttlefish ink and gnocchi—a true symphony in black and white—prove that his fertile inspiration is still alive and doing fine, thank you. He was said to be too expensive. Here again, he pops another one, a 240 F à la carte market set-price meal, featuring the best of Maximin, who can make a simple tomato burst with flavors we never imagined. Eggplant terrine with tapenade croutons, anchovy sauce and mixed salad with his marvellous Maximim-style seasoning; pig's head with green beans or white broad bean au gratin with bacon; transfigured peasant dishes. The celebration of life continues with dessert: gingery candied eggplant and white-peach gazpacho, apricots and roast almonds and foamy apricot cappucino. Maximin decided to take a drive down tastebud lane, and is it ever to our delight. So much so, that we forgot to tell you about the charming bourgeois house, Provençal-style, filled full of his buddies' works—Novaro, Arman and César. But really, you should just go see for yourself... C 400. M 240-450.

Relais Cantemerle

258, chemin Cantemerle
04 93 58 08 18, fax 04 93 58 32 89
Closed mid Oct-beg Apr. 19 stes 950-1,030. 1 rm 600. Restaurant. Half-board 560-775. Rm ser. Air cond. Pool. Garage pkg.

A gorgeous Provençal garden surrounds the Relais with tranquility. Inside, you'll find a 1930s–style bar and lounge, and bright guest rooms with private terraces.

Le Vieux Couvent

37, av. Alphonse-Toreille - 04 93 58 78 58
Closed Wed, Sun dinner (Oct-Mar). Open until 9:15pm (10pm in summer). Terrace dining.

You might dine in the former chapel of a seventeenth-century convent in a prettily decorated dining room with stone walls that speak out their history, but chef Jean-Jacques Bissières suffers from the lack of light and space. It's a pity, because he turns a dandy sauce and masters his cooking times to perfection. For less than 250 F including wine, you can make a superb culinary trip between Provence and the Southwest: stuffed zucchini blossoms, hot foie gras with grapes, roast pigeon and scrumptious desserts. Bissières is a candid chef with a steady professionalism, he just needs a few rays of sunlight. After Maximin, this is the best restaurant in Vence. C 210-300. M 150-295.

VIDAUBAN   83550
Paris 846 - Cannes 65 - Fréjus 29 - Toulon 64   Var

Château Les Lonnes

3 km NW on D 84, chemin des Moulins-d'Entraigues
04 94 73 65 76, fax 04 94 73 14 97
Open year-round. 2 stes 1,200-3,600. 12 rms 550-1,400. Rms for disabled. Pool. Tennis. Garage pkg.

The streetlights light up one by one as you drive down the private driveway to the château. This superb eleventh-century dwelling lost in the middle of its 55-acre woods offers tastefully decorated rooms with thoroughly unpretentious luxury—Provençal furniture weathered with age, marble bathrooms and a bucolic view.

VILLEFRANCHE-SUR-MER   06230
Paris 935 - Monaco 16 - Nice 6   Alpes-Mar.

La Flore

Bd Princesse-Grace-de-Monaco
04 93 76 30 30, fax 04 93 76 99 99
Open year-round. 31 rms 300-1,060. Restaurant. Half-board 500-1,260. Pool. Pkg.

A modern hotel that is renovated every few years. Lovely pastel colors in daintily decorated rooms doted with wide private loggia.

Welcome

1, quai de l'Amiral-Courbet
04 93 76 76 93, fax 04 93 01 88 81
Closed Nov 20-Dec 20. 32 rms 425-625. Half-board 425-625. Rm ser. Air cond. Pkg.

This former convent where writer Jean Cocteau liked to stay has been modernized, adding bedside quotations from Cocteau to serve as food for your dreams. The rooms are comfortable and air conditioned, with some spectacular ones on the fifth floor overlooking the sea.

See also: **Beaulieu-sur-Mer**

SHOPS

FOOD

Here in the land of the sun, the air and light have a singular character. The locals have plenty of character, too, and a lilting accent that is a joy to hear. When in the South, do as the Southerners do: take the time to enjoy life and appreciate nature's bounteous gifts: aromatic olive oil, taut-skinned vegetables, luscious fruits, a glass of cool pastis served on a shaded terrace, sweets made from local fruits and almonds...

• CHARCUTERIE

ARLES   13200 – B./Rhône

Charcuterie Milhau

11, rue Réattu - 04 90 96 16 05
Open Tue-Sat 6:30am-1pm & 3:30pm-8pm, Sun 9am-12:30pm. Closed Mon.
Mr. Milhau makes the longest sausage in the world, and it's certainly more than a foot long. In fact, it weighs in at some 770 pounds and covers a length of more than 263 feet! His real specialty is saucisson d'Arles, a spiced-up mixture of lean beef and pork, bull sausage, and spit-roasted bull, in keeping with the long tradition of Arlesian bullfighting.

NîMES   30000 – Gard

Jean-Pierre Marcon

Halles Centrales - 04 66 67 55 22
Open 7am-12:30pm. Closed Mon, Sun, hols.
Hams, large sausages and headchesses made out of farm-raised hogs. The *rayolette d'Anduze*, a small dry horseshoe-shaped sausage, and the saucisson d'Arles, a large pork-based sausage mixed with Camargue beef, herbes de Provence and large peppercorns, are a must.

VAISON-LA-ROMAINE   84110 – Vaucluse

Millet

14, place Monfort - 04 90 36 05 76
Open 8:30am-12:30pm & 4pm-7:30pm. Closed Sun, Mon.
Mr. Millet is the inventor of *Pontias*, a large sausage flavored with the famous Nyons olives.

Looking for a winery? Refer to the index.

• CHOCOLATE & CANDY

AIX-EN-PROVENCE   13100 – B./Rhône

Brémond Confiseur

2, rue Cardinale - 04 42 38 01 70
Open 9am-noon & 2pm-7pm. Closed Sun, Mon.
No surprises here, just traditional and more traditional, but oh so faultlessly fresh calissons.

Calissons du Roy René

La Pioline, rue Guillaume du Vair,
13 Les Milles - 04 42 39 29 89, fax 04 42 24 41 94
E-mail: royrene@calisson.com
Open Mon-Fri 9am-noon & 2pm-7pm, Sat 10am-noon & 2pm-7pm. Closed Sun.
Calissons are a famed local specialty: a tender, aromatic sweet based on almond paste.

Chocolaterie de Puyricard

7, rue Rifle-Rafle - 04 42 21 13 26, fax 04 42 21 55 61
Also in Arles, Avignon, Marseille, Nice, Toulon
Open 9am-7pm. Closed Sun.
Good chocolates, with classic and unusual varieties on offer. Delicious calissons, too.

Léonard Parli

35, avenue Victor-Hugo - 04 42 26 05 71
Open Tue-Sat 8am-noon & 2pm-7pm, Sun 10am-noon. Closed Mon.
The traditional diamond-shaped marzipan sweet consists of almonds, candied melon and two thin layers of unleavened bread. There are variations on this, of course, but what's most important is the freshness, and that's what you'll find here, because it's made right before your very eyes. Don't pass up the crispy little Aix cookies (*biscotins*) and the crystallized fruit.

CANNES   06400 – Alpes-Mar.

Confiserie Bruno

50, rue d'Antibes
04 93 39 26 63, fax 04 92 99 07 64
Open 9am-12:30pm & 2:30pm-7:30pm. Closed Sun.
A rainbow of gorgeous candied fruits. We particularly recommend the Vaucluse apricots and the sweet local tangerines.

CARPENTRAS 84200 – Vaucluse

Confiserie Bono

282, allée Jean-Jaurès - 04 90 63 04 99
Open Mon-Fri 9am-noon & 2:30pm-7pm, Sat 10am-noon. Closed Sun.
Fruits candied the old-fashioned way, over low heat for a long time. The most succulent (in our estimation) are the Provençal figs, the Alpine pears, and the local plums, melons, tangerines, and lemons. The delicious fruit jams are also worth trying.

GRÉOUX-LES-BAINS 04800 – Alpes/H.-P.

Pâtisserie Durandeu

46, rue Grande - 04 92 78 00 01
Open Tue-Sat 8am-1pm & 3pm-7pm, Sun 8am-1pm. Closed Mon.
The specialties are ultra-fresh marzipan sweets, almond croquants, homemade nougat and the more unusual homemade butter cookies all well worth the calories.

MARSEILLE 13004 – B./Rhône

Biscuiterie Orsoni

4th arr. - 7, bd Botinelly - 04 91 34 87 03
Open 8am-7pm. Closed Sat, Sun.
The great specialist of *navettes*, small Marseille cookies flavored with orange-flower water; these are totally made by hand. Taste the crispy almond croquants, macaroons and *canistrelli* (anise seed cookies).

Facor

4th arr. - 13-15, rue Xavier-Progin - 04 91 49 38 07
E-mail: facor.corsiglia@wanadoo.fra
Open 8am-noon & 2pm-6pm. Closed Sat, Sun.
It would be hard to find better candied chestnuts (marrons glacés): these are succulent, aromatic little morsels!

MONACO 98000 – Principality of Monaco

Pâtisserie Canet

4, bd de France
(377) 93 30 82 94, fax (377) 93 30 28 91
Open Tue-Sat 7:30am-12:30pm & 3pm-7:30pm, Sun 7:30am-12:30pm. Closed Mon.
Very good fruit jellies (pâtes de fruits) and excellent chocolates.

Chocolaterie de Monaco

7, rue Biovès - (377) 93 15 00 55
Open 9am-noon & 2pm-7pm. Closed Sun & Mon (hols).
Refined, very well crafted chocolates, filled with delicately flavored ganaches, a rich blend of chocolate and thick cream.

MUY (LE) 83490 – Var

Nougat Cochet

709, bd de la Libération - 04 94 45 97 90
Open 8:30am-noon & 2pm-5:30pm. Closed Sun, Mon.
Real nougat made from pure honey and Provence almonds, right here on the premises.

NICE 06300 – Alpes-Mar.

Confiserie Auer

7, rue Saint-François-de-Paule
04 93 85 77 98, fax 04 93 62 07 17
Open 8am-12:30pm & 2:30pm-7pm. Closed Mon (exc Jun-Sep).
Come to this charming Rococo shop for toothsome fruits confits, candied by hand the old-fashioned way.

Confiserie Florian du Vieux Nice

14, quai Papacino
04 93 55 43 50, fax 04 93 55 21 46
Open daily 9am-noon & 2pm-6:30pm.
Watch as fruits confits are candied before your eyes by experts. An enormous variety to choose from. Take a look at the chocolates, as well as candied rose petals, jasmine flowers, and crystallized flowers.

ORAISON 04700 – Alpes/H.-P.

Confiserie François Doucet

Z.A. - 04 92 78 61 15
Open 8am-noon & 2pm-6pm. Closed Sat, Sun.
Fruit jellies are the specialty here, and they are some of the best in all of France. It would be too bad to miss out on the chocolate sugar-coated almond pralines as well.

PEYRUIS 04310 – Alpes/H.-P.

Manon et Cie

2, Espace Saint-Pierre - 04 92 68 00 13
Open Mon-Fri 8am-noon & 2pm-6:30pm, Sat 9am-noon & 2pm-6:30pm. Closed Sun.
One-stop shopping for regional sweets such as nougat, marzipan, fruit jellies and honey. You can visit the laboratories on certain days, but you should make an appointment beforehand.

SAULT 84390 – Vaucluse

André Boyer

Porte des Aires - 04 90 64 00 23, fax 04 90 64 08 99
http://www.epicuria.fr/boyer-nougat/
E-mail: boyer-nougat@epicuria.fr
Open daily 6:30am-7pm.

What could be more Provençal than nougat? here you'll find white nougat, black (because it's caramelized) nougat, as well as crunchy pralines, candied fruits, marzipan, and a host of other sweet indulgences. An excellent address.

SÉDERON   26560 – Drôme

Nougats Boyer

Pl. de la Poste - 04 75 28 51 60
Open daily 8am-8pm.
Great Grandma Juliette tends this old-world boutique where you can stock up on nougat, macaroons and other crispy almond cookies. It's made just on the outskirts of the village.

SORGUES   84700 – Vaucluse

Au Petit Prince

52, pl. de la République
04 90 83 00 29, fax 04 90 39 24 99
Open Mon-Sat 7:30am-12:30pm & 2pm-7:30pm, Sun 7am-7pm.
A typically Provençal sweet shop, stocked with nougat, pralines, candied fruit, and candies made with almond paste. Everything's delicious, so just follow your fancy!

TOURRETTES-SUR-LOUP   06140 – Alpes-Mar.

Confiserie Florian des Gorges du Loup

Le Pont du Loup - 04 93 59 33 20
Open daily 9am-6:30pm.
Excellent candied fruits prepared with sun-ripened fruits, as well as candied rose petals and jasmine flowers, crystallized rose petals, violets and verbena, acid drops and citrus fruit jams.

• GOURMET SPECIALTIES

AUPS   83630 – Var

Voirin-Mailaender

Domaine de la Tuillère - 04 94 70 00 59
Open Mon-Sat 8am-8pm, Sun & hols 3pm-8pm.
Good farm-raised products from the region: jam, chutney, canned goods, olive oil (Paris Gold Medal in 1998) and assorted olives.

COGOLIN   83130 – Var

Au Bec Fin

Parc d'Activités Artisanales - 04 94 55 74 44
Open 8am-noon & 1pm-6pm. Closed Sat, Sun.
All sorts of Provence-inspired canned goods: fish soup, anchovy paste, pistou, and much more.

MARSEILLE   13005 – B./Rhône

Terre d'Épices

5th arr. - 43, pl. Jean-Jaurès - 04 91 42 06 36
Open 9am-1pm & 4pm-8pm. Closed Sun, Mon.
Specialties from all over the world. For example: here nougat does not come from Montélimar, but from the Middle East. The interesting recipe cards they include with your purchases will give you a wealth of ideas.

MOUGINS   06250 – Alpes-Mar.

La Boutique du Moulin

Pl. du Commandant Lamy (in Vieux-Village)
04 93 90 19 18
Open mid May-mid Sep daily 11am-midnight; mid Sep-mid May: Sun-Thu 11am-8pm, Fri-Sat 11am-10pm.
This is the boutique of the talked-about chef Roger Vergé. Lots of finds: unexampled jams, a whole range of ready-cooked dishes, select foies gras, wine, champagne and hard-to-find brandies, table dressings and antiques.

TOURTOUR   83690 – Var

La Ferme de Tourtour

Route de Villecroze - 04 94 70 56 18
Open daily 8am-5pm.
Provençal specialties such as jams and canned dishes. Also foies gras and terrines, puréed fruit sauces and various other sauces.

VALLAURIS   06200 – Alpes-Mar.

Coopérative Agricole Nérolium

12, av. Georges-Clémenceau - 04 93 64 27 54
Open Tue-Fri 8am-noon & 2pm-6pm, Sat 8am-noon & 3pm-6pm, Sun 9am-noon & 2pm-6pm. Closed Mon.
You can buy regional products here, especially the excellent citrus fruit jams, but the number one specialty is the distillation of *néroli*, the essential oil of the orange flower.

Honey & Jams

BRAS-D'ASSE   04270 – Alpes/H.-P.

Miellerie de l'Asse

04 92 34 44 04
By appt.
This red-label (a seal of quality) honey is made with all the nectars of the region with a predominance of lavender.

COTIGNAC   83570 – Var

Les Ruchers du Bessillon

2, rue des Naïs - 04 94 04 60 39, fax 04 94 04 62 06
Open Mon-Sat 9am-noon & 1:30pm-6pm, Sun 10am-noon.
Provençal honeys in an array of subtly nuanced flavors: acacia, lavender, linden-blossom, etc. Also on offer are candies, gingerbread, and other honey-based delicacies.

MENTON   06500 – Alpes-Mar.

L'Arche des Confitures

2, rue du Vieux-Collège - 04 93 57 20 29
Open 9am-noon & 3pm-7pm, Sun 10am-noon & 3pm-6pm.
8, rue Ardoïno - 04 93 28 47 70
Open 9am-noon & 3pm-6pm. Closed Sat, Sun.
More than twenty years of experience have made these jams famous. They're especially well known for unheard-of combinations that work like magic: melon and lemon; tomato, eggplant and ginger; apricot and banana, among many others. Their fruit syrups are also excellent. You can visit the factory at rue Ardoïno on Wednesdays at 10:30am; groups on reservation.

ROBION   84440 – Vaucluse

La Roumanière

Pl. de l'Église - 04 90 76 41 40, fax 04 90 76 41 41
Open Mon-Fri 8:30am-5pm. Closed Sat (exc Apr-Oct: 10am-7pm), Sun.
The luscious fruit jams (many original varieties) are all made by hand, and are prettily presented in jars capped with Provençal print fabrics.

TIGNET (LE)   06530 – Alpes-Mar.

Jean-Louis Lautard

343, av. Docteur Belletrud - 04 93 66 46 57
Open Mon-Fri 8am-4pm. Call for appt for the other days or hours.
J.-L. Lautard's honeys cover the whole gamut of Provence scents: lavender, chestnut, rosemary. The nectar is gathered and kept in accordance with the strict rules of the trade.

Mushrooms

ALÉS   30312 – Gard

Au Champignon Cévenol

1091, av. des Maladreries - 04 66 86 11 41
Open 9am-noon & 2pm-5:30pm. Closed Sat, Sun.
Mushroom paradise: cèpes, chanterelles, morels and dried woodland mushrooms galore.

Other regional products as well; the jams are especially worth mentioning.

Pasta & Ravioli

CANNES   06400 – Alpes-Mar.

Aux Bons Raviolis

31, rue Meynadier - 04 93 39 36 63
Open Mon-Sat 8am-12:30pm & 3:30pm-7:30pm, Sun 8am-12:30pm.
All sorts of freshly-made pasta. Excellent ravioli stuffed with vegetables, meat, herbs, etc.

FLAYOSC   83780 – Var

Les Pâtes Flayoscaises

23, bd Jean-Moulin - 04 94 70 41 52
Open Tue-Sat 8am-12:30pm & 3:30pm-7:30pm, Sun 8am-12:30pm. Closed Mon.
Freshly-made cèpe, meat and foie gras ravioli and other pasta, really the freshest around.

MARSEILLE   13006 – B./Rhône

Raviolis Francis Denier

6th arr. - 5, rue Saint-Michel - 04 91 48 48 88
Open 8am-12:30pm & 4pm-7pm. Closed Sun, Mon.
Cèpe, meat, fresh goat cheese, ricotta and other kinds of ravioli. Lots of care goes into the appearance.

NICE   06300 – Alpes-Mar.

Barale

7, rue Sainte-Réparate - 04 93 85 63 08
Open 6am-12:30pm. Closed Mon.
Georges Barale's son-in-law, Éric Guernion, was elected Craftsman of the Year in 1995 for his fresh stuffed pasta, ravioli, gnocchi and panisses. The place is extremely well kept and boasts a jolly good reputation. Watch out for the time: they're only open in the morning.

Truffles

ST-PAUL-TROIS-CHÂTEAUX   26130 – Drôme

Maison de la Truffe et du Tricastin

Rue de la République - 04 75 96 61 29
Open Nov-Mar: Mon 2pm-6pm, Tue-Sat 9am-noon & 2pm-6pm, closed Sun; Apr & Oct: Mon 2pm-6pm, Tue-Sat 9am-noon & 2pm-6pm, Sun 10am-noon & 2pm-6pm; May-Sep: Mon 3pm-7pm, Tue-Sat 9am-noon & 3pm-7pm, Sun 10am-noon & 3pm-7pm.

Truffle-lovers' heaven. You can buy truffles here all year long, because they sell them canned (fresh ones are normally only sold to dealers). You can also sip some of the wine they sell and learn the A to Z of truffles in their little museum. The best time to visit is the second Sunday of February during the truffle festival.

• OLIVE OIL

ANTIBES 06600 – Alpes-Mar.

Crème d'Olive

29, rue James Close - 04 93 34 08 55
Open Tue-Sat 9am-12:30pm & 3pm-7:30pm, Sun 9am-12:30pm. Closed Mon.
Olive oil and olives made merrier with Balsamic vinegars and olive ravioli.

BEAUMES-DE-VENISE 84190 – Vaucluse

Coopérative Oléicole la Balméenne

Avenue Jules Ferry - 04 90 62 94 15
Open 8am-12pm & 2pm-6pm (7pm in seas). Closed Sun (exc Apr-Aug & Dec).
An extremely full-flavored oil marked by a strong accent of Verdale olives, which are harvested in the autumn.

COLLORGUES 30190 – Gard

Soulas

In Saint-Chaptes - 04 66 81 21 13
Open Mon-Fri 8:30am-noon & 2pm-6pm, Sat 9am-11:30am. Closed Sun.
A lovely full-flavored oil made a touch pungent by the Picholine green olives, which are a tasty complement to apéritifs as well.

GRASSE 06130 – Alpes-Mar.

Moulin à Huile Sainte-Anne

138, route de Draguignan - 04 93 70 21 42
Open 9am-noon & 2pm-6pm (7pm in seas). Closed Sun.
Only pukka goes for the Conti family. The olives may be full-flavored, more subdued in flavor or outright rustic, but you can be sure they choose only the best quality to make their oils.

MANOSQUE 04100 – Alpes/H.-P.

Coopérative Oléicole de Manosque

Place de l'Olivette - 04 92 72 00 99
Open 8am-noon & 2:30pm-6:30pm. Closed Sun.
Aglandau olives give this oil its rich bouquet.

MARSEILLE 13001 – B./Rhône

L'Oliveraie

1st arr. - 2, rue Halles Delacroix - 04 91 55 04 55
Open Mon 7am-12:30pm, Tue-Sat 7am-6:30pm. Closed Sun.
Mild- or stronger-tasting virgin oils and whole olives perked up with a variety of different aromatics.

MAUSSANE-LES-ALPILLES 13520 – B./Rhône

Moulin Jean-Marie Cornille

Coopérative Oléicole de la Vallée des Baux, rue Charloun-Rieu - 04 90 54 32 37, fax 04 90 54 30 28
Open Mon-Thu 9am-noon & 2pm-6pm, Fri until 5pm. Closed Sat, Sun. But openings can vary depending on stock.
The highly unique flavor of the Vallée des Baux oil is produced by mixing 4 or 5 different varieties of olives.

MEES (LES) 04190 – Alpes/H.-P.

Huile d'Olive du Moulin des Pénitents

Parc d'Activités - 04 92 34 07 67
Open Mon-Tue & Thu-Sat 8:30am-noon, Wed 8:30am-noon & 2:30pm-6pm. Closed Sun.
The best restaurants in Provence argue over who will get the most of this glorious golden oil so full of flavor.

MOURIES 13890 – B./Rhône

Christian Rossi

Cours Paul Révoil - 04 90 47 50 40
Open 9am-noon & 3pm-6pm. Closed Sun, Mon.
This old oil mill has been completely restored. You can even visit it free of charge in November and December when it is in full operation (just ask!). You will then be tempted to purchase some of the miller's olive oil so full of character.

NICE 06300 – Alpes-Mar.

Escale en Provence

7, rue du Marché - 04 93 85 23 90
Open 9am-7pm. Closed Sun.
Here's an interesting shop, stocked with top-quality, handmade Provençal sweets and condiments: olive oil, Niçois olives, jams, honeys, vinegars (flavored or not). But also Provençal apéritifs and spirits, mustards and teas.

Huilerie Alziari

14, rue Saint-François-de-Paule - 04 93 85 76 92
Open 8:15am-12:30pm & 2:15pm-7:15pm. Closed Sun, Mon.

Stop at this pretty, old-fashioned shop to purchase wonderfully fragrant olive oil, excellent tapenade, and other interesting condiments. Another address at 318, bd de la République, tel 04 93 44 45 12; open 8am-noon & 2pm-6pm, closed Sat, Sun.

Huilerie des Caracoles

5, rue Saint-François-de-Paule - 04 93 62 65 30
Open 9:30am-1pm & 2:30pm-6:30pm. Closed Sun.
You can buy olive oil from the Moulin de la Brague in Opio (see below), as well as other regional products.

NÎMES   30000 – Gard

Olives Daniel

202, route de Beaucaire - 04 66 02 94 50
Open 8:30am-noon & 2pm-6pm. Closed Sat, Sun.
You can buy olive oil from the Vallée des Baux and Nyons, as well as other Provençal specialties: different varieties of olives from the region, salt cod, brandade, vinegars, and much more. Their traditional smoke- and salt-cured products are so good that even the famous chefs in the region stock up here. You can also find all these products at the markets in Nîmes, Montpellier and Avignon.

NYONS   26110 – Drôme

Coopérative du Nyonsais

Place Olivier-de-Serres - 04 75 26 03 44
Open Mon-Sat 8:30am-12:30pm & 2pm-7pm, Sun & hols 9:30am-12:30pm & 2:30pm-6:30pm.
Only Nyons olives and nothing else are used to make this oil donning a guaranteed vintage sticker. Incredibly fresh and kept under optimal conditions. A few local wines and some Côtes-du-Rhône.

Huilerie Ramade

7, impasse du Moulin - 04 75 26 08 18
Open Mon-Fri 9am-noon & 2pm-7pm, Sat 10am-noon & 2pm-6:30pm. Closed Sun.
This is the place to come to learn everything there is to learn about olives. Not only a guided tour, but documentary films teaching you the A to Z of olives and olive trees. You can also buy pickled olives.

Moulin Autrand Dozol

Le Pont Roman - rue du Bas Bourg - 04 75 26 02 52
Open 9am-12:15pm & 2pm-6:45pm. Closed Sun.
The regional olives, the black Tanches, are the basis of this vintage Nyons oil. The mill itself is a real marvel—you can see it from the foot of the Roman bridge. You can even watch them crushing the olives with the millstone.

OPIO   06650 – Alpes-Mar.

Moulin de la Brague

2, route de Châteauneuf - 04 93 77 23 03
Open 9am-noon & 2pm-7pm. Closed Sun.
This ancient fifteenth-century mill also sells seasoned olives and various virgin oils, and other Provençal products and objects.

RAPHÈLE-LES-ARLES   1328 – B./Rhône

Moulin la Cravenco

Route d'Eyguières - 04 90 96 50 82
Open Mon-Fri 8am-noon & 2pm-6pm, Sat 8am-noon. Closed Sun.
The best chefs in France buy their oil here. It is made from four different species of olives, giving it its own very unique personality, and is often prize-winning.

SAINT-SATURNIN-D'APT   84490 – Vaucluse

Maurice Jullien

1, rue Albert-Tronchet - 04 90 75 45 80
Open Mon-Sat 9am-noon & 3pm-7pm, Sun 9am-noon.
You can make your purchases in the little shop smack in the middle of town after you've visited the oil mill.

• *PASTRY & COOKIES*

MARSEILLE   13007 – B./Rhône

Four des Navettes

7th arr. - 136, rue Sainte - 04 91 33 32 12
Open Mon-Sat 7am-8pm, Sun until 2pm.
You can taste *navettes*, the famous little boat-shaped cakes flavored with orange-flower water, hot from the oven, or if you don't arrive at the right time, slightly warmed. The shop is always full!

MORIÈRES-LÈS-AVIGNON   84310 – Vaucluse

Croquettes Aujoras

Route de Saint-Saturnin
04 90 32 21 40, fax 04 90 31 30 97
Open 8am-noon & 2pm-6pm. Closed Sat, Sun (exc hols).
Here we discovered crunchy cookies with true almond flavor, as well as lemon croquettes, delicious macarons, and all manner of tempting treats. Don't miss the *papaline*, a liqueur-filled rocher.

ST-RÉMY-DE-PROVENCE · 13210 – B./Rhône

Le Petit Duc Pâtissiers

7, bd Victor-Hugo · 04 90 92 08 31
Open 10am-1pm & 3pm-7:30pm. Closed Wed off-seas.
Anne Daguin, André Dauguin's daughter, and her husband offer an assortment of baked sweets using recipes gathered from unpublished historical documents. Natural products have precedence. In the summertime, Sainte Hildegarde de Binguen's zucchini and walnut cakes.

SAINT-TROPEZ · 83990 – Var

Micka–La Tarte Tropézienne

36, rue Clémenceau, pl. Louis Blanc · 04 94 97 71 42
Open 7:30am-8pm. Closed Mon (exc Jun-Sep).
You can find St-Tropez pies just about anywhere, but this one has a distinct edge on the others. It's only normal that it's the best around. After all, it was invented here!

• WINE & SPIRITS

AIX-EN-PROVENCE · 13100 – B./Rhône

Bacchus

27, rue d'Italie · 04 42 38 07 41
Open Tue-Fri 8am-12:30pm & 4pm-7:30pm, Sat 8am-12:30pm & 3pm-7:30pm, Sun 9am-12:30pm. Closed Mon.
Only available here, the apéritif wine that you drink with the traditional Provençal Christmas dessert the «13 desserts»—each of them symbolizing Christ and the twelve apostles—along with a highly admirable selection of local wines.

Jacquèmes

9, rue Méjanes · 04 42 23 48 64
Open Mon 2:30am-7:15pm, Tue-Sat 8:30am-12:15pm & 2:30am-7:15pm. Closed Sun.
Wines from the world over, hard liquors and whiskies in the smartest of gourmet groceries.

ANTIBES · 06600 – Alpes-Mar.

Cave La Treille d'Or

12, rue Lacan · 04 93 34 33 87
Open Sun-Mon 9am-noon, Tue-Sat 8:30am-noon & 2:30pm-7pm.
Another excellent wineseller where you can try out all the local wines, including the very best.

CANNES · 06400 – Alpes-Mar.

Caves de Forville

3, pl. du Marché Forville · 04 93 39 45 09

Open Mon-Sat 7:30am-1pm & 3pm-7:30pm, Sun 7:30am-1pm.
A good selection of the best regional wines in this shop just a step away from the best market in town.

CASTILLON · 06500 – Alpes-Mar.

Boisson du Soleil

In Lieu-dit Comairasse · Tel/fax 04 93 28 39 61
By appt.
The name «sunny drink» refers to the artisanally-made citrus fruit apéritifs they make here. You can taste them along with some local specialties such as chickpea pancakes cooked over a wood fire.

FORCALQUIER · 04300 – Alpes/H.-P.

Distilleries et Domaines de Provence

Av. St-Promasse · 04 92 75 15 41, fax 04 92 75 11 85
Open Apr-Dec 9am-noon & 3pm-7pm. Closed Tue, Sun.
This distillery produces Pastis Bardouin, the most refined and subtly flavored of all the anise-flavored spirits on the market. Also on hand is a selection of Provençal wine- and spirit-based specialties (wine punch, walnut wine, peach wine, almond cordial, fruits preserved in brandy) that make wonderful gifts.

MARSEILLE · 13000 – B./Rhône

Le Sommelier

1st arr. - 42, rue de Rome · 04 91 33 53 53
Open 9:45am-1pm & 2:30pm-7pm. Closed Sun, Mon.
6th arr. - 69, rue de la Palud · 04 91 33 77 87
Open 9:30am-1pm & 2:30pm-7pm. Closed Sun, Mon.
Maurice Richard is an amateur with a diploma; he was named Best Amateur Sommelier in France in 1980. He not only selects the best, but teaches his customers the art of wine-tasting.

SISTERON · 04200 – Alpes/H.-P.

Cave des Alpes Provençales

29 bis, av. Jean-Jaurès · 04 92 61 29 80
Open Tue-Sat 9am-12:30pm & 2pm-7pm, Sun 9:30am-12:30pm. Closed Mon.
First-rate wineseller who musters the gems of Provence wine as well as from the Southwest.

TOULON · 83000 – Var

Caves Saint-Louis

6, rue Louis Jourdan · 04 94 92 31 27
Open 8am-noon & 3pm-7pm. Closed Sun.
All the wines from the region are especially well represented.

PROVENÇAL GIFTS

• *BASKETS*

ST-RÉMY-DE-PROVENCE 13210 – B./Rhône

La Fabrique

25, av. de la Libération - Tel./fax 04 90 92 02 27
Open 9am-noon & 3pm-6:30pm. Closed Sun, Mon (Christmas-Easter).
There aren't many basket-makers left in France, but there are still a lot of basket-lovers. These basket-weavers specialize in made-to-measure wicker baskets and the famous *banastes* from Provence, which are elongated wicker fruit baskets. Customers come from literally all over the world to buy them.

• *CANDLES*

AURIBEAU-SUR-SIAGNE 06810 – Alpes-Mar.

Le Cirier d'Auribeau

RD 9, Moulin du Sault - 04 93 40 76 20
Open Mon-Fri 9am-12:30pm & 1:30pm-6:30pm, Sat & Sun 10am-12:15pm & 2:30pm-6pm.
You can visit wax chandler Didier Bianchi's studio, where he makes beautiful hand-made candles.

• *FABRICS*

ARLES 13200 – B./Rhône

Les Campagnardes

17, rue de la République - 04 90 18 95 23
Open 9:30am-12:30pm & 2:30pm-7:30pm. Closed Sun.
Marie makes one collection of lingerie and embroidered table linens per year. She also makes things to order on request.

L'Arlésienne
(Maryse Mincarelli)

12, rue Président Wilson - 04 90 93 28 05
Open Mon 2:30pm-7pm, Tue-Sat 9am-noon & 2:30pm-7pm. Closed Sun.
For traditional cowherders' clothes and traditional Arlesian costumes. Can be bought or rented.

ST-ÉTIENNE-DU-GRÈS 13103 – B./Rhône

Les Olivades

Av. Barberin - 04 90 49 19 19, fax 04 90 49 19 20
E-mail: les-olivades@provence-fabrics.com
Open 9am-noon & 2pm-6pm. Closed Sat, Sun.
These genuine printed calicoes are distributed all over the world, but the famous plantlife designs that made them famous are designed and made here. Salesroom at the parent company as well as addresses of all the boutiques that distribute the brand.

TARASCON 13150 – B./Rhône

Souléïado

39, rue Proudhon - 04 90 91 08 80
Open Mon-Tue 8am-noon & 1:30pm-5:30pm, Fri until 4:30pm. Closed Sat, Sun.
These Provence fabrics are known worldwide, and they have just opened a shop in New York. Their Indiana line has just won a prize (again!). Showroom at the parent company, where you can also find the addresses of their shops located in other towns in France and across the globe.

• *FAIENCE & POTTERY*

BASTIDE-DES-JOURDANS (LA) 84240 – Vaucluse

Faïence d'Art
Nicole de la Bastide

04 90 77 82 54
Open 10am-noon & 2:30pm-6:30pm (in summer 4pm-8pm), Sun upon appt. Closed Tue & Fri mornings.
Earthenware showroom and workshop. Plates, soup tureens, apothecary jars, vases and lamps.

MARSEILLE 13008 – B./Rhône

Figuères et Fils

8th arr. - 12, av. Lauzier - 04 91 73 06 79
Open Mon-Fri 9am-noon & 1pm-6pm, Sat 9am-noon. Closed Sun.
Authentic ceramics basically of fruits, flowers and vegetables found on the Mediterranean

coast. You can visit the workshop or the Château Pastré just a step away, where there is a Faïence Museum.

RAPHÈLE-LES-ARLES 13280 – B./Rhône

Faïencerie Provençale de Raphèle

Albert Rixin, N 453, mas de la Bienheureuse
04 90 98 48 50
Open 9am-7pm. Closed Sun.
This studio makes mainly decorative and dining faïence in the Old Marseille style, which is a floral design on a yellow background.

ST-RÉMY-DE-PROVENCE 13210 – B./Rhône

Les Bouquets de Provence

27, bd Victor-Hugo - 04 90 92 60 53
Open Mon 3pm-7pm, Tue-Sat 10:30am-12:30pm & 3pm-7pm, Sun 11am-1pm.
The name is misleading, because you won't find bouquets of any shape or form here, only the renowned Moustier earthenware.

VALLAURIS 06220 – Alpes-Mar.

Céramiques Natoli

Av. Jérôme Massier/bd des Deux Vallons
04 93 63 90 14, fax 04 93 63 23 62
Open 8am-noon & 2pm-6pm. Closed Sat, Sun.
You find pottery and ceramics on every street corner in this village so dear to Picasso, but here, you can visit the workshops where they make it and take part in turning and decorating demonstrations.

• GLASS

BIOT 06410 – Alpes-Mar.

It was Éloi Mondor who opened the first glassware shop in 1956, the Verrerie de Biot®. Inspired by the work of glassmakers in Venice, Majorca and Barcelona, he started with glass objects for domestic use. Don't miss the famous **Fernand Léger Museum** in Biot (Chemin du Val de Pôme, tel 04 92 91 50 30, fax 04 92 91 50 31, open 10am-12:30pm & 2pm-5:30pm, until 6pm in summer, closed Tue). A few of these famous Biot glassmakers have both a workshop and a storefront.

La Verrerie de Biot

Chemin des Combes
04 93 65 03 00, fax 04 93 65 00 50
http://www.biot.verre.fr
Open Mon-Sat 9am-6:30pm, Sun & hols 10:30am-1pm & 2:30pm-6:30pm. Workshop closed Sun & hols 10:30am-1pm.

Verrerie Farinelli

465, route de la Mer
04 93 65 17 29, fax 04 93 65 50 84
http://www.biot.edit.fr/biot
(then click on Verrerie)
Open Mon-Sat 10am-7:30pm, Sun 10am-noon & 1pm-7:30pm.

Verrerie du Village

16, rue Saint-Sébastien
04 93 65 06 50, fax 04 93 65 55 99
Open 2pm-6:30pm. Closed Mon.

Verrerie du Vieux Moulin

Route de la Mer, 9, chemin du Plan
04 93 65 01 14, fax 04 93 65 19 54
Open Mon 2pm-6pm, Tue-Fri 10am-noon & 2pm-6pm, Sat-Sun 3pm-6pm.

• PERFUME

GRASSE 06332 – Alpes-Mar.

Parfumerie Galimard
Le Studio des Fragrances

Les 4 Chemins - 04 93 09 20 00, fax 04 93 70 36 22
http://www.galimard.com
Open daily 9am-12:30pm & 2pm-6pm.
Parfumerie Galimard opens its «Fragrance Studio» for an introductory course on perfume creation in just two hours. The *Nez* (nose) will teach you the intimate details of designing the «architecture» of a good perfume. And they keep the formula for future orders.

Molinard

60, bd Victor-Hugo
04 93 36 01 62, fax 04 93 36 03 91
http://www.molinard-parfums.com
Open Apr-Sep daily 9am-6:30pm; Oct-Mar Mon-Sat 9am-12:30pm & 2pm-6pm, Sun by appt.
Since 1849, Molinard perfumes have been perpetuating the French family tradition of perfume in Grasse. They use the most exclusive raw materials, such as Rosa Centifolia and the jasmine of Grasse. Possibility of creating a personalized perfume which will be offered free of charge at the end of the course.

NICE 06000 – Alpes-Mar.

Au Parfum de Grasse

10, rue Saint-Gaétan - 04 93 85 60 77
Open Tue-Sat 9:30am-noon & 2:30pm-6:30pm, Sun 9:30am-noon. Closed Mon.
Breathe in a little of the world's capital of perfume and take a little home with you. It's a must, even if you're short on time.

Looking for a chic souvenir? Refer to the **Index.**

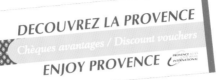

The Good Life.

Forbes *FYI*

"Forbes FYI is the magazine that
GQ and Esquire want to be."

• *SANTONS*

You must not leave Provence without buying some of the *santons*, so typical of the region, to decorate your nativity scene at Christmas or just for gifts.

AIX-EN-PROVENCE   13100 – B./Rhône

Santons Fouque

65, rue Gambetta - 04 42 26 33 38
http://www.laprovence.com
E-mail: a4a@enprovence.com
Open 8am-noon & 2pm-6pm. Closed Sun (exc Dec).
All the professions of yesteryear are represented—the butcher, the baker and the candlestick-maker, as well as the knife-and-scissors grinder and the miller—with more than 1,800 models of *santons*, the nativity scene figurines traditional in Provence, and made by Paul Fouque, inventor of the «mistral gale» *santon* in 1952.

AUBAGNE   13400 – B./Rhône

Maison Louis Sicard-Amy L'Atelier d'Art

2, bd E.-Combes - 04 42 70 12 92
Open Mon-Fri 8am-noon & 1:30pm-6pm, Sat 9am-noon & 2:30pm-6pm. Closed Sun (exc: Aug 9am-noon & 2:30pm-6pm).
Provençal grasshoppers created by Louis Sicard at the end of the nineteenth century, as well as *santons* (nativity scene figurines), either painted or dressed in costumes, and traditional earthenware.

Scaturro Daniel

20, av. de Verdun - Tel./fax 04 42 84 33 29
Open Mon 2:30pm-6pm, Tue-Fri 10am-noon & 2:30pm-6pm. Closed Sun.
Daniel Scaturro gets the inspiration for his *santons* from Pagnol characters. You can buy them entirely dressed in clothes, or completely molded in clay or painted.

BAUX-DE-PROVENCE   13520 – B./Rhône

Jacqueline Peyron-Campagna

Rue de l'Orme - 04 90 54 41 78, fax 04 90 54 53 26
Open daily 8am-6:30pm.
A workshop where they make Provençal *santons*, the little sculptures of shepherds, the Wise Men and other figures to put in your nativity scene.

NICE   06000 – Alpes-Mar.

Au Cœur de Nice

11, rue Mascoïnat - 04 93 13 88 11
E-mail: joel.garrigues@hol.fr
Open Mon-Fri 10am-1pm & 3pm-7pm, Sat-Sun 11am-1pm & 3pm-6pm.

La Couquetou

8, rue Saint-François-de Paule - 04 93 80 90 30
Open Mon-Sat 8am-7pm, Sun 10am-1pm.

Les Poupées Yolande

4, rue A.-Gautier - 04 93 55 56 00, fax 04 93 26 71 28
Open Mon-Fri 8am-noon & 2pm-7pm, Sat 8am-noon. Closed Sun.

WINE

In Provence, winemaking is a tradition rooted deep in antiquity. Grapes flourished here even before the Greeks landed in what is now Marseille, around 600 BC. Wine and its culture are woven into the fabric of daily life in Provence, and the vine has indelibly marked the countryside: even now vineyards carpet the hillsides, from the southern Rhône Valley downriver to the delta, and east to the Italian border.

Though they are actually situated in Provence (and so will be included in this chapter), Châteauneuf-du-Pape, Gigondas, Tavel, and several other prestigious *appellations* are considered Rhône Valley wines—for reasons that have as much to do with «image» as with geography and grape varieties!

In official terms, the wine-growing region of **Provence** covers the coast and the mountainous hinterland between **Arles** and **Nice**. The region's two largest AOCs, the Coteaux-d'Aix and the gigantic Côtes-de-Provence area, are surrounded by a string of more or less smaller cousins: the Coteaux Varois (recently promoted to AOC status), Cassis, Bandol, and the tiny AOCs of Palette (near Aix) and Bellet (next to Nice). Many different types of grapes are cultivated, but lately the Southern workhorse varieties—Carignan for red, Cinsault for rosé, and Ugni for white—are yielding to Grenache, for powerful, fruity reds; Tibouren for deeply colored and flavorful rosés; Bourboulenc and Rolle for clean, aromatic whites. Bellet is planted with its own distinctive varieties (Braquet, Folle Noire...), and Bandol's long-lived red wines owe their velvety texture and inky hue to the Mourvèdre grape. Marsanne and Syrah (white and red varieties, respectively) recently migrated from the northern Rhône, and are thriving in Provence.

Provence still suffers from an out-dated image as a wellspring of highly alcoholic, slightly oxidized rosés. In fact, since the mid-'80s the region's most talented vintners have concentrated on producing premium reds. The results are impressive: certain red wines from the Coteaux-d'Aix and Côtes-de-Provence can rival many a fine bottle from Bordeaux or the northern Rhône. First-rate white wines are less common, but they do exist; and the Institut du Rosé in Vidauban is dedicated to refurbishing the image of Provençal rosés.

SOUTHERN RHÔNE VALLEY

BEAUMES-DE-VENISE　　84190 – Vaucluse

Cave Castaud
Domaine des Bernardins
Route Lafare - 04 90 62 94 13, fax 04 90 65 01 42
Open 8am-noon & 2pm-6pm. Closed Sun & hols.
The place to go for the famous Muscat, so full of the fragrance of fresh grapes, and which slides down so easily with desserts.

BOLLÈNE　　84500 – Vaucluse

Château la Croix Chabrière
Route de Saint-Restitut
04 90 40 00 89, fax 04 90 40 19 93
Open daily 9am-noon & 2pm-6:30pm.
This Côtes-du-Rhône and Côteaux du Tricastin wine grower will let you visit his cellars and give you a 101 course in wine tasting, along with a guided tour of the château's *orangeraie* and stables. Count an hour and a half for the works.

CAIRANNE　　84290 – Vaucluse

Caveau du Belvédère
04 90 30 85 71
Open daily 9am-12:30pm & 1:30pm-7pm.
This is *the* showcase for Cairanne wines. Twenty-two independent Cairanne vine growers are represented along with those of the cooperative cellar. Free wine tastings, which last about one hour and a half, are organized in the spring and summer.

CHÂTEAUNEUF-DU-PAPE　　84230 – Vaucluse

Château Mont-Redon
04 90 83 72 75, fax 04 90 83 77 20

Open daily 8am-7:30pm.
Here, all thirteen traditional grape varieties are cultivated for an ever-distinguished Châteauneuf-du-Pape. Notable white Châteauneuf as well, and a spectacular Côtes-du-Rhône AOC produced with as much care as a Grand Cru. Tour of the cellar on reservation only.

COURTHÉZON
84350 – Vaucluse

Château de Beaucastel

J.-P. et F. Perrin - 04 90 70 41 00, fax 04 90 70 41 19
Open Mon-Fri 9am-11:30am & 2pm-5:30pm. Closed Sat, Sun?
Beaucastel continues to cultivate all thirteen of the grape varieties that traditionally compose Châteauneuf-du-Pape (elsewhere Syrah, Mourvèdre, and Grenache predominate); and each variety is vinified separately. Come here for consistently superb, concentrated Châteauneufs, and a lovely second wine, Le Coudoulet de Beaucastel.

GIGONDAS
84190 – Vaucluse

Cave des Vignerons de Gigondas

04 90 65 86 27, fax 04 90 65 80 13
Open Mon-Sat 8am-noon & 2pm-6pm, Sun & hols 10am-noon & 2:30pm-6:30pm.
This coop is one of the very few that offers wines as interesting as those of a top-quality individual producer. The secret? Rigorous selection. Look for the Seigneurie de Fontange/Vieilles Vignes cuvée: brawny, but balanced and fragrant Gigondas from older vines.

MALAUCENE
84340 – Vaucluse

Cave de Beaumont-du-Ventoux

Route de Carpentras
04 90 65 11 78, fax 04 90 12 69 88
Open daily 9am-noon & 2pm-6:30pm.
The vine growers of this cellar have recreated a *vin de liqueur* (sweet wine) that existed during Roman times! It is made with grapes harvested late (in October) and dried for three and one half months before being pressed. It then has to be aged for the same amount of time before being drunk, preferably with dessert.

TAIN-L'HERMITAGE
26600 – Drôme

Cave de Tain l'Hermitage

22, route de Larnage
04 75 08 20 87, fax 04 75 07 15 16
Open Sep-Jun: Mon-Sat 8am-noon & 2pm-6pm, Sun 9am-noon & 2pm-6pm; Jul-Aug: Mon-Sat

8am-noon & 1:30pm-7pm, Sun 9am-noon & 2pm-7pm.
The French wine review elected this cellar Cellar of the Year in December '95. You'll find all the Rhône Valley wines from the Syrah vines (reds) and Marsanne vines (whites).

TAVEL
30126 – Gard

Château d'Aquéria

04 66 50 04 56, fax 04 66 50 18 46
Open Mon-Fri 8am-noon & 2pm-6pm & by appt.
Tavel is the only Grand Cru of rosé, yielding a spicy, solid, aromatic wine that can stand up to food. Vincent and Bruno de Bez, a devoted pair of winemakers, produce one of the *appellation's* most consistently remarkable wines: brimming with fruit and menthol nuances that evolve into resinous aromas with age. Also: splendid white and red Liracs.

VACQUEYRAS
84190 – Vaucluse

Domaine Le Clos des Cazaux

Maurice et Jean-Michel Vache
04 90 65 85 83, fax 04 90 65 83 94
Open Mon-Sat 9am-noon & 2pm-6:30pm. Closed Sun.
Tannic by definition, Vacqueyras (now a cru, like Gigondas and Châteauneuf) is a quality wine for long keeping. Maurice and Jean-Michel Vache's firmly structured Cuvée des Templiers fits the description. Also: a charming white Vacqueyras redolent of ferns and almonds.

PROVENCE

ARCS-SUR-ARGENS (LES)
83460 – Var

Maison des Vins des Côtes de Provence

N 7 - 04 94 99 50 20, fax 04 94 99 50 29
Open Mon-Sat 10am-1pm & 1:30pm-6pm (7pm in May-Jun), Sun & hols until 5pm.
You'll find a selection of Côtes-de-Provence wines as well as artisanal products and a restaurant.

BAUX-DE-PROVENCE (LES)
13520 – B./Rhône

Mas Sainte-Berthe

04 90 54 39 01, fax 04 90 54 46 17
Open daily 9am-noon & 2pm-6pm.
At a site long famed for its pure spring water, Hélène David cultivate old Grenache vines

along with newer plantings of Syrah and Rolle to make their Cuvée Louis David, a superb red Coteaux-d'Aix with heady aromas of fruit, spice, and herbs.

CADIÈRE-D'AZUR (LA)　　83740 – Var

Château de Pibarnon

04 94 90 12 73, fax 04 94 90 12 98
Open Mon-Sat 8am-noon & 2pm-6:30pm. Closed Sun.
Bandol produces mostly rosés, but true wine buffs really get excited over the *appellation's* spicy, intense, and long-lived red wines (dominated by the Mourvèdre grape), perfect partners for red meats and game. Pibarnon is one of Bandol's top estates, with exceptional soil (the owner, Count Henri de Saint-Victor, is particularly proud of his land's blue marl). The wonderfully powerful red wines are aged for nearly two years in wood before bottling, and require several more years in the cellar. Memorable rosés, too.

CASSIS　　13260 – B./Rhône

Clos Sainte-Magdeleine

Av. du Revestel - 04 42 01 70 28, fax 04 42 01 15 51
Open Mon-Fri 10am-noon & 3pm-7pm. Closed Sat, Sun.
Only a dozen growers work the Cassis AOC region, making famous white wines that are lively and fresh, ideal companions to seafood and bouillabaisse. This estate, perched in a dreamy setting above the Mediterranean, makes one of France's greatest white wines, from a blend of grapes dominated by Marsanne, along with Ugni and Clairette. Excellent rosé, too.

FLASSANS-SUR-ISSOLE　　83340 – Var

Domaine de Saint-Baillon

N 7 - 04 94 69 74 60, fax 04 94 69 80 29
Open Mon-Sat 8am-1pm & 2pm-7pm. Closed Sun.
Hervé Goudard, a former lawyer, is now one of the top winemakers in the Côtes-de-Provence region. He only makes his Cuvée du Roudaï (60 percent Cabernet, 40 percent Syrah) in ideal years. But what a wine! Powerful, smoky, full-bodied, and long... The rosé Opale is also a winner, as the pure Rolle white wine (aged in oak).

LONDE-LÈS-MAURES (LA)　　83250 – Var

Château Sainte-Marguerite

04 94 66 81 46, fax 04 94 66 51 05
Open 8:30am-noon & 2:30pm-6pm. Closed Sun.
The estate's Ugni Blanc vines are over 100 years old. They yield exceptional white Côtes-de-Provence wines, particularly the Cuvée M de Marguerite and the floral, supple Grande

Réserve. Jean-Pierre Fayard also presents vivacious, full-bodied rosés and reds that benefit from a few years in the cellar.

LUC (LE)　　83340 – Var

Domaine La Bernarde

04 94 60 71 31, fax 04 94 47 96 04
Open 8:30am-noon & 1:30pm-5:30pm. Closed Sun.
Guy Meulnart's Côtes-de-Provence wines don't come cheap, but they compare favorably in quality to some of Médoc's Crus Bourgeois. The reds (made from Cabernet, Syrah, Mourvèdre, Grenache) are splendid: Le Clos La Bernarde is undoubtedly one of the region's top wines. Sémillon grapes give his whites a heady perfume, and his rosés are ripe and spicy (Guy serves them with caviar...).

MEYREUIL　　13590 – B./Rhône

Château Simone

René Rougier - 04 42 66 92 58, fax 04 42 66 80 77
Open 8am-noon & 2pm-6pm. Closed Sun.
Palette is a minuscule AOC near the city of Aix, and Château Simone is Palette's best-known estate, whose very old vines benefit from a favorable microclimate. The red wines are bottled only after three years in wood and should age another ten years before they are uncorked. Even the whites and rosés can reach a ripe old age, with no danger of oxidation. No need to worry about vintage years here: the wines are always wonderful.

NICE　　06000 – Alpes-Mar.

Château de Bellet

Quartier Saint-Roman de Bellet
04 93 37 81 57, fax 04 93 37 93 83
Open by appt only.
Just a few hundred yards (straight up!) from Nice's Promenade des Anglais, the AOC vineyards of Bellet produce a small quantity of estimable wine. Ghislain de Charnacé, owner of this estate, makes his white wines from Rolle grapes, which seem to have more character here than elsewhere in Provence. The cuvée aged in new oak is remarkable, but the finest of all is the white Cuvée Baron G, made from a single vineyard.

PLAN-DU-CASTELLET (LE)　　83330 – Var

Domaine Tempier

EARL Peyraud - 04 94 98 70 21, fax 04 94 90 21 65
Open Mon-Fri 9am-noon & 2pm-6pm, Sat 9am-noon. Closed Sun.
Jean-Marie and François Peyraud are grand masters of the historic Tempier estate. They are not interested in making popular wines; in the

past ten years they have reduced yields to obtain more concentrated, richer wines with a strong regional character. Five different cuvées of red Bandol are elaborated—none is cheap, and none is for early drinking!

ROQUEBRUNE-SUR-ARGENS 83520 – Var

Domaine des Planes

04 94 82 90 03, fax 04 94 82 94 76
http://www.dom-planes.com
E-mail: info@dom-planes.com
Open 9am-noon & 2pm-6:30pm. Closed Sun.
Tour of the cellar Tue & Fri at 5:30pm.
  Come here to taste a red Côtes-de-Provence made from 100 percent Mourvèdre grapes, and an array of delicious white wines. The new tasting cellar is most welcoming (regional specialties are also on sale), and there is a furnished rental (*gîte*) on the property.

ROQUEBRUSSANNE (LA) 83136 – Var

Domaine du Loou

04 94 86 94 97, fax 04 94 86 80 11
Open Mon-Sat 9am-noon & 2:30pm-6:30pm, Sun 11am-noon & 4:30pm-6:30pm.
  The Coteaux Varois is a small, new AOC area in the center of the Var *département*. Unlike most of the red wines made in this area, Daniel di Placido's wines are structured, powerful, and destined for a stint in the cellar before they reach the table. He also makes a fine rosé firm enough to stand up to food, and a fresh, aromatic white.

ST-RÉMY-DE-PROVENCE 13210 – B./Rhône

Château Romanin

04 90 92 45 87, fax 04 90 92 24 36
Open Mon-Fri 8:30am-1pm & 2pm-6:30pm, Sat-Sun & hols 11am-7pm.
  The château's spectacular cellars are carved out of solid rock. Therein you may sample elegant Coteaux-d'Aix wines made with state-of-the-art methods and equipment. The Château Romanin Rouge is typical of the region's new wave of spicy, well-crafted reds.

Domaine de Terres Blanches

D 99 - 04 90 95 91 66, fax 04 90 95 99 04
Open daily 10am-1pm & 2pm-6pm.
  Organically grown vines and the vintners' know-how produce super Les-Baux-de-Provence AOC wines.

VILLECROZE 83690 – Var

Domaine de Saint-Jean

04 94 70 63 07, fax 04 94 70 67 41
Open in seas: daily 9am-7:30pm; off-seas: daily 9am-noon & 2pm-6pm.
  The estate's American owner leaves the winemaking chores to French winemakers. Most of the property's Coteaux Varois are meant to be consumed in their youth, but the Cabernet Sauvignon de Saint-Jean is a keeper, with wonderful aromas of truffles and thyme.

BASICS

■ GETTING AROUND

■ AT YOUR SERVICE

GETTING AROUND

• AIRPORT

AVIGNON 13200 – B./Rhône

Aéroport d'Avignon-Caumont

In Montfavet
04 90 81 51 51, fax 04 90 84 17 23

MARSEILLE 13000 – B./Rhône

Aéroport International Marseille-Provence

In Marignane
04 42 14 14 14

NICE 06000 – Alpes-Mar.

Aéroport Nice Côte d'Azur

04 93 21 30 30

• HELICOPTER

Héli Air Monaco

Héliport, av. de Ligures
(377) 92 05 00 50, fax (377) 92 05 76 17
Open daily 7am-9:30pm.
Six minutes from the Nice airport to Monaco: no one can beat that (401 F one way). Héli Air Monaco also offers numerous packages on helicopter-theme excursions in the area (golf, children's birthdays, off-shore boating, canoeing, St-Tropez beaches, etc.).

• LIMOUSINES

See *Alliance Autos*, p. 139.

• TRAIN

SNCF

08 36 35 35 35
Open daily 7am-10pm.

AT YOUR SERVICE

• ENGLISH-LANGUAGE BOOKS

AIX-EN-PROVENCE 13090 – B./Rhône

Aix Paradox

15, rue du 4-Septembre
04 42 26 47 99, fax 04 42 38 54 93
Open Dec-Sep 9am-12:30pm & 2pm-6:30pm, Oct-Nov 9am-6:30pm. Closed Sun.
This international bookstore carries books in almost all matters, not only in English, but also in German, Spanish, Italian and Russian, as well as videos.

ANTIBES 06600 – Alpes-Mar.

Antibes Books

24, rue Aubernon - Tel/fax 04 93 34 74 11
Open daily 10am-7pm.
Thirteen years ago, Heidi Lee came to the old town of Antibes for a vacation and never left. The first one to open an English bookshop on the Côte d'Azur 8 years ago, people affectionately refer to her as the *doyenne*. With over 20,000 titles in stock, she offers a wide selection of new and used books at great prices, all under medieval vaulted ceilings. Also known in the area for being a community center for the large English-speaking community, Antibes Books hosts art exibitions or one-man theatre shows, and carries stationery, greeting cards and candles.

AVIGNON 84000 – Vaucluse

Shakespeare

155, rue Carreterie
04 90 27 38 50, fax 04 90 27 17 07
Open 9:30am-12:30pm & 2pm-6:30pm. Closed Sun, Mon.
A very extensive selection of English books: over 10,000 titles of new and used books in stock. Even though the books are imported, they sell them at jacket price, and even manage to give discounts on their already low prices. The jacket price is simply converted into French francs. Linger in the tea roomwhere you can lap up tea or coffee with home-made scones, or in summer, take them on the patio with its ivy-covered walls.

CANNES 06400 – Alpes-Mar.

Cannes English Bookshop

11, rue Bivouac Napoléon
04 93 99 40 08, fax 04 93 66 46 31

Open 10am-1pm & 2pm-7pm. Closed Sun. During the Festival daily 9:30am-8pm.
Christel Storier is the owner of the only English bookstore in Cannes. It carries some 7,000 titles covering a full range of subjects.

Rubis Presse

12, rue Jean de Riouffre - 04 93 68 15 75
Open daily 7:15am-7:45pm.
After a tour in this *maison de la presse*, you will be well stocked with English newspapers and magazines.

FAYENCE   83440 – Var

Librairie du Château

1, rue Saint-Pierre - Tel/fax 04 94 84 72 00
Open Mon 2:30pm-7pm, Tue-Sat 9am-12:30pm & 2:30pm-7pm (in summer 9am-7pm). Closed Sun.
Christine Buisson, of English descent, has been in France for more than 30 years and knows the area very well. An emphasis on books about the region in this cozy two-room store.

MONACO   98000 – Principality of Monaco

Scrupules

9, rue Princesse Caroline
Tel/fax(377) 93 50 43 52
Open Mon-Fri 9:30am-noon & 2:30pm-7pm, Sat until 6:30pm. Closed Sun.
Despite her name, Madame France is English and only sells books in her mother tongue. She was one of the first ones in the Côte d'Azur to do so in a small, but well-stocked boutique (from Virgil to Jacky Collins). You will also find greeting cards for any occasion, gifts, and children's things for parties.

NICE   06000 – Alpes-Mar.

Cat Whiskers

26, rue Lamartine
Tel/fax 04 93 80 02 66
Open Mon-Fri 9:30am-noon & 2pm-6:45pm, Sat 9:30am-noon & 3pm (3:30pm in summer)-6:30pm. Closed Sun.
English owner Linda Pickering will help choose you find your heart's desire amid all the books that she has so carefully selected.

Maison de la Presse

1, pl. Masséna
04 93 87 79 42, fax 04 93 16 09 23
Open Mon-Sat 8:45am-7:30pm, Sun 9:30am-noon & 3:30pm-7:30pm.
All you have always wanted to know, in English of course, in newspapers and magazines.

VALBONNE   06560 – Alpes-Mar.

English Reading Centre

12, rue Alexis Julien - 04 93 12 21 42
Open 9:30am-12:30pm & 3pm-6pm (6:30pm in summer). Closed Sun, Mon.
About 5,000 references to choose from. You will also find videos for rainy days.

• *ORIENTATION*

See p. 142.

• *TOURIST INFORMATION*

For all the brochures and other «literature» that the sage sightseer might need about major cities (listed alphabetical order).

Aix-en-Provence

2, pl. du Général-de-Gaulle
04 42 16 11 61, fax 04 42 16 11 62
http://www.aix-en-provence.com/aixofftour/
E-mail: aixtour@aix.pacwan.net
Open Sep-Jun: Mon-Sat 8:30am-8pm, Sun 10am-1pm & 2pm-6pm; Jul-Aug daily 8:30am-10pm.

Antibes

11, pl. du Général-de-Gaulle
04 92 90 53 00, fax 04 92 90 53 01
Open Mon-Fri 9am-12:30pm & 2pm-6:30pm, Sat 9am-noon & 2pm-6pm. Closed Sun (exc in summer 9am-noon).

Arles

35, pl. de la République
04 90 18 41 20, fax 04 90 93 17 17
http://www.arles.cci.fr
E-mail: contact@arles.cci.fr
Open Oct-Mar Mon-Sat 9am-6pm, Sun 10am-noon; Apr-Sep Mon-Sat 9am-7pm, Sun 9am-1pm, hols 9am-7pm.

Avignon

41, cours J.-Jaurès - 04 90 82 65 11, fax 04 90 82 95 03
http://www.avignon-tourisme.com
E-mail: information@ot-avignon.fr
Open Mon-Fri 9am-1pm & 2pm-6pm, Sat-Sun until 5pm.

Baux-de-Provence (Les)

Ilôt «Post Tenebras Lux»
04 90 54 34 39, fax 04 90 54 51 15
Open Easter-Oct: daily 9am-7pm; Nov-Easter: 9am-dawn.

Beaulieu-sur-Mer

Pl. Georges-Clémenceau
04 93 01 02 21, fax 04 93 01 44 04
http://www.compuserve.com/homepage/beaulieu-sur-mer
Open 9am-12:15pm & 2pm-6pm (in summer until 7pm). Closed Sun.

Cannes

SEM «Palais des Festivals»
04 93 39 24 53, fax 04 93 99 84 23
http://www.cannes-on-line.com
E-mail: semaftou@palais-festivals-cannes.fr
Open 9am-7pm. Closed Sun (exc during conventions).

Grasse

22, cours H.-Cresp
04 93 36 03 56, fax 04 93 36 86 36
E-mail: Tourisme.Grasse@wanadoo.fr
Open Jul-mid Sep daily 9am-7pm; mid Sep-Jun Mon-Sat 9am-12:30pm & 13:30pm-6pm. Closed Sun (mid Sep-Jun).

Juan-les-Pins

51, bd Ch.-Guillaumont - 04 92 90 53 05
Open Mon-Fri 9am-noon & 2pm-6pm, Sat 9am-8pm, Sun 9am-noon. Closed off-seas Sat pm & Sun.

Marseille

1st arr. - 4, la Canebière
04 91 13 89 00, fax 04 91 13 89 20
E-mail: destination-marseille@wanadoo.fr
Open summer daily 8:30am-8pm; winter daily 9am-7pm.

Monaco (Principalty of)

2, bd des Moulins
(377) 92 16 61 66, fax (377) 92 16 60 00
http://www.monaco.mc/usa/
E-mail: mgto@monaco1.org
Open Mon-Sat 9am-7pm, Sun & hols 10am-noon.

Mougins

Av. J.-Ch. Mallet - 04 93 75 87 67, fax 04 92 92 17 08
Open 10am-5:30pm. Closed Sun, Mon (Oct-Jun).

Ramatuelle

1, rue Georges Clémenceau
04 94 79 26 04, fax 04 94 79 12 66
http://www.nova.fr/ramatuelle
http://www.franceplus.com/golfe.de.saint-tropez
Open in summer: daily 9am-1pm & 3pm-7:30pm; off-seas: 8:30am-12:30pm & 2:30pm-6:30pm. Closed Sat & Sun off-seas.

Saint-Paul-de-Vence

Rue Grande, maison Tour
04 93 32 86 95, fax 04 93 32 60 27
Open daily 10am-noon & 2pm-6pm; in summer until 7pm.

Saint-Rémy-de-Provence

Pl. Jean-Jaurès - 04 90 92 05 22, fax 04 90 92 38 52
Open daily 9am-noon & 2pm-6pm. Closed Sun.

Saint-Tropez

Quai Jean-Jaurès - 04 94 97 45 21, fax 04 94 97 82 66
http://www.nova.fr/saint-tropez
E-mail: tourisme@nova.fr
Open beg Apr-end Jun daily 9am-12:30pm & 2:30pm-7pm; end Jun-beg Sep daily 9:30am-1pm & 3pm-10:30pm; beg Sep-Nov 1 daily 9am-12:30pm & 2:30pm-7pm; Nov 2-Dec 20 daily 9am-noon & 2pm-6pm; Dec 21-Jan 3 daily 9am-1pm & 2pm-7pm; Jan 4-beg Apr daily 9am-noon & 2pm-6pm.

Saintes-Maries-de-la-Mer

5, av. V.-Van Gogh
04 90 97 82 55, fax 04 90 97 71 15
http://www.visitprovence
Open daily 9am-7pm.

Salon-de-Provence

56, cours Gimon - 04 90 56 27 60, fax 04 90 56 77 09
http://www.salon-de-provence.org
http://www.visitprovence.com
Open Mon-Sat 9am-noon & 2pm-6:30pm; in summer 9am-noon & 2:30pm-7pm.

Nice

5, Promenade des Anglais
04 92 14 48 00, fax 04 92 14 48 03
http://www.nice-coteazur.org
E-mail: otc@nice-coteazur.org
Open in summer: daily 8am-7pm; rest of the year: 9am-6pm, closed Sun.

Vence

Pl. Grand Jardin - 04 93 58 06 38, fax 04 93 58 91 81
Open Mon-Fri 9:30am-12:30pm & 2pm-6pm, Sat 9:30am-12:30pm & 2pm-5pm. Closed Sun.

• USEFUL ADDRESSES

Here are some addresses and phone numbers of particular interest to English-speaking travelers:

Consulates

MARSEILLE   13006 – B./Rhône

American Consulate

6th arr. - 12, bd Paul Peytral
04 91 54 92 00, fax 04 91 55 09 47
Open 8:30am-12:30pm & 1:30pm-5:30pm. Closed Sat, Sun.

British Consulate

6th arr. - 24, av. Prado - 04 91 15 72 10

Open 9am-noon & 2pm-6pm. Closed Sat, Sun.

NICE   06000 – Alpes-Mar.

American Consulate

31, av. du Maréchal Joffre - 04 93 88 89 55
Open 9am-11:30am & 1:30pm-4:30pm. Call for appt. Closed Sat, Sun.

British Consulate

Le Palace, 8, rue Alphonse Carr
04 93 82 32 04, fax 04 93 82 48 24
Open Tue, Wed, Thu 10am-noon. Closed Mon, Fri, Sat, Sun.

Canadian Consulate

64, av. Jean Médecin
04 93 92 93 22, fax 04 93 92 55 51
Open 9am-noon. Closed Sat, Sun.

English-speaking Organizations

American Chamber of Commerce

Monaco (Principalty of - 98000)
7, rue Gabian, Gildo Pastor Center
(377) 92 05 79 99, fax (377) 92 05 77 22
Open 9am-6pm. Closed Sat, Sun.

• *PHONE DIRECTORY*

Fire Department

18
Open daily 24 hours.

Police

17
Open daily 24 hours.

Medical

Centre Anti-Poisons

In Marseille - 04 91 75 25 25
Open daily 24 hours.
Poison Control Center.

SAMU (Ambulance)

15
Open daily 24 hours.

S.O.S. Médecins

Aix-en-Provence (13100) - 04 42 26 24 00
Antibes (06600) - 04 93 67 20 00

Avignon (84000) - 04 90 82 65 00
Cannes (06400) - 04 93 38 39 38
Marseille (13000) - 04 91 52 91 52
Menton (06500) - 04 93 41 41 41
Nice (06000) - 04 93 85 01 01
Saint-Raphaël (83700) - 04 94 95 15 25
Open daily 24 hours.
These doctors make house calls at any hour of the day or night.

Miscellaneous

Nationwide Traffic

08 36 68 20 00
Open daily 24 hours.
All day, all night, an answering machine will keep you abreast of traffic problems on the highways (and byways) of France.

Telegrams

36 55
Open Open daily 24 hours.
Messages for France are relayed by phone, then the hard copy is sent by mail. The minimum charge is 65 F for 25 words (not including the address) and 12.20 F for each ten-word addition. To send a telegram abroad, call the toll-free number 0 800 33 44 11, (135.24 F for 15 words, including the address, and 27.46 F for each five-word addition).

Time

36 99
Open daily 24 hours.
Feeling disoriented? Call this number to learn the date and time, anytime.

Wake-up Call

55 or 36 88 if 55 doesn't work with the phone you are using.
From any voice-tone phone you can schedule a wake-up call: to be awakened at 7:45am, for example, dial *55* 0745#. To cancel, dial #55*0745#. But remember: don't try to schedule a call more than 24 hours ahead! It will cost you 3.71 F.

Weather

08 36 68 00 00
Open daily 24 hours.
No need to stick your head out the window! To find out how the weather is or is likely to be in the Ile-de-France, just pick up your phone.

• *DUTY-FREE SHOPPING*

See p. 146.

GAYOT PUBLICATIONS

on the Internet

GAYOT PUBLICATIONS/GAULTMILLAU IS PROUD TO FEATURE
RESTAURANT, HOTEL AND TRAVEL INFORMATION FROM OUR
BOOKS AND UPDATES ON MANY INTERNET WEB SITES.

We suggest you start surfing at:
http://www.gayot.com

We welcome your questions and comments at our e-mail address:
gayots@aol.com

FOOD NOTES

MENU SAVVY

A

Agneau: lamb
Aïoli: garlicky mayonnaise
Américaine or armoricaine: sauce of white wine, Cognac, tomatoes, and butter
Ananas: pineapple
Andouille: smoked tripe sausage, usually served cold
Anglaise (à l'): boiled meats or vegetables
Anguille: eel
Asperges: asparagus
Aumônière: literally means «alms-purse»; usually savory or sweet wrapped in a thin pastry in the shape of a purse or bag

B

Bar: bass
Ballottine: boned, stuffed, and rolled poultry
Bavarois: Bavarian cream
Béarnaise: sauce made of shallots, tarragon, vinegar, and egg yolks, mixed with butter
Béchamel: white sauce made of flour, butter, and milk
Beurre blanc: sauce of wine and vinegar boiled down with finely chopped shallots, then thickened with butter
Beurre noisette: lightly browned butter
Bière: beer
Bigarade: bitter orange used in sauces and marmalade
Bisque (crayfish, lobster, etc.): rich, velvety soup, usually made with crustaceans, flavored with white wine and Cognac
Blinis: small, thick crêpes made with eggs, milk, and yeast
Bœuf: beef
Bœuf bourguignon: beef stewed with red wine, onions, and lardoons
Bombe glacée: molded ice cream dessert
Bordelaise: fairly thin brown sauce of shallots, red wine, and tarragon
Boudin noir: blood sausage or black pudding
Brioche: a soft, often sweet yeast bread or roll enriched with eggs and butter
Brochet: pike
Brochette: on a skewer, shish kebab
Biscuits: cookies

C

Caille: quail
Calvados: distilled apple cider
Canard: duck
Carbonnade: pieces of lean beef, first sautéed then stewed with onions and beer
Carrotte: carrot
Carré d'agneau: rack of lamb
Cèpe: prized wild mushroom, the same as the Italian porcini
Cerise: cherry
Champignon: mushroom
Chanterelle: prized wild mushroom, trumpet-shaped; also called *girolle*
Charlotte: dessert of flavored creams and/or fruit molded in a cylindrical dish lined with ladyfingers (if served cold) or strips of buttered bread (if served hot)
Chasseur: brown sauce made with shallots, white wine, and mushrooms
Chèvre (fromage de): goat (cheese)
Chevreuil: venison
Chou: cabbage
Choucroute: sauerkraut; often served with sausages, smoked bacon, pork loin, and potatoes
Citron: lemon; **Citron vert:** lime
Chou-fleur: cauliflower
Clafoutis: a dessert of fruit (usually cherries) baked in an eggy batter
Confit: pork, goose, duck, turkey, or other meat cooked and sealed in its own fat; when the term is used with a fruit or vegetable, it simply means that it becomes glazed or candied by cooking in its own juices
Coquilles St-Jacques: scallops
Côte d'agneau: lamb chop
Coulis: thick sauce or purée, often of vegetables or fruits
Court-bouillon: stock in which fish, meat, and poultry are cooked
Crème chantilly: sweetened whipped cream
Crêpes Suzette: crêpes stuffed with a sweetened butter mixture and ground almonds, Grand Marnier, tangerine juice, and peel
Crevette: shrimp
Croque-monsieur: grilled ham and cheese sandwich
Croustillant: crispy or crisp
Croûte (en): in pastry crust
Crudités: raw vegetables
Crustacé: shellfish

D

Daube: beef braised in red wine
Daurade: sea bream

E

Écrevisse: crayfish
Entrecôte: beef rib steak
Épinards: spinach
Escalope: slice of meat or fish, flattened slightly and sautéed
Escargots (à la bourguignonne): snails (with herbed garlic butter)

F

Faisan: pheasant
Financière: Madeira sauce enhanced with truffle juice
Fish: poisson
Florentine: with spinach
Foie: liver
Foie gras: liver of a specially fattened goose or duck
Forestière: garnish of sautéed mushrooms and lardoons
Fraise: strawberry
Framboise: raspberry
Frangipane: almond pastry cream

G

Galantine: boned poultry or meat, stuffed and pressed into a symmetrical shape, cooked in broth and coated with aspic
Gâteau: cake

Gelée (en): in aspic; gelatin usually flavored with meat, poultry, or fish stock
Génoise: sponge cake
Gibier: game
Glace: ice cream
Granité: lightly sweetened fruit ice
Gratin: for savory dishes, topped with cheese or bread crumbs and browned under broiler; for sweet dishes, the cheese or bread crumbs are replaced by thick cream
Gratin dauphinois: sliced potatoes baked in milk, sometimes with cream and/or grated Gruyère
Grenouille: frog (frogs' legs: cuisses de grenouilles)

H

Hollandaise: egg-based sauce thickened with butter and flavored with lemon
Homard: lobster
Huître: oyster

J

Jambon: ham
Julienne: shredded vegetables; also a consomme garnished with shredded vegetables
Jus: juice; also a reduction or essence used as a sauce

L

Lait: milk
Langouste: rock or spiny lobster
Langoustine: saltwater crayfish or Dublin bay prawn
Lapereau: young rabbit
Lapin: rabbit
Lièvre: hare
Lotte: monkfish or anglerfish; sometimes called «poor man's lobster»

M

Magret (Maigret): breast of fattened duck, cooked with the skin on; usually grilled
Médaillon: food, usually meat, fish, or foie gras, cut into small, round «medallions»
Mirabelle: yellow plum
Moelleux: literally means «soft and springy»; often refers to a type of cake, usually chocolate, that is velvety in texture and runny in the middle
Morue: salt cod
Moules (marinière): mussels (cooked in the shell with white wine, shallots, and parsley)

N

Nantua: sauce of crayfish, white wine, butter, and cream with a touch of tomato
Navets: turnips
Noisettes: hazelnuts; also, small, round pieces of meat (especially lamb and veal)
Nougat: sweet made with roasted almonds, egg whites, honey, and sugar

O

Œuf: egg

P

Pain: bread
Parfait: sweet or savory mousse; also a layered ice cream dessert
Parisienne: garnish of fried potato balls
Pâtisserie: pastry
Paupiette: thin slice of meat stuffed with forcemeat and shaped into rolls
Pêche: peach

Pigeonneau: squab
Pintade: guinea hen
Poireau: leek
Poire: pear
Pomme: apple
Pomme de terre: potatoe
Poulet: chicken
Provençale (à la): with garlic or tomato and garlic
Prune: Plum

Q

Quiche: savory tart filled with a mixture of eggs, cream, and various fillings (such as ham, spinach, or bacon)

R

Raisin: grape
Ratatouille: stew of eggplant, tomatoes, bell peppers, zucchini, onion, and garlic, all sautéed in oil
Rémoulade: tangy cold sauce often flavored with capers, onions, parsley, gherkins, or herbs
Ris de veau: sweetbreads
Rissole: type of small pie filled with forcemeat
Rognon: kidney
Rouget: red mullet
Rouille: a Provençal sauce, so called because of the red chiles and sometimes saffron which give it a «rust» color; chiles are pounded with garlic and breadcrumbs and blended with olive oil; the sauce being served with bouillabaisse, boiled fish or octopus

S

Sabayon: fluffy, whipped egg yolks, sweetened and flavored with wine or liqueur and served warm
Saint-Pierre: John Dory; a white-fleshed fish
Sandre: pikeperch
Saumon: salmon
Soissons: garnished with white beans
Sole meunière: sole dipped in flour and sautéed in butter, served with parsley and lemon
Steak au poivre: pepper steak; steak covered in crushed peppercorns, browned in a frying pan, flambéed with Cognac, often served with a cream sauce
Steak tartare: chopped raw steak mixed with onion, anchovy, seasonings, and egg yolk

T

Tapenade: a paste of black olives, often with capers and anchovies, crushed in a mortar with lemon juice and pepper
Tartare: cold sauce for meat or fish: mayonnaise with hard-boiled egg yolks, onions, and chopped olives
Tarte: tart, round cake or flan; can be sweet or savory
Tarte Tatin: upside-down apple tart invented by the Tatin sisters
Tortue: turtle, also, a sauce made with various herbs, tomato, Madeira
Tourteau: large crab
Truffe: truffle; highly esteemed subterranean fungus, esp. from Périgord
Truite: trout

V

Vacherin: ice cream served in a meringue shell; also, creamy, pungent cheese from Switzerland or eastern France
Viande: meat
Volaille: poultry

REGIONAL SPECIALTIES

A

Aïgo bouido or boulido or bullido (Provence): garlic soup with oil served over slices of bread

Aïoli or aïlloli (Provence): sauce (mayonnaise with garlic) has lent its name to this dish of dried cod, various vegetables, snails, and hard-boiled eggs

Aligot (Auvergne): mashed potatoes combined with garlic and Cantal or fresh Tomme cheese; has a very elastic consistency

Anchoïade (Provence): purée of anchovy fillets combined with garlic and olive oil; accompanies crudités

Andouille de Guémené (Brittany): andouille (tripe sausage) with a characteristic marking of concentric rings

Andouille de Vire (Calvados): andouille (pork tripe sausage) with irregular marbling

Andouillette de Troyes (Champagne): small andouille made of pork in rather broad and alternating strips

Anguille au vert (Lille): eel in a green sauce flavored with thirteen herbs

B

Baba (Lorraine): a small yeast cake soaked in a rum syrup; said to have been invented by King

Bæckeoffe (Alsace): hot terrine made with alternating layers of beef, mutton, and pork, marinated in wine with sliced potatoes and onions

Beignets de fleurs de courge (Provence, Nice): squash blossoms (pistils removed) dipped in batter and deep fried

Beurre blanc nantais (Nantes, Loire, Anjou): sauce consisting of minced shallots cooked in a reduction of Muscadet and/or vinegar, with butter whisked in until the consistency is perfectly creamy; most often accompanies pike. The sauce often lends its name to the dish itself

Bireweck (Alsace): sweet, moist bread studded with dried fruit, flavored with Kirsch and spices

Bœuf gardiane (Camargue): marinated beef stewed with bacon, onions, garlic, tomatoes, olives, and red wine

Boles de picoulat (Roussillon): meatballs made of minced beef, pork, garlic, and eggs, accompanied by parsleyed tomatoes

Boudin blanc (Normandy and all of France): sausage of pork fat, milk, eggs, bread, starch, and rice flour; often includes truffles, trimmings or leftover bread

Bouillabaisse (Provence): various fish (including scorpionfish) in a soup of olive oil, tomatoes, garlic and saffron

Bouilleture or bouilliture (Anjou, Aunis): eel stewed in red wine with onions or shallots, prunes, and (optionally) garlic and egg yolk

Bouillinade (Roussillon): a sort of bouillabaisse made of pieces of fish (lotte, turbot, John Dory, sea bass) with potatoes, oil, onions, and garlic; the broth is thickened with egg yolk and oil

Bourdelot (Normandy): a whole apple baked in a pastry crust

Bourride (Provence): a sort of bouillabaisse usually made with large white fish (lotte, turbot); the creamy broth is thickened with aïoli and poured over slices of bread

Boutifare or boutifaron (Catalonia, Roussillon): boudin with bacon and herbs

Brandade de morue (Nîmes): salt cod puréed with olive oil, truffles (optional) and milk or cream

Broufado (Provence): layers of thin slices of marinated beef and chopped onions with vinegar, capers, and anchovies

Bugnes (Lyonnais, Burgundy): a sweet dessert fritter

C

Cabassol (Languedoc): lamb tripe

Cagouille or luma (Charentes): local name for snail; (cagouillard, the nickname for natives of the Charentes, comes from cagouille)

Caillette (Ardèche, Drôme): chopped spinach, chard, onion, parsley, garlic, bread, minced pork, and egg formed into fist-sized balls, baked, and served hot or cold

Carbonnade (Flanders): pieces of lean beef, first sautéed then stewed with onions and beer

Cargolade (Languedoc, Roussillon): snails simmered in wine, or cooked over charcoal, with salt and pepper, flavored with bacon fat

Casserons en matelote (Ile de Ré, Charente-Maritime): squid in a sauce of red wine (from the island), garlic, shallots, a bit of sugar, and butter

Cassoulet (Toulouse, Castelnaudary and other regions): white Cazères or Pamiers beans and various meats (mutton, preserved goose or duck, sausage, salt brisket, pig's trotters) cooked at length in an earthenware casserole

Caudière or chaudrée (Flanders): fish soup with potatoes, for which there are numerous recipes(it is the origin of American chowder)

Cervelas de Lyon (Lyonnais): fat, short pork sausage, often flavored with truffles or pistachios and placed in a brioche crust

Cervelas de Strasbourg (Alsace): sausage in a red-colored casing, eaten hot or cold (in a salad)

Cervelle de canut (Lyonnais): white cheese mixed with shallots, herbs, and chives, cream, white wine, and a bit of oil

Chaudrée (Poitou, Saintonge, Aunis): soup or stew of various fish cooked in white wine, with shallots, garlic, and butter

Chipirons à l'encre (Pays Basque): cuttlefish stuffed with onions, bread, and cuttlefish meat, served in a sauce of its own ink with tomatoes

Confit (Périgord, Quercy, Béarn): wings, thighs, and other pieces of duck, pork, or goose (or, rarely, turkey or chicken), cooked in their own fat and stored in a stoneware jar

Cornics (Brittany): type of croissant

Cotriade (Brittany): fisherman's soup, infinitely variable, composed of delicate fish simmered with potatoes, onions, garlic, parsley, and butter; served over croûtons

Cou d'oie farci (Périgord): mixture of sausage meat, duck liver, and a small amount of minced truffle, stuffed in the skin of a fatted goose. The whole is cooked in boiling fat, like a confit, and eaten hot or cold, accompanied by a salad dressed with walnut oil

Cousina or cousinat (Vivarais, Auvergne): chestnut soup made with cream, butter, onions, and leeks, or sometimes with prunes or apples

Cousinat (Pays Basque): a stew of Bayonne ham, small artichokes, beans, carrots, tomatoes and various other vegetables

Craquelot (Flanders): herring smoked over walnut leaves

Crémet (Loire): whipped cream and stiffly beaten egg whites placed in a mold lined with muslin; served with cream and sprinkled with sugar

Crémet (Nantes): molded cheese covered with sweetened whipped cream; Normandy has an almost identical recipe for white cheese that bears the same name

Crêpes dentelle (Brittany): crêpes that are extremely thin, almost like lace (dentelle), and flaky, served rolled up. Originally from Quimper

Criques (Vivarais): grated potatoes mixed with eggs and fried like pancakes. Related to the râpée and grapiau (Morvan) and truffiat (Berry)

D

Daube (Provence, Languedoc): beef or mutton marinated in red wine with oil and onions, then braised in an earthenware pot

Diots (Savoie): sausages made with chard, spinach, cabbage, and leeks, mixed with pork and pork fat; they are preserved in oil and are often cooked in white wine with shallots and minced onions

Douillon (Normandy): a whole pear baked in a pastry crust

E

Éclade de moules or fumée or térée (Saintonge): mussels laid out on a board with their tips up, roasted over a fire of pine needles

Escargots à la bourguignonne (Burgundy): snails stuffed with butter, garlic, and parsley

F

Farci poitevin (Poitou): pâté of greens (spinach, chard, sorrel, cabbage) mixed with bacon and eggs, wrapped in cabbage leaves and cooked in bouillon; eaten hot or cold

Farcis niçois: see *Petits farcis*

Farçon (Auvergne): large pancake made of sausage meat, sorrel, onions, eggs, flour, and white wine

Farçon (Savoie): potatoes, bacon, prunes, and eggs, or mashed potatoes, milk, and eggs, mixed and gratinéed in the oven

Ficelle picarde (Picardie): crêpe rolled with ham, mushrooms, and grated cheese, gratinéed in the oven

Flamique or flamiche (Picardie): sort of tart-flan with leeks, onion, or squash

Flammekueche or tarte flambée (Alsace): a rectangle of bread dough with raised edges, filled with cream, bacon, onions, and (sometimes) white cheese, then baked

Flamusse (Nivernais, Morvan): fruit (often apple) omelet

Flognarde or flaugnarde (Auvergne): a type of flan

Fougassette (Provence): oval-shaped bread made with oil and flavored with orange or lemon rind and orangeflower water

G

Galettes and crêpes (Brittany): galettes are made of buckwheat flour and are usually savory; crêpes are made of wheat flour and are usually sweet

Garbure (Southwest): soup prepared with fat (sometimes with streaky bacon and sausage), green beans, thinly sliced cabbage, beans, garlic, marjoram, thyme, and parsley; a piece of preserved duck, turkey, goose, or pork (tromblon or trébuc) is added and the soup is served over slices of bread

Gâteau basque (Pays Basque): thick torte stuffed with pastry cream

Gâteau breton (Brittany): type of pound cake or a large, somewhat hard and crumbly cake

Gaufres (Flanders, Artois): waffles

Grattons (Lyonnais): rillettes; browned but not molded cubes of bacon

Grillons (Périgord): bits of goose (or pork) meat left over from preparation of confit

H

Hochepot (Flanders): sort of pot-au-feu made with oxtails

Huîtres à la bordelaise (Bordelais): oysters accompanied by sausages with optional truffles

J

Jambon persillé (Burgundy): ham cooked in white wine, cut into pieces, and mixed with aspic and parsley; served cold molded in a salad bowl

Jésus de Morteau (Franche-Comté): large pork sausage with a small wooden peg at one end—a sign that it has been smoked over pine and juniper

K

Kouing amann (Douarnenez, Brittany): a rich, buttery cake

Kugelhopf (Alsace): a sort of brioche with raisins and almonds, cooked in a characteristic fluted mold

L

Langues d'avocat (Bordelais): «lawyer's tongues»—the local name for small sole

M

Madeleine de Commercy (Lorraine): small, fluted, and domed cake; said to have been created by King Stanislaw Leszczynski's cook, Madeleine

Millia (Périgord): a pumpkin-and-cornflour flan; a very similar dish is made in the Limousin

Mogette or mojette, Mougette, Mohjette (Angoûmois): a small bean that reminds natives of Charente of the humble, curled-up posture of a nun (mougette) at prayer

Mouclade (Charentes): mussels cooked with cream, egg yolks, white wine, and butter, to which Pineau des Charentes can also be added

O

Osso buco (Provence): Italian stew made with veal shanks braised in olive oil, white wine, broth, onions, garlic, tomatoes, carrots, celery and lemon peel

P

Panisses (Provence): chickpea flour made into a porridge, then fried in oil

Pastis (Pays Basque): cake flavored with orangeflower water

Petits farcis (Provence): squash, eggplant, tomatoes, and onions stuffed with their own pulp mixed with chopped pork or veal, eggs, and garlic, then baked in the oven with oil

Pieds et paquets (Marseille, Provence): stuffed lamb tripes simmered in white wine and broth with lard and sheep's trotters

Pissaladière (Nice): tart topped with onions, black olives, and anchovy fillets

Pistou (Provence): condiment made up of a mixture of crushed basil, garlic and olive oil and sometimes tomatoes and Parmesan, France's version of Italy's pesto; or a French vegetable soup made with includes green beans, white beans, onions, potatoes, tomatoes and vermicelli and seasoned with the pistou above, similar to Italian minestrone.

Pogne (Dauphiné): brioche loaf studded with candied fruit

Pommes de terre sarladaise (Périgord): raw potatoes cut into thin slices and baked with goose fat and (optional) truffles

Pompe (Auvergne, Nivernais, Morvan): sort of torte or turnover filled with fruit (such as apples)

Pompe de Noël or gibassié (Provence): bread made with oil and orange rind or lemon, perfumed with orangeflower water

Porchetta (Nice): a small pig stuffed with its offal mixed with herbs and garlic, then roasted on a spit

Potée (multiregional): various vegetables and meats boiled together

Potjevfleisch (Dunkirk, Nord): terrine of veal, pork, and rabbit

Pounti (Auvergne): meatloaf made with ground pork and chard; eggs or cream can also be added, or grapes, prunes, and herbs

Poutargue (Provence): red or gray mullet roe, salted, pressed and served in the form of slightly flattened sausages

Presskopf or tête roulée (Alsace): cubes of pig's head or veal and pieces of pork in wine aspic with (optionally) shallots and gherkins. Often served with an herbal vinaigrette

Q

Quenelles (Lyonnais, Bugey, Alsace): fowl or pike made with a mousseline stuffing thickened with eggs and shaped into small cylinders or dumplings

R

Raisiné (Aunis, Saintonge, Burgundy): jam made with grape juice or must, reduced until it has the consistency of jelly or marmalade

Ravioles (Dauphiné): pasta stuffed with goat cheese

Ravioli à la niçoise (Nice): pasta stuffed with meat (veal, pork, or beef), poached and minced chard, and a bit of grated cheese

Rillettes du Mans (Sarthe): shredded pork spread with some rather large bits left in

Rillettes de Tours (Touraine): darker in color than the previous type, with a rather delicate texture; often contain pork liver

Rillons or rillauds (Touraine, Anjou): pieces of pork brisket and shoulder cut into large cubes and cooked in pork fat

Rosette (Lyonnais): large dry sausage of pure pork (usually wrapped in a net)

Rouille (Provence): rust-colored mayonnaise flavored with chilis, garlic, bread soaked in bouillon, olive oil, and saffron; often accompanies bouillabaisse

S

Salade niçoise (Nice): salad of tomatoes, hard-boiled egg, anchovy fillets, tuna, sweet peppers, celery, and olives (also can include green beans, potatoes, basil, onions, and/or broad beans)

Saladier lyonnais (Lyonnais): salad of sheep's trotters, chicken **Spätzle (Alsace)**: round noodles, sometimes made with egg

T

Tablier de sapeur (Lyonnais): pieces of tripe browned and cut into triangles, dipped in beaten eggs, then breaded; often served with snail butter or with mayonnaise containing shallots and tarragon

Tapenade (Provence): black olives from Nice, capers, and anchovies, crushed in a mortar with lemon juice and pepper. Can be eaten as an hors d'œuvre on toast, or used as a stuffing for hard-boiled eggs

Tergoule or teugoule, torgoule, terrinée (Normandy): rice cooked with sweetened milk, a dash of cinnamon, baked for a long time in an earthenware dish

Tian (Provence): usually refers to a dished of mixed vegetables au gratin.

Tourin or tourain (entire Southwest): onion soup made with bacon and a small clove of garlic, thickened with egg yolk and a dash of vinegar, then poured over thin slices of bread

Touron (Languedoc, Roussillon): sort of almond paste, with different flavors, containing pistachios, hazelnuts, or candied fruit

Tourteau fromagé (Poitou): a round cheese-flavored cake with a very dark brown top

Tripes à la mode de Caen (Caen, Calvados): beef tripe cooked (for about twelve hours) with calf's feet, onions, carrots, herbs, and (optionally) Calvados, in a clay pot

Tripoux or tripous (Auvergne, Rouergue, Cévennes): mutton or calf's tripe in the shape of small bundles, stuffed with meat from the trotters, cloves, and lots of pepper

Truffade (Auvergne): a large pancake of sautéed potato, with or without bits of bacon, and Tomme cheese; another recipe calls for the Tomme to be served separately, cut into cubes

Truffiat (Berry): grated potato mixed with flour, eggs, and butter, then baked. Related to criques and râpée (Vivarais) and grapiau (Morvan)

Trulet (Nice): blood sausage typical of Nice, made with pork's blood, chard, onion, sweetbreads, and bacon

Ttoro (Pays Basque): slices of various fish baked or fried with minced onion, tomato, and garlic

W

Waterzooï or waterzoï de poulet (or poisson) (Flanders): chicken (or fish) braised with whites of leek, bouillon, cream, and egg yolk

INDEX

Entries in CAPITALS are names of cities and localities.
Entries in **BOLD CAPITALS** are subject headings.
Entries in **bold print** are regional food specialties.

"Gault Millau is provocative and frank."
—*Los Angeles Times*

"You will enjoy their prose."
—*US News & World Report*

"Gault Millau is the toque of the town."
—*San Francisco Examiner*

Please send me the "The Best of" books checked below:

❏ Chicago $18.00
❏ Florida $17.00
❏ France $25.00
❏ Germany $20.00
❏ Hawaii $18.00
❏ Italy $20.00

❏ London $20.00
❏ Los Angeles $20.00
❏ New Orleans $17.00
❏ New York $18.00
❏ Paris $20.00
❏ Paris Ile-de-France & The Loire Valley ...$15.00

❏ Paris & Provence ..$15.00
❏ San Francisco $18.00
❏ Wineries of North America $18.00
❏ LA Restaurants $14.00
❏ NYC Restaurants ..$12.00
❏ SF Restaurants $12.00

Mail to:
Gault Millau, Inc., P.O. Box 361144, Los Angeles, CA 90036

Order toll-free:
1 (800) LE BEST 1 • FAX: (213) 936-2883 • *E-mail:* gayots@aol.com
In the U.S., include $5 (shipping charge) for the first book, and $4 for each additional book. Outside the U.S., $7 and $5.

❏ Enclosed is my check or money order made out to Gault Millau, Inc. for $ _____.

❏ Please charge my credit card: ❏ VISA   ❏ MC   ❏ AMEX

Card # _____ Exp. ___/___

Signature_____ Telephone _____

Name _____

Address _____

City _____ State_____ ZIP_____

Country _____

324/98

GAYOT PUBLICATIONS

**GAYOT PUBLICATIONS GUIDES ARE AVAILABLE AT
ALL FINE BOOKSTORES WORLDWIDE.**

**INTERNATIONAL DISTRIBUTION IS COORDINATED
BY THE FOLLOWING OFFICES:**

MAINLAND U.S.
Publishers Group West
1700 Fourth St.
Berkeley, CA 94710
(800) 788-3123
(800) 528-3444
Fax (510) 658-1834

CANADA
Publishers Group West
543 Richmond St. West
Suite 223, Box 106
Toronto, Ontario
M5V 146 CANADA
(416) 504-3900
Fax (416) 504-3902

HAWAII
Island Heritage
99-880 Iwaena
Aiea, HI 96701
(800) 468-2800
Fax (808) 488-2279

AUSTRALIA
Little Hills Press Pty. Ltd.
Regent House, 37-43 Alexander St.
Crows Nest (Sydney) NSW 2065
Australia
(02) 437-6995
Fax (02) 438-5762

TAIWAN
Central Book Publishing
2nd Floor, 141, Section 1
Chungking South Rd.
Taipei, Taiwan R.O.C.
(02) 331-5726

Fax (02) 331-1316
HONG KONG & CHINA
Pacific Century Distribution Ltd.
G/F No. 2-4
Lower Kai Yuen Ln.
North Point, Hong Kong
(852) 2811-5505
Fax (852) 2565-8624

UK & EUROPE
World Leisure Marketing
Downing Rd.
West Meadows Industrial Estate
Derby, Derbyshire
DE21 6HA England
(01) 332-343-332
Fax (01) 332-340-464

FRANCE
■ GaultMillau, Inc.
01.48.08.00.38
Fax 01.43.65.46.62

SOUTH AFRICA
Faradawn C.C.
P.O. Box 1903
Saxonwold 2132
Republic of South Africa
(11) 885-1787
Fax (11) 885-1829

**TO ORDER THE GUIDES FOR GIFTS, CUSTOM EDITIONS OR
CORPORATE SALES IN THE U.S., CALL OUR TOLL-FREE LINE.**

ORDER TOLL-FREE
1 (800) LE BEST 1

RECEIVE
3 FREE
ISSUES OF

André Gayot's

TASTES
THE WORLD DINING & TRAVEL CONNECTION

- New Restaurants, Hotels, Shops & Wines
- Travel Tips & Bargains
- Events in the Food World
- Special Places & Resorts

(A $15 VALUE)

BY FILLING OUT THIS QUESTIONNAIRE, YOU'LL RECEIVE 3 COMPLIMENTARY ISSUES OF "TASTES," OUR INTERNATIONAL NEWSLETTER.

NAME _____

ADDRESS _____

CITY _____ STATE _____

ZIP _____ COUNTRY _____

PHONE ( )   –

The Gayot/GaultMillau series of guidebooks reflects your demand for insightful, incisive reporting on the best that the world's most exciting destinations have to offer. To help us make our books even better, please take a moment to fill out this anonymous (if you wish) questionnaire, and return it to:

GaultMillau, Inc., P.O. Box 361144, Los Angeles, CA 90036;
Fax: (213) 936-2883.

1. How did you hear about the Gayot guides? Please specify: bookstore, newspaper, magazine, radio, friends or other.

2. Please list in order of preference the cities or countries which you would like to see Gayot cover.

3. Do you refer to the AGP guides for your own city, or only when traveling?

A. (Travels) ………   B. (Own city) ………   C. (Both) ………

(Please turn)

4. Please list by order of preference the three features you like best about the Gayot guides.

A. ....

B. .... C. ....

5. What are the features, if any, you dislike about the Gayot guides?

6. Please list any features that you would like to see added to the Gayot guides.

7. If you use other guides besides Gayot, please list below.

8. Please list the features you like best about your favorite guidebook series, if it is not Gayot/GaultMillau.

A. ....

B. .... C. ....

9. How many trips do you make per year, for either business or pleasure?

Business: International .... Domestic ....

Pleasure: International .... Domestic ....

10. Please check the category that reflects your annual household income.

$20,000–$39,000 .... $40,000–$59,000 ....
$60,000–$79,000 .... $80,000–$99,000 ....
$100,000–$120,000 .... Other (please specify) ....

11. If you have any comments on the AGP guides in general, please list them in the space below.

12. If you would like to recommend specific establishments, please don't hesitate to list them:
   Name   *City*   *Phone*

_____

_____

_____

13. Do you often/sometimes use the Internet to buy goods & services? ❑ Yes ❑ No

We thank you for your interest in the Gayot guides, and we welcome your remarks and recommendations about restaurants, hotels, nightlife, shops, services and so on.